The **Council of Europe**, founded in 1949, is an intergovernmental organisation of 39 member states which has among its aims to protect and strengthen pluralist democracy and human rights, to promote the emergence of a genuine European cultural identity, to seek solutions to the problems facing society (the position of minorities, xenophobia and intolerance, environmental protection, bioethics, drugs, Aids, etc.), to develop a political partnership with the new democracies and to help them with their political, legislative and constitutional reforms.

European Union LIFE-Nature is the financial instrument supporting European Union environmental policy. LIFE-Nature co-finances action in nature conservation and in other fields of environmental protection. In practice, LIFE-funded projects must contribute to the implementation of EU Birds and Habitats Directives and, in particular, to contribute to establishing the European network of protected areas – Natura 2000.

BirdLife International is the global partnership of bird conservation NGOs. Its European Programme includes research and action for Important Bird Areas, globally threatened species and conservation of key habitats for birds. Its publications programme has contributed enormously to conservation in recent years through works such as *Important Bird Areas in Europe* (1989: revised version in preparation), *Birds in Europe: their conservation status* (1994) and the forthcoming *Habitats for Birds in Europe*. BirdLife International is represented throughout Europe and has programmes in 34 European countries.

The Royal Society for the Protection of Birds is the United Kingdom Partner of BirdLife International. The three-year programme *Action plans for globally threatened birds in Europe* was funded by the RSPB and the European Union.

Wetlands International is the world's leading non-profit organisation concerned with the conservation and wise use of wetlands. Its network extends to 120 countries worldwide, with co-ordination through three regional headquarters – in the Netherlands, Malaysia and Canada. Wetlands International co-ordinated the workshops, compilation, consultation and drafting of six action plans: Dalmation Pelican, Pygmy Cormorant, Lesser White-fronted Goose, Red-breasted Goose, Marbled Teal and White-headed Duck.

Contents

Foreword by J.-P. Ribaut

The Council of Europe welcomes this excellent work on the most threatened birds of Europe by BirdLife International and other non-governmental organisations. It underlines the role of voluntary bodies both in developing public awareness and in producing scientifically sound conservation material.

Birds have always interested man for their beauty, but are also wonderful biological indicators: their rareness or abundance tells us much about the way we manage our forests, water and countryside. In this respect, the list of 23 species threatened on a world scale is very instructive. The message is that human activities are affecting every piece of land and water, causing an impoverishment of its biological richness and diversity. We have long known that wetlands and wetland birds were severely endangered. Yet the presence on this list of species such as the Great Bustard (*Otis tarda*) or the Corncrake (*Crex crex*) raises fundamental environmental questions as these species are just the tip of a large iceberg. Many countryside bird species are in serious decline. Let us mention the shirks, the warblers ... so abundant 30 years ago, so rare today.

The urgency of the situation demands both broad measures (such as a new approach to regional planning and better regulation of pollutants and other hazardous substances) and very specific measures, like those contained in these action plans.

The Standing Committee of the Bern Convention recognised this urgency when it encouraged (in its Recommendation No. 48 of 26 January 1996) the states that are parties or observers to the convention to work for the implementation of national action plans on the 23 species mentioned. The Bern Convention has developed in the past year numerous action plans on threatened species and these plans provide an extraordinary opportunity to focus more on birds. New activities will be co-ordinated with the implementation of a European Threatened Species Programme to be developed in the framework of the recently developed Pan-European Strategy on Biological and Landscape Diversity. The Strategy includes a detailed vade-mecum on biological management for European ministers of the environment. Chapter 11 of the action plan is especially devoted to threatened species.

Let us hope that all the different measures envisaged or in hand will definitely preserve our natural heritage not only for us, but for future generations.

Jean-Pierre Ribaut
Head of Environment Conservation and Management Division

Foreword by B. Julien

Restrained only by their natural boundaries, birds have come to symbolise the importance of international co-operation in the conservation of our natural heritage. If we are to respond effectively to the dramatic decline we are currently witnessing amongst some of our birds, we not only need to have a good understanding of the ecological requirements of each species, we must also assume our collective responsibility for their future by collaborating in ways that will make our actions as tangible as possible.

This ambition has now been made more attainable through the elaboration of this unique publication prepared by Birdlife International with the financial support of the European Union's Directorate for Environment. Focusing on 23 of Europe's most endangered species, each action plan gives us an indispensable tool in identifying priority measures for conservation action needed to halt their decline. What makes them even more useful is the fact that they result from an extensive process of consultation, consent and as far as possible consensus between government agencies, NGOs and individuals throughout Europe. This should help pave the way for their implementation at all appropriate levels, whether local, national, European or global.

All 23 species are listed in the European Union's Birds Directive. The action plans will therefore facilitate member states' tasks in implementing the legal provisions for the conservation of these species. They will also be put to immediate use in the allocation of funds under the European Union's LIFE-Nature programme which was initially established to assist the application of the Birds Directive. Given that all these birds are considered priority for funding, the plan will help focus the limited resources to those areas where financing is most urgent. Already several projects involving these species have received financial support under LIFE, including the elaboration of the action plans themselves.

We all recognise that actions plans are only the start of the process. They need to be translated into real conservation if they are to achieve their objective. This is the challenge we now face and by which we will be judged. With these plans we cannot say that we did not know what measures to take to make Europe a safer haven for our most endangered wild birds.

Bruno Julien

Head of Unit for Nature Conservation
Directorate General for Environment
European Commission

Introduction

Threatened species

Of some 10 000 bird species in the world, over 1100 are believed to be threatened with extinction (Collar et al., 1994). A great many of these are endemic to small areas, such as oceanic islands or mountains, and the vast majority are in tropical regions. Europe has a relatively small share of the world's avifauna – some 514 regularly occurring species – and of its threatened species.

A recent survey, country by country, species by species, of the conservation status of Europe's birds, was carried out by BirdLife International in collaboration with the European Ornithological Atlas project. This showed (Tucker and Heath, 1994) that of the 514 European bird species, 195 have an unfavourable conservation status. This refers to the rate of decline of a species, and/or to its rarity (for a full explanation, see Tucker and Heath (1994) pp. 27-31). These 195 species can be divided into three groups, according to the importance of their European populations in relation to the world total. A fourth group contains species which, while not having an unfavourable conservation status, are concentrated in Europe. These are therefore also of interest, since any future change in their conservation status in Europe may be of wider importance. Together, these four groups, totalling 278 species or 54% of Europe's avifauna, are therefore classified as *Species of European Conservation Concern*, or SPECs. The four SPEC categories are:

SPEC 1: Species of global conservation concern. Species which are globally threatened, conservation dependent or data deficient according to Collar et al. (1994) which applied new IUCN criteria (24 species).

SPEC 2: Species whose world populations are concentrated in Europe (ie. over 50% of the total population or range occurs in Europe) and which have an unfavourable conservation status (41 species).

SPEC 3: Species whose world populations are not concentrated in Europe, but which have an unfavourable conservation status in Europe (130 species).

SPEC 4: Species which have a favourable conservation status but whose populations are concentrated in Europe (83 species).

Arguably, the ultimate goal of the conservation community is to prevent extinctions. Thus, particular attention is drawn to species in category SPEC 1. For these species, piecemeal actions are unlikely to be sufficiently strong or coherent to prevent extinctions. It is therefore necessary to define in some detail specific actions which are required to prevent further deterioration in their status and, where appropriate, to begin their recovery. This report represents the first step in this task.

The twenty-four European globally threatened species are:

Fea's Petrel	*Pterodroma feae*
Zino's Petrel	*Pterodroma madeira*
Dalmatian Pelican	*Pelecanus crispus*
Lesser White-fronted Goose	*Anser erythropus*
Red-breasted Goose	*Branta ruficollis*
Marbled Teal	*Marmaronetta angustirostris*
Ferruginous Duck	*Aythya nyroca*
Steller's Eider	*Polysticta stelleri*
White-headed Duck	*Oxyura leucocephala*
Greater Spotted Eagle	*Aquila clanga*
Imperial Eagle	*Aquila heliaca*
Spanish Imperial Eagle	*Aquila adalberti*
Lesser Kestrel	*Falco naumanni*
Corncrake	*Crex crex*
Great Bustard	*Otis tarda*
Sociable Plover	*Chettusia gregaria*
Slender-billed Curlew	*Numenius tenuirostris*
Audouin's Gull	*Larus audouinii*
Madeira Laurel Pigeon	*Columba trocaz*
Dark-tailed Pigeon	*Columba bollii*
White-tailed Pigeon	*Columba junoniae*
Aquatic Warbler	*Acrocephalus paludicola*
Blue Chaffinch	*Fringilla teydea*
Scottish Crossbill	*Loxia scotica*

Action plans

Action plans are the start of a process, not an end in themselves. Their purpose is to define the actions needed to reach a given set of goals, and, crucially, to build consensus among the organisations and individuals who are in a position to influence the outcome. The process should facilitate an exchange of experience between countries and establish best practice in specific areas. These plans should form the basis for decisions at international level, and provide a framework for more detailed planning at national level.

In most cases, therefore, the actions called for are intended as guidelines for more detailed development. For the species which are not endemic to a single country it will be necessary to define more detailed actions for each country, and in most cases, national action plans will be needed, in turn achieving consensus among national and local players, and setting ambitious but achievable targets.

International plans were developed in the 1970s for several populations of North American waterfowl because of this group's economic and social importance. A framework for these plans was developed by the North American Waterfowl Management Plan, which represents a rationale for international co-operation between Canada, the United States and Mexico in the conservation of wetlands and waterfowl. The Bonn Convention (Convention on the Conservation of Migratory Species of Wild Animals) is preparing an action plan for Anatidae, Storks, Ibises and Spoonbills, under the framework of the African/Eurasian Migratory Waterbirds Agreement. The IUCN has also embarked on the preparation of action plans for several taxonomic groups of animals, including, so far, three bird families produced by BirdLife International and the Species Survival Commission of the IUCN. These are broad plans dealing with whole taxonomic groups, and point out general steps needed rather than give detailed prescriptions.

Wetlands International and the Wildfowl and Wetlands Trust have produced several action plans for globally threatened Anatidae in recent years. The plan published for the White-headed Duck in 1989 was accompanied by a series of

educational booklets in local languages, and has led to successful implementation in the species' main wintering region in Turkey. A plan published for the White-winged (Wood) Duck *Cairina scutulata* in 1992 has led to successful implementation in Thailand and Indonesia. A plan was published for the Marbled Teal as recently as 1993. These reports are produced through the network of the Wetlands International Threatened Waterfowl Research Group and include very thorough reviews of the status of the species accompanied by recommendations for conservation action at a national level. Recommendations for the European species were reformulated and strengthened during the current project.

European action plans

In 1993, BirdLife International undertook to draw up action plans for twenty-three species. Several key organisations and individuals came together to form an advisory committee (see above). The Royal Society for the Protection of Birds and the European Commission's LIFE programme provided the necessary funds for the three-year programme, which was to involve over 370 experts from almost every European country.

The species covered by this project comprise nineteen SPEC 1s, one SPEC 2 and two SPEC 3s. The three latter species were included on the grounds that they were considered globally threatened at the time the project started, and remain near-threatened.[1] The endemic Azorean Bullfinch, *Pyrrhula (p.) murina*, is included on the grounds that it is widely believed to be a full species, and if so, is among the rarest birds in the world. Its taxonomic status needs to be clarified.

Five SPEC 1s are not included in this project at this stage. The Sociable Plover *Chettusia gregaria* is highly marginal in Europe, being essentially restricted to Asian Russia and Kazakhstan. Scottish Crossbill *Loxia scotica* is a United Kingdom endemic for which an approved action plan exists; furthermore its taxonomic status is somewhat unclear. The remaining three species were

---

1. *Phalacrocorax pygmeus*: SPEC 2, vulnerable (moderate decline, <10000 pairs); *Aegypius monachus*: SPEC 3, vulnerable (<2500 pairs); *Chlamydotis undulata*: SPEC 3, endangered endemic subspecies (<250 pairs).

not included solely because when the project began, their status as globally threatened species was not recognised. These species, Steller's Eider *Polysticta stelleri*, Ferruginous Duck *Aythya nyroca* and Spotted Eagle *Aquila clanga* will be covered in a second phase of the project commencing in 1996.

For each species, a workshop of experts and interested parties from as many range states as possible was held. This ensured that the latest information on the status, distribution, limiting factors, threats and other key data concerning the species was readily available. For each species a compiler, or team of compilers, was appointed. These would normally be technical experts in the species. A first draft action plan would bring together all the information obtained at the workshop, along with a synthesis of relevant written material. The draft would be circulated to workshop participants, other known experts and relevant NGOs and public bodies. Depending on the species, there may have been several successive drafts in light of comments and new information. In each country the BirdLife partner or representative would provide a further consultation channel for information and comments.

Wetlands International (formerly IWRB) co-ordinated the workshops, compilation, consultation and drafting of the six waterfowl species: Dalmatian Pelican, Pygmy Cormorant, Lesser White-fronted Goose, Red-breasted Goose, Marbled Teal and White-headed Duck.

Following consultation on a round of first drafts, advanced drafts were prepared by June 1995. These were discussed at a specially-convened seminar at the Council of Europe, Strasbourg. This was attended by national and headquarters' delegates of BirdLife International and Wetlands International, action plan compilers and several delegates of national governments. Representatives of the European Commission and the Bonn Convention also participated. This led to agreement on the structure of the plans, and comments on further drafts were encouraged.

The resulting drafts were presented to a meeting of the European Union's Committee for the Adaptation to Technical and Scientific Progress under the EU Birds Directive in December 1995.

Finally, the Standing Committee of the Bern Convention discussed the plans in January 1996. Endorsement by the competent authorities of the countries concerned was sought at these meetings, and obtained. Final editing, mainly to take account of the most recent information, was completed in April 1996.

Geographical scope

The plans cover all European states west of the Ural Mountains including the islands of Madeira, Azores and the Canaries, the whole of Turkey and the Caucasian republics of Georgia, Armenia and Azerbaijan.

Three of the species covered (Lesser Kestrel, Corncrake and Aquatic Warbler) are long-distance migrants whose wintering grounds lie mostly in Africa, south of the Sahara. Their winter quarters are not covered in the action plans. Exceptionally, however, the geographical scope has been extended beyond Europe (See Table 1). This is the case for the Slender-billed Curlew plan which includes prescriptions for the breeding grounds in Siberia and the Imperial Eagle plan which covers the Middle East. The plans for Audouin's Gull, Marbled Teal and White-headed Duck include recommendations for North African countries because these populations are biogeographically linked with their European counterparts and constitute a Mediterranean unity.

Format

Each plan consists of three main sections. Part 1 deals with basic information about status, ecology, threats and current conservation measures. The threats have been rated according to the following categories:

- critical: a factor that could lead to the extinction of the species in 20 years or less;

- high: a factor that could lead to a decline of more than 20% of the population in 20 years or less;

- medium: a factor that could lead to a decline of less than 20% of the population over significant parts of its range in 20 years or less;

- low: a factor that only affects the species at a local level;

Table 1

Non-European countries for which actions are included in the action plans

Species	DZ	EG	IR	IQ	IL	KZ	LB	MA	SY	TN
Lesser White-fronted Goose						•				
Red-breasted Goose						•				
Marbled Teal	•	•	•	•	•		•	•	•	•
White-headed Duck	•		•	•	•			•	•	•
Imperial Eagle		•	•	•	•	•				
Lesser Kestrel	•	•			•	•		•		•
Slender-billed Curlew	•		•	•			•		•	•
Audouin's Gull	•						•	•		•

DZ Algeria - EG Egypt - IR Iran - IQ Iraq - IL Israel - KZ Kazakhstan - LB Lebanon - MA Morocco - SY Syria - TN Tunisia

– unknown: a factor that is likely to affect the species but it is not known to what extent.

Part 2 includes the aims and generic objectives of the plan. The objectives are grouped under the following headings:

– policy and legislation;
– species and habitat protection;
– monitoring and research;
– public awareness.

Each objective is broken down into a series of actions followed by a brief description. These actions are generic and do not make reference to any particular country or geographical region except for species which are found in only one European country. Each action is given a priority rating and time-scale in which it ought to be carried out using the following categories:

Priority

– essential: an action that is needed to prevent a large decline in the population which could lead to the species' extinction;

– high: an action that is needed to prevent a decline of more than 20% of the population in 20 years or less;

– medium: an action that is needed to prevent a decline of less than 20% of the population in 20 years or less;

– low: an action that is needed to prevent local population declines or which is likely to have only a small impact on the population across the range.

Time-scale

– immediate: completed within the next year;

– short: completed within the next 1-3 years;

– medium: completed within the next 1-5 years;

– long: completed within the next 1-10 years;

– ongoing: an action that is currently being implemented and should continue;

– completed: an action that was completed during the preparation of the action plan (such actions may nevertheless need reviewing or carrying out again as circumstances develop in the future).

Priority actions for each European country within the species range, cross-referenced to the numbered objectives, are listed in an annex to the plans (with the exception of plans involving one country only) to act as a guide for the preparation of national action plans.

Overview of the species

Fea's Petrel

Fea's Petrel Pterodroma feae is an extremely rare and threatened Macaronesian endemic petrel, known to exist only on Bugio and some of the Cape Verde Islands. Not much is known about the population on the Cape Verde Islands, though there are estimates of a total population of up to 1000 breeding pairs. In the Madeira archipelago it nests only on Bugio.

Over the years, the birds have suffered predation by fishermen, but since the whole land surface of the Desertas was made a strict reserve this situation has improved dramatically. Current threats include degradation of habitat due to grazing by goats and rabbits.

The study of this bird is particularly important as it may well give very important insights to the life history of Zino's Petrel, whose status is precarious.

Zino's Petrel

Zino's Petrel or Madeira Freira *Pterodroma madeira* is Europe's rarest breeding seabird. It is endemic to the island of Madeira where it breeds in the central mountain massif. The breeding population is estimated to be down to a precarious 20 to 30 pairs.

By 1960, there were so few records of this species many believed it to be extinct. It was rediscovered in 1969 by a local ornithologist, P. A. Zino. The breeding colony remained under discrete study and in 1986 the colony was found not to be breeding successfully due to predation by rats. As a result a Freira Conservation Project was set up with support from BirdLife International and commercial sponsors to try and contain the rat problem. The situation was further aggravated in 1990 when a cat (or cats) killed 10 adults, probably breeding birds, on one ledge.

Pygmy Cormorant

The Pygmy Cormorant *Phalacrocorax pygmaeus* is considered as Near-threatened within its whole geographical distribution, and is listed as Vulnerable at European level (Tucker and Heath, 1994). Its present world breeding population is currently estimated at 13 000 pairs, and probably half of this number is in Europe, where the largest colonies are still found in Romania, Turkey and Greece. Data on the distribution, biology and ecology of this species are most inadequate.

Since the second half of the nineteenth century, the Pygmy Cormorant has been in continuous decline due to drainage, persecution by fishermen, destruction of breeding colonies and degradation of wetlands.

Dalmatian Pelican

The Dalmatian Pelican *Pelecanus crispus* is classified as Vulnerable within its whole geographical range. Its present world breeding population is estimated at 3215 to 4280 pairs, more than 80% being in the former Soviet Union – Kazakhstan, Russian Federation, Turkmenistan, Ukraine and Uzbekistan. The European population occupies Albania, Bulgaria, Greece, Romania, Russian Federation, Turkey, Ukraine and Federal Republic of Yugoslavia (Serbia only).

Since the second half of the nineteenth century, the Dalmatian Pelican has never stopped declining, due to disturbance and degradation of wetlands, hunting and colony destruction by fishermen.

Lesser White-fronted Goose

During the twentieth century, populations of the Lesser White-fronted Goose *Anser erythropus* have undergone drastic declines in numbers everywhere even in the breeding and wintering ranges. Since the 1940s, the population has probably fallen by more than 90% to fewer than 50 000. Indeed, a recent follow-up meeting of experts on the species could account for no more than 2000 birds throughout its entire West Palaearctic range. The reasons for this are virtually unknown, the combination of negative factors acting on the breeding grounds (e.g. habitat loss, disturbance, shooting, increased predation) being insufficient to explain the rapid decline of recent years. More information is needed on numbers, distribution, habitat requirements and threats in the central part of the species' breeding range in north Siberia as well as on its wintering grounds.

Red-breasted Goose

The Red-breasted Goose *Branta ruficollis* is not only one of the rarest goose species in the world, it is also one of the most attractive, making it highly suitable as a "flagship" species for conservation throughout its range. It nests in the Russian arctic and winters in temperate regions along the

Black Sea coast (Bulgaria, Romania, Ukraine and Turkey). Existing data suggest that the population suffered a dramatic decline from 60 000 to 25 000 during the late 1950s and 1960s, but recent comprehensive counts of over 70 000 geese may indicate that a sizeable proportion of the population was overlooked and that previous estimates were too low. The decline during the 1960s was accompanied by, and possibly due to, large-scale re-distribution from the wintering grounds on the Caspian Sea coast, where massive land-use changes occurred, to the Black Sea coast.

Marbled Teal

The Marbled Teal *Marmaronetta angustirostris* is undergoing rapid declines throughout its remaining range, which extends in a band from Senegal and North Africa eastwards to China; in Europe it is found in Spain, Turkey, Azerbaijan and, in small numbers, Russia and Armenia. Destruction and degradation of habitats (particularly breeding habitats) is the most important cause; hunting and a range of other factors also contribute to this decline. The most important need is the effective conservation of wetlands of importance for the species, paying particular attention to the special features of their breeding sites.

Ferruginous Duck

This species was not included in the current phase of action planning, but will be treated in 1996/97. The breeding range of the Ferruginous Duck *Aythya nyroca* comprises wetlands in the steppe, desert and southern forest zones of Eurasia, extending from the Mediterranean basin to central China. Although the total population size is unclear, it is estimated that roughly half of its global breeding range is within Europe, largely concentrated in the south-east with strongholds in Romania, Ukraine, Turkey, Moldova, Hungary and southern Russia.

The Ferruginous Duck has severely declined in population size and range in Europe. During the late 1960s the total population of the former Soviet Union was estimated at 75 000 pairs. However, by the early 1980s, just 12 000 to 14 000 pairs were estimated in the European part of the former Soviet Union, falling further to around 6 000 pairs by the early 1990s.

It is essential that the remaining wetlands which are important are conserved and the reduction and strict control of hunting would be beneficial.

Steller's Eider

This species was not included in the current phase of action planning, but will be treated in 1996/97. Steller's Eider *Polysticta stelleri* breeds along the Arctic cost of Alaska and the eastern half of Siberia, including the Taymyr peninsula of north-central Siberia. Most birds winter in the northern Pacific, but the main European areas for both non-breeders in summer and for wintering birds are the Varangerfjord in northern Norway and the Murmansk coast of north-east Russia which together hold more than two-thirds of the Steller's Eiders in Europe.

The species is increasingly found in all countries around the Baltic Sea with large numbers wintering in Estonia, especially on Soaremaa Island in the Vilsandi State Nature Reserve.

The number wintering in Europe appears to be increasing but due to its concentration at few sites the species remains vulnerable to oil spills and to accidental trapping in gill-nets. The wintering population of Steller's Eiders in Alaska has declined seriously and the species is therefore now regarded as globally threatened.

White-headed Duck

The White-headed Duck *Oxyura leucocephala* has undergone a considerable decline in range and population size this century, with the destruction and degradation of habitat and hunting being the causes. The Spanish population has recently recovered after being near to extinction in the 1970s. There has been considerable attention paid to the species in Turkey since 1989 which has led to conservation measures being taken at Burdur Gölü, a site that holds most of the world population in winter.

The spread of introduced North American Ruddy Ducks (*Oxyura jamaicensis*) poses the most severe threat to the White-headed Duck, owing to the free hybridisation between the two species. The Ruddy Duck has now been recorded in 20 European countries, with the United

Kingdom holding by far the largest population, and hybridisation already posing a serious problem to White-headed Duck sites in Spain. The extinction of the White-headed Duck is only likely to be prevented if rapid action is taken to control Ruddy Ducks in all European countries where it occurs.

The conservation of the White-headed Duck in Europe also requires the effective conservation of wetlands of importance for the species, together with the effective control of hunting on these wetlands.

Cinereous Vulture

The Cinereous Vulture *Aegypius monachus* is classified as Near-threatened at world level (Collar et al., 1994) and Vulnerable at European level (Tucker and Heath, 1994). It has a discontinuous distribution in Europe, where it is present in the Caucasus mountains (190 pairs shared among Russia, Georgia, Armenia and Azerbaijan), Greece (20), Spain (1000), Turkey (100–500) and Ukraine (6).

Populations are considered to be increasing in Spain and Greece, stable in Turkey and declining in Ukraine and the Caucasus. The widespread use of poison baits to control foxes is a major threat; the species' increase in Spain is partly due to better control of poisons. Here, as elsewhere, the loss of Mediterranean forest and scrub is becoming significant.

Greater Spotted Eagle

This species was not included in the current phase of action planning, but will be treated in 1996/97. The major part of the world range of the Greater Spotted Eagle *Aquila clanga* extends through the southern forest zone in north European Russia and south-central Siberia as far east as the lower Amur river. About a quarter of the range lies within Europe, in a band from the Poland/Belarus border, extending eastwards between 64°-65° N in the north and the edge of the forest zone in the south. The species is migratory, with regular wintering areas lying around the eastern Mediterranean, including Egypt and the Middle East, as well as in southern Asia.

The European range of this globally threatened species contracted between 1970 and 1990. The species' total European population is very small, amounting to about 1000 pairs. The majority are in Russia but even here the species occurs in extremely low densities and numbers continue to decline, mostly due to habitat destruction and human disturbance. Additional protected areas are required with measures designed to conserve meadows and marshes alongside blocks of undisturbed forest. Nest sites should be guarded to prevent disturbance.

Imperial Eagle

The Imperial Eagle *Aquila heliaca* is classified as Vulnerable at the global level (Collar et al., 1994) and Endangered at the European level (Tucker and Heath, 1994). In Europe it occurs in the Carpathian mountains and basin, the southern and eastern Balkan peninsula, the hills and steppes of south-east Ukraine and south Russia, and the Caucasus mountains. The population in Slovakia and Hungary has begun to increase as a result of intensive conservation efforts. Total numbers are estimated at 363 to 604 pairs. Threats include habitat alteration, poisoning and shooting.

Spanish Imperial Eagle

The Spanish Imperial Eagle *Aquila adalberti* is endemic to the western Mediterranean, and currently breeds only in Spain and Morocco, although dispersing or nomadic juveniles regularly appear in Portugal. At international level it is considered Vulnerable (Collar et al., 1994; Tucker and Heath, 1994), although in Spain it is legally classified as Endangered. Threats include poisoning, electrocution and collision with powerlines, and habitat alteration. Since 1986 an intensive conservation programme has been underway, involving the participation of DGN (Directorate-General for Nature Conservation) and the regional governments of Castilla-León, Castilla-La Mancha, Madrid, Extremadura and Andalucía.

Lesser Kestrel

The Lesser Kestrel *Falco naumanni* is a globally threatened species classified as Vulnerable by

Collar et al. (1994). It has shown major population declines in large parts of its western Palaearctic breeding range and has disappeared from several countries where it bred until recently. The western Palaearctic population (Europe and North Africa) was estimated to be 10000 to 17000 pairs in 1994. The species is affected by the transformation of grassland breeding habitat to other land-uses and prey reduction due to pesticide use.

Comprehensive knowledge of the migration routes of different breeding populations and their wintering grounds is still lacking. Knowledge of the species' migration and winter ecology and of possible threats in Africa is incomplete.

Corncrake

The Corncrake *Crex crex* is a globally threatened species, classified as Vulnerable at both world and European level due to the long-term and very steep decline of the species across its range. The Corncrake's breeding range extends over much of northern and central Europe and into Asia. It migrates in autumn, especially through Egypt, to winter in sub-Saharan Africa. The current estimate of the total European population is 92000 to 233000 singing males, breeding in 34 countries. This figure may, however, be revised substantially upwards. Only 10 states, nine of which are in central and eastern Europe, now have populations of more than 1000 singing males, and only Russia, Belarus and Ukraine have more than 10000 males. Corncrakes have been declining in Europe since the last century, on average by about 20%–50% over the last 10 years. This is due primarily to changes in land-use and farming practices.

Great Bustard

The Great Bustard *Otis tarda* is a globally threatened species listed as Vulnerable by Collar et al. (1994). In Europe it is present in Austria, Bulgaria, Croatia, the Czech Republic, France, Germany, Greece, Hungary, Italy, Moldova, Portugal, Romania, Russia, Slovakia, Spain, Turkey, Ukraine and the former Yugoslavia. The European population is estimated to be between 23790 and 30483 individuals (at least half in Spain) but there

has been a rapid decline in much of central and eastern Europe. Its habitat is dry grass agricultural land and mixed extensive agricultural and pasture/fallow land. The most significant threat is the conversion of extensive grassland systems to more intensive use. Conservation measures must focus on active habitat management and on the maintenance of large areas of non-intensive farming systems.

Houbara Bustard

This species is widespread across subtropical latitudes in semi-desert from the Canary Islands to central Asia. Although no longer considered globally threatened, this species was retained in the programme due to the precarious status of the Canary Islands Houbara Bustard *Chlamydotis undulata fuertaventurae*. This is a subspecies endemic to the islands of Fuerteventura, Lobos, Lanzarote and Graciosa. The total population is estimated at 700 to 750 birds. The species is protected under Spanish legislation and classed as Endangered in the national Red Data Book; there has been a recovery plan in existence since 1985. Loss, alteration and degradation of habitat and disturbance by tourists are serious problems.

Sociable Plover

The Sociable Plover *Chettusia gregaria* breeds in Russia and Kazakhstan, the small numbers occurring within Europe occupying the steppes between the Volga and the Ural rivers. It was decided not to include this species in the project, due to its marginal European status. Birds winter in desert regions from Israel and north-east Africa to north-west India. In the nineteenth century, the species had a more westerly breeding distribution, extending across the steppe to the Dnieper river (Ukraine) and the Crimea. It was also common in the Volga region and, up to the mid-twentieth century, occurred in the Kalmykia region, west of the Volga river.

The species is rare and declining in Europe due mainly to the conversion of grass steppes into arable agriculture and the consequent increase in grazing pressure on remaining grasslands. Areas of natural steppe in Europe need to be conserved, and breeding colonies must be protected from disturbance, trampling by cattle, excessive predation by Rooks, and destruction by agricultural machinery. The Sociable Plover is considered to have declined over the period 1970 to 1990 to no more than 2100 pairs in Europe.

Slender-billed Curlew

The conservation status of the Slender-billed Curlew *Numenius tenuirostris* is classified as Critical at a global level. Along with Zino's Petrel it is the rarest and most poorly known bird in Europe, where it occurs as a passage migrant and occasional winter visitor. The population is estimated to be 50 to 270 birds. The most significant threats are habitat loss on its wintering and passage sites, possible habitat loss in its breeding range and, historically at least, hunting.

Conservation of the Slender-billed Curlew is a truly formidable task. With populations now so low, a significant problem may be the breakdown in social behaviour patterns. Although major gaps remain in our knowledge of the species in large parts of its range, certain actions can be taken immediately (and some have already been achieved). Effective conservation action will depend largely on a high degree of co-operation and commitment among those responsible, and on medium to long-term funding.

Audouin's Gull

Audouin's Gull *Larus audouinii* is a rare and localised species with a breeding population of about 15000 pairs limited to the Mediterranean Sea. Because of the population increase in the western Mediterranean in the last twenty years it is now classified as Conservation Dependent. Most breeding sites are rocky cliffs and offshore islands or islets, the exception being the colony in the Ebro delta (Spain) which is on a mainland saltmarsh/sandy seashore habitat. The most important colonies (approximately 90% of the total population) lie within protected areas. Wintering areas are poorly known and include Algeria, Mauritania, Morocco and Senegal.

Madeira Laurel Pigeon

The Madeira Laurel Pigeon *Columba trocaz* is an endemic bird of the island of Madeira and is under strict national and international protection.

In the earlier days of man's colonisation of the island it was a very abundant bird but due to very heavy persecution and dramatic loss of its habitat it has become a threatened species. The remaining laurel forest (an area of about 12000 ha) is now under the jurisdiction of the Parque Natural da Madeira. Thanks to the very intense management carried out by the natural park, the population of the Madeira Laurel Pigeon is now increasing, and has reached numbers that give great optimism for its future if, and only if, the management, protection and research are continued.

Dark-tailed Pigeon

The Dark-tailed Laurel Pigeon *Columba bollii* is endemic to the Canary Islands occurring in the laurel forests of Tenerife, La Palma, La Gomera and El Hierro with an estimated population of 1700 individuals.

The range of this species has contracted substantially since the nineteenth century. The Dark-tailed Laurel Pigeon now occupies just 35%-40% of its original area, which gives an idea of the scale of the destruction and alteration of laurel forests on the island.

White-tailed Pigeon

The White-tailed Laurel Pigeon *Columba junoniae* is a species endemic to the Canary Islands archipelago, being found only on the islands of Tenerife, La Palma and La Gomera. It occurs in laurel forests and has an estimated population of about 1200 to 1480 birds. The species is considered as globally threatened.

The enormous reduction in laurel forest cover over the last 500 years has resulted in a substantial contraction of the species range. Numbers are, however, believed to have been stable from 1970 to 1990 although insufficient data are available to confirm this.

Aquatic Warbler

The Aquatic Warbler *Acrocephalus paludicola* is a globally threatened species which breeds in Belarus, Germany, Hungary, Latvia, Lithuania, Poland, Russia and Ukraine. The European population is estimated between 2900 and 8600 singing males, with major populations in Belarus, Poland, Hungary and Russia. Migration has been recorded in 13 European countries, mainly in the west and south-west of the continent. Habitat loss due to drainage, burning or abandonment of agriculture are important threats. It winters in south-west Africa south of the Sahara but little more is known about the species during winter. There is also a lack of knowledge about its habitat requirements during migration.

Blue Chaffinch

The Blue Chaffinch *Fringilla teydea* is endemic to the Canary Islands and comprises two sub-species, one found on Tenerife and the other on Gran Canaria. Its habitat is Canary pine *Pinus canariensis*. Although there has not been a census of the Tenerife population, its situation is thought to be stable, while the estimated population on Gran Canaria is 185 to 260 birds, which means that the latter subspecies is classified as Endangered both nationally and internationally.

Azores Bullfinch

The Azores Bullfinch *Pyrrhula (p.) murina* is a very distinct form occurring in the east of the island of São Miguel. It was a locally abundant pest of fruit orchards in the nineteenth century but became rare after 1920. The present population of about 120 pairs is largely confined to around 500 ha of native vegetation, which has been reduced and invaded by aggressive exotic plants.

Scottish Crossbill

Not included in this report, this species is a single-country endemic, *Loxia scotica*. A national action plan for this species was published in 1996 by the biodiversity steering group set up under the United Kingdom Biodiversity Action Plan (1994). The population is believed to be between 300 and 1300 pairs, but trends are unclear. Over the past few hundred years the original habitat of the Caledonian pine forest has declined seriously, by over 99.9%, to only 12000 ha.

Measures to increase the area and quality of such forest are required, as is research into the species' habitat use. The Forestry Agency of the United Kingdom is a grant-aiding native pinewood establishment.

Overview of threats and actions

Policy and legislation

The plans highlight significant gaps in the legal basis for species conservation in several countries. This is particularly true for the newly democratic states, many of which are in the process of reforming legislation. For these countries, accession to international treaties such as the Bern, Bonn and Ramsar Conventions will undoubtedly assist in establishing effective national legislation. However, several countries remain without adequate legislation being implemented even after having ratified these conventions.

At both national and pan-European level, biodiversity strategies provide a further stimulus to effective, co-ordinated efforts for threatened species conservation. The Pan-European Landscape and Biodiversity Strategy (1995) highlights the need for international co-operation through species action plans backed by legislation.

Important Bird Areas (IBAs)

Conservation of sites of particular importance for birds is central to any effort to conserve threatened species. Such sites have been identified by BirdLife International on the basis of bird numbers and species complements they hold, as Important Bird Areas – IBAs (Grimmett and Jones, 1989). A fundamental tenet of conservation, and of these action plans, is that such sites are subject to both legal protection and appropriate active management.

Since publication of the original European IBA list a considerable amount of new information has become available. In Germany (NABU, 1991), France (Rocamora, 1993), Italy (Lambertini et al., 1991), Netherlands (van den Tempel and Osieck, 1994), Spain (SEO, 1992) and United Kingdom (Pritchard et al., 1992) inventories have been completely revised. In total, national programmes have so far identified over 500 new IBAs in Europe, especially in the south and east of the region.

Table 2

Legal status of European globally threatened birds under international instruments

Species	World status (a)	European status (b)	SPEC category	Birds Directive Annex	Bern Conv. Annex	Bonn Conv. Annex	AEWA
Fea's Petrel	V	E	I	I	II		
Zino's Petrel	C	E	I	I	II		
Pygmy Cormorant	NT	V	2	I	II		•
Dalmatian Pelican	V	V	I	I	II	I/II	•
Lesser White-fronted Goose	V	V	I	I	II	II	•
Red-breasted Goose	V	L	I	I	II	II	•
Marbled Teal	V	E	I	I	II	II	•
Ferruginous Duck	V	V	I	I		II	•
Steller's Eider	V	L	I		II	II	•
White-headed Duck	V	E	I	I	II	II	•
Cinereous Vulture	NT	V	3	I	II	II	
Spotted Eagle	V	E	I	I	II	II	
Imperial Eagle	V	E	I	I	II	II	
Spanish Imperial Eagle	V	E	I	I	II	II	
Lesser Kestrel	V	(V)	I	I	II	II	
Corncrake	V	V	I	I	II		
Great Bustard		E	3	I	II	I/II	
Houbara Bustard	V	D	I	I	II	II	
Slender-billed Curlew	C		I	I	II	I/II	•
Audouin's Gull	CD	L	I	I	II	I	•
Madeira Laurel Pigeon	CD	V	I	I			
Dark-tailed Laurel Pigeon	V	V	I	I	II		
White-tailed Laurel Pigeon	V	V	I	I	II		
Aquatic Warbler	V	E	I	I	II	II	
Blue Chaffinch	CD	V	I	I	II		
Azores Bullfinch	(C)	(E)					

(a) as listed in *Birds to Watch 2* (Collar et al., 1994) and the IUCN Red List: Critical; Vulnerable; Conservation Dependent; Near-threatened
(b) as listed in *Birds in Europe* (Tucker and Heath, 1994): Endangered; Vulnerable; Declining; Localised
AEWA: African-Eurasian Migratory Waterbirds Agreement under the Bonn Convention
(brackets: provisional status)

Therefore, a complete pan-European review of the Important Bird Areas inventory is needed: this started in October 1994. The review will be published in a revised inventory in 1998. In the meantime Grimmett and Jones (1989) and subsequent national IBA books list some 347 sites holding globally threatened birds in the 15 member states of the European Union alone (BirdLife International, 1995).

At European level, key sites for threatened species enjoy legal protection under both the Bern Convention and the European Union's Birds and Habitats Directives (Directives 79/409/EEC and 92/43 EEC). Implementation of these provisions at national level is patchy, however. The action plans therefore lay considerable emphasis on legal protection for IBAs. This is backed by calls for safeguards such as environmental impact assessment to be built into planning systems, and for active habitat management.

Habitat conservation strategies

About half the species concerned in this report are dependent primarily on habitat conservation measures that apply across wide areas. Thus site-based conservation alone may be inadequate for these species. This applies in particular to birds of agricultural, wetland or marine habitats.

BirdLife International will therefore be publishing conservation strategies for those habitats which hold particularly high numbers of species of European conservation concern (SPECs – see above). In drawing up each habitat strategy, an assessment has been made of the importance of habitat change for each SPEC affected; particularly vulnerable species are accorded priority in considering the conservation measures to be prescribed. Where SPEC1 (globally threatened) species are concerned, they are listed in Table 3.

Table 3

Globally threatened species accorded priority in drawing up habitat conservation strategies for birds

Species	Priority	Habitat conservation strategies
Fea's Petrel	A	Marine (Macaronesian seas)
Zino's Petrel	A	Marine (Macaronesian seas)
Pygmy Cormorant	B	Coastal wetlands
Dalmatian Pelican	A A	Inland wetlands Coastal wetlands
Lesser White-fronted Goose	A A	Inland wetlands Agricultural habitats (dry grass and ext cereals)
Red-breasted Goose	A A	Inland wetlands Agricultural habitats (int arable and grass)
Marbled Teal	A A	Inland wetlands Coastal wetlands
Ferruginous Duck	A A	Inland wetlands Coastal
Steller's Eider	A	Marine (NW and European seas)
White-headed Duck	A	Inland wetlands
Cinereous Vulture	D	Agricultural habitats (alpine grass)
Greater Spotted Eagle	A	Agricultural habitats (wet grass)
Imperial Eagle	A	Agricultural habitats (pastoral woodland)
Spanish Imperial Eagle	A B	Agricultural habitats (pasture woods) Coastal wetlands

Lesser Kestrel	B	Agricultural habitats
Corncrake	A	Agricultural habitats
Great Bustard	A	Agricultural habitats (dry grasslands)
Slender-billed Curlew	A A	Inland wetlands Coastal wetlands
Audouin's Gull	A A	Marine (Mediterranean and Black Sea) Coastal wetlands
Aquatic Warbler	A A B	Agricultural habitats (wet grassland) Inland wetlands Coastal wetlands

The habitat conservation strategies are:
Marine: *i. NW and European Seas; ii. Macaronesian Atlantic; iii. Mediterranean and Black seas*
Coastal wetlands
Inland wetlands
Moorland, mires and tundra
Lowland Atlantic and central heathlands
Boreal and temperate forests
Mediterranean forests and heathlands
Agricultural habitats: *i. intensive arable and mixed farmland; ii. perennial crops; iii. pastoral woodland; iv. rice cultivations; v. wet grassland; vi. dry grasslands; vii. pseudo-steppe and arid habitats; viii. mountains, rocky hills and alpine grasslands*

The action plans highlight the importance of agricultural habitats, and therefore agricultural practices. Gross changes in habitat stimulated by market or policy shifts clearly have an impact on species such as Great Bustard, Corncrake and Lesser Kestrel. However, some species are extraordinarily sensitive to apparently minor alterations such as changes to stocking density or hay mowing methods. The impact of relatively small policy decisions can be very significant on the ground, and our understanding of these effects in detail remains inadequate.

The plans do, however, make detailed recommendations on agriculture policy and practice where research has been undertaken and understanding permits. In any case, they draw attention to a range of general measures aimed at reversing or mitigating the negative impact of general trends in agriculture.

Most work to date has been on changes necessary to agriculture policy in the European Union. Here the greatest scope for conservation is through payments to farmers for sympathetic management, whereby specific environmental goals are delivered. Policies such as the Agri-environment Regulation 2078/92 and related measures are increasingly applied, although often the measures prescribed are in insufficient detail or the incentives inadequate to ensure maximum conservation benefit.

Political and economic developments in Europe, including accession of more countries to the European Union, will lead to further development of the economies of "marginal" areas through financial assistance. As central and east European countries undergo transition to a market economy, pressure on natural and farmed habitats and intensification or abandonment of farmed land may be expected. However, policies that are being pursued to adjust farming structures, for example, granting aid for farm amalgamation and development, could be used to benefit the environment, and avoid causing incidental damage.

Implementation at national level

In at least three European states, national action planning is an established basis for the conservation of threatened species.

In the Netherlands, the Ministry of Agriculture, Nature Management and Fisheries has issued species conservation plans for Wall plants, Butterflies, Grey Partridge *Perdix perdix*, Black Grouse *Tetrao tetrix*, Spoonbill *Platalea leucorodia* and Otter *Lutra lutra* following the prescriptions of the Nature Policy Plan of the Netherlands. Plans for Crane *Grus grus* and Barn Owl *Tyto alba* are presently being prepared. In most cases a small working group is formed in which the plan is discussed. Once confirmed by the Minister of Agriculture, Nature Management and Fisheries, the conservation plans become official governmental plans. However, it is uncertain whether this approach will be continued in future (Winkelman, *in litt.*).

In the United Kingdom, Species Action Plans are being produced for 188 bird species by the RSPB (the BirdLife partner in the United Kingdom), in association with the Joint Nature Conservation Committee, the three country conservation agencies and, where appropriate, the Wildfowl and Wetlands Trust. The species covered are of particular conservation importance due to their rare, localised, declining or internationally important populations. The statutory conservation agencies have agreed to use these plans as a starting point for the development of their own species action plans. In the case of the three globally threatened species which occur in the United Kingdom, outline plans have been published by the body set up by the government to advise on its implementation of the Biodiversity Convention.

The Spanish Law for Nature Conservation of 1989 has established a process of listing threatened species under different levels of threat, and requires the preparation of recovery plans for endangered species. These plans are regional and once finalised they are published as a Royal Decree and become legally binding. In 1995 a recovery plan for the White-headed Duck in Castilla-La Mancha entered into law. This is the first legally recognised plan to be explicitly derived from the European action plans presented here. When all the regional plans for one species are in place, the Directorate-General for Nature Conservation (DGN, formerly ICONA) organises a working group with experts and administrators from the different regions, and puts together a co-ordinated action plan which serves as the basis for the regional recovery plan. An official recovery plan has already been produced for the Lammergeier *Gypaetus barbatus*, as have co-ordinated action plans for the Spanish Imperial Eagle, White-headed Duck, Cinereous Vulture and Black Stork *Ciconia nigra*.

One of the most important limiting factors in implementing the plans is funds. The role of international agencies and bilateral arrangements between states is thus crucial. The European Union has funded work on 16 of the 23 species under consideration since 1989 (See Table 4). The introduction of the LIFE fund from 1992 has ensured that funding is increasingly priority-driven.

Whilst implementation of the plans is largely in the hands of national and local players, some international co-ordination is needed. It is suggested that the international institutions with primary responsibility for species conservation in Europe participate in promoting and reviewing implementation. In particular, the European Commission and appropriate European Union agencies, the Council of Europe through the Bern Convention, and the Bonn Convention are encouraged to co-ordinate their responses to this challenge.

Review

Finally, it must be emphasised that the action plans presented here are not the final word on the conservation of these species. Most of these species are in rapid decline, or are highly vulnerable to future changes in their environment, or are showing early signs of recovery from a parlous situation. Thus it is essential that the action plans are reviewed in the light of future changes to their conservation status.

Furthermore, some of the species are very poorly known in terms of their population sizes, geographical ranges or the factors affecting them. As our understanding improves, so the plans should be modified to take this into account.

Each plan has a suggested review period. This is based on the likelihood of changes occurring in the near future affecting each species status or our understanding of them.

Table 4

European Union funding for actions for globally threatened birds allocated the period 1986-95 (B = Belgium, D = Germany, E = Spain, F = France, GR = Greece, I = Italy, IR = Republic of Ireland, UK = United Kingdom)

Fund Commencement date	ACE/ACNAT 1986-92	LIFE 1992	LIFE 1993	LIFE 1994	LIFE 1995	LIFE 1996
Fea's Petrel					P	P
Zino's Petrel				P		
Dalmatian Pelican	GR					
White-headed Duck	E, GR					
Cinereous Vulture	E, GR	GR				
Spanish Imperial Eagle		E				
Lesser Kestrel					I	
Corncrake				B, F, IR, UK		
Great Bustard	E	D	P			
Houbara Bustard				E		
Slender-billed Curlew		all				GR, I
Madeira Laurel Pigeon			P	P		
Dark-tailed Laurel Pigeon				E		
White-tailed Laurel Pigeon				E		
Blue Chaffinch				E		
Azores Bullfinch				P		

Source: European Commission

Acknowledgements

This project is a collective effort which would have not been possible without the collaboration of numerous people and organisations. BirdLife International wishes to thank the European Commission for its financial support and for actively promoting the planning process among European Union member states. The Council of Europe provided a very effective means of consulting non-European Union range states; publication of the plans by the Council of Europe is particularly welcome.

The following BirdLife partners, NGOs and institutions organised and in some cases provided financial assistance for workshops: OTOP (Poland), Universidad de La Laguna (Spain), SEO (Spain), WWF Greece, HOS (Greece), MME (Hungary), CPCN (Morocco), LIPU (Italy), SPNE (Greece), RSPB (UK), and Ecosystems (Poland).

The following people were particularly instrumental in one way or another: Lesley Ashcroft, Yvonne Bagnall, Gerard Boere, Nicola Crockford, Martin Davies, Eladio Fernandez-Galiano, Vladimir Galushin, Petar Iankov, Pavol Kanuch, Carol Kemp, Barbara Lombatti, Carlos Martin-Novella, Alexander Mischenko, Szabolcs Nagy, Micheál Ó Bríain, Jacek Szostakowski, Graham Tucker, Carlota Viada and Murat Yarar.

Staff of the BirdLife International Secretariat provided invaluable assistance in various ways, with thanks in particular to Colin Bibby, Duncan Brooks, Beverley Childs, Lindsay Derry, Melanie Heath, Kathleen Rosewarne and Zoltán Waliczky.

Janine van Vessem co-ordinated the input of Wetlands International and special thanks are due to her and her colleagues.

Leighton Bell, Joan Bird and Susan Cherry helped as volunteers with subediting.

Finally, we are indebted to the steering committee, the action plan compilers and no less than 370 contributors for their invaluable contributions to the conception, development and drafting of the plans.

Action plan for Fea's Petrel (*Pterodroma feae*)

Reviews

This document should be reviewed and updated by BirdLife International every four years. An emergency review will be undertaken if sudden major environmental changes, liable to affect the population, occur within the species' range.

Geographical scope

Mainly the island of Bugio in the archipelago of the Desertas (Madeira, Portugal), but action is also to be undertaken in the other islands of the Desertas, especially Deserta Grande, and potentially, the Azores.

Summary

Fea's Petrel *Pterodroma feae* is an extremely rare and threatened Macaronesian endemic petrel, known to exist only on Bugio and some of the Cape Verde Islands.

The first record of this petrel was of two specimens obtained by Dr Robert Frere from his correspondent in Madeira in 1853, though there is a specimen in the Natural History Museum (Tring, UK), collected in 1852, whose origin is uncertain. Fea's Petrel is almost impossible to distinguish at sea from Zino's Petrel *P. madeira*.

Not much is known about the population on the Cape Verde Islands, though there are estimates of a total population of up to 1000 breeding pairs. In the Madeira archipelago it nests only on Bugio, and the greatest concentration is on the southern plateau of this island. A few nest on the northern plateau, but, as this is not accessible by foot and extremely difficult to reach even by helicopter, that area is almost impossible to study.

Over the years, the birds have suffered predation by fishermen, but since the whole land surface of the Desertas was made a strict reserve this situation has improved dramatically.

The study of this bird is particularly important as it may well give very important insights to the life history of Zino's Petrel, whose status is precarious.

Threats and limiting factors

Degradation of habitat due to overgrazing by goats and rabbits – high

Predation by Yellow-legged Gulls –– unknown, potentially high

Disturbance caused by rabbits – unknown, potentially high

Human predation – low, historically high

Conservation priorities

Ensure continued financial support for the work on the Desertas from the European Union – high

Removal of goats, rabbits and cats from Deserta Grande and Bugio – high

Biological studies including annual monitoring of the breeding population – high

Provide shelter facilities on Bugio for wardens and researchers – high

Introduction

Fea's Petrel, also called Bugio Freira in Madeira and Gongon in the Cape Verde Islands, is considered to be a globally threatened species classified as Vulnerable in *Birds to Watch 2* (Collar et al., 1994). Previously, it was listed as Rare in the African Red Data Book (Collar and Stuart, 1985) and in the *IUCN Red List of Threatened Animals* (Groombridge, 1993). It is included in Annex I of the European Union's Wild Birds Directive and in Appendix II of the Bern Convention.

A very significant step towards the conservation of Fea's Petrel was the declaration in 1990 of the Nature Reserve of the Desertas Islands, which falls under the umbrella of the Natural Park of

Madeira. Legal protection is effective now and human predation of the islands' seabirds has been halted through the wardening of the breeding colonies.

The real challenge is to manage the habitat in order to restore the natural conditions that existed on the Desertas prior to the arrival of man and domestic animals in 1420. This entails promoting the regeneration of the natural vegetation and thus enhancing its capacity to provide a breeding place for large numbers of seabirds. If this goal is achieved the Desertas will become one of the finest bird sanctuaries in the world.

This action plan is targeted at any organisations or individuals that wish to undertake conservation or research work in the area, and provides a technical framework for future management.

Background information

Distribution and population

The only known place in Europe where Fea's Petrel breeds is on Bugio, southernmost island of the Desertas. The majority of burrows are to be found on the southern plateau, despite the fact that the northern plateau is more extensive, though more arid and with less vegetation (Zino and Zino, 1986). On the basis of sub-fossil *Pterodroma* bones, the species is believed formerly to have bred on Deserta Grande, Porto Santo and the main island of Madeira (Pieper, 1985). It seems increasingly likely that it breeds in the Azores (Bibby and del Nevo, 1991). Outside Europe it breeds in the Cape Verde Islands, where the population is believed to be of 1000 breeding birds or roughly 500 pairs (Hazevoet, 1994).

The population on Bugio is considered to be around 150 to 200 breeding pairs and appears to be stable (Zino and Biscoito, 1994).

Life history

Taxonomic status

The species belongs to the gadfly-petrels *Pterodroma*, the largest group of tubenosed birds, with 25 species (Warham, 1990). Within the gadfly-petrels it forms part of the Soft-plumaged

Petrel complex, with two distinct forms in the North Atlantic, *feae* and *madeira*, and one, *mollis*, in the southern oceans (Bourne, 1983).

Fea's Petrel was originally identified as *Pterodroma mollis* by Harcourt in 1855, then included in a distinct species, *P. feae*, by Salvadori in 1900, and then described as a dubious race *P. m. deserta* by Mathews in 1934 (Mathews, 1934; W. R. P. Bourne, *in litt.*, 1993). More recently it has been proposed as a separate species under the name of *P. feae* (Bourne, 1983). Zino and Zino (1986) showed that Fea's Petrel is heavier and considerably bigger, especially in bill size, than its relative Zino's Petrel *P. madeira*, and endorsed the proposal to treat this bird as a different species.

Breeding

On Bugio, the birds return to their breeding grounds at about the end of June and laying starts about 20 July, with breeding activity reaching its peak during early August. Birds enter the breeding sites after dark and call loudly if there is no moon, falling silent when the moon rises (Zino and Zino, 1986). The nesting burrows have varying entrance sizes and depths: the majority are more than one metre in length, the nest-chamber being 30 to 60 cm below the surface (Zino and Zino, 1986).

Feeding

The species is essentially pelagic and highly adapted for living out of contact with land. Food is likely to consist of fish, cephalopods and crustaceans, often as plankton, but there is very little specific information available on diet and feeding behaviour. The birds can often be seen from the shore by day, flying and sometimes feeding.

Habitat requirements

On the Desertas, Fea's Petrel breeds in areas where there is a thick layer of earth covered with grass and *Mesembryanthemum*. On and around the southern plateau of Bugio there are places with earth more than one metre thick, and it is essential that a sufficient depth is available for the birds to construct burrows (Zino and Zino, 1986).

Threats and limiting factors

Availability of breeding grounds limited by habitat degradation

Bugio is heavily overgrazed by goats and rabbits, which are responsible for the loss of vegetation and the consequent soil erosion by wind and rain (Zino and Biscoito, 1994). On Bugio, the main breeding grounds lie on the southern plateau. The northern plateau is very much larger, but there is much more erosion and less vegetation cover. It has also been suggested that regeneration of the flora would make the ground softer for the petrels to burrow into.

There is fossil evidence that Fea's Petrel was once dispersed more widely within the archipelago, for fossils have been found on Deserta Grande, Madeira and Porto Santo. Whether or not their disappearance from areas other than Bugio is due to alterations in the habitat is not known.

Importance: high

Disturbance by rabbits

Rabbits are abundant on Bugio and have been shown to cause much disturbance to breeding burrows of *Pterodroma* species in New Zealand (invading and modifying burrows, digging new entrances and inter-connections), causing considerable stress to breeding pairs and resulting in the abandonment of breeding sites (Chappuis et al., 1994).

Importance: unknown, potentially high

Predation and disturbance by Yellow-legged Gulls

The Yellow-legged Gull (*Larus cachinnans atlantis*) population in the Desertas has increased markedly, with some 500 to 700 pairs on Bugio and approximately 4 000 pairs on Ilhéu Chão. There are also big colonies on the main island of Madeira. This is largely due to the poorly controlled dumping of rubbish in Madeira. In 1986 one netted Fea's Petrel was released at sea in daylight off Bugio; a Yellow-legged Gull immediately dived down from the cliffs above and attacked the bird, which managed to escape only with the greatest difficulty (Zino and Zino, 1986). The gulls hunt by day and – more dangerously for Fea's Petrel – by night. Young birds that leave their

burrow to exercise their wings are thus exposed to predation by them. Gulls are a problem throughout the archipelago; they have been observed taking Bulwer's Petrels on many occasions and hunting by moonlight (Zino and Biscoito, 1994).

Importance: unknown, potentially high

Human predation

Since the Desertas became a total land reserve this threat has been much reduced, but continued wardening is still of the utmost importance.

Importance: low, historically high

Conservation status and recent conservation measures

Fea's Petrel is classed as Vulnerable in the Portuguese Red Data Book (Cabral et al., 1990). It is a protected species in Portugal under Decreto-Lei 75/91. The establishment of the nature reserve of the Desertas Islands in 1990 was followed by an increase in wardening and surveillance. The reserve has been financed by the European Union from the beginning. The island of Bugio is listed as an important bird area (Grimmett and Jones, 1989) and the Desertas have been designated as a special protection area by the Portuguese Government under Article 4 of the European Union's Wild Birds Directive.

A survey of the breeding population has been carried out on a regular basis since 1967 through the mapping and recording of active burrows. Up to 1994, more than 400 birds were ringed (F. Zino, *in litt.*, 1993).

In 1993, a feasibility study on the removal of problem animals from the islands of Madeira was carried out by Management International Ltd (New Zealand) at the request of BirdLife International (Bell, 1993).

Aims and objectives

Aims

To protect and maintain the breeding population of Fea's Petrel and to promote its expansion to all the available habitat on the island of Bugio and, eventually, to Deserta Grande.

Objectives

1. **Policy and legislation**

1.1. *To ensure an adequate legal and financial framework for the conservation of threatened species in Portugal*

1.1.1. Incorporate species recovery plans into regional and national legislation

Recovery plans are included as legal measures in other countries. Consideration should be given to incorporating the action plan for this species into appropriate legislation.

Priority: low
Time-scale: medium/long

1.1.2. Ensure continued financial support from the European Union for the Desertas and that some funds are directed towards the conservation of this species

The management of the Nature Reserve of the Desertas Islands has received financial support from the European Union during the period 1986-96 through the ACNAT and LIFE programmes. A further application to the European Union should be prepared to make sure that this funding continues in the future.

Priority: high
Time-scale: ongoing

1.1.3. Develop and implement a strategy for addressing the issues affecting this species while at sea

A Conservation Strategy for Birds of Marine Habitats in Europe is currently being prepared by BirdLife International, to be published in 1996. It will identify broad measures for the conservation of birds in their marine habitats, including Fea's Petrel in the Macaronesian Seas. This strategy should be used as a basis for additional actions for this species.

Priority: medium
Time-scale: ongoing

2. **Species and habitat conservation**

2.1. *To improve conditions for the breeding birds by removing herbivores and predators*

2.1.1. Undertake a feasibility study for the eradication of problem animals from Deserta Grande and Bugio

An assessment of the rabbit and goat populations on Deserta Grande and Bugio was made by Wildlife Management International Ltd in 1993. The rabbits are short of food and would be very susceptible to a poisoning campaign. Brodifacum, which is effective against rats, can be used against rabbits. Part of the terrain is easy but the cliff faces are a major challenge. The eradication of rabbits is a practical objective and could be achieved to a level of 95% in three months. Follow-up spot poisoning and shooting would complete the task.

Goats were presumably introduced to the Desertas by seafarers to provide food for future visits. As on many oceanic islands, these mammals now threaten the indigenous plants and animals. Overgrazing is leading to serious soil erosion and the majority of the indigenous flora is restricted to inaccessible cliffs. Goat control should be carried out in combination with rabbit control; removal of just one species would lead to a population increase of the other.

Goat numbers are estimated by reserve wardens and local observers at 250 on Deserta Grande and 80 to 100 on Bugio. The islands have no woody cover so the goats are very vulnerable to shooting. Their only escape is to take to inaccessible cliffs, where they could still be shot from a helicopter.

Priority: high
Time-scale: Completed

2.1.2. Pursue the eradication of rabbits, goats and cats from Deserta Grande

Following the recommendations of the feasibility study, a control programme should be carried out humanely and in a way which is compatible with the conservation of the seabirds and other species that exist on the island and in the surrounding waters. This programme should be managed by a specialist team under close supervision from the Nature Reserve. It is recommended that this starts with Deserta Grande, since access is easier and it offers accommodation facilities. Rabbit control would be beneficial not only to Fea's Petrel and other petrel species, but also to the flora of the island.

The small population of feral cats on Deserta Grande should be removed as soon as possible and certainly not later than the removal of the rabbits. If cats are not removed at this time it is likely that they will change from their present food source (rabbits) to others, such as birds and lizards.

Priority: high
Time-scale: short/medium

2.1.3. Pursue the eradication of goats and rabbits from Bugio

There is a population of about 80 to 100 goats on Bugio. Unlike the "mixed bag" which is present on Deserta Grande, those on Bugio are all-black and appear to be different from the normal feral goats. They are rumoured to be of very old stock, and whilst this is doubtful, their origins are being investigated.

Priority: high
Time-scale: medium

2.1.4. Explore potential destinations for relocated goats

Some specimens should be taken into captivity before eradication, for research and tourist purposes. The possibility of sending some to other countries upon request should also be explored.

Priority: high
Time-scale: medium

2.1.5. Develop a contingency plan for the accidental introduction or reintroduction of problem animals (particularly rats)

The Natural Park of Madeira should prepare a contingency plan for use in emergencies (e.g. shipwrecks on the Desertas Nature Reserve) to prevent unwanted animals becoming established.

Priority: medium
Time-scale: short/medium

2.1.6. Prevent the expansion of the Yellow-legged Gull population on the Desertas

The population explosion of Yellow-legged Gulls over the last 10 to 15 years now poses a serious threat to Fea's Petrel and to other seabirds such as Bulwer's Petrel *Bulweria bulweri*. A culling programme should be started at the gull colonies of Ilhéu Chão and Bugio by narcotising birds and sterilising eggs.

Priority: medium
Time-scale: medium

2.2. *To prevent human disturbance and disruption to the breeding cycle*

2.2.1. Wardening of breeding colonies

The Desertas are already wardened and this has significantly reduced the killing of seabirds by man. The presence of permanent wardens must be maintained and increased, under the auspices of the Natural Park of Madeira.

Priority: medium
Time-scale: ongoing

2.2.2. Provide shelter facilities in Bugio

It would be extremely useful to reconstruct the old whale lookout at Ponta da Agulha. This would provide shelter for the wardens during their missions and also for the researchers or other visitors to the island. On the southern plateau of Bugio a small stone shelter would be very useful for work on Fea's Petrel. The existing facilities on Deserta Grande have proved to be essential for the wardening and management of the Nature Reserve.

Priority: high
Time-scale: medium

2.3. *To promote the expansion of Fea's Petrel to other suitable areas in the Desertas*

2.3.1. Enhance the regeneration of natural vegetation

The natural vegetation must be allowed to regenerate in order to build up enough soil to permit the digging of burrows by the petrels. Replanting of selected species native to the island should be done experimentally; seeds or cuttings should be used wherever possible, but if this is not feasible then whole plants should be brought from the nearest source. In some areas supporting dry walls could be built to slow down erosion and loss of topsoil.

Priority: low/medium
Time-scale: medium/long

2.3.2. Provide artificial burrows for breeding

An experiment should be undertaken to construct artificial burrows in selected areas on both Deserta Grande and Bugio after the rabbits have been removed. The artificial burrows should be carefully designed to fit the species' needs. Care needs to be taken not to cause disturbance or make the erosion problems worse.

Priority: medium
Time-scale: medium

3.   Monitoring and research

3.1. *To undertake an annual monitoring programme of the Fea's Petrel breeding population*

3.1.1. Monitoring of breeding numbers and breeding success

Monitoring has been going on for several years and needs to be continued. Ideally, two surveys should be carried out annually, at the beginning and at the end of each breeding season. During the first survey the number of pairs that attempt to breed should be recorded by counting occupied burrows. The second survey serves to determine the breeding success, that is the number of fledged young. However, it is recognised that this may prove impracticable given the difficulty of the terrain. Maps should be made, at the appropriate scale, of the distribution of seabird breeding colonies on Bugio.

Priority: high
Time-scale: ongoing

3.1.2. Monitoring the effectiveness of the habitat management experiments

The areas where artificial burrows are made should be visited at the beginning of the breeding season to verify acceptance by Fea's Petrels or other species.

Priority: medium
Time-scale: medium/long

3.2. *To evaluate the efficiency of the control programme for problem animals and to monitor the regeneration of vegetation*

The process of eradicating goats and rabbits provides an excellent opportunity to follow the evolution of the ungrazed vegetation. Photographs from fixed points need to be taken to show the landscape before and after eradication. The whole process of vegetation recovery should be monitored with scientific accuracy. Wardens on Deserta Grande should maintain constant vigilance for rabbit and goat signs after the eradication campaign, and take appropriate action to remove any remaining animals. Specialists should pay annual visits to the island for two years following the main campaign.

Priority: medium
Time-scale: medium/long

3.3. *To promote research initiatives which are of direct application for the conservation of Fea's Petrel*

3.3.1. Determine taxonomic status

The relationships between the forms of *Pterodroma* from Bugio, the Cape Verde Islands and Madeira need to be clarified by means of the most recent taxonomic techniques, that is DNA fingerprinting or mitochondrial DNA analysis. This study has already started, but must be continued until some conclusions are reached and published.

Priority: low
Time-scale: ongoing

3.3.2. Determine population dynamics and predict the species' capacity to expand and colonise new areas

Ongoing studies on population dynamics should continue and be reported. Regular analysis of recapture data should enable the population to be assessed and monitored more precisely in the future.

Priority: low
Time-scale: medium

3.3.3. Carry out searches of other potential breeding areas

Recent records of the species from the Azores (Bibby and del Nevo, 1991; Luis Monteiro, *in litt.*)

give some hope that new European colonies may be found. The University of the Azores is undertaking small-scale efforts to obtain further records under a seabird conservation project funded by the LIFE fund and the RSPB. If this leads to significant further records, a larger, systematic survey should be carried out.

Priority: medium
Time-scale: medium

4.   Public awareness and training

4.1.   *To increase the awareness of the Madeiran public of Fea's Petrel and the Desertas Nature Reserve, and to improve their attitude towards their conservation*

4.1.1. Launch a public relations campaign prior to the beginning of the programme to eradicate goats and rabbits

A public relations campaign, accompanied by the production of suitable materials (leaflets, posters, etc.), will be necessary to ensure that the reasons for the eradication programme are well understood. This is important to prevent local opposition to the eradication programme.

Priority: high
Time-scale: short/medium

4.1.2. Increase public awareness

The natural values of the Nature Reserve should be publicised and promoted, and the possibility of organised visits by boat for a limited number of people should be explored. A small information centre about the archipelago of the Desertas should be set up either on Deserta Grande or on Madeira, including information on Fea's Petrel.

Priority: medium
Time-scale: medium/long

4.1.2 Training of wardens

The wardens should be given a more positive role than just policing. They should be trained to carry out monitoring, management and some of the technical aspects of research programmes.

Priority: medium
Time-scale: short/medium

Action plan for Zino's Petrel (*Pterodroma madeira*)

Reviews

This document should be reviewed and updated by BirdLife International every two years. An emergency review will be undertaken if sudden major environmental changes, liable to affect the population, occur within the species' range.

Geographical scope

The island of Madeira in the Madeiran archipelago (Portugal).

Summary

Zino's Petrel or Madeira Freira *Pterodroma madeira* is Europe's rarest breeding seabird. It is endemic to the island of Madeira where it breeds in the central mountain massif. The breeding population is estimated to be down to a precarious 20 to 30 pairs.

By 1960, there were so few records of this species many believed it to be extinct. It was rediscovered in 1969 by a local ornithologist, P. A. Zino, after some fascinating detective work using the tape-recorded calls of Fea's Petrel. Immediately following the rediscovery the newly found breeding ledges were plundered by a visiting (and accredited) specimen- and egg-collector who took three adult breeding birds and six eggs. At a later date the eggs of Fea's Petrel and Zino's Petrel in the collection of the Museu Municipal do Funchal were also stolen.

The reduced breeding colony remained under discrete study in an attempt not to publicise the breeding location which might again fall foul of collectors. In 1986, the colony was found not to be breeding successfully due to predation by rats. As a result a Freira Conservation Project was set up with outside help to try and contain the rat problem. The situation was further aggravated in 1990 when a cat (or cats) killed 10 adults, possibly breeding birds, on one ledge.

Despite current efforts, the position of these beautiful birds is still very precarious and they need all the help available to save them from extinction.

Threats and limiting factors

Predation by rats and cats – critical

Habitat degradation limiting availability of suitable nest sites – high

Human predation and disturbance – high

Conservation priorities

Continue and increase the rat and cat control programmes – essential

Establish a management plan for the National Park of Madeira – high

Seek funds from relevant international organisations, especially the European Union – high

Purchase of the breeding area to ensure its appropriate management – high

Removal of herbivores from the breeding area – high

Increase wardening, particularly during the breeding season – high

Continue research, especially monitoring of the breeding population – high

Introduction

Zino's Petrel *Pterodroma madeira*, also known as Madeira Freira, or just as Freira, is one of the most threatened birds in the world. It is classified as Endangered in the African Red Data Book (Collar and Stuart, 1985) and in the *IUCN Red List of Threatened Animals* (Groombridge, 1993), and as Critical in *Birds to Watch 2* (Collar et al., 1994). It is included in Annex I of the European Union's Wild Birds Directive and in Appendix II of the Bern Convention.

By 1960, there were so few records of the bird that many believed it to be extinct. It was rediscovered in 1969 by P. A. Zino, who played a tape of the Bugio birds to a shepherd from Curral das Freiras; he immediately recognised the call, and led the researchers to the only known breeding area.

Given the species' rarity and the threat posed by cats and rats, the Freira Conservation Project was launched in 1986 and has continued until the present day. Despite the limited funds available, the project has achieved much, with no fewer than eight chicks being reared in 1993 after the failed breeding attempts in the mid-eighties.

This action plan provides a technical framework for future management. Although not a legally binding document, it is hoped that the Madeiran and Portuguese authorities will accept its recommendations, and that it will help to integrate the different institutions and organisations involved, so that effective measures are taken to prevent the extinction of Zino's Petrel.

Background information

Distribution and population

Zino's Petrel is restricted to the island of Madeira, where it breeds in a relatively small area in the high central massif. Breeding has been recorded on three ledges, the "main ledge", the "small ledge" and the "1987 ledge", which can only be reached with the help of climbing equipment. Breeding on the small ledge stopped several years ago. When feeding, and throughout the non-breeding period, the birds are dispersed at sea, although the distribution is not known.

The breeding population is currently very small and estimated to be no more than 30 pairs (Zino and Zino, 1986). Imber (1989) suggested a total population of 250 to 400 birds, based on the number of birds flying over the colony on three nights in June 1989 and on comparing this with work carried out on the Taiko P. magentae. This could be an overestimate and should be treated cautiously.

H. Pieper has found subfossil bones together with those of Fea's Petrel in a low-level cave in eastern Madeira, so Zino's Petrel was doubtless originally more numerous and widespread (W. R. P. Bourne, in litt., 1993).

Life history

Taxonomic status

The bird was first discovered by Schmitz in 1903, and described as a race of P. mollis by Mathews (1934), together with P. m. deserta in the Desertas Islands and P. m. feae in the Cape Verde Islands, although most subsequent authors considered P. m. deserta and P. m. feae to be inseparable. More recently Bourne (1983) suggested that the three subspecies be treated as separate species, P. mollis, P. feae and P. madeira, on the basis of their size and behavioural differences.

Zino and Zino (1986) compared measurements of Fea's and Zino's Petrels and found Fea's to be heavier and larger in all respects, especially bill size and wing length. They concluded that the two should be treated as separate species. Also, there is a difference of about two months in their laying periods, even though their nesting sites are only about 50 km apart.

Breeding

The gadfly-petrels, to which Zino's Petrel belongs, are highly social and when courting tend to congregate at night in one particular area and call repeatedly, although they also call elsewhere. In the case of Zino's Petrel, courting occurs over the main breeding area, during the late evening and early morning hours (Zino and Zino, 1986).

The birds return from sea to their breeding grounds in late March or early April and laying takes place from mid-May to early June. Nests are located in burrows about 140 cm deep, situated on well vegetated ledges which are generally inaccessible to man, goats and sheep. A single egg is laid, and hatching takes place in late July and early August, with the young usually fledging in late September or early October (Zino and Zino, 1986). Breeding performance on the main ledge in previous years is shown in Table 2.1. Breeding success on the 1987 ledge before the destruction of the colony by a cat is not known.

Table 2.1

Breeding performance of Zino's Petrel (Zino et al., 1993). In 1987 one bird fledged from the "1987 ledge"

Year	No. of chicks fledged on "main ledge"
1985	0
1986	0
1987	0
1988	0
1989	2
1990	3
1991	4
1992	4
1993	8
1994	5
1995	4

Feeding

Zino's Petrel, as with other *Pterodroma* species, probably feeds on small squid and fish. The vomit of one bird handled in 1987 contained remains of cephalopods, bioluminescent myctophid fish *Electrona rissoi*, and amphipod and isopod crustaceans (Zino et al., 1989).

Habitat requirements

The breeding areas are ledges at 1600 metres altitude in the central mountain massif, which are still rich in endemic flora because they are inaccessible to goats. It is essential that there is sufficient earth on the ledges to allow the birds to burrow and make their nests (Zino et al., 1994). Little is known about this species' location and requirements outside the breeding season.

Threats and limiting factors

Mortality caused by predators

i.   Rats

Madeira is severely infested with rats *Rattus rattus* and this problem extends to the high-altitude mountain areas (Zino and Zino, 1986). The first evidence of rat predation was obtained in 1985, when the remains of an egg eaten by rats were

found. In 1986 a dead chick was found, clearly eaten by rats (Zino, 1991). Rats abound in the forest below the bird colonies.

Clearing all the rats from the area is not a practical solution and is probably not even possible. It has therefore been the policy of the Conservation Project to protect the known breeding ledges as much as is possible, using poison (Klerat), and this has met with success. Unfortunately not all the breeding areas are known, but it would no doubt be beneficial if the protected area were to be increased. Poison should certainly be put down around those ledges where the petrels are known to have nested in the past but no longer do.

Importance: critical

ii.   Cats

In July 1991, the remains of 10 dead Zino's Petrels were found on the 1987 ledge, all of them apparently killed by cats. Given the small size of the petrel's population and the ability of cats to hunt by both night and day and to reach the most inaccessible places, these predators are now a significant threat.

Importance: critical

Habitat degradation limiting availability of suitable nest sites

The two known Zino's Petrel colonies are located in places which are totally inaccessible to goats and sheep. Although it may appear that there is plenty of suitable nesting habitat, heavy grazing by these animals has caused large reductions in its availability (Zino et al., 1994). Freira burrows are very vulnerable to trampling by goats and sheep, which cause erosion and reduce soil depth (Imber, 1989).

Importance: high

Human predation and disturbance

In the past, shepherds are known to have taken juveniles to eat. Collectors now pose a much more significant threat and are known to have taken adults and eggs in recent years. Following the discovery of the breeding site in 1969, a visiting ornithologist collected three birds and six eggs, and in 1970 the site was raided again (Zino and Zino, 1986). This problem appears to be under control. Limited funds have made it possible to have the area wardened, but more manpower is needed to increase this wardening.

Importance: high

Conservation status and recent conservation measures

This species is classified as Endangered in the Portuguese Red Data Book (Cabral et al., 1990). It is also a protected species under Portuguese law (Decreto-Lei 75/91).

Given the species' rarity and the threat posed by rats, the Freira Conservation Project was launched in 1986 with the participation of the Madeira Natural Park, the Funchal Municipal Museum, ICI Agro-Chemicals, Agricultural Development and Advisory Service (ADAS) and the International Council for Bird Preservation (ICBP, now BirdLife International). The project is run by the BirdLife International representative in Madeira, Dr Francis Zino, and has been funded by Zeneca Agro in Lisbon and the RSPB. The project has concentrated on reducing the threat of predation of eggs and the young by rodents, but has also involved wardening, studies of the birds themselves and cat control.

There is also a LIFE-funded project running from October 1994 to December 1996: Conservação e Recuperação de Espécis e Habitats na Madeira covering a range of complementary conservation activities in the National Park.

Rat control

Following evidence of predation by rats, a rodent control programme was initiated in 1987, with the aim of reducing the population of rats in the vicinity of the birds' breeding ledges. Bait boxes have been positioned on, above, and below the main ledge. Overall, the rodent control campaign is effective, substantially reducing and controlling the rat population throughout the egg-laying and incubation periods, and during the first weeks after hatching (Swash and Zino, 1991).

Cat control

Following the damage caused by cats on the 1987 ledge in 1991, a trapping scheme was started using Fuller cat traps. Up to 1993, four cats had been captured.

Site protection

The breeding site is an Important Bird Area (Grimmett and Jones, 1989) which has been designated as a Special Protection Area under the European Union's Wild Birds Directive by the Portuguese Government. The whole area is included in the Madeira Natural Park.

Biological studies

Bird studies include examination of Zino's Petrels' nesting burrows, ringing of birds, and observations at night. The birds are captured during the night and ringed with incoloy rings provided specifically for the project. The chicks are also ringed if they can be safely removed from their burrows.

Aims and objectives

Aims

To increase the breeding population to at least 40 pairs by the year 2000, by eliminating the factors which are adversely affecting the species.

Objectives

1. **Policy and legislation**

1.1. *To ensure an adequate legal and financial framework for the conservation of Zino's Petrel*

1.1.1. Incorporate species recovery plans into regional and national legislation

Recovery plans are included as legal measures in other countries. Consideration should be given to incorporating the action plan for Zino's Petrel into appropriate legislation.

Priority: low
Time-scale: medium/long

1.1.2. Establish the management plan for the Natural Park of Madeira

A comprehensive management plan should be developed for approval by the regional authorities, and an adequate budget allocated for species and habitat conservation. Ideally, the Zino's Petrel action plan would become a part of this management plan as would the action plan for the Madeira Laurel Pigeon.

Priority: high
Time-scale: short

1.1.3. Attract funding from relevant international organisations, especially the European Union

A general application for the conservation and management of the Natural Park of Madeira should be submitted to the European Union under the LIFE regulation, including a chapter on financing the Freira Conservation Project in the years to come. This would also benefit the conservation of the endemic flora.

Priority: high
Time-scale: ongoing

1.1.4. Develop and implement a strategy for addressing the issues affecting this species while at sea

A Conservation Strategy for Birds of Marine Habitats in Europe is currently being prepared by BirdLife International to be published in 1996. It will identify broad measures for the conservation of birds in their marine habitats including Zino's Petrel in the Macaronesian Seas. This strategy should be used as a basis for additional actions for this species.

Priority: medium
Time-scale: ongoing

2.   Species and habitat protection

2.1. *To control mammalian predators*

2.1.1. Prevent predation by rodents

The programme for the control of rats on the breeding ledges and in surrounding areas, which started in 1987, should be continued and reinforced. Increased wardening would contribute to the control programme which should be expanded to all known colonies, including the 1987 ledge. The control is carried out with the anticoagulant rodenticide brodifacoum (Klerat), by placing boxes containing 1 kg of the material in 320 g wax blocks on the large ledges. The baits are checked approximately every month, and those on the main ledge are checked whenever visits are made. If new colonies are found, a preventive baiting scheme must be established.

Priority: essential
Time-scale: ongoing

2.1.2. Maintain the breeding areas free of rats

To keep the area where Zino's Petrels breed free of rats, it is necessary to take action on the likely sources of rats. Most come from the forest below, but one source in the vicinity of the breeding area is likely to be the restaurant at Pico de Areeiro, which is accessible via a tarmac road. The Madeiran authorities should inform this establishment about the potential danger of rats for the surrounding wildlife, prevent random dumping of waste and consider the provision of equipment for adequate waste management. A "take your litter home" policy should be encouraged among hikers on the Areeiro–Pico Ruivo path.

Priority: high
Time-scale: ongoing

2.1.3. Control predation by feral cats

The cat control measures implemented to date have proved very effective but the trapping effort should be considerably increased. The use of paddled leg-hold traps or kill traps, which are less conspicuous than the traditional traps and could be used more extensively, could be considered if herbivores were removed from the area.

Priority: essential
Time-scale: ongoing

2.2. *To control human access and disturbance*

2.2.1. Warden the breeding area

Wardening of the site is thought to have been an effective way of protecting the area in previous years. It is recommended that the employment of a full-time warden to patrol the area is continued, particularly during the breeding season (April to October). This person could also check the bait boxes and traps and assist when required during visits to the breeding ledges.

Priority: high
Time-scale: ongoing

2.2.2. Protect the current breeding area through purchase and management

The known breeding colonies are located on land which is private property at present, and although the land is within the Parque Natural da Madeira, there can be a conflict of interests. Efforts should be made to acquire the property where the birds breed, which would make it possible to control livestock, carry out habitat management and restrict access where necessary. The ownership of all existing and potential nesting sites should be determined.

Priority: high
Time-scale: medium/long

2.3. *To encourage an expansion of the breeding area to other suitable ledges*

2.3.1. Create and expand nesting habitat at designated sites

The feasibility of undertaking an experiment to facilitate colonisation of new breeding areas should be explored. This could be done by digging artificial burrows in potentially suitable areas, and monitoring their acceptance by petrels. Recorded calls could be broadcast at night and material from old nests (thus likely to smell of petrels) could be spread around to help attract birds. Prior to any experimentation, a thorough review of such actions for *Pterodroma* species in other parts of the world (e.g. Galapagos, Bermuda, New Zealand) should be undertaken.

Priority: low
Time-scale: medium/long

2.4. *To exclude grazing stock from the breeding area*

2.4.1. Reduce goat numbers

This would greatly benefit the natural regeneration of vegetation, including the endemic flora, and soil in the breeding area and could be achieved through a compensation scheme to the owners of livestock. Funding for such a scheme should be sought from the European Union through the Agri-environment regulation 2078/92. Ideally, the area would be fenced off and all livestock removed.

Priority: high
Time-scale: medium/long

3.   Monitoring and research

3.1. *To determine population status and distribution*

3.1.1. Try to locate new breeding colonies

Surveys should be made for other breeding sites in the vicinity of the known breeding colonies, and other suitable places on the island of Madeira. Extensive listening searches should be carried out in the mountains by people acquainted with the calls of Zino's Petrel, combined with visual searches for likely breeding ledges and followed by verification by climbing parties. The use of automatic recorders to detect and amplify calls should be explored. The advice and experience of the local experts needs to be followed when choosing places to check for breeding colonies. Given the difficulties of the terrain, at least two experienced climbers with adequate equipment are needed. Any search for breeding colonies must be co-ordinated by the Freira Conservation Project.

Priority: high
Time-scale: ongoing

3.1.2. Monitor population numbers and trends

The breeding ledges should be visited once a month, between mid-April and mid-October, to verify the occupation of burrows. Details of the state of activity at each burrow should be recorded on a standard form whenever a visit is made to the ledges. Since the available ground must be a major limiting factor for the population, a great deal of care is needed to avoid physical damage to the burrows when working on the ledges.

Priority: high
Time-scale: ongoing

3.2. *To promote scientific investigations that enhance and facilitate recovery effort*

3.2.1. Investigate population dynamics and survival rates

The capture (with mist-nets) and ringing of birds above the breeding sites, as well as that of chicks in the nest, should continue. When sufficient data are available, the capture/recapture method could be applied to estimate the total number of birds, although there are liable to be many biases affecting this technique. In any case, the existing data on survival rates should be analysed. There is also the possibility of using fibreoptics and miniature television cameras to study incubation and fledging if funding can be obtained.

Priority: medium
Time-scale: ongoing

3.2.2. Characterise habitat selection at nest sites

A habitat evaluation study should be undertaken to determine the special habitat requirements and to compare habitat selection among colonies. The results of this study should allow the precise identification of the most suitable areas for Zino's Petrel in Madeira.

Priority: low
Time-scale: medium

3.2.3. Study the diet of predators living around the breeding area

Faeces of cats should be regularly collected around the breeding area and subsequently analysed for Zino's Petrel remains.

Priority: low
Time-scale: ongoing

3.2.4. Investigate the birds' feeding and non-breeding range

The possibility of attaching data-loggers to birds caught at burrows during the breeding season should be explored. Satellite tracking would be another possibility, although the technology for a bird of this size is not yet available. The non-breeding range of this species is currently unknown and these techniques could identify areas to target for more detailed study. Any technique would first have to be tested on a less endangered species.

Priority: medium
Time-scale: long

3.2.5. Continue research on the taxonomic status of Zino's Petrel

The research already started to determine the genetic affinities of the *Pterodroma* petrels occurring in Madeiran waters should be continued and finalised, with the help of DNA fingerprinting and mitochondrial DNA analysis.

Priority: low
Time-scale: ongoing

3.2.6. Initiate a general investigation about rat ecology and population dynamics in Madeira

Rats in Madeira, as elsewhere, appear subject to population cycles. A more detailed knowledge of the length of these cycles and of the factors triggering population explosions would be helpful in preventing sudden increases in rat numbers in Zino's Petrel breeding areas.

Priority: low
Time-scale: long

4.   **Public awareness and training**

4.1.   *To increase awareness of the need to protect Zino's Petrel*

4.1.1. Develop and distribute educational material and upgrade the image of Zino's Petrel among the islanders of Madeira

A leaflet including information about Zino's Petrel should be published (but keeping the breeding areas confidential), in order to raise awareness among the local population about the need to protect this species. The special importance of Zino's Petrel should be promoted as a symbol among the inhabitants of the island of Madeira, with the aim of ensuring that it is adopted as part of the island's cultural identity.

Priority: medium
Time-scale: short/medium

4.1.2. Provide adequate facilities to the visitors of the Natural Park of Madeira

An information centre should be built to promote a better understanding of the natural values of the park, including Zino's Petrel. The breeding season coincides with the period when tourists visit the mountains. Once the area is well controlled and wardened, it may be possible to take tourists to hear the birds at night. This would bring in funds for the continued conservation of the area.

Priority: medium
Time-scale: medium

Action plan for the Pygmy Cormorant (*Phalacrocorax pygmeus*) in Europe

Reviews

This action plan should be reviewed and updated by BirdLife International every five years. An emergency review will be undertaken if sudden major environmental changes, liable to affect the population, occur within the species' range.

Geographical scope

The action plan needs implementation in Albania, Bulgaria, Federal Republic of Yugoslavia (Serbia only), Greece, Moldova, Romania, Russian Federation, the former Yugoslav Republic of Macedonia, Turkey and Ukraine.

Acknowledgements

We wish to thank Janine van Vessem, Paul Rose, Gernant Magnin and Petar Iankov who have made useful comments on the draft of this action plan.

Summary

The Pygmy Cormorant is considered today as Near-threatened within its whole geographical distribution, from Serbia to the Russian Federation (Collar et al., 1994), and is listed as Vulnerable at European level (Tucker and Heath, 1994). Its present world breeding population is estimated at 13 000 pairs, and probably half of this number is in Europe, where the largest colonies are still found in Romania, Turkey and Greece. Recent surveys in Azerbaijan suggest a substantial additional population there. Data on the distribution, biology and ecology of this species are most inadequate.

Since the second half of the nineteenth century, the Pygmy Cormorant has never stopped declining – due to drainage, persecution by fishermen, destruction of breeding colonies and degradation of wetlands.

In view of the limited knowledge available on this species, it is important to take a cautious approach and not to recommend possibly counter-productive measures.

Threats and limiting factors

Drainage and habitat degradation of breeding and wintering habitats – critical

Disruption of the hydrological regime – high

Disturbance and shooting – medium

Fishing nets – unknown

Contamination with heavy metals – unknown

Climatic change – unknown

Conservation priorities

Effective legislation to protect the species and its habitat from hunting, disturbance and development – essential

Appropriate management of wintering and breeding sites, particularly vegetation, water levels and access – essential

Monitoring of wintering and breeding populations – essential

Monitoring of water levels and water quality at Pygmy Cormorant sites – essential

Development and implementation of national action plans for the species and for the conservation of wetlands – high

Research into dispersal and feeding ecology – high

Public awareness campaign aimed at hunters, fishermen, local communities, politicians and civil servants – high

Introduction

The Pygmy Cormorant *Phalacrocorax pygmeus* was, until recently, classified by the IUCN as globally threatened in the category Insufficiently Known (Groombridge, 1993). According to the new criteria developed by the IUCN (Mace and Stuart, 1994), it has been re-classified as Near-threatened (Collar et al., 1994). At European level it is considered Vulnerable (Tucker and Heath, 1994). It is listed in Appendix II of the Bern Convention, Annex I of the European Union's Wild Birds Directive, Appendix II of the Bonn Convention and in the African-Eurasian Migratory Waterbirds Agreement (AEWA) developed under the Bonn Convention.

This action plan includes approximately 50% to 60% of the species' world breeding population and less than 80% of its wintering population.

This action plan is a framework document which identifies the main threats and the main actions to be taken in order to enhance the population of this species and restore its habitat. It is therefore recommended that a body is designated in each country to prepare a detailed national action plan for the species; the same body will also be responsible for implementing this. The preparation of such a plan will provide an opportunity to further develop objectives involving integrated and interdisciplinary work as well as specific policies.

Background information

Distribution and population

The Pygmy Cormorant is the smallest of the three European cormorants. It is restricted to the south-east of the western Palaearctic but has occurred accidentally in Austria, Czech Republic, France, Germany, Hungary, Italy, Poland, Slovakia, Sweden, Switzerland and Tunisia (Cramp and Simmons, 1977; Johnsgard, 1993).

Today, it breeds in Albania, Bulgaria, Greece, Moldova, Romania, Russian Federation, Turkey, Ukraine and Federal Republic of Yugoslavia (in Serbia), mainly along the coast of the Caspian Sea (Cramp and Simmons, 1977; Nankinov, 1989; Johnsgard, 1993: Table 3.1). It is not known whether it still breeds today in south-east Iraq and Iran. The world population is estimated to be approximately 13 000 pairs (Nazirides and Papageorgiou, in press). Rose and Scott (1994) estimate the world population at approximately 30 000 individuals.

According to Cowles (1981), the species was more widespread during the Middle Ages, even including the British Isles. It stopped breeding in

Table 3.1

The European breeding populations of *Phalacrocorax pygmeus* (modified from Nazirides and Papageorgiou, in press)

Country	Breeding pairs (year of census)	References
Albania	100–300 (1990s)	D. Vangeluwe, pers. comm.
Bulgaria	60–180 (1990s)	T. Michev, pers. comm.
Federal Republic of Yugoslavia (Serbia only)	150 (1980s)	Grimmett and Jones, 1989
Greece	557–590 (1990s)	Nazirides and Papageorgiou, in press
Moldova	200–500	Tucker and Heath, 1994
Romania	4000 (1990s)	M. Marinov, pers. comm.
Russian Federation	150–250	Tucker and Heath, 1994
Turkey	1000–1500 (1990s)	Dogal Hayati Koruma Dernegi, pers. comm.
Ukraine	10–30	Tucker and Heath, 1994
Total	6227–7500	

the Aral Sea area in the 1970s. It is extinct in Hungary (although apparently bred again there in 1988) and was considered to be a breed species in Algeria in the nineteenth century (Hudson, 1975; Cramp and Simmons, 1977). In 1940 it probably bred for the last time in Israel (S. Ashkenazi, verbally, 1994), but may be breeding again, although nests have still not been found (S. Ashkenazi, verbally, 1994). It bred in Italy in 1980 (Ortali, 1981), 1981 (Fasola and Barbieri, 1981) and 1994, when three breeding pairs were discovered (Volponi, verbally, 1994).

Pygmy Cormorants winter mostly in the Balkans (Albania, Greece, the former Yugoslavia), western Turkey, Cyprus, Iraq, Iran and recently in Israel, Bulgaria and Romania. Many birds are also wintering along the Azerbaijan and Iranian coasts of the Caspian Sea.

During the 1993 midwinter counts in the Black and Mediterranean Seas, 5240 individuals were recorded. In Asia (including the Middle East), 912 were counted (Perennou et al., 1994). These numbers are obviously too low which may be because the species is difficult to count and often winters along rivers (e.g. Axios, Danube) where it can be overlooked.

Life history

Breeding

Pair-bonding activity takes place in the wintering areas (Straka, 1990), and eggs are laid between the end of March and early July (Cramp and Simmons, 1977; Johnsgard, 1993; Nazirides and Papageorgiou, in press). Pygmy Cormorants breed in colonies, often with other species (cormorants, herons, Spoonbill Platalea leucorodia, Glossy Ibis Plegadis falcinellus, etc.). Nests are in dense trees or bushes on medium to high branches or in thick reedbeds 1 to 1.5 metres above water-level (Cramp and Simmons, 1977; Johnsgard, 1993). At Lake Kerkini in Greece, birds nest in mixed colonies in flooded forest; nests are 2.2 to 5.5 metres above ground (Nazirides and Papageorgiou, in press). Old nests are often repaired and re-used (Cramp and Simmons, 1977; Johnsgard, 1993), and if nests are destroyed the birds will build anew (Nazirides and Papageorgiou, in press). Clutch size is 2 to 8

(Cramp and Simmons, 1977). Mean hatching success is 77.1% (74.0%–78.7%), and the mean survival rate to three weeks old is 69.1% (68.1%–69.9%) (Nazirides and Papageorgiou, in press). The young fledge at 6 to 7 weeks old.

Feeding

The diet is primarily fish, though small mammals, crustaceans, leeches and large insects are occasionally taken (Cramp and Simmons, 1977; Johnsgard, 1993; A. J. Crivelli and G. Catsadorakis, verbally, 1994). Andone et al. (1969) found 15 fish species in 130 birds collected in the Danube delta; these included perch Perca fluviatilis 18.8%, roach Rutilus rutilus 14.8%, carp Cyprinus carpio 10.8%, spined loach Cobitis taenia 9.7% and pike Esox lucius 5.6%; average weight of the fish was 15 g (7–71 g). Pygmy Cormorants feed exclusively in shallow water.

Habitat requirements

The Pygmy Cormorant is a species of warm climates, mainly restricted to lowland freshwater and brackish habitats. It has been recorded in: open water with sizeable trees in the proximity; fresh or brackish marshes with thick reedbeds; open water or slow-flowing fresh water, including oxbows, backwaters, ricefields, swamps and flooded fields where fish can be easily caught in shallow water; densely vegetated areas with trees, bushes and even small floating islets of dead plants.

Wintering is mainly in coastal lagoons and deltas, and along rivers in riparian forest, but also in inland wetlands (e.g. at Lakes Prespa, Kerkini and Kastoria in Greece; Ovcharitza in Bulgaria; Sultan marshes, Lakes Uluabat and Isikli in Turkey).

There is no information available on passage habitats.

Threats and limiting factors

Drainage and habitat degradation of breeding and wintering areas

In most countries this is the most important factor in the decline. Drainage of wetlands and development schemes (for land reclamation and irrigation) were responsible for the abandonment of many colonies and reduced considerably the number of wetlands which can be used by Pygmy Cormorants. A decrease in the availability of shallow waters (e.g. through drainage or water extraction) might be detrimental to breeding success or to winter survival.

Importance: critical

Disruption of the hydrological regime of wetlands

Disruption of the natural pattern of water quantity, hydrology and flow distribution has a negative affect on the functioning of wetlands and on the birds which depend on them.

Importance: high

Contamination by heavy metals and pesticides

The single study available (Fossi et al., 1984) found rather low concentrations of heavy metals and chlorinated hydrocarbons in eggs collected in the Danube delta.

Importance: unknown

Disturbance and shooting

In many countries, fishermen view Pygmy Cormorants as competitors (like other species of cormorants) and destroy colonies. Winter shooting of Pygmy Cormorants is common in several areas. Disturbance by birdwatchers at the colonies, especially for photography, may cause serious problems (e.g. Lake Prespa, Lake Kerkini). Disturbance might also increase predation.

Importance: medium

Fishing nets

In some areas where fishermen set their nets close to the colonies (e.g. Kerkini in Greece), Pygmy Cormorants, especially juveniles, are caught in nets and drowned. Such mortality also occurs in winter.

Importance: unknown

Climatic changes

Climatic change has been an important influence on the geographical distribution of the species. During the Middle Ages, the climate in Europe reached its warmest for thousands of years, and the temperate conditions with mild winters helped Pygmy Cormorants to become established in England (Cowles, 1981). The subsequent change to severe winters restricted its range.

Importance: unknown

Conservation status and recent conservation measures

Albania

Legislation:
Protected since 1988 by the Hunting Law.

Distribution:
Breeding: probably still breeding at Albanian coastal wetlands.
Wintering and migration: all along the Adriatic coast and at a few inland wetlands.

Key sites:
Breeding: formerly in Kune and Vain marshes and in Velipoja marshes; today probably along the Bojana river (unprotected).
Wintering and migration: Lake Skadar (Skodra), Drin delta and Prespa lakes.

% of population included in protected areas:
Breeding: none.
Wintering: <5%.

Conservation efforts:
None.

Research:
See Whistler (1936), Lamani (1989), Gjiknuri and Peja (1992), Hagemeijer (1994) and Vangeluwe et al. (in press).

Bulgaria

Red Data Book:
Listed as Threatened (Anon., 1985).

Legislation:
Protected by law since 1962. The species is listed in Act 342/2104.86 of the Ministry of Environment (fine of US$ 2.20 for damaging birds or eggs). A fine of US$ 460 for any killed bird is planned together with an additional penalty.

Distribution:
Breeding: areas along the Danube river, areas along the Black Sea coast and a few inland sites such as Kaiadjik and Maritza rivers.
Wintering and migration: Black Sea coast area and Danube river.

Key sites:
Breeding: Burgas area, Belene Marshes Nature Reserve, banks and islands of Maritza river, Srebarna Nature Reserve.
Wintering and migration: lakes in Burgas area, Lakes Durankulak and Varna, Ovcharitza and Rozov reservoirs, Danube and Maritza rivers.

% of population included in protected areas:
Breeding: 56%–61%.
Wintering: 20%–30%.

Conservation efforts:
• Protected area designated for the conservation of Pygmy Cormorants in winter (e.g. no hunting).
• A poster calling for the preservation of the Pygmy Cormorant produced by BSPB.
• Update of the act protecting the species and increase of fine from US$ 2.20 to US$ 445 per specimen killed.
• National Wetlands Plan including priority actions for the conservation of the most important wetlands in Bulgaria prepared in 1993 (Ministry of Environment and BSPB).
• Preparation of management plans for several important wetlands (Ministry of Environment and BSPB).

Research:
See Anon. (1985), Nankinov (1989) and Simeonov et al. (1990).

Federal Republic of Yugoslavia (Serbia only)

Distribution:
Breeding: in Vojvodina and in Lake Sasko and along the Bojana river (Montenegro).
Wintering and migration: Montenegro.

Key sites:
Breeding: Bojana river and Obedska Bara marshes (unprotected).
Wintering and migration: Lake Skadar (National Park).

% of population included in protected areas:
Breeding: none.
Wintering: 60%.

Conservation efforts:
None.

Research:
See Boswall and Dawson (1975), Vizi (1979) and Soti et al. (1981).

Greece

Red Data Book:
Included as Endangered, category 2 ("The danger they face is not immediate for the present") (Handrinos, 1992).

Legislation:
Declared as "species of high protection" (Decision of Ministry of Agriculture, 414985/ 1985). Hunting is thus forbidden.

Distribution:
Breeding: northern Greece (breeds regularly at Prespa, Petron and Kerkini, irregularly at Porto-Lago, Kastoria, Axios and Ismaris).
Wintering and migration: northern and south-west Greece (Kalamas delta and Kastoria lake).

Key sites:
Breeding: Lakes Prespa and Kerkini (Ramsar Sites).
Wintering and migration: Lake Kerkini, Porto-Lagos area, Nestos, Evros and Axios deltas (Ramsar Sites).

% of population included in protected areas:
Breeding: 90%.
Wintering: 90%.

Conservation efforts:
None.

Research:
• Major research project at Kerkini by T. Nazirides (University of Thessaloniki, dissertation in preparation).
• See also Jerrentrup et al. (1988), Pyrovetsi and Crivelli (1988), Handrinos (1993), Crivelli et al. (1995a,b), Catsadorakis et al. (in press) and Nazirides and Papageorgiou (in press).

Moldova

Red Data Book:
Listed as Vulnerable in the Red Data Book of the USSR (Borodin, 1984).

Legislation:
Not known.

Distribution:
Breeding: Moldova.
Wintering and migration: none.

Key sites:
Breeding: Danube area.
Wintering and migration: none.

% of population included in protected areas:
Breeding: not known.
Wintering: none.

Conservation efforts:
None.

Research:
Not known.

Romania

Legislation:
Laws concerning the Biosphere Reserve of the Danube delta.

Distribution:
Breeding: Danube delta and Danube river.
Wintering and migration: Danube delta.

Key sites:
Breeding: Bondar, Obrelin Mic, Clinova, Purcelu and Braila (Biosphere Reserve).
Wintering and migration: Danube delta.

% of population included in protected areas:
Breeding: 100%.
Wintering: 20%–40%.

Conservation efforts:
Unknown.

Research:
• Monitoring of the breeding colony (M. Marinov).
• See also Paspaleva et al. (1985), Anon. (1992) and annual reports of the Danube Delta Institute.

Russian Federation

Red Data Book:
Listed as Vulnerable in the Red Data Book of the USSR (Borodin, 1984).

Legislation:
Unknown.

Distribution:
Breeding: Russian Federation.
Wintering and migration: Caspian Sea coast.

Key sites:
Breeding: Terek delta.
Wintering and migration: not known.

% of population included in protected areas:
Breeding: not known.
Wintering: not known.

Conservation efforts:
Unknown.

Research:
See Sapetin (1968) and Bondarev (1975).

The former Yugoslav Republic of Macedonia

Legislation:
Not known.

Distribution:
Breeding: none.
Wintering and migration: Lake Ohrid, Vardar river, Lake Doiran, Bitola fish-ponds.

Key sites:
Breeding: none.
Foraging: Lake Megali Prespa (unprotected).
Wintering and migration: Lake Megali Prespa (unprotected), Ohrid (unprotected), Lake Doiran (unprotected), Bitola fish-ponds (unprotected).

% of population included in protected areas:
Breeding: none.
Wintering: none.

Conservation efforts:
None.

Research:
None.

Turkey

Red Data Book:
Listed as Vulnerable in the Draft List of Threatened Animals of Turkey (Ministry of Environment).

Legislation:
Protected by law since 1975.

Distribution:
Breeding: mainly central Anatolia.
Wintering and migration: mainly at coastal wetlands.

Key sites:
Breeding: Eregli marshes, Sultan marshes (National Park), Lakes Uluabat, Aksehir and Eber.
Wintering and migration: Goksu, Büyük Menderes (National Park) and Meric deltas, Sultan marshes, Lakes Uluabat, Bafa and Isikli, and Camalti Tuzlasi (Nature Reserve).

% of population included in protected areas:
Breeding: <20%.
Wintering: <60%.

Conservation efforts:
None.

Research:
See Géroudet (1977) and Kasparek (1992).

Ukraine

Red Data Book:
Listed as Vulnerable in the Red Data Book of the USSR (Borodin, 1984).

Legislation:
Unknown.

Distribution:
Breeding: Ukraine.
Wintering and migration: none.

Key sites:
Breeding: Dniester delta and Oysul lagoon in Crimea.
Wintering and migration: none.

% of population included in protected areas:
Breeding: not known.
Wintering: none.

Conservation efforts:
Unknown.

Research:
See Buzun and Grinchenko (1991).

Aim and objectives

Aim

1.   In the short term to prevent any further declines below the 1994 levels in the population size and distribution of the Pygmy Cormorant.

2.   In the medium to long term to increase the population size of the Pygmy Cormorant to a level at which it no longer qualifies as Near-threatened.

Objectives

1.   **Policy and legislation**

1.1.   *Promote policies at international level which benefit the Pygmy Cormorant*

1.1.1.   Promote the maximum protection of the Pygmy Cormorant and its habitat through international conventions

The Barcelona Convention should seek to include all Pygmy Cormorant colonies in the Mediterranean as SPAs.

National strategies drawn up under the Biodiversity Convention should promote the conservation and sustainable management of coastal and inland wetland ecosystems.

Priority: medium
Time-scale: medium

1.1.2.   Encourage international policies and legislation which promote the conservation of suitable wetlands within the Pygmy Cormorant's range

The Ramsar Convention, MEDWET programme, European Union and other international aid and subsidy programmes have a role to play along with international policies and legislation on agriculture, transport, tourism, etc. International co-operation and exchange of information should be encouraged.

Priority: medium
Time-scale: medium

1.2.   *Encourage policies at national and regional (within country) level which benefit the Pygmy Cormorant*

1.2.1   Promote the development and implementation of a national action plan for the Pygmy Cormorant

All range states should be encouraged to address in more detail the actions highlighted in this action plan including identifying organisations which will be responsible for implementing each action.

Priority: high
Time-scale: short

1.2.2.   Promote the development and implementation of a national action plan for the conservation of wetlands

All range states should be encouraged to set clear targets and priorities for the protection and integrated management of wetlands important for the Pygmy Cormorant and other species. Adjustments needed in national policies and legislation on water, agriculture, tourism, etc. can be identified through this process. The habitat conservation strategies for coastal and inland wetlands, to be published by BirdLife International in

1996 will provide a framework for detailed action plans at national level.

Priority: high
Time-scale: short

1.2.3. Promote full protection of key sites

National policies and legislation should promote the protection of sites important for the Pygmy Cormorant.

Priority: essential
Time-scale: short

1.2.4. Promote hunting legislation

Legal protection for the Pygmy Cormorant should be encouraged in all range states (breeding or wintering).

Priority: essential
Time-scale: short

1.2.5. Promote non-intrusion zones around breeding colonies

All breeding range states should be encouraged to ensure that the appropriate legislation exists to allow for the enforcement of statutory permanent or temporary non-intrusion zones around breeding colonies, excluding all human access (including fishermen, birdwatchers and photographers). Scientists should be allowed to visit colonies only with permission of the appropriate national body.

Priority: essential
Time-scale: short

2.   **Species and habitat protection**

2.1. *Seek protected area designation for all sites important for the Pygmy Cormorant*

Sites important for the Pygmy Cormorant should be effectively protected from damage or loss through drainage, land reclamation, water extraction, pollution and other damaging developments. Riparian forests, particularly those already known to be used by the Pygmy Cormorant, should be given priority when planning the designation of new protected areas. Heronries should also be protected as they play an important role in attracting Pygmy Cormorants to breed.

Priority: essential
Time-scale: short

2.2. *Promote the enforcement of legislation and prevent disturbance*

It is recommended that a ban on hunting should be implemented in all areas where Pygmy Cormorants winter in large numbers (>100). Adequate levels of wardening will be needed to ensure that hunting controls in wintering areas and protection of breeding colonies are effective. Hunting controls should also be widely publicised (see 4.1.).

Priority: essential
Time-scale: short/ongoing

2.3. *Promote appropriate management of wetlands important for the Pygmy Cormorant*

2.3.1. Enhance proper management of vegetation in breeding areas

Tree cutting in breeding areas should be avoided.

Priority: essential
Time-scale: short/ongoing

2.3.2. Promote proper water management of wetlands

Favour the creation of shallow waters to improve feeding areas for Pygmy Cormorant. Pollution and drainage should be prevented.

Priority: essential/high
Time-scale: ongoing

3.   **Monitoring and research**

3.1. *Monitor numbers at breeding and wintering sites*

The number of breeding pairs should be monitored annually (by qualified people only; when a colony is located in reedbeds, the arrival-departure method should be used during the incubation period). Wintering birds should be counted in mid-January each year.

Priority: essential
Time-scale: ongoing

3.2. *Monitor water-level and water quality of key Pygmy Cormorant wetlands*

Priority: essential
Time-scale: ongoing

3.3. *Monitor ecological change at key Pygmy Cormorant wetlands*

This can be done by computer-aided techniques like geographical information systems.

Priority: medium
Time-scale: ongoing

3.4. *Undertake studies on dispersal, winter movements and the origins of nesting birds*

Priority: high
Time-scale: ongoing

3.5. *Study feeding ecology*

Undertake studies on feeding ecology and fishery catches, especially in relation to potential conflicts between Pygmy Cormorants and commercial fishermen, and assess the impact of the birds on the fish community.

Priority: high
Time-scale: short

3.6. *Study interspecific relationships*

Undertake studies of the relationships between Pygmy Cormorants and other colonial waterbirds in breeding and feeding areas.

Priority: medium
Time-scale: medium

4. **Public awareness and training**

4.1. *Raise public awareness of the importance of the Pygmy Cormorant and its habitat*

Undertake public awareness campaigns at all key sites, targeted mainly at hunters, fishermen and local communities as well as civil servants responsible for Pygmy Cormorant conservation.

Priority: high
Time-scale: short/ongoing

4.2. *Promote training for those involved in the management and protection of Pygmy Cormorant sites*

Promote training courses on wetland issues and provide training for the trainers.

Priority: medium
Priority: ongoing

Annex
Recommended conservation actions by country

Albania

1.2.5./2.2. Promote the establishment of a non-intrusion zone around all the colonies during the breeding period.

2.1/2.3.1. Prevent tree cutting in the existing breeding colonies.

3.1. Undertake yearly surveys of the breeding colonies and mid-winter counts.

3.3. Monitor ecological change at key sites.

3.4. Undertake a ringing programme.

3.5. Carry out studies on the feeding ecology in the breeding areas.

4.1. Undertake public awareness campaigns and training at all key sites, targeted mainly at hunters, fishermen and local communities.

Bulgaria

1.2.2. Encourage the implementation of the National Action Plan for Conservation of the Wetlands (1993).

1.2.4./2.2. Promote strong control on hunting and wardening at all sites where Pygmy Cormorants winter and migrate in large numbers, especially Ovcharitza and Rozov reservoirs and Lakes Durankulak, Varna, Atanasovo, Burgas and Mandra.

1.2.5./2.2. Promote the establishment of temporary non-intrusion zones around breeding colonies of the Pygmy Cormorant

2.2. Careful consideration will have to be given to the risk to Pygmy Cormorants from potential control measures for Cormorants *P. carbo*. Any damage to the Pygmy Cormorant and its habitat should be avoided.

2.2. Promote the preservation of the feeding grounds and their fish populations, especially around the breeding colonies.

2.2. Reduce pollution in the wetlands around the Burgas area.

2.3.2. Encourage the restoration of the hydrological regime of the Srebarna and Belene Reserves.

3.1. Undertake surveys of the breeding colonies and mid-winter counts.

3.3. Monitor ecological change at key sites.

3.5. Undertake studies on feeding ecology, especially in the light of potential conflicts between Cormorants (*P. carbo* and Pygmy Cormorant) and commercial fishermen, and assess the impact of the birds on the fish community. This study could provide additional information for the public awareness campaign (see 4.1).

4.1. Undertake public awareness campaigns and training at all key sites, targeted mainly at hunters, fishermen and local communities.

4.2. Produce educational materials on the species.

Greece

2.2. Enhance the enforcement of existing hunting regulations.

1.2.2. Encourage the implementation of the Action Plan for the Conservation and Management for Greek Wetlands (1989).

1.2.2./2.3.1./2.3.2. Restore freshwater marshes.

1.2.5./2.2. Encourage the establishment of a non-intrusion zone (at least 50 metres) around all colonies during the breeding period.

2.3.1./2.3.2. Recommended management at Lake Ismaris: prevent saltwater intrusion and restore the reedbeds and freshwater marshes.

2.3.1./2.3.2./2.2. Recommended management at Lake Kerkini: (1) find practical alternatives to the planned construction of new dikes; (2) lower the present maximum water-level to 35 metres a.s.l. by solving the sediment problem (Psilovikos, 1992) through finding new sources of water for agriculture and improving the efficiency of the irrigation network (Bartzoudis and Pyrovetsi, 1994); (3) enforce and implement the ban on hunting; (4) enforce the ban on cutting the riparian forest.

2.3.1./2.3.2. Recommended management at Lake Prespa: (1) ensure the maintenance of an April–June water-level of at least 854.6 metres a.s.l. favouring spawning of fish and producing shallow-water feeding areas; careful thought should be given to making a new link between Mikri and Megali Prespa including a strict management plan for the use of the new sluice in order to ensure a high water-level in spring; (2) manage the reedbeds and restore the wet meadows.

3.1. Census the breeding colonies in Lakes Prespa, Kerkini, Petron and Kastoria, and carry out mid-winter counts.

3.3. Monitor ecological change at key sites.

3.4. Undertake a ringing programme.

3.5. Undertake studies on feeding ecology, especially in the light of potential conflicts between Pygmy Cormorants and commercial fishermen, and assess the impact of the birds on the fish community.

4.1. Undertake public awareness campaigns and training at all key sites, targeted mainly at hunters, fishermen, local communities and civil servants.

4.2. Produce educational materials on the species.

Moldova

1.2.5./2.2. Promote the establishment of a non-intrusion zone around all colonies during the breeding period.

2.3.2. Oppose drainage and water extraction and/or water diversion at wetlands.

3.1. Undertake surveys of the breeding colonies and mid-winter counts.

3.3. Monitor habitat changes at key sites.

3.4. Monitor movements of ringed birds.

3.5. Undertake studies on feeding ecology, especially in the light of potential conflicts between Pygmy Cormorants and commercial fishermen, and assess the impact of the birds on the fish community.

4.1. Undertake public awareness campaigns and training at all key sites, targeted mainly at hunters, fishermen and local communities.

Romania

1.2.5./2.2. Promote the establishment of a non-intrusion zone around all colonies during the breeding period.

2.3. Encourage the restoration of the floodplains within the Danube delta by partial or total destruction of the dikes along the canals.

3.1. Undertake surveys of breeding colonies and mid-winter counts.

3.3. Monitor ecological change at key sites.

3.4. Undertake a ringing programme.

3.5. Undertake studies on feeding ecology, especially in the light of potential conflicts between Pygmy Cormorants and commercial fishermen, and assess the impact of the birds on the fish community.

4.1. Undertake public awareness campaigns and training at all key sites, targeted mainly at hunters, fishermen and local communities.

Russian Federation

1.2.5./2.2. Promote the establishment of a non-intrusion zone around all colonies during the breeding period.

2.3.2. Oppose drainage and water extraction and/or water diversion at wetlands.

3.1. Undertake surveys of breeding colonies and mid-winter counts.

3.3. Monitor habitat changes at key sites.

3.4. Monitor the movements of ringed birds.

3.5. Undertake studies on feeding ecology, especially in the light of potential conflicts between Pygmy Cormorants and commercial fishermen, and assess the impact of the birds on the fish community.

4.1. Undertake public awareness campaigns and training at all key sites, targeted mainly at hunters, fishermen and local communities.

The former Yugoslav Republic of Macedonia

1.2.5./2.2. Promote the establishment of a non-intrusion zone around all colonies during the breeding period.

3.1. Undertake surveys of the breeding colonies and mid-winter counts.

3.3. Monitor ecological change at key sites.

3.4. Undertake a ringing programme.

3.5. Carry out studies on feeding ecology in the breeding areas.

4.1. Undertake public awareness campaigns and training at all key sites, targeted mainly at hunters, fishermen and local communities.

Turkey

1.2. Promote the preparation and publication of a Red Data Book for Turkey.

1.2.4./2.2./4.1. Improve and publicise the hunting legislation and secure better enforcement.

2.1. Encourage the designation of protected areas (breeding and wintering areas) for the species.

2.2. Increase wardening at the breeding colonies.

2.3.1./2.3.2. Improve the water management of each wetland and secure the minimum habitat requirements for the survival of the Pygmy Cormorant.

2.3.2. Prevent wetland drainage and water extraction and/or water diversion, etc.

2.3.2. Encourage the necessary measures to prevent pollution throughout the catchment areas of wetlands.

3.1. Undertake surveys of the breeding colonies and mid-winter counts.

3.3. Monitor ecological change at key sites.

3.4. Undertake a ringing programme.

3.5. Undertake studies of feeding ecology, especially in the light of potential conflicts between Pygmy Cormorants and commercial fishermen, and assess the impact of the birds on the fish community.

4.1. Undertake public awareness campaigns and training at all key sites, targeted mainly at hunters, fishermen and local communities.

Ukraine

1.2.5./2.2. Promote the establishment of a non-intrusion zone around all colonies during the breeding period.

2.3.2. Prevent drainage and water extraction and/or water diversion at wetlands.

3.1. Undertake surveys of breeding colonies and mid-winter counts.

3.3. Monitor habitat changes at key sites.

3.4. Monitor the movements of ringed birds.

3.5. Undertake studies of feeding ecology, especially in the light of potential conflicts between Pygmy Cormorants and commercial fishermen, and assess the impact of the birds on the fish community.

4.1. Undertake public awareness campaigns and training at all key sites, targeted mainly at hunters, fishermen and local communities.

Action plan for the Dalmatian Pelican (*Pelecanus crispus*) in Europe

Reviews

This action plan should be reviewed and updated every five years. An emergency review will be undertaken if sudden major environmental changes, liable to affect the population, occur within the species' range.

Geographical scope

The action plan needs to be implemented in Albania, Bulgaria, Federal Republic of Yugoslavia (Serbia), Greece, Romania, Russian Federation, Turkey and Ukraine.

Acknowledgements

We wish to thank Janine van Vessem, Paul Rose, Gernant Magnin and Petar Iankov for making useful comments on the draft of this action plan.

Summary

The Dalmatian Pelican *Pelecanus crispus* is classified today as Vulnerable within its whole geographical distribution, from the Federal Republic of Yugoslavia to Mongolia (Collar et al., 1994). Its present world breeding population is estimated at 3215 to 4280 pairs, more than 80% being in the former Soviet Union – Kazakhstan, Russian Federation, Turkmenistan, Ukraine and Uzbekistan. The European population occupies Albania, Bulgaria, Federal Republic of Yugoslavia (Serbia only), Greece, Romania, Russian Federation, Turkey and Ukraine.

Rose and Scott (1994) estimate the world population to be approximately 12000 to 16000 individuals. Since the second half of the nineteenth century the Dalmatian Pelican has never stopped declining, due to disturbance and degradation of wetlands, hunting and colony destruction by fishermen.

Threats and limiting factors

Drainage and habitat degradation in breeding and wintering areas – critical

Powerlines – high

Disturbance, nest destruction and shooting – high

Contamination by heavy metals and pesticides – medium to low

Climatic changes – unknown

Conservation priorities

Legal protection of the species and its habitat during breeding and wintering in all range states – essential

Sustainable management of wetlands – essential

Establishment of wardened non-intrusion zones around breeding colonies – essential

Appropriate vegetation and hydrological management – essential

Monitoring of breeding, wintering numbers and ecological change at key sites – essential

Burial of powerlines or replacement with thick cable – high

Monitoring of conservation measures taken and hydrological studies – high

Public awareness campaign aimed at decision makers, hunters, fishermen and local communities – high

Introduction

The Dalmatian Pelican *Pelecanus crispus* is classified by the IUCN as globally threatened in the category Vulnerable (Groombridge, 1993), and this is unchanged under the new criteria (Category C2a: small population and declining with severe fragmentation) (Collar et al., 1994; Mace and Stuart, 1994). At European level it is considered Vulnerable (Tucker and Heath, 1994).

The species is included in Appendix II of the Bern Convention, in Annex I of the European Union's Wild Birds Directive, in Appendix I of CITES, in

Appendix II of the Bonn Convention and in the Agreement for the Conservation of African-Eurasian Migratory Waterbirds (AEWA) under the Bonn Convention.

This action plan identifies the main threats and the main actions to be taken in order to enhance the population of this species and restore its habitat. It covers approximately 30% of the species' world breeding population and 25% to 30% of its wintering population. It is therefore necessary to implement the plan not only in Europe, but over the whole distribution of the species. Crivelli and collaborators (pers. comm.) have hypothesised that there are several subpopulations almost totally isolated from each other; it is thus practicable to implement the action plan as a first step in Europe only, and subsequently to extend it to the whole range of the species.

Background information

Distribution and population

During ancient times pelicans appear to have been spread widely through western Europe. Considering that the temperature during the Palaeolithic period was 2°C–3°C higher than today it is possible that the Dalmatian Pelican bred over a large part of western Europe at this time (Crivelli and Vizi, 1981). During this century and last, a strong decline has occurred in Europe with breeding colonies disappearing in the former Yugoslavia, Hungary, Albania, Greece, Mongolia, the former Soviet Union, Romania and Turkey (Crivelli and Vizi, 1981). Today, the species breeds in Albania, Bulgaria, Federal Republic of Yugoslavia (Serbia only), Greece, Kazakhstan, Mongolia, Romania, Russian Federation, Turkey, Turkmenistan, Ukraine and Uzbekistan (Crivelli, 1994).

The best estimate of the world population is 3215 to 4280 pairs (Crivelli, 1994). The former Soviet Union (Kazakhstan, Russian Federation, Turkmenistan, Ukraine and Uzbekistan) harbours 80% to 84% of this, and the next most important country, Greece, has 6% to 8%. European numbers (Table 4.1) are estimated at 886 to 1204 pairs (c. 30% of the world population).

The wintering sites of the Dalmatian Pelican in south-east Europe, Turkey and the former Soviet Union are well-known (Crivelli et al., 1991a), but

Table 4.1

Numbers of breeding Dalmatian Pelicans *Pelecanus crispus* in Europe (modified from Crivelli, 1994)

Country	Breeding pairs (year of census)	Number of breeding sites	References
Albania	40–70 (1990s)	1	Peja et al., in press
Bulgaria	70–90 (1990s)	1	T. Michev, pers. comm.
Fed. Rep. of Yugoslavia (Serbia only)	10–20 (1980s)	1	O. Vizi, pers. comm.
Greece	190–260 (1990s)	2	Catsadorakis et al., in press, A. J. Crivelli and D. Hatzilacou; unpubl. data
Romania	70–150 (1990s)	1	B. Kiss and M. Marinov, pers. comm.
Russian Federation	400–450	4–5	Crivelli et al., 1994
Turkey	100–150 (1990s)	4–5	Peja et al., in press
Ukraine	6–14	1	Lysenko, 1994
Total	886–1204	15–17	

this does not apply to the Middle East (Iran, Iraq) or Asia (Pakistan, India, China) (Crivelli et al., 1991b), and several sites in these areas probably remain to be discovered. The January 1993 mid-winter counts in the Black Sea and Mediterranean (Albania, Bulgaria, Greece, Syria and Turkey) gave a figure of 1463 individuals (P. Rose, pers. comm.) and in the Middle East and Asia 4803 individuals (Perennou et al., 1994). These numbers are low considering that the world population in January (including immatures) should be 12 000 to 16 000 individuals.

Life history

Breeding

Breeding colonies are located on lakes, deltas and estuaries, preferably within reedbeds. Breeding birds usually arrive in February, and laying generally occurs 10 days later. The birds lay up to four eggs and the average clutch is 1.8. Incubation lasts 31 to 32 days and fledging takes 11 to 12 weeks (Crivelli et al., 1991b). The main mortality during breeding is at the egg stage (Crivelli, 1987); hatching success varying from 35% to 70%. Contrary to common belief, the Dalmatian Pelican can easily rear two chicks and fledging success in a well-protected colony is over one chick per nest, up to a maximum of 1.35 (Catsadorakis et al., in press). Even in a protected area, however, breeding success can be less than one chick fledged per nest. At Srébarna, a Nature Reserve in Bulgaria, for example, average success between 1955 and 1993 was 0.84 chicks per nest with a coefficient of variation of 30% (T. Michev, verbally, 1994); this lower success might be explained by predation, especially by wild boars Sus scrofa destroying nests with eggs or killing chicks.

With the present state of knowledge of the population dynamics of pelicans it would appear that a success rate in the Dalmatian Pelican of 0.8 chicks per nest should be at least sufficient to keep the population stable. A success rate of over one chick per nest should ensure an increasing population (Crivelli, 1987).

Wintering

The breeding areas are vacated in autumn, and the main winter quarters are located in coastal areas of the Mediterranean and Caspian Seas and the Persian Gulf, often in deltas. Unfrozen water and a rich food supply are the key factors, and so there are few wintering sites inland. Suitable sites for night-roosting, safe from terrestrial predators, are also an important requirement.

Feeding

Dalmatian Pelicans eat only fish and feed alone or in groups (Crivelli et al., 1991b). The composition of the diet depends almost entirely on the relative abundance of prey species, on their spatial and temporal distribution, and to a lesser extent on their behaviour. In lagoon systems the birds will catch mainly migratory fish such as eels Anguilla anguilla, mullets Mugil and sedentary fish such as gobies Gobius and sand-smelts Atherina (Crivelli, 1987; Peja et al., in press; A. Crivelli, D. Hatzilacou and Ebert, verbally). In inland fresh waters, preferred species are Cyprinidae such as roach Rutilus, bleak Alburnus, rudd Scardinius, carp Cyprinus carpio and others (Andone et al., 1969; Crivelli and Vizi, 1981; Crivelli, 1987; Romashova, 1994). Fish taken range in length from 3 to 50 cm. Birds sometimes feed far away from the breeding colony.

Habitat requirements

Dalmatian Pelicans are absent from cold regions, although they will tolerate temperatures below 0°C for short periods (7–10 days). Originally, the species was probably found only in fresh water inland, but today there are a few colonies in brackish lagoon ecosystems in the Mediterranean region (Peja et al., in press).

For breeding and roosting the birds need areas totally isolated from the mainland by water (e.g. islands, sand banks, reedbeds surrounded by water) in order to avoid predation by mammals (foxes, dogs, wolves, wild boars, jackals, etc.) and disturbance. The absence of adequate roosting areas can prevent pelicans using a site at any time of year.

The hydrological regime within wetlands is a further key factor in successful breeding (Catsadorakis et al., in press), and also in the pelicans' use of wetlands for other purposes. For example, the presence of shallow water is important for the successful spawning of fish which form the birds' food, and Dalmatian

Pelicans need wetlands with a rather high density of fish. Water transparency and depth are not important factors for successful foraging.

Threats and limiting factors

Disruption of hydrological regimes and habitat degradation in breeding and wintering areas

This is the most important factor in the decline in most countries. Drainage of wetlands and development schemes (land reclamation and irrigation) caused the abandonment of many breeding colonies and has considerably reduced the number of wetlands which can be used by Dalmatian Pelicans. Burning of reedbeds in spring is a common practice which could be very detrimental to the breeding habitat. Long-term eutrophication of wetlands is also considered a negative factor.

Water management is a common feature in all wetlands today. Such management and exceptional climatic events (drought or flood) have important impact on the breeding of pelicans (Catsadorakis et al., in press) and on their use of wetlands (e.g. Lake Kerkini in Greece: Pyrovetsi, 1990; Pyrovetsi and Papastergiadou, 1992; Crivelli et al., 1995a,b). Other striking examples are the recent ecological changes in the Aral Sea in Kazakhstan or at Lake Lop in China which have led to the disappearance of the breeding populations of Dalmatian Pelicans.

Importance: critical

Contamination by heavy metals and pesticides

High concentrations of DDE were found in eggs collected at Lake Prespa (northern Greece) between 1984 and 1986, eggshell thickness being 12% to 20% less than pre-1947 values, dating from before DDT was in use (Crivelli et al., 1989). Later investigations (1989) showed a sharp decrease in the concentrations of chlorinated hydrocarbons. Other recent studies have also detected concentrations of heavy metals and chlorinated hydrocarbons in Dalmatian Pelican eggs (Cook, 1992; Albanis, 1993; T. Michev, verbally, 1994). Poslavski and Chernov (1994) showed that hatching success is very low mainly due to a low eggshell thickness, a direct consequence of the heavy use of pesticides for cotton cultivation in the Aral Sea area.

Importance: medium to low

Powerlines

Crivelli et al. (1988) identified powerlines as a significant cause of mortality in one wintering area, mainly through collision, and the problem was also encountered subsequently at a breeding site (Crivelli et al., 1991b) and in many other areas. Removal of powerlines, the addition of plastic flags as markers, and the use of thick cables have been tested with successful results (Crivelli et al., 1991a; G. Catsadorakis and A. Crivelli, verbally, 1994; H. Jerrentrup, verbally, 1994).

Importance: high

Disturbance, nest destruction and shooting

In many countries, disturbance is a major threat, especially in the breeding season (e.g. birdwatchers and photographers, normally from western countries). Destruction of colonies by fishermen still occurs, though it is becoming rarer. Shooting, mainly from autumn to spring, is still common in all countries, and it is not unusual to find shot birds in most of the wetlands used by Dalmatian Pelicans. There are also numerous reports of pelicans shot at fish-farms or aquaculture installations in Greece, Israel, Romania, the former Soviet Union and the former Yugoslavia (Heins et al., 1990; Pyrovetsi, 1990; G. Handrinos, verbally, 1994; T. Nazirides, verbally, 1994; G. Catsadorakis, verbally, 1994; D. Hatzilakou, verbally, 1994; Society for the Protection of Nature in Israel, verbally, 1994). Such shooting is a threat which has not been correctly assessed up to now.

Importance: high

Climatic changes

Krivenko et al. (1994) have shown that cyclical changes in climate could be important in determining distribution and abundance of pelicans in arid and semi-arid regions (e.g. Kazakhstan). In terms of short-term climatic cycles, an increase in pelican numbers is observed in cool, wet periods and a decline in warm, dry periods. With global warming, and an increase of man's influence on water management, the importance of this limiting factor could increase in the future.

Importance: unknown

Conservation status and recent conservation measures

Note: "protected area" means "designated as protected area".

Albania

Legislation:
The Dalmatian Pelican has been protected since 1988 by the "Hunting Law".

Distribution:
Breeding: Karavasta lagoon.
Wintering and migration: all along the Adriatic coast and lakes in central Albania.

Key sites:
Breeding: Karavasta lagoon (unprotected).
Foraging: Lake Megali Prespa.
Wintering: Karavasta and Narta lagoons.

% of population in protected areas:
Breeding: 0%.
Wintering: 0%.

Conservation efforts:
• Warden hired during the breeding season (April–July) since 1992 at Karavasta lagoon under the International Pelicans Research, Management and Conservation Programme (Project leader: A. J. Crivelli).

Research:
See Barbieri et al. (1986), Lamani (1989), Gjiknuri and Peja (1992), Hagemeijer (1994), Peja et al. (in press), Vangeluwe et al. (in press).

Bulgaria

Red Data Book:
Listed as Threatened (Anon. 1985).

Legislation:
Protected by law since 1948. The species is listed in the Act 342/21.04.1986 of the Ministry of Environment and a fine of US$ 460 plus an additional penalty is planned for any killed bird or collected egg. Hunting is banned at all wintering or passage sites.

Distribution:
Breeding: Lake Srébarna.
Wintering and migration: Black Sea coast area and a few inland wetlands.

Key sites:
Breeding: Lake Srébarna (Nature Reserve).
Foraging: Danube river, Romanian wetlands north of Srébarna.
Wintering and migration: Lakes Burgas, Atanasovo and Mandra, and Ovcharitza and Studen kladenetz reservoirs.

% of population in protected areas:
Breeding: 100%.
Wintering: 25%.

Conservation efforts:
• Building one artificial raft; no successful breeding (T. Michev and colleagues).
• Burning the reedbed and fencing the breeding colony as measures against predators, mainly wild boars and jackals (T. Michev and colleagues, BSPB); led to an increase in the number of breeding birds.
• Public awareness programme with a permanent television display of the breeding colony at Srébarna (Srébarna Nature Reserve Authorities).
• Educational and public awareness materials involving the media to create a positive attitude towards the species.
• Updating the act, protecting the species by increasing the fine to US$ 447.80 for killing a bird and collecting eggs.
• National Wetlands Plan including priority actions for the conservation of the most important wetlands in Bulgaria (1993) (Ministry of Environment and BSPB).
• Preparation of a management plan for Srébarna Nature Reserve with the support of the Ramsar Convention (Ministry of Environment).
• Attempts to improve the enforcement of the legislation and to ensure wardening of the pelican colony at Srébarna by employing four wardens (Ministry of Environment).

Research:
• Monitoring and ringing at the Srébarna colony.
• Monitoring of the Dalmatian Pelicans migrating in autumn over the Burgas area since 1978 (T. Michev and colleagues, BSPB).
• Midwinter counts since 1977 (T. Michev and colleagues, BSPB).
See also Michev (1981), Anon. (1985), Simeonov et al. (1990), Crivelli et al. (1991b).

Federal Republic of Yugoslavia (Serbia only)

Legislation:
Legally protected in Serbia.

Distribution:
Breeding: Lake Skadar (Montenegro).
Wintering and migration: none.

Key sites:
Breeding: Lake Skadar (National Park)
(Montenegro Province).
Foraging: Lakes Skadar and Megali Prespa
(the former Yugoslav Republic of Macedonia).
Wintering and migration: none.

% of population in protected areas:
Breeding: 100%.
Wintering: no wintering.

Conservation efforts:
• Creation of a National Park at Lake Skadar.

Research:
See Crivelli and Vizi (1981), Vizi (1975, 1979a,b,
1981).

Greece

Red Data Book:
Listed as Endangered, category 1 (in immediate
danger of extinction) (Handrinos, 1992).

Legislation:
Declared a "species of high protection" (Decision
of Ministry of Agriculture, 414985/1985); hunting
of it is thus prohibited.

Distribution:
Breeding: northern Greece (Prespa) and south-
west Greece (Amvrakikos).
Wintering and migration: northern Greece, and
south-west Greece.

Key sites:
Breeding: Prespa lakes (National Park) and
Amvrakikos Gulf (Tsoukalio and Logarou
lagoons, Ramsar Site).
Wintering and migration: Kerkini, Lakes Langada
and Kastoria, Porto-Lagos area, Evros and Axios
deltas, Amvrakikos Gulf and Mesolonghi.

% of population in protected areas:
Breeding: 100%.
Wintering: 90%.

Conservation efforts:
Two round-table meetings of experts and interested parties were held in 1990 with a view to
drawing up a national action plan. Although this
has not been published, it remains the main single
source of information on the species in Greece.
Specific conservation measures have included:

• Surveillance of the Tsoukalio breeding colony
(Amvrakikos area) over three years (HOS).
• Dismantling of a powerline in Porto-Lagos
(Crivelli et al., 1988).
• Installing thick cable at Porto-Lagos (H.
Jerrentrup, verbally, 1994).
• Continuing efforts to remove all pelicans held
illegally as pets or as tourist attractions (Forestry
Service, Ministry of Agriculture, verbally, 1994).
• Building of three artificial islands at Kerkini by
the Sidirokastro Forest Service in 1993: no
breeding attempts in 1994 (T. Nazirides, verbally,
1994).
• Publication of a leaflet, a poster and other rel-
evant awareness materials by the Society for the
Protection of Prespa (M. Malakou, verbally, 1994).
• A study for the zoning of Prespa National Park
according to the European Union's Wild Birds
Directive (Catsadorakis et al., 1988).
• A study at Lake Kerkini, 1982-94, on the effects
on vegetation, fisheries and waterbirds of raising
water-levels at this Ramsar Site (Crivelli et al.
1995a,b).
• Education programme at Amvrakikos (HOS).
• In Prespa, which holds the largest colony in
Greece, a continuous effort has been made since
1983 by IPRMCP in collaboration with local
authorities, public services and NGOs (especially
the locally based SPP) to ensure the safety and
increase of the breeding Dalmatian Pelicans.
Among numerous activities, the following should
be mentioned:

– Continuous monitoring, 1983-94, of pelican
numbers, nesting attempts, breeding success and
population dynamics; environmental factors are
also monitored in order to understand the causes of population change.
– Long-term study, 1984-94, on the fish populations of Lake Prespa in parallel with the study of
the diet of pelicans.
– In 1988 and 1989 in collaboration with the
Greek National Power Corporation, the marking
of powerlines with plastic flags. In 1990, because
the flags had deteriorated, the conventional dangerous powerlines were substituted with one
thick (and thus more visible) insulated cable; this
has proved very effective, and no collisions have
occurred since.
– From 1988 to 1994 a detailed survey and
study of each pelican breeding site was carried
out to identify nest-site preferences in order to

permit construction of artificial nest-sites.

– In 1987 a series of artificial rafts, 3 x 4 metres and made with timber and reeds, were built during the winter. In 1988, one raft was installed, but was used only for roosting; in 1989, four pairs bred successfully on it. In 1990, three rafts were installed and 21 nests were made on them; eggs were laid, but were abandoned due to human disturbance. In 1991, nine rafts were installed, and these successfully hosted 52 nests of White Pelicans *P. onocrotalus* and Dalmatian Pelicans.

– 1985-86, 1990–94: pelicans monitored at Lake Kastoria, an important wetland for these birds during the breeding season.

– 1993-94: education programme with a focus on pelicans, by SPP with IPRMCP as consultants; more than 7000 students attended.

– 1993-94: education programme of the SPP on the values of Prespa and the pelicans for all schools of Prespa (IPRMCP collaborators as consultants).

– Wardening of the breeding colony by volunteers in 1989 (at the request of the Prespa Centre for Man and Nature) organised by IPRMCP. From 1990 to 1994 a warden was hired with funds from WWF and IPRMCP at the request of SPP.

– 1994: publication of an awareness leaflet on pelicans for visitors, by SPP written by IPRMCP scientists with data from 1983-94.

– 1994: publication of a poster on pelicans by SPP.

– 1994: hiring of a local fisherman by SPP for three months during the breeding season to distribute awareness materials to visitors to prevent disturbance of the pelican colony.

– 1983-94: continuous collaboration of SPP and IPRMCP scientists with local fishermen to minimise disturbance during the breeding season.

– Continuous collaboration of SPP and IPRMCP scientists with the Florina Forest Service to stop disturbance of the breeding colonies by visitors.

– 1991: installation of signs with information on the vulnerability of pelican colonies and the ban on approaching them, by the Florina Forest Service, at the request of and with the advice of SPP and IPRMCP.

– 1991-94: marking a non-intrusion zone around the main pelican breeding island with the installation of floating buoys in collaboration with the Forest Service and SPP and IPRMCP scientists.

– 1994: study of the management of wet meadows for fish and waterbirds (SPP, Tour du Valat, RSPB, WWF, IPRMCP).

• Actions carried out by the Aristotle University team to create a new breeding habitat at Lake Kerkini (project leader M. Pyrovetsi, funded by ACNAT). The management measures were accompanied by the following actions to promote successful implementation:

– Building of artificial structures at Lake Kerkini: one dredged-soil islet (1987); two floating rafts (1988); two platforms made of tree branches and two dredged-soil islets (1991); one metal stable structure with floating platform (1992). Dalmatian Pelicans nested on the dredged-soil islet in 1990, but breeding was interrupted as a result of egg theft. The structures have been used extensively by pelicans and other waterbirds for roosting.

– 1988-89: socio-ecological research among fishermen of Lakes Kerkini, Vistonis and Prespa to identify the nature of conflicts between them and pelicans.

– 1989-90: seminars with fishermen of three villages around Lake Kerkini and Porto-Lagos by the Greek Secretariat of Youth and the Society for the Conservation and Ecodevelopment of Wetlands in Northern Greece.

– 1991: production of a poster about management at Kerkini by the above organisation and NGOs. Production of six posters about Dalmatian Pelicans at Lake Mikri Prespa, thanks to the British Council.

– 1987-88, 1993-94: education programmes at primary schools of all villages around Kerkini; preparation of printed materials.

– 1991-94: environmental education programmes at secondary schools in four villages around Kerkini and Thessaloniki high schools.

– 1991-94: review of the management structures at Lake Kerkini.

– 1991: assistance in organising local NGOs for the protection of Lake Kerkini at Lithotopos and Kerkini.

– 1993-94: agro-ecological study at Lakes Prespa and Kerkini concerning the impact of agricultural practices on pelicans and wetlands.

– 1993-94: study of the wise use of irrigation water at Kerkini.

- Actions undertaken by the HOS for the conservation of Dalmatian Pelican in Greece:
  - A study funded by the RSPB entitled "The distribution of the globally endangered Dalmatian Pelican (*Pelecanus crispus Bruch*) in Greece: threats pertaining to its habitats and recommendations for protection" (Hatzilacou, 1993) The aim of this study, which was an initial step in the preparation of this action plan, was to provide detailed up-to-date information on the distribution of the Dalmatian Pelican in Greece, to outline current and imminent threats pertaining to the species' habitats and to recommend actions for protection. It has been widely distributed to NGOs, the Ministries of Environment and Agriculture and to the environment services of prefectures where the Dalmatian Pelican's habitat is present (Evros, Rodopi, Xanthi, Serres, Kastoria, Florina, Thesprotla, Arta, Preveza, Agrinio) in order to inform the local authorities about the specific problems of the Dalmatian Pelican in each region and to highlight sensitive issues which must be taken into consideration during the drafting of local management plans.

Research:
Present projects:
- Management and development of biotopes of the Dalmatian Pelican in northern Greece (project leader M. Pyrovetsi).
- IPRMCP (project leader A. J. Crivelli).
A great number of publications exist, but only those published since 1990, or in press, are listed here: Pyrovetsi and Daoutopoulos (1990), Daoutopoulos and Pyrovetsi (1990), Pyrovetsi (1990), Pyrovetsi and Daoutopoulos (1991), Crivelli et al. (1991a,b), Psilovikos (1992), Pyrovetsi and Papastergiadou (1992), Cook (1992), Pyrovetsi et al. (1993a,b), Hatzilacou (1993), Pyrovetsi and Dimalexis (1994), Bartzoudis and Pyrovetsi (1994), Catsadorakis et al., in press), Crivelli et al. (1995a,b), Pyrovetsi and Papazahariadou (in press).

Romania

Legislation:
Protected by law as a National Monument.

Distribution:
Breeding: Danube delta (Biosphere Reserve, Ramsar Site).
Wintering and migration: none.

Key site:
Breeding: Danube delta (Lake Lejai in Sf Gheorghe area).
Wintering and migration: none.

% of population in protected areas:
Breeding: 100%.
Wintering: None.

Conservation efforts:
- Educational material on the species.
- Public awareness programme for the Danube delta (ROS/BirdLife International)

Research:
See Rudescu (1955), Korodi (1962–1963), Catuneanu et al. (1978), Paspaleva et al. (1985), Crivelli et al. (1991b), Anon. (1992).

Russian Federation

Red Data Book:
Listed as Vulnerable in the Red Data Book of the USSR (Borodin, 1984).

Legislation:
Ban on hunting.

Distribution:
Breeding: Russian Federation.
Wintering and migration: Caspian sea coast (Russian Federation and Azerbaijan) and Turkmenistan.

Key sites:
Breeding: Terek delta (Local Reserve), Kirov Bay area, Kura delta, Kuban delta (Hunting Reserve), Volga delta (Hunting Reserve) and Lake Manych-Gudilo (State Reserve).
Wintering and migration: Kura delta, Bol'shoi Kyzyl-Agachsky Gulf.

% of population in protected areas:
Breeding: <45%.
Wintering: <20%.

Conservation efforts:
- Building artificial rafts in the Volga delta; successful breeding for several years until rafts deteriorated (Bondarev, 1976).

Research:
See Bondarev (1976), Borodin (1984), Crivelli (1994), Kazakov et al. (1994), Khokhlov and Melgunov (1994), Krivenko et al. (1994), Krivonosov et al. (1994), Linkov (1994), Litvinova (1994), Romashova (1994).

Turkey

Red Data Book:
Listed as Endangered in the Draft List of Threatened Animals of Turkey (Ministry of Environment).

Legislation:
Protected by law since 1974.

Distribution:
Breeding: Mainly western Anatolia, also along Black Sea coast and in central Anatolia.
Wintering and migration: Mainly coastal wetlands in western and southern Turkey and a few inland wetlands.

Key sites:
Breeding: Büyük Menderes delta (National Park) and Kizilirmak delta (unprotected), Lakes Manyas (National Park) and Aksehir and Camalti Tuzlasi (Nature Reserve).
Wintering and migration: Goksu, Büyük Menderes and Meric deltas, Lakes Manyas, Bafa, Marmara and Isikli, and Camalti Tuzlasi.

% of population in protected areas:
Breeding: >90 %.
Wintering: >75%.

Conservation efforts:
• Building of artificial platforms in trees at Lake Manyas; successful breeding for more than 25 years (T. Gurpinar).
• Education and conservation programme in several wetlands (DHKD) including the Menderes delta for four years.
• After three years of campaigning by DHKD, Menderes delta has been declared a National Park and Lake Bafa a Nature Park.
• DHKD employed and supervised a warden for the conservation of the pelican colonies in the Menderes delta for three breeding seasons.
• Printing of a pelican poster and brochure (DHKD).

Research:
• Monitoring and ringing in Menderes and Kizilirmak deltas (DHKD).
• Monitoring and ringing at Camalti Tuzlasi (M. Siki).
• Search for colonies (DHKD).
See also Vielliard (1968), Lehmann (1974), Heins et al. (1990), Crivelli et al. (1991b), Kasparek (1992), Peja et al. (in press).

Ukraine

Red Data Book:
Listed as Vulnerable in the Red Data Book of the USSR (Borodin, 1984).

Legislation:
Ban on hunting only.

Distribution:
Breeding: Danube delta.
Wintering and migration: Caspian Sea coast (Russian Federation and Azerbaijan) and Turkmenistan.

Key sites:
Breeding: Lake Kugurlui (unprotected) in the Danube delta.
Wintering and migration: Kura delta, Bol'shoi Kyzyl-Agachsky Gulf.

% of population in protected areas:
Breeding: 0%.
Wintering: 0%.

Conservation efforts:
None.

Research:
See Crivelli (1994), Litvinova (1994), Lysenko (1994).

Aims and objectives

Aims

1. In the short term, to prevent any further declines below 1994 levels in the population size and distribution of the Dalmatian Pelican.

2. In the medium to long term, to increase the population size of the Dalmatian Pelican to a level at which it no longer qualifies as a globally threatened species.

Objectives

1. **Policy and legislation**

1.1. *Legislation*

The legal protection during breeding and wintering of Dalmatian Pelicans and key sites for the species should be encouraged in all range states.

Priority: essential
Time-scale: short

1.2. Taking of birds

Establish a total ban on catching chicks or adults for zoos or tourist purposes.

Priority: essential
Time-scale: short

1.3. Promote sustainable development in wetlands

An integrated approach to the conservation of wetlands should be promoted which will also benefit the conservation of other species. Such an approach will need to address the protection of sites from development, pollution, changes in the hydrological regime, tourism and fishing policy, etc. The welfare of the local people should also be taken into account. The involvement of local communities in conservation and management measures is of critical importance.

The Dalmatian Pelican is considered as a priority species in the coastal and inland wetland European conservation strategies currently being prepared by BirdLife International (Tucker et al., in press)

Priority: essential
Time-scale: short/ongoing

1.4. International co-operation

Establish and enhance co-operation on the conservation of trans-border wetlands. Promote international collaboration and information exchange.

Priority: medium
Time-scale: ongoing

1.5. National species action plan

It is recommended that in each country a body is designated to prepare a detailed national action plan for the species. The same body would also be responsible for co-ordinating the implementation of the national action plan. Preparation of such plans will provide an opportunity to further develop objectives involving further integrated and interdisciplinary work as well as specific policies. Organisations responsible for the implementation of each action should be identified at this stage.

Priority: medium
Time-scale: short

2. Species and habitat protection

2.1. Site protection

2.1.1. Designation as protected areas

The designation of all breeding, key feeding areas and wintering sites should be promoted in all range states.

Priority: essential
Time-scale: medium

2.1.2. Hunting

The implementation of the ban on hunting in all wintering and staging areas where Dalmatian Pelicans occur in large numbers should be encouraged with high penalties for those found guilty of harming Dalmatian Pelicans.

Priority: essential
Time-scale: short

2.1.3. Wardening

Encourage the establishment of statutory temporarily or permanently wardened zones around the colonies, forbidding human intrusion including fishermen, birdwatchers and photographers. Scientists should be allowed to visit breeding colonies only with permission of the appropriate national body.

Priority: essential
Time-scale: short

2.2. Site management

2.2.1. Vegetation management

Promote a ban on burning (or cutting) of reedbeds in spring within the breeding areas. Encourage measures to restore wetland sites within the range of the Dalmatian Pelican.

Priority: essential.
Time-scale: short/ongoing

2.2.2. Hydrological management

Carry out proper water management of the wetlands in which a breeding colony is located and/or in important staging and wintering areas. Promote the restoration of the hydrological regime within the range of the Dalmatian Pelican.

Priority: essential
Time-scale: short/ongoing

2.2.3. Powerlines

Dismantle or bury powerlines identified as dangerous for pelicans. If this is not feasible, powerlines should be made visible to the birds in order to avoid collisions.

Priority: high
Time-scale: short

2.2.4. Artificial structures

When appropriate, and only in fully protected areas, provide adequate artificial structures to facilitate breeding or roosting.

Priority: low
Time-scale: ongoing

2.2.4. Residues and pollution

Prevent dumping of residues, chemical pollution and eutrophication at Dalmatian Pelican sites. Promote the restoration of sites which have suffered from pollution.

Priority: low
Time-scale: ongoing

3.   Monitoring and research

3.1. Breeding birds

Monitor the number of breeding pairs annually using trained people only.

Priority: essential
Time-scale: short/ongoing

3.2. Wintering birds

Monitor the number of wintering birds every mid-January, preferably by counting birds at roosting sites.

Priority: essential
Time-scale: short/ongoing

3.3. Ecological change

Monitor water-level, water quality and ecological change at key wetland sites.

Priority: essential
Time-scale: short/ongoing

3.4. Undertake hydrological studies

These should include the whole water catchment and especially the effects of river diversions and pumping of underground water for irrigation.

Priority: high
Time-scale: medium

3.5. Conservation measures

Regularly monitor and assess the effects of the conservation and management measures taken, and, when necessary, steer actions as appropriate.

Priority: high
Time-scale: short/ongoing

3.6. Prey populations

Monitor fishery catches at the key Dalmatian Pelican sites in collaboration with the official services responsible for collecting such data.

Priority: medium
Time-scale: medium/ongoing

3.7. Causes of mortality

Monitor dead pelicans and undertake research on causes of death.

Priority: low
Time-scale: medium/ongoing

3.8. Socio-ecological aspects

Undertake socio-ecological studies on key wetlands for the species in order to identify existing or potential conflicts between people and pelicans.

Priority: low
Time-scale: medium

3.9. Feeding ecology

Undertake studies on feeding ecology, where this has still not been done, especially in relation to potential conflicts between Dalmatian Pelicans and commercial fishermen, and assess the impact of the birds on the fish populations.

Priority: low
Time-scale: medium

3.10. *Dispersal*

Monitor and study the dispersal of Dalmatian Pelicans throughout the year by surveys and colour-ringing.

Priority: medium
Time-scale: ongoing

4.   **Public awareness and training**

4.1. *Public awareness*

The users of wetland resources and decision-makers at local, regional, national and international level should be informed about the plight of the Dalmatian Pelican. Public awareness campaigns should be undertaken with hunters, fishermen, local communities, civil servants and officials involved in Dalmatian Pelican conservation.

Priority: high
Time-scale: short

4.2. *Training*

Promote training courses and environmental education on wetland issues, and provide training for the trainers.

Priority: medium
Time-scale: short/ongoing

Annex
Recommended conservation actions by country

Albania

1.1./2.1.1. Promote the creation of a Nature Reserve or a National Park at Karavasta lagoon. It is recommended that only professional fishermen of the local co-operative be allowed to fish, using fixed traps only and with a ban on fishing within the lagoon. Independent fishing should be totally forbidden.

1.4 Develop co-operative links with NGOs and public bodies in Greece and the former Yugoslav Republic of Macedonia for the conservation of the Prespa Lakes.

2.1.3. Promote the establishment of a non-intrusion zone of 200 metres around the colony at Karavasta.

2.1.3. Hire two wardens from March to July to guard the colony against disturbance and destruction by local people.

2.2.2. Encourage the maintenance of the three connections between the sea and the lagoon by dredging them regularly.

3.1. Census the colony.

3.2. Undertake mid-winter counts, not only on coastal wetlands but also in inland wetlands.

3.3. Monitor ecological change.

3.9. Continue the study of feeding ecology in the breeding area.

3.10. Carry out colour-ringing.

4.1./4.2. Undertake public awareness campaigns and training at all key sites, targeted mainly at hunters, fishermen and local communities.

Bulgaria

1.3. Promote the implementation of the national Action Plan for the Conservation of Wetlands in Bulgaria.

1.1./2.1. Establish appropriate protection of the wetlands where pelicans roost, migrate or winter or where they forage during the breeding season.

1.3. Promote sustainable development within the framework of the management plan for Srébarna, including improvement of the conditions for the breeding colony, identifying the main feeding grounds of the pelicans around Srébarna and applying to all conservation projects in Bulgaria.

1.4. Establish co-operation between Bulgarian and Romanian organisations for the preservation of the wetlands northwards of Srébarna where pelicans feed.

2.2.2. Promote restoration of the former hydrological regime at Srébarna Nature Reserve.

2.2.5. Decrease the pollution in the wetlands around the Burgas area.

3.1. Monitor the breeding colony including ringing young birds with colour rings.

3.2. Undertake mid-winter counts.

3.3. Monitor ecological change at key wetland sites.

3.9. Identify the main feeding grounds of pelicans nesting in Srébarna.

3.10. Undertake colour-ringing of chicks at the Srébarna colony.

4.1./4.2. Undertake public awareness campaigns and training at all key sites, targeted mainly at hunters, fishermen and local communities.

Federal Republic of Yugoslavia (Serbia only)

2.1.1. Promote implementation and enforcement of the existing law relevant to the National Park of Lake Skadar.

2.1.3. Prevent disturbance at the colony in spring.

2.2.3. Through proper water management, ensure the spring flooding of Lake Skadar in order to favour fish spawning.

3.1. Census the colony.

3.2. Undertake mid-winter counts.

3.3. Monitor ecological change.

3.9. Carry out studies on feeding ecology in the breeding areas.

3.10. Carry out colour-ringing.

4.1./4.2. Undertake public awareness campaigns and training at all key sites, targeted mainly at hunters, fishermen and local communities.

Greece

1.3. Promote implementation of the Action Plan for the Conservation and Management for Greek Wetlands (1989).

1.4. Develop co-operative links with NGOs and public bodies in Albania and the former Yugoslav Republic of Macedonia for the conservation of the Prespa Lakes.

1.5. Re-establish discussions on a national action plan for the Dalmatian Pelican in order to bring this project to fruition.

1.1./2.1.2. Encourage enforcement and implementation of the ban on hunting.

2.1.3. Promote establishment of a non-intrusion zone around all colonies during the breeding period. If needed, such measures could also be implemented in other non-breeding areas important for the species (e.g. Lakes Kastoria and Kerkini).

2.2.1. Encourage enforcement and implementation of the ban on cutting of the riparian forest at Lake Kerkini and restoration of the reedbeds.

2.2.1. Promote management of the reedbeds and restoration of the wet meadows at Lake Prespa.

2.2.2. Recommended hydrological management at Lake Kerkini: (1) find practical alternatives to the planned construction of new dikes; (2) lower the present maximum water-level to 35 metres a.s.l. by solving the sediment problem (Psilovikos, 1992) through finding new sources of water for agriculture and improving the efficiency of the irrigation network (Bartzoudis and Pyrovetsi, 1994).

2.2.2. Recommended hydrological management at Lake Prespa: ensure the maintenance of an April – June water-level of at least 854.6 metres a.s.l. favouring efficient spawning of fish and shallow-water areas as feeding grounds. Careful thought should be given to making a new link between Mikri and Megali Prespa including a strict management plan for the use of the new sluice in order to ensure a high water-level in spring.

2.2.3. Promote burial of all powerlines located on the isthmus between the two Prespa Lakes or at least install a thick cable along the full length of the powerlines.

2.2.3. Promote installation of thick cable on several powerlines which are dangerous for Dalmatian Pelicans in other areas (Amvrakikos, Kerkini, etc.).

3.1. Census colonies in Lakes Prespa and Amvrakikos.

3.2. Undertake mid-winter counts.

3.3. Monitor ecological change.

3.3. Monitor water quality at wetlands.

3.5. Monitor existing and future management measures at Kerkini, Prespa, Amvrakikos and Porto-Lago.

3.5. Assess and review the management measures taken during recent years at Lake Kerkini, before any new management is initiated.

4.1./4.2. Undertake public awareness campaigns and training at all key sites, targeted mainly at civil servants, hunters, fishermen and local communities.

4.2. Promote environmental education within the framework of the national educational programme emphasising Dalmatian Pelican conservation.

Romania

2.1.3. Promote establishment of a non-intrusion zone around all colonies in the Danube delta during the breeding period.

2.2.2. Encourage restoration of the floodplains within the delta by partial or total destruction of the dikes along the canals.

3.1. Census the colony.

3.2. Undertake mid-winter counts.

3.3. Monitor ecological change at key wetland sites.

4.1./4.2. Undertake public awareness campaigns and training at all key sites, targeted mainly at hunters, fishermen and local communities.

Russian Federation

1.1./2.1.1. Encourage the designation as protected area of the whole of Lake Manych-Gudilo and the Kura delta, and enlargement of the protected areas in the Kuban and Volga deltas.

2.1.3. Promote establishment of a non-intrusion zone around all colonies during the breeding period.

2.2.2. Protect the remaining wetlands with breeding colonies from drainage and water abstraction and/or water diversion.

2.2.4. Build and establish floating rafts in the Volga delta.

3.1. Census the colonies.

3.2. Undertake mid-winter counts.

3.3. Monitor ecological change at key wetland sites.

4.1./4.2. Undertake public awareness campaigns and training at all key sites, targeted mainly at hunters, fishermen and local communities.

The former Yugoslav Republic of Macedonia

1.4. Develop co-operative links with Albanian and Greek NGOs and public bodies for the conservation of Prespa Lakes.

2.2.2. Promote measures to stop eutrophication at Lake Megali Prespa by building treatment plants and sewage systems.

Turkey

1.1. Promote improvement and updating of the National Red List of Threatened Animals.

1.3./2.2.2. Encourage measures to stop drainage and water extraction and/or water diversion and other damage at Turkish wetlands.

1.3./2.2.5. Prevent pollution in the catchment areas of the wetlands.

2.1.1. Promote the designation of wintering sites as protected areas.

2.1.2. Promote improvement and publicise the hunting legislation and secure better enforcement.

2.1.3. Encourage improved wardening of the colonies.

2.2.2. Improve the water management of each wetland and secure the minimum habitat requirements for the survival of the species.

3.1. Census the colonies.

3.2. Undertake mid-winter counts.

3.3. Monitor ecological change at key wetland sites.

4.1. Undertake public awareness campaigns and training at all key sites, targeted mainly at hunters, fishermen and local communities.

Ukraine

1.3./2.2.3. Promote measures to stop drainage and water extraction and/or water diversion at the remaining wetlands with breeding colonies.

2.1.1. Encourage the designation of Lake Kugurlui as a protected area.

2.1.3. Encourage establishment of a non-intrusion zone around all colonies during the breeding period.

3.1. Census the breeding colonies.

3.2. Undertake mid-winter counts.

3.3. Monitor ecological change at key wetland sites.

4.1./4.2. Undertake public awareness campaigns and training at all key sites, targeted mainly at hunters, fishermen and local communities.

International action plan for the Lesser White-fronted Goose (*Anser erythropus*)

Reviews

This action plan should be reviewed and updated every three years. An emergency review will be undertaken if sudden major environmental changes, liable to affect the population, occur within the species' range.

Geographical scope

The action plan needs to be implemented in Azerbaijan, Bulgaria, Finland, Germany, Greece, Hungary, Kazakhstan, Lithuania, Norway, Romania, Russia, Sweden, Turkey and Ukraine.

Summary

During the twentieth century, populations of the Lesser White-fronted Goose *Anser erythropus* have undergone drastic declines in numbers everywhere, even in the extent of the breeding and wintering ranges. Since the 1940s, the population has probably fallen by more than 90% to fewer than 50000 individuals (Europe c.1000 wintering; Caspian region possibly 30000; eastern Palaearctic c. 6000), and the decline is apparently continuing. Indeed, a recent follow-up meeting of experts on the species could account for no more than 2000 birds throughout its entire West Palaearctic range (Lorentsen and Madsen, 1995). The reasons for this are virtually unknown, the combination of negative factors acting on the breeding grounds (e.g. habitat loss, disturbance, shooting, increased predation) being insufficient to explain the rapid decline of the 1950s, and the apparent catastrophic decline of recent years. Damaging factors at staging areas and in the winter quarters, for example, habitat loss and shooting, appear to be key factors. More information is needed on numbers, distribution, habitat requirements and threats in the central part of the species' range.

In all European range states except Romania, the Lesser White-fronted Goose is protected. Recently, increased habitat protection and a general shooting ban on geese in Greece and Hungary, where geese are protected within Ramsar Sites, have probably been a cause of increasing numbers of Lesser White-fronted Geese staging and wintering there. In Sweden, a re-introduction programme where young Lesser White-fronted Geese are fostered by adult Barnacle Geese has had some success.

The short-term aim of this action plan is to maintain the current population of the Lesser White-fronted Goose in known areas throughout its range and to locate and assess the existing poorly known breeding and (especially) staging and wintering areas of the species, and, if possible, remove the current threats. In the longer term, the aim is to conserve and manage all major sites to encourage increased use by the species and ultimately a population recovery.

Threats and limiting factors

Hunting – unknown, probably high

Predation – unknown, probably high

Disturbance and habitat loss on the breeding grounds – unknown, probably low; helicopter disturbance – locally high

Habitat loss on the staging/wintering grounds – unknown

Conservation priorities

Locate and assess key areas – essential

Promote the use of international conventions for the protection of the species together with direct discussions between range states – high

Promote the legal protection of the species and key sites – high

Reduce the hunting pressure – high

Manage habitats and prevent further losses in the staging and wintering grounds – high

Monitor the remaining populations and carry out research on the biology of the species – high

67

Raise public awareness of the species, particularly amongst hunters and landowners – high

Introduction

The world population of the Lesser White-fronted Goose *Anser erythropus* breeds in a belt from northern Fennoscandia and northern Russia to far east Siberia. The population winters from the Balkans in the west to the Caspian Sea; further east, wintering grounds are found in China and the Korean peninsula.

Throughout its range the population has undergone a dramatic decrease within the last 50 years (Fennoscandia: Soikkeli, 1973; Norderhaug and Norderhaug, 1982; Hungary: Sterbetz, 1982; Russia: Vinogradov, 1990; Rogacheva, 1992); A. Andreev unpubl. report. The reasons for the decline are not known, but are generally believed to be found in the staging or wintering areas (Madsen et al., 1993).

The Lesser White-fronted Goose is classified by the IUCN as globally threatened in the category Rare (Groombridge, 1993). According to the new criteria developed by IUCN (Mace and Stuart, 1994), it is classified as globally threatened in the category Vulnerable (Collar et al., 1994), and at the European level it is also considered Vulnerable (Tucker and Heath, 1994). The Lesser White-fronted Goose is listed in Annex I of the European Union's Wild Birds Directive and is protected under the Bonn Convention (Appendix II) and the Bern Convention (Appendix II).

The present size and trend of the Lesser White-fronted Goose population wintering in the western Palaearctic is unknown, because recent counts are not available from what is thought to be the main winter quarters, in Azerbaijan and Russia. Probable total numbers during mid-winter are now well below 50000 birds, and this estimate is now considered to be far too optimistic. A recent meeting of experts could account for no more than 2000 birds throughout its entire West Palaearctic range (Lorentsen and Madsen, 1995). The population wintering in China and the Korean peninsula probably only numbers around 6000 individuals (A. Andreev unpubl.).

Action must be taken now, firstly to locate and evaluate the remaining staging and wintering sites of the Lesser White-fronted Goose, secondly to safeguard the population from pressures which may adversely affect it.

Background information

Distribution

Breeding range

The Lesser White-fronted Goose breeds in the sub-arctic/low-arctic zone from northern Scandinavia in the west to eastern Siberia in the east, with the range's centre of gravity lying in central Siberia. Within the western Palaearctic the Lesser White-fronted Goose breeds in the Scandinavian mountain ranges (Norderhaug and Norderhaug, 1984). In Russia, the species used to breed in a belt extending from the Kola peninsula to the Bolshezemelskaya tundra, but at present it is suggested that a viable breeding population is found only in the Bolshezemelskaya tundra.

The range in Fennoscandia has contracted markedly during the twentieth century. The distributions in the western and eastern parts of the range have become fragmented: in northern Scandinavia only small groups (loose associations of a few pairs/families) are found in Finnmark, and the situation in Russia is likely to be the same (Rogacheva, 1992).

Staging areas and winter quarters

The autumn staging areas and winter quarters of the Scandinavian population are poorly known. Autumn and spring staging areas are found in Hungary (Sterbetz, 1982), and from late autumn to early spring small numbers are observed in Romania (Munteanu et al., 1991 and unpubl.), Bulgaria (Boev, 1985; Georgiev et al., 1994) and Greece (Handrinos and Goutner, 1990; Handrinos, 1991). Further to the east, staging areas are found in the Ob valley in Kazakhstan, and major wintering grounds are found in Azerbaijan (Vinogradov, 1990), and possibly in Iran and Iraq. According to Vinogradov (1990) massive shifts in winter distribution have occurred in the Caspian region within the last 30 to 40 years. Wintering areas in Iran have been abandoned, and the status of wintering sites in Iraq is unknown. Spring staging areas are poorly known. In western Finland, small flocks stage in May (Soikkeli, 1973; J. Markkola, pers. comm.). Recent use of satellite tracking has enabled important staging areas to be located on the Kanin peninsula, Russia. Potentially important staging areas have been found in Brandenburg, Germany, southwest Lithuania, the Azov Sea and in northern Kazakhstan. There is unconfirmed information that further staging areas exist in the Baltic republics.

Population

Numbers and trends on breeding grounds

The Fennoscandian breeding population was estimated at more than 10000 individuals in the first half of the twentieth century (Norderhaug and Norderhaug, 1984), but since then the population has crashed, and by 1992 numbers were estimated at around 50 pairs. In Sweden the population is considered close to extinct (Sweden: von Essen, 1993; Norway: Øien and

Aarvak, 1993; Finland: J. Markkola, pers. comm.). In the early 1990s, 30 to 60 birds gathered in a post-moulting site in Porsanger Fjord in Norway (August–September) (Aarvak and Brøseth, 1994).

Drastic reductions in population size and range have also been recorded in northern Russia since the middle of the twentieth century (Vinogradov, 1990), and in European Russia the population is estimated at 3500 to 5500 individuals (Vinogradov, 1990), but this information has to be regarded as a guess only, and V. Morozov (pers. comm.) considers this figure too high.

From surveys on the breeding grounds Vinogradov (1990) estimated the total population in Russia to exceed 100000 individuals; according to Vinogradov (1990) the population in Taimyr has been stable during recent decades. However, these figures have not been confirmed by recent winter counts, as only approximately 30000 were accounted for in the Caspian region in the 1980s (Vinogradov, 1990). Rogacheva (1992) and V. Morozov (pers. comm.) question

Figure 1

Distribution of breeding areas and staging and wintering grounds of the Lesser White-fronted Goose in the former Soviet Union (redrawn from Vinogradov 1990)

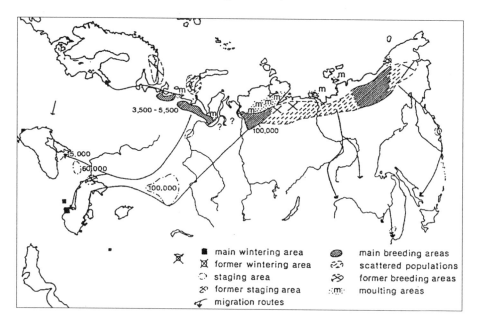

the high estimate and state that in many regions of central Siberia and northern Russia the population has decreased. The far east Siberian population has declined sharply in recent decades (A. Andreev, pers. comm.).

Numbers and trends in staging and wintering areas

The declines recorded on the breeding grounds have been reflected at the Hungarian autumn staging areas; before the 1950s the autumn population was suggested to have numbered around 100000 birds; in the late 1960s this had fallen to around 5000 (Sterbetz, 1982), and the decrease has continued since, so that in the late 1980s only 200 to 600 birds were observed annually (Farago et al., 1991 and unpubl.). Encouragingly, in the winters of 1992-93 and 1993-94, increasing numbers (up to 1200) had been observed wintering/staging in Hungary (S. Farago, pers. comm.).

A decrease has also been observed in the spring staging areas in Finland. Before the 1950s several hundred birds were observed each spring, but numbers have declined sharply (Soikkeli, 1973) and now only small flocks (usually fewer than 50 birds) are seen (Norderhaug and Norderhaug, 1982; J. Markkola, pers. comm.). In recent years, up to 97 different individuals have been observed on a pre-nesting staging area at the Porsanger Fjord in northern Norway (Aarvak and Øien, 1994).

In Romania and Bulgaria, fewer than 10 Lesser White-fronted Geese are usually observed during mid-January waterfowl censuses, though in January 1992 a total of 900 was estimated in Romania (D. Munteanu, pers. comm.), and Lesser White-fronted Geese are generally overlooked in the large flocks of wintering White-fronted Geese *Anser albifrons*. Nankinov (1993) has described a hitherto unknown wintering site of up to 1000 Lesser White-fronted Geese in northern Bulgaria, but these numbers need to be confirmed.

In Ukraine, only small groups or single birds are observed in flocks of White-fronted Geese (T. Ardamatskaya and V. Serebryakov, pers. comm.).

In Greece, up to 1600 were observed in the 1960s, but since then numbers have declined, and January counts in the 1980s have varied from none to 142 (Handrinos and Goutner, 1990; Handrinos ,1991). In recent winters, a small but stable winter population of up to 140 birds has become established in north-east Greece (H. Jerrentrup and G. Handrinos, pers. comm.).

In Azerbaijan, 30000 birds have been reported wintering, though this information is not supported by more recent data. A partial survey in February 1996 suggested only 1085 birds, of which only 2.7% - 5.6% were immatures, suggesting poor breeding success in 1995 (Fauna and Flora International, unpubl.). The survey did not include the southern shore of Sarasuy lake, where in the past, huge numbers of unspecified geese have been seen from the air (E. Sultanov, pers. comm. and *in litt.*). This area is difficult to access. Other former mass wintering sites in the Caspian region have been completely abandoned (Vinogradov, 1990; V. Morozov, pers. comm.). In Iran, former wintering sites have also been abandoned (Wetlands International, unpubl.).

The status of the Lesser White-fronted Goose in Turkey is uncertain. Few specimens have been observed among wintering White-fronted Geese (L. von Essen, pers. comm.).

In summary, the breeding and wintering population of Lesser White-fronted Goose in the western Palaearctic has undergone an alarming decline (more than 90%) and range contraction in the second half of this century, and this is apparently continuing. The eastern Palaearctic population is now estimated at around 6000 birds, based on mid-winter counts (Rose and Scott, 1994; J. Lu, pers. comm.). Hence, it is realistic to assume that the population decline has affected the whole of the world population and that the total has declined to fewer than 50000 individuals, a figure which must be treated as an absolute maximum (Europe fewer than 1000 wintering; Caspian region possibly 30000 and almost certainly far fewer; eastern Palaearctic 6000).

Life history

Very little information is available about the life history of the species in the wild.

Migration

In Hungary, the last birds of winter/spring are usually seen in late March (Sterbetz, 1982). In western Finland and Norway the first birds usually arrive in early May and migration continues until early June (Norderhaug and Norderhaug, 1982; T. Aarvak, pers. comm.). The geese arrive on the breeding grounds from late May to mid-June and leave the breeding areas from mid-August through September (Norderhaug and Norderhaug, 1982; Rogacheva, 1992). In Siberia, non-breeding birds undertake a moult-migration to areas north of the breeding range (Rogacheva, 1992), while non-breeders in Fennoscandia moult at high altitudes (Ekman, 1922; T. Aarvak and J. Markkola, pers. comm.). The first autumn influx of birds in Hungary usually occurs in September (Sterbetz, 1982).

Feeding and habitat requirements

Nesting habitat includes the taiga and tundra zone, in particular the scrub ecotone (Uspenski, 1965; Rogacheva, 1992). In Scandinavia, the geese nest inland at relatively high altitudes, up to 700 metres (Ekman, 1922). The species is strictly herbivorous, foraging on a variety of plants along lake and river margins and in marshes (Lorentsen and Spjøtvoll, 1990). During pre-nesting in northern Norway the geese feed on saltmarshes (Aarvak and Øien, 1994).

In winter, the geese traditionally occurred in the steppe zone/semi-arid zone, foraging on short grassy, so-called sodic-pasture, vegetation (Sterbetz, 1968; 1990). In Hungary, Lesser White-fronted Geese feed predominantly in this habitat, using other types only when there is no steppe available (Sterbetz, 1990). Kovács (1995) observed that the species uses pioneer vegetation at the bottom of recently-drained fishponds in the Hortobágy. Because of lack of recent knowledge about winter occurrence, present habitat usage is poorly known.

Threats and limiting factors

The reasons behind the dramatic population decline are not known, so the causes can only be guessed at.

Disturbance on the breeding grounds

Conditions have been relatively stable throughout the century, but, especially in Scandinavia, increasing tourism and angling cause disturbance in some breeding areas. The pre-nesting staging area in Porsanger Fjord, Norway, is next to a helicopter airport which causes much disruption of the activities of the geese.

Importance: unknown, but probably low;
helicopter disturbance, locally high

Habitat loss and physical development on the breeding grounds

Habitat loss through the creation of reservoirs for hydroelectric power has occurred in Scandinavia. Intensification of reindeer-rearing by the Laps and consequent increased grazing pressures on the tundra may also have had negative influences.

Importance: unknown

Predation

The arctic fox *Alopex lagopus* probably causes some nest predation, but the level is unknown. A recorded spread of the red fox *Vulpes vulpes* at higher levels in mountains into the breeding range of the Lesser White-fronted Goose, may have played a role in the decline. In Fennoscandia, red foxes appear to be a severe threat (J. Markkola, pers. comm.).

Importance: unknown, but probably high

Habitat loss and modification on the staging/wintering grounds

The traditional feeding conditions have deteriorated through the transformation of the steppes, the former wintering habitat of the birds (Sterbetz, 1968; 1990), into cultivated land. This development has happened throughout most of the assumed wintering range. In Greece, marshland habitat, which is favoured for feeding, is converted into agricultural land (Handrinos and Goutner, 1990; H. Jerrentrup and T. Nazirides, pers. comm.). The spring staging areas in western Finland are grasslands (salt and fresh) traditionally extensively used for hay cutting and livestock grazing. However, the condition of the grasslands as goose feeding habitat has deteriorated because of lack of cutting and grazing, which has caused much of the formerly short-grazed vegetation to grow too tall (J. Markkola, pers. comm.).

Importance: unknown, but probably high

Hunting

Over-exploitation from hunting has perhaps played a role, but there is scant information about former hunting pressures on the geese. Despite the fact that the Lesser White-fronted Goose is protected throughout its range in the western Palaearctic, birds are still shot because of misidentification with other quarry species of geese or because of indiscriminate waterfowl shooting. This is known to be the case in Russia where spring hunting of waterfowl is allowed (Rogacheva, 1992), and in Finland (J. Markkola, pers. comm.), and undoubtedly in the other range states as well. It was formerly a problem in Greece (Handrinos and Goutner, 1990; H. Jerrentrup and T. Nazirides, pers. comm.) but since 1993 all goose hunting has been banned in key sites, and any remaining threat would be from illegal goose hunting. Apart from the direct negative impact, hunting in or near roosting and feeding sites causes disturbance which can reduce the availability of suitable habitat. In northern Scandinavia, and probably also in the Russian breeding range, mass capture of moulting Lesser White-fronted Geese took place at certain sites as late as in the 1950s (Curry-Lindahl, 1959).

Importance: unknown, but probably high

To summarise, the combination of negative factors potentially acting on the breeding grounds is probably not sufficient to explain the rapid rate of decline that took place in the 1950s. Probably the sharp decline has been caused primarily by negative factors in the winter quarters, namely habitat loss and excessive hunting.

Vulnerability indices

Assessed on the basis of a declining population and the lack of recent knowledge about the status of breeding and wintering areas throughout the world range, the species appears to be highly vulnerable.

Extinction risk

The fragmentation of the breeding range and the continued population decline greatly increase the risk of local and regional extinctions. For the world population the extinction risk is assessed to be medium to high.

Conservation status and recent conservation measures

Azerbaijan

Protected. The major wintering area in Azerbaijan was formerly a reserve with some shooting regulations and with farmland managed especially to attract Lesser White-fronted Geese, for example, unharvested seed crops (V. Vinogradov, pers. comm.). The status of these regulations under the new Azerbaijan regime is unknown. A partial survey was carried out in January - February 1996.

Bulgaria

The species is protected by the Act 342 (1986), and is listed as Endangered in the Red Data Book of Bulgaria (Boev, 1985). The major certain staging area, Shabla Lake, has recently been designated as protected. Goose hunting is not permitted at Ramsar Sites. Action is taken to give better protection and habitat management to Lake Shabla (prepared by the Ministry of Environment, the Bulgarian Academy of Science and the Bulgarian Society for the Protection of Birds). A penalty, soon to be increased from US$ 2.30 to US$ 460, is imposed for shooting a Lesser White-fronted Goose.

Finland

Protected. Staging areas near Oulu are protected. Marshes are managed for the Lesser White-fronted Geese (grazing and mowing). See also actions undertaken in Sweden.

Germany

Strictly protected. A regular visitor on passage in very small numbers. The main sites are Unterer Niederrhein (Nordrhein Westfalia), wetlands in northern Germany (Schleswig-Holstein, Lower Saxony) and eastern Germany (e.g. Galenbecker See in Brandenburg). The main sites are protected as nature reserves and Unterer Niederrhein and Galenbecker See are Ramsar Sites. Illegal hunting and shooting in error through misidentification are likely threats.

Greece

Protected. The three most important sites, Evros delta, Lake Kerkini and Lake Mitrikou, are Ramsar Sites and European Union Special Protection Areas (RCB, 1990). Since 1993, hunting of all goose species has been banned, and this has probably led to the recent establishment of a small wintering population. However, hunting of other game species continues in areas used by the Lesser White-fronted Geese. Habitat restoration is carried out in the Evros delta, with the aim of maintaining its lagoon characteristics.

Hungary

Strictly protected. The major autumn staging areas in Hungary are protected, including a general shooting ban on waterfowl. Goose hunting is no longer permitted at Ramsar Sites, and this may be the cause of the recent increase in wintering and staging numbers of the Lesser White-fronted Goose. However, illegal hunting away from these areas may pose a threat. The hydrology of the fishpond system in the Hortobágy is managed specifically to create conditions for feeding Lesser White-fronted Geese as well as roosting Cranes *Grus grus*.

Kazakhstan

Protected.

Lithuania

Recent information suggests there is an important staging area in the south-west, with counts of 200 to 500. Several birds have been reported shot (Svasas, in press).

Norway

Protected. Pre-nesting staging areas in the Porsanger Fjord, northern Norway, are protected; breeding areas are partly within national parks. See also actions undertaken in Sweden.

Romania

Presently a quarry species but likely to become protected in the near future.

Russian Federation

Protected. Part of the central breeding area in Taimyr is within the Taimyr State Reserve.

Sweden

Protected. Former breeding areas are partly within National Parks. A reintroduction project was launched in 1981 (von Essen, 1991; 1993). Semi-captive Barnacle Geese *Branta leucopsis* are used as foster parents to goslings of Lesser White-fronted Geese and these families are released into former breeding areas of Lesser White-fronted Geese. The intention is to restore a breeding population in Sweden by reducing winter mortality through the change of migration routes of the Lesser White-fronted Geese from the original south-easterly direction to the southwest, towards wintering grounds of the Barnacle Geese in the Netherlands. In Finland, a restocking project has been underway since 1989 in which juvenile birds are released in areas with a dispersed breeding population. The Swedish project has had some success: introduced birds have established a migration to the Netherlands, have reappeared in the release areas, and a small breeding population has been established (von Essen, 1993 and pers. comm.). It is too early to evaluate the Finnish project. Observations on the wild population in Norway have the aim of pin-pointing possible limiting factors and threats.

Turkey

Protected. The species occurs only occasionally.

Ukraine

Protected.

International

In Scandinavia, different initiatives, under the auspices of an informal Nordic Lesser White-fronted Goose working group, have been taken to meet the decline of the breeding population.

Aims and objectives

Aims

1. In the short term, to maintain the current population of the Lesser White-fronted Goose in known areas throughout its range.

2. In the medium to long term, to ensure an increase in the Lesser White-fronted Goose population.

Objectives

1. **Policy and legislation**

1.1. *To finalise detailed conservation planning with member states in the fly way of the Lesser White-fronted Goose*

The signing, ratification and implementation of the relevant international wildlife conventions (especially Ramsar and Bonn, and the Agreement on the Conservation of African-Eurasian Migratory Waterbirds under the Bonn Convention) by range states should be encouraged and pursued. However, this process may take several years; because of the urgency of action for the Lesser White-fronted Goose direct negotiations with range states about the conservation of the species and its habitat will be required.

Priority: high
Time-scale: short

1.2. *To protect the Lesser White-fronted Goose and its habitat through national and international legislation*

Encourage actions to ensure that the species receives the fullest possible legislative protection in all range states. Where the current protection is inadequate, sites of international importance should be given more protection, including the creation of refuge areas with feeding and roosting opportunities.

Priority: high
Time-scale: short

1.3. *To promote agricultural and other land use policies that benefit the species*

It is anticipated that agricultural practices in eastern Europe will change because of the change in political systems. The effect on the habitat of the Lesser White-fronted Goose is unclear but the problem should be addressed once the major staging and wintering sites have been located.

The Lesser White-fronted Goose is considered a priority in the conservation strategies for European inland wetlands and agricultural habitats currently being prepared by BirdLife International (Tucker et al., in press). These will address habitat-wide measures which could be implemented to benefit this and other species.

Priority: high
Time-scale: medium

2. **Species and habitat protection**

2.1. *To prevent hunting and associated disturbance*

Despite the fact that the Lesser White-fronted Goose is protected in all European range states except Romania, birds are still shot. At key sites, all waterfowl shooting should be regulated to prevent avoidable mortality of Lesser White-fronted Geese. To minimise the disturbance effect of hunting, core zones with no shooting should be designated at all key sites, including roosting and feeding habitats. In core breeding areas in Russia, spring shooting should be prevented. Generally, harmonisation of hunting seasons between neighbouring range states should be promoted in order to reduce hunting during late winter and spring.

Priority: high
Time-scale: short

2.2. *To prevent further loss of habitat on the breeding grounds*

Promote protection of core breeding areas through designation as protected areas and the diversion of industrial development and tourism to other areas.

Priority: medium
Time-scale: medium

2.3. *To manage habitat on staging and wintering grounds*

For known staging and wintering areas, management plans should be prepared, prioritising the conservation needs and habitat requirements of Lesser White-fronted Geese. Sites in the Kanin peninsula, Russia and Brandenburg, Germany should be protected and adequately managed.

Priority: high
Time-scale: short, ongoing

2.4. To reintroduce and restock populations when other conservation measures fail

Reintroduction and restocking may be accepted as an alternative way to minimise the risk of extinction of the species but should be applied only when other efforts to conserve the wild population appear to fail and the IUCN criteria for reintroductions are met (Kleiman et al. 1994). Reintroduction should only be carried out in areas where the species has disappeared, and measures should be taken to minimise risks to natural populations. As long as captive stocks of Lesser White-fronted Geese exist and can be maintained, there is no urgency for reintroduction and restocking. Therefore, these activities should have lower priority compared to measures focusing on the remaining wild populations. Reintroduction and restocking should be discontinued if a natural recovery of the wild population can be verified.

Priority: low
Time-scale: long

3.   Monitoring and research

3.1. To locate and assess key areas

Key staging and wintering sites of the populations breeding in Fennoscandia and Russia should be located and carefully monitored. The status of staging and wintering sites in Kazakhstan and Azerbaijan should be checked. Use of satellite-tracking on individuals from Scandinavia and central Siberia may give the most efficient first answers about winter dispersal and migratory movements. The tracking could be followed up by ground surveys, with the Azov Sea an early target. Moulting grounds should be located.

Priority: essential
Time-scale: short/medium

3.2. To monitor remaining populations

The monitoring of the remaining breeding population in Scandinavia and the staging and wintering populations in Hungary, Greece, Romania and Bulgaria (and Turkey) should continue in order to assess the trends of the wild population. Counts of age ratios and brood size should be carried out; this has been done successfully in Hungary for some years (Sterbetz, 1986) but unfortunately has now stopped. Distribution, habitat use and threats should be described.

Priority: high
Time-scale: short/ongoing

3.3. To conduct studies relevant to the conservation of the species

Comprehensive field studies of the habitat and behavioural ecology of the Lesser White-fronted Goose throughout its annual cycle should be carried out in order to permit greater understanding of the species' habitat requirements. This will create an informed basis for site and habitat protection and management. On the breeding grounds, factors affecting breeding success should be studied.

Priority: high
Time-scale: short

4.   Public awareness and training

4.1. To increase awareness of the importance of the Lesser White-fronted Goose and the threats facing the species

Relevant government departments and NGOs should be encouraged to raise public awareness of the importance of the Lesser White-fronted Goose within their range states.

Priority: high
Time-scale: short

4.2. To educate hunters and landowners

An internationally co-ordinated education programme aimed at hunters and landowners should be developed to make them aware of the vulnerability of the species, the problems in identification and the need to avoid hunting in key areas.

Priority: medium
Time-scale: medium

4.3. To train reserve wardens in census techniques

In particular, distinguishing Lesser White-fronted Geese in mixed Anser flocks and distinguishing different age-classes.

Priority: medium
Time-scale: medium

Annex
Recommended conservation actions by country

Azerbaijan

1.2. Promote fullest possible protection of all key sites.

2.1. Encourage positive habitat management to maintain and increase use by the Lesser White-fronted Goose.

3.1. Assess status of wintering sites; carry out a full survey of the Sarasuy lake.

3.2. Monitor the use of sites by geese and carry out research into habitat requirements and threats to wintering birds.

4.1. Raise public awareness of the threats faced by the species and its importance.

4.3. Encourage and train reserve staff to count Lesser White-fronted Goose separately in mixed flocks, and to monitor age ratios.

Bulgaria

1.2./1.3. The conservation of the Lesser White-fronted Goose should be considered when new agricultural legislation and policies are prepared and appropriate measures for ensuring the quality of the feeding habitats should be promoted in agricultural practices.

2.2. Promote the designation of Lake Shabla as a Ramsar Site and an increase in the no-hunting zone around the lake.

3.1./2.2./2.3. Confirm the status of the newly described sites for the species in northern Bulgaria. In case it is regularly used, designation as a protected area should be promoted and habitats managed to the benefit of the geese.

3.2. Monitor the use of sites by geese and carry out research to determine habitat requirements of the geese and local threats.

4.1. Raise public awareness of the threats faced by the species and its importance.

4.2. Raise awareness amongst hunters of the importance of the species, the problems in identifying it and the need to avoid hunting in key areas.

Finland

2.2. Promote the full protection of the remaining breeding area from development and tourism.

2.3. Promote management of the spring staging areas near Oulu for the benefit of the geese.

3.2. Continue annual monitoring of numbers of geese utilising the site.

3.2. Regularly monitor the breeding population.

4.2. Raise awareness amongst hunters of the importance of the species, the problems in identifying it and the need to avoid hunting in key areas.

Germany

2.2./3.1. Locate and assess key staging areas, and promote fullest possible protection.

3.3. Initiate studies of the habitat requirements during staging; local threats should be determined.

Greece

1.2./1.3./2.2./2.3. Promote the fullest possible protection of key sites in north-east Greece in order to maintain and increase wintering numbers.

2.3. Continue with the implementation of core zones where the geese can feed and roost undisturbed.

3.2. Continue monitoring of the species.

3.3. Initiate studies of habitat and behavioural ecology.

4.2. Raise awareness amongst hunters of the importance of the species, the problems in identifying it and the need to avoid hunting in key areas.

Hungary

3.2. Continue monitoring of the species.

3.3. Studies of the habitat and behavioural ecology of the geese should be initiated; age ratios and brood size should be assessed annually; threats to the geese should be determined.

4.2. Raise awareness amongst hunters of the importance of the species, the problems in identifying it and the need to avoid hunting in key areas.

Kazakhstan

1.2./2.2. Promote fullest possible protection of key sites and manage habitats for the benefit of the Lesser White-fronted Goose.

2.1. Promote control of hunting in areas used by the Lesser White-fronted Goose.

3.1. Locate staging areas.

3.2./3.3. Monitor the use of sites by geese and carry out research to determine habitat requirements and threats to the staging population.

4.1. Raise public awareness of the threats faced by the species and its importance.

4.2. Raise awareness amongst hunters of the importance of the species, the problems in identifying it and the need to avoid hunting in key areas.

Lithuania

1.2./2.2. Promote fullest possible protection of key sites.

2.1. Promote control of hunting in areas used by the Lesser White-fronted Goose.

3.1. Locate staging areas.

3.2./3.3. Monitor the use of staging sites by geese and establish the extent of any shooting problems.

4.2. Raise awareness amongst hunters of the importance of the species, the problems in identifying it and the need to avoid hunting in key areas.

Norway

2.2. Promote fullest possible protection for the remaining breeding areas, pre-nesting and post-nesting staging areas, from development and tourism.

2.3. Promote regulation of helicopter flights in the pre-nesting area in Porsanger Fjord.

3.2. Monitor annually the population of pre-nesting and post-nesting staging geese, as well as the breeding population.

Romania

1.2. Promote full protection from hunting for the species.

3.2./3.3. Monitor wintering numbers annually and determine habitat use.

4.1. Raise public awareness of the threats faced by the species and its importance.

4.2. Raise awareness amongst hunters of the importance of the species, the problems in identifying it and the need to avoid hunting in key areas.

Russian Federation

2.2. Promote fullest possible protection for key areas for breeding, staging or wintering from physical development and hunting.

3.1. Locate and assess core areas for nesting, moulting, and pre-nesting and post-breeding staging.

3.3. Initiate studies of factors affecting breeding success.

3.3. Initiate studies of the habitat requirements during staging; local threats should be determined.

4.1. Raise public awareness of the threats faced by the species and its importance.

4.2. Raise awareness amongst hunters of the importance of the species, the problems in identifying it and the need to avoid hunting in key areas.

Sweden

2.2./2.3. Although the wild population is regarded as practically extinct, the relevant authorities should keep the conservation focus on former breeding areas, in case the wild population may recover and return, or in case sites may be used as centres of reintroduction.

Ukraine

3.1. Possible wintering sites should be located and assessed.

4.1. Raise public awareness of the threats faced by the species and its importance.

4.2. Raise awareness amongst hunters of the importance of the species, the problems in identifying it and the need to avoid hunting in key areas.

International action plan for the Red-breasted Goose (*Branta ruficollis*)

Reviews

This action plan should be reviewed and updated every five years and/or when agricultural practices in Bulgaria and Romania change significantly. An emergency review will be undertaken if sudden major environmental changes, liable to affect the population, occur within the species' range, and/or goose numbers decline.

Geographical scope

The action plan needs to be implemented in Azerbaijan, Bulgaria, Greece, Kazakhstan, Romania, Russian Federation, Turkey and Ukraine.

Summary

The Red-breasted Goose *Branta ruficollis* is not only one of the rarest goose species in the world, it is also one of the most attractive, making it highly suitable as a "flagship" species for conservation throughout its range. It nests from June to July in the Russian arctic and winters in temperate regions along the Black Sea coast (Bulgaria, Romania, Ukraine and Turkey). The total number and distribution of Red-breasted Geese has puzzled scientists for many years, as counting them in their vast range (c. 1 200 000 km²) is often difficult. Since the early 1900s, population estimates have been based on incomplete data resulting in information which was either geographically incomplete or simply non-existent for years at a time (see Annex 2). Existing data suggest that the population suffered a dramatic decline from 60 000 to 25 000 during the late 1950s and 1960s, but recent comprehensive counts of over 70 000 geese may indicate that a sizeable proportion of the population was overlooked and that previous estimates were too low. The decline during the 1960s was accompanied by, and possibly due to, large-scale re-distribution from the wintering grounds on the Caspian Sea coast, where massive land-use changes occurred, to the Black Sea coast.

Threats and limiting factors

Potential land-use changes – high

Hunting and disturbance – high

Wetland habitat loss in non-breeding areas – medium

Climate change – unknown, probably medium

Predation – unknown

Industrial development at breeding sites – unknown

Rodenticides – unknown

Conservation priorities at European level

Maximum protected status of the Red-breasted Goose and its habitats – essential

Future agricultural policies which are sympathetic to the needs of the geese by providing suitable feeding habitat – essential

Adequate population monitoring on staging and wintering grounds – essential

Adequate monitoring of current threats including changes in agricultural practice and hunting pressure in the wintering grounds and industrial developments in the Russian breeding grounds – essential/high

Adequate protection and management for key sites – high

Public awareness campaign particularly in wintering and staging states – high

Setting up of a multinational Red-breasted Goose Working Group to organise monitoring schemes and research effort, and to co-ordinate conservation efforts throughout the species' range – high

Introduction

The Red-breasted Goose *Branta ruficollis* is the smallest goose in the western Palaearctic and easily distinguishable by its pattern of black, white and chestnut-red. It is also one of the rarest Palaearctic geese, and breeds on the tundra between the Arctic Circle and 78°N in west-central Siberia, mostly on the Taimyr peninsula. Disturbance from hunting and oil exploration may pose threats to the breeding population (Vinokurov, 1990). The species winters predominantly on the western Black Sea coast where the greatest threats are illegal and unregulated hunting and potential changes in agricultural practices in Bulgaria and Romania.

The Red-breasted Goose is classified by the IUCN as globally threatened in the category Insufficiently Known (Groombridge, 1993). According to the new criteria developed by IUCN (Mace and Stuart, 1994) the Red-breasted Goose is still classified as globally threatened and is listed as Vulnerable (Collar et al., 1994). At European level it is considered Localised (Tucker and Heath, 1994). The Red-breasted Goose is listed in Annex I of the European Union's Wild Birds Directive and in CITES, Appendix II. It is protected under the Bonn Convention (Appendix II) and the Bern Convention (Appendix II).

The total number of Red-breasted Geese has been something of a mystery for many years (Owen, 1980). Between 1956 and 1969 the population may have declined from 60000 to 25000, although other explanations of the disparity in counts are plausible (see "Population", below). During this period the majority of the geese switched wintering sites from the coasts of the Caspian Sea, where their habitat was lost and hunting pressure may have been great, to the western coast of the Black Sea. Recent co-ordinated, mid-winter counts approached 75000 individuals (Black and Madsen, 1993), though it is likely that there are as many as 78000 (D. Vangeluwe, pers. comm., 1994). As much as 90% of the population winters at only three or four sites in Bulgaria and Romania, and if current pressures result in these areas becoming unsuitable, the population could once more be displaced, and may decline as a result.

Based on two counts in the 1990s, Callaghan and Green (1993) ranked the species, according to the Mace-Lande criteria, as Safe, that is, not meeting the threatened species criteria. However, our understanding of the status of the Red-breasted Goose is still very poor: firstly, population estimates are too variable, suggesting instability, and only three of the last 10 mid-winter counts approached 70000; secondly, the species may be susceptible to massive population decline due to habitat loss in the winter quarters;

and thirdly, potent, man-made limiting factors including changes in agricultural policy, hunting and oil exploration, are in operation. Action must be taken to ensure that current pressures on the Red-breasted Goose are monitored and quantified throughout the range states so that their effects on the species can be adequately assessed and removed where necessary.

An international Red-breasted Goose workshop took place in Strasbourg on 5 December 1994 (WWT/IWRB Threatened Waterfowl Research Group and IWRB Goose Research Group).

Background information

Distribution

Breeding range

The breeding range of the Red-breasted Goose is restricted to the arctic tundra of the Taimyr, Gydan and Yamal peninsulas (see Figure 1). In all, 70% of the breeding population nests in the Taimyr (Kostin, 1985), the rest in Gydan and Yamal. For detailed accounts of breeding sites within these areas see Krivenko (1983), Vinokurov (1990) and Kostin and Mooij (in press). The breeding range in the Taimyr area is thought to be expanding (E. Syroechkovski, Jr., pers. comm., 1994). Small numbers may be breeding in the tundra west of the Ural mountains (Vinokurov, 1990), but this is not likely to be a significant proportion of the population.

Staging areas

Almost all Red-breasted Geese migrate down the eastern side of the Urals, pass through the Turgay lowlands between the southern end of the Urals and the Kazakh uplands, turn southwest over the northern Caspian Sea, and then move on towards the western Black Sea coast (Owen, 1980).

Staging areas are thought to be the same for both spring and autumn migration, and the available literature indicates that there appear to be four major ones. From the breeding grounds, the birds migrate south along a corridor only 100 to 150 km wide (Red Data Book of the Kazakh SSR), across the Nadym and Pura basins, to the first staging area at the Ob floodplains on the Arctic Circle (V. Krivenko, pers. comm., 1994). The next site is on the middle Ob near Khanty-Mansisk,

Russia. A small number have been known to stage in the region between Surgut and the River Vakh. From the middle Ob, the birds move south-west across the south of the west Siberian plain, over the town of Kustanai to the third major staging area on the Tobol-Ishim forest-steppe and the watersheds of the Ubagan, Ulkayak and Irgizin rivers in the Kazakh uplands (Krivenko, 1983). Passing over the towns of Orsk and Aktyubinsk, they then move across the north of the Caspian Sea to stage in the Manych valley, Russia. Some may stop off at the Azov Sea and may remain to winter on the northern Black Sea coast in Ukraine, but it seems that the next stop is generally the main wintering grounds in Bulgaria and Romania (see Figure 2).

Winter quarters

Prior to 1950, the main wintering areas were the southern coasts of the Caspian Sea, particularly the south-west coast. In 1968, counts indicated that about half the wintering population shifted to the west coast of the Black Sea (Annex 2) which is approximately 1800 km west of the Caspian. In the 1970s, very few Red-breasted Geese were found on the traditional sites on the Caspian, presumably because of reduced food availability and hunting pressure (Grimmett and Jones, 1989). Scattered records of small flocks further south may indicate that the birds ranged much further before monitoring began. The earliest known records of Red-breasted Geese are from Egyptian friezes about 6000 years old (Kohl, 1958), perhaps suggesting that they were once frequent visitors to that area.

The current wintering areas on the Black Sea coast are the Shabla and Durankulak lakes of Bulgaria, the lagoon/steppe complex of the Danube delta in Romania, and the Dobrodgea plateau which lies between the Danube and the coast and spans the Bulgaria/Romania border (Michev et al., 1991; Munteanu et al., 1991; P. Iankov, *in litt.*, 1995). In recent winters, 80% to 90% of the world population of Red-breasted

Figure 1
Summer distribution of the Red-breasted Goose *Branta ruficollis* in the Russian tundra (based on Vinokurov, 1990, new breeding sites by E. Syroechkovski, Jr., location of reserves from WWF Arctic Bull. 3: 17).
Ramsar Sites: 1. Gorbita delta, 2 Yenisey inner delta, 3 upper Dvuobye.

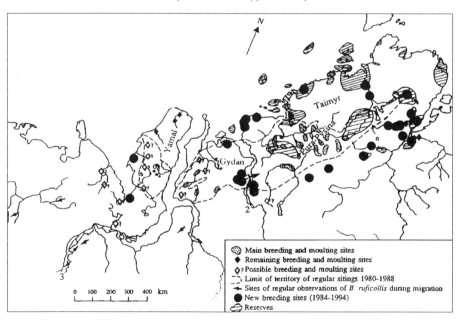

Geese wintered in Bulgaria (B. Ivanov, P. Iankov and G. Dandliker, *in litt.*, 1994). Small flocks winter in Ukraine and possibly Azerbaijan while others may visit Greece (IWRB, 1994; D. Vangeluwe, pers. comm., 1994). Occasionally very small numbers reach Hungary, Turkey, Iraq and Iran. The species is accidental in the United Kingdom, Belgium, Netherlands, Norway, Sweden, Denmark, Finland, Germany, France, Poland, Czech Republic, Slovakia, Austria, Italy, Spain, Albania, Serbia, Israel, Cyprus, Egypt and southeast China (Cramp and Simmons, 1977).

Figure 2

Map showing the main fly way and staging areas of the Red-breasted Goose *Branta ruficollis*

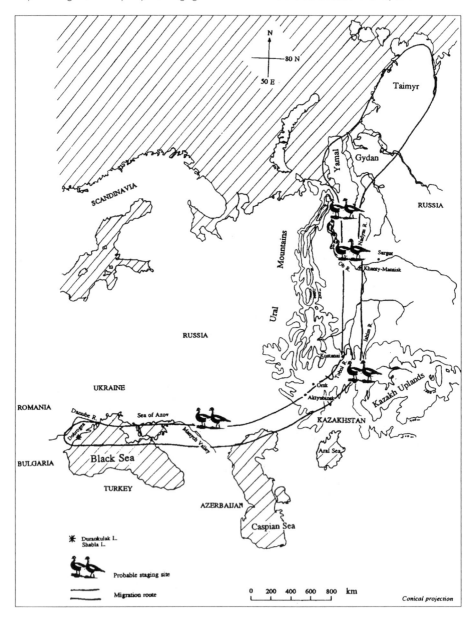

Population

It has been difficult to monitor changes in Red-breasted Goose numbers as the birds range across a wide wintering area (approximately 1 200 000 km²) and counts have been infrequent. The maximum population estimates and counts (where available) for each year since 1899 are given in Annex 2. Prior to 1954, records were scarce, but it is thought that numbers were larger than, or similar to, those of today. In 1899 "many tens of thousands of Red-breasted Geese were seen in their wintering sites" (Krivenko, 1983). Between 1956 and 1967 numbers were estimated at around 50 000 to 60 000; the best coverage was achieved in the winters of 1967 and 1968 when a total of 49 000 were counted in the Black and Caspian Sea regions, divided equally between the two. Between 1969 and 1989 count totals did not exceed 30 000, and ornithologists suggested that the population might have crashed due to the birds being forced from their traditional wintering area at the Caspian Sea and/or the effects of DDT on Peregrines *Falco peregrinus* which protect nesting geese from arctic foxes *Alopex lagopus* (see "Life history", below). Recent counts, which included coverage throughout the Black Sea wintering range, gave population estimates of 70 000 to 74 000 in three consecutive years. However, the overall count for 1993/94 was only 37 400 (Table 6.1), in spite of near-optimum count coverage (excluding the Caspian region), illustrating the erratic nature of population estimates.

The 1991 to 1993 counts indicate, therefore, either that the population doubled in size in just a few years (i.e. from 25 000 in 1989 to 70 000 in 1991) or, more likely, that significant proportions of the population were not recorded in previous years, especially in the late 1980s. Indications from other, well studied, goose populations (Owen and Black, 1990) suggest that the former hypothesis is unlikely. It is also possible, therefore, that the apparent decline in the Red-breasted Goose population in the 1970s may have been much less dramatic.

The apparent increase in Red-breasted Goose numbers may be due to improved monitoring, but as information is limited it may also be the result of improved conservation in both the breeding and wintering ranges and/or possibly the recovery of populations of birds of prey. Recent world population estimates are 70 000 to 74 000 (Table 6.1; Annex 2).

Table 6.1

Population size of the Red-breasted Goose in Europe, 1992-94. Figures refer to the numbers of individuals, from mid-winter counts and observations (see Annex 2 for details)

	No. of individuals		
	1992	1993	1994
Bulgaria	42 816	59 206	30 000
Romania	26 913	14 650	4 308
Ukraine	0	0	3 038
Greece	0	0	9
Others	10	0	0
Total	69 739	73 856	37 355

Life history

Breeding

Red-breasted Geese arrive on the breeding grounds in early June, around the time that the snow on the tundra melts. They nest in colonies averaging five to six pairs (Kostin and Mooij, in press). Laying begins in the second half of June and the clutch contains 3 to 10 eggs, most commonly 4 to 5. Incubation lasts 25 days and the fledging period 5 to 6 weeks (Owen, 1980). Clutch loss is usually less than 15% to 20% (Borodin, 1984). Breeding success fluctuates from year to year and depends mainly on the birds' condition when they arrive on the breeding grounds, as well as on climate, predation and population levels of birds of prey (Kostin and Mooij, in press). Severe climatic conditions can inhibit all recruitment. The arctic fox is the main predator, the degree of predation depending largely on the cyclical variation in abundance of the fox's main prey, the lemming, and on the proximity of nests to those of Peregrines, Rough-legged Buzzards *Buteo lagopus* and gulls which are thought to impart protection from the fox. Observations showed a correlation between the presence of nests of these birds and the average number of nests of Red-breasted Geese (Kostin, 1985; Kostin and Mooij, in press).

Moult

Red-breasted Geese moult on, or near, the breeding grounds (Figure 1). The flightless stage of moult lasts for 15 to 20 days between mid-July and late August. Non-breeders moult two weeks earlier (Uspenski, 1965).

Feeding

During breeding, grass leaves and the shoots of cotton-grass Eriophorum angustifolium make up the bulk of the diet (Uspenski, 1965). Grass shoots may be supplemented with tubers and rhizomes on steppe habitats during migration (Dementiev and Gladkov, 1952). Historically, when the geese wintered on the Caspian Sea coast, they fed on glasswort Salicornia from coastal mudflats and steppe pasture/stubble (Cramp and Simmons, 1977; Owen, 1980), but loss of these natural habitats may have forced the geese onto the agricultural lands of the Black Sea coast. On the main wintering sites in Romania and Bulgaria the geese now feed predominantly on winter wheat, barley, maize, some pasture grasses and spilt grain (Sutherland and Crockford, 1993; D. Munteanu, in litt., 1994). In Bulgaria in March, the geese will feed on grass shoots in ploughed fields (B. Ivanov, P. Iankov and G. Dandliker, in litt., 1994). Other plants taken include pondweed Potamogeton and seeds of Galium and Bolboschoenus (Owen, 1980).

Migration

The spring migration starts in March. There are three to four main staging areas (see "Distribution", above, and Figure 2). In early May the birds reach the Kazakh uplands and by early June have reached the breeding grounds. Autumn migration starts in mid-September, birds reaching Kazakhstan by the end of September (Cramp and Simmons, 1977; Owen, 1980). A few may continue south to the Aral Sea, while the majority travel south-west towards the Caspian. Small flocks may remain to winter on the Caspian Sea coast in Azerbaijan and some individuals continue south to Iran and Iraq. The majority, however,

travel on to the western Black Sea coast, arriving in October-November and are usually found with White-fronted Geese Anser albifrons. Small numbers may visit Greece from the main winter quarters in Bulgaria and Romania (D. Vangeluwe, pers. comm., 1994).

Habitat requirements

Nesting is mostly in tundra and sometimes in open parts of northern shrub tundra, where the species favours high and dry situations on steep river banks, steep rocky slopes, low rocky crags or gulleys. Cover is usually thin and includes dwarf birch Betula, willow Salix or dead grass (Cramp and Simmons, 1977). Proximity to the nests of Peregrines, Rough-legged Buzzards or gulls may improve breeding success (see above). The geese usually nest close to adequate water, to provide a refuge for the young (Cramp and Simmons, 1977).

There is little information available on the habitat and its use at staging sites, though steppe habitats are apparently used during migration (Cramp and Simmons, 1977).

On the western Black Sea coast, the winter feeding habitat comprises agricultural land dominated by cereal crops and grassland (Sutherland and Crockford, 1993). The birds periodically fly to coastal lakes to drink. These lakes, situated up to 50 km from the feeding areas, are also safe night-roosts. The proximity of drinking and roosting sites to feeding areas may influence winter distribution (D. Munteanu, in litt., 1994). In Bulgaria, Red-breasted Geese roost on water; usually in the middle of lakes, but occasionally, or in times of high hunting pressure, on the sea if it is calm. When the lakes freeze (which is rare) they roost on the ice (B. Ivanov, P. Iankov and G. Dandliker, in litt., 1994; D. Vangeluwe, pers. comm., 1994). Roost sites in Romania are in remote parts of wetlands where the geese utilise shallow water, and muddy and sandy beaches with low aquatic vegetation (D. Munteanu, in litt., 1994). On the Evros delta in Greece, the Red-breasted Goose feeds, and possibly roosts, on a specific area of natural vegetation (G. Handrinos, in litt., 1994).

Threats and limiting factors

Land-use changes

Due to recent political changes, there are now proposals for abandonment, division and privatisation of land in Romania and Bulgaria (Crockford (1991), Black and Madsen (1993)). This may lead to changes from the cereals favoured by the geese to cash crops such as vines and vegetables, which Red-breasted Geese do not utilise. Land-use change on the Caspian Sea coasts was the likely cause of the massive re-distribution to the Black Sea coast and apparent decline in numbers during that time. Land-use changes in Bulgaria and Romania may result in a similar loss of wintering habitat, thereby causing another re-distribution event which may in turn lead to further population decline.

Although preliminary enquiries suggest that only one third of arable land in South Dobrodgea may be privatised (B. Ivanov, P. Iankov and G. Dandliker, *in litt.*, 1994), the threat lies in whether privatisation will lead to unforeseen land-use change, such as large-scale conversion to cash crops, development or increased hunting; and/or intensification of existing arable land, which in turn may lead to conflict between geese and landowners as happens in western Europe (J. Mooij, pers. comm., 1994).

Importance: high

Hunting and disturbance from other human activities

The Red-breasted Goose is protected throughout its range except in Romania. Although Romanian legislation prohibited the hunting of the species during the 1993/94 season (D. Munteanu, *in litt.*, 1993), there has so far been no similar provision for 1994/95 onwards. The number of geese shot (of any species) is not monitored in any of the range states. This, together with the lack of regular productivity estimates (proportion of young birds in flocks, brood sizes, population estimates), makes it difficult to assess the impact that hunting may have.

In the highly populated area of the Yenisey inner delta (71°N 82°E) south of the Gydan and Taimyr peninsulas, the Red-breasted Goose is the most abundant goose species and is consequently hunted (E. Syroechkovski, Jr., pers. comm., 1994).

Disturbance caused by the hunting of closely associated species, particularly the White-fronted Goose, may influence the foraging performance, distribution and reproductive success of the Red-breasted Goose, as is evident in other goose species (Madsen, 1995). On the Black Sea coast, shooting is concentrated near the roost sites (coastal lakes) for about one hour at dawn and one hour at dusk, although shooting on inland feeding areas during the day also occurs. As many as 300 to 500 shots per hour have been counted as the birds arrive at and depart from the roost sites at Lake Shabla, Bulgaria (T. Michev, pers. comm., 1994). Privatisation of land around Lake Shabla has altered the boundaries of the government residence situated there, and as a result hunters now have access to areas much closer to the roost sites (B. Ivanov, P. Iankov and G. Dandliker, *in litt.*, 1994).

Visiting hunters from countries such as Italy, Spain and France are becoming an increasing problem in Bulgaria and Romania. Such tourist hunters do not respect quotas, hunt at night and hunt on every day of the week (local people hunt only on three days of the week) thus extending the time that the geese are disturbed and shot. Tourist hunters also make little effort to distinguish between the White-fronted Goose and the protected Red-breasted Goose (B. Ivanov, P. Iankov and G. Dandliker, *in litt.*, 1994).

In Romania, wintering geese are intentionally and illegally poisoned, and the carcasses are then sold at markets as food (D. Munteanu, *in litt.*, 1994).

In Russia, Red-breasted Geese are known to nest on river banks and some of the best fishing areas are also along these rivers. Consequently, disturbance from boat traffic, fishermen and their dogs is perhaps becoming an increasing problem (V. Flint, pers. comm., 1994). Human depopulation of the northern areas means, however, that access is more difficult and expensive, thereby reducing the number of people visiting these regions (E. Syroechkovski, Jr., pers. comm., 1994).

Importance: high

Loss of wetland habitats in non-breeding areas

In addition to land-use changes in the winter quarters (see above), further sources of habitat loss are given here.

In Romania, the Dobrodgea lagoons are being artificially separated from the Black Sea. The resulting decrease of salinity may increase freezing, thereby reducing available roosting and drinking areas, which in turn may push geese further south to less suitable sites (Crockford, 1991).

In Greece, degradation of habitats through drainage and development has left few habitats for wintering geese (Handrinos, 1991). In Macedonia alone, 40% of the area of inland lakes has been drained and 95% of the marshland has been reclaimed for agriculture. These changes are affecting the ground water balance and promoting salinisation of the remaining area, thereby furthering habitat loss (Handrinos, 1991).

Importance: medium

Climate change

On the Russian tundra, severe weather can prevent 80% of the potential breeding population from nesting (Kostin, 1985) and, in some years, may result in no recruitment of offspring whatsoever. The percentage of geese which breed and the number of nests per colony seem to be determined by conditions at the beginning of June, namely temperature, precipitation and snow cover of the cliffs (Kostin and Mooij, in press).

Deteriorating weather and consequent reduction of food availability on migratory routes and at staging areas may lead to increased mortality in autumn/winter (Krivenko, 1983) and reduced breeding success in spring/summer (Kostin and Mooij, in press).

In the winter quarters, severe weather reduces growth of winter wheat, an important part of the Red-breasted Goose diet (Borodin, 1984). Drought conditions in autumn can cause reduced growth of cereal crops resulting in reduced quantity and quality of goose food during the winter (B. Ivanov, P. Iankov and G. Dandliker, *in litt.*, 1994; D. Munteanu, pers. comm., 1994).

If climate change were to lead to severe weather on the breeding or wintering grounds, in several successive years, it could cause a significant decline in the population.

Importance: unknown, probably medium

Predation

Reproductive success of the Red-breasted Goose is partly influenced by predation by the arctic fox. The degree of predation is dependent on population levels of birds of prey (see 'Life history', above). During the 1950s, numbers of Peregrines declined as a result of organochlorine pesticides (DDT) and disturbance (Cramp and Simmons, 1980). The consequent loss of protection for Red-breasted Geese during the nesting period could have resulted in a decline in breeding success either through increased predation or lack of suitable nesting sites (Isakov, 1972; Kostin, 1985). Red-breasted Goose numbers apparently increased during the time that populations of these birds of prey were recovering.

Importance: unknown

Industrial development

Development of oil and gas depots, and the consequent disturbance from land and air, may have forced the Red-breasted Goose to abandon many breeding sites in Gydan and Yamal (Vinokurov, 1990).

Importance: unknown

Rodenticides

In Bulgaria, use of rodenticide has in the past (especially the winter of 1988/89) caused the deaths of many wintering geese, including Red-breasted Geese (B. Ivanov, P. Iankov and G. Dandliker, *in litt.*, 1994).

Importance: unknown

Conservation status and recent conservation measures

Only those range states of past or present international importance for the Red-breasted Goose are listed below. See Annex 2 for detailed counts and estimates for each country.

Azerbaijan

The current status of the species is unclear. While some suggest that around 500 individuals (0.6% of the population) regularly winter there (D. Vangeluwe, pers. comm., 1994), others say that the species probably no longer occurs in the area and has not done so in any significant numbers for the last 20 to 30 years (see Annex 2) (M. Patrikeev, pers. comm., 1995).

Until the 1970s, the coasts of the Caspian Sea were the main wintering site for the Red-breasted Goose. In 1956, a maximum of 60 000 were thought to use this site (100% of the then-known population) (Cramp and Simmons, 1977). Drainage for market gardening and a change from cereal and rice crops to cotton and vines (Grimmett and Jones, 1989) reduced the area of suitable habitat and may have forced the geese to abandon this area. In 1989, 500 birds were reported in the south-west of the Caspian (Vinokurov, 1990), but this observation was never confirmed and it is unlikely that the habitat, which is unsuitable, could support these geese (M. Patrikeev, pers. comm., 1995).

Prior to 1990, the species had threatened status and was protected by law. The Kisil-Agach State Reserve gave protection to the species, and hunting and trapping were prohibited. Annual waterfowl counts were carried out by Russian ornithologists. However after 1990, when Azerbaijan declared its independence from the Soviet Union, the Russian ornithologists left and it is likely that all conservation laws were annulled (M. Patrikeev, in litt., 1994).

Bulgaria

The species is listed as Endangered in the Red Data Book of Bulgaria (Botev and Peshev, 1985), and protected under the Law for the Conservation of Nature (1967) whereby a fine soon to be increased from US$ 4.60 to US$ 460, is imposed for damage to a protected species (Michev et al., 1991; B. Ivanov, P. Iankov and G. Dandliker, in litt., 1994).

The hunting season is restricted from 1 September to 31 January, with hunting permitted on Saturdays, Sundays and Wednesdays, though few local people hunt on Wednesdays (Wilson and Moser, 1994; B. Ivanov, in litt., 1995).

As much as 90% of the world population of Red-breasted Geese winters on Shabla and Durankulak lakes (T. Michev, unpublished results in Wilson and Moser, 1994). Lake Durankulak is a Ramsar Site and Lake Shabla is protected by Bulgarian law (B. Ivanov, in litt., 1995). There used to be a 500 metre zone around Lake Shabla in which shooting was prohibited (Ivanov and Pomakov, 1981), but privatisation of the land has changed the borders of the protected zone (B. Ivanov, P. Iankov and G. Dandliker, in litt., 1994; D. Vangeluwe, pers. comm., 1994). In 1995, Shabla Lake was designated as protected (510.8 ha through Act 31, 24 January 1995). The biggest part of the protected area is now fenced. Up to 60000 Red-breasted Geese have been recorded on Lake Shabla in late January from 1991 to 1994 (77% of the population) (B. Ivanov, pers. comm., 1994). The Committee on Forests is responsible for enforcing hunting laws, but violations are increasing as a result of poor enforcement, and shooting regularly occurs from within the 500 metre zone and even from the lake itself (Black and Madsen, 1993; Wilson and Moser, 1994; D. Vangeluwe, pers. comm., 1994; P. Iankov, in litt., 1995). Legislation to control hunting by tourists is in preparation.

Special programmes are underway to protect the Red-breasted Goose and eight other species in Bulgaria, supported by BirdLife International and IWRB (Wilson and Moser, 1994). A joint project of the Ministry of the Environment and the Swiss Association for the Protection of Birds (SVS, the BirdLife Partner organisation in Switzerland) on the coastal wetlands of the Black Sea includes the preparation and implementation of a management plan for Lakes Shabla and Durankulak. The Red-breasted Goose will be the main focus of these management plans. The project started in 1994 and will last three years (funded by the Swiss Government). Since January 1995, a privately run conservation organisation, Le Balkan, has been renting 197 ha of land for wintering geese.

Extensive monitoring of the population, co-ordinated with counts in Romania, was initiated in winter 1990-91 (D. Vangeluwe, pers. comm.,

1994), and in January 1993 ornithologists from the United Kingdom and Denmark joined Romanian and Bulgarian teams to conduct co-ordinated surveys and for discussions on Red-breasted Goose conservation (Black and Madsen, 1993). Another survey was carried out in 1994 by a team from the RSPB.

Educational materials such as posters depicting the Red-breasted Goose have been prepared.

Greece

Legislation to protect the Red-breasted Goose was instigated in 1985. The species is listed as Endangered in the Greek Red Data Book (Handrinos, 1992). Since 1993, hunting of all goose species has been banned.

The Evros delta is the most important site in Greece for wintering Red-breasted Geese and has Ramsar and European Union Special Protection Area status. Though degradation of the habitat has resulted in fewer birds wintering there, small flocks of around 50 birds visit regularly. Regular counts of wintering geese are conducted, and numbers since 1963 have typically ranged from 0 to 116 (0-0.2%). In relatively cold periods larger numbers migrate from Romania/Bulgaria to Greece (D. Vangeluwe, pers. comm., 1994). A maximum of 2000 Red-breasted Geese was recorded in the severe winter of 1984-85 (2.7% of the population) (Handrinos, 1991). Hunting is permitted in a small part of the Evros delta, away from the areas usually used by Red-breasted Geese.

Efforts have been made to regulate the influx of salt water into lagoons on the Evros delta by constructing a temporary earth dam in the river. A full management and delineation study for the Evros delta has now been completed (G. Handrinos, in litt., 1994).

Hungary

Up to 16 birds have been reported annually since 1984 in Hortobagy and Kiskunsag National Parks.

Kazakhstan

The Red-breasted Goose is protected and included in the Red Data Book (1991). There is reported to be a major staging area on the Tobol-Ishim forest steppe and the watersheds of the Ubagan, Ulkayak and Irgizin rivers in the Kazakh uplands (52.5°N 65°E), but its current importance is not known and there are no resources for carrying out basic survey work (Zhatkanbayev, pers. comm., 1995). A maximum of 3000 birds was recorded during spring in the period 1972 to 1977 (8.6% of the 1972-77 population) and a maximum of 15 000 in autumn (42.5% of the 1977 population) (Krivenko, 1983).

Romania

For the winter of 1993-94 Red-breasted Geese were completely protected by Decision No. 501/14 July 1993 by the Ministry of Waters, Forests and Environment Protection (D. Munteanu, in litt., 1993), but this law was not automatically renewed for 1994-95, so currently the geese are not protected. Conservationists await the ministry's decision on a new proposal put forward for future years (D. Munteanu, pers. comm., 1994). The hunting season, formerly 15 August to 31 March, has been shortened to cover 10 September to 1 March (D. Munteanu, in litt., 1993).

The recently adopted law for the Danube Delta Biosphere Reserve (Ramsar Site) will give strict control to all forms of wildlife utilisation by a system of permits, administered and enforced by the reserve administration (Wilson and Moser, 1994).

The Danube delta, the Razelm-Sinoie complex and the Dobrodgea plateau are the most important sites in Romania for the Red-breasted Goose (Madsen, 1994). On the Dobrodgea plateau, the main feeding site, the geese are not protected; a maximum of 33 830 was recorded feeding there in the winter of 1990-91 (45.7% of the population) (Sutherland and Crockford, 1993).

Extensive monitoring of the population, co-ordinated with counts in Bulgaria, was initiated in the winter of 1990-91 (D. Vangeluwe, pers. comm., 1994), and in January 1993 ornithologists from the United Kingdom and Denmark joined Romanian and Bulgarian teams to conduct co-ordinated surveys and for discussions on Red-breasted Goose conservation (Black and Madsen, 1993).

Educational materials such as posters depicting the Red-breasted Goose have been prepared.

Russian Federation

The Red-breasted Goose is protected in Russia. It is listed as Rare in the Red Data Book of the USSR (Borodin, 1984). In 1970 an export ban was declared.

On 13 September 1994, Russia ratified the Ramsar Convention. The Gorbita and Yenisey inner deltas were designated Ramsar Sites (Figure 1). Also included were the Ob floodplains (upper Dvuobye), just north of Khanty-Mansisk (62.5°N 67°E), where a maximum of 10 000 Red-breasted Geese have been recorded (13.5% of the 1993 population), and Lake Manych-Gudilo (47°N 42°E) where 25 000 were recorded in autumn 1976 (62.5% of the 1976 population) (Krivenko, 1983).

Up to 70% of the breeding population nests on the Taimyr peninsula (Kostin, 1985). Large areas of this region have been given reserve status, but only about 20% of the known breeding sites lie within these reserves (Figure 1). The percentage of breeding pairs which this represents is unknown. In 1978, the largely unprotected Pura-Pysina watershed in the Taimyr held the highest concentration of breeding birds (Kostin, 1985). Ramsar status was proposed for part of this area, but was not ratified.

Since the changes in the communist administration, reserves and the enforcement of hunting legislation are now controlled by regional authorities. Consequently, there is less communication with a central administration and less monitoring and regulation of activities in remote areas (I. Kostin, pers. comm., 1994) (Figure 1).

An extensive study of the Red-breasted Goose's breeding biology and the implications for its conservation was carried out from 1977 to 1983 (Kostin, 1985). Recent analyses of some aspects of the breeding biology and breeding success have been made (Kostin and Mooij, in press).

Over the past 10 years, surveys have discovered several new breeding sites beyond the known range (E. Syroechkovski, Jr., pers. comm., 1994).

In November 1994, the Working Group on Geese of Eastern Europe and Northern Asia was established with the aim of supporting and developing studies on Red-breasted and Lesser White-fronted Geese in Russia and of planning conservation measures to protect the most important areas for these species. An international goose research project, based in the Russian arctic and including studies on the Red-breasted Goose, is planned for 1995. Participants include the Russian Academy of Sciences, Wildfowl and Wetlands Trust, the Dutch Institute for Forestry and Nature Research, and the Danish National Environmental Research Institute (funded by the European Union).

Educational materials such as posters depicting the Red-breasted Goose have been prepared.

Ukraine

The Red-breasted Goose is protected. The species is thought to use the Azov Sea as a staging area, and flocks of 2000 to 3000 winter on the Ukrainian coast of the Black Sea. The most important sites are the Yagorlystski and Tendra Bays (Madsen, 1994). During mild periods birds will migrate from Romania/Bulgaria to Ukraine (D. Vangeluwe, pers. comm., 1994). Regular counts of wintering geese are conducted, and a maximum of 3038 Red-breasted Geese were recorded in the winter of 1993-94 (4.1% of the population) (IWRB, 1994).

Aims and objectives

Aims

In the short term, to maintain the Red-breasted Goose population at no less than 70 000 individuals.

Objectives

1. **Policy and legislation**

1.1. *To protect wintering Red-breasted Geese from adverse changes in agricultural policy*

The effects of agricultural policies in Bulgaria and Romania are crucial to wintering Red-breasted Geese. Under the former Soviet administration large "bread basket" areas of winter-wheat were farmed, and it is these which are now supporting thousands of wintering Red-breasted Geese. If current policies on privatisation allow large-scale intensification and/or change to cash crops, the geese could be displaced to other, less favourable habitats and decline as a result. New agricultural policies should be sympathetic to the species.

The Red-breasted Goose is considered a priority species in the European agricultural and inland wetlands conservation strategies currently being prepared by BirdLife International (Tucker et al., in press).

Priority: essential
Time-scale: short

1.2. *To ensure that all range states give the maximum appropriate legal protection to the Red-breasted Goose and its habitat*
Legislation banning all hunting of the species should be promoted in Romania and maintained in all other range states. Regulations to control tourist hunters should be promoted as necessary. New legislation to protect sites used by the species should be encouraged where required. Penalties should be sufficiently high to be an effective deterrent against offences.
Priority: essential
Time-scale: short

1.2.1. Synchronise the waterfowl hunting seasons between neighbouring range states
Reducing the hunting season to a minimum period in all states (end of January) would help to lower hunting pressure on Red-breasted Geese and reduce conflict between hunters and the authorities.
Priority: medium
Time-scale: medium

1.3. *To involve international conventions in ensuring international co-operation over the conservation of the Red-breasted Goose*
All range states should be encouraged to participate in joint international actions under the auspices of the Agreement on the Conservation of African-Eurasian Migratory Waterbirds (AEWA) under the Bonn Convention.
Priority: high
Time-scale: short

2. **Species and habitat protection**

2.1. *To prevent shooting and other destruction or disturbance of Red-breasted Geese*

Full enforcement of legislation protecting the Red-breasted Goose should be promoted. To minimise direct mortality from hunting and other activities (including poisoning), complete wildfowl shooting bans should be introduced at all key sites during the times when the geese are present. Where possible, non-hunting buffer zones should be created around these sites.

Adequate wardening should be promoted at all vulnerable key wintering sites to protect Red-breasted Geese from threats such as illegal shooting, the use of poison and unnecessary disturbance.

Prosecution of any offenders should be sought with penalties which are sufficiently high to deter future offences.
Priority: essential
Time-scale: ongoing

2.2. *To ensure adequate protection for key Red-breasted Goose sites*

2.2.1. Ensure optimum statutory protection for important sites

Promote the designation as protected areas of any sites identified as nationally or internationally important for the species, especially key roost sites.
Priority: high
Time-scale: short

2.2.2. Prevent further loss of Red-breasted Goose habitats both in the breeding and wintering grounds

Promote full environmental impact assessments for development proposals which may have a negative impact on the species, including wetland loss in wintering areas and habitat fragmentation and degradation by mining and exploration for oil and gas. These developments should be monitored and diversion to less important areas should be encouraged.
Priority: high
Time-scale: ongoing

2.3. *To prevent further deaths from rodenticides*

If the use of rodenticides in the winter quarters is found to be a problem (see 3.6.) measures to control their use should be put into place.

Priority: medium
Time-scale: medium

2.4. *Where applicable, to enhance staging and wintering habitats by "farming" the land for the geese in areas currently used by the species*

If the results of the research on the feeding and distribution studies listed below (3.2., 3.2.1., 3.2.2., 3.3.1. and especially 3.3.2.) show it to be necessary, feeding habitat management strategies based on the results of this research should be considered. Habitat enhancement can increase the chance of survival and the reproductive success of the birds. These measures should be initiated in key sites and if appropriate extended to areas regularly, but less commonly used for wintering.

Priority: unknown
Time-scale: medium

2.5. *To promote international co-operation for conservation of the Red-breasted Goose*

A multilateral agreement for the conservation of Red-breasted Geese should be pursued with the aim of finalising detailed conservation planning with member states in the species' fly way.

The elaboration of such an agreement as well as the co-ordination of research on the species could be conducted within the framework of a Red-breasted Goose working group which would include representatives of each of the main range states.

Priority: high
Time-scale: short/medium

3.   Monitoring and research

3.1. *To monitor, annually, population size and structure*

Co-ordinated winter counts in Bulgaria, Romania, Ukraine, Greece and Azerbaijan, similar to the one conducted in 1992-93 (Black and Madsen, 1993), would give an indication of the stability of the population. The frequency of these counts

should be increased to up to twice per month in the peak season. Age ratio and brood size should be included in the counts to give an indication of recruitment, survival rates and age structure (Black and Madsen, 1993).

Distribution and numbers of breeding Red-breasted Geese should also be monitored.

Priority: essential
Time-scale: ongoing

3.2. *To assess the current status of areas reported to be important for Red-breasted Geese but for which there is little or no information*

3.2.1. Current status of spring and autumn staging areas

Little is known about the staging areas. The most important staging areas should be identified; distribution of geese, habitat use and threats in these areas should be determined. Marking birds with rings, collars or satellite transmitters may help to determine migration routes and staging areas.

Priority: essential
Time-scale: short

3.2.2. Current status of traditional wintering sites

It is not known whether some traditional wintering sites are still being utilised by the species. Distribution and numbers of geese and habitat use in these areas should be determined.

Priority: high
Time-scale: short

3.2.3. Current status of traditional breeding sites

Periodically update information on the breeding areas.

Priority: medium
Time-scale: medium

3.3. *To conduct research relevant to the conservation of the species*

3.3.1. The relationship between spring fattening and breeding success

Studies on this matter are required to determine from which habitats the geese are obtaining adequate resources for nesting.

Priority: medium
Time-scale: medium

3.3.2. Feeding and behavioural ecology during migration and in winter

These studies are necessary to ensure that any habitat enhancement projects optimise survival and reproductive rates.
Priority: medium
Time-scale: medium

3.3.3. Feeding ecology of breeding females

These studies are required to determine constraints on nesting success imposed by the phenology, availability and value of the food resources and the potential dependence on protection from birds of prey, especially Peregrines.
Priority: medium
Time-scale: medium

3.4. *To monitor changes in land use in the winter quarters*

Following the changes in agricultural policies and practices, the Red-breasted Goose's habitat in Bulgaria and Romania should be monitored and, if changes are seen to be affecting the suitability of the land for the geese, actions to prevent displacement of the species should be taken (see 1.1.).
Priority: essential
Time-scale: ongoing

3.5. *To monitor and assess the impact of mortality and disturbance caused by hunting, including the hunting of White-fronted Geese*

Particular attention should be focused on assessing the impact of tourist hunting on the Red-breasted Goose so as to make recommendations on any necessary regulations to control their activities (see 1.2. and 2.1.).
Priority: high
Time-scale: short

3.6. *To monitor the possible impacts on the Red-breasted Goose of the use of rodenticides*

This research is needed to determine if actions are needed (see 2.3.).

Priority: medium
Time-scale: medium

4.   Public awareness and training

4.1. *To promote awareness of the conservation needs of the species among people using Red-breasted Goose habitats*

4.1.1. Increase public awareness of the importance of the species

Relevant government departments and non-government organisations should be encouraged to raise the profile of the Red-breasted Goose in their range states, particularly where illegal shooting has been reported.

Priority: high
Time-scale: ongoing

4.1.2. Initiate education/awareness programmes

Especially for hunters, particularly tourist hunters, fishermen and farmers in each range state, designed to inform them of the status of the species and the need for protection.

Priority: high
Time-scale: ongoing

4.2. *To promote the conservation of areas used by the Red-breasted Goose and other species of threatened waterbird*

The Red-breasted Goose could be used as a flagship species to promote the conservation of the habitat which is valuable to several threatened species including the Dalmatian Pelican *Pelecanus crispus*, Pygmy Cormorant *Phalacrocorax pygmeus*, Lesser White-fronted Goose *Anser erythropus*, Marbled Teal *Marmaronetta angustirostris*, Ferruginous Duck *Aythya nyroca* and White-headed Duck *Oxyura leucocephala*.

Priority: high
Time-scale: ongoing

Annex I
Recommended conservation actions by country

Azerbaijan

2.5./3.1. Efforts should be made to find a Red-breasted Goose working group member for Azerbaijan who will co-ordinate regular winter counts. It has been suggested that a Turkish ornithologist could monitor Azerbaijan as an interim solution until a representative can be found.

3.2.2. The current status of Azerbaijan as a wintering site should be clarified as soon as possible.

Bulgaria

1.1. Consideration should be given to the conservation of the Red-breasted Goose when new agricultural legislation and policies are drawn up.

1.2. The Ministry of the Environment and Committee for Forestry should encourage the parliament to adopt the newly proposed legislation for the control of tourist hunters.

2.1. The no-hunting buffer zones around Lakes Shabla and Durankulak should be redefined and perhaps enlarged to 500 metres. Key sites should be actively guarded during critical periods.

2.1./3.5. Disturbance and mortality caused by hunting should be monitored and regulated.

2.1. Tourist hunters should be restricted to areas where they will not disturb Red-breasted Geese or where disturbance is not a problem.

2.2.1./2.4. Promote the designation of Lake Shabla as a Ramsar Site and reserve status and the feasibility of establishing an adjacent refuge that is "farmed" for the geese should be assessed.

2.5. An ornithologist from a Bulgarian agency (possibly BSPB) should be formally selected to represent Bulgaria in a multinational Red-breasted Goose working group.

2.3./3.6. Encourage the stricter control of rodenticide use and promote a complete ban in core feeding areas for Red-breasted Geese, where

alternative methods should be implemented and monitored.

3.1. Co-ordinated winter counts between Bulgaria, Romania, Ukraine, Greece and Azerbaijan should be conducted once to twice monthly on a formal and annual basis.

3.3.1. Ecological and behavioural studies of Red-breasted Geese in the winter quarters should be initiated.

4.1. Public awareness of the importance of the species and the threats it faces should be raised.

Greece

1.2.1. It is recommended that the end of the hunting season should be brought forward to the end of January.

2.1./3.5. Promote a review of hunting regulations and activities. Where necessary, disturbance and mortality caused by hunting should be monitored and regulated.

2.5. An ornithologist from a Greek agency (possibly the Ministry of Agriculture) should be formally selected to represent Greece in a multinational Red-breasted Goose working group.

2.2.2. The use of European Union Structural Funds should be evaluated to prevent further habitat loss in wetlands used by the Red-breasted Goose.

2.4. Promote further protection and enhancement of habitats used by wintering Red-breasted Geese, particularly in the Evros delta, to enable them to support larger numbers of geese and in order to provide suitable alternative wintering sites.

3.1. More frequent winter counts, co-ordinated with those in Bulgaria, Romania, Ukraine and Azerbaijan, would be valuable for determining movements of Red-breasted Geese.

Kazakhstan

2.5. An ornithologist from a Kazakhstan agency (possibly the Institute of Zoology) should be formally selected to represent Kazakhstan in a multinational Red-breasted Goose working group.

3.1. Regular counts of goose numbers utilising the staging areas should be initiated.

3.2.1. The current importance of Kazakhstan staging areas should be determined as soon as possible.

3.3.1. Studies on goose ecology and behaviour in the staging areas should be initiated.

Romania

1.1. Consideration should be given to the conservation of the Red-breasted Goose when new agricultural policies are drawn up.

1.2. Promote permanent protected status throughout Romania, including a total ban on shooting, for the Red-breasted Goose.

1.2. Encourage an annual hunting close season policy.

1.2.1. It is recommended that the hunting season should close at the end of January.

2.1. Shooting of Red-breasted Geese should be prevented.

2.1. The problems of mortality and disturbance caused by tourist hunters should be addressed.

2.1. Deliberate poisoning of feeding geese must be prevented.

2.1./3.5. Disturbance caused by the hunting of other goose species should be assessed and regulated where necessary.

2.2.1. Promote protected status for areas of the Dobrodgea plateau used by the geese.

2.2.2. The rate and effects of isolation of the Dobrodgea lagoons from the sea should be assessed and, where appropriate, counter-measures taken.

2.4. Some areas of the Dobrodgea plateau could be farmed for the geese.

2.5. An ornithologist from a Romanian agency (possibly ROS) should be formally selected to represent Romania in a multinational Red-breasted Goose working group.

3.1. Co-ordinated winter counts between Romania, Bulgaria, Ukraine, Greece and Azerbaijan should be conducted once to twice monthly on a formal and annual basis.

3.3.1. Ecological and behavioural studies of Red-breasted Geese in the winter quarters should be initiated.

4.1. Public awareness of the importance of the species and the threats it faces should be raised.

Russian Federation

1.2./2.1./3.5. Promote a review of hunting regulations and activities. Where necessary, disturbance and mortality caused by hunting should be monitored and regulated.

2.2.1. Encourage the extension of the existing Taimyr reserves to include the most important Red-breasted Goose nesting sites.

2.2.2. Efforts should be made to limit disturbance caused by oil/gas in the breeding range.

2.4. Staging areas on the Ob river and in the Manych valley should be assessed and, where necessary, protected and enhanced.

2.5. An ornithologist from a Russian agency (possibly CSRLGMNR) should be formally selected to represent Russia in a multinational Red-breasted Goose working group.

2.5. Encourage improved communications with the more remote regional authorities regarding conservation matters.

3.2.1. The current importance of staging areas in Russia should be assessed.

3.2.3. The distribution of breeding colonies should be monitored, particularly in the relatively unknown western part of the breeding range (E. Syroechkovski, Jr., pers. comm., 1995).

3.3.3. Breeding ecology studies should be initiated to determine the constraints on breeding success.

4.1. Public awareness of the importance of the species and the threats it faces should be raised.

Turkey

1.2.1. Promote the closing of the hunting season at the end of January.

Ukraine

2.1./3.5. Encourage a review of hunting regulations and activities. Where necessary, disturbance and mortality caused by hunting should be monitored and regulated.

2.5. An ornithologist from a Ukrainian agency (possibly Shevchenko University) should be formally selected to represent the Ukraine in a multinational Red-breasted Goose working group.

3.1. Co-ordinated winter counts between Ukraine, Romania, Bulgaria, Greece and Azerbaijan should be conducted once to twice monthly on a formal and annual basis.

3.2.1. Surveys of location, goose numbers and habitat use should be carried out in staging areas.

3.3.1. Ecological and behavioural studies of Red-breasted Geese at the staging sites should be initiated.

Annex 2

Maximum counts or rough estimates of numbers of Red-breasted Goose *Branta ruficollis*, 1899–1994 (where data are available)

For winter counts, data are given for January or February of that year. * on migration, + breeding
For table references see overleaf

Year	Romania	Bulgaria	Caspian Sea	Greece	Turkey	Iran	Hungary	Ukraine	Russia	Azerbaijan	Other	Estimated total
1899			tens of thousands[24]							huge flocks[40]		Tens of thousands[24]
1930	small flocks[45]	solitary birds and small flocks[46]										
1936	14[2]											
1939		15–20[11]								dozens to thousands[40]		
–1950		"rare"[11]										
1954				300[16]								
1955												
1956										60000[27]		60000[27]
1957										40000[20]		50000[25]
1958										2400[41]		
1959												
1960									10000[45/+]	11000[41]		
1961									"	4200[43]		
1962									"	8000[41]		
1963				40[17]					"	4800[43]		25000[21]
1964				45[17]					"	4500[43]		
1965									"	3300[43]		50000[19]
1966									"			
1967	25000[3]								"	23800[42]		48800
1968	25000[27]		24000[24]	12[17]					"			49012
1969	25000[22]			54[17]					"			25054
1970	4080[4]	1000[11]	25000[24]	12[17]		16[35]						30108
1971	9300[5]			200[29]								
1972	6000[5]			4[12]			7[13]					
1973							14[13]		7500[prs28/+]	4[42]		25000[28]
1974				7[17]			41[13]	40000[33/*]				
1975	6000[6]						10[13]	"	15000[28]	50[42]		
1976	5500[6]	1500[12]	20000[45/*]	2[17]				"	25000[24]			
1977	1000[7]	1274[26]					1[13]	"				
1978	4250[8]	1580[11]					86[14]	"	3250[prs23/+]			27500[23]
1979	200[45]	1507[26]		<50[29]			43[13]	"	27000[24]	65[42]		
1980		16566[26]					60[13]	"		23[42]		
1981		2306[26]	<10[30]					"	1500[24]	31[42]		30000[23]
1982		12243[10]						"		45[42]		
1983	6000[28]	9948[10]						"			Netherlands = 2[44]	
1984	"	6890[10]					47[15]	"				
1985	"	14047[10]		2000[17]								
1986	"											
1987	"	13800[10]										
1988	2400[9]	3093[10]										
1989	11630[9]	12548[10]		500[32]	116[35]							24794
1990	4310[10]							86[35]	30000[31]		Turkmenia = 48	35000[32]
1991	36335[1]							717[35]				70000[39]
1992	26913[18]	42816[18]			9[35]		1[35]					69727[18]
1993	14650[34]	59206[35, 34]										73856
1994	4308[35]	30000[37]		9[38]					3038[35]			37355

1. Vangeluwe, D. and Stassin, P. (1991) Hivernage de la Bernache à cou roux *Branta ruficollis* en Dobroudja septentrionale, Roumanie et revue du statut hivernal de l'espèce. *Gerfaut* 81: 65–99.

2. Scott, P. (1939) *Wild chorus*. Glasgow: University Press.

3. Ciochia, V. and Hafner, H. (1969) Observations sur quelques espèces d'oiseaux qui hivernent sur le littoral de la mer Noir at dans le delta de Danube. *Lucr. Stat. Cerc. Mar.* 3: 307–313.

4. Scott, P. (1970) Redbreasts in Rumania. *Wildfowl* 21: 37–41.

5. Dijksen, A. J., Lebret, T., Ouwened, G. L. and Philippona, S. (1973) Ornithological observations in the lagoons of the Dobrodgea, Rumania, in autumn and winter of 1969, 1970 and 1971. *Ardea* 61: 159–178.

6. Puscariu, V. (1983) La présence de *Branta ruficollis* pendant l'hiver en Roumanie. *Aquila* 90: 23–27.

7. Puscariu, V. (1977) Roumanie. *IWRB Bull.* 43/44: 32–33.

8. Lebret, T. (1978) Roemeens dagboek op zoek naar de laatste Roodhalsganzen. *Lepelaar* 55: 14–17.

9. Munteanu, D., Tonuic, N., Weber, P., Seabo, J. and Marinov, M. (1989) Evaluarea efetivelor pasarilov acvatice in cartierele lor de ierare din Romania (1988–1989). *Ocrot. Nat.* 33: 105–112.

10. Cracknell, G. (1990) Reports and news. *IWRB Goose Res. Group Newsl.* 3: 4–10.

11. Ivanov, B. E. and Pomakov, V. A. (1983) Wintering of the Red-breasted Goose (*Branta ruficollis*) in Bulgaria. *Aquila* 90: 29–34.

12. Anon. (1978) European news. *Brit. Birds* 71: 582–587.

13. Sterbetz, I. (1982) Migration of *Anser erythropus* and *Branta ruficollis* in Hungary 1971–1980. *Aquila* 89: 107–114.

14. Sterbetz, I. (1980) Occurrence of the Red-breasted Goose (*Branta ruficollis*) at Kardoskut in 1978–1979. *Aquila* 87: 141–142.

15. Farago, S., Kovcacs, C. and Sterbetz, I. (1991) Goose populations staging and wintering in Hungary 1984–1988. *Ardea* 79: 161–164.

16. Coombes in Bannerman, D. A. (1957) *The birds of the British Isles*, 6. Edinburgh: Oliver and Boyd.

17. Handrinos, G. I. (1991) The status of geese in Greece. *Ardea* 79: 175–178.

18. Vangeluwe, D. and Snethlage, M. (1992) Rapport des investigations sur l'écologie et la conservation de la Bernache à cou roux *Branta ruficollis* en Dobroudja (Roumanie et Bulgarie) Janvier 1992. Institut Royal des Sciences Naturelles de Belgique.

19. Uspenski, S. M. (1965) *Die Wildgänse nordeurasiens*. Wittenberg-Lutherstadt: Neue Brehm-Bücherei.

20. Uspenski, S. M. and Kishko, Y. K. (1967) Winter range of the Red-breasted Goose in eastern Azerbaidzhan. *Problemy Severa* 11: 235–243.

21. Green, A. G. (1992) Wildfowl at risk. *Wildfowl* 43: 160–184.

22. Johnson, A. and Hafner, H. (1970) Winter wildfowl counts in south-east Europe and western Turkey. *Wildfowl* 21: 22–36.

23. Borodin, A. M., ed. (1984) [*Red data book of the USSR: rare and endangered species of animals and plants*, 1: *animals*]. Second edition. Moscow: Promyshlennost. (In Russian.)

24. Krivenko, V. G. (1983) *The Red Data Book of the RSFSR*.

25. Uspenski, S. M. (1966) Verbreitung and ökologie der Rothalsgans. *Falke* 13: 83–85.

26. Michev, T. M., Naninkov, D. N., Ivanov, B. E. and Pomakov, V. A. (1981) Midwinter numbers of geese in Bulgaria. IWRB Symposium on Population Ecology of Geese. Hungary 26–30 October 1981.

27. Cramp, S. and Simmons, K. E. L., eds. (1977) *The birds of the western Palearctic*, 1. Oxford: Oxford University Press.

28. Madge, S. and Burn, H. (1988) *Wildfowl*. London: Christopher Helm.

29. Scott, D. A. (1980) *A preliminary inventory of wetlands of international importance for waterfowl in West Europe and Northwest Africa*. Slimbridge, U.K.: International Waterfowl and Wetlands Research Bureau (Spec. Publ. 2).

30. Krivonosov, G. A. and Rusanov, G. M. (1990) Wintering waterfowl in the north Caspian. In G. V. T. Matthews, ed. *Managing waterfowl populations. Proc. IWRB Symp., Astrakhan 1989*. Slimbridge, U.K.: International Waterfowl and Wetlands Research Bureau (Spec. Publ. 12).

31. Flint, V. Y. and Krivenko, V. G. (1990) The present status and trends of waterfowl in the USSR. In G. V. T. Matthews, ed. *Managing waterfowl populations. Proc. IWRB Symp., Astrakhan 1989*. Slimbridge, U.K.: International Waterfowl and Wetlands Research Bureau (Spec. Publ. 12).

32. Vinokurov, A. A. (1990) *Branta ruficollis* in the USSR. Pp.197–198 in G. V. T. Matthews, ed. *Managing waterfowl populations. Proc. IWRB Symp., Astrakhan, 1989*. Slimbridge, U.K.: International Waterfowl and Wetlands Research Bureau (IWRB Spec. Publ. 12).

33. Lysenko, V. I. (1990) Current status of waterfowl in Ukraine. Pp.43 in G. V. T. Matthews, ed. *Managing waterfowl populations*. Slimbridge, U.K.: International Waterfowl and Wetlands Research Bureau (Spec. Publ. 12).

34. Black, J. M. and Madsen, J. (1993) Red-breasted Goose: conservation and research needs. *IWRB Goose Res. Group Bull.* 4: 8–15.

35. IWRB Database of the International Waterfowl Census (IWC). Accessed 1994. Slimbridge, U.K.: International Waterfowl and Wetlands Research Bureau.

36. Kohl, I. (1958) The Red-necked Goose (*Branta ruficollis*) in Rumania. *Larus* 9–10: 184–187.

37. Michev, T. (1994) pers. comm.

38. Handrinos, G. (1994) *in litt.*

39. Vangeluwe, D. (1994) pers. comm.

40. Verestchagin 1950; via Patrikeev, M. (1995) *in litt.*

41. Vinogradov and Tcherniavskaya 1965a; via Patrikeev, M. (1995) *in litt.*

42. Vinogradov and Morozkin 1979, Babaev 1984; via Patrikeev, M. (1995)*in litt.*

43. Vinogradov 1967; via Patrikeev, M. (1995) *in litt.*

44. Madsen, J. (1994) Red-breasted Goose *Branta ruficollis*. Pp.116–117 in G. M. Tucker and M. F. Heath *Birds in Europe: their conservation status*. Cambridge, U.K.: BirdLife International (BirdLife Conservation Series No. 3).

45. Anon.

46. Anon. (1995) National Bank for Ornithological Information, Bulgarian Society for the Protection of Birds, Sofia, Bulgaria.

International action plan for the Marbled Teal (*Marmaronetta angustirostris*)

Reviews

This action plan should be reviewed and updated every four years. An emergency review will be undertaken if sudden major environmental changes, liable to affect the population, occur within the species range. As far as possible, this action plan is intended to achieve the aims of the Agreement on the Conservation of African-Eurasian Migratory Waterbirds under the Bonn Convention for the species. This agreement is likely to influence the need for and timing of future reviews.

Geographical scope

The action plan needs implementation in the following range states of the Marbled Teal: Algeria, Armenia, Azerbaijan, Egypt, Georgia, Israel, Lebanon, Morocco, Russian Federation, Spain, Syria, Tunisia and Turkey.

Summary

The Marbled Teal *Marmaronetta angustirostris* is undergoing rapid declines throughout its remaining range, with the destruction and degradation of habitats (particularly breeding habitats) being the most important cause; hunting and a range of other factors also contribute to this decline. The conservation of the species in Europe and the Mediterranean region requires action on several fronts.

The most important need is the effective conservation of wetlands of importance for the species, paying particular attention to breeding sites. A large proportion of these breeding sites already have some form of protection status but are still being degraded by a variety of factors, such as hydrological changes within their catchments. In the face of the ongoing loss of the major breeding grounds of the Marbled Teal in southern Iraq it is imperative that this action plan be implemented successfully to conserve the populations remaining in the west and east Mediterranean.

Threats and limiting factors

Habitat loss – high

Habitat degradation – high

Hunting – medium

Trapping in nets set for crayfish and fish – medium

Brood mortality in concrete canals – low to medium

Introduction of other species – unknown

Disturbance – low

Lead poisoning – unknown

Warfare – unknown

Conservation priorities

Habitat protection at all sites regularly holding Marbled Teal – essential

Prevent Marbled Teal mortality from causes other than hunting – essential

Increase public awareness of the need to protect the Marbled Teal and its habitat – essential

Regular breeding surveys and monitoring – essential/high

Research into the species ecology, habitat requirements and movements – essential/high

Legal protection for the species and key sites in all range states – high

Development of national and regional action plans and recovery programmes for the species – high

Establish hunting bans at all sites where the species is regularly recorded and enforce restrictions. Where this cannot be achieved implement measures to reduce the number of Marbled Teal shot – high

Secure financial support for implementation of hunting laws – high

Introduction

The Marbled Teal *Marmaronetta angustirostris* is a globally threatened species classified as Vulnerable by the IUCN (Groombridge, 1993) and BirdLife International (Collar et al., 1994). It is listed in Annex I of the European Union's Wild Birds Directive, in Appendix II of the Bonn Convention and Appendix II of the Bern Convention. It is not listed in the Washington Convention (CITES). It is classified as Endangered at European level by BirdLife International (Tucker and Heath, 1994).

On 6 December 1994, a workshop took place in Strasbourg (France) to discuss the situation of the Marbled Teal in the Mediterranean and Black Sea region and to agree a conservation strategy for the future. The workshop was organised by the Wildfowl and Wetlands Trust and Wetlands International. It was attended by experts from Israel, Morocco, Netherlands, Pakistan, Spain, Tunisia, Turkey and United Kingdom, as well as by a representative of UNEP/CMS. This action plan is based on discussions held during the workshop, a recent comprehensive report on the species (Green, 1993) and on further information received by correspondence before and after the workshop.

A limitation of this plan is that its scope does not include south-west Asia, which holds the majority of the remaining world population of the Marbled Teal and is a region where the species is now extremely threatened by the destruction of the marshes in southern Iraq. Another weakness is that it was not possible at the time to gain the active involvement of representatives from Azerbaijan and Algeria, two countries within the scope of this plan that support very important breeding populations of the species. In contrast, the sections for Spain, Morocco and Turkey follow extensive consideration and discussion.

Background information

Distribution and population

The current global distribution of the Marbled Teal is fragmented (Green, 1993), with major centres of distribution in the western Mediterranean and tropical Africa (Spain, Morocco, Algeria, Tunisia, Senegal, Mali, Nigeria and Chad), the eastern Mediterranean (Turkey, Israel, Egypt and Syria) and western and southern Asia (Azerbaijan, Armenia, Russian Federation, Turkmenistan, Uzbekistan, Tajikistan, Kazakhstan, Iraq, Iran, Afghanistan, Pakistan, India, China). The first and last of these regional populations are found partly within the western Palaearctic, while the second lies wholly within it. The movements that occur within and between these regional populations are very poorly understood and open to speculation (Green, 1993). The only ringing data for Marbled Teal comes from the western Mediterranean.

Table 7.1

Estimates of current sizes of Marbled Teal wintering and breeding populations in Europe, North Africa and the Middle East, based on data collected from 1985 to 1994

Country	Winter population	Breeding pairs
Algeria	350–400	20–50
Armenia	-	2–15
Azerbaijan	-	70–200
Egypt	10–100	-
Israel	80–200	35–50
Iran	25 000–30 000[2]	2000–4000
Iraq	>200[2]	1000–6000[2]
Morocco	2000–3000	30–50
Russian Federation	-	?
Spain	50–500	30–250
Syria	?	>20
Tunisia	200	100–150
Turkey	5–20	150–250

? figures unknown.
1. Wintering may occur only exceptionally.
2. These numbers may now be far too high, owing to the destruction of the Iraqi marshes.
Figures for Spain indicate the range observed over the last decade. Figures for other countries indicate conservative estimates of the numbers present in a good year.

On the basis of recent mid-winter counts, the current world wintering population of Marbled Teal has been conservatively estimated at 34000 birds (Green, 1993). The western Mediterranean/tropical African population can be estimated at 3000, with a 1993 IWC count of 2435 in Morocco and Algeria and several hundred birds probably wintering in tropical Africa. The eastern Mediterranean wintering population must be at least 600, given the fact that 200 pairs or more currently breed in Turkey and Israel. The south-west and southern Asian wintering population can be conservatively estimated at 30000, with a 1992 IWC count of 26275 in Iran and Pakistan. Numbers present at many potential wintering sites in Asia are still unknown, particularly in Iraq, Afghanistan and the former Soviet Union, and this population is likely to have been underestimated.

The actual total world population immediately prior to the destruction of the marshes of southern Iraq was most likely to lie in the range 34000 to 40000, with a total breeding population of 8000 to 13000 pairs (Green, 1993). Like those of other duck species, Marbled Teal populations must fluctuate considerably from one year to the next, and the above figures refer to estimates of peak population size within the range of current fluctuations. There are insufficient data to estimate the lower limit of this range, but it is likely to be less than 50% of the peak population. However, these figures for population size may already be out of date and a population crash is likely to result from the destruction of the Iraqi marshes since 1991 (Pearce, 1993), as this area may have supported over 10000 Marbled Teal in the breeding season. Most birds breeding in Iraq were thought to winter in Iran, and there is evidence for such a population crash from the extremely low recent winter counts from Iran of 5021 in 1993 and 1919 in 1994 (Wetlands International International Waterfowl Census).

Life history

Breeding

The mating system is monogamous, but is still poorly understood. Very few paired birds are observed in winter, and pairing occurs in early spring (A. J. Green, unpublished). The species is sexually monomorphic, and field observations in Spain suggest that males remain with females and their broods, playing a guarding role. The timing of nesting is variable, with 4 to 14 eggs laid from late April to the first half of July. Incubation takes 25 to 27 days. The time from hatching to fledging has not been recorded, but is probably 8 to 9 weeks. Brood amalgamation has often been observed, up to 32 ducklings having been recorded with one female (Green, 1993). Communal nesting was formerly known (Valverde, 1964; Cramp and Simmons, 1977).

Feeding

The very few data on diet indicate a mixture of invertebrates and plant material (seed, shoots, leaves, roots, tubers) being taken (Green, 1993). Marbled Teal feed mainly by dabbling, with upending observed very occasionally. Feeding activity is concentrated in beds of submerged macrophytes when these are available. The filter in the bill is not very fine, suggesting that Marbled Teal do not feed on plankton.

Moulting

There are very few data, but there is probably a full, flightless moult in late summer, followed by a partial moult into breeding plumage in late autumn/early winter, as with other dabbling ducks and pochards. Moulting flocks have been reported in Tunisia in the first half of July (F. Maamouri in Green, 1993), while 10 moulting birds were reported in Uzbekistan on 17 June 1982 (Mukhina and Lukashevich, 1989).

Habitat requirements

Habitat needs are poorly understood. Marbled Teal mainly use shallow, eutrophic wetlands, typically with dense emergent and submerged vegetation. Fresh to saline wetlands are used, but there is some evidence of a preference for slightly brackish sites. More permanent wetlands seem to be favoured for breeding while newly flooded areas seem to be preferred outside the breeding season. *Phragmites*, glasswort (e.g. *Salicornia*) or *Typha* are typically dominant in favoured wetlands, especially when they offer densely vegetated, shallow areas that provide good cover (Green, 1993). Many temporary wetlands that flood only in years of high rainfall are used throughout the life cycle. This is particularly true in North Africa, where some of the most important breeding sites are dry most years.

Movements

The Marbled Teal is migratory across its range in the sense that it undergoes frequent movements across national frontiers, but it is largely nomadic, making unpredictable, non-cyclical and opportunistic movements in relation to rainfall and flooding patterns that are themselves highly unpredictable over most of the range. There is a general migration southwards in winter, but the timing and extent of such movements varies considerably between years (Green, 1993; Navarro and Robledano, in press).

Threats and limiting factors

Habitat loss

This century, very large areas of wetlands of great importance for breeding and wintering Marbled Teal have been completely destroyed, or degraded to such an extent that they have lost their value. This habitat loss has occurred across the species' range and is probably the single major cause of the decline in world population and in distribution (Green, 1993).

Drainage by agricultural schemes has resulted in a catastrophic decrease in the area of Marbled Teal habitats across the former Soviet Union, including Azerbaïjan, where drainage of Marbled Teal sites is continuing (M. Patrikeev, in litt., 1992). In Turkey, there has been extensive drainage in the Çukurova deltas, Göksu delta and elsewhere, including the loss of the Aynaz swamp area which was an important breeding site and held over 1 200 birds in winter 1967 (Aukes et al., 1988). In Israel, the area of the Hula marshes where Marbled Teal were once very abundant has been reduced from around 6 000 ha to 200 ha (Carp 1980). Other important breeding sites that have been destroyed include a major part of Lake Fetzara in Algeria and Lac Iriki in Morocco. Many sites are currently facing new threats from development proposals. Drainage schemes are planned that will destroy part of the seasonal wetlands of the Göksu delta (V. van den Berk, in litt., 1992). Huge areas of breeding habitat are currently being drained in Iraq (Pearce, 1993).

No figures for the overall rates of habitat loss are available, but the destruction of Marbled Teal breeding habitats may well have exceeded 50% this century. In the eastern Mediterranean, there was probably a crash in the Marbled Teal population prior to 1960 largely as a result of the war against brackish-water malaria, which led to the drainage of large areas of habitat in Turkey, Israel and elsewhere (V. van den Berk and D. Allon, verbally, 1994).

Importance: high

Habitat degradation

Many important wetlands have been severely degraded, reducing their value for Marbled Teal without being totally destroyed. In Tunisia, upstream barrages have severely affected several breeding sites, increasing the frequency of desiccation of Sebkha Kelbia by two and a half times and increasing the salinity at Lac Ichkeul where further upstream dams are planned (Hughes and Hughes, 1992). Most key sites in Turkey are affected by drainage/irrigation schemes in the surrounding areas. The construction of dams and other hydrological work carried out within the catchments of the Hotamis and Eregli marshes in Turkey has led to them both being drastically reduced in size, and caused the Sultan marshes to be completely dry in 1991 (DHKD, in litt., 1994). A similar process has happened in the Marismas del Guadalquivir (Spain) where a variety of problems has markedly reduced the frequency, extent and duration of flooding of the seasonal marshes of the National Park and other areas (Castroviejo, 1993). The quality of remaining habitats in the marismas also appears to have been affected by the high densities of herbivorous mammals, whose grazing and movement have reduced the amount of aquatic vegetation.

There are numerous other causes of degradation of wetlands important for Marbled Teal. Intensive reed-cutting, reed-burning and overgrazing are commonplace and reduce the amount of habitat available for nesting. Pollution from agricultural, industrial and domestic sources is a threat at many sites (see Green, 1993). In Azerbaïjan, oil drilling threatens Lakes Bos-Koba and Saraesy with pollution (M. Patrikeev, in litt., 1994). In

Tunisia, major urbanisation at Lake Tunis during the 1980s stopped Marbled Teal from breeding along the north shore (M. Smart, *in litt.*, 1992), while Oued Sed, an important breeding site, is heavily polluted by olive-oil residues, other industrial waste and domestic effluent, and is also affected by reed-cutting (H. Hamrouni, verbally, 1994).

Importance: high

Hunting

The Marbled Teal is considered a relatively tame duck that is easy to shoot, particularly in the breeding season (Phillips, 1923; Green, 1993). Furthermore, it is a relatively inconspicuous and unknown bird, and very few hunters are able to identify it. Although in winter the Marbled Teal is typically found on wetlands that support many more ducks of other species, in summer it is one of only a handful of wildfowl species occurring within its range. As a result, it is particularly vulnerable to shooting and egg collection through the breeding season.

An increase in hunting pressure after the French occupation is said to have caused a significant decline in the numbers of Marbled Teal in Algeria as early as 1867 (Phillips, 1923). Intense hunting pressure is likely to have eliminated the breeding population in Egypt (P. L. Meininger, *in litt.*, 1992). Egg collection at Sebkha Kelbia in Tunisia was so severe in the 1960s that very few young reached maturity (Smart, 1970). In Turkey, extreme hunting pressure has been held responsible for the decline of the species in the southern coastlands by 1970 (Gürpinar and Wilkinson, 1970).

Hunting, illegal or legal, is thought to be a continuing problem in every major range state, although there is very little quantitative information. In Morocco, although the Marbled Teal is protected from hunting, several Marbled Teal sites such as lower Loukos suffer intense hunting pressure and illegal hunting in winter (Beaubrun et al., 1986). Hunting at lower Loukos starts at sunrise, making accurate identification of ducks impossible (J. Franchimont, *in litt.*, 1994). Hunting is still a problem in Spain, particularly in the El Hondo/Salinas de Santa Pola complex where official records showed that 74 birds were shot in

the 1981-82 season (Green, 1993; Navarro and Robledano, in press). The number of birds shot in recent years is unknown, although at least four were shot in the first week of the 1992-93 season (J. D. Navarro, *in litt.*, 1994). Hunting still occurs regularly during the breeding season in unprotected parts of the Marismas del Guadalquivir (A. J. Green pers. obs., 1994). The species is protected in Algeria but lack of knowledge about its identification amongst hunters could be leading to some losses which cannot be estimated at present.

Importance: medium

Trapping in nets set for crayfish and fish

In the Marismas del Guadalquivir, nets set to catch crayfish are causing high mortality to Marbled Teal ducklings and adults, particularly in the Brazo del Este area (Asensio, 1991). The drowning of young birds in fishing nets has been observed in the Göksu delta (V. van den Berk, *in litt.*, 1992).

Importance: medium

Brood mortality in concrete canals

In El Hondo and Salinas de Santa Pola, Spain, a network of concrete canals is causing significant mortality in Marbled Teal broods which fall into the canals and cannot get out. Many of these broods are taken home by local people. In 1994, the Azarbe del Convenio canal alongside El Hondo was patrolled, and at least 118 Marbled Teal chicks from at least 12 broods fell in, representing an extremely high proportion of the broods hatching in the area.

Importance: low to medium

Introduction of other species

In the most important area for the species in Spain, the Guadalquivir marshes, the breeding success of the Marbled Teal has probably been adversely affected by the introduction of the Louisiana crayfish *Procambarus clarkii* which has had an immense impact on wetland communities (Montes et al., 1993) and may have greatly reduced the food supply for the Marbled Teal. The introduction of fish has occurred in various parts of the range (e.g. Lake Parishan in Iran) and has had an unknown effect. High fish densities generally reduce the breeding success of dabbling ducks.

Importance: unknown

Disturbance

Disturbance may have a negative impact on survival or breeding success at a number of sites. This includes disturbance from the normal activities of a high human population (e.g. at the Sidi Moussa-Oualidia wetlands in Morocco, A. J. Green, pers. obs., 1995) and disturbance from tourism (e.g. at Sidi Bou Ghaba in Morocco).

Importance: low

Lead poisoning

There are no data on the importance of lead poisoning as a cause of the mortality of Marbled Teal, but hunting is intense at many key sites, and the ingestion of lead shot could result in significant mortality at some of these sites (see Pain, 1992).

Importance: unknown

Warfare

War is having an unknown effect on the species in Azerbaijan, where the area of warfare (1992-93) is very close to the key site of Lake Aggel (M. Patrikeev, *in litt.*, 1994). The Iran/Iraq war and the Gulf War could also have affected the species in the western Iranian wetlands and Iraqui marshes.

Importance: unknown

Conservation status and recent conservation measures

Algeria

There is no national Red Data Book. The species has been fully protected since August 1983 by Decree No. 83–509.

Marbled Teal were formerly "very common … in summer" (Hume and Marshall, 1880) and breeding in "countless numbers" in Lac Fetzara (Phillips, 1923) which is now largely drained. There are few recent data, but breeding is currently thought to occur at four sites in the El Kala, Centre and West-Oranie regions (Ledant et al., 1981) with at least 50 breeding pairs in wet years. Since most of

the birds currently wintering in Morocco must breed in North Africa, it is likely that there are many important breeding sites in Algeria still to be identified (e.g. in the Biskra region), and Marbled Teal may still be breeding in what is left of Lake Fetzara (D. Boukhalfa, *in litt.*, 1995). Wintering is concentrated in West-Oranie with up to 360 birds recorded in the 1970s, divided between Grande Sebkhet d'Oran, Lac des Gharabas and Marais de la Macta (Wetlands International International Waterfowl Census). Occasional records from southern Algeria suggest that the little-known wetlands of this region may support a significant wintering population (B. Chalabi, pers. comm., 1992). A record of 12 spring migrants on the Moroccan border (Smith, 1968) suggests that some Algerian breeders winter in Morocco. A record from the southern Algerian Sahara suggests that some wintering occurs south of the Sahara in the Chad basin (Ledant et al., 1981).

The six known key sites are Grande Sebkhet d'Oran (unprotected), Lac des Gharabas (unprotected), Marais de la Macta (unprotected), Barrage de Boughzoul (unprotected), Lac de Réghaïa (unprotected) and Lac Bou Lhilet (unprotected). See Green (1993) for further details, for example, threats to each site. No specific conservation programmes have yet been conducted for the species in Algeria, and current levels of conservation activities are minimal.

Armenia

No information is available concerning Red Data Books and current legal status.

Marbled Teal were formerly reported as common in spring in the Erevan region but were not found breeding (Dementiev and Gladkov, 1952). The species was reported as rare in the Araks valley alongside the Iranian border in the 1950s, and has been recorded in spring and summer at the Armashski carp farm in the valley since 1984 (Adamyan, 1989). In June 1987, 32 birds were flushed from this site and two nests found (Adamyan, 1989). Birds breeding in Armenia are likely to winter in Iran, and birds breeding in Azerbaijan are reported to use the Araks valley in

Armenia as a spring migration route (M. Patrikeev, *in litt.*, 1992).

The only known key site is Armashski carp farm (unprotected). See Green (1993) for details. No specific conservation programmes have yet been conducted for the species in Armenia.

Azerbaijan

The species is listed in the Red Data Book of Azerbaijan published in 1990 (no details available). It was fully protected in the former Soviet Union, but its current legal status in Azerbaijan is unclear.

The Marbled Teal was formerly reported to be "common" in Transcaucasia by Phillips (1923). According to a report prepared by M. V. Patrikeev (*in litt.*, 1992), in the nineteenth century it was common in summer in the Kura valley from Ganja to Lenkoran. Following a decline in range and population size, it is thought to have disappeared from the left bank of the Kura valley and the Mugan and Lenkoran lowlands. It now breeds in Lakes Aggel and Saraesy and in Kizil Agach State Reserve. Breeding probably also occurs in Lakes Bos-Koba and Shorbet-Koba (Krivenko and Vinokurov, 1984; V. Vinogradov, verbally, 1991). According to Patrikeev (in Green, 1993), the whole Mil steppe lake system (including Lakes Aggel, Bos-Koba, Shorbet-Koba and Saraesy) is thought to contain about 200 pairs in summer. Breeding has only been confirmed at Aggel, where broods have been seen (M. Patrikeev, *in litt.*, 1992).

In the breeding season in 1989, 30 birds were also recorded at Lakes Mahmud-Chala in the south-east Mugan steppe. In July 1990, birds were seen at Lakes Mahmud-Chala and Third Chala (Novogolovskaya Chala). It is possible that the Marbled Teal still occurs elsewhere in the Kura valley but has been overlooked. It is seen during spring migration along the Arars river valley. In autumn the Marbled Teal are thought to fly towards Iran and winter there, and are sometimes recorded at Divichi Liman on passage (M. Patrikeev, *in litt.*, 1992). There are occasional records from winter and a few hundred were seen in early February at Aggel in the very cold winter of 1972 (Tuaien and Kurbanov, 1984).

The six key sites are Lake Aggel (State Reserve), Lake Saraesy (unprotected), Kizil-Agach State Reserve (also Ramsar Site), Lake Bos-Koba (unprotected), Lake Mahmud-chala (unprotected) and Lake Shorbet-Koba (unprotected). See Green (1993) for further details. No specific conservation programmes have yet been conducted for the species in Azerbaijan, and current levels of conservation activities are minimal. The protected status given to two key sites is not currently thought to be effective, and illegal hunting is probably intense all year round.

Egypt

The Marbled Teal does not feature in a National Red Data Book and is not legally protected.

Marbled Teal formerly bred in the Western Desert and in the Nile valley. They were "quite common" at Lake Qarun in the Nile valley but elsewhere the numbers were small (Goodman et al., 1989). In winter they were "often obtained" in the Nile delta and Suez Canal area (Meinertzhagen, 1930). The Marbled Teal is now only a winter visitor to the Nile valley and delta in very small numbers (Goodman et al., 1989; Green, 1993). A record of one migrant in northern Sinai in September 1990 (G. Atta, *in litt.*, 1992) suggests that these birds breed in Israel or Turkey. Observations from Israel suggest an autumn passage of birds migrating south into Egypt (see above); these seem most likely to be Turkish breeders. There are no known key sites.

Georgia

Georgia is listed as a breeding area by Inskipp and Collins (1993), based on a distribution map in Flint et al. (1984). However, no records of the species have been traced from this area. Despite this, former or current presence seems likely owing to presence in neighbouring states. No information is available concerning Red Data Books and current legal status.

Israel

There is no Red Data Book for Israel, but there is an official report on the status of all vertebrates, which lists Marbled Teal as Endangered (no details available). The species is fully protected under the 1955 Wildlife Protection Law.

In Israel in the last century, Marbled Teal bred "in great numbers" in the Hula valley (Tristram, 1887), where 100 to 200 pairs were breeding in the 1950s (Paz, 1987). Numbers have been greatly reduced by the drainage of most of these marshes (Green, 1993) and during the 1970s and 1980s only 15 to 35 pairs bred in the valley (Shirihai, 1995). E. Shy (in litt., 1992) now reports 45 to 50 pairs breeding in the Hula Nature Reserve and nearby fish ponds, while Blitzblau (1992) records lower numbers with only 8 to 11 pairs in 1990. There is currently a trend for breeding birds to desert the fish ponds and to become more concentrated within the Hula Reserve. This is likely to continue in the future as the number of fish ponds is now decreasing (E. Shy, verbally, 1994). During the 1970s and 1980s, two to three pairs were also reported breeding at the Golan reservoirs (Shirihai, 1995). The birds breeding in Israel are reported to concentrate from September to November (250 in the Hula valley in late November 1991) and to disperse somewhat towards mid-winter, when they also appear to be augmented by foreign breeders arriving in the Hula valley and other areas in northern and sometimes west-central Israel (Green, 1993; Shirihai, 1995). In 1993, a record 168 birds were recorded in Israel in mid-winter, with 138 in the Hula valley (IWC). A concentration of 150 to 200 birds is sometimes recorded in the Hula valley in March (E. Shy in Green, 1993), probably on spring passage. Tishlovet Hakishon is another important site for autumn passage, with concentrations of up to 60 birds recorded between June and December (D. Alon, verbally, 1994; Green, 1993). Israel may be a passage area for birds moving between Turkey and Egypt.

It is possible that the species is still breeding in the Golan Heights (D. Alon, verbally, 1994). In April 1994, approximately 24 km² of the drained Hula marshes was reflooded (see Watzman, 1993), and vegetation is now developing in the area. It is possible that this re-created wetland will provide suitable breeding habitat for Marbled Teal (E. Shy verbally, 1994). The three key sites are now Hula reserve (Nature Reserve), Hula valley fish ponds (unprotected but hunting forbidden) and Tishlovet Hakishon (unprotected but hunting forbidden). See Green (1993) for further details (e.g. threats to each site). The species is recorded from IBAs 002, 003, 005, 007, 008 and 012 (Evans, 1994). No specific conservation programmes have yet been conducted for the species in Israel.

Lebanon

There is one autumn record of Marbled Teal from the 1970s from Lake Qaraoun, a reservoir on the River Litani (A. M. Macfarlane, in litt., 1983). If birds are moving between Turkey and Israel, Lebanon is likely to be an important passage area.

Morocco

There is no national Red Data Book. The Marbled Teal has been fully protected since 1992 (J. Franchimont, in litt., 1993).

Marbled Teal were formerly very abundant in winter when they were exceeded in number around Tangier only by the Common Teal *Anas crecca*. They were also a "common breeder" (Phillips, 1923). Numbers have clearly declined significantly as Marbled Teal are now heavily outnumbered in winter by many duck species (Rose, 1992), but IWC counts show there remains a regular wintering population of at least 2000 to 3000 (Green, 1993). The count in January 1993 was the highest yet with a total of 2410 including 1973 counted at Barrage Al Massira (M. Dakki and IWC). This was the first time that this site had been accurately counted (M. Dakki, verbally, 1994), suggesting that the Moroccan wintering population may be considerably underestimated by IWC data. Breeding is currently known to occur at eight sites in the north-west, north-east and south regions, but no more than 60 breeding pairs were recorded in total. Seven breeding sites are described in Green (1993), the eighth site being Barrage Mohammed V where 12 possible breeding pairs were recorded in June 1994 (Schollaert et al., in prep.). The large numbers counted in winter cannot be explained by an influx of Spanish breeding birds, and there must be unknown breeding sites of great importance in Morocco or elsewhere in North Africa.

The 14 key sites are Oued Massa delta (Biological Reserve and National Park), Lagunes de Sidi Moussa-Oualidia (unprotected), Merja de Sidi Bou Ghaba (National Monument and Ramsar Site), Merja Zerga (Biological Reserve and Ramsar Site), Sebkha Zima (Hunting Reserve), Merja de Douyiet (Royal Reserve), Moulouya delta (unprotected), Dayet Ifrah (unprotected), Dayet Merzouga (unprotected), Dayet al Hafa (unprotected), lower Loukos marshes and estuary (unprotected), Barrage Al Massira (unprotected), Barrage Mohammed V (unprotected) and Barrage d'Ouarzazate (unprotected). See Green (1993) for further details. No specific conservation programmes have yet been conducted for the species in Morocco.

Russian Federation

The Marbled Teal is listed as "Category I: Endangered" in the Russian Red Data Book (Krivenko, 1983). The species was fully protected in the former Soviet Union, but its current legal status in the Russian Federation is unclear.

The Marbled Teal formerly bred on western sub-steppe *ilmenni* (shallow, generally temporary lakes) in the Volga delta, on wetlands of the Trans-Volga and along the western coast of the Caspian in the Terek and Samur deltas, but was extremely rare in these areas (Dementiev and Gladkov, 1952; Krivenko, 1983). The last record from the Volga delta was in 1953 when two moulting birds were caught (Krivenko, 1983). In the northern Caucasus, there have been recent records from Ardon (seven in December 1986), Elkhotovo on the Terek river (three in January 1981), Lake Solyonoe in Anzgizsky, (two in April 1985) and Lake Dadynskoe, Stavropol (one in October 1981) (Komarova and Komarova, 1988; Khoehlov, 1989). These recent records suggest there may still be a small breeding population in the region.

There are no known key sites. No specific conservation programmes have yet been conducted for the species in the Russian Federation. It is considered that the problems identifying the species are an important factor, as is habitat change caused by changes in water levels. The

population is declining in Uzbekistan (A. Golovkin, pers. comm.).

Spain

The Marbled Teal is listed as Endangered in the national Red Data Book (Blanco and González, 1992) and it has been protected from hunting across Spain under national law since 1980. It is listed as Endangered in the National Catalogue of Threatened Species (Royal Decree 439/90) and hence the preparation of regional recovery plans is obligatory under Law 4/89.

There are two main centres of Marbled Teal distribution in the south (western Andalucía) and in the east (Alicante province, Valencia). Full details of past and current status are given by Navarro and Robledano (in press). The most important area is the Marismas del Guadalquivir in Andalucía. The Marbled Teal was formerly a very abundant breeder in the marismas: several thousand breeding pairs were thought to be present at the turn of the century, and flocks of over 1000 were still common in the 1920s (Valverde, 1964). Numbers in the marismas have always been subject to major fluctuations between years but there has been a long-term decline throughout this century (Valverde, 1964). Numbers fell very low during the drought of the late 1970s and early 1980s (Hidalgo, 1991) but recovered between 1983 and 1989. The breeding population from 1984 to 1988 was an estimated 150 to 250 pairs (Máñez, 1991). Since 1989 there has been a marked and consistent decline in numbers, with less than 20 breeding pairs in 1994 when numbers were lower than in any year since records began (Estación Biológica de Doñana, unpublished data).

In the eastern region, the most important breeding sites are the El Hondo and the adjacent Salinas de Santa Pola complexes in the province of Alicante. Marbled Teal were probably formerly very abundant in southern Alicante where there were originally very large areas of marshland habitat at Albufera de Elche and between the mouths of the Segura and Vinalopo rivers. An estimated 200 pairs were present at El Hondo reservoirs in the mid-1960s (J. D. Navarro, *in litt.*, 1992). A major decline has since occurred and 15 to 25 breeding pairs have been recorded at El Hondo and Salinas de Santa Pola from 1988 to 1994.

Nomadic movements occur and small numbers still breed at a number of other sites in Andalucía, Valencia, Castilla la Mancha and Murcia. Outside the breeding season, important concentrations occur in Andalusian lagoons and the species has been recorded in many parts of Spain. Several hundred birds sometimes winter in the Marismas del Guadalquivir, but four ringing recoveries from Morocco and one from Algeria confirm that most birds winter in North Africa.

The key sites are now Doñana National Park (also Ramsar Site, Biosphere Reserve and SPA), Parque Natural del Entorno de Doñana, Paraje Natural del Brazo del Este, unprotected parts of the Marismas del Guadalquivir (particularly las Cantaritas, el Reboso del Brazo del Este, the northern section of Brazo de la Torre), Laguna de Medina (Reserva Natural, Ramsar Site and SPA), Espera lagoon complex (Reserva Natural and Ramsar Site), Puerto de Santa María lagoon complex (Reserva Natural and SPA), Cañada de las Norias (Hunting Reserve), Salinas de Santa Pola (Parque Natural, Ramsar Site and SPA), El Hondo (Parque Natural, Ramsar Site and SPA), Marjal del Moro (unprotected), Marjal de Pego-Oliva (Ramsar Site, Parque Natural) and Albufera de Valencia (Parque Natural, Ramsar Site and SPA). See Green (1993) and Navarro and Robledano (in press) for further details.

Although most sites are protected, they still face very serious threats exacerbated by successive years of low rainfall since 1991. The situation is particularly serious in the Marismas del Guadalquivir, where a reduction in suitable habitat has led to the abandonment of the National Park in recent breeding seasons with birds confined to surrounding areas offering little nesting habitat or having high densities of lethal crayfish traps. The Generalitat Valenciana has prepared a regional recovery plan for the conservation of Marbled Teal in the Community of Valencia (Ambiental, 1992), although this plan awaits approval and implementation. Focused research into the status and ecology of the species has been undertaken in Valencia since 1991 and in Andalucía since 1993, and is still under way.

Regional agencies in Andalucía and Valencia pledged to commence conservation actions in 1995.

Syria

The status of Marbled Teal in any national Red Data Book is unknown, as is its legal status.

One was seen in June 1975 at Shumaytiyah pond 20 km north-west of Deir Ez Zor (A. M. Macfarlane, in litt., 1983) and there are three summer records from 1994 (G. Kirwan, in litt., 1994; Orn. Soc. Middle East Bull. 33), suggesting the existence of a breeding population. There appears to be a regular wintering population, and at Lake Quattine, 20 were recorded in 1993 and 10 in 1994 (IWC). Lake Quattine (unprotected) is the only key site identified so far. The species is recorded from IBAs 003, 006, 010 and 017 (Evans, 1994). It is possible that the species is still breeding in the Golan Heights (D. Alon, verbally, 1994).

Tunisia

There is no national Red Data Book. The species is fully protected.

Hume and Marshall (1880) described Marbled Teal as "very common … in winter", but wintering has been very occasional in recent decades, with an exceptional concentration of 200 at Sebkhet Sidi Mansour in 1971 (Wetlands International International Waterfowl Census). Breeding is thought to occur at 10 sites (see Green, 1993), and is mainly divided between large, natural lakes (particularly Sidi Mansour and Sebka Kelbia) and artificial reservoirs such as Barrage el Haouareb. In July 1991, 318 birds were seen at Sidi Mansour (F. Maamouri, verbally, 1993). Sidi Mansour and Kelbia are dry for years at a stretch, and the size of the breeding population fluctuates accordingly but probably peaks at over 100 pairs (Green, 1993). In August 1993 an exceptional post-breeding concentration of 620 birds including at least six large broods was observed at Barrage el Haouareb (Meininger et al., 1994). Wintering of Tunisian breeders is thought mainly to occur south of the Sahara (M. Smart, in litt., 1992). However, 250 birds were recorded at Oasis Noueil in January 1994 (J. van der Winden, in litt., 1994), and 140 in February

1994 (F. Maamouri, *in litt.*, 1994), and the oases in southern Tunisia may be important wintering and/or passage sites.

The eight key sites are now Sebkhet Sidi Mansour (unprotected), Sebkha Kelbia (Natural Reserve), Lake Ichkeul (National Park, World Heritage Site, Biosphere Reserve and Ramsar Site), Oued Sed (unprotected), Barrage el Haouareb (Hunting Reserve), Sebkhet Ariana (unprotected), Lake Tunis (National Reserve) and Oasis Noueil (unprotected). See Green (1993) for further details. No specific conservation programmes have yet been conducted for the species in Tunisia.

Turkey

There is no national Red Data Book. The "Draft Red List of Threatened Animals of Turkey" published by the Ministry of Environment in 1990 gives the status of the Marbled Teal as Endangered (see Porter, 1991). The species has had full legal protection since the 1984-85 hunting season, when the Bern Convention came into force.

Turkey is a major range state, although there is no information on the status of the species in the first half of this century. In the early years of the IWC, between 1967 and 1971, large numbers of Marbled Teal were recorded in winter at the Çukurova deltas, with 2660 in 1968. Over 2000 were seen in the deltas in August 1967 (*Orn. Soc. Turkey Bird Rep.*). The Marbled Teal is now almost entirely a summer visitor and breeding birds in about 12 sites split between the southern coastlands, central plateau, east and south-east. There are an estimated 150 to 250 breeding pairs in total, with the majority found in the Çukurova and Göksu deltas in the southern coastlands, where breeding occurs annually (Green, 1993). In April 1990, 106 were seen in the Çukurova deltas (L. J. Dijksen, *in litt.*, 1991), and in 1991, 31 broods were seen at the Göksu delta (V. van den Berk, *in litt.*, 1992). Much breeding habitat in both of these deltas and elsewhere has been lost, and winter counts suggest an apparent decline in the population of more than 65% in the last 25 years. Winter records are now exceptional.

The six key sites are now the Çukurova deltas (partly a Hunting Reserve but the areas most

important for Marbled Teal are not protected), Göksu delta (Special Protected Area and Ramsar Site), Hotamis marshes (Natural Heritage Site), Eregli marshes (Natural Heritage Site), Sultan marshes (Strict Nature Reserve, Natural Heritage Site and Ramsar Site) and Van marshes (unprotected). Many important sites for the species have been destroyed and all other sites have been degraded. The Çukurova deltas and Hotamis marshes have been drastically degraded, while the Sultan marshes, Eregli marshes and Göksu delta are severely threatened (Green, 1993). See Green (1993) for further details (e.g. threats to each site). No specific conservation programmes have yet been conducted for the species in Turkey. There has been no education work, and the species is totally unknown to the general public (DHKD, *in litt.*, 1994).

Aims and objectives

Aims

1.   In the short term, to maintain the current population and area of occupancy of the Marbled Teal throughout its range (based on 1985-94 figures).

2.   In the medium term, to promote the population increase of the species within its current range.

3.   In the long term, to promote the expansion of the breeding population to other suitable areas.

Objectives

1.   **Policy and legislation**

1.1.   *To ensure that policies at an international level benefit the Marbled Teal*

1.1.1. Ensure that all relevant international conventions give Marbled Teal maximum protection

Range states should be encouraged to sign the Agreement on the Conservation of African-Eurasian Migratory Waterbirds (under the Bonn Convention), which will provide a framework for international co-operation for the conservation of the Marbled Teal. The Marbled Teal should be promoted to Annex I of the Bonn Convention (currently in Annex II).

Priority: medium
Time-scale: medium

1.1.2. Ensure that international policies and legislation promote the conservation of suitable wetlands within the Marbled Teal's range

The Ramsar Convention, MEDWET programme, European Union and other international aid and subsidy programmes have a role to play along with international policies and legislation on agriculture, transport, tourism, etc. International cooperation and exchange of information should be encouraged.

Priority: medium
Time-scale: medium

1.2. *To ensure that policies at national and regional (i.e. sub-national) level benefit Marbled Teal*

1.2.1. Promote the development and implementation of national and regional action plans and recovery programmes
Priority: high
Time-scale: short

1.2.2. Ensure that the Marbled Teal receives maximum legal protection in all range states
Priority: high
Time-scale: short

1.2.3. Promote the integrated management of wetlands and ensure that broad policies such as agriculture, transport, tourism, etc., do not have a negative impact on the Marbled Teal and its habitat

All range states should be encouraged to develop and implement an effective national wetland conservation strategy. Such a strategy should set clear targets and priorities for the protection and integrated management of potential Marbled Teal habitats. National policies and legislation on agriculture, transport and tourism should all be finely tuned to the needs of wetland conservation.

The Marbled Teal is a priority species in the European inland wetlands and coastal Conservation Strategies currently being prepared by BirdLife International.

Priority: medium
Time-scale: medium/ongoing

2.   **Species and habitat protection**

2.1. *To ensure adequate protection for key Marbled Teal sites*

2.1.1. Seek protected-area designation for all sites regularly holding Marbled Teal

This is particularly important for sites where Marbled Teal breed regularly.

Priority: high
Time-scale: medium

2.1.2. Prevent destruction or degradation of all sites regularly holding Marbled Teal

This is particularly important for sites where Marbled Teal breed regularly. Legal protection should be enforced where it exists, and developments damaging the hydrology, vegetation, water quality, etc., of key sites should be prevented whenever possible. Full environmental impact assessments should be conducted for any new development schemes at these sites.

Priority: essential
Time-scale: short/ongoing

2.1.3. Ensure maximum benefit is obtained from international conventions in protecting sites for Marbled Teal

All key sites should be designated as Ramsar Sites. The conservation status of many of the existing Ramsar Sites needs urgently to be improved.

Priority: high
Time-scale: medium

2.2. *To manage habitats to increase Marbled Teal breeding success and reduce mortality*

Wetland management can readily increase breeding success, for example, by providing more vegetation for nesting, by maintaining stable water-levels during the breeding season or by reducing disturbance. It can also reduce mortality, for example, by providing more shallow, vegetated, undisturbed areas suitable for feeding. These needs should be addressed by the production and implementation of management plans for key sites, which include specific objectives and prescriptions for Marbled Teal.

Priority: medium
Time-scale: medium/ongoing

2.3. *To create new breeding and wintering habitats for the Marbled Teal*

Many artificial wetlands are now important for the Marbled Teal, and if new wetlands are being created within the range they should be designed so as to provide suitable habitats for the species. For example, in Spain several new wetlands have been created by sand extraction, and the creation of a shallow profile with well-vegetated, shallow borders is essential if a site is to be used by Marbled Teal. The area of suitable breeding habitat now remaining in Andalucía (Spain) in years of low rainfall is so limited that there is a very strong case for the creation of artificial sites specifically designed for the species.

Priority: low
Time-scale: long

2.4. *To actively prevent the hunting of the Marbled Teal at key sites throughout the range*

2.4.1. Seek permanent hunting bans at all sites where the species is regularly recorded
Priority: high
Time-scale: short

2.4.2. Increase wardening at key sites and levy penalties on offenders

This is particularly important for sites where hunting occurs during the breeding season. Wardens should enforce hunting bans or, at sites where hunting is permitted, ensure that no Marbled Teal are shot.

Priority: high
Time-scale: short

2.4.3. Where hunting bans cannot be achieved, use other methods to minimise the number of Marbled Teal shot

It will be politically impossible to ban hunting totally at all sites where Marbled Teal occur regularly. Various mechanisms can reduce the number of Marbled Teal shot, including effective hunter education (see 4.1), restricting the number of hunters, restricting the hunting season to periods when the number of Marbled Teal present is minimal, and banning the hunting of look-alike species such as Common Teal and Red-crested Pochard *Netta rufina*. Marbled Teal are readily confused with female and juvenile Red-crested

Pochard under normal hunting conditions, owing to their similar body colour and dark eye patch. In winter, Marbled Teal often form mixed flocks with Common Teal, and are a similar size. The hunting of Red-crested Pochard should be prohibited in all Marbled Teal range states.

Priority: high
Time-scale: short

2.4.4. Secure financial support for countries with less funds to aid the implementation of their hunting laws
Priority: high
Time-scale: short

2.5. *To phase out the use of lead shot at all key sites throughout the range*

It is important to minimise the threat to Marbled Teal resulting from lead poisoning, using voluntary bans where necessary.

Priority: medium
Time-scale: medium

2.6. *To prevent mortality of Marbled Teal from other causes*

Crayfish nets, concrete drains and other factors are causing significant mortality in certain areas. These problems are relatively easy to solve in many cases. For example, alternative net designs exist which are just as effective for catching crayfish but which catch no ducks at all, while fencing could prevent birds from falling into concrete drains.

Priority: essential
Time-scale: short

3. **Monitoring and research**

3.1. *To develop and implement national and international programmes to monitor the status and distribution of the Marbled Teal*

3.1.1. Conduct regular surveys at known breeding sites

While many wintering sites are censused annually in mid-winter during the International Waterfowl Census, less attention is given to surveys of breeding sites, and data on breeding numbers and distribution are collected in an unsystematic and unco-ordinated fashion. Regular monitoring would allow the calculation of trends in breeding numbers for each site, and would help identify local declines in time to address the causes.

Priority: high
Time-scale: short/ongoing

3.1.2. Conduct surveys at possible breeding sites

High numbers recorded in winter in North Africa show that very important breeding sites remain to be discovered in that region, and additional breeding sites are likely to be still undiscovered elsewhere in the range. In order to conserve these sites, they must first be located.

Priority: essential
Time-scale: short/ongoing

3.1.3. Extend the Wetlands International International Waterfowl Census to cover all sites where the Marbled Teal is recorded

There are many known or potential wintering sites not regularly covered in the midwinter census.

Priority: medium
Time-scale: ongoing

3.1.4. Conduct regular, simultaneous surveys of all important sites at a national level

Simultaneous surveys of all important sites at different times of the year are a useful tool in clarifying population size, the importance of different sites, and the nature of movements between them. This was done successfully in Spain in 1994, and should be extended to Morocco as soon as possible.

Priority: medium
Time-scale: ongoing

3.1.5. Encourage foreign birdwatchers to survey Marbled Teal sites where the status of the species is uncertain, and to submit their records to national BirdLife Partners or to the Wildfowl and Wetlands Trust

In Turkey, visiting birdwatchers are successfully being encouraged to visit known or possible IBAs and send their observations to DHKD. This could be done in many other Marbled Teal range states.

Priority: medium
Time-scale: ongoing

3.2. *To promote biological and other research which is useful for the conservation of the Marbled Teal*

3.2.1. Undertake studies of the species' ecology and habitat requirements

Very little research has been conducted on the species, and our understanding of habitat requirements throughout the life cycle must be improved in order to aid habitat conservation and management. For example, the availability of suitable breeding habitat is probably acting as a factor limiting the population, but the nature of "suitable breeding habitat" is not yet understood at a fine level.

Priority: essential
Time-scale: short/ongoing

3.2.2. Promote a better understanding of the movements of Marbled Teal by marking and monitoring individuals

The species is very nomadic, at least in the western Mediterranean, and ringing recoveries prove that birds move regularly between Spain, Morocco and Algeria. Movements are also suspected between Turkey, Israel and Egypt. Once an effective and harmless marking method has been found, the marking of individuals will allow a much greater understanding of the nature of these movements.

Priority: high
Time-scale: medium/ongoing

3.2.3. Undertake applied studies of hydrology, pollution impacts, socio-economic needs, etc., at key sites

At many key sites, the nature and significance of threats are poorly understood, and specific research is needed to assess changes to the hydrology, the impact of agrochemicals or the use of the site by local people. The results of all such studies should be fed into management plans for the sites (see 2.2).

Priority: medium
Time-scale: medium

4. Public awareness and training

4.1. To increase awareness of the need to protect the Marbled Teal and its habitat

The species and its plight are poorly known at all levels of society, and the Marbled Teal has never been used as a flagship for conservation as has, for example the White-headed Duck *Oxyura leucocephala* or the Greater Flamingo *Phoenicopterus ruber*. There is an urgent need to educate administrators, hunters and the local population surrounding all sites that regularly support the species. An educational booklet on the conservation of the Marbled Teal should be produced in all major languages within the range of the species. Wide and effective distribution of this booklet should be done by BirdLife Partner organisations.

An international education campaign is needed to educate hunters in all Marbled Teal range states as well as hunters from other countries who visit range states to shoot ducks. Hunters need to be educated about the importance of the Marbled Teal and how to identify it. The Conseil International de la Chasse et de la Conservation du Gibier (CIC) should assist in promoting such a campaign through national, regional and local hunting organisations. Such a programme should use educational materials such as a video, emphasising the status and plight

of the species across the whole Mediterranean, translated into all major languages (e.g. Spanish, Turkish, Arabic, English, French, Italian). A practical brochure for hunters could also be prepared. This could be combined with similar programmes to reduce the hunting pressure on other globally threatened waterfowl occurring in the same region, particularly the White-headed Duck and the Ferruginous Duck *Aythya nyroca*. This educational work at an international level could be combined with a programme established at a national level and should include targets that can be evaluated.

The contacts between scientists and technical staff (including members of hunting organisations) working in different Marbled Teal range-states should be promoted. A working group of researchers interested in the species should be formed, with regular exchange of research results and methods (e.g. sexing of birds in the field). Those interested in the species are already receiving the biannual newsletter of the Wetlands International/IUCN Threatened Waterfowl Research Group, which is an ideal forum for the exchange of information between researchers, etc.

Priority: essential
Time-scale: short

Annex
Recommended conservation actions by country

Algeria

1.2.1. Encourage the preparation of a joint fly way management plan between Morocco, Spain, Algeria and Tunisia.

2.1.1. Promote the protection of Lac de Boughzoul, Lac de Réghaïa, Marais de la Macta and Lac Bou Lhilet. Protection should also be considered for Grande Sebkhet d'Oran and Lac des Gharabas. Grande Sebkhet d'Oran would be suitable as a Réserve Nationale because of its relative intactness and proximity to a large university city (Morgan, 1982).

2.2. Encourage the preparation of adequate management plans for key sites

3.1.1./3.1.2. Prepare an inventory of known and potential sites for the species.

3.1.1./3.1.2. Breeding surveys of wetlands in the El Kala, Centre, Oranie, Hauts Plateaux and Biskra regions, especially Boughzoul, Réghaïa, Lake Fetzara and Marais de la Macta. Surveys of wetlands in the southern Sahara, which may hold many, as yet unknown, breeding sites. The Oued Khrouf is one area that should be surveyed.

3.1.3. Improved coverage of Ouest-Oranie wetlands; surveys of *chotts* and *sebkhas* of the south (e.g. Chotts Helrhir, bou Djeloud, de Merouane, de Kerdache and de Ouargla: see Jacobs and Ochando, 1979).

3.2.1. Undertake studies on the biology and ecology of the species in different areas of the country.

4.1. Carry out a public awareness campaign and educate hunters in the identification of the species particularly in the area of the El-kala National Park (PNEK).

Armenia

2.1.1. Promote protection of Armashski carp farm.

3.1.1./3.1.2. Survey of known and potential breeding sites to establish current status.

Azerbaijan

1.2.2. Promote the full legal protection of the species.

1.2.3./2.1.2./3.2.3. Promote improved water management at a national level. The following specific measures are recommended: chemical pollution from cotton fields surrounding the Kizil Agach marshes and Lakes Aggel, Saraesy, Shorbet-Koba and Bos-Koba should be investigated and controlled; water extraction for irrigation from Lakes Aggel, Saraesy, Shorbet-Koba and Bos-Koba should be prevented; the original links between the Kura river and each of these lakes should be restored to ensure a clean supply of water; a water supply should be provided to the western part of Lake Aggel (Kichik Aggel or Malyi Aggel), which is now drained.

2.1.1./2.1.2. Promote the protection of all key sites from poaching and habitat degradation.

2.1.2./2.4.2. Promote extension of the protected areas at Lake Aggel well beyond the edges of the lake, and facilities and training for the reserve guards should be improved.

2.1.3. Promote the designation of Lakes Aggel, Saraesy, Bos-Koba and Mahmud-Chala as Ramsar Sites.

2.4.2. Promote strict enforcement of hunting restrictions particularly in protected areas.

3.1.1./3.1.2. Survey of former and current breeding sites to establish current status. Winter surveys are also required.

Egypt

1.2.2. Encourage the legal protection of the Marbled Teal.

3.1.3. Develop an annual International Waterfowl Census which covers all potential wintering sites, including the lakes of the Western Desert.

Georgia

3.1.2. Survey of potential breeding sites to establish current status.

Israel

2.1.1. Encourage the declaration of Tishlovet Hakishon as a Nature Reserve.

2.2. Promote careful management to ensure that the newly restored section of the Hula valley marshes provides suitable breeding habitat for Marbled Teal.

2.2. The cutting of bankside vegetation, human disturbance and water-levels in the Hula fish ponds should be carefully managed to improve the area of habitat available to Marbled Teal and to improve their breeding success.

3.1.1./3.1.2. Conduct annual breeding surveys at all suitable sites in the Hula valley.

3.2.2. Conduct a detailed study of changing numbers of birds at Tishlovet Hakishon from 1 June to 1 December in order to clarify the nature of passage movement.

3.2.2. Co-ordinate studies of marked individuals together with Turkey.

Lebanon

3.1.2. Conduct surveys of potential breeding sites.

3.1.3. Develop an International Waterfowl Census to cover potential wintering sites.

Morocco

1.2.1. Encourage the preparation of a joint fly way management plan between Morocco, Spain, Algeria and Tunisia.

2.1.1. Encourage the protection of additional sites: Moulouya delta, lower Loukos marshes and estuary, Sidi Moussa-Oualidia complex, Barrage Al Massira, Barrages Mohamed V and Mansour Eddehbi and Dayet Merzouga.

2.2. Promote the establishment of management plans for key sites and the implementation of existing plans.

2.2. Recommended management at Sidi Bou Ghaba: management should prevent the loss of habitat through siltation and eutrophication, and reduce the impact of disturbance from tourism.

2.4.2. Encourage the strict application of the hunting legislation.

2.4.3./4.1. Educate hunters and the general public about the importance of the Marbled Teal and its habitat.

3.1.1./3.1.2. Survey known and possible breeding sites: to clarify the size and distribution of the breeding population and discover, as yet unknown, sites.

3.1.4. Conduct simultaneous censuses with those co-ordinated across Spain in order to improve our understanding of movements within and between the countries.

3.2.1. Conduct research into the biology of Marbled Teal, especially into winter ecology (at Sidi Bou Ghaba) and breeding ecology. Merja de Douyiet is a suitable site for research.

3.2.1. Define the ecological requirements of Marbled Teal that need to be addressed in the various management plans for key sites.

3.2.2. Study the movements of marked birds within and beyond Morocco once a safe marking technique has been developed.

4.1. Use the Marbled Teal as the flagship species in the National Conservation Education Centre at Sidi Bou Ghaba, making it the symbol of the site and developing an education programme for the species.

4.1. A display about the Marbled Teal should be developed as one of the central features of the National Conservation Education Centre at Sidi Bou Ghaba.

Russian Federation

3.1.2. Survey of suitable sites in the northern Caucasus to establish the current status of Marbled Teal.

Spain

1.2.1. Encourage the approval and implementation of the recovery plan prepared for the species in the Autonomous Community of Valencia (Ambiental, 1992) by the Consellería de Medi Ambient.

1.2.1. Prepare a joint fly way management plan between Spain, Morocco, Algeria and Tunisia.

1.2.1. Encourage preparation, approval and implementation of recovery plans for the Marbled Teal in the Autonomous Communities of Andalucía and Murcia.

1.2.1. Encourage the preparation of a co-ordinated action plan for the conservation of the Marbled Teal between the central and regional administrations, in which local experts and NGOs are involved.

1.2.1. Promote the creation of a Comité de Especies Amenazadas, within the Comisión Nacional de Protección de la Naturaleza stipulated by Article 36 of Law 4/1989, charged with promotion and co-ordination of the Autonomous Communities of Recovery Plans, Management and Conservation for the species listed in the Catálogo Nacional de Especies Amenazadas.

2.1.1. Encourage the following designations:

(a) Provide legal protection to the following wetlands as a Reserva Natural or a Paraje Natural: Cañada de Las Norias, Laguna de los Tollos, Marjal de Pego-Oliva, Marjal del Moro.

(b) Include the area of El Reboso within the Paraje Natural of the Brazo del Este.

(c) Include the areas of las Cantaritas and the northern part of Brazo de la Torre within the Parque Natural del Entorno de Doñana.

2.1.1. Encourage the designation of the following sites as Special Protection Areas (SPAs) under the European Union's Wild Birds Directive: Parque Natural del Entorno de Doñana, Brazo del Este, Cañada de las Norias, Laguna de los Tollos, Marjal de Pego-Oliva, Marjal del Moro, Salinas de San Pedro y Playa de la Hita, Lagunas de Lebrija-Las Cabezas.

2.2./2.6. Promote regulation and substantially reduce the level of fishing activity in the following wetlands: Paraje Natural de El Hondo, Paraje Natural de las Salinas de Santa Pola.

2.2. Promote improved habitat management in existing wetlands within the Marismas del Guadalquivir: create more suitable breeding habitat through the management of water-levels and provision of islands and appropriate vegetation for nesting at Veta la Palma, Salinas de Sanlúcar, Lucio de la FAO and Salinas de San Rafael.

2.2./2.3. Promote restoration and creation of suitable habitat in El Hondo and Salinas de Santa Pola: recover former marshes converted into crops that have now been abandoned or are of little financial value; adequately manage the vegetation, hydrology and structure of pools and reservoirs.

2.2./2.3. Promote restoration of wetlands along the margin of Mar Menor, Murcia. Management should improve the habitat available to the species in areas where the species already occurs (Playa de la Hita y Marina del Carmolí), as well as restoring other sites (abandoned salinas) to increase the area of habitat available to the species.

2.3. Promote the creation of more wetlands suitable for breeding within the Marismas del Guadalquivir by recovering lakes which have been drained and by creating artificial lakes.

2.4.1. Promote a ban of hunting in those parts of the following wetlands where Marbled Teal are recorded: Paraje Natural de El Hondo, Paraje Natural de las Salinas de Santa Pola, Parque Natural del Entorno de Doñana.

2.4.3./4.1. Carry out effective hunter education and ban hunting of the look-alike Common Teal *Anas crecca* and Red-crested Pochard *Netta rufina* in and around all key sites.

2.6. Promote reduced mortality caused by crayfish nets in the Brazo del Este and other parts of the Marismas del Guadalquivir by banning these nets in areas used for breeding and by enforcing the modification of net design.

2.6. Encourage action to avoid the falling of broods into concrete drains within the Parque Natural de El Hondo and Salinas de Santa Pola, and increase guarding to prevent the capture of these broods by the public.

3.1.4. Conduct simultaneous spring, summer and autumn censuses at Marbled Teal sites in Spain and Morocco and joint research in the two countries.

3.2.1./3.2.2. Conduct research into the ecology and biology of the Marbled Teal, especially into habitat requirements, breeding ecology and the nature of movements within and beyond Spain.

Syria

3.1.3. Extend the International Waterfowl Census to cover all potential wintering sites.

3.1.2. Conduct surveys of potential breeding sites.

Tunisia

1.2.3./2.1.2./2.4.2./3.2.3. It is recommended that at Oued Sed, the disposal of industrial and domestic effluents, reed-cutting, snail-collecting and hunting of all bird species should be totally banned. A guard should be employed during the breeding season, and all domestic animals should be removed from the site. A socio-economic study of the area should be carried out and ecotourism should be promoted.

2.1.1. Encourage the designation of Oued Sed, Sebkhet Sidi Mansour, Barrage El Haouareb, Oasis Noueil and Sebkhet Ariana sedimentation ponds as protected areas.

2.2. It is recommended that at Barrage El Haouareb, the area of emergent vegetation suitable for nesting should be increased by management. Hunting should be banned around the lake, and access tightly controlled.

3.1.1./3.1.2. Conduct breeding surveys of the key sites listed above plus the following additional sites in order to clarify distribution and numbers, particularly in wet years: Barrage Bir M'Cherga, Oasis de Zaafrane, Salins de Monastir, Marais de Soliman, Barrage Lebna, Barrages Gdir el Ghoul and Mornaguia, Chott Blidette, Barrage Chiba, Hadj Kacem marshes.

4.1. Guards working at the Barrages El Haouareb, Bir M'Cherga, Lebna and Gdir el Ghoul and Mornaguia should be educated about the need to protect these sites and their Marbled Teal, given training in ornithology, and provided with binoculars and telescopes.

4.1. Education programmes should be carried out around key sites and targeted at schools, colleges, farmers and hunters.

4.1. National and regional workshops should be organised to promote an understanding of the importance of the Marbled Teal.

Turkey

2.1.1. Promote the effective protection of all key sites and the designation of the Van marshes as a protected area.

2.1.2./3.2.3. Recommended management for the Eregli marshes: restore the former water-level; control reed-cutting and stop reed-burning. Studies of pollution and hydrology are needed.

2.1.2./2.2. Recommended management for the Sultan marshes: a hydrological management plan for the reserve and surrounding areas is needed to ensure that water-levels inside the reserve are maintained.

2.1.2./2.4.2./3.2.3. Recommended management for the Çukurova deltas: control illegal and excessive hunting; control agricultural expansion; control tourist development (second homes); assess

the impact of the drainage of agrochemicals from surrounding land, especially into Akyatan Gölü, Tuzla Gölü and meanders between the lakes.

2.1.2. Recommended management for the Göksu delta: stop marsh reclamation; control agricultural expansion/development; supply clean water from the river to Akgöl.

2.1.2. Recommended management for the Hotamis marshes: stop reed-burning and control reed-cutting.

2.1.3. Promote improvements in the conservation status of the existing Ramsar Sites (Göksu delta and Sultan marshes).

2.4.2. Promote enforcement of hunting legislation.

3.1.1. Detailed breeding surveys should be carried out at all key sites to assess the status of the breeding population.

3.1.1./3.1.5. Visiting foreign birdwatchers should be encouraged to visit key sites and to submit their records to DHKD using their standard site recording forms.

3.1.2. Search for further breeding sites in eastern Turkey.

3.2.1. A detailed study of the breeding ecology and habitat use of the species should be conducted in the Göksu delta and/or Çukurova deltas.

3.2.2. Marking programme: to be carried out in the Göksu delta and/or Çukurova deltas in co-ordination with ornithologists in Israel to attempt to identify the wintering grounds.

4.1. The species should be used as a flagship for the protection of the Eregli marshes, Hotamis marshes, Göksu delta and Çukurova deltas.

4.1./2.4.3. An education programme should be carried out to raise the awareness of the species among hunters.

Action plan for the White-headed Duck (*Oxyura leucocephala*) in Europe

Reviews

This action plan should be reviewed and updated every four years. An emergency review will be undertaken if sudden major environmental changes, liable to affect the population, occur within the species' range. As far as possible, this action plan is intended to achieve the aims of the Agreement on the Conservation of African-Eurasian Migratory Waterbirds (currently under development under the Bonn Convention) for the species. This agreement is likely to influence the need for and timing of future reviews.

Geographical scope

The action plan needs implementation in the following range states of the White headed Duck: Algeria, Azerbaijan, Bulgaria, Greece, Israel, Romania, Russian Federation, Spain, Tunisia, Turkey and Ukraine. In addition, it should be implemented in the following range states of the introduced North American Ruddy Duck *Oxyura jamaicensis*: Austria, Belgium, Denmark, Finland, France, Germany, Hungary, Iceland, Ireland, Italy, Morocco, Norway, Netherlands, Portugal, Sweden, Switzerland, United Kingdom. Implementation is also required in any other countries where the Ruddy Duck is found in captivity.

Summary

The White-headed Duck *Oxyura leucocephala* has undergone a considerable decline in range and population size this century, with hunting and the destruction and degradation of habitat being the causes. The Spanish population has recently recovered after being near to extinction in the 1970s. There has been considerable attention paid to the species in Turkey since 1989 which has led to conservation measures being taken at Burdur Gölü, a site that holds most of the world population in winter. Numbers appear to be roughly stable in most countries, but many key sites are not effectively protected, and the threats to them have the potential to cause rapid population declines in the near future. The species is incredibly easy to shoot, making hunting a much more significant threat than for most waterbirds.

In recent years, it has become clear that the spread of introduced North American Ruddy Ducks (*Oxyura jamaicensis*) poses the most severe threat to the White-headed Duck, owing to the free hybridisation between the two species. A concerted, co-operative international effort is urgently required to stop and reverse the spread of the Ruddy Duck across the western Palaearctic before this becomes impossible. The species has now been recorded in 20 countries, with the United Kingdom holding by far the largest population, and hybridisation is already posing a serious problem in White-headed Duck sites in Spain. The extinction of the White-headed Duck is only likely to be prevented if rapid action is taken to control Ruddy Ducks (which may include eradication) in all countries where it occurs. Both action in the field to remove wild individuals, and in captivity to prevent the escape of more birds, is essential.

The conservation of the White-headed Duck in Europe also requires the effective conservation of wetlands of importance for the species, together with the effective control of hunting on these wetlands.

Threats and limiting factors

Introduction of the North American Ruddy Duck – critical

Habitat loss – high

Habitat degradation – high

Hunting – high

Introduction of other species – low

Trapping in fishing nets – low

Lead poisoning – unknown

Warfare – unknown

Conservation priorities at European level

Promote and develop national and international policies to control (which can include eradication) the Ruddy Duck – essential

Control Ruddy Ducks and Ruddy Duck/White-headed Duck hybrids – essential

Promote adequate protection for key sites – essential

Postpone reintroductions of White-headed Duck until the Ruddy Duck problem has been solved – essential

Improve national and international monitoring of the status and distribution of the Ruddy Duck – essential

Monitor and improve effectiveness of suitable control measures for the Ruddy Duck – essential

Monitor the number of stifftails kept in captivity – essential

Increase awareness of the need to control the spread of the Ruddy Duck – essential

Promote national and international policies which specifically favour the protection of the White-headed Duck and its habitat – high

Actively prevent hunting of White-headed Duck at key sites throughout its range – high

Develop and implement national and international programmes to monitor the status and distribution of the White-headed Duck – high

Increase awareness of the need to protect the White-headed Duck and its habitat – high

Introduction

The White-headed Duck *Oxyura leucocephala* is a globally threatened species classified as Vulnerable by the IUCN (Groombridge, 1993) and BirdLife International (Collar et al., 1994). It is listed in Annex I of the European Union's Wild Birds Directive. It has recently been placed on Appendix I of the Bonn Convention, and it is listed in Appendix II of the Bern Convention and in Appendix II of CITES. It is listed as Endangered at European level by BirdLife International (Tucker and Heath, 1994).

The White-headed Duck is the only stifftail (*Oxyurini*) indigenous to the Palaearctic, and has attracted a great deal of interest from the international conservation community in recent years. Concern over marked declines of the species led to the production of national (Spanish) and international conservation plans in the late 1980s.

In recent years, there has been growing concern about the threat posed to the species by the introduced North American Ruddy Duck *O. jamaicensis jamaicensis* which has brought the species to the forefront of conservation issues in many countries, particularly in Spain and the United Kingdom. An international workshop into the problem posed by the spread of the Ruddy Duck was held in Arundel (UK) in March 1993 and the relevant recommendations from that meeting are incorporated into this action plan. Another workshop on the Ruddy Duck problem took place on 29 and 30 September 1994 in Córdoba (Spain), and was organised by the Andalusian Agencia de Medio Ambiente.

On 8 December 1994, a workshop, organised by the Wildfowl and Wetlands Trust and IWRB, took place in Strasbourg (France) to discuss the action plan for the White-headed Duck in Europe. It was attended by experts from Bulgaria, Denmark, Germany, Greece, Israel, Italy, Morocco, Netherlands, Pakistan, Romania, Spain, Switzerland, Tunisia, Turkey and United Kingdom. This action plan is based on discussions held during this workshop, on conclusions of other workshops organised on the Ruddy Duck problem, and on further information received by correspondence before and after the workshop. A great deal of background information used in this document has previously been compiled for other publications on the White-headed Duck (e.g. Anstey, 1989; Green and Anstey, 1992; Green, 1994). Information on the number of Ruddy Duck records comes largely from a database managed by the Wildfowl and Wetlands Trust, and from Martí (1993).

A limitation of this plan is that its scope does not include western Asia, which probably holds the majority of the remaining world population of the White-headed Duck during the breeding season, including most of the birds wintering in Turkey and other parts of the eastern Mediterranean. Successful implementation of this plan thus cannot guarantee effective conservation of the east Mediterranean population. In addition, the separate population wintering in Pakistan is highly threatened and urgently requires conservation attention. Another weakness of this plan is that we have failed to gain the active involvement of representatives from Azerbaijan and the Russian Federation, two countries within the scope of this plan that support important populations of the species.

Background information

Distribution and population

The present distribution of the White-headed Duck is fragmented, with a small resident population in the western Mediterranean (Spain, Tunisia, Algeria) and a larger, mainly migratory population in the eastern Mediterranean and Asia (Green and Anstey, 1992). The majority of the birds in this latter population breed outside the western Palearctic in Kazakhstan and the Russian Federation and winter inside the western Palaearctic in Turkey (Table 8.1).

There are now at least two subpopulations, one being centred around the western Mediterranean and the other centred around the eastern Mediterranean and the coasts of the Black Sea and Caspian. The nature of movements within each of these regions is very poorly understood, with a total lack of ringing data, and it is possible that there are more than two subpopulations isolated from each other by a lack of interchange. The global population was probably over 100 000 originally. Concentrations of about 50 000 wintering on the Caspian coast of Turkmenistan until the 1930s have since disappeared (Poslavski, 1992). On the basis of recent mid-winter counts, the present world wintering population of the White-headed Duck can be conservatively estimated at 19 000 birds (Green and Anstey, 1992). The western Mediterranean winter population can be estimated at 1 000 with a 1992 count of 836. The wintering population in countries bordering the eastern Mediterranean and Black Sea can be estimated at 13 000 with a 1991 count of 11 507. The wintering population in countries further east can be conservatively estimated at 5 000, with a 1991 count of 3 904, 3 620 of these being found within the western Palaearctic (Azerbaijan).

Like all animal populations, the size of the White-headed Duck population must fluctuate, and the above figure represents a minimum estimate for the peak of these fluctuations (namely, the size of the population in a very good year). The coverage of wetlands during mid-winter counts is too incomplete in most areas to be able to assess the nature and extent of fluctuations with confidence. However, the count of only 3576 in Turkey in 1993, including an extremely low but certainly accurate count of 3010 at Burdur Gölü (Green et al., 1993), suggests that the world wintering population of White-headed Ducks could be well under 19 000 in some years.

Table 8.1

Estimates of current sizes of White-headed Duck wintering and breeding populations in Europe, North Africa and the Middle East. The years of peak winter counts are given in brackets

? historical records only, current status unclear.
* mainly important as a passage area.

Country	Peak winter count (1984–1994)	No. of breeding females
Algeria	220 (1984)	40+
Azerbaijan	3620 (1991)	–
Bulgaria	233 (1993)	–
Greece	850 (1994)	–
Iran	628 (1988)	100+
Iraq	?	?
Israel	620 (1988)	–
Romania	18* (1990)	occasional
Russian Federation	?*	50+
Spain	786 (1992)	100–200
Syria	35 (1994)	–
Tunisia	182 (1989)	occasional
Turkey	10 927 (1991)	200–300
Ukraine	?*	?

Within the western Palaearctic, there has been a drastic historical decline in range. Former breeding populations have become extinct in Italy, Corsica (France), Morocco, Hungary, Albania, Serbia, Greece, Israel and Egypt, and probably also Ukraine and Armenia (Phillips, 1923; Green and Anstey, 1992).

Life history

Breeding

The mating system is polygamous, and nesting occurs in dense reedbeds, often on top of old Coot *Fulica atra* nests (Amat and Sánchez, 1982; Torres et al., 1986). The timing of breeding is variable, with 4 to 9 eggs laid from April to early July. Incubation takes 22 to 24 days and fledging occurs within 8 to 9 weeks (Anstey, 1989).

Feeding

Chironomid larvae are probably the major component of the diet, both for adults and ducklings (Torres and Arenas, 1985; Green et al., 1993), but a variety of other invertebrates are eaten, as well as seeds and vegetative parts of *Potamogeton*, *Ruppia* and other plants (Anstey, 1989).

Moulting

Flightless moult occurs twice a year, after breeding and in late winter (Anstey, 1989).

Habitat requirements

White-headed Ducks prefer freshwater or brackish, alkaline, eutrophic lakes, which often have a closed basin hydrology and are frequently semi-permanent or temporary. Breeding sites have dense emergent vegetation around the fringes and are small, or are enclosed areas within larger wetland systems. They typically have extensive areas of 0.5 to 3 metres depth (Matamala et al., 1994). Stable water-levels during the incubation period are vital for successful breeding. Wintering sites are generally larger, deeper and often have little emergent vegetation (Anstey, 1989). Freshwater habitats are used more in winter than in the breeding season. The availability of chironomid larvae is likely to be a key feature in habitat selection (Green et al., 1993).

Threats and limiting factors

Introduction of the North American Ruddy Duck

The greatest threat to the survival of the White-headed Duck is undoubtedly that resulting from hybridisation and competition with the North American Ruddy Duck introduced into the United Kingdom in the 1950s and now spreading across the western Palaearctic as it undergoes population growth in the UK (Hughes, 1991; Arenas and Torres, 1992; Green and Anstey, 1992; Pintos and Rodríguez de los Santos, 1992; Anon., 1993; ICONA, 1993; Rose, 1993; Torres et al., 1994a,b). The population in the UK increased tenfold between 1975 and 1990 and is now estimated at over 3 500 birds in winter, with the number of records on the European continent and the species' distribution increasing in parallel as birds spread outwards from the UK. The spread of the Ruddy Duck is also partly due to continuous escapes from waterfowl collections in the Netherlands and probably other countries (Rose, 1993). The Ruddy Duck has now been recorded in 20 western Palaearctic countries (including the UK) plus an unconfirmed record from Ukraine; breeding has been confirmed in six countries. This introduced species threatens to drive the White-headed Duck to extinction through hybridisation, which readily occurs between them. The hybrids are fully fertile: second-generation birds have already been collected in Spain (Urdiales and Pereira, 1993) and third-generation hybrids have been bred in captivity at the Wildfowl and Wetlands Trust, Slimbridge. The majority of hybrids shot in 1993 and 1994 were young birds, showing that the continuing intensive control efforts in Spain are not sufficient to prevent hybridisation.

The threat from the Ruddy Duck is extremely serious, given the nature of the problem and the fact that, if allowed to proceed beyond a certain point, the Ruddy Duck's spread across the Palaearctic will become unstoppable. This would certainly be the case if the species was allowed to become established in White-headed Duck range states such as Algeria, Turkey or the Russian Federation, where the huge size and area of the wetlands and their infrequent monitoring would make control impossible.

Importance: critical

Habitat loss

Drainage of numerous shallow lakes, marshes and other wetlands of former importance for breeding and wintering has occurred across the range (Green and Anstey, 1992), and it has been estimated that the area of suitable breeding habitat has been roughly halved this century (Anstey, 1989). Whole wetland systems have been transformed in the former Soviet Union. More quantitative information is available for Spain, where 60% of the endorreic lagoons in Andalucía have been drained this century. Amongst the most recent sites to be destroyed is Çorak Gölü in Turkey, an important wintering site which has been permanently dry since 1987.

In some areas (e.g. Spain, Tunisia) the White-headed Duck is now making extensive use of artificial lagoons and reservoirs and these are partially compensating for the loss of natural habitats. In 1993, about a third of the ducklings recorded in Spain were bred on wetlands of a completely artificial nature (Matamala et al., 1994), a particularly high figure owing to drought conditions affecting many natural, temporary sites.

Importance: high

Habitat degradation

Many important wetlands have been severely degraded, reducing their value for the White-headed Duck without being totally destroyed. The fact that many of the wetlands are endorreic makes them particularly vulnerable to hyper-eutrophication and pollution. Fortunately, the species seems to be more resistant to eutrophication than many other waterbird species (Green et al., in press).

The range of threats facing sites important for the White-headed Duck is well illustrated by the existing threats from industrial, domestic and agricultural pollution, sedimentation and water extraction from the catchment that face the most important wintering site, Burdur Gölü (Anon., 1993b; Green et al., 1993; in press). Furthermore, the construction of an international airport has started on the shores of the lake, and there are plans to build a huge industrial complex of 160 factories (mainly textiles) without assessment of their impact on the lake. Similar factors threaten to destroy or degrade numerous important sites in most major range states of the White-headed Duck (Anstey, 1989). Some further examples follow.

The construction of dams and other hydrological work carried out within the catchments of the

Hotamis marshes and Eregli marshes in Turkey has led to them both being reduced drastically in size, and caused the Sultan marshes to be completely dry in 1991 (DHKD, *in litt.*, 1994). At Lake Vistonis in Greece, there are plans for the construction of a large dyke to reclaim the marshes adjacent to the south-east part of the lake where the White-headed Duck winters (Handrinos, 1995). Plans to raise the water levels at Lake Kerkini will have unknown effects on the species. In Tunisia, upstream barrages have severely affected the breeding site Sebkha Kelbia, increasing the frequency of desiccation by two and a half times (Hughes and Hughes, 1992). Severe pollution has led to the recent abandonment of Menzel Bourguiba, another breeding site, and reed-cutting is severely limiting the area of vegetation available for nesting, for example, at Barrage Sidi Abdelmonaam (Z. Benaïssa, *in litt.*, 1994).

Importance: high

Hunting

The White-headed Duck is an incredibly easy bird to shoot given its lack of ability to escape when facing hunters (Torres et al., 1986; Green et al., 1993; in press). Hunting has therefore undoubtedly played an important role in its decline. Hunting and egg-collection were probably the final causes of extinction in France, Italy, the former Yugoslavia and Egypt. Hunting is still a major threat across most of the species' range, although its impact has rarely been quantified. An investigation into illegal hunting at Burdur Gölü in winter 1993 found that an estimated 4.5 birds per day were being shot within a limited study area that held 25% of the lake's White-headed Duck population. This death rate almost certainly exceeded the limits of "sustainable harvest" of the lake's population (Green et al., 1993; in press). The White-headed Duck formerly suffered significant hunting pressure in Spain, and Torres et al. (1986) considered hunting to be "the principal cause of the drastic decline in numbers prior to 1978". Hunting is no longer a threat in Andalucía, although it still applies in the newly colonised areas of Castilla-La Mancha (Esparvel, 1993) and Valencia (Dolz et al., 1991). White-headed Ducks are shot in Greece each winter (Handrinos, 1995) and are often shot in Bulgaria

(Iankov, 1994). Numerous birds were shot at Menzel Bourguiba lagoon in Tunisia in April 1985 (Z. Benaïssa, *in litt.*, 1994). White-headed Ducks are regularly shot at Lake Saraesy, Azerbaijan (M. Patrikeev, *in litt.*, 1995).

Importance: high

Introduction of other species

In the lagoons of Córdoba, Spain, breeding success is thought to have been adversely affected by the introduction of carp which are believed to affect the birds' foraging success through direct competition for food and by causing ecological change. The removal of carp from Laguna del Rincón led to a dramatic recovery in White-headed Duck numbers and breeding success (Torres et al., undated).

Importance: low

Trapping in fishing nets

White-headed Ducks have been found trapped in fishing nets in Iran (D. A. Scott, *in litt.*, 1995), and this is possibly a widespread problem.

Importance: low

Lead poisoning

There are no data on the importance of lead poisoning as a cause of mortality, but hunting is intense at many key sites, and the ingestion of lead shot could result in significant mortality (see Pain, 1992).

Importance: unknown

Warfare

War is having an unknown effect on the species in Azerbaijan, where the area of warfare (1992-1993) is very close to the key site of Lake Aggel (M. Patrikeev, *in litt.*, 1994).

Importance: unknown

Conservation status and recent conservation measures

White-headed Duck range states

Algeria

There is no national Red Data Book. The White-headed Duck is fully protected under Decree No. 83–509 of 20 August 1983.

Algeria has a resident population of White-headed Ducks in the El Kala wetland complex in the north-east, which is also thought to have been the main area for the species in the last century. However, the species probably also bred in Lac Fetzara (Annaba region) and Lac Holloula (Alger region) before these sites were transformed in the 1930s (Heim de Balsac and Mayaud, 1962; van Dijk and Ledant, 1983). The White-headed Duck is currently breeding in Lac Tonga, Lac des Oiseaux and Lac de Ben Azzouz, and about 37 nests were located in 1991 (Boumezbeur, 1992). Breeding probably also occurs in Marais de la Mekhad. Non-breeders and wintering birds occur on Lac des Oiseaux and Lac Oubeira (Chalabi, 1990). The highest count ever recorded was 220 on Lac Oubeira in January 1984 (M. Smart, *in litt.*, 1989) with 209 on Lac des Oiseaux in March 1992 (Boumezbeur, 1992).

Key sites are Lac des Oiseaux (unprotected), Lac Tonga (National Park and Ramsar Site), Lac Oubeira (National Park and Ramsar Site) and Lac Ben Azzouz (unprotected).

No specific conservation programmes have been conducted for the species. There are no Ruddy Duck records.

Armenia

Breeding was formerly recorded in the Lake Sevan area (Dementiev and Gladkov, 1952). There are no recent records. The legal status and status in national Red Data Books for the species are unclear. There are no Ruddy Duck records.

Azerbaijan

The species is listed in the Red Data Book of Azerbaijan published in 1990 (no details available). The species was fully protected in the former Soviet Union, but its current legal status in Azerbaijan is unclear.

Breeding may have occurred in lakes of the southern Mugan and Kura valley until the early part of this century, but there is no evidence of breeding in recent years (M. Patrikeev, *in litt.*, 1995). In winter, Azerbaijan is of major importance for the species, at least in some years, and in 1991 over 3100 birds were counted in Lake

Aggel and 520 in Kizil Agach Bays (IWRB's International Waterfowl Census, IWC). Lake Aggel thus seems to be the most important wintering site for the species after Burdur Gölü, although there is no mention of the species from previous censuses at the site in the 1960s. There is, however, an unconfirmed record of 5000 birds in Kizil Agach Bays in 1962 (M. Patrikeev, in litt., 1991).

Key sites are Lake Aggel (State Reserve), Kizil Agach Bays (State Reserve and Ramsar Site) and Lake Saraesy (unprotected).

No specific conservation programmes have yet been conducted for the species. There are no Ruddy Duck records.

Bulgaria

The White-headed Duck has been fully protected under the law since 1962. It is listed as Rare in the national Red Data Book (Botev and Peshev, 1985).

From the 1890s to the 1940s the White-headed Duck was recorded wintering or on passage in the west of Bulgaria (around Sofia) and along the Black Sea coast (Botev and Peshev, 1985). Important numbers continue to winter along the Black Sea coast with record counts of 214 at Lake Durankulak in January 1983 (B. Ivanov, in litt., 1994) and 233 birds on 29 and 30 November 1993 (188 at Lake Mandra complex and 45 at Lake Burgas). The birds arrive in November and are sometimes recorded until the end of March (B. Ivanov, in litt., 1994).

Key sites are Lake Mandra, especially the Uzungeren zone (unprotected), Poda (Protected Site), Lake Burgas (partly protected) and Lake Durankulak (Natural Monument and Ramsar site).

The species is included on a poster on globally threatened waterbirds produced by the Bulgarian Society for the Protection of Birds (BSPB), but no other specific conservation programmes have yet been conducted for the species. There are no Ruddy Duck records. The Ruddy Duck is not legally protected, and is not found in private waterfowl collections. The identification guide to Ruddy Ducks and hybrids (Urdiales and Pereira, 1993) has been circulated by the BSPB, and the

need to search for these birds has been stressed in the BSPB magazine Neophron. The BSPB has taken the first steps towards active guarding at Uzungeren zone near Burgas.

France

Small numbers of White-headed Ducks were recorded breeding on Lake Biguglia and other Corsican wetlands until the 1960s (P. Dubois, in litt., 1989). Recent proposals for a reintroduction project in Corsica have been postponed (Perennou and Cantera, 1993).

There are a total of 85 Ruddy Duck records, mainly during the winter, plus two breeding records from 1988 and 1993. Breeding probably now takes place annually in small numbers. An informal working group made up of the Ministry of the Environment, the Office National de la Chasse (ONC) and various NGOs was established in December 1994 to address the Ruddy Duck problem. No control measures against Ruddy Ducks have yet been implemented. A ministerial decree needs to be issued before control measures are legal.

Greece

The White-headed Duck is listed as Endangered in the national Red Data Book (Handrinos, 1992). It is legally protected by Joint Ministerial Decision 414985/85.

In the last century, the White-headed Duck was reported to be common in Epirus and resident in the Louros delta, Amvrakikos, although no nest has ever been found (Handrinos, 1995). Cramp and Simmons (1977) reported that breeding may have occurred in Greece in the 1950s, but this is open to question (Handrinos, 1995). In recent years, a significant wintering population has developed in Macedonia and Thrace, with a peak mid-winter count of 423 in January 1990 (G. Handrinos and IWRB International Waterfowl Census). A record count of 850 to 900 was made at Lake Vistonis on 12 December 1994 (P. Pergantis and S. Grigoropoulos, verbally, to G. I. Handrinos, 1994). All records since 1960 are for December to early April, although the birds probably start to arrive in November. Since 1982, there has been the trend for wintering numbers to increase, to spread to the west and to become more concentrated in Lake Vistonis (Handrinos, 1995). It is not known whether these birds come from the north (through Bulgaria) or from Turkey; the shooting of a female in December 1991 on Lesbos supports the latter possibility.

Key sites are Lake Vistonis (Ramsar Site and SPA), Lake Ismaris/Mitrokou (Ramsar Site and SPA) and Lake Kerkini (Ramsar Site and SPA). Hunting is permanently banned at Kerkini (Ministry of Environment, *in litt.*), but is permitted at Vistonis and Ismaris. There are significant threats to the habitat at all three sites (Handrinos, 1995).

No specific conservation programmes have yet been conducted for the species. There are no Ruddy Duck records.

Hungary

Strictly protected, and listed in the Hungarian Red Data Book. Breeding of the White-headed Duck was recorded in Hungary from 1853 onwards around the northern Danube and between the Danube and the Tisza. The last confirmed breeding was at Lake Kondor in 1961 although breeding may have occurred at Lake Nádas in 1971 (Green and Anstey, 1992). The species is now considered extinct as a breeding bird in the country, although there are records for 1995 of vagrants.

A reintroduction of the White-headed Duck in Hungary was conducted in 1988 by the Hungarian Ornithological Society and the Wildfowl and Wetlands Trust, but this failed to establish a population in the wild (Anstey, 1989). There is one unconfirmed record of a Ruddy Duck, from November 1994. No action has yet been taken to control Ruddy Ducks. The legal status of the Ruddy Duck is unclear, but plans exist for enlisting hunters in agreement with the hunting authorities to prevent Ruddy Ducks becoming established should they arrive in the country (Min. Environment, *in litt.*).

Israel

There is no Red Data Book in Israel, but there is an official report on the status of all vertebrates, which lists the White-headed Duck (no details

available). The species is fully protected under the 1955 Wildlife Protection Law.

In the last century the White-headed Duck was considered a common resident on Lakes Tiberias and Hula, but breeding has not been recorded for at least 50 years (Paz, 1987). A wintering population has remained, and the known wintering population increased markedly following the creation of a reservoir, Tishlovet Hakishon, in 1984. Numbers have increased steadily each winter, from 70 in 1986 to 514 in 1994 (D. Alon, verbally, 1994). It is likely these increasing numbers reflect a relocation of birds from other wintering sites in the Middle East. The breeding grounds of these birds are unknown, but could be eastern Turkey.

Key sites are Tishlovet Hakishon, Ma'ale Kishon reservoir, Yesodot reservoir and Hula valley (including Hula Reserve), and data from the IWRB International Waterfowl Census supplied on a regional level show there are important numbers wintering in the wetlands of the valley of Yesreel, northern Negev, Jordan valley, foothills of Judea and the Galilee coastal plain.

No specific conservation programmes have yet been conducted for the species in Israel. There is one Ruddy Duck record from April 1983. The legal status of the Ruddy Duck is unclear.

Italy

The White-headed Duck is strictly protected under Law No. 157 of 11/2/92. It is listed as Endangered in the national Red Data Book (Schenk, 1976).

Breeding and wintering of White-headed Ducks was formerly recorded in Puglia, Sardinia and probably Sicily until 1977 (Brichetti et al., 1992), but the species is now only a vagrant. There are currently two plans to develop reintroduction projects, co-ordinated separately by WWF Italy (Vitaloni, 1994) and Lega Italiana Protezione Uccelli (LIPU).

There have been eight Ruddy Duck records, all in winter. No actions have yet been taken to control Ruddy Ducks, although conservationists and aviculturalists have already held meetings to discuss the Ruddy Duck issue in relation to plans to reintroduce the White-headed Duck. There are plans to set up a working group and to introduce a monitoring system for captive stifftails (M. Grussu, in litt., 1994).

Morocco

There is no national Red Data Book. The White-headed Duck is fully protected (M. Dakki, verbally, 1994).

The White-headed Duck bred in northern Morocco at the turn of the century and was regarded as "common" (Phillips, 1923). Only vagrant birds have been recorded since the 1950s (Louette, 1973). There is no evidence that birds from the currently expanding Spanish population have dispersed to Morocco.

Groups of up to 12 Ruddy Ducks have been present regularly since November 1992 and all year round in 1994, mainly at Merja Barga and Merja Haloufa. There is a growing awareness among Moroccan ornithologists and the government of the need to take action to deal with this problem. Two adult males were shot at Merja Barga by Eaux et Forêts guards in March 1994. The Ruddy Duck is effectively granted legal protection because the protective legislation cites les erismatures without specifying the species.

Romania

There is no national Red Data Book. The species is not currently protected, but a proposed new hunting law would list the species as fully protected. This new law has yet to be approved by parliament.

The White-headed Duck formerly bred in the lakes of Transylvania, with the last record of breeding from Sculia in 1908 (D. Munteanu, in litt., 1989). Breeding was recorded in the Danube delta, Dobrodja, in May 1986, when eight adults and three young were seen on channels between Crisan and Maliuc (D. Ilhes, in litt., 1991). It is possible that breeding occurs regularly, although the last previous breeding record in the Danube delta was from Lake Agigea in 1957 (D. Munteanu, in litt., 1989). Lake Techirghiol and the Danube delta have been used as wintering sites since at least the 1960s with up to 37 birds in mid-winter

(1969), Lake Techirghiol being the major site. These sites are also important for passage (D. Munteanu, in litt., 1989), with autumn passage beginning about 10 October and probably ending about the end of November, and spring passage occurring in March (D. Munteanu, in litt., 1994). The highest numbers recorded are 218 on Lake Techirghiol in November 1982 (D. A. Scott, in litt., 1983), with 75 seen on 25 November 1993 (D. Munteanu, in litt., 1994).

Key sites are the Danube delta (Ramsar Site, Biosphere Reserve, World Heritage Site) and Lake Techirghiol (unprotected).

No specific conservation programmes have yet been conducted for the species. There are no Ruddy Duck records. The Ruddy Duck is not legally protected.

Russian Federation

The White-headed Duck is listed as Category IV: Rare in the Russian Federation Red Data Book (Ivanov, 1983). The species was fully protected in the former Soviet Union, but its current legal status in the Russian Federation is unclear.

In that part of the Russian Federation which lies within the scope of this action plan, the species was formerly a common breeder in the Sarpa lowlands between Volgograd and the Caspian and in the Volga/Ural steppes (Dementiev and Gladkov, 1952). The species has also been recorded historically in the northern Caucasus and along the western coast of the Caspian. In 1992, breeding occurred in one to three sites alongside the Volga and Uzen rivers in the Volga delta area, when 40 to 70 adults and three broods were recorded (V. Moseikin, verbally, to G. Tucker, 1993). The Manych and Gudilo reservoirs are major spring and autumn migration sites for the species, probably for birds wintering in Turkey. In October 1980, 1 200 birds were counted at these lakes (Ivanov, 1983; Linkov, 1984).

Key sites identified so far are the Manych and Gudilo reservoirs and the Volga delta. Specific sites within these large wetland complexes and their precise legal status have yet to be identified.

No specific conservation programmes have yet been conducted for the species. There are no Ruddy Duck records.

Spain

Spain holds a secure, resident population of White-headed Ducks which has recovered from a low point of only 22 birds recorded in 1977 to 786 birds in January 1992. The majority of the population has always been found in Andalucía. However, the increase in numbers has been accompanied by an expansion in distribution both within and beyond the former strongholds of lagoons in the Córdoba, Cadiz, Sevilla and Huelva provinces of Andalucía (Torres et al., 1986; AMA Córdoba, 1991; Green, 1994; Matamala et al., 1994), and nowadays the species can also be found in the provinces of Almería, Ciudad Real, Toledo, Madrid, Alicante and Mallorca.

Since 1984, breeding has been recorded in Málaga and for the first time in Almería and Jaén provinces. Breeding has also been recorded outside Andalucía in Alicante province (Valencia) and Toledo and Ciudad Real provinces (Castilla-La Mancha). Since 1992, the majority of breeding birds have been in Almería, mainly due to the severe drought which has affected most of the traditional breeding sites in western Andalucía. Since 1984, birds have also been recorded in Cuenca (Castilla-La Mancha), Madrid and Santander (Cantabria).

The White-headed Duck has been protected from hunting across Spain under national law since 1973. It is listed as Endangered in the Spanish Red Data Book (Blanco and González, 1992). The White-headed Duck is also listed as Endangered in the National Catalogue of Threatened Species (Royal Decree 439/90) and hence it is compulsory to prepare regional recovery plans under Law 4/89.

A highly effective conservation programme initiated in Andalucía in 1979 has led to the dramatic population recovery. This programme involved the protection of all the major Andalusian sites for White-headed Ducks (AMA Córdoba, 1991; ICONA, 1993). In the early 1980s, ICONA (now DGN) initiated a working management plan.

Since 1992, DGN has led a series of technical co-ordination seminars in which all communities where White-headed Ducks are recorded have participated. No communities have satisfied their legal requirement by developing their own recovery plans. Effective protection from illegal hunting in Andalucía has undoubtedly played the most important role in the population recovery. Other habitat protection measures taken include the removal of introduced fish (from Laguna del Rincón and Laguna de Zoñar, Córdoba), the control of pollution and sedimentation, and the regeneration of the natural surrounding vegetation. The species has recently become established in Valencia and Castilla-La Mancha. The principal site in Valencia, El Hondo, was declared a Paraje Natural in 1988. Of five sites important for the species in Castilla-La Mancha, only one is protected, as a Hunting Refuge (ESPARVEL, 1993). However, over 75% of the Spanish population occurs in protected areas at any one time. Since 1982 there has been a captive breeding programme for the White-headed Duck run by DGN, with 79 birds being released into the wild by the end of 1990 (Pereira, 1991) and at least 85 additional birds released since then (ICONA, 1993). In 1993, an additional 36 birds were released in Mallorca with eight birds still present in the area after nine months (Mayol, 1994).

The shooting of North American Ruddy Ducks and hybrids began in 1989 and has usually been conducted independently by the environmental agencies of each autonomous community. However, from June to December 1993, DGN contracted a specialised team to control the birds on a national level. DGN has published an identification guide with the aim of aiding the detection of Ruddy Ducks (Urdiales and Pereira, 1993). In 1993, SEO/BirdLife prepared a report commissioned by the European Union (DG XI) and DGN which compiled data on the spread of the Ruddy Duck in Spain and beyond and suggested conservation measures (Martí, 1993). Data on the spread of the Ruddy Duck are also presented by Matamala et al. (1994) and Torres et al. (1994a,b). In Spain, the incidence of hybridisation has increased very rapidly since hybrids were first recorded in 1991, and a total of 53 hybrids and Ruddy Ducks had been shot at White-headed

Duck sites by the end of 1994. In order to prevent escapes of Ruddy Ducks from collections within Spain, the individuals and organisations holding the bird in captivity have been identified and contacted individually to request that all reproduction and escape of the species is prevented (Rose, 1993). In the Balearic Islands the trade in and possession of live birds or eggs of any species of *Oxyura* (apart from *O. leucocephala*) has been prohibited.

Numerous small wetlands are important sites (e.g. breeding recorded in 23 to 27 wetlands since 1984), and for a list see Matamala et al. (1994). However, the key sites are Albufera de Adra (IBA 230, SPA, Ramsar Site, Natural Reserve), Salinas de Cerrillos (IBA 230, SPA, Nature Reserve), Cañada de la Norias (SEO/BirdLife Ornithological Reserve), Veta la Palma (IBA 247, Natural Park), Lebrija-Las Cabezas complex (IBA "U", Nature Reserve), Embalse de la Coronela (unprotected), Laguna del Gosque (IBA 267, Nature Reserve), Laguna de Arjona (Nature Reserve), Lagunas del Tarelo (IBA 247, Natural Park), Puerto de Santa María complex (IBA 250, Nature Reserve, SPA), Espera complex (IBA 249, Nature Reserve, SPA), Laguna de Medina (IBA 252, SPA, Nature Reserve), Laguna Amarga (IBA 242, SPA, Nature Reserve), Laguna de Zoñar (IBA 242, SPA, Nature Reserve), Laguna del Rincón (IBA 243, SPA, Nature Reserve), Embalse de Malpasillo (IBA 243, Ramsar Site, Natural Site), Laguna Honda (Nature Reserve), Laguna del Acebuche (IBA 247, Natural Park), Dehesa de Monreal (IBA 084, unprotected), Laguna de Pedro Muñoz (IBA 082, Hunting Reserve, SPA) and Embalse de El Hondo (IBA 215, SPA, Natural Site).

Syria

The status of the White-headed Duck in any national Red Data Book is unclear, as is its legal status.

There is one June record of the White-headed Duck from 1994 (G. Kirwan, *in litt.*, 1994, *Orn. Soc. Middle East Bull.* 33). There appears to be a regular wintering population, and at Lake Quattine 30 were recorded in 1993 and 35 in 1994 (IWRB

International Waterfowl Census). Lake Quattine (unprotected) is the only key site identified so far.

No specific conservation programmes have yet been conducted for the species. There are no Ruddy Duck records.

Tunisia

There is no national Red Data Book. The White-headed Duck is fully protected.

The species winters regularly in northern Tunisia, but breeding has only been occasionally recorded, suggesting exchange of birds with Algeria. The first breeding record, near Gabès in 1957 (Castan, 1958), was during an unusually wet year. Winter numbers have declined after over 500 birds were recorded in the IWRB censuses in 1968, 1969, 1971 and 1973 and a flock of 1550 was recorded at Lac de Tunis in February 1969 (M. Smart, *in litt.*, 1989). Following major floods in 1969, the winter distribution expanded to southern Tunisia as more wetlands became available, but from the late 1970s the range has been restricted to the north-east (M. Smart, *in litt.*, 1989). Breeding is irregular and in small numbers and since 1980 has been recorded at Barrage El Houareb, Barrage Sidi Abdelmoneim, Barrage Besbessia and Menzel Bourguiba lagoon (Green and Anstey, 1992; Z. Benaïssa, *in litt.*, 1994).

Key sites are Lake Ichkeul (National Park, World Heritage Site, Biosphere Reserve, Ramsar Site), Barrage el Haouareb (Hunting Reserve), Lake Tunis (National Reserve), Gdir El Ghoul 1 (unprotected), Gdir El Ghoul 2 (unprotected), Barrage Lebna (unprotected), Barrage Sidi Abdelmoniem (unprotected), Sebkha Kelbia (Natural Reserve), Barrage Besbessia (unprotected), Salines de Soliman (unprotected), Oued El Kebir (unprotected), Barrage Mornaguia (unprotected), Barrage Mlaabi (unprotected), Menzel Bourguiba lagoon (unprotected) and Lake Hammam Jedidi (unprotected).

The distribution of educational booklets summarising the previous action plan (Anstey, 1989) in French in 1990 is reported to have brought clear benefits in educating *Eaux et Foréts* guards responsible for controlling hunting on reservoirs occupied by the species (F. Maamouri, verbally,

1993). No other specific conservation programmes have yet been conducted for the species in Tunisia. There are no Ruddy Duck records.

Turkey

There is no national Red Data Book. The Draft Red List of Threatened Animals of Turkey published by the Ministry of Environment in 1990 gives the status of the White-headed Duck as Vulnerable to Endangered (see Porter, 1991). The species has had full legal protection since the 1984-1985 hunting season, when the Bern Convention came into force.

Turkey has the largest wintering population of the White-headed Duck of any range state, and also holds a major breeding population. The southern coastlands and central plateau have major breeding and wintering sites, eastern Turkey has breeding and passage sites, and the Black Sea coastlands hold major passage sites. Wintering is also recorded in the Black Sea coastlands and western Anatolia (see Beaman, 1986 for definitions of regions). The peak wintering population is at least 11000 birds, while Green et al. (1989) estimated a total of 150 to 200 breeding pairs. The number of Turkish breeding pairs is likely to be higher than this figure, as in 1991 the breeding population was about 150 pairs in the central plateau alone (Kirwan, in press).

The most important site in Turkey is Burdur Gölü which often holds over 50% of the known world population during winter. In February 1991 there was a record count of 10927 birds on the lake (Berrevoets and Erkman, 1991), but numbers fluctuate markedly and only 3010 were recorded in February 1993 (Green et al., 1993, in press). About 500 birds were recorded on 27 July 1994 (J. Petit, in litt., 1994), and the lake is probably vitally important all year round. Other recent counts include 1246 at Cernek Gölü in the Kizilirmak delta in March 1992 (Hustings and van Dijk, 1994), which is an extremely important passage site.

Key sites are the Çukurova delta (particularly Akyatan Gölü and Akyayan Gölü, Hunting Reserve and unprotected respectively), Arin Gölü (unprotected), Burdur Gölü (Ramsar Site and Hunting Reserve), Hotamis marshes (Natural Heritage Site), Eregli marshes (Natural Heritage Site), Kizilirmak delta (particularly Cernek Gölü, Hunting Reserve), Kulu Gölü (Natural Heritage Site), Marmara Gölü (unprotected), Salda Gölü (Natural Heritage Site), Sultan marshes (Strict Nature Reserve, Natural Heritage Site and Ramsar Site), Van Gölü (unprotected), Van marshes (unprotected), Horkum Gölü (unprotected), Edremit marshes (unprotected), Bendimahi marshes (unprotected), Uyuz Gölü (unprotected), Yarisli Gölü (unprotected), Kozanli Saz Gölü (unprotected), Hirfanli reservoir (unprotected) and Akkayi Baraji (unprotected). Many important sites for the species have been destroyed and most other sites have been degraded. Several former key sites listed by Anstey (1989) seem to have lost their importance for the species due to habitat degradation (Karamik Gölü, Corak Gölü, Eber Gölü, Cavuscu Gölü).

Considerable conservation work on the species has already been done by DHKD, the Wildfowl and Wetlands Trust and the Burdur Municipality, using the species as a successful flagship for wetland conservation. Distribution of educational booklets summarising the previous international action plan for White-headed Ducks (Anstey, 1989) in Turkish led to the imposition of temporary hunting bans at Burdur Gölü and Yarisli Gölü from December 1990 onwards. An international symposium on Burdur Gölü and the White-headed Duck was organised in December 1991 (DHKD and Burdur Municipality, 1993), and DHKD produced an attractive poster in Turkish and English in 1993. The steps necessary to prepare a management plan have been identified (Salathé and Yarar, 1992), and a detailed ecological study of White-headed Ducks was completed at the lake in 1993 (Green et al., 1993; in press). In 1993, the lake was declared a Game and Waterbird Conservation Area and Ramsar Site principally to protect the species. The White-headed Duck is now being used as a flagship in the current campaign against development proposals at the lake, and has become a symbol for nature conservation in Turkey. There is one record of a Ruddy Duck from April 1988. The Ruddy Duck is not legally protected.

Ukraine

The White-headed Duck is included in the national Red Data Books published in 1980 and 1995, but details are not known. Its legal status is unclear.

Both breeding and wintering were historically recorded in the Azov Sea area (Valkh, 1900; Phillips, 1923) and passage was recorded in the Crimean region (Nikolskyi, 1891). In the past 100 years there have been only 19 records of the species from Ukraine, mainly of single birds (Lysenko, 1991; I. Gorban, in litt., 1995), but it seems extremely likely that important numbers of birds seen on passage in Romania and wintering in Bulgaria and Greece pass through Ukraine along the Black Sea coast.

No specific conservation programmes have yet been conducted for the species. There is one unconfirmed Ruddy Duck record from 1992. The legal status of the Ruddy Duck is unclear.

Ruddy Duck range states with no White-headed Duck

Austria

There are two winter records of Ruddy Ducks, both from Lake Constance. No action has yet been taken to control Ruddy Ducks and the legal status of the species is unclear.

Belgium

Most of the 79 Ruddy Duck records refer to winter, plus two breeding records from 1991 and 1993. A small number of breeding attempts are now known to take place annually. No action has been taken to control Ruddy Ducks although aviculturalists have been informed of the need to prevent their escape.

Denmark

There have been eight Ruddy Duck records, mainly in summer. No action has yet been taken to control Ruddy Ducks and the legal status of the species is unclear.

Finland

There have been three Ruddy Duck records, mainly in summer. No action has yet been taken to control Ruddy Ducks and the legal status of the species is unclear.

Germany

Ruddy Ducks have been recorded on 41 occasions throughout the year and throughout the country. No action has yet been taken to control Ruddy Ducks despite the committed actions of conservationists to raise awareness of the problem. There would be considerable difficulties in introducing country-wide control measures for the Ruddy Duck due to the fact that current national laws do not give clear directives on how to treat the species (Bauer, 1994). Federal laws may be applicable, though these differ considerably between the 16 federal ministries, suggesting that negotiations over the introduction of control measures may be time-consuming and complicated.

Iceland

Ruddy Ducks migrate to Iceland to breed, with a total of 21 records by the end of 1994 (with a combined total of 42 birds). Three confirmed breeding attempts are known, the first of which took place in 1990 (Nielsen, 1994; 1995). The first young were successfully fledged in 1994. No measures to control Ruddy Ducks have yet been taken although the species is well monitored and the distribution and status are well known.

Ireland

There are about 30 Ruddy Ducks wintering annually and five breeding records. It is likely that one or two pairs breed every year. No measures to control Ruddy Ducks have yet been taken although conservationists are well informed of the problem.

Netherlands

Ruddy Ducks occur mainly in winter, with at least 175 records to date. Records throughout the summer since 1988 (when two pairs are known to have bred successfully) suggest that a small number of pairs breed annually. There is currently a proposal to designate the Ruddy

Duck under Article 54 of the Hunting Law which will allow licensed control of the species (A. Binsbergen, *in litt.*, 1994). There are also plans to designate the Ruddy Duck under Article 24.a of the Nature Conservation Act which would prohibit trade in, the release of, and/or the keeping of the species. No control measures against Ruddy Ducks have yet been implemented.

Norway

There have been 20 Ruddy Duck records, mainly in summer. No action has yet been taken to control the species, and its legal status is unclear.

Portugal

Two Ruddy Ducks have occurred in winter, and, despite this small number of records, the Portuguese have already acted positively by setting up a Ruddy Duck control team which is prepared to control any Ruddy Ducks which occur on Nature Reserves. There are four records of White-headed Duck (L. Costa, pers. comm., 1994). The Ruddy Duck is not legally protected.

Sweden

There have been 24 Ruddy Duck records, mainly in summer. No action has yet been taken to control Ruddy Ducks. The Ruddy Duck is legally protected, since it is not listed in the hunting legislation.

Switzerland

There have been at least nine Ruddy Duck records, mainly in winter. No action has yet been taken to control Ruddy Ducks. The legal status of the species is unclear.

United Kingdom

The current Ruddy Duck population is estimated at 3500 wintering birds and at least 700 breeding pairs (Hughes and Grussu, 1994). Realising the potential threat which the UK Ruddy Duck population posed to the White-headed Duck, the UK set up a Ruddy Duck working group (RDWG) in September 1992. This group, comprising representatives from government, conservation and research organisations, and aviculturalists, has the role of devising a strategy for dealing with the Ruddy Duck problem in the UK (Holmes and Galbraith, 1994). The RDWG immediately identified the need for research into possible control measures for Ruddy Ducks in the UK, and this work, which is being carried out by the Wildfowl and Wetlands Trust, funded mainly by the UK Government, started in 1993. The research has shown that shooting (with shotguns and rifles) and nest trapping of breeding females are effective control measures (Hughes and Grussu, 1994). The RDWG therefore plans to proceed to a phase of regional control in two areas of the UK in order to assess the practicality of controlling Ruddy Ducks throughout the UK. The other major role of the RDWG is to raise awareness of the Ruddy Duck problem both nationally and internationally, and a national public relations strategy is currently being implemented.

The Ruddy Duck is legally protected by the 1981 Wildlife and Countryside Act, and prior to November 1995 killing was only possible under scientific licence. Recent changes remove all legal constraints to organised control for the purposes of conserving the White-headed Duck. Other changes mean that a licence is now required to trade in captive-bred Ruddy Ducks, thus restricting this trade.

Aims and objectives

Aims

In the short term, to maintain the current population and area of occupancy of the White-headed Duck throughout its range. In the medium term, to promote the population increase of the White-headed Duck within its current range. In the long term, to promote the expansion of the White-headed Duck breeding population to other suitable areas. In addition, to prevent hybridisation of the White-headed Duck by eradicating the introduced North American Ruddy Duck in the western Palaearctic.

Objectives

I. Policy and legislation

I.I. *To promote and develop national and international policies to control (which can include eradication) the Ruddy Duck*

I.I.I. Promote and develop national control strategies in all western Palaearctic countries supporting Ruddy Ducks

All countries should be encouraged to follow the lead of Spain and the United Kingdom in formulating their own national strategies for the control of Ruddy Ducks.

Priority: essential
Time-scale: ongoing

I.I.2. Encourage national legislation which permits the control of Ruddy Ducks in all western Palaearctic countries

In some countries, there are currently legal barriers to the control of Ruddy Ducks, which urgently need to be removed.

Priority: essential
Time-scale: ongoing

I.I.3. Promote national legislation in all western Palaearctic countries which prohibits the escape or release of Ruddy Ducks from captivity

It is imperative that populations of Ruddy Ducks in the wild are not augmented by escapes from captivity. Ruddy Ducks from captive collections are still being allowed to fly free in a number of European countries, even though this is illegal in some of them. It is currently unclear in which countries the release of Ruddy Ducks has been made illegal, but they include the United Kingdom.

Priority: essential
Time-scale: ongoing

I.I.4. To develop strategies to prevent the escape of Ruddy Ducks from collections

Making the escape or release of Ruddy Ducks illegal will not be sufficient to prevent it from happening, and other policies are required. It is recommended that legally enforceable registers for captive individuals of all stifftail species should be established. Legislation to prohibit the keeping of Ruddy Ducks in captive waterfowl collections should also be considered since this would provide a guarantee that no birds could escape. Trade in Ruddy Ducks should be phased out, and waterfowl keepers should be encouraged to phase out Ruddy Ducks from their collections.

Priority: essential
Time-scale: ongoing

I.I.5. Involve international conventions in solving the Ruddy Duck problem, particularly the Bonn, Bern and Biodiversity Conventions

All contracting parties to the Bonn Convention should provide the legislative means for the control of Ruddy Ducks in order to comply with Article III (4.c) which states that "to the extent feasible and appropriate, [contracting parties should endeavour] to prevent, reduce or control factors that are endangering or are likely to further endanger the [White-headed Duck], including strictly controlling the introduction of, or controlling or eliminating, already introduced exotic species".

Article II (2.b) of the Bern Convention requires Contracting Parties "to strictly control the introduction of non-native species".

Article 8 (h) of the Biodiversity Convention requires Contracting Parties to "prevent the introduction of, control or eradicate, those alien species which threaten ecosystems, habitats or species".

Priority: medium
Time-scale: medium

I.2. *To promote national and international policies which specifically favour the protection of the White-headed Duck and its habitat*

I.2.I. Promote the full protection through national and international legislation of the White-headed Duck and its habitat

Priority: high
Time-scale: short

I.2.2. Involve international conventions in protecting the White-headed Duck and its habitat, especially the Ramsar, Bonn and Bern Conventions

All key sites for the White-headed Duck should be designated as Ramsar Sites. Parties should be encouraged to sign the Agreement on the Conservation of African-Eurasian Migratory Waterbirds (under the Bonn Convention), which will provide for further protection to the White-headed Duck.

Priority: medium
Time-scale: medium

1.2.3. Promote the development and implementation of national and regional action plans and recovery programmes

Range states and regions are encouraged to follow the timely lead of the Spanish Autonomous Region of Castilla-La Mancha, which has given statutory approval for a recovery plan for the species, citing an earlier draft of this European action plan (Decree 183/1995 of 28 November 1995).

Priority: high
Time-scale: short

1.3. *To promote the integrated management of wetlands and ensure that broad policies such as agriculture, transport, tourism, etc. do not have a negative impact on the White-headed Duck and its habitat*

It is recommended that all range states should develop and implement an effective national wetland conservation strategy. Such a strategy should set clear targets and priorities for the protection and integrated management of White-headed Duck's habitat. National policies and legislation on agriculture, transport and tourism should all be finely tuned to the needs of wetland conservation.

Priority: medium
Time-scale: medium

2. Species and habitat protection

2.1. *To control Ruddy Ducks and Ruddy Duck/White-headed Duck hybrids*

2.1.1. Reduce the size of the UK Ruddy Duck population as quickly as possible

In order to safeguard the White-headed Duck, in the long term it is essential that the spread of North American Ruddy Ducks from the UK to the European continent is stopped completely. However, given the large size and wide distribution of the UK population, the only realistic objective for the four-year duration of this action plan is to reduce the size of this population as quickly as possible.

Priority: essential
Time-scale: ongoing

2.1.2. Eliminate all small populations of Ruddy Ducks from the western Palaearctic

Every effort should be made to remove the small numbers of Ruddy Ducks present in other countries in the western Palaearctic in order to prevent the establishment of further self-sustaining populations. The European Union should promote the adoption of a common approach to stopping and reversing the spread of the North American Ruddy Duck within the EU. The first priority is to prevent feral breeding populations from becoming established outside the UK. However, in order to ensure that no Ruddy Ducks reach White-headed Duck populations, all individuals need to be controlled. It is more important to control adult birds than juveniles, female birds than males, and hybrids than pure birds. It is more important to control long-staying than short-staying individuals.

It takes time to develop the necessary national control strategies, which often require careful planning and negotiation and/or legislative changes. Given the urgency of the current situation, those countries which cannot introduce unconditional control immediately should attempt to implement control in stages. For example, measures to prevent breeding (e.g. by nest destruction or the coating of eggs with liquid paraffin) could be undertaken immediately, proceeding to the control of all adult birds as soon as possible. The general objectives, in order of priority, should be:

a. Total prevention of breeding.

b. Control of all Ruddy Ducks which occur between March and September inclusive and thus have the potential to breed. Note that it is preferable to control potential breeding birds in April while they are in conspicuous courtship display and before the females begin incubation.

c. Control of all Ruddy Ducks which occur between October and February inclusive.

Priority: essential
Time-scale: ongoing

2.1.3. Eliminate all Ruddy Duck/White-headed Duck hybrids

Where hybrids are recorded, they should be controlled in the same way as Ruddy Ducks. This is in fact even more important.

Priority: essential
Time-scale: ongoing

2.2. *To promote adequate protection for key White-headed Duck sites*

2.2.1. Seek protected-area designation for all sites regularly holding White-headed Ducks

Priority: essential
Time-scale: medium

2.2.2. Prevent destruction or degradation of all sites regularly holding White-headed Ducks

Legal protection should be enforced where it exists, and developments damaging the hydrology, vegetation, water quality, etc., of key sites should be prevented. Full environmental impact assessments should be conducted for any new development schemes at these sites.

Priority: essential
Time-scale: ongoing

2.3. *To manage habitats to increase White-headed Duck breeding success and reduce mortality*

Wetland management can readily increase breeding success, for example, by providing more emergent vegetation for nesting, by maintaining stable water-levels at artificial breeding sites or by reducing disturbance. The reduction of fish densities reduces competition for food and increases duckling survival. These needs should be addressed by the production and implementation of management plans for key sites, which include specific objectives and prescriptions for the White-headed Duck.

Priority: medium
Time-scale: ongoing

2.4. *To create new breeding and wintering habitats for the White-headed Duck*

Many artificial wetlands are now important for the species, and if new wetlands are being created within the range they should be designed so as to provide suitable habitats for the species.

Priority: low
Time-scale: ongoing

2.5. *To actively prevent the hunting of White-headed Ducks at key sites throughout the range*

2.5.1. Seek permanent hunting bans at sites where the species is regularly recorded

The White-headed Duck is one of the easiest of all waterbirds to shoot and hunting pressure is still high at many important wintering sites.

Priority: high
Time-scale: short

2.5.2. Increase wardening at key sites and apply penalties to offenders

In many parts of the range, where legal protection of the species and/or hunting bans at sites are not very effective in preventing hunting, active guarding is essential if hunting is to be minimised. Wardens should enforce hunting bans or, at sites where hunting is permitted, ensure that no White-headed Ducks are shot.

Priority: high
Time-scale: ongoing

2.5.3. Where permanent hunting bans cannot be achieved, use other methods to minimise the number of White-headed Ducks shot

It will be politically impossible to ban hunting totally at all sites where White-headed Ducks occur regularly. Various mechanisms can reduce the number of White-headed Ducks shot, including effective hunter education (see 4.2.3), restricting the number of hunters and restricting the hunting season to periods when the number of White-headed Ducks present is minimal.

Priority: high
Time-scale: ongoing

2.5.4. Secure financial support for countries with less funds to aid the implementation of their hunting laws

This is particularly important for countries in the eastern Mediterranean region.

Priority: high
Time-scale: ongoing

2.5.5. Harmonise hunting seasons between neighbouring range states

The hunting season in Bulgaria ends at the end of January, while it continues for a month or more in the neighbouring countries Romania and Turkey. Reducing the hunting season to a minimum period in all states would help to lower the hunting pressure on White-headed Ducks.

Priority: low
Time-scale: short

2.6. *To phase out the use of lead shot at all key sites throughout the range*

It is important to minimise the threat to the White-headed Duck resulting from lead poisoning, using voluntary bans where possible.

Priority: medium
Time-scale: ongoing

2.7. *To postpone any reintroductions of the White-headed Duck until the Ruddy Duck problem has been solved*

Although there have been proposals to reintroduce White-headed Ducks in France and Italy, it is essential that these do not proceed until Ruddy Ducks have been successfully eliminated in these countries and controlled in other countries. Such reintroductions would simply increase the possible zone of hybridisation between the two species and thus escalate the problem of identifying and removing these hybrids. Ruddy Ducks have already been recorded at sites in Corsica and Sardinia. Experience in Spain suggests that Ruddy Ducks are concentrated at sites where White-headed Ducks are present, hence it can be predicted that releases of White-headed Ducks would increase the number of Ruddy Ducks recorded at these sites. All future reintroduction programmes should follow the IUCN guidelines for reintroductions (Black, 1991; Kleiman et al., 1994).

Priority: essential
Time-scale: ongoing

3. **Monitoring and research**

3.1. *To improve national and international monitoring of the status and distribution of the Ruddy Duck*

Although international and national mechanisms to monitor the Ruddy Duck have been in place since the Arundel meeting, there is still work to be done to improve these. For example, experience in Morocco and Turkey shows that records from

holidaying birdwatchers are not reaching the "national focal points" appointed at the Arundel meeting to monitor the status of Ruddy Ducks in each country. There is a need to ensure that birdwatchers are aware of the need to look for Ruddy Ducks and are informed of the focal point or person to whom the relevant information should be reported. In some countries, records of Ruddy Ducks have not been submitted as they were viewed as escapes from captivity.

Priority: essential
Time-scale: ongoing

3.2. *To monitor and improve the effectiveness of suitable control measures for Ruddy Ducks*

The United Kingdom Ruddy Duck research programme has shown that shooting with rifles and shotguns, nest-trapping of breeding females, and the dipping of eggs in liquid paraffin can all be used to control Ruddy Duck populations. This research should remove the need for other countries to assess control methods independently.

Priority: essential
Time-scale: ongoing

3.3. *To develop and implement national and international programmes to monitor the status and distribution of the White-headed Duck*

3.3.1. Conduct regular breeding surveys in known breeding sites

While many wintering sites undergo an annual census in mid-winter during the IWRB International Waterfowl Census, less attention is given to breeding surveys, and data on breeding numbers and distribution are collected in an unsystematic and unco-ordinated fashion. Regular monitoring would allow the calculation of trends in breeding numbers for each site, and would help identify local declines in time to address the causes.

Priority: high
Time-scale: ongoing

3.3.2. Conduct breeding surveys at possible breeding sites

Potential additional breeding sites in Turkey, the Russian Federation and elsewhere in the range are not likely to be discovered unless a special effort is made to locate them. Obviously, any such sites cannot be conserved until they are located.

Priority: high
Time-scale: ongoing

3.3.3. Extend the International Waterfowl Census to cover all sites where the White-headed Duck is recorded

There are many known or potential wintering sites that are not covered in the mid-winter census on a regular basis.

Priority: medium
Time-scale: ongoing

3.3.4. Identify major passage sites

In most of the range, many wetlands only have a census in mid-winter, and the route between breeding and wintering sites remains unclear. Autumn and spring surveys should be organised in possible passage areas.

Priority: high
Time-scale: short

3.3.5. Monitor key sites throughout the year

In many cases, key sites have always been monitored at the same time of year (typically mid-winter) and their importance during other seasons remains unclear. Regular surveys at different times will improve our understanding of seasonal distribution and movements.

Priority: high
Time-scale: ongoing

3.3.6. Encourage foreign birdwatchers to submit their records

Foreign birdwatchers can be encouraged to survey White-headed Duck sites where the status of the species is uncertain, and to submit their records to national organisations (e.g. BirdLife Partner organisations) or to the IWRB/IUCN Threatened Waterfowl Research Group at the Wildfowl and Wetlands Trust or to the IWRB. In Turkey, visiting birdwatchers are successfully being encouraged to visit designated or possible Important Bird Areas and send their observations to DHKD; this could be done in many other White-headed Duck range states.

Priority: medium
Time-scale: ongoing

3.4. *To promote biological and other scientific research useful for the conservation of the White-headed Duck*

3.4.1. Undertake studies of the biology of captive-bred, released White-headed Ducks in Spain in order to aid and evaluate possible future reintroduction programmes for this and other duck species

Priority: medium
Time-scale: short

3.4.2. Promote a better understanding of the movements of White-headed Ducks by marking and monitoring individuals

There are very few data on the movements of White-headed Ducks, and the nature of migration routes and movements between range states remains very unclear. For example, it is not known whether there are movements between Spain and North Africa, or if the birds wintering in Greece are migrating through the northern Black Sea or through Turkey. An effective and harmless method of marking (once found) will allow a much greater understanding of the nature of these movements. Satellite transmitters should be developed to reduce their size, and such transmitters could be applied to White-headed Ducks in the eastern Mediterranean region (subject to available funds).

Priority: medium
Time-scale: medium

3.4.3. Undertake studies of the species' ecology and habitat requirements

A reasonable amount of ecological research has already been conducted in Spain and Turkey, but local studies will provide an important aid to the development of site management plans, etc.

Priority: low
Time-scale: medium

3.4.4. Provide blood or tissue samples from Ruddy Ducks for DNA analysis to attempt to identify their place of origin

All countries should send blood or tissue samples from Ruddy Ducks and hybrids taken from the wild to Leicester University for DNA analysis in order to attempt to identify their place of origin (see Rose, 1993, for more details).

Priority: essential
Time-scale: ongoing

3.4.5. Undertake applied studies of hydrology, pollution impacts, socioeconomic needs, etc., at key sites

At many key sites, the nature and significance of threats are poorly understood, and specific research is needed to assess changes to the hydrology, the impact of agrochemicals or the use of the site by local people. The results of all these studies should be incorporated in management plans for the sites (see 2.2).

Priority: medium
Time-scale: ongoing

3.5. *To monitor the number of stifftails kept in captivity*

Such monitoring is important in assessing the numbers and distribution of Ruddy Ducks and other stifftails in captivity, and hence the extent to which escapes or releases may be a problem now or in the future. It is also important for assessing progress of objective 1.1.4.

Priority: essential
Time-scale: ongoing

4. **Public awareness and training**

4.1. *To increase awareness of the need to control the spread of the Ruddy Duck*

Priority: essential
Time-scale: ongoing

4.2. *To increase awareness of the need to protect the White-headed Duck and its habitat*

4.2.1. Ensure development of a strong network of organisations and individuals committed to the conservation of the White-headed Duck

People interested in the species have already contributed to a series of publications (e.g. Anstey, 1989; Green and Anstey, 1992) and are recipients of the biannual newsletter of the IWRB/IUCN Threatened Waterfowl Research Group, which is an ideal forum for the exchange of information between researchers, etc. Contacts between scientists and technical staff (including representatives of hunters' organi-

sations) working in different White-headed Duck range states should be improved, for example, through the IWRB/IUCN Threatened Waterfowl Research Group and the BirdLife network.

Priority: high
Time-scale: ongoing

4.2.2. Use the White-headed Duck as a flagship species to enhance protection of wetlands

This has already been done successfully in Spain (particularly in Andalucía) and Turkey (particularly around Burdur Gölü).

Priority: high
Time-scale: ongoing

4.2.3. Conduct education programmes to promote and inform about the White-headed Duck

Educational programmes should be carried out, using posters, stickers, T-shirts, etc. Such programmes are particularly important in and around key sites. An educational booklet on the conservation of the White-headed Duck should be produced in all major languages within the range of the species. Wide and effective distribution of this booklet should be done by national organisations.

An international education campaign is required to educate hunters in all White-headed Duck range states as well as hunters from other countries who visit range states to shoot ducks. Hunters need to be educated about the importance of the White-headed Duck and how to identify it. The Conseil International de la Chasse et de la Conservation du Gibier (CIC) should assist in promoting such a campaign through national, regional and local hunting organisations. A hunter education programme should use means such as a video, translated into all major languages (e.g. Turkish, Spanish, Arabic, English, French, Italian), emphasising the status and plight of the species across the whole Mediterranean. A practical brochure for hunters could also be prepared. This could be combined with similar programmes to reduce the hunting pressure on other globally threatened waterbirds occurring in the same region, particularly the Marbled Teal *Marmaronetta angustirostris* and the Ferruginous Duck *Aythya nyroca*.

Priority: high
Time-scale: ongoing

Annex I
Recommended conservation actions by country

White-headed Duck range states

Algeria

2.2.1. Promote the official protection of Lac des Oiseaux and Lac Ben Azzouz.

3.1./2.1.2./2.1.3. Given the presence of Ruddy Ducks in neighbouring Morocco, close monitoring of the White-headed Duck is essential to ensure the detection of hybrids and Ruddy Ducks.

3.3.1./3.3.2. Breeding surveys of key sites and other wetlands that could be important for the species (e.g. Garaet El Mekhada).

3.3.5. Constant monitoring of the population in the El Kala wetlands.

4.2.2./4.2.3. A public awareness campaign should be conducted, using the White-headed Duck as a flagship for wetland conservation.

Azerbaijan

1.2.1. Promote full legal protection for the species.

1.2.2. Promote designation of Lakes Aggel and Saraesy as Ramsar Sites.

1.3./2.2.2./3.4.5. Promote improved water management at a national level. Chemical pollution from cotton fields surrounding the Kizil Agach marshes and Lake Aggel should be investigated and controlled. It is recommended that water extraction for irrigation from Lake Aggel should be prevented. The original links between the Kura river and the lake should be restored to ensure a clean supply of water. A water supply should be provided to the western part of Lake Aggel (Kichik Aggel or Malyi Aggel) which is now drained.

2.2.1./2.5.2. At Lake Aggel it is recommended that the protected area should be extended well beyond the edges of the lake, and facilities for and training of the reserve guards should be improved.

2.2.2./2.5.2. Encourage protection of all key sites from poaching and habitat degradation.

2.5.2. Hunting restrictions should be tightly enforced.

3.3.2./3.3.3. Winter surveys of key sites and other possible sites are needed to establish current status. Breeding surveys are also required.

Bulgaria

2.2.1. Promote the protection of Uzungeran (Lake Mandra).

2.5.2. It is recommended that guards should be employed to prevent hunting of White-headed Ducks at Durankulak, Mandra/Uzungeren and Poda.

3.3.4./3.4.2. A collaborative monitoring programme should clarify numbers and distribution, and study the nature and timing of movements between Bulgaria, Romania, Greece and Turkey.

4.2.2. Use the White-headed Duck as a flagship for the conservation of key sites, using posters, badges, etc.

4.2.3. A hunter education programme centred around the key sites.

Greece

2.2.1./2.3. Promote the adequate protection of all key sites by definition of their boundaries, development of management plans and adequate wardening.

2.2.2. It is recommended that the proposed reclamation of the marshes in the south-east of Lake Vistonis should be cancelled.

2.5.1. It is recommended that hunting on the eastern shore of Lake Vistonis should be prohibited immediately.

2.5.2. Illegal hunting should be stopped at all key sites.

3.3.3./3.3.4./3.3.5. The White-headed Duck should be monitored regularly at all key sites, with additional surveys to locate important passage sites (e.g. possibly Lesbos) and possibly further wintering sites.

3.3.4./3.4.2. A collaborative monitoring programme is required to establish the nature and timing of movements between Greece, Bulgaria, Romania and Turkey.

3.4.3. Research should be undertaken in wintering ecology (e.g. diet).

3.4.5. All key sites should be closely monitored to detect possible changes in their ecological character.

4.2.2./4.2.3. Education programme for the species at all key sites, targeting hunters, fishermen, etc.

Israel

2.2.1. Promote the declaration of Tishlovet Hakishon as a Nature Reserve and the designation of key sites as Ramsar Sites.

Italy

2.2.1. The Gargano complex (including Lago di Lesina and Varano) in Apulia and the Po delta in Emilia Romagna and Veneto were historically important sites for the White-headed Duck and consideration should therefore be given to declaring them National Parks.

2.2.1. Promote the protection of historical breeding sites in Apulia (Daunia Risi, Valle Carapelle and S. Floriano) and in Sicily (Lentini, Gela and Catania).

2.7. No reintroductions of the White-headed Duck should be carried out until the Ruddy Duck problem has been solved. Any reintroductions should be organised through a national and international agreement.

Morocco

1.2.1. The White-headed Duck should not be deleted from the list of legally protected species.

2.2.1. Promote the effective protection of the Moulouya delta to allow its possible future recolonisation by White-headed Ducks.

Romania

1.2.1. Promote the legal protection of the White-headed Duck.

2.2.1. Promote the legal protection of Lake Techirghiol.

2.5.3. Promote the reduction of the hunting season to that operating in Bulgaria.

3.3.1. A summer survey of the Danube delta should be conducted to clarify the breeding-season status of the species.

3.3.4./3.4.2. Autumn and spring surveys are needed in order to clarify the nature and timing of passage movements through Lake Techirghiol and the Danube delta. A collaborative monitoring programme should establish the nature and timing of movements between Bulgaria, Greece, Romania and Turkey.

4.2.2./4.2.3. Education programme in the Danube delta using posters, etc., targeted at hunters.

Russian Federation

3.3.1./3.3.2. Breeding survey of suitable wetlands in the Volga delta to clarify breeding numbers and identify key sites.

3.3.3. Increased participation in the International Waterfowl Census should be promoted if the resources become available.

3.3.4./3.3.5. Spring and autumn surveys of the Manych and Gudilo reservoirs are needed to clarify the numbers and distribution of White-headed Ducks during passage.

Spain

1.1.3./1.1.4. Legal mechanisms should be promoted to prohibit the trade in and possession of *Oxyurini* other than the White-headed Duck, as has already been effected in the Balearic Islands.

1.2.3. Promote legal implementation of recovery plans in all communities with regular presence of White-headed Ducks. Co-ordination between DGN and autonomous communities should be improved. NGOs (such as SEO/BirdLife) should be official participants in such co-ordination meetings.

2.2.1./2.2.2./2.3. Promote the conservation of all sites with regular presence of White-headed

Ducks. Both legal protection measures and effective implementation of management plans are required.

2.5.3. Temporary banning of hunting when White-headed Ducks are recorded at sites where hunting is normally permitted, particularly at Dehesa de Monreal and El Hondo, should be encouraged.

3.4.1. A thorough programme to monitor White-headed Ducks released from captivity should be carried out and the results published. Further research should assess how well the captive-bred released White-headed Ducks have integrated into the wild population. A broad assessment of the role of captive breeding should be carried out, including the need to diversify the captive population and the size of this population required to maintain genetic diversity in the long term.

Syria

3.3.2. Conduct surveys of potential breeding sites.

3.3.3. Promote the extension of the International Waterfowl Census to cover all potential wintering sites.

Tunisia

2.2.1. Promote the declaration as protected areas of key sites, particularly breeding sites.

2.3. Promote management of emergent vegetation at key sites which increases the area of nesting habitat.

2.5.1./2.5.2. Promote the tight control of hunting at all key sites, particularly breeding sites.

3.3.1./3.3.2. A survey of all known and potential breeding sites is required.

4.2.2./4.2.3. Education programmes should be carried out around key sites and targeted at schools, colleges, farmers and hunters, using posters and other media.

Turkey

2.2.1./2.2.2. Promote the effective protection of all the key sites.

2.2.2. Promote the improvement of the conservation status of existing Ramsar Sites (Burdur Gölü and Sultan marshes).

2.2.2./2.5.2./3.4.5. The following conservation measures are urgently recommended at Burdur Gölü:

• Complete environmental impact assessment of the various existing pollution problems. Modern treatment plants should be incorporated in the Burdur sewage system and in factories dumping waste into the lake.
• The hunting ban should be tightly enforced throughout the year.
• Improved sedimentation control is required, for example, with afforestation schemes and restrictions on grazing.
• A detailed hydrological study is required at Burdur Gölü to identify the reasons for the drop in water-level.

2.5. Promote improved enforcement of hunting legislation.

2.5.3./4.2.2./4.2.3. Education programmes should be continued in order to raise the awareness of the species among hunters.

3.3.1. Detailed surveys should be carried out at all breeding sites to assess the status of the population.

3.3.2. Search for further breeding sites in eastern Turkey.

3.3.4. Detailed surveys should be carried out to identify all important passage sites.

3.3.4./3.4.2./4.2.1. A collaborative monitoring programme is required to establish the nature and timing of movements between Bulgaria, Greece, Romania and Turkey.

3.3.5. Monitoring of all waterbirds at Burdur Gölü should be improved, with at least four complete counts a year.

3.3.6. Visiting birdwatchers should be encouraged to visit key sites and to submit records to DHKD using their standard Site Recording Forms.

Ukraine

3.3.4. Autumn and spring surveys should be conducted to identify passage sites for birds moving to and from Romania, Bulgaria and Greece.

Ruddy Duck range states

Countries with large populations: United Kingdom

1.1.3. The UK Government should ensure enforcement of Section 14 (1.b) of the Wildlife and Countryside Act which prohibits the release or escape of Ruddy Ducks into the wild.

1.1.4. The UK Government should consider adding the Ruddy Duck to Schedule 4 of the Wildlife and Countryside Act 1981 which requires the ringing and registration of all birds kept in captivity.

2.1.1. The UK should undertake its planned regional control programme as soon as possible. This control programme will attempt to control two different regional populations of Ruddy Ducks. If the results suggest that it is possible to control Ruddy Ducks on a large scale, the UK should undertake country-wide control measures for Ruddy Ducks as soon as possible.

3.2. The current UK Ruddy Duck research programme should proceed and the process of making the results available to all countries considering control measures should continue.

3.5. The UK Government should consider whether there should be monitoring of captive Ruddy Ducks if the option of placing the bird on Schedule 4 is discounted.

4.1. The UK RDWG should continue its public relations strategy to inform the British public of the necessity for Ruddy Duck control.

Countries with small populations: Austria, Belgium, Denmark, Finland, France, Germany, Hungary, Iceland, Ireland, Israel, Italy, Morocco, Netherlands, Norway, Portugal, Spain, Sweden, Switzerland, Turkey and Ukraine

These countries can be divided into five different categories depending on the status and pattern of occurrence of Ruddy Ducks. These categories are listed in order of priority in terms of the urgency with which the actions listed below need to be implemented:

a. Countries with annual breeding attempts: Belgium, France, Iceland, Ireland, Netherlands and Spain.

b. Countries where birds have been present throughout the year: Germany and Morocco.

c. Countries where birds have been present for prolonged periods (two months or more) during the summer: Norway and Sweden.

d. Countries where birds have been present for prolonged periods (two months or more) during winter: Italy.

e. Countries with fewer than 10 records (of birds present for short periods): Austria, Denmark, Finland, Hungary, Israel, Portugal, Switzerland, Turkey and Ukraine.

The following recommendations apply to all the above countries. Countries where action is needed most urgently are mentioned by name.

1.1.1. All 20 countries are encouraged to develop national control strategies for Ruddy Ducks. This is most urgent for Belgium, Germany, Iceland, Ireland and Morocco. Norway and the other Scandinavian countries should also address the issue of Ruddy Duck control as there are indications that birds are remaining for long periods during the breeding season.

1.1.2. All 20 countries are encouraged to ensure provision for control of Ruddy Ducks under national laws as quickly as possible. The German Government should urgently investigate possible legal mechanisms to allow country-wide control of Ruddy Ducks.

2.1.2. All 20 countries are encouraged to take active control measures as soon as possible. Only Spain is carrying out such measures at present. The target should be to control all Ruddy Ducks which exist, but the highest priority should be the control of breeding birds and long-staying individuals.

3.1. All countries are encouraged to establish and maintain national monitoring systems to record the status and distribution of Ruddy Ducks throughout the year. Such monitoring systems should contain the following information: geographical co-ordinates and name of site, number, sex and age of individuals, date, habitat, protected status of site, evidence and outcome of breeding, recorder and degree of reliability of record. Where necessary, technical assistance for the establishment and maintenance of national schemes can be sought from IWRB.

3.1. All countries are encouraged to report annually the results of national monitoring schemes to IWRB which collates an international summary for dissemination to the appropriate body within each country.

3.1. Encourage the submission of winter records of Ruddy Ducks through the International Waterfowl Census network (IWRB).

3.1. Encourage birdwatchers to submit records of Ruddy Ducks from their own country to national rarities committees or official Ruddy Duck contacts (see Annex 2), especially in those countries where submission of records has not taken place through confusion over the feral status of Ruddy Ducks.

3.2. Any control measures undertaken should be adequately monitored and the results and outcome should be reported annually to IWRB for dissemination to the appropriate body within each country.

3.4.4. All countries are encouraged to send blood or tissue samples from Ruddy Ducks and hybrids taken from the wild to Leicester University for DNA analysis in order to attempt to identify their place of origin (see Rose 1993).

4.1. All countries are encouraged to increase public awareness of the need to control the spread of the Ruddy Duck through the development and implementation of national public relations strategies. Experiences gained through public relations exercises should be disseminated to other countries.

All western Palaearctic countries (including those above)

1.1.4. All countries where Ruddy Ducks are found in collections are encouraged to seek to reduce as much as possible the keeping of Ruddy Ducks in captivity. Consideration should also be given to introducing a legally enforceable register for captive individuals of Ruddy Ducks as well as considering restrictions on trade in Ruddy Ducks where appropriate.

1.1.4. In countries where Ruddy Ducks are not held in collections, consideration should be given to prohibiting the importation of the species and the keeping of it in collections.

1.1.4. Waterfowl keepers in all countries should be encouraged to follow a code of conduct for keeping stifftails, as outlined in a booklet produced by the UK Ruddy Duck Working Group. This booklet advises the pinioning and ringing of all birds and the keeping of accurate records.

3.1. Encourage birdwatchers travelling to foreign countries to submit records of Ruddy Ducks to national rarities committees or official Ruddy Duck contacts (see Annex 2).

3.5. Those countries where stifftails are kept in collections are encouraged to establish an annual monitoring scheme for these populations.

Annex 2
IWRB Official Ruddy Duck contacts

Algeria: Djahida Boukhalfa, Chef de Service des Parcs, Nationaux et Zones Humides à l'ANN, Jardin botanique du Hamma, BP 115, El Annasser, Alger, Algeria.

Austria: Gerard Aubrecht, PA OO Landesmuseum/Zoology, Museumstr. 14, Linz A-4010, Austria.

Belarus: Yuri Viazovich, Head Researcher, Insitute of Zoology, Academy of Sciences, F. Skorina Str. 27, BY-Minsk 220733, Belarus.

Belgium: Sophie Bouche, CEC DG XI, 200 Rue de la Loi, B-1049 Brussels, Belgium.

Koen Devos, Institute of Nature Conservation, Kiewitdreef 5, B-3500 Hasselt, Belgium.

Croatia: Jozsef Mikuska, Union of Ornithological Societies of Yugoslavia, Illraki trg 9, HR-41000 Zagreb, Croatia.

Czech Republic: Jitka Pellantova, Czech Institut of Nature Protection, Lidicka 25/27, pp 120, CZ-602 00 Brno, Czech Republic.

Denmark: Pelle Andersen-Harild, Ministry of Environment, Agency for Forest and Nature, Haraldsgade 53, DK-2100 Copenhagen, Denmark.

Estonia: Andres Kuresoo, Zoology and Botany Institute, Estonian Academy of Sciences, c/o Ministry of Environment, Toompuiestte 24, EE-0100 Tallinn, Estonia.

Finland: Tapani Veistola, Association of Orni-thological Societies in Finland, PL 17 (Vesitorni, 4.krs), SF–18101 Heinola, Finland.

France: J.-P. Cantera, AGENC, 3 Luce de Casablanca, F-20200 Bastia, France.

Philippe Dubois, LPO, La Corderie Royale, BP 263, F-17305 Rochefort, France.

Bertrand Trolliet, Office National de la Chasse, Chanteloup, F-85340 Ile d'Olonne, France.

Germany: Hans-Gunther Bauer, Max Planck Institute, Vogelwarte Radolfzell, AM Obstberg 1, D–7760 Radolfzell, Germany.

Greece: George Handrinos, Ministry of Agriculture, Game Management Section, 3–5 Ippokratous St., Athens, Greece.

Iceland: Olaf Nielson, Icelandic Museum of Natural History, PO Box 5320, IS-125 Reykjavik, Iceland.

Ireland: Oscar Merne, Office of Public Works, 51 St Stephens Green, Dublin, Ireland.

Italy: Nicola Baccetti, INFS, Via Ca'Fornacetta 9, I-40064 Ozzano dell Emilia, Bologna, Italy.

Giullano Tallone, LIPU, Vicolo S tiburzio 5/A, I-43100 Parma, Italy.

Michele Vitaloni, WWF-Italy, Via Salaria 290, I-00199 Roma, Italy.

Latvia: Antra Stipniece, Laboratory of Ornithology, Institue of Biology, Academy of Science of Latvia, LV-229021 Salaspils-Miera 3, Latvia.

Lithuania: Saulius Svazas, Laboratory of Ornithology, Institute of Ecology, Akademijos Str. 2, LT-232 600 Vilnius, Lithuania.

Luxembourg: J.-C. Heidt, Fondation Hellef fir d'Nature, BP 709, L-2017 Luxembourg, Luxembourg.

Morocco: Mohammed Dakki, Institut Scientifique, Dept de Zoologie/Ecolgie, Charia Ibn Batouta, BP 703 Rabat, Morocco.

Netherlands: Vincent van den Berk, National Reference Centre for Nature Forest and Landscape, PO Box 30, NL-6700 A Wageningen, Netherlands.

Norway: Øystein Storkersen, NINA, Tungasletta 2, N-7004 Trondheim, Norway.

Portugal: Luis Costa, CEMPA, Rua Filipe Folque 46, 3, P-1000 Lisboa, Portugal.

Romania: Dan Munteanu, Centrul de Cercetari Biologice, RO-3400 Cluj, Str. Republicii 48, Romania.

Slovakia: Alzbeta Darolova, Ustav Zoologie a Ekosozologie SAV, Manesovo nam 2, SK-8510 01 Bratislava, Slovakia.

Spain: DGN, Gran Via de San Francisco 4, 28005 Madrid, Spain.

Ramon Marti, SEO/BirdLife Spain, Facultad de Biologia, E-28040 Madrid, Spain.

José Antonio Torres-Esquivias, El Director Provincial, Junta de Andalucía, Agencia de Medio Ambiente, Avd. Gran Via Parque (Edificio Delfin), E-14071 Córdoba, Spain.

Sweden: Gustaf Aulén, Sveriges Ornitologiska Forening, Box 14219, S-104 40 Stockholm, Sweden.

Torsten Larsson, Department of Natural Resources, Swedish Environmental Protection Agency, S-17185 Solna, Sweden.

Leif Nielson, Ecology Building, S-22362 Lund, Sweden.

Switzerland: Nicklaus Zbinden, Schweizerische Vogelwarte, CH-6204 Sempach, Switzerland.

Tunisia: Faouzi Maamouri, Bureau 15 Imm. B. Sassi, Rue de Carthage, 2080 Ariana, Tunisia.

Turkey: Gernant Magnin, Dogal Hayati Koruma Dernegi, pk 18 Bebek, TR-80810-Istanbul, Turkey.

Ukraine: Valentin Serebryakov, Biological Department, Kiev State University, Vladimirskaya St. 64, UA-Kiev 252017, Ukraine.

United Kingdom: John Holmes, Ruddy Duck Working Group, JNCC, City Rd., Peterborough PE1 1JY, UK.

John Milburne, Department of the Environment for Northern Ireland, Calvert House, Belfast BT1 1FY, UK.

Action plan for the Cinereous Vulture (*Aegypius monachus*) in Europe

Reviews

This action plan should be reviewed and updated every four years. An emergency review will be undertaken if sudden major environmental changes, liable to affect the population, occur within the species' range.

Geographical scope

The action plan needs active implementation in: Albania, Armenia, Azerbaijan, Bulgaria, Croatia, France, Georgia, Greece, Italy, Portugal, Russian Federation (Europe only), Spain, the former Yugoslav Republic of Macedonia, Turkey and Ukraine.

Summary

The Cinereous Vulture *Aegypius monachus* formerly known as the Black Vulture, is classified as Near-threatened at world level (Collar et al., 1994) and Vulnerable at European level (Tucker and Heath, 1994). It has a discontinuous distribution in Europe, where it is present in the Caucasus mountains (190 pairs shared among Russia, Georgia, Armenia and Azerbaijan), Greece (20), Spain (1000), Turkey (100-500) and Ukraine (6). Populations are considered to be increasing in Spain and Greece, stable in Turkey and declining in Ukraine and the Caucasus.

Threats and limiting factors

Habitat alterations in the breeding areas – critical

Poisoning – high

Food shortage – medium, potentially high

Forest fires – medium

Persecution and illegal trade – low

Human disturbance – low

Conservation priorities

Prevent the use of toxic chemicals for predator control and undertake a public awareness campaign about the dangers of this practice – essential

Protected area status for breeding areas and prevention of damaging developments or disturbance – essential/high

International and national forestry policies and practices which are compatible with the conservation of the Cinereous Vulture – high

National legislation which includes provisions for the protection of the species and key sites – high

Introduction

The Cinereous Vulture *Aegypius monachus*, formerly known as the Black Vulture, is classified as Near-threatened at world level (Collar et al., 1994) and as Vulnerable at European level (Tucker and Heath, 1994). It is included in Annex I of the European Union's Wild Birds Directive and in Appendix II of the Bern, Bonn and CITES Conventions.

Being a predatory bird with a long life span and a huge home range it needs vast areas of unspoiled landscape, and these are becoming increasingly rare in Europe. The designation of protected areas is not enough to guarantee the survival of such dispersed species which exploit a variety of biotopes. Broad policies which are sensitive to the environment are necessary to ensure that the countryside outside protected areas retains the capacity to sustain Cinereous Vulture populations.

The recovery that the species has undergone in Spain shows that it is still possible to have large numbers of Cinereous Vultures if the appropriate conservation measures are put in place. A highly encouraging experiment has been undertaken in France to restore the species to an area where it disappeared a hundred years ago; if this succeeds, as it has with the Griffon Vulture *Gyps fulvus*, the future of the Cinereous Vulture in other European countries where it is now extinct may rely on similar reintroduction schemes, as long as the required habitats for breeding and foraging still exist and persecution is no longer a significant threat.

In September 1993, a workshop took place in Dadiá (Greece) to discuss the conservation of the Cinereous Vulture in Europe and adjacent regions. This action plan relies largely on the results of that workshop and on a process of wide consultation among experts and competent authorities. It intends to provide a general framework for future work and to stimulate active conservation management at national level.

Background information

Distribution and population

The global range extends from the Iberian peninsula across southern Europe and through the central Asian plateau to Mongolia and China.

In Europe, the Cinereous Vulture breeds in Armenia, Azerbaijan, Bulgaria, Georgia, Greece, Russia, Spain, Turkey and Ukraine. It may occasionally breed in Portugal, the former Yugoslav Republic of Macedonia and Albania. It is now extinct in France (1800s), Italy (1950), Poland (1800s), Slovakia (1800s), Austria (1800s), Croatia (early 1900s), Yugoslavia (1956), Romania (1964), Moldova (1929) and Cyprus (1960) (Cramp and Simmons, 1980; Meyburg and Meyburg, 1984). The population status is given in Table 9.1.

Life history

Breeding

The Cinereous Vulture breeds in loose colonies or solitarily. Age of first breeding is usually between 5 and 6 years. It builds a huge nest on top of a tree (Pinus, Quercus, Juniperus, etc.) where it lays one egg. Laying usually starts at the beginning of February and finishes at the end of April, with the maximum number of clutches between the last week of February and the beginning of March. Incubation is by both adults and lasts 50 to 54 days. The chick usually spends more than 100 days in the nest and remains with the adults 2 to 3 months after fledging before moving away. Breeding success is very high (up to

90%) in areas with low human disturbance. The chick is fed with meat regurgitated by the adults. The maximum daily energy requirements of a breeding pair, between the end of June and the beginning of July, are 2200 g; the yearly needs of a successful pair would be approximately 600 kg (Hiraldo, 1983). Cinereous Vultures breed regularly in captivity in several European and North American zoos.

Table 9.1

Breeding population of the Cinereous Vulture in Europe, 1994. Based on Tucker and Heath (1994), Galushin and Abuladze (in press) and data gathered during the Dadiá workshop (1993)

Country	No. of pairs
Armenia	15 – 25
Azerbaijan	100 – 100
Bulgaria	0 – 1
Georgia	10 – 20
Greece	20 – 21
Russia	30 – 50
Spain	1050 – 1150
Turkey	100 – 500
Ukraine	4 – 6
Total	1329 – 1873

Feeding

Birds feed on medium to large carcasses, only rarely taking live prey. They search at lower altitudes and often over more wooded country than do Griffon Vultures (Cramp and Simmons, 1980). In southern Spain the Cinereous Vulture feeds basically on mammals, especially rabbits and sheep (90%), but insects and lizards also appear in the diet; the remarkable increase of populations of wild ungulates such as deer and wild boar has changed its diet towards these (González, 1994). Individual pairs nesting no more than 3 km apart can show differences in diet, suggesting different foraging areas (Hiraldo, 1976). Tortoises Testudo are also eaten, and in the Caucasus a significant part of the diet consists of dead sheep and other livestock which die in large numbers following overgrazing (Galushin, 1995).

Habitat requirements

Breeding requires quiet slopes covered with forest in open valleys and low sierras, occasionally in open parkland; also subalpine forests of *Pinus* spp., up to 2000 metres. Birds forage over forested areas, but also in many types of open terrain from steppe to upland grasslands.

Threats and limiting factors

Habitat alterations in the breeding areas

These are usually related to forestry operations, including destruction of native forests for afforestation with exotic species, tree-felling during the breeding season, undergrowth clearing, construction of new tracks to extract timber, opening up of fire breaks, etc. Apart from the direct effect on the habitat, these activities cause disturbance to the breeding pairs and facilitate access to otherwise inaccessible areas.

Importance: critical

Forest fires

The dry weather which has predominated in Europe in recent years has led to an increase in forest fires, especially in the Mediterranean region. Socio-economic changes and abandonment have also affected the frequency of forest fires. Fire can have a devastating effect on the habitat of the Cinereous Vulture; one fire in 1992 in Andalucía destroyed eight nests containing young, as well as 21 empty breeding platforms (Andalus, 1993).

Importance: medium

Poisoning

Unintentional poisoning resulting from the use of poison baits for vertebrate control is responsible for the loss of a number of Cinereous Vultures every year. Although prohibited by the Bern Convention, this method of killing is occasionally applied throughout the species' range in Europe. Chemicals used include strychnine, luminal and pesticides. In 1993 an official poisoning campaign was launched in Bulgaria for wolf control by the Committee of Forestry, but this was stopped thanks to actions by the Ministry of Environment and NGOs.

Importance: high

Shortage of food

There is a correlation between the distribution and relative abundance of the Cinereous Vulture and cattle. Changes in traditional farming practices are likely to have a negative effect on this species, for example, a decrease in the numbers of livestock, the keeping of sheep and cattle inside during winter, and removal of carcasses by man. Wild ungulates and rabbits also play an important role in the diet and should be promoted.

Importance: medium, potentially high

Persecution and illegal trade

Direct persecution from hunters and collectors was a problem in the past. Nowadays some Cinereous Vultures are still occasionally shot but not in significant numbers. In countries of the former Soviet Union the illegal trade of live specimens taken from the wild to zoos or for private collections in western Europe is becoming a particular problem.

Importance: low

Human disturbance

This has been described as a limiting factor in the Caucasus, where mountain tourism has been very popular. Human disturbance during incubation often results in loss of the egg due to predation by crows. Recently the region has not been attractive to tourism because of the existing conflicts, and soldiers have replaced tourists in mountain forests.

Importance: low

Conservation status and recent conservation measures

Armenia

Included in the Armenian Red Data Book (1987) as Rare. It occurs in Khosrov Forest south of Yerevan and in the far south along the borders with Iran and Azerbaijan.

Azerbaijan

The population has been decreasing over the last 10 years. It occurs in the north-western districts along the borders with Georgia and Armenia, as well as in the central mountains and in the north-east, near the border with Russia. A preliminary inventory of Important Bird Areas lists the species as being present at the following sites: 003 Alty Agach (Nature Reserve), 006 Mount Babadag (partly a Game Reserve), 009 Bosdag Mountains (unprotected), 013 Mount Giamish (unprotected), 024 Lachin (Game Reserve), 034 Shahbuz (unprotected) (Patrikeev, 1993).

Bulgaria

The Cinereous Vulture is listed as Extinct as a breeding species in the Red Data Book (1985). However, it occurs regularly in the eastern Rhodope mountains, where two pairs probably bred for the last time in the period 1980 to 1982. In 1993 a nest was found and a chick fledged successfully (S. Marin, pers. comm., 1993), and 10 to 13 birds are regularly seen at the feeding stations which are maintained in the area (Iankov et al., 1994). Within the area there are two protected sites for birds: Valchi Dol Nature Reserve (IBA 013) and the Kovan Kaia Protected Natural Landmark. In 1992 and 1993, Cinereous Vultures were seen in the Sakar Mountain and eastern Balkan Range, which is more than 200 km north of the eastern Rhodope area.

The Bulgarian Society for the Protection of Birds is carrying out a conservation project in the eastern Rhodope mountains, with special emphasis on the Cinereous Vulture. The project started on a voluntary basis but has been financed by the Bulgarian-Swiss Biodiversity Conservation Programme since the end of 1994 and three members of staff are now employed. In 1984, a feeding station was started and two Cinereous Vultures poisoned with barbiturates were successfully treated and released. There are now two feeding stations in operation, and 10 artificial nests have been built to attract the vultures. A poster calling for the protection of birds of prey has been printed and distributed, and a documentary about Bulgarian vultures has been produced (Iankov, 1993).

France

In 1992, the Fonds d'Intervention pour les Rapaces started a reintroduction programme in the Grand Causses (Cevennes National Park), at the request of the Black Vulture Conservation Foundation. In that same year six young born in captivity were released, as were three more in 1993 (Tariel, 1993). A pair was observed building a nest in 1995.

Georgia

The Cinereous Vulture is included in the national Red Data Book. It occurs in the south-eastern part of the country where it breeds in Vashlovani State Reserve (8–14 pairs) and Chachuna Game Reserve (2–5 pairs). A reservoir on the Iori river has recently flooded 11 nests (A. Abuladze, pers. comm., 1993). The total number in Georgia is estimated to be 17 to 19 pairs (A. Abuladze, pers. comm., 1994).

Greece

It is listed as Endangered in the Greek Red Data Book (Handrinos, 1992) and occurs only in the north-eastern part of the country, in the forest of Dadiá, district of Evros. The habitat is an open pine forest of *Pinus brutia* and *P. nigra* with a dense undergrowth of oak brushwood. The present population amounts to over 100 individuals with about 20 active breeding pairs. Breeding also occurred in the mountains of Olympos and Kato Olympos until 1987 (two pairs), and seven birds were present in the area up to 1989 but had all gone by 1991 (Hallmann, in prep.).

Dadiá Forest was given protection by the Greek Government in 1980 as an outstanding biotope for birds of prey. Actual conservation management started in 1987 with the appointment of two guards, the opening of the feeding station, the construction of a hide for observing the vultures on the feeding station, and the building of a visitor centre and ecotourism hostel near Dadiá. In 1992, WWF Greece undertook a new project for the management and wardening of the reserve, and the development of ecotourism there; an operational management plan is currently being prepared (Katsadorakis et al., in prep.). This work has benefited from European Union funds through the ACNAT programme.

In 1994, the Specific Environmental Study for Dadiá Reserve was completed. This study focused on the conservation of the site's biodiversity and of its population of birds of prey in the whole of the protected area (core areas and buffer zone), with particular emphasis on the Cinereous Vulture.

The population of the Cinereous Vulture has increased from 9 pairs in 1988 to 20 pairs in 1994 (WWF Greece, in prep.). The main reasons for this increase have been:

– The absolute protection of the main breeding colonies in Dadiá Reserve;

– The operation of the feeding place and the regular supply of carcasses;

– The positive attitude of the local people towards the protection of the birds of prey as a result of the development of ecotourism and its resulting social and financial benefits.

Italy

A feasibility study on the reintroduction of the Cinereous Vulture in Sardinia is under way. This project is being carried out under an agreement between LIPU, the Black Vulture Conservation Foundation and the Junta de Extremadura (which will provide birds to be used in the reintroduction programme).

Portugal

The Cinereous Vulture is classified as Endangered in the Portuguese Red Data Book, although considered probably to have become extinct as a breeding species in recent years (Cabral et al., 1990).

Russian Federation

Classified as Endangered in the Red Data Book of 1983 and recommended for inclusion in the next edition which is now being prepared. It occurs along the north slope of the Caucasus, mostly in its eastern part but some pairs are also recorded in the centre and west of the range. There are about 10 pairs in Dagestan Autonomous Republic and probably a few pairs in Chechen and Kalmikia Autonomous Republics; a small population has recently been discovered in the Caucasus Nature Reserve (Abuladze, 1994; Khokhlov, 1995). It is declining due to habitat

destruction, human disturbance, persecution and poisoning (Galushin, 1995).

Spain

Classified as Vulnerable in the Red Data Book (Blanco and González, 1992). It occupies the south-western part of the country, breeding in lowland sierras and subalpine forests. The population has increased from 200 pairs in 1970 to about 1000 in 1992 (Hiraldo, 1974; González 1994). National surveys were also carried out in 1982 (370 pairs) and 1989 (774 pairs) (González, 1990). In Mallorca the population has increased from 20 to 22 individuals in 1986 to 57 birds in 1991, thanks to the release of rehabilitated birds from continental Spain and captive-bred chicks from several European zoos and other institutions; a total of 33 birds have been released over eight years (Tewes, 1994). Supplementary feeding and a reduction in the number of birds poisoned also contributed to the increase in the Mallorcan population.

The main reasons for the recovery in Spain have been: the protection of the breeding colonies and the regulation of forestry activities, the reduction in mortality due to a ban on poisoning, and the undertaking of awareness campaigns by the administration and local NGOs (González, 1990).

Most of the breeding population (87%) is included in Special Protection Areas under the Birds Directive. These include: Encinares Río Alberche y Río Cofio, Alto Lozoya (Madrid); Valsaín, Valle de Iruelas, Batuecas, Arca y Buitrera (Castilla-León); Cabañeros (Castilla-La Mancha); Monfragüe, Sierra de San Pedro (Extremadura); Sierra de Hornachuelos, Sierra Pelada y Ribera del Aserrador (Andalucía); Sierra de Alfabia (Mallorca). In the Sierra de Gata (Extremadura) there has been a project funded by ACNAT for habitat restoration and food restocking.

Key sites for the Cinereous Vulture in Spain are Monfragüe Natural Park in Extremadura with about 230 pairs, and Cabañeros National Park in Castilla-La Mancha with about 190 pairs (Jiménez, 1990). In November 1995, under law 33/95, Cabañeros was delared a national park, the first in Spain to cover Mediterranean forest habitat.

There is a worrying return of poisoning as a method of predator control in Spain, as shown by the numbers of birds of prey found poisoned in the regions of Madrid, Castilla-La Mancha and Castilla-León in the years 1990 to 1994.

Turkey

It is classified as Endangered in the Draft Red List of Threatened Animals of Turkey (1991), and is legally protected. It is confined mainly to the large forests of northern Anatolia, the Kizilcahamam area to the north of Ankara, the eastern Pontic Mountains and the Uludag (M. Kasparek, *in litt.*, 1993). It is present in the following Important Bird Areas: 010 Uludag (presumably breeds), 012 Ilgaz Daglari, 013 Kackar Daglari (presumably breeds), 014 Kizilcahamam Mountains including Soguksu National Park (6 nests), 043 Acigol and Calti Golu (possibly breeds) (Grimmett and Jones, 1989). Three new breeding areas were discovered during a small survey in 1995 (Murat Yarar, *in litt.*)

Ukraine

Included in the national Red Data Book as Endangered. The only place where it occurs is in the Crimean Game Reserve (IBA 045), including the northern and southern slopes of the main Crimean range. In the beginning of the 1980s the population was estimated at 5 to 8 breeding pairs (Meyburg and Meyburg, 1984). In 1990 six pairs bred, each raising one chick, and a further 13 non-breeding individuals were observed in the area. Nests are built in *Pinus* spp. and *Juniperus foetidissima*, on steep slopes. The main threats are: lack of food, shooting and poisoning outside the reserve, and disturbance related to forestry (Appak, 1992). Exceptionally cold winters, such as that of 1988-89, reduce the breeding performance. The Cinereous Vulture is considered to be decreasing in Crimea, whereas the Griffon Vulture appears to be stable (Appak, 1992).

Aims and objectives

Aims

1. In the short term, to maintain and enhance the existing Cinereous Vulture populations in Europe.
2. In the long term, to encourage the recolonisation of the former range.

Objectives

1. **Policy and legislation**

1.1. *To promote national and international broad policies which are compatible with the conservation of the Cinereous Vulture and its habitat*

1.1.1. Forestry

The conservation of the Cinereous Vulture in Europe is intimately related to the conservation of forests. Forestry policies, at both national and international levels, should guarantee that forest management is based on the principles of sustainability and ensure the long-term survival of all native forests. Management activities should take full account of the presence of Cinereous Vultures and other threatened species, avoiding disturbance of them during the breeding period. Guidelines for forest management in areas of exceptional natural value should be prepared at national level.

Priority: high
Time-scale: short

1.1.2. Agriculture

Agriculture policies can have an influence on Cinereous Vulture conservation as far as livestock is concerned. As an example, the European Union's Agri-environment Regulation 2078/92 sets up aid schemes for farmers who undertake a reduction in stocking levels of sheep and cattle. Overall, this regulation will be beneficial to steppe and dry grassland birds, but it could be detrimental to vultures and other scavengers. In the long term, agricultural policies must ensure the sustainability of stock-raising and the long-term survival of traditional extensive livestock practices and conditions which favour adequate populations of other key prey species such as rabbits.

The Cinereous Vulture is one of the species included as dependent on agricultural habitats in the European Agricultural Habitats Conservation Strategy currently being prepared by BirdLife International (Tucker et al., in press).

Priority: medium
Time-scale: medium

1.1.3. International co-operation

Most of the remaining Cinereous Vulture populations in Europe are located in countries which lack the financial resources needed to undertake comprehensive conservation measures. It is not so much the know-how, but rather funds and equipment (computers, telescopes, vehicles, etc.) that are urgently needed. International help from wealthier countries and organisations is essential to strengthen institutions and support NGOs.

Priority: essential
Time-scale: short/ongoing

1.2. To ensure maximum legal coverage of the Cinereous Vulture and its habitat in national and international legislation

1.2.1. National legislation

Where appropriate, the range states should review their legislation on nature conservation to include provisions for the conservation of species and sites, in addition to conservation measures in the wider environment. It is recommended that a species listing process is established and that recovery plans or action plans are foreseen for the most threatened taxa. In parallel with nature conservation law, impact assessment regulations should also be developed.

Importance: high
Time-scale: short/medium

2. Species and habitat protection

2.1. To protect all the existing breeding colonies and isolated nests against habitat alterations and human disturbance

2.1.1. Protected area status

The breeding colonies should be included as core zones in larger protected areas, in order to ensure the long-term conservation of these areas. The declaration as a protected area allows the administrators to establish a protection regime and to regulate the uses of the land and the access of people. The management plans of existing protected areas should take into account the presence of the Cinereous Vulture and provide precise recommendations for its conservation.

Priority: essential
Time-scale: short/medium

2.1.2. Prevention of damaging or disturbing developments and activities near nest sites

If a breeding colony cannot be legally protected, any proposed activities in its immediate vicinity must be carefully evaluated to assess the impact they have on Cinereous Vultures. During the breeding season, all motorised activity and blasting should be restricted within 2.5 km of nest sites. The minimum distance between lightly used dirt roads and nests should be 1.5 km. All human activity within 1 km of the nests should be restricted, including tourism and recreation.

Priority: high
Time-scale: short/ongoing

2.1.3. Forestry operations

As the Cinereous Vulture breeds in forests there can be a conflict between the species and forestry operations. As a rule, forest exploitation should not be allowed from January to September within 1 km of any nest. If forest management operations are necessary around the nest, these should take place from October to December. As a rule, trees containing nests should never be cut down. Plans should be developed for preventing and controlling wildfires in areas inhabited by Cinereous Vultures.

Priority: high
Time-scale: short/ongoing

2.2. To provide optimum food availability

2.2.1. Encourage a continuing livestock economy

The preservation of an extensive livestock economy is essential to the survival of the Cinereous Vulture in the wild. At local level, regular contacts with land managers and stockbreeders should be maintained to encourage them to leave dead stock for the vultures, although this has to be done under careful supervision of local veterinarians.

Priority: medium
Time-scale: medium/ongoing

2.2.2. Encourage repopulation of native wild ungulates

Wild ungulates such as red deer Cervus elaphus, roe deer Capreolus and fallow deer Dama dama constitute a valuable source of food for the Cinereous Vulture, especially during the hunting season when the remains of game animals are regularly left out in the wild. Any reintroduction or restocking schemes with wild ungulates should involve native species, and should be done according to the IUCN guidelines for reintroductions (Kleiman et al., 1994). Particular attention needs to be given to avoiding overgrazing and competition with other key prey species such as rabbits.

Priority: low
Time-scale: long

2.2.3. Provide supplementary food at specific sites

Supplementary feeding has proved to be a very useful way of boosting vulture populations. It has the advantages of providing both extra and safe, poison-free, food supplies. Experiments carried out in Spain show that Cinereous Vultures prefer feeding sites which are in areas of open forest with undergrowth brush rather than in open space (Jiménez, 1990). Also, they prefer small carcasses of the size of a sheep or goat rather than large carcasses such as those of cows or horses. These characteristics are of importance when providing additional food in regions where the Griffon Vulture is still numerous, as that species generally prefers feeding on large carcasses in open areas.

Priority: low
Time-scale: ongoing

2.3. To prevent the use of toxic chemicals for predator control

The use of poisons such as strychnine, barbiturates and other chemicals for predator control programmes, largely against wolves and foxes, has been one of the factors responsible for the disappearance of the Cinereous Vulture from large areas of Europe. The use of poisoned baits for predator control is now illegal in most European countries and is also prohibited by the Bern Convention. If it is suspected that poisoning is taking place it is necessary to gather information about the products being used and the individual people using them illegally. The competent authorities should be encouraged and assisted to enforce the existing regulations. Public awareness should be raised about the unacceptability of poisoning (see 4.2.).

Priority: essential
Time-scale: short/ongoing

2.4. To restore the Cinereous Vulture to those areas from which it has disappeared

Reintroduction schemes should be considered in those countries which can guarantee suitable conditions for supporting the species. These conditions should comply with the IUCN criteria for reintroductions (Kleiman et al., 1994), which can be summarised as follows: there has to be good historical evidence of former presence; the factors responsible for the extinction should no longer be in existence; and the habitat has to be adequate in area and quality to meet the species' requirements. The Cinereous Vulture is bred in captivity in several European zoos, and the techniques for the reintroduction of captive-bred birds have been greatly refined and successfully applied in recent years (Tariel, 1993; Tewes, 1994). Countries that, in principle, could be considered for reintroduction include Italy (Sardinia, where a feasibility study is already in progress), Croatia and Romania.

Priority: low
Time-scale: long

3.   Monitoring and research

3.1.   To monitor regularly the status and population trends of Cinereous Vultures in Europe

3.1.1. Regular national monitoring schemes

A complete national survey should take place at least every four years in each range state, and colonies situated in protected areas should be monitored annually. Usually it is sufficient that one visit is made to each nest site at the end of the breeding season when the chicks are well grown. National surveys should be co-ordinated internationally by BirdLife International.

Priority: medium
Time-scale: short/ongoing

3.1.2. Surveys to establish the status of Cinereous Vultures

All the range states should establish a clear idea of the population size and distribution of the species. There is an urgent need for an inventory of all breeding colonies within the range, including data on location, habitat, number of breeding pairs, protection status, threats, etc. If necessary, these surveys could be carried out by international teams involving nationals and expatriates. These surveys can also take place within the framework of broader Important Bird Area surveys.

Priority: medium
Time-scale: short/medium

3.1.3. Monitor causes of mortality

Whenever a Cinereous Vulture or any other bird of prey is found dead or with symptoms of poisoning, it should be taken to the appropriate institution for examination, including X-ray and toxicological analysis. The statutory nature conservation authorities of each country should pay for these analyses.

Priority: medium
Time-scale: short/ongoing

3.1.4. Monitor results of reintroduction efforts

In all cases where Cinereous Vultures have been released in a particular area with the aim of establishing a new population it is essential that the birds are individually marked and monitored. The results should be well documented and evaluated, including a description of the techniques used and success achieved. Information about ongoing efforts will greatly enhance the likelihood of success for new initiatives.

Priority: low
Time-scale: ongoing

3.2. *To undertake studies about home range, habitat use and dispersal*

There is very little information about the ecological requirements of the Cinereous Vulture especially with regard to home range and habitat use. Individual marking of young and adults with radio-transmitters, wing tags, colour rings or decoloration of feathers would provide very useful information about activity patterns, habitat selection, home-range, foraging areas and movements of the young after leaving the nest, as well as pointing out some causes of mortality. These studies should be done in countries where the Cinereous Vulture still enjoys a favourable conservation status.

Priority: medium
Time-scale: medium

4.   **Public awareness and training**

4.1.   *To inform the public and increase general awareness of the need to protect Cinereous Vultures and their habitat*

Education and awareness campaigns about the ecological role of scavengers as sanitarians of the environment, and their vulnerability to poisoning and land-use changes, should be carried out nationally according to the requirements of each country. Successful reintroduction and restocking projects, such as the ones in Mallorca and France, should be widely publicised and used as a means of increasing the public's appreciation of this species. The Cinereous Vulture should be considered as a "flagship" species to promote the conservation of forests and traditional farming practices throughout its range in Europe.

Priority: low
Time-scale: medium/ongoing

4.2.   *To undertake national and international anti-poisoning awareness campaigns*

These campaigns, led by the government where possible, should seek to increase public opinion against persecution and also encourage peer pressure amongst farmers against poisoning. Where appropriate, any prosecutions should be used to raise public awareness through media coverage. The scientific facts about the devastating effects that illegal poisoning is having on Cinereous Vultures and other wildlife should be promoted. Alternative safe, target-specific methods of vertebrate predator control, and improved methods of stock control to reduce predation risk, should also be promoted to farmers in target areas.

Priority: essential
Time-scale: short/ongoing

Annex
Recommended conservation actions by country

Armenia

Under the existing economic and social conditions field research is virtually impossible in the country. In future, when conditions improve, international help will be needed.

Azerbaijan

As above.

Bulgaria

1.1.3. Provide long-term support for the work in the Rhodope mountains being carried out by BSPB. Funding is currently available until 1997.

2.1.1. Promote the declaration of the core part of the eastern Rhodope mountains as a Nature Park, according to the new Nature Protected Areas Law. The local population must be consulted and involved in the process to establish protected areas, and "green tourism" should be considered as a priority for the sustainable development of the whole region.

2.1.3. Encourage the Forest Committee and the local forest service to avoid clearance of the forest and the cutting of old trees in areas which have already been identified as former breeding grounds of the Cinereous Vulture, as well as other suitable areas which may be identified in the near future.

2.3. Constant monitoring of the Cinereous Vulture population is needed in order to detect any poisoning incidents. The authorities should be encouraged to implement a strict ban on this kind of activity and to take immediate action should the problem recur.

Georgia

Under current conditions field research is practically impossible. Nevertheless, this action plan acknowledges the research and monitoring carried out up to 1991 by the Institute of Zoology and A. Abuladze in particular. Once the social and economic situation in the country has settled this work should continue. In future, when conditions improve, international help will be needed.

Greece

1.2.1. The authorities responsible for nature conservation should draw up a recovery plan for the Cinereous Vulture with the aim of re-establishing the species throughout its former range in the country. This recovery plan should be officially endorsed, and a specific budget allocated for its implementation.

2.1.1. Promote the provisions of qualified staff and wardens for protected areas.

2.1.1. Promote the completion and implementation of the management plan for Dadiá Forest being prepared by WWF Greece and the Ministry of Environment.

2.1.3. Promote forestry operations in Dadiá Forest that are fully compatible with the conservation of the Cinereous Vulture. No forestry activities have been undertaken within the core areas since 1980. The specific environmental study delimits the highly sensitive zone, which includes those sections of the core areas and the buffer zone where the main nesting habitats of the Cinereous Vulture (and also the Griffon Vulture and Golden Eagle *Aquila chrysaetos*) are known to exist. It is recommended that all human activities, except traditional grazing and bird monitoring, be forbidden in these areas throughout the year. For the two isolated nests which lie in the southern buffer zone, outside the highly sensitive zone, it is recommended that no forestry activity takes place during the breeding season within 1 km of the nests.

The following measures are recommended to conserve suitable forests for the breeding of the Cinereous Vulture and other raptors in the Evros Prefecture:

– Definition of areas with particular ecological value for nesting, in which strict protection measures should be enforced.

– Management for the creation of uneven-aged forest areas while preserving mature stands at all times.

– Special management of evergreen broad-leaved stands with large isolated pine trees; these trees must be safeguarded as nest-sites.

3.1.1. Continue the yearly monitoring of the population as it has been since 1987 by the local team at Dadiá.

Russian Federation

3.1.2. Undertake national surveys to draw up a precise distribution map, including the relevant breeding nuclei. Field surveys should concentrate in the Nature Reserves (Zapovedniks) and other protected areas along the Caucasus. These surveys could be carried out within the framework of broader Important Bird Area surveys. NGO development in Russia should be promoted.

Spain

1.2.1. Promote completion of the National Catalogue for Threatened Species under Law 4/89 for the Conservation of Natural Areas and Wildlife. This should include those species in need of specific protection measures. The Cinereous Vulture is currently classified as Of Special Interest in the preliminary Catalogue (Royal Decree 439/90), which means that management plans should be prepared at regional level. However it should be reclassified to a more appropriate category of Threatened according to the national Red Data Book.

2.1.1. Ideally all breeding colonies should be included within protected areas, and these should have management plans to regulate forestry and hunting. Some new protected areas need to be declared.

2.1.2./2.1.3. Private landowners should be provided with precise guidelines to prevent disturbance and alterations of the breeding range. These include forestry activities such as the establishment of tracks for cork or timber extraction, clearance of woodland and cutting of scrubland. In some areas the habitat is intensively managed for game species such as red deer and wild boar, and new tracks are made to permit easy access for hunting which can increase disturbance.

2.1.2. Monitor the use of the European Union's Structural and Cohesion Funds. Planned infrastructural and hydrological development in Spain continues to threaten nesting and the feeding habitat of Cinereous Vultures through flooding, increase of disturbance and ease of access to the breeding colonies.

2.3./4.2. Careful surveillance by official wardens and NGOs is necessary to detect instances of poisoning, and each case should be thoroughly investigated and fines imposed as appropriate. If a particular hunting estate offends, the required hunting permit should be withdrawn by the regional authorities. A study of the socio-economic factors inducing gamekeepers to use poison for predator control should be undertaken, as should an awareness campaign about the risks of poisoning for protected wildlife and human welfare.

3.1.1. A national survey should be carried out every four years, which could be co-ordinated by DGN. Colonies in protected areas should be monitored yearly.

3.2.1. A comprehensive research project should be undertaken to determine food and habitat requirements, home-range, dispersion, survival rates and patterns of colonisation of new territories, with the help of individual marking. The expanding population of the Cinereous Vulture now offers ideal conditions for such a study, which would permit better management of the population and establish principles for reintroduction schemes in other countries.

Turkey

3.1.2. There is a lack of baseline information about population status, distribution and trends. Field surveys are necessary to locate the main breeding areas and assess population size. These surveys could be carried out in the framework of broader Important Bird Area surveys. A comprehensive inventory of all the existing colonies and isolated pairs is urgently needed.

3.1.3. In parallel with the surveys above, information needs to be gathered about the factors likely to affect the population: poisoning, destruction of forests, habitat alterations, persecution, etc.

Ukraine

2.2.3. A feeding station should be set up in the Crimea Game Reserve and supplied regularly.

3.1. Being the only population in Ukraine, it is essential that monitoring of numbers, breeding success, causes of mortality and population trends is carried out yearly.

International action plan for the Imperial Eagle (*Aquila heliaca*)

Reviews

The action plan should be reviewed and updated every four years. An emergency review will be undertaken if sudden major environmental changes, liable to affect the population, occur within the species' range.

Geographical scope

This action plan is primarily targeted at those European countries where the Imperial Eagle breeds or occurs on migration or in winter. However, given the significance of the Middle East for migration and/or wintering, and the conservation problems which affect migratory birds of prey in that region, the geographical scope of the action plan was extended to include the Middle East as well. The action plan needs active implementation in: Armenia, Azerbaijan, Bulgaria, Croatia, Cyprus, Federal Republic of Yugoslavia (Serbia and Montenegro), Georgia, Greece, Hungary, Iran, Iraq, Israel, Jordan, Kuwait, Lebanon, Moldova, Oman, Romania, Russian Federation (European part), Saudi Arabia, Slovakia, the former Yugoslav Republic of Macedonia, Turkey, Ukraine and Yemen.

Summary

The Imperial Eagle *Aquila heliaca* is classified as Vulnerable at the global level (Collar et al., 1994) and Endangered at the European level (Tucker and Heath, 1994). In Europe it occurs in the Carpathian mountains and basin, the southern and eastern Balkan peninsula, the hills and steppes of south-east Ukraine and south Russia, and the Caucasus mountains. Total numbers are estimated at 363 to 604 pairs.

Threats and limiting factors

Habitat alterations caused by forestry operations – critical

Shooting and human disturbance – high

Poisoning – medium, potentially high

Nest robbing and illegal trade – high

Shortage of key prey species – medium

Collision with, and electrocution by, powerlines – unknown, potentially high

Conservation priorities

Forestry policies compatible with the conservation of the species – high

Legal protection for the species and key sites – high

Designate protected areas – high

Implementation of international conventions and treaties – high

Appropriate habitat management – high

Increase availability of key prey species, particularly suslik – high

Prevent mortality due to nest robbing, illegal trade and poisoning – high

Reduce mortality caused by powerlines – high

National surveys to identify breeding sites and monitoring of key sites – high

Locate wintering areas and migration routes – high

Introduction

The Imperial Eagle *Aquila heliaca* is a migratory species classed as Vulnerable at the world level (Collar et al., 1994) and Endangered at a European level (Tucker and Heath, 1994). It is listed as Rare in the *IUCN Red List of Threatened Animals* (Groombridge, 1993) and is also included in Annex I of the European Union's Wild Birds Directive, in Appendix I of CITES and in Appendix II of both the Bern and Bonn Conventions.

In Europe it has suffered a rapid decline in recent decades and is now very rare or extinct in many areas. It is known to be increasing only in Hungary and Slovakia, thanks to specific conservation programmes undertaken in those countries.

In December 1993, the third meeting of the Eastern Imperial Eagle Working Group took place in Királyrét (Hungary), hosted by the Hungarian Ornithological and Nature Conservation Society (MME) and organised by the MME and BirdLife International. Representatives from Bulgaria, Croatia, Georgia, Germany, Greece, Hungary, Romania, Slovakia and Ukraine were present. The Imperial Eagle's situation was thoroughly discussed and the most important actions to safeguard its future in Europe were outlined.

This action plan relies mainly on the information gathered during that meeting, but also on literature sources and the comments of other experts consulted. It intends to provide a framework of action for statutory agencies, conservation organisations and individuals responsible for, or interested in, the conservation of the species.

Background information

Distribution and population

The Imperial Eagle is sparsely distributed from central, south-east and eastern Europe eastwards to Lake Baikal in Russia. In Europe it occurs as a breeding species in Armenia, Azerbaijan, Bulgaria, Croatia, Cyprus, Georgia, Greece, Hungary, Moldova, Romania, Russia, Slovakia, the former Yugoslav Republic of Macedonia, Turkey and Ukraine. Population figures for each of these countries have been gathered from several presentations during the workshop at Királyrét and from the Dispersed Species Project of BirdLife International (Table 10.1).

The adult eagles are partially migratory, with some birds moving south or south-east, though in severe winters Europe may be totally vacated. The young are fully migratory and winter in Egypt, Greece, Iraq, Iran, Israel, Jordan, Kuwait, Lebanon, Oman, Saudi Arabia, Sudan, Turkey and Yemen (Cramp and Simmons, 1980; Evans, 1994).

In the Middle East the species occurs widely on passage and in winter. The migrant/wintering population has been estimated at 500 to 1 000 birds between October and March. During the winter it occurs regularly at 79 sites (Table 10.2), numbers at each varying from one to about 15 birds. In the marshes of southern Iraq the total

wintering population probably exceeds 100 (Evans, 1994; R. F. Porter, in litt., 1994).

Table 10.1

Breeding population of the Imperial Eagle in Europe, based on data gathered during the workshop carried out in Hungary in December 1993. The figure for Russia is from Galushin (1995)

Country	No. of pairs
Armenia	8–10
Azerbaijan	35–40
Bulgaria	20–25
Croatia	1–2
Cyprus	2–4
Georgia	8–11
Greece	0–2
Hungary	34–36
Moldova	3–3
Romania	10–20
Russian Federation	150–300
Slovakia	30–35
The former Yugoslav Republic of Macedonia	4–6
Turkey	10–50
Ukraine	40–50
Yugoslavia (Serbia and Montenegro)	8–10
Total	363–604

Table 10.2

Occurrence of the Imperial Eagle in Middle Eastern countries in winter. Based on Evans (1994)

Country	No. of sites
Iran	28
Iraq	10
Israel	7
Jordan	9
Kuwait	3
Lebanon	1
Oman	7
Saudi Arabia	5
Yemen	9
Total	79

Some important migration bottlenecks are in Burgas (Bulgaria), north-east Turkey, the eastern shore of the Mediterranean (Syria, Lebanon, Israel) and Elat (Israel). The highest concentration of passage birds is over Elat where up to 90 have been recorded on migration in spring.

Life history

Taxonomic status

The Imperial Eagle was formerly considered a species comprising two races: *adalberti* in the Iberian peninsula and *heliaca* in central and eastern Europe and Asia. In recent years, evidence has been put forward to support their separation as distinct species (Hiraldo et al., 1976; González et al., 1989), and cytochrome b sequences endorse this (Wink and Seibold, 1994). This plan deals only with *A. heliaca* and, since the Spanish Imperial Eagle *A. adalberti* is also globally threatened, there is an action plan for this species in the same series.

Breeding

The Imperial Eagle builds a large stick nest on the tops of trees; these may be solitary or in shelterbelts in flat landscapes, or in deciduous or coniferous forests; very occasionally nests are built on electricity pylons. The clutch is completed in late March or early April and usually consists of 2 to 3 eggs; breeding success is around 1.5 young per successful pair, but can vary a great deal depending on food availability. The young remain with their parents throughout the summer and then migrate. Adult plumage is acquired at 5 to 6 years old but pairs with both birds in immature plumage have successfully reared young. Birds will accept purpose-built, artificial nest structures. Captive breeding has been achieved in France since 1986.

Feeding

The diet is largely mammals, mainly suslik *Citellus citellus*, hamster *Cricetus cricetus* and hare *Lepus*, but also small rodents (*Microtus, Apodemus*), and carrion. Birds comprise 15%–25% of the diet and include Quail *Coturnix coturnix*, Pheasant *Phasianus colchicus*, Partridge *Perdix perdix*, domestic chicken and passerines (Simeonov and

Petrov, 1980). Imperial Eagles in the Caucasus feed largely on rodents, corvids, lizards and carrion (Abuladze, in prep.).

Habitat requirements

The Imperial Eagle is predominantly a lowland species but has been pushed to higher altitudes by persecution. In central and eastern Europe the breeding habitat consists of forests in mountains, hills and along rivers, at an altitude of up to 1000 metres, but also steppes, open landscapes and agricultural areas (Petrov et al., in prep.). In the Caucasus it occurs in lowland and riverine forests, semi-deserts and old forests (Abuladze, in prep.). It hunts in open areas and wetlands. A variety of habitats are used during migration, though birds seem to prefer wetlands for wintering.

Threats and limiting factors

Habitat alterations caused by forestry

Forestry operations affecting breeding areas are possibly the most important threat. These consist of the cutting of the forest for reafforestation with alien species; cutting of large, old trees in forest and along field edges; disturbance by logging during the breeding season; and destruction of lowland forest. In Greece, old low-altitude forests have been intensively exploited, and some have been turned into pine plantations (Hallmann, 1985). An important side effect of forestry is the increased human disturbance in previously isolated areas due to the construction of tracks.

Importance: critical

Human disturbance

The Imperial Eagle is a species sensitive to human activities in its nesting area. Disturbance, both intentional and unintentional, is a major cause of breeding failure.

Importance: high

Nest robbing and illegal trade

The disintegration of the Soviet Union in 1991 has led to a decline of the general control of the laws protecting wildlife; control by customs has relaxed considerably and there is a general lack of enforcement of the CITES regulations (Flint and Sorokin, 1992). In 1992, 12 Imperial Eagles from Kazakhstan and Azerbaijan were confiscated by customs officers in Germany and sent to Hungary, where they were successfully released in 1993. A further 11 birds are still being held in Slovakia awaiting a destination, and there are at least two further consignments (of two and four birds) that have gone to Germany or Belgium. The methods used for smuggling birds of prey out of the former Soviet Union are clearly very efficient and there are good grounds for believing that the extent of trapping and smuggling will increase further in the near future if no immediate national and international actions are taken to prevent this. Many of the birds taken from the wild are brought into zoos where they are registered as "legal" and then put on the market as captive-bred (Abuladze and Shergalin, in prep.). Unsuccessful fledglings and other young birds are sometimes taken and kept in captivity with no specific objective (P. Iankov, in litt., 1994).

Importance: high

Shooting

Persecution is still a problem in Romania and Greece. After habitat destruction, shooting is considered the second most important threat to birds of prey in Greece, contributing substantially to the decline of the Imperial Eagle (Hallmann, 1985). Shooting of birds of prey on migration is common practice in north-east Turkey, Lebanon and Syria (Magnin, 1988; Baumgart, 1991), and an Imperial Eagle carrying a satellite transmitter was shot in Saudi Arabia in 1993 (B.-U. Meyburg, pers. comm., 1993). The military in the Middle East often use birds of prey for target practice (R. F. Porter, verbally, 1995). There are also instances of shooting in Georgia and Azerbaijan, and the problem of expatriate hunters shooting indiscriminately in east European countries is increasingly reported.

Importance: high

Poisoning

This problem involves secondary or unintentional ingestion of poisons which are being used for the control of other species. Poisoning for wolves is one of the reasons for the decline of the Imperial Eagle in eastern Europe and Greece. The use of strychnine was regular in the Caucasian republics but this has now ceased due to social and economic problems. In Bulgaria, luminal was officially used in 1993 against wolves by the Committee for Forestry, but this was stopped due to actions by the Ministry of Environment and NGOs. Poisoning is also a problem in the Middle East, where poison is used on rubbish tips to control crows, foxes, jackals, dogs, rats, etc.

Importance: medium, potentially high

Shortage of key prey species

The Imperial Eagle is a specialised predator, tending to concentrate on one or a few prey items such as, in eastern Europe, the suslik. Susliks have virtually disappeared from Hungary due to over-hunting and habitat loss. The removal of this food source affects the Imperial Eagle by substantially decreasing its productivity and increasing the likelihood of sibling aggression.

Importance: medium

Trapping

The capture of full-grown Imperial Eagles in Europe appears to be an incidental result of mammal trapping, usually by the exposed bait method; it is generally sporadic and of local significance. Imperial Eagles are known to have been caught in mammal leg-hold traps only in the Caucasus, where trapping is widespread – though it is likely that similar incidents do happen occasionally in other countries. Trapping is also a problem in the Middle East, and in Syria large numbers of birds of prey, including Imperial Eagles, are trapped and sold in markets around Damascus (R. F. Porter, in litt., 1994).

Importance: low

Collision with, and electrocution by, powerlines

Collision with powerlines is only occasional but electrocution can be a very important factor. In the case of the Spanish Imperial Eagle it proved to be the main source of mortality of young birds during dispersion. With the Imperial Eagle some instances have occurred in Georgia, but more research is needed to clarify its importance here and elsewhere.

Importance: unknown, potentially high

Conservation status and recent conservation measures

Armenia

The Imperial Eagle is included in the Armenian Red Data Book of 1987. There are only a few breeding records from the north of the country, near the border with Georgia and Azerbaijan. Information on the species is very sparse (A. Abuladze, pers. comm., 1993). The country is suffering from armed conflict.

Azerbaijan

The species is legally protected but not included in the Red Data Book. Most of the population is in the west near the border with Georgia, along the lowland forests of the Kura river. At least two pairs are included in a protected area, the Karaijaz Game Reserve (A. Abuladze, pers. comm., 1993; Abuladze, in prep.). The country is suffering from armed conflict.

Bulgaria

The species is protected by the Law for the Conservation of Nature of 1962 and is listed as Endangered in the Red Data Book of 1985. It occurs in mountains, hills and agricultural areas. The largest part of the population (56%) lies along the middle course of the Tundzha river including the Strandzha mountains. Next in importance is the Rhodope mountains (22%), with the remainder occupying the area between the Sredna Gora mountains and the fore-Balkan range (Petrov et al., in prep.). One of the known breeding pairs is within a protected area, Sashtinska Sredna Gora mountain. The Strandzha mountains were designated as a National Park (116 000 ha) in 1995. The main limiting factors are loss of breeding and feeding habitat, the felling of old solitary trees in the plains, forestry, poaching, nest robbing and human disturbance (Petrov and Iankov, 1993).

The Imperial Eagle is currently the main target of a raptor conservation programme in the eastern Rhodopes being carried out by the BSPB. The population is monitored, breeding success assessed and supplementary feeding provided. This is organised mainly for vultures, but is also used by Imperial Eagles. There are proposals for a new protected area (including the critical areas for the species) in preparation, in collaboration with the Ministry of Environment. There is no specific conservation programme or regular monitoring for the remainder of the population.

Croatia

Imperial Eagles are protected under the Croatian Law of Nature Protection of 1994: any disturbance, persecution, killing and trade are strictly prohibited. Present status is unknown, but there is a possibility that some pairs still nest in eastern Slavonia (around Ilok) and in Spačva forests; none of these areas is covered by the IBA network. There have been recent observations in Kopački rit (IBA 014) and eastern Slavonia (Dugo Cerje and Ilok) during migration and in winter. The species has not been monitored because of the armed conflict affecting Croatia for much of the last few years.

Cyprus

The Imperial Eagle was formerly common but is now a very scarce resident in the Troodos range, where it usually breeds on Aleppo pine *Pinus halepensis*. It migrates regularly over Cyprus (Flint and Stewart, 1992).

Federal Republic of Yugoslavia (Serbia and Montenegro)

The Imperial Eagle is legally protected and included in the Red Data Book of the former Yugoslavia. It occurs in hilly areas with deciduous forest and in grazing pastures/steppes. Most of the population is in Vojvodina, divided between two sites: Fruska gora (four pairs) and Deliblatska Pescara (6–7 pairs). The proportion within protected areas is good, Fruska Gora being a National Park and Deliblatska Pescara, a Special Reserve, although the latter site is severely threatened by afforestation schemes. Imperial Eagles formerly occurred in southern Serbia but there are no recent breeding records (Vasic et al., 1985; Grimmett and Jones, 1989; I. Ham, pers. comm., 1993). Due to the current armed conflict in the area there is no monitoring of the species.

Georgia

The species is legally protected and is listed as Endangered in the Georgian Red Data Book of 1982. It occurs in the south-east of the country, in lowland forest along the Kura, Alazani, Iori and Khrami rivers, on the Iori plateau, and in the eastern slopes of the Trialethi range in the Caspian Sea catchment area. As a wintering species it occurs in the semi-desert zone and in the extreme south-east. Some pairs are covered by protected areas in Gardabani and Chachuna Game Reserves and a few birds winter in the Vashlovani Reserve. The main limiting factors are destruction of nesting habitat, human disturbance, predation of clutches by corvids, shooting, electrocution and poisoning (Abuladze, in prep.). Between 1981 and 1991 the Imperial Eagle was monitored regularly by biologists of the Institute of Zoology of Georgia, as part of a broader programme; this has now stopped because of the armed conflict from which the country is suffering.

Greece

The Imperial Eagle is legally protected and classified as Endangered in the Greek Red Data Book. In the past it has bred in single trees or remnant riparian woods of deltas (Axios, Evros). It is now virtually extinct but may breed occasionally in Evros, Thessaly and on the border with the former Yugoslav Republic of Macedonia. The decline is attributed to the cutting of old forests for reafforestation, incidental poisoning linked to the poisoning of wolves, and shooting (B. Hallmann, pers. comm., 1993).

Hungary

The species is in the highest category of legal protection and also in the Hungarian Red Data Book. The population lies mainly in the mountain areas along the border with Slovakia, although in recent years a few pairs have become established on the plain. It occurs in the following Important Bird Areas: 004 Börzsöny (Landscape Protection Reserve), 006 Vértes (Landscape Protection Reserve), 012 Zemplén (Landscape Protection Reserve), 013 Bükk (National Park), 028 Aggtelek (National Park), 029 Gerecse (Landscape Protection Reserve), 030 Mátra (Landscape

Protection Reserve) (Grimmett and Jones, 1989). The proportion within protected areas is reasonably good although some areas deserve stricter protection. Main conservation problems include the privatisation of land, hunting and game management, human disturbance, and the intensification of agriculture. The population is very well monitored by the Hungarian Ornithological and Nature Conservation Society (MME), and conservation action undertaken includes nest surveillance, suslik reintroduction and restocking, construction of artificial nests, and the reintroduction of confiscated birds (Haraszthy et al., in prep.).

Moldova

There are only very small numbers and the species is included in the Red Data Book. It is present in the Kapriyanovsko-Lozovo forest in central Kodry, an unprotected IBA (Grimmett and Jones, 1989). Main threats are the reduction of food, the felling of old trees, and persecution and disturbance during the breeding season (N. Zubcov, in litt., 1994).

Romania

The Imperial Eagle is legally protected and included in the Red Data Book. Occurring in lowland forest near the Black Sea coast and along the Carpathians and Transylvanian Alps, it is present in the following IBAs: 002 Padurea Niculitel-Babadag (4–6 pairs, unprotected), 007 Canaraua Fetii (partially Nature Reserve, 2 pairs), 011 Cheile Bicazului and Lacul Rosu (Nature Reserve, 1–2 pairs), 022 Domogled Mountain (Nature Reserve) (Grimmett and Jones, 1989). There are other breeding pairs which are included neither in IBAs nor in protected areas. The main threats to the species are forest management, persecution, egg-collecting, and general negative attitudes towards birds of prey. Knowledge about the population is scarce and there is no regular monitoring (Kalabér, in prep.).

Russian Federation

Included as Vulnerable in the Russian Red Data Book of 1983 and expected to remain in the same category in the new edition. Existing conservation legislation is poorly enforced, and as a result young Imperial Eagles and other rare raptors are illegally taken and smuggled abroad (Raptor-Link, 1993). The Imperial Eagle inhabits steppes, forest edges, semi-deserts and mountains between the Black and Caspian seas, and extends into central Asia and southern Siberia as far as Lake Baikal. In European Russia, it is present in the northern Caucasus (30–40 pairs), Don river (40–50), Volga river and western Ural mountains (100–200) (V. Galushin, 1995). It is a rare bird and is declining locally due to habitat destruction, shortage of key prey (susliks), disturbance, nest robbing, electrocution and smuggling. There is no current monitoring but a two year study programme is planned in the border area with the Ukraine.

Slovakia

The Imperial Eagle is legally protected by the Law for the Conservation of Nature and is classified as Endangered in the Red Data Book of 1988. It occurs in southern parts of the country along the Hungarian border, mainly in areas of old deciduous forest but in recent years some pairs have also become established in agricultural areas. It is present in the following important bird areas: 05 Malé Karpaty mountains (Protected Landscape Area), 11 Poana mountains (Protected Landscape Area Biosphere Reserve), 13 Slovensky kras karst (Protected Landscape Area Biosphere Reserve), 14 Slanské vrchy mountains (unprotected), 15 Vihorlatské vrchy mountains (Protected Landscape Area) (Hora and Kanuch, 1992). It is also present in the Vychodoslovenská nízina lowlands (unprotected), Kosická kotlina basin (unprotected), Slovenské rudohorie mountains (unprotected), Stiavnické vrchy hills (Protected Landscape Area), Vtáčnik mountains (Protected Landscape Area), Tríbec mountains (Protected Landscape Area), Povazsky Inovec mountains (unprotected). The main conservation problems are associated with destruction of breeding and feeding habitats, human disturbance, nest robbing, illegal shooting and (potentially) electrocution. The population is very well monitored by the Group for the Protection of Birds of Prey and Owls of the Slovak Ornithological Society, and conservation action undertaken includes nest wardening, the securing of unstable nests and suslik reintroductions (Danko, 1993; P. Kanuch, in litt., 1994).

The former Yugoslav Republic of Macedonia

Breeding continues, but numbers have decreased considerably, and breeding no longer occurs in the north and east (Vasic et al., 1985). At least two pairs nest on electricity pylons (I. Ham, pers. comm., 1993).

Turkey

The Imperial Eagle is legally protected and is classed as Rare in the Draft Red List of Threatened Animals of Turkey. Except in the south and south-east of the country, it is a very rare and local breeder and the decline in recent decades has been drastic. On migration and in winter it can occur anywhere across southern and western Turkey, and in central Anatolia (Kasparek, 1992); the north-east of the country along the Black Sea coast is an important migration corridor. It is present as a breeding bird in the following IBAs: 008 Meriç Deltasi (probably one pair, unprotected), 012 Ilgaz Daglari (probably breeds, partially National Park), 017 Yeniçaga Gölü (Grimmett and Jones, 1989; M. Yarar, in litt., 1994). Two further sites are important, and are candidates for inclusion in the revised IBA inventory: Beynam forest, a Forestry Recreation Area, and Yozgat forest, a National Park. The number of Imperial Eagles within IBAs and protected areas is very low. The reasons for the decline are not well understood although they are probably related to habitat alteration and poisoning. In north-east Turkey migrating raptors are regularly shot to feed the decoys used to trap Sparrowhawks Accipiter nisus for falconry; illegal shooting is a regular feature of several Turkish wetlands (Magnin, 1988).

Ukraine

The Imperial Eagle is protected by the Law for Nature Conservation and included in the Ukrainian Red Data Book of 1979. It occurs mainly in the north-east along the Seversky Donets river and in the Poltawa lowlands (35 pairs), breeding in small old woodland plots of Scots pine Pinus sylvestris; also in the Dnieper and

Podol highlands (10 pairs) and in Crimea (five pairs). The coverage under protected areas is quite low and there is a problem of enforcement in the existing ones. The main conservation problems are logging of old forests (especially the felling of old trees), illegal shooting, human disturbance at breeding sites, changes in food availability, and pollution. There is no regular monitoring (Vetrov and Gorban, 1994; V. Vetrov, pers. comm., 1994).

International

The Eastern Imperial Eagle Working Group was created in 1990 at the headquarters of the MME; it involves Bulgaria, Croatia, Greece, Hungary, Romania and Slovakia, and has held three meetings so far. Co-operation between Hungary and Slovakia on Imperial Eagle protection is very close (Bagyura, 1993; L. Haraszthy, pers. comm., 1993).

Aims and objectives

Aims

1. In the short term, to maintain the present numbers of the Imperial Eagle throughout its present range.

2. In the medium to long term to ensure range expansion.

Objectives

1. **Policy and legislation**

1.1. *To promote policies which ensure long-term conservation of the Imperial Eagle and its habitat*

1.1.1. Forestry

Forest management can conflict with Imperial Eagle conservation in several European countries. Governments should review their forestry policies to ensure that they are compatible with the conservation of the Imperial Eagle. It is recommended that such policies should incorporate the following elements:

a. Priority for the protection of the wildlife resources;
b. Where the logging of indigenous forest is seen as acceptable, commercial forestry opera-

tors should allow some part of their holdings to evolve naturally without felling or planting;
c. The presence of the Imperial Eagle and other threatened birds should be taken into account in yearly forestry plans, and human activity should be prevented within 300 metres of an active nest;
d. Agreements with landowners for appropriate management of forest areas should be pursued. This co-operation is essential to retain and, where possible, to enhance the value of forest remnants as refuges for biological diversity;
e. Precise guidelines for forest management in areas where sensitive species occur should be produced and disseminated.
Priority: high
Time-scale: medium

1.1.2. Farming and agriculture

The recent colonisation of agricultural areas by the Imperial Eagle in several east European countries shows the potential of such habitats to hold expanding populations. However, there can be conflict between the human activities which need to be carried out periodically in these areas and the Imperial Eagle's breeding success. With this in mind it is important to prepare guidelines for farming which are compatible with the presence of this species as a breeding bird.

The Imperial Eagle is a priority species in the European Agriculture Conservation Strategy currently being prepared by BirdLife International (Tucker et al., in press).

Priority: medium
Time-scale: short/medium

1.1.3. Protected areas

Protected-area policies and regulations should promote the following:

a. Conservation management of all the Important Bird Areas where the Imperial Eagle occurs;
b. Areas holding at least one pair of this species should be eligible for protected status designation;
c. Conservation of remaining original forest cover, particularly in lowland forests;
d. Endorse and implement the IUCN Action Plan for Protected Areas in Europe.

Priority: high
Time-scale: short/medium

1.1.4. International co-operation

The experience gathered in countries, such as Hungary and Slovakia, in designing and implementing successful conservation programmes for the Imperial Eagle should be acknowledged and exported to neighbouring range states (e.g. Bulgaria, Romania, the former Yugoslav Republic of Macedonia and Ukraine) at their request. Bilateral co-operation among these countries should be pursued. The Eastern Imperial Eagle Working Group could play an important role.

In more general terms, international support will be required to initiate or re-establish conservation programmes in those countries presently suffering from armed conflict or in great economic and social difficulties. Such help should focus on:

a. Assessing the damage to Important Bird Areas.
b. Strengthening legislation and institutions;
c. Training conservation specialists;
d. Research and monitoring;
e. Provision of funds and equipment.

Priority: high
Time-scale: short/medium

1.2. *To promote national legislation which adequately protects the species and its habitat*

Where appropriate, a review and update of national laws and regulations relating to nature conservation should be encouraged to ensure that:

a. the Imperial Eagle is given the maximum level of protection, and heavy penalties are instated for shooting, trapping, taking, poisoning, disturbing, possessing or trading specimens or their eggs;
b. recovery plans and habitat management plans are foreseen for endangered species;
c. environmental impact assessment is required for afforestation schemes, dam construction, powerlines or any other infrastructure likely to affect the habitat of the Imperial Eagle;
d. poisoning is totally banned or strictly regulated.

Priority: high
Time-scale: medium

1.3. *To promote implementation of international conventions and treaties*

There are three major international treaties which list the Imperial Eagle: the Convention on the Conservation of European Wildlife and Natural Habitats (Bern Convention); the Convention on the Conservation of Migratory Species of Wild Animals (Bonn Convention) and the Convention on International Trade in Endangered Species of Wild Fauna and Flora (Washington Convention or CITES). These conventions, together with the Biodiversity Convention, provide an adequate framework for the conservation of the Imperial Eagle and its habitat, and all the countries where the species occurs are encouraged to sign, ratify and implement them.

Priority: high
Time-scale: long

2. **Species and habitat protection**

2.1. *To ensure that the Imperial Eagle habitat retains the necessary conditions for the presence of the species*

2.1.1. Promote the designation of all the Important Bird Areas where the species occurs as protected areas

The compilation of the directory of IBAs (Grimmett and Jones, 1989) allowed the identification of many sites for the Imperial Eagle in Europe. In the short term, protection of those sites containing three or more pairs should be given priority; in the long term all sites holding breeding birds should be designated as protected areas.

Priority: high
Time-scale: short/long

2.1.2. Encourage appropriate habitat management in unprotected sites

There are a number of IBAs in forests where the Imperial Eagle occurs which usually fall under the jurisdiction of forestry departments and are regularly exploited for timber production. These sites are not likely to be declared protected areas in the short term but it must be ensured that they retain their capacity to sustain Imperial Eagle populations. Careful monitoring is necessary to highlight any potentially harmful activities, and regular contact needs to be established between NGOs and the forestry authorities to inform them about the location of breeding pairs and ensure that buffer zones are declared to prevent disturbance during the critical periods of incubation and rearing.

Priority: high
Time-scale: short/ongoing

2.1.3. Encourage appropriate habitat management at privately owned sites

In the case of areas which are unprotected and privately owned, landowners must be made aware of the existence of the Imperial Eagle and encouraged to manage the habitat according to the species' needs and to emphasise the importance of the conservation of biodiversity. Guidelines for habitat management should be provided for these landowners and state-supported environmentally sensitive management schemes should be launched. The possibility of giving a bonus to those properties where the Imperial Eagle successfully rears its young should also be explored.

Priority: medium
Time-scale: medium/ongoing

2.1.4. Provide artificial nest structures to avoid the loss of clutches and chicks due to bad weather

If manpower and expertise are available, nests belonging to pairs attempting breeding for the first time should be secured to the supporting tree to ensure that they do not fall. It will occasionally be necessary to provide artificial nest structures to encourage birds away from areas prone to human disturbance. This sort of management activity should take place outside the breeding season, within the framework of a wider conservation programme, and by experienced personnel.

Priority: low
Time-scale: long

2.1.5. Increase abundance and availability of key prey species

In eastern Europe the suslik is a basic prey item for the Imperial Eagle. Attempts to restore suslik populations in Imperial Eagle areas should be undertaken whenever possible, and technical guidelines for such restoration should be produced by those organisations and agencies which already have the expertise. These attempts should be aimed at establishing viable suslik colonies in areas where they formerly occurred, and should take into consideration the principles of any reintroduction or restocking project including screening of the health of the released stock and monitoring of the results (Kleiman et al., 1994).

Priority: high
Time-scale: short/medium

2.2. *To eliminate or control non-natural factors which are affecting the Imperial Eagle*

2.2.1. Prevent nest robbing and illegal trade

The following actions are suggested:

a. Increased surveillance and wardening of those nest sites which are regularly robbed;
b. Heavy fines for taking birds should be included in national law and adequately publicised;
c. Stricter controls on captive-breeding centres;
d. The Eurogroup Against Bird Crime, national customs authorities, CITES Secretariat and TRAFFIC offices should be made aware of the illegal trade in Imperial Eagles and encouraged to take action. A permanent liaison and information exchange between the above organisations is essential;
e. European and former Soviet Union zoos must be warned about the risks of accepting birds of uncertain origin;
f. More information needs to be gathered about the way nest robbers operate and the routes of the illegal trade.

Priority: high
Time-scale: short

2.2.2. Prevent mortality by poisoning

The use of poison or anaesthetic to kill or capture birds and mammals is specifically prohibited by Appendix IV of the Bern Convention. The occurrence of poisoning must be permanently monitored in each European country, and the authorities must be alerted against the issuing of permits to poison wolves. If chemical analyses of corpses prove that secondary poisoning is responsible for the deaths of Imperial Eagles or other birds of prey, a case should be brought to the courts of justice. Alternative methods for the selective control of species which are causing damage to livestock or agriculture must be brought to the attention of the authorities and farmers.

Priority: high
Time-scale: short/ongoing

2.2.3. Control illegal hunting

Governments should be urged to enforce hunting regulations and increase surveillance in protected areas where Imperial Eagles occur, especially wetlands. Awareness campaigns targeted at hunters' associations should be undertaken in those areas where the problem is especially acute. At migration bottlenecks, public education among the local population is also necessary (see 4.1.); the acquisition or leasing of land at mountain passes should be explored, as it has proved an effective way of preventing shooting at Orgambidexka in the western Pyrenees.

Priority: medium
Time-scale: medium/ongoing

2.2.4. Reduce mortality from electrocution by powerlines

For a species which hunts in open landscapes, electricity poles and pylons are an attractive perch, and mortality due to electrocution probably has a significant effect on Imperial Eagle populations in Europe. It is essential to locate the actual pylons where electrocution occurs most often and then urge the companies owning the lines to undertake appropriate modifications. In the case of lines under construction, it has to be ensured that the routing does not affect areas critical for the Imperial Eagle and that corrective measures against electrocution are incorporated. Much expertise has been developed in the field of designing electricity pylons to make them safe for birds, both in western Europe and in the United States, and this information must be made available to those organisations and agencies involved in Imperial Eagle conservation.

Priority: high
Time-scale: short/ongoing

2.2.5. Prevent human disturbance

In cases where human disturbance is a persistent cause of breeding failure, wardening should be organised to prevent both intentional and unintentional disturbance to nesting birds. Such schemes can be carried out with the help of volunteers who must be adequately briefed to avoid becoming a disturbance themselves. Nest wardening also provides the opportunity to gather information about the species' biology. It is essential that wardens provided with equipment to carry out their observations from a long distance, and with radios to seek assistance from the authorities if required.

Priority: medium
Time-scale: medium/ongoing

2.2.6. Reduce incidental mortality from trapping

The use of leg-hold traps for the commercial capture of fur-bearing animals is widespread in several countries across the Imperial Eagle's range. This method of trapping is prohibited by the Bern Convention, and enforcement should be encouraged in all signatory countries where the Imperial Eagle occurs. The use of sight-baited leg-hold traps should be discouraged in all areas frequently used by eagles.

Priority: low
Time-scale: medium/ongoing

3. Monitoring and research

3.1. *To initiate a monitoring programme for the Imperial Eagle*

In each country where the species breeds, a network of competent field ornithologists needs to be developed for monitoring of the Imperial Eagle. During March and April all nesting areas should be checked to locate active nests and verify incubation; in May all the nests should be visited again to see whether the young have hatched and how many there are; the final visit is undertaken at the end of July to count the fledglings. Exceptional care must be taken in order not to disrupt the reproduction process and cause desertion, especially during the incubation and early rearing periods. Climbing of the nest trees should be avoided except for ringing or marking purposes, and in this case it should only be done by experienced personnel with the appropriate licence.

Priority: high
Time-scale: short/ongoing

3.2. To undertake national surveys

In 1995 and 1996 special efforts are needed to clarify the population status of the Imperial Eagle. This has to be done through surveys at national level, involving the optimum number of professional and amateur ornithologists. Guidelines for all the participants in these surveys must be produced by the co-ordinators of the survey in each country. The expertise in Imperial Eagle conservation which exists in countries such as Hungary and Slovakia must be brought into these surveys and it would be desirable that experts from those countries participate in them.

Priority: high
Time-scale: short

3.3. To gather new data about the location of wintering areas and migration routes

Satellite-tracking of migratory eagles has proved an effective way to delineate the migration route, to identify mortality factors during migration, and to locate the wintering areas of particular populations. Current studies about this topic should be continued and expanded, with a special emphasis on the Imperial Eagle.

Priority: high
Time-scale: ongoing

3.4. To promote research which helps identify limiting factors and causes of mortality

A better understanding of the species' habitat use, the home range of adult pairs, and the movements of the young after leaving the nest would be very helpful for future conservation efforts. Radio-tracking is easily available now and provides these kinds of data; marking and tracking a few fledglings in the nest, as well as some breeding adults, with radio-transmitters would enable the gathering of very useful information about the risks and threats that these birds undergo in their day-to-day life.

Priority: medium
Time-scale: medium

3.5. To update and complete national IBA inventories

The European IBA inventory of 1989 is being reviewed and updated by BirdLife Partners and representatives, and an IBA database is being established at the BirdLife Secretariat. There are plans to publish a new inventory by 1996. National IBA inventories are also being reviewed and published separately.

Priority: high
Time-scale: ongoing

4. Public awareness and training

4.1. To improve and maintain awareness, concern and support for the protection of the Imperial Eagle and its habitat

The Imperial Eagle has great potential to be used as a symbol of the lowland forests which covered Europe in the past. Public information programmes should be geared to provide updated, accurate information on the status and needs of eagles and the relationship between eagle recovery and the well-being of man. While support must be sought from the general public, specific problems such as indiscriminate shooting, the use of poison and traps must be resolved by focusing efforts on specific groups. The costs associated with the species' recovery must be supported by an informed public.

Priority: medium
Time-scale: medium/ongoing

Annex
Recommended conservation actions by country

Armenia

Recent international ornithological surveys have begun to clarify the status of several species. At present there is insufficient information on the Imperial Eagle to make recommendations, but future reviews should aim to give recommendations for this and other globally threatened species.

Azerbaijan

At present there is insufficient information on the Imperial Eagle to make recommendations, but future reviews should aim to give recommendations for this and other globally threatened species.

Bulgaria

1.1.1. Prepare guidelines to avoid disturbance by forestry, farming and agricultural operations in Imperial Eagle areas, and disseminate them to local forestry offices and landowners.

1.1.4. Assist neighbouring countries, at their request, with surveys and with the setting up of monitoring programmes.

1.2. Promote strengthened legal protection of the Imperial Eagle and increase the penalty for killing or taking specimens or eggs.

Promote protection by law of those solitary trees which hold Imperial Eagle nests.

2.1.1. Promote designation of protected areas to cover Imperial Eagle territories in the eastern Rhodope mountains, Strandzha mountains, Sakar, Sredna Gora mountains and other regions of importance for the species.

2.1.4. Provide artificial nest structures and prevent human activities during the incubation and early rearing periods within 300 metres of nest sites of pairs attempting to breed in agricultural areas.

2.1.5. Undertake the restoration of suslik populations in appropriate areas where the Imperial Eagle occurs.

2.2.1. Organise wardening for nests which are regularly robbed or disturbed.

Promote enforcement of CITES and the establishment of stricter customs controls to prevent the smuggling of Imperial Eagles and other threatened species out of Bulgaria.

2.2.2. Promote a total ban on the use of poisoned bait.

3.1. Initiate a long-term conservation programme including year-to-year monitoring of all the pairs and their breeding success.

3.3. Carry out research on the impact of electrocution on, and the habitat requirements of, the Imperial Eagle, and use the data from the monitoring programme to establish the population dynamics of the species.

4.1. Initiate a public awareness campaign and produce educational materials to achieve in particular, a positive response to the eagles' return to the populated lowlands.

Croatia

1.1.3./3.2. During 1996 an international team should visit the occupied areas of Croatia and carry out a survey of potential breeding and feeding sites.

2.1.1. Promote the protection of key migrating and wintering sites (e.g. Kopački rit) which are currently occupied and inaccessible to Croatian scientists and conservation authorities.

3.2. Assess the current situation of the Imperial Eagle outside the occupied territories and start a monitoring programme if a resident population is still present.

3.5. The Croatian IBA inventory needs to be updated and completed, especially in respect of mountain and forest areas.

Cyprus

3.2. Assess the current situation of the Imperial Eagle and start a monitoring programme if a resident population is still present.

Georgia

1.1.1. Promote restrictions in the exploitation of forests in floodlands, arid woodlands and low mountains, and provide legal protection to old forests.

1.1.4. Promote better co-ordination among ornithologists working in the Caucasus in order to undertake joint efforts for the conservation of the Imperial Eagle in central Transcaucasia.

1.2. Discourage the use of traps for mammals and ban the use of poisoned baits.

2.1.1. Promote the protection of all Imperial Eagle territories.

2.2.3. Promote enforcement of hunting regulations to prevent illegal shooting.

2.2.5. Promote restrictions to human activities around active nests during the breeding season.

3.2. Undertake a national survey.

4.1. Use the media to raise public awareness about nature conservation in general and the Imperial Eagle in particular.

Greece

1.1.2./2.1. Promote extension of the protected-area network and management of key sites for the species.

1.2. Promote preparation of a comprehensive recovery plan for the Imperial Eagle.

2.1.1. Promote designation as Special Protection Areas of all those sites where the Imperial Eagle occurs as a breeding or wintering species.

2.2.2. Promote a complete ban on, or strictly control the use of, poisoned bait.

3.1. Research the past distribution of the species.

3.2. Monitor closely any possible breeding attempts.

4.1./2.2.3. Increase public awareness of the problem of hunting in wintering areas in and around major wetlands, especially along the west coast and in Peloponnesus, and promote increased surveillance.

Hungary

1.1.1. Prepare precise guidelines for forest management in areas where the Imperial Eagle and other sensitive forest species occur, delimiting the periods when forest activities can take place and establishing buffer zones around nest sites.

1.1.3. Promote legal protection to lowland habitats where Imperial Eagles forage and which are rich in susliks.

1.1.4. Assist neighbouring countries, at their request, with surveys of the Imperial Eagle and with the development of conservation and monitoring programmes for the species.

1.2. Promote preparation of a comprehensive recovery plan.

2.1.1. Encourage the extension of Zemplén Landscape Protection Reserve to encompass those Imperial Eagle pairs which lie outside the existing protected area.

2.2.4. Undertake an inventory of critical localities for the electrocution of birds of prey and urge the companies responsible for the powerlines to adopt corrective measures.

3.1. Continue and strengthen the project for the conservation and monitoring of the Imperial Eagle that has been successfully implemented by MME during recent years.

Middle East

1.2. Promote legal protection of all birds of prey.

2.2.2. Promote bans or strict controls on the use of poisons for mammal control (e.g. foxes, rats) at sites where Imperial Eagles congregate.

3.1. Monitor all sites where Imperial Eagles occur regularly.

4.1. Raise awareness amongst military leaders in Middle East countries of the importance of Imperial Eagles and other birds of prey.

Moldova

1.2. Promote strengthening and enforcement of existing bird protection legislation.

2.1.1. Encourage improved protection status of the Kodri forest and promote the creation of a National Park in the centre of the republic.

3.2. Establish contact with the local ornithologists, gather available information and undertake a national survey.

Romania

3.2. Undertake a national survey of the Imperial Eagle and start a monitoring programme; international co-operation for this survey should be sought if necessary.

4.1./2.2.2. Carry out an awareness campaign highlighting the role of birds of prey as ecological regulators of rodents and other potential pest species. Stress the threat posed by the use of poisoned bait for wolf control and illegal shooting.

Russian Federation

1.2. Promote strengthening of existing legislation for the protection of rare birds.

Encourage the development of a comprehensive recovery plan for the Imperial Eagle through co-operation between government, ornithological NGOs, etc.

2.2.1. Promote enforcement of CITES and stricter customs controls to prevent the smuggling of Imperial Eagles and other threatened species out of Russia.

3.1. Establish a network of contacts throughout the country and carry out thorough population surveys and regular monitoring, seeking international co-operation if required.

Slovakia

1.1.1. Promote a review of forestry policies to ensure long-term protection of forests as a habitat of the Imperial Eagle and other threatened species.

Encourage the preparation of precise guidelines for forest management in areas where the Imperial Eagle and other sensitive species occur, delimiting the periods when forest activities can take place and establishing buffer zones around nest sites.

1.1.3. Promote appropriate conservation management in all protected areas where the Imperial Eagle occurs.

1.1.4. Assist neighbouring countries, at their request, with surveys of the Imperial Eagle and with the development of conservation and monitoring programmes.

1.2. Promote preparation of a recovery plan for the Imperial Eagle through collaboration between the conservation bodies and authorities concerned.

2.1.1. Promote the designation as protected areas of the most important sites for the Imperial Eagle in Slovakia.

2.1.3. Establish regular contacts with private landowners and encourage them to manage the habitat for the benefit of the Imperial Eagle.

2.1.4. Undertake work to repair or fix in place those nests which are threatened by weather damage.

2.1.5. Encourage the restoration of suslik populations in appropriate areas where the Imperial Eagle occurs.

2.2.1. Promote enforcement of CITES and stricter customs controls to prevent the smuggling of Imperial Eagles and other threatened species out of Russia.

2.2.1. Encourage wardening schemes for nests which are regularly robbed and/or disturbed.

2.2.4. Undertake an inventory of critical localities for the electrocution of birds of prey and encourage the adoption of corrective measures.

2.2.5. Encourage restrictions on human activities during the incubation and early rearing periods within 300 metres of nest sites of pairs attempting to breed in agricultural areas.

3.1. Continue and expand the existing monitoring and management programme to the whole range of the Imperial Eagle in Slovakia.

3.2. Carry out a national survey involving an optimum number of ornithologists.

3.4. Carry out research on population dynamics and habitat requirements, paying special attention to the recolonisation of agricultural areas.

3.5. Review and update the Slovak IBA inventory to include areas where the Imperial Eagle occurs.

4.1. Raise public awareness and support for the protection of the Imperial Eagle, especially in areas where its conservation comes into conflict with the interests of local landowners.

4.1./2.2.3. Undertake an education campaign about the threat of shooting birds of prey in Slovakia.

The former Yugoslav Republic of Macedonia

1.1.4. Seek international support to assess the situation of the Imperial Eagle and to start a monitoring programme.

3.2./3.4./3.5 Evaluate the status and condition of IBAs.

Turkey

2.1.1. Promote the designation as protected areas of those IBAs where the Imperial Eagle occurs.

3.2. Undertake surveys in appropriate areas.

3.5. Update and complete the IBA inventory, especially with respect to mountain and forest areas.

4.1. Undertake an education campaign about the shooting of migratory birds of prey in north-east Turkey.

Ukraine

1.2. Promote the development of new legislation for nature conservation.

2.1.1. Promote the designation as protected areas of IBAs containing Imperial Eagles.

3.2. Undertake a national survey and initiate a monitoring programme.

3.5. Review and update the existing IBA inventory.

Action plan for the Spanish Imperial Eagle (*Aquila adalberti*)

Reviews

This action plan should be reviewed and updated every four years. An emergency review will be undertaken if sudden major environmental changes, liable to affect the population, occur within the species' range.

Geographical scope

The plan mainly covers Spain, the only country with a stable breeding population. However, some recommendations for Portugal and Morocco have been included.

Summary

The Spanish Imperial Eagle *Aquila adalberti* is endemic to the western Mediterranean, and currently breeds only in Spain and Morocco, although dispersing or nomadic juveniles regularly appear in Portugal. At international level it is considered Vulnerable by BirdLife International (Collar et al., 1994; Tucker and Heath, 1994), although in Spain it is legally classified as Endangered. Since 1986 an intensive species conservation programme has been underway, involving the participation of DGN (Directorate-General for Nature Conservation) and the regional governments of Castilla-León, Castilla-La Mancha, Madrid, Extremadura and Andalucía. Since 1992 this programme has received financial support from the European Union within the framework of the LIFE programme.

This action plan recognises the important efforts being made in Spain to protect the Imperial Eagle and highlights the aspects that would have to be given special emphasis in order for the species to recover fully. Some recommendations for measures in Portugal and Morocco are also included with a view to future reintroductions there.

Threats and limiting factors

Alterations to breeding and feeding habitat – critical

Poisoning – critical

Electrocution – critical

Shortage of key prey species – high

Illegal shooting – medium

Human disturbance during breeding – medium

Chemical contamination (heavy metals, pesticides, etc.) – medium

Nest collapse – low

Nest robbing – low

Conservation priorities

Maintain an adequate area of protected habitat for the species including nesting, dispersal and recolonisation areas – essential

Location, description and modification of powerlines which are potentially dangerous or which have caused Spanish Imperial Eagle deaths. Further research into the design of electricity pylons safe for eagles – essential/high

Modify technical regulations concerning the installation of high voltage powerlines – high

Include in the network of protected areas all known nesting sites and draw up management plans for these – high

Environmental Impact Assessment for any project which might affect the Spanish Imperial Eagle habitat in nesting, dispersal or recolonisation areas – high

Strict application of hunting legislation – high

Where possible, temporal and spatial restrictions on rabbit hunting – high

Restrict quarrying and other activities near nests to reduce human disturbance – high

Increase rabbit population including the use of restocking. Carry out research into the most effective restocking techniques – high

Return any Spanish Imperial Eagle chicks to the wild – high

Annual surveys of the breeding population – high

Monitoring of tagged individuals – high

Monitor the use of poisoned bait and its impact on the species – high

Introduction

The Spanish Imperial Eagle *Aquila adalberti* is one of the rarest birds of prey in the world and is endemic to the west Mediterranean region. Studies of morphology and plumage (Hiraldo et al., 1976), zoogeography (González, 1991) and genetics (Wink and Seibold, 1995) have established conclusively that it is a different species from the Eastern Imperial Eagle *Aquila heliaca*.

BirdLife International classifies it as Vulnerable at world and European level (Collar et al., 1994; Tucker and Heath, 1994) and it is listed as Threatened by IUCN (Groombridge, 1993).

In Spain it is classed as Endangered in the National Red Data Book (Blanco and González, 1992) and in the National Catalogue of Threatened Species (Royal Decree 439/90). It is also listed in Annex I of the European Union's Wild Birds Directive and in the Habitats Directive, and in Appendix II of the Bern Convention, the Bonn Convention and CITES. Under EU CITES law it is classified as a C1 species.

The Spanish Imperial Eagle is now well known in scientific terms, and is the subject of an intensive conservation programme. In this action plan its conservation status is analysed, indicating its current situation in comparison with that of 20 years ago, and highlighting the measures needed for its total recovery.

Background information

Distribution and population

Breeding birds, totalling about 150 pairs, are found only in Spain. The range includes the Sierras of Guadarrama and Gredos, the plains of the Tajo and Tiétar rivers, the central hills of Extremadura, Montes de Toledo, Alcudia valley, Sierra Morena and the Guadalquivir marshes (Doñana). In addition there are occasional nesting reports from Salamanca and Málaga.

During this century the range has been considerably reduced. In Morocco, the Spanish Imperial Eagle has disappeared as a breeding species (Bergier, 1987), although one pair was found recently (Fouarge, 1992) and juveniles are regularly reported, some of them ringed as chicks in Doñana National Park (Calderón et al., 1988). In Portugal it is now very rare, with occasional observations, but no breeding has been recorded in recent years (Rufino, 1989).

In Spain it was a relatively common raptor at the beginning of this century, with a range extending over most of the country where habitat was available (except the Cantabrian mountains and the Pyrenees). The population has declined drastically over the last 80 years, birds having disappeared from central and southern Portugal, northern and eastern Spain and the Penibetic Sierras (González et al., 1989b). It was close to extinction in the 1960s when only 30 pairs were found (Garzón, 1974). Recovery started in the early 1980s at a rate of five new breeding pairs per year up to 1994.

The breeding population is monitored annually in the main protected areas (Jiménez, 1990; Cadenas, 1992; Sánchez and Rodríguez, 1992) and every 4 to 5 years nationally. There have been four national surveys (Garzón, 1974; González et al., 1987, 1990; ICONA, 1994).

Thirty-three percent of the breeding territories are included in protected areas. The main breeding populations are in Monfragüe Natural Park (Cáceres), Doñana National Park (Huelva) and Monte del Pardo (Madrid) (González, 1991).

Life history

Breeding

The Spanish Imperial Eagle nests in trees, normally pine *Pinus* or oak *Quercus*. Most clutches are laid between 21 February and 20 March, the earliest date recorded being 15 February and the latest 28 April. The average clutch is 2.47, two eggs being most common. Hatching success is 71.7%, with 1.36 chicks fledging per occupied nest and 1.7 fledging per successful nest. Of the total number of birds that attempt to breed, 80% breed successfully.

Prevalence of rabbits *Oryctolagus cuniculus* and the age of the paired birds are the factors that most affect breeding success. Success is greater in areas with more rabbits, and in adult pairs compared with sub-adult pairs. The degree of human activity and influence in the nesting territories and the associated disturbance may, in some way, affect breeding performance. A decrease in breeding success has been noted with increasing proximity to roads and people.

Cainism (aggression between siblings) is common in Spanish Imperial Eagles and frequently leads to the death of the youngest chick. The young fledge at 65 to 78 days old and remain 3 to 6 weeks in a small area near the nest, dependent on their parents to provide food. Parental negligence and aggression determine the move to independence and the start of juvenile dispersal. Once independent, the juveniles leave the area in which they were reared and make ever-greater dispersal movements.

During dispersal the young tend to concentrate in a few specific localities with an extraordinary abundance of rabbits, moving between the various sites. These focal areas, which are very important for the survival of the species, are located in the south-west of Madrid, the Tiétar valley (Toledo), south-east of La Mancha (Ciudad Real), south-west of Badajoz, the Guadalquivir marshes (Huelva) and El Andévalo and Medina-La Janda plains (Cádiz).

Feeding

Rabbits generally make up half the prey items and in some cases as many as 70%. Other prey worth mentioning are hares *Lepus*, pigeons, partridges, Corvidae, reptiles and ungulate carrion of both domestic and wild species. In Doñana the most important prey items, apart from rabbits, are aquatic birds (wildfowl, coots *Fulica*, herons, egrets and waders).

Habitat requirements

Spanish Imperial Eagles are found in three types of landscape: alluvial plains and dunes in the Guadalquivir marshes, plains and hills in central Spain and high mountain slopes in the Sistema Central (González, 1991). Except for four pairs that have used electricity pylons, nesting is in trees, with up to 16 tree species known to have been used, most frequently cork oak *Quercus suber* and stone pine *Pinus pinea*.

The average distance between nests of different pairs is 6.5 km and the average density is one pair per 52 km². The highest density is in Doñana and the lowest in the Tajo valley; breeding density in protected areas is four times greater than in unprotected areas.

The abundance and distribution of rabbits are two of the main factors influencing population density, range and reproductive performance, while a low incidence or absence of irrigated farmland is the best predictor of the eagle's presence. Nests tend to be located in zones with abrupt relief, far from roads, tracks, towns and powerlines and where access is difficult. However, newly settled and sub-adult pairs show greater tolerance of human presence.

The Spanish Imperial Eagle prefers areas with a Mediterranean climate – relatively hot, dry summers and warm, rainy winters. The breeding territories are regularly dispersed which indicates that neither food resources nor nest sites are limiting.

Threats and limiting factors

Habitat alterations

The history of forest cover in Spain holds some of the keys to the current scarcity of Spanish Imperial Eagles. The species needs a habitat with considerable tree cover in order to breed and the number of birds has thus always been related to the extent of woodland.

Holm oak *Q. ilex* forms perhaps the most extensive and representative forests in Spain. They have been intensively exploited for agriculture, timber and, in former times, for reasons of war and have therefore undergone a great decline in

Spain to the extent that well-preserved woods remain only in a few areas with minimal population density or irregular relief, or are used for livestock farming or hunting. For example, the lowland oakwoods that in the past formed an almost uninterrupted natural corridor in the depressions of the Tajo and Tiétar rivers are now fragmented and reduced to a few isolated and threatened enclaves. These woods hold some of the densest populations of Spanish Imperial Eagles currently found. The woods of holm oak and cork oak on the plains of the Guadiana and Guadalquivir basins are in the same situation.

Irrigation has a greater impact on the Spanish Imperial Eagle habitat than other agricultural activities, although their effects are rather similar. Irrigation schemes have been carried out where the greatest breeding densities of Spanish Imperial Eagles occur on plains with oakwoods and a Mediterranean climate. Between 1970 and 1985, the irrigated area on the lowland grasslands of the Guadiana and Guadalquivir rivers increased from 316 000 to 507 000 ha, resulting in a significant decrease in forest cover.

In the south-east of Spain, irrigation projects have been accompanied by the establishment of 29 new towns, which has increased the number of people in the countryside. Where this coincides with Spanish Imperial Eagle nesting areas, it has been proven that human disturbance brings about a significant decrease in breeding success.

Importance: critical

Poisoning

The second most important cause of death in the Spanish Imperial Eagle at present is poisoning in Hunting Reserves. In these areas the habitat is flat with little or no tree cover and large areas given over to the hunting of small game. Eagles and other birds of prey are often still considered harmful to local hunting interests and are poisoned.

Of all poisoning cases, 80% occurred in just five provinces, Madrid, Toledo, Ciudad Real, Huelva and Cádiz; these have the largest areas given over to small game Hunting Reserves with commercial exploitation of rabbit and Red-legged Partridge

Alectoris rufa. There is a significant correlation between the numbers of these species and recorded eagle deaths per province.

In recent years deaths by poisoning have risen considerably, not only for the Spanish Imperial Eagle but also for other species, and it seems obvious that poisons are being more widely and intensively used to control predators in the countryside.

Importance: critical

Electrocution

Of 112 Spanish Imperial Eagles found dead over the last 30 years, 62% were electrocuted. This occurs through contact with two conductors or through contact with a conductor and an earthed metal post. Due to the size of the posts, the distance between the conductors and the length of the insulators, electrocution is only frequent on powerlines with voltages of 15 to 45 kV. Various studies have indicated that the danger of electrocution depends on the design of the post, the layout of the insulators being the most important characteristic. In general, posts with rigid insulators, free upper bridges and with functions other than alignment (crosspiece anchor supports, transformers, disconnecting switches in portico and with horizontal upper bridges) are the most dangerous. On the other hand, alignment supports in quincunxes with hanging insulators, domed supports with suspended insulators and wooden posts in quincunxes with rigid insulators are the least dangerous (Ferrer et al., 1990). Plumage is ten times more conductive when wet rather than when dry.

Lines near roads and tracks cause far fewer deaths than those sited away from them, and a strong positive correlation has been found between the number of rabbits in the vicinity of a powerline and the number of eagles electrocuted there. The greatest number of deaths by electrocution occurs in juveniles because of their greater difficulty in perching due to lack of flying experience, lower selectivity in their choice of perch, and more frequent use of populated areas.

Importance: critical

Shortage of key prey species

Myxomatosis is a viral disease that has caused massive falls in rabbit numbers throughout Spain since 1957 and has had catastrophic consequences for the Spanish Imperial Eagle, which had to change its diet. In places where substitute prey existed, such as Doñana, the eagles ate aquatic birds instead of rabbits. There are no data for the rest of Spain, but it is thought that many pairs stopped breeding when suddenly deprived of their main food while not having access to any abundant substitute prey.

In recent years a new viral disease (haemorrhagic pneumonia) has also been affecting rabbit populations and causing high mortality. This, added to the existing myxomatosis, has brought about a very big drop in rabbit numbers over wide areas where the Spanish Imperial Eagle is found. Although there are still no accurate quantifiable data available on the magnitude of the rabbit decline, studies in Doñana and Navarra indicate a decrease of around 80%. The reduction in the number of breeding Spanish Imperial Eagles recorded in a 1989 census appears to be related to the decline in rabbits.

The number of brood reduction cases was greater in habitats with few rabbits than in those with plenty of rabbits. In 19.5% of cases the loss of two chicks from the same nest due to sibling aggression was recorded (80% of those cases were in areas with low rabbit densities). In the light of the recent drop in rabbit numbers, it is to be expected that sibling aggression will increase in future.

In recent years there have been cases of young fledglings found dead or dying, and analyses have revealed that they were in an advanced state of malnutrition associated with several infectious diseases. In some cases, the adults were present in the territory but did not feed the chicks, causing the chick to become independent earlier than normal. The possibility of a link between this abnormal behaviour and the recent fall in rabbit numbers due to viral pneumonia in the territories of these pairs has not been ruled out.

Importance: high

Illegal shooting

Of 112 birds found dead or wounded over the last 30 years, 35% had been shot. Nevertheless, it is thought that the numbers shot have fallen considerably in recent years.

Importance: medium

Human disturbance

Every year a certain number of breeding failures are recorded due to disturbance by people near the nest or forestry work going on nearby during incubation, and it is to be expected that further such failures go undetected. This is probably one of the main reasons for the low breeding success of some populations such as those in the Sierra de Guadarrama and in oakwoods south-east of Madrid.

Importance: medium

Chemical contamination

Infertile Spanish Imperial Eagle eggs that have been analysed to date contain a wide range of chemical pollutants, especially heavy metals (copper, zinc, mercury, lead and cadmium) and organochlorine compounds (DDT, DDE, aldrin, dieldrin, HCHs and PCBs). Comparison of eggshells from the last century with recent ones, and fertile and infertile eggs, revealed that shell thickness has decreased by 12.6% in the first comparison and the degree of shell crystallisation has decreased in both. This is associated with the presence of abnormal quantities of chlorine, potassium, magnesium and copper, as well as the increase in the percentage of phosphorous and sulphur in the shells of recent eggs, a large increase in the amount of phosphorous in the egg contents and a deficiency in the degree of crystallisation in infertile eggs. This all indicates that the shells of contaminated eggs are more fragile and breakable, and there are more often deformities that make the egg unviable. Some pairs in Doñana, Extremadura and Guadarrama had contamination levels that were high enough to lead to breeding failure. However, the levels of these products that have been detected so far are not high enough to have a significant effect, and a decrease in levels has even been recorded in recent years.

Importance: medium

Lead intoxication

In studies of raptors that feed on aquatic birds, lead shot has quite often been found in their digestive systems as a result of eating prey which had been wounded or killed by it. Lead shot also appeared in 4.4% of Spanish Imperial Eagle pellets in Doñana, and one live specimen that was rescued could not fly and was a very obvious clinical case of lead poisoning (M. Hernandez, pers. comm.). It is likely that the species is suffering from lead poisoning from unknown causes.

Importance: medium

Nest collapse

Some pairs that seek to nest in the highest branches, or use unstable branches simply because they are the only ones available, select flimsy trees such as Eucalyptus and poplar Populus in which their nests easily overturn or collapse in high winds. The collapse of the whole or part of a nest has been the cause of 45% of chick deaths in some years (Cadenas, 1995; L. García, pers. comm., 1994; J. Oria pers. comm., 1994).

Importance: low

Nest robbing

All the chicks in a nest may be lost (total brood loss) or partial brood reduction may occur. There are few cases of total brood loss (4.9%), which are caused by people robbing the nest or by the nest falling. Partial brood loss is much more frequent and occurred in 55.7% of monitored breeding attempts, representing the loss of 26.2% of chicks that hatched in broods of more than one (González, 1991).

Importance: low

Conservation status and recent conservation measures

Since 1987, DGN and the Madrid, Castilla-León, Castilla La Mancha, Extremadura and Andalucía regional governments have been implementing a co-ordinated plan of action for Imperial Eagle conservation which, in general terms, consists of the monitoring and the carrying out of a census of the nesting population, identification of limiting factors and causes of mortality, the promotion of measures to improve the status of the species and the co-ordination of the bodies and groups involved in its study and conservation. The main measures are as follows.

Legal measures

The Spanish Imperial Eagle was classified as Endangered in Royal Decree 439/90, and it is thus obligatory to prepare recovery plans for it at regional level. Royal Decree 873/90 allows non-governmental organisations to participate in conservation work as beneficiaries of state grants. The European Union's Habitats Directive includes the Spanish Imperial Eagle as a priority species and identifies a large part of its habitat as of special interest.

As a complementary measure to this legislation the regional governments have drawn up a series of regional laws that have benefited the Spanish Imperial Eagle, especially Law 2/91 on the protection of wildlife in the Madrid region, the law on the protection of vegetation cover in Castilla-La Mancha, the law that approves the list of protected areas in Andalucía, the Law on the Dehesa of Extremadura, Decree 45/91 on the protection of ecosystems in Extremadura, the rules for promoting prey availability in Castilla-León, etc.

The Andalusian Regional Government passed Decree 194/90 to protect birds from high-voltage electrical installations with non-insulated conductors in protected natural areas. The Extremadura and Madrid regional governments passed a law and a decree making any kind of powerline subject to an environmental impact survey.

Between September 1992 and December 1995 habitat leasing, food restocking and powerline isolation have been supported by LIFE funds.

The passing of legislation forbidding or regulating the use of certain organochlorine and organophosphate products in agricultural treatments (Ministerial Order of 1975 and European Union directives) has helped a great deal in reducing the use of these pollutants.

Surveys and monitoring

To date, four national censuses have been carried out: between 1971 and 1974 (Garzón, 1972, 1974), in 1986 (González et al., 1987), in 1989

(González, 1991) and in 1994 (DGN/CCAA, 1995). The central and regional governments are responsible for co-ordinating and conducting these censuses. The information is centralised in DGN's Wildlife Service.

Habitat protection

About 33% of the total nesting population is found in the 10 protected natural areas (Doñana National Park, Cuenca Alta del Manzanares Regional Park, Entorno de Doñana, Cabañeros, Monfragüe, Cardeña-Montoro, Sierra Norte de Sevilla, Despeñaperros, Hornachuelos and Andújar Natural Parks), a National Heritage Site (Monte del Pardo) and a DGN site (Pinar de Valsaín). All these areas have been declared Special Protection Areas (SPAs). In addition, eight other areas have been designated as SPAs, although they are still not protected by additional measures. There are, therefore, 20 areas protected by law containing 78 nesting pairs or 62% of the total breeding population.

The Spanish Imperial Eagle is one of the species included as dependent on agricultural habitats (wood-pasture systems) in the European Agricultural Habitats Conservation Strategy currently being prepared by BirdLife International (Tucker et al., in press).

Reduction of mortality by electrocution

Identification and modification of powerlines. At present the powerlines that cause deaths, or the potentially dangerous ones crossing home ranges and dispersal zones, are being identified and modified, either by installing dome supports or by insulating cables. This work has already been completed in Madrid, Avila, Segovia, Cáceres, Badajoz, Ciudad Real, Toledo, Cádiz and Sevilla. No deaths have been reported since modifications were carried out.

Repairing nests and installing platforms. Whenever it looks as if a nest is unstable or has fallen, the nest is either reinforced or an artificial platform in the form of a replacement nest is installed. High occupation rates have been achieved in Extremadura, Guadarrama and Doñana (Cadenas, 1995).

Nest surveillance. Since 1989 several nests in Guadarrama and Doñana have been guarded, as they are in areas with many passers-by or are readily visible. Human disturbance and theft have in the past led to lost clutches or broods, but not a single clutch or brood has been lost since monitoring started.

Reduction in chick mortality due to sibling aggression. The technique consists of removing the weakest chick from the nest, building it up for a few days in captivity, and then reintroducing it into another nest with a sibling of similar age and at a similar stage of development. Since 1983 the deaths of at least 25 chicks have been avoided using this method (González et al., 1989a, J. Oria, pers. comm., 1994).

Supplementary feeding. Every year, live or dead prey (mainly rabbits and wildfowl) are provided at feeding stations for pairs that often have problems with sibling aggression or whose young suffer nutritional deficiencies. In this way, the deaths of quite a number of chicks and fledglings have been avoided in Doñana (Cadenas, 1995) and Guadarrama (J. Oria, pers. comm., 1994). Also, in recent years, and in order to improve the availability of natural food for some pairs, experimental restocking with rabbits in the home ranges of breeding pairs in the Sierra de San Pedro, Monfragüe, Guadarrama and Gredos has been carried out by providing protected burrows or by setting up release enclosures (Aparicio, pers. comm., 1994).

Radiotracking juveniles. Since 1984 in Doñana (González et al., 1985; Ferrer, 1992; Cadenas, 1995) and since 1990 in the centre of Spain (J. Oria, pers. comm., 1994), juveniles have been tagged and tracked using radiotransmitters in order to find out about their dispersal routes, temporary dispersal zones, survival and causes of death.

Captive breeding. There are at present two Spanish Imperial Eagle captive breeding centres in operation, one at the Quintos de Mora estate (Toledo) and the other in Sevilleja de la Jara (Toledo). At present there are about 20 pairs in captivity.

Awareness-raising and publicity. Several articles, photographic spreads, a leaflet, posters and calendars, etc., concerning the Spanish Imperial Eagle have been published.

Aims and objectives

Aims

To increase the population and distributional range of the Spanish Imperial Eagle to a degree that will allow its reclassification as a species that is not threatened.

Objectives

1. **Policy and legislation**

1.1. *To improve habitat quality*

1.1.1. The habitat requirements of the Spanish Imperial Eagle should be included in management and utilisation plans for natural protected areas, forestry and agriculture, in management plans for protected areas, public utility land or countryside administered by the state, and in the natural resource management plans
Priority: medium
Time-scale: medium/ongoing

1.1.2. Promote the regeneration of forest cover with native species, especially holm oak, cork oak and stone pine, within the eagle's distributional range where the local ecology, soil and climate are suitable
Priority: medium
Time-scale: long

1.1.3. Prepare an environmental impact assessment for any work or project that might alter or have a negative effect on the Spanish Imperial Eagle or its habitat in the nesting, dispersal and recolonisation areas
Priority: high
Time-scale: short/ongoing

1.1.4. Establish agreements with private landowners on whose land the Spanish Imperial Eagle occurs in order to advise on habitat management; include non-monetary compensation and improvements for proper-

ties that co-operate in protecting the species
Priority: medium
Time-scale: medium

1.2. *Establish, where possible, spatial and temporal restrictions on rabbit hunting*

These measures would facilitate the recovery of rabbit populations that have been most affected by disease, and promote the spread of immune individuals. There should be designation of close season orders or complementary legal measures and of areas where rabbit hunting is restricted or prohibited except as permitted by law. Restocking and other measures that will boost prey numbers should be subsidised (for example, the Order of 20 May of the Castilla-León regional government), conditioned by the close season in restocked zones.
Priority: high
Time-scale: short

1.3. *Modify technical regulations concerning the installation of high-voltage powerlines*

The measures noted under 2.6.2 need to be introduced into Regulation 3115/68 of the Ministry of Industry and Energy. Moreover, new powerlines should avoid breeding areas and dispersal and recolonisation zones. The electricity companies will be provided with the necessary information and guidance.
Priority: high
Time-scale: short

1.4. *Restrict quarrying and rural activities near nests*

Concessions and permits for agriculture, forestry work, collection of firewood, cork or pine cones, etc., will include clauses expressly giving those responsible for Spanish Imperial Eagle conservation the power to exclude the aforementioned safety zones from said concessions between February and July with the possibility of compensating those affected if it is deemed necessary. In general, it is advisable that any activity that may disturb the normal progress of the eagles' breeding be prevented or interrupted.

Priority: high
Time-scale: short/ongoing

2. Species and habitat protection

2.1. *To increase habitat availability*

2.1.1. Maintain a suitable area of protected habitat for the species – including nesting, dispersal and recolonisation areas – in order to improve the quality of the habitat through appropriate management
Priority: essential
Time-scale: short/ongoing

2.1.2. Include in the network of protected natural areas all known nesting sites and draw up natural resource management plans in accordance with Law 4/89
Priority: high
Time-scale: short/ongoing

2.1.3. Establish suitable conservation regimes and implement natural resource management (Law 4/89) in the juvenile dispersal and recolonisation areas
Priority: medium
Time-scale: medium

2.1.4. Regional administrations should acquire (or rent) and consolidate property in the most important Spanish Imperial Eagle areas
Priority: medium
Time-scale: medium

2.2. *To reduce mortality due to hunting activities*

The measures centre on reducing mortality, especially in the provinces of Madrid, Toledo, Ciudad Real, Huelva, Sevilla and Cádiz, and specifically in the districts where there are many Hunting Reserves devoted to the exploitation of game species.

2.2.1. Strict application of hunting legislation

The deliberate killing of a Spanish Imperial Eagle is considered a serious offence under Law 4/89. It is necessary to apply the sanctions laid down in national and regional legislation as rigorously as possible on those who kill eagles (private wardens, pest-control officers, hunters) as well as on those who encourage this shooting.

Priority: high
Time-scale: short/ongoing

2.2.2. Withdraw the reserve licence in areas where dead eagles are found

Article 48 of the Hunting Law (Decree 506/71) includes provision for annulment of the declaration of reserve status when species in a Hunting Reserve are not exploited in a correct manner, or when the conservation and hunting plans are not respected.

The relevant authorities must require that holders of hunting rights and lessees of Hunting Reserves which include Spanish Imperial Eagle nesting and dispersal areas have a scientifically correct technical plan for hunting exploitation. This plan must include a section about the protected species in the reserve, expressing a formal commitment to conserve them as well as to make known immediately anything that could negatively affect them.

If a Spanish Imperial Eagle is shot dead in the common hunting areas, hunting should be banned temporarily and the area declared a regulated hunting zone as an interim measure.

Priority: high
Time-scale: short/ongoing

2.2.3. Death from poisoning

In areas where it is suspected or proved that poison has been put down to control predators the same measures as in 1.2.2 should be taken. If the use of poison is proven, health legislation must be applied to forbid the consumption or commercial exploitation of game from the area where poison was used.

Priority: high
Time-scale: short/ongoing

2.2.4. Deaths in traps

In areas where it is suspected or proven that traps have been illegally set, the same measures as in 1.2.2 should be taken. Similarly, no exceptions should be made to those in Article 28 of Law 4/89 in the nesting and juvenile dispersal zones.

Priority: medium
Time-scale: short/ongoing

2.2.5. Surveillance in Hunting Reserves

Most deaths of juveniles from shooting or poisoning occur in dispersal areas. In Hunting Reserves the dates of these offences usually coincide with the close season so it is essential that surveillance be increased in those reserves, especially at times of year when peak numbers of eagles are present.

Priority: medium
Time-scale: short/ongoing

2.3. *To improve food availability for the species throughout the year*

The measures planned within this objective would have a positive effect on the Spanish Imperial Eagle population in the medium and long term. An increase in food availability would improve the chances of success in any recolonisation of potential areas and would increase the survival chances of the sub-adult population.

2.3.1. Increase rabbit numbers

Rabbit populations need to be boosted efficiently and quickly, at least up to a level that will serve to sustain the number of eagles that the plan seeks to achieve.

Priority: high
Time-scale: short/medium

2.3.2. Restock areas with rabbits where there has been a decline in their numbers and evidence of a decrease in the breeding success of the Spanish Imperial Eagle

This should be a priority action for populations in the north of the Sierra de Guadarrama, Gredos, and in some parts of Sierra de San Pedro, Monfragüe, Sierra Morena and Doñana. A vaccine test programme must be designed and oriented towards the criteria for restocking with rabbits that are resistant to diseases.

Priority: high
Time-scale: short/medium

2.4. *To increase the annual productivity of the population*

The aim of the actions below is to stop the downward trend in productivity and return to normal population breeding performance via an increase in the number of productive pairs to 80%, in order to ensure a hatching rate of 70% and a fledging rate of 1.3 young per occupied nest and 1.7 per successful nest.

2.4.1. Reinforce and prop-up precarious nests

Unstable nests must be secured using supports both for the tree and for the nest itself. In exceptional cases newly constructed nests could be treated in the same way, but always before the nest is completely finished.

Priority: medium
Time-scale: short/ongoing

2.4.2. Install artificial nests

In nesting areas or the territories of established pairs where there is no suitable natural support, or to replace insecure nests in unfavourable areas, artificial nests on suitable supports should be installed so that there is no risk of collapse.

Priority: medium
Time-scale: short/ongoing

2.4.3. Reduce chick mortality in the nest

When chicks in the same nest are known to be very different in age and size, and it is suspected that one may die due to aggression by siblings, it is advisable to avoid death by all means available. Food should be provided at the nest site, and if the chick has wounds or is badly malnourished or underdeveloped it should be removed from the nest to be treated under veterinary control so that, once recovered, it can be returned to the wild.

Priority: medium
Time-scale: medium

2.4.4. Return chicks to the wild

Once in a good physical state, chicks taken temporarily from the nest, and others from elsewhere (captive-bred, stolen, victims of falls, etc.), must be returned to the wild, preferably to the original nest or another nearby. If this is not possible:
• Chicks that are completely feathered and fully capable of flight should be reintroduced into family groups with fledglings that have just reached the independent phase.
• In other cases, the technique of "hacking" should be used in suitable recolonisation areas.

Priority: high
Time-scale: ongoing

2.4.5. Provide supplementary feeding when appropriate

Supplementary feeding should be implemented when there is evidence of retarded development, risk of sibling aggression, malformations, etc., that indicate deficient feeding. The following techniques are recommended.
• Provide prey by placing it in the usual hunting area, on perching places or directly in the nest.
• The provision of rabbit burrows and the setting up of artificial enclosed feeding stations stocked with rabbits in the eagles' hunting area. At the same time, the feeding stations will serve as a restocking focus for the area. The station must be kept under surveillance and the rabbits provided with food and water.

Priority: medium
Time-scale: short/ongoing

2.4.6. Eliminate human disturbance in the breeding season

As a general rule, access will be restricted (including closure of tracks and paths as necessary) within a suitable radius known as a "safety zone" that will vary according to the characteristics of the land near each nest; 300 to 500 metres is recommended.

Priority: high
Time-scale: short/ongoing

2.4.7. Restrictions on movement near nests

All roads open to vehicles and people (whatever the reason for travel) in Spanish Imperial Eagle safety zones will be cut and signposted so that they are used only under strict supervision. As a general rule, it is advisable that as many roads as possible are closed to through traffic within the safety zone.

Priority: medium
Time-scale: short/ongoing

2.4.8. Nest surveillance

Surveillance can be carried out in two ways.
• General surveillance: by the wardening staff of each area.
• Individual surveillance: where necessary, due to poor siting of a nest. If it cannot be covered by wardening staff, nature conservation organisations can be called upon to organise nest surveillance campaigns.

Priority: medium
Time-scale: short/ongoing

2.5. *To increase breeding success artificially*

Should captive-reared chicks be available, they can be used to strengthen the productivity of pairs and populations where the IUCN criteria for reintroductions are met (Kleiman et al., 1994). Their reintroduction to the wild should be carried out as follows.
• Unfledged chicks should be placed in nests which are unsuccessful due to hatching failure or negligence in chick care. Special care should be taken to do it as quickly as possible, without increasing the size of the normal brood. The outcome should be monitored closely.
• Should fledglings be available (captive-bred or accident victims) they should be introduced into a family group.

Priority: medium
Time-scale: medium/ongoing

2.6. *To reduce the number of deaths from electrocution*

Fatal accidents due to electrocution are frequent, especially among juveniles and immature birds. Particular types of pylon are more dangerous than others: information is easily available on anti-electrocution measures and modifications, some of which are easy to apply and inexpensive.

2.6.1. Location, description and upgrading of powerlines that are potentially dangerous or have been proven to cause deaths

There will be periodic surveys of the lines that cross the eagle's distribution area, and especially the juvenile dispersion zones in order to locate pylons that cause deaths or are potentially dangerous. This information will be supplied to the relevant bodies so that anti-electrocution measures can be applied.

Priority: high
Time-scale: short/ongoing

2.6.2. Apply corrective measures to pylons

In the absence of better solutions, technically possible corrective anti-electrocution measures will be applied to existing lines and to those under construction. The following measures are recommended, in order of priority.

1. In no case should rigid insulators on the crosspiece on supports be installed. This does not include insulating crosspieces. Chains of insulators should always be used.
2. Uninsulated free bridges over struts and post heads should not be installed.
3. In exposed transformers, the crossbridge between the conductor and the transformer should be made with insulated cable and connected via devices that have been proved effective in insulating and preventing electrocution.
4. Exposed switches should not be installed in a horizontal position on top of the supports.
5. The alignment supports must meet the following minimum safety access distances: 0.75 metres between conductor and perch on the crosspiece; 1.5 metres between conductors.
6. The anchor, angle, line end and, generally, all those supports with a chain of horizontal insulators must have a minimum safety access distance of 1 metre between the perching zone and the conductor.
7. Quincunxes or "Canadian" type supports should be used in preference to any other kind of overhead post with exposed conductors for lines with nominal voltages equal to or lower than 36 kV.

Priority: essential
Time-scale: short/medium

2.7. *Extension of the current distribution area*

Based on available knowledge of the historical distribution of the species and its habitat requirements, certain areas where recolonisation would be possible can be delimited. The establishment of new breeding areas would facilitate genetic exchange between subpopulations.

2.7.1. Inventory and mapping of potential recolonisation areas

All the possible recolonisation areas need to be identified before any juveniles can be released.

The information could be compared with or complemented by ground surveys to check the current status of these populations and draw up a list of possible areas with details about their conservation status.

Priority: low
Time-scale: long

2.8. *Captive breeding programme*

In the event of a natural catastrophe or disease bringing population levels dangerously low, it is necessary to have access to a captive-breeding stock to provide for reintroduction or population-boosting projects.

Priority: medium
Time-scale: medium

3.   Monitoring and research

3.1. *Monitoring*

3.1.1. Annual surveys of the breeding population

There is a fundamental need for continuous monitoring of the size and distribution of the population in order to establish the population trends and problems and to evaluate the effectiveness of conservation measures adopted. To do this, it is advisable that every year a survey be done on as many territories as possible to identify pairs during the breeding season. When censuses are carried out, areas where new pairs are suspected and where potential habitat exists should be surveyed. It is advisable to do a national census every four years.

Priority: high
Time-scale: ongoing

3.1.2. Monitor breeding

It is recommended that regular monitoring of breeding pairs be carried out in order to check that nesting is progressing well and to detect any threats to breeding success.

Priority: medium
Time-scale: ongoing

3.1.3. Tag juveniles

It is advisable that, where possible, radio or satellite transmitters be fitted to chicks and juveniles for management and research purposes including those subject to the supplementary feeding programme. It is also important to use radio-telemetry to monitor juveniles that have been reintroduced to the wild in order to confirm success or to rescue the birds in the event of failure.

Priority: medium
Time-scale: medium/ongoing

3.1.4. Monitor tagged individuals

Radiotracking of tagged birds provides useful information on dispersal, mortality and conservation problems in both juveniles and adults, and this work should therefore continue, collecting further information from areas already studied and looking for new dispersal areas.

Priority: high
Time-scale: ongoing

3.1.5. Monitor levels of chemical pollutants in eggs

As part of the monitoring of breeding, unhatched eggs will be removed for analysis for organochlorines and heavy metals in both the shell and egg contents.

Priority: medium
Time-scale: ongoing

3.1.6. Survey and monitor supplementary feeding

Nests involved in the supplementary feeding programme should be constantly and rigorously monitored to check that all is well and to obtain information with a view to future improvement.

Priority: low
Time-scale: ongoing

3.1.7. Monitor deaths on powerlines

It is recommended that modified powerlines be checked periodically, particularly in nesting, dispersal and recolonisation areas.

Priority: medium
Time-scale: ongoing

3.1.8. Monitor the use of poisons

In order to detect and confirm the use of poisons in the countryside, any live birds, corpses or remains showing symptoms or signs of poisoning must be subjected to toxicological analysis and the origin and causes of the poisoning should be monitored.

Priority: high
Time-scale: short/ongoing

3.2. *Research*

3.2.1. Use of space and energy budgets of breeding adults

Knowledge of the home range, hunting areas, etc., is necessary in order to decide how much land needs to be protected. The mechanisms regulating population density and requirements for settlement of new pairs in potential habitats are also important. Similarly, the energy requirement of breeding birds needs to be investigated: the number of chicks that can be produced, the cost to the adults and the amount of food required.

Priority: medium
Time-scale: medium

3.2.2. Juvenile dispersal

It is necessary to improve knowledge of the ecology of juvenile dispersal (feeding, movements, use of space, intra- and inter-specific relationships, etc.), as well as establishing dispersal movements for populations not yet studied.

Priority: medium
Time-scale: medium

3.2.3. Pair formation and population renewal

Factors involved in the formation of new pairs and the integration of immatures into the population are unknown and need to be investigated in order to evaluate the mechanisms regulating populations and to establish the minimum population size needed to ensure that the species is out of danger.

Priority: low
Time-scale: long

3.2.4. Design of harmless electricity pylons

Technical solutions for modifying pylons are largely complete, but their variety means that it would be better to design a new type of pylon which would be economical for electricity companies and safe for birds.

Priority: high
Time-scale: short

3.2.5. Techniques and methods for rabbit restocking

Few attempts at restocking have been made, so there is little information on methods, and the results have not been properly evaluated. An experimental study would serve as a method-ological guide and help to make restocking finan-cially viable.

Priority: high
Time-scale: short

3.2.6. Chemical contamination of eggs

More needs to be known about the effects of organochlorines, phosphates and heavy metals used in agriculture, on the shell and contents of unhatched eggs. This would permit a more accu-rate idea of the extent to which these products affect infertility in some pairs. It would be worth-while also to monitor the levels of chemical pol-lutants in Spanish Imperial Eagle habitats.

Priority: medium
Time-scale: medium

3.2.7. Identification, mapping and updating of the inventory of nesting, dispersal and recoloni-sation areas

It is recommended that the existing inventory be updated with suitable maps of all the nesting, dis-persal and recolonisation areas compiled from information provided by the yearly monitoring and national censuses.

Priority: low
Time-scale: short/medium

3.2.8. Determine the population size which is necessary to remove the species from the list of threatened birds

Nowadays, the concept of minimum viable popu-lation is used as an important parameter in designing management plans for threatened species. Knowing this parameter for the Spanish Imperial Eagle population, including geographic, demographic, and genetic variables, would be very useful in establishing more accurately the main aim of the recovery plans and finding out how close the objectives come to achieving it.

Priority: low
Time-scale: medium/long

4. Public awareness and training

4.1. *To increase the level of information and awareness among the public*

All the above-mentioned measures will only achieve maximum efficacy when there is a suffi-cient level of awareness at all social levels involved.

4.1.1. Initiate awareness-raising and publicity cam-paigns

These campaigns must consist of two separate and complementary phases. The first is aimed at rural schoolchildren, the second at the general public and large centres of population in the provinces, with special emphasis on those sectors most directly concerned with Spanish Imperial Eagle problems (hunters, electricity companies, landowners and managers of Hunting Reserves, forestry representatives, the Civil Guard, conser-vation organisations, judges, taxidermists and administrative organisations responsible for moni-toring poisonous and toxic products). The public should be made aware of the importance of modifying electricity pylons so that they under-stand the need for power cuts.

Priority: medium
Time-scale: medium/ongoing

4.1.2. Prepare educational materials

These would include educational and interpretive notebooks that cover activities related to the biology, management and conservation problems of the Spanish Imperial Eagle. In this way, it is hoped that the public will come to know better the species and its importance; also that the pub-lic will be encouraged to participate actively by offering them the necessary resources and tools. There would also be talks, lectures, round tables and film shows.

Priority: medium
Time-scale: medium/ongoing

4.1.3. Travelling exhibition

This would tour within the geographical range of the Spanish Imperial Eagle and would deal with the species' past, present and future. A comple-mentary edition of a general informative and educational leaflet would also be published with the aim of letting people know about the different aspects of the species, making them aware of its importance and problems and encouraging them to participate in the groups most involved in its conservation.

Priority: low
Time-scale: medium/long

Annex
Recommended conservation actions by country

Morocco

3.1.1. Carry out an exhaustive census of the species.

Portugal

2.4.5. Restore rabbit populations.

2.7.   Initiate viability studies with a view to possible reintroductions.

2.7.1. Identify potential areas for recolonisation.

3.1.1. Carry out an exhaustive census of the species.

Spain

All the objectives listed under "Aims and objectives" can be considered as actions relevant to Spain.

International action plan for the Lesser Kestrel (*Falco naumanni*)

Reviews

This action plan should be reviewed and updated by BirdLife International every five years. An emergency review will be undertaken if sudden major environmental changes, liable to affect the population, occur within the species' range.

Geographical scope

This action plan needs implementation in Albania, Algeria, Armenia, Azerbaijan, Bosnia-Herzegovina, Bulgaria, Croatia, Cyprus, Czech Republic, Egypt, the Federal Rebublic of Yugoslavia (Serbia and Montenegro), France, Greece, Hungary, Iran, Iraq, Israel, Italy, Jordan, Kazakhstan, Lebanon, Libya, Moldova, Morocco, Oman, Poland, Portugal, Romania, Saudi Arabia, Slovakia, Slovenia, Spain, Syria, the former Yugoslav Republic of Macedonia, Tunisia, Turkey, Ukraine, Uzbekhistan and Yemen. During migration and winter, most African countries – notably South Africa where large numbers winter – are visited by the Lesser Kestrel, and parts of the action plan will also need implementation in the Afro-tropics.

Summary

The Lesser Kestrel *Falco naumanni* is a globally threatened species classified as Vulnerable by Collar et al. (1994). It has shown major population declines in large parts of its western Palaearctic breeding range and has disappeared from several countries where it bred until recently. The western Palaearctic population (Europe and North Africa) was estimated to be between 10 000 and 17 000 pairs in 1994 (Biber, 1994).

In many countries, data on Lesser Kestrel breeding populations are still deficient. Our knowledge of the species' ecology also shows some gaps (e.g. maximum distances of foraging grounds from breeding colonies). In particular, a comprehensive understanding of the migration routes of different breeding populations and their wintering grounds is still lacking. Knowledge of the species' migration and winter ecology and of possible threats in Africa is incomplete.

Threats and limiting factors

Habitat loss in breeding areas – critical

Reduction in the availability of prey due to pesticide use – critical

Habitat loss in winter quarters and stopover sites – unknown

Loss of nest sites – low/medium

Interspecific competition – low/medium

Pesticide toxicity – low

Human persecution and disturbance – low

Conservation priorities

Promote appropriate agricultural policy including low-density grazing, low use of fertilizers and suitable cultivation practices – high/critical

Promote a zoned forestry policy – high

Encourage full legal protection for Lesser Kestrel and the designation of protected areas – high

Promote the production of a national species action plan – high

Protect colonies from accidental and deliberate disturbance – high

Development of standard survey methodology and surveys to identify important areas – high

Research into limiting factors and appropriate habitat management – high

Introduction

Since the 1960s, populations of the Lesser Kestrel *Falco naumanni* throughout the western Palaearctic have declined dramatically. This decline may be attributed to a number of factors including restoration and demolition of older buildings (reducing nest site availability), the urbanisation of formerly open areas (destroying important feeding areas) and intensification of agricultural practices (loss of feeding sites and a reduction in prey availability). These factors have led to similar declines in the populations of a number of insectivorous bird species, such as the Hobby Falco subbuteo, Great Bustard Otis tarda, Little Owl Athene noctua, Roller Coracias garrulus and others. Other threats to the Lesser Kestrel include poisoning by pesticides, human persecution and interspecific competition.

The Lesser Kestrel is a globally threatened species listed as Vulnerable by Collar et al., (1994). It is included in Annex I of the European Union's Wild Birds Directive, Appendix II of the Bern Convention, Appendix II of the Bonn Convention, Appendix II of CITES and Annex B of the African Convention on the Conservation of Nature and Natural Resources.

A first action plan for the Lesser Kestrel was compiled in 1990 (Biber, 1990) on behalf of the Commission of the European Communities and the International Council for Bird Preservation (now BirdLife International). Three workshops have been held so far to identify priority actions necessary for the conservation of the Lesser Kestrel: 7 September 1991, Canterbury, UK; 14 May 1992, Berlin, Germany; 20 September 1994, Palma de Mallorca, Spain. They were all attended by people from most of the main range states. The last of these, which set the basis for this action plan, was attended by 20 people from 10 range states.

Background information

Distribution

Breeding range

The Lesser Kestrel has a Palaearctic breeding distribution, south of 55°N. It breeds from the Iberian peninsula east to Afghanistan, Mongolia and north-east China. In Europe it breeds in Albania, Armenia, Azerbaijan, Bosnia-Herzegovina, Bulgaria, Croatia, France, Georgia, Greece, Italy, Kazakhstan, Moldova, Portugal, Romania, Russia, Slovenia, Spain, Turkey and Ukraine (Biber, 1994). In North Africa, it breeds in Algeria, Morocco, Tunisia and occasionally in Egypt. In the Middle East, the breeding range includes Afghanistan, Iran, Iraq, Israel, Jordan and Syria (Evans, 1994).

Winter range

The bulk of the western Palaearctic population winters in Africa south of the Sahara, excluding the Congo basin and Cameroon (Louette, 1981). However, a proportion of adults winter in southern Spain (Negro et al., 1991), southern Turkey and north-west Africa (Cade, 1982; Bergier, 1987). The number of birds wintering in Spain appears to depend upon the availability of food, which is in turn dependent upon climatic factors (Negro et al., 1991).

Information on wintering numbers in west Africa is limited, but it is possible that this region holds lower densities than other African winter quarters (Moreau, 1972; Cade, 1982). However, J. M. Thiollay (verbally, 1992) believes that the species has never been looked for in this region, and that numbers could in fact be higher.

In eastern Africa, Lesser Kestrels winter from Ethiopia (Moreau, 1972) and possibly Somalia (Ash and Miskell, 1983), south to South Africa, with large numbers occurring in the highlands of western and central Kenya and in the less arid parts of eastern Kenya and northern Tanzania. The main wintering areas lie from Zimbabwe south to Botswana and, especially, South Africa (Cade, 1982).

Population

Cade (1982) estimated the world breeding population of the Lesser Kestrel to be 650000 to 800000 pairs. The European population is now estimated at only 15000 to 20000 pairs, and all west Palaearctic breeding populations for which data are available have declined during the last 30 years, some dramatically. Population data for Turkey and the former Soviet Union are very sparse.

Table 12.1

Population status of the Lesser Kestrel *Falco naumanni* in Europe and North Africa. Countries listed are those where breeding has been recorded in recent years (unconfirmed for those countries in brackets). The figure for Turkey covers central Anatolia only. Based on Biber (1994) and on information gathered at the workshop in Palma de Mallorca. Figure for Georgia from Abuladze (1994)

Country	Breeding pairs	Year
Albania	100–1000	1994
Bulgaria	57–100	1994
Croatia	(5–10)	1994
France	31–33	1994
Georgia	700	1994
Greece	2700–3240	1994-95
Italy	1300–1500	1994
Moldova	7–12	1989
Morocco	1000–1000	1990
Portugal	150–150	1994
Romania	120–130	1989
Russian Federation	(70–150)	1994
Slovenia	5–10	1994
Spain	8000–8000	1994
Tunisia	100–100	1994
Turkey	1500–3500	1994
Ukraine	(200–300)	1994
Total	15045–19935	

Life history

Breeding

The Lesser Kestrel normally breeds in colonies in walls or roofs of old houses, stables, barns, castles or churches; also in tree holes, earth cliffs and in rocks, quarries or heaps of stones. Breeding occurs within and outside cities, but often in the vicinity of human settlements (González et al., 1990). With the decline of the species, small colonies of fewer than 10 pairs, and single pairs, have become more and more common. There are also mixed colonies, with Jackdaws *Corvus monedula*, and less frequently with Kestrels *F. tinnunculus*. Lesser Kestrels are monogamous, and the male and female take an equal share in incubation and feeding the young. Clutch size is 2 to 8, usually 3 to 5. Some breeding sites are abandoned by late July, and most by mid-August. Lesser Kestrels are gregarious all year; they migrate and winter in flocks and roost communally in single trees or groups of trees.

Feeding

The main food consists of invertebrates, chiefly large Orthoptera: field-crickets (Gryllidae), grasshoppers (Acrididae), bush-crickets (Tettigoniidae), mole-crickets (Gryllotalpidae) and beetles (Coleoptera). At some locations small lizards may form an important part of the diet (Cheylan, 1991; Parr and Naveso, 1994), though small mammals and birds are only rarely taken. In winter the Lesser Kestrel relies largely on swarms of locusts, mainly the large gregarious *Shistocerca* and *Locusta* species where available, and flying termites (Isoptera) (Brown and Amadon, 1968). During breeding, as well as in winter, the Lesser Kestrel requires high densities of available prey concentrated in small areas.

Habitat requirements

Throughout its range, the Lesser Kestrel occurs in open areas, avoiding closed forest, wetlands and farmland with tall crops. In the western Palaearctic it is found in continental and forest steppes and semi-deserts at up to 500 metres, primarily within the Mediterranean zone (Cade, 1982). In these areas it forages in meadows, pastures, steppe-like habitats, non-intensively cultivated land and occasionally in scrub (garrigue) and open woodland. It prefers warm or hot areas with short vegetation and patches of bare ground where it can easily find its prey.

In southern Spain the Lesser Kestrel forages in areas of non-intensive herbaceous dry cultures, avoiding areas with scrub and trees (Donázar et al., 1994). In its North African breeding areas and in its winter quarters, it forages in savanna, steppe and thornbush vegetation, and on open grassland or farmland (sorghum, peanut, wheat and bean crops).

Threats and limiting factors

Habitat loss in the breeding areas

Habitat loss through urbanisation and modification of agricultural practices has reduced the availability of food and forced Lesser Kestrels to abandon many traditional colony sites (González et al., 1990; Donázar et al., 1993). Pasture grasslands and non-intensively cultivated farmland with fallows are threatened by agricultural policies in Europe; grassland is being converted into intensively cultivated farmland (e.g. sunflowers in Spain or maize in Bulgaria), while non-intensively farmed areas are losing their uncultivated patches. Irrigation schemes and the disappearance of formerly traditional culture rotation have serious effects on the Lesser Kestrel's habitat. The abandonment of agricultural land causes habitat loss through the growth of scrub and trees. Afforestation on agricultural land can also lead to loss of habitat.

In the last 30 years, the number of sheep grazing in La Crau (southern France) has halved. As a consequence vegetation grows higher and more densely, with a detrimental effect on Orthoptera populations. Overgrazing is also known to have damaging consequences, notably in Italy, Kazakhstan and in eastern Africa.

In North Africa the drought of the early 1980s caused severe habitat deterioration which had negative effects on the Lesser Kestrel. The building of dams has lead to the loss of inundation zones and thus to the destruction of grasslands with the consequent disappearance of food sources.

Importance: critical

Habitat loss in the winter quarters and at stopover sites

The increasing desertification in the Sahel zone since 1968 has caused the loss of large areas of savanna, an important habitat for migrating and wintering Lesser Kestrels. This has been compounded by overgrazing and by increasing human use of the already stressed watertable. Dams and other hydrological works have destroyed large areas of river floodplains (e.g. Senegal and Niger) which are important foraging areas for the Lesser Kestrel as soon as they dry out after the wet season (Ledant et al., 1986).

Locusts which form such an important part of the diet in the west African savannas formerly occurred in large swarms, but have disappeared from many areas, partly because of the destruction of grassland as a consequence of drought and overgrazing, and partly due to heavy pesticide application throughout their range.

Importance: unknown

Loss of nest sites

The most important cause of nest-site loss in man-made structures is the obstruction or destruction of cavities during renovation or demolition. Such action generally results in the colony being deserted or at least a reduction in the number of breeding pairs, both in Europe (Cheylan, 1990; González et al., 1990; Negro and Hiraldo, 1993) and in North Africa. Many old tiled roofs are replaced with flat roofs which no longer provide nest sites. However, recent work by Forero et al. (in prep.) in Andalucía and Aragón (Spain) showed that nest-site cavities were not a scarce resource even in decreasing Lesser Kestrel populations.

Importance: low/medium

Pesticides

The results of a study analysing residues of organochlorines, PCBs and heavy metals in Lesser Kestrel eggs from Spain showed that, although contaminants were detected in all eggs, the levels were generally below those known to have negative effects on reproduction (Negro et al., 1993).

An important consequence of pesticide use is the reduction in prey populations (Palma, 1985; Negro et al., 1993). Decline in invertebrates in

Africa has been attributed to large-scale locust control schemes (J. P. Ledant, pers. comm.).

Importance: direct influence, low;
influence on prey, critical

Interspecific competition

Jackdaws may contribute to colony desertion through disturbance of nesting birds, egg predation and kleptoparasitism of adults feeding young, these having been noted in both Spanish and French colonies (Cheylan, 1990). Competition for nest sites has been demonstrated between Lesser Kestrel and Jackdaw (Hallmann, 1985; Bijlsma et al., 1988; Lucchesi, 1990). However, in Andalucía and Aragón (Spain), the presence of presumed competitors (Jackdaws and feral pigeons) did not limit nest site availability, and breeding success was not lower in colonies with competitors than in colonies without (Forero et al., in prep.). Predation by rats has been noted in Portugal, and was averted in 1995 by more careful siting of artificial nest sites (A. Araújo, pers. comm., 1995).

Importance: low/medium

Human persecution and disturbance

In the Mediterranean, the main direct destruction of Lesser Kestrels by man is for sport (Greece, Italy, Malta, Morocco, Spain), out of tradition (Malta, Spain) and for sale of live or mounted birds (Malta, the former Yugoslavia).

Egg-collecting has been a major problem in Morocco, Portugal, Slovenia and Spain (Andalucía). In Portugal it has been reported that up to 200 eggs have been taken from one colony in a single season (Palma, 1985).

In Russia, Ukraine, Kazakhstan and the Caucasian Republics small colonies are sometimes disturbed by shepherds and tourists (V. Galushin, pers. comm., 1995). In several range states, renovation of historic buildings can also be a source of disturbance.

Importance: low

Conservation status and recent conservation measures

Albania

The population of the Lesser Kestrel in Albania is believed to be between 100 and 1000 pairs (Tucker and Heath, 1994) but little is known of its present status. Surveys and clarification of its legal status and any threats are needed.

Bulgaria

The Lesser Kestrel has been protected under the Hunting Law since 1962 and by the Special Act 342 of 1986 with a fine of US$ 460 for killing a bird plus an additional penalty. It is included in the national Red Data Book (1985) as Endangered. About 10% of the breeding population is located in protected areas (Iankov et al., 1994). During the period 1992 to 1994 some new Lesser Kestrel breeding sites have been included in protected areas.

The BSPB started a complete survey in 1995. A project to provide artificial nest boxes has already started in some regions of the Trakia lowlands and the eastern Rhodopi mountains. The BSPB has been conducting a study on the autumn migration of birds of prey along the Black Sea coast for the past 18 years.

Croatia

The legal status is unknown at the moment. Two of the IBAs where the Lesser Kestrel occurs are National Parks: Nacionalni Park Kornati (IBA 020) and Nacionalni Park Krka (IBA 021), and two are proposed ornithological reserves: Klisura reke Babune i Topolke i Crn Kamen (IBA 050) and Demir kapija (IBA 053) (Grimmett and Jones, 1989).

France

The only breeding area is in the plain of La Crau, east of the Rhône delta. The Lesser Kestrel has been legally protected in France since 1972. It was included in the Red Data Book in 1983 as a species having reached a critical population level.

The population of La Crau is in a specially protected area (11 500 ha), and steps have been undertaken to declare it a Natural Reserve. Agri-environment measures have been taken and 250 ha have been bought by NGOs, the Conservatoire du Littoral and Conseil Général des Bouches du Rhône. The site is being wardened. Artificial nests have been provided in several places, with holes small enough to prevent Jackdaws from entering. The population has been monitored and studied since 1984, and a ringing programme was started in 1994. Relations with landowners are good.

Greece

Breeding occurs mainly in Thessaly, the biggest colony being of 200 pairs. The species is legally protected and included in the Red Data Book (1990) as Vulnerable. It is present in Kalamas Gorge (Thesprotia, IBA 050) and Mount Dirfis and the peaks of Xirovouni, Skotini, Mavrovouni, Alokteri, Ortari and the vicinity of Kimi (Evvia, IBA 071) (Grimmett and Jones, 1989). A full survey involving schoolchildren was carried out in 1994, as well as a study on sexual dimorphism, including ringing. A complete survey of Thessaly in 1995 identified 104 colonies containing 2679 pairs (Hallmann, 1996)

Israel

All birds of prey have been protected since 1955 by the Wild Animal Protection Law. The Lesser Kestrel breeds mainly in the Jordan valley. Prior to 1950 it was the most common breeding bird of prey in Israel, but from the 1960s became extremely rare though remaining a common migrant.

Italy

The Lesser Kestrel has been protected under the hunting law since 1976. Three separate populations can be identified: Sicily (320 pairs, decreasing), Sardinia (c. 100 pairs, decreasing) and Apulia-Basilicata (500–1000 pairs, increasing/fluctuating). LIPU carried out a census in Sicily, Apulia and Basilicata in 1994. With European Union financial support, a census in Sardinia is planned. Artificial nests were provided in Matera (Basilicata) but these have not been successful. New designs are being tested by LIPU in Apulia

and Basilicata. A public awareness campaign has been launched in this area involving local communities. A national action plan has been drafted by LIPU and is being considered for adoption by local authorities in Apulia and Basilicata.

Morocco

The Lesser Kestrel has been legally protected since 1980. There has been a strong decline since the beginning of the century, and this continues.

Portugal

The Lesser Kestrel is legally protected and classified as vulnerable in the Portuguese Red Data Book (1990). Mértola and Castro Verde are the most important areas for the species, with up to 100 pairs. The population is concentrated in two major colonies, Mértola with 60 pairs and Belver with 17 pairs. Productivity in Mértola is causing concern and research into limiting factors at the site is underway. Some juveniles have been colour-ringed. The Belver colony is on land recently purchased by LPN with assistance from the European Union.

Romania

The Lesser Kestrel is legally protected under Law 26/1976, covering all birds of prey. It breeds in one IBA, Padurea Niculitel-Babadag (Tulcea, IBA 002).

Russian Federation

It is proposed that the species be listed as Endangered in the new edition of the Red Data Book. The species is considered a high priority; therefore an action plan and national programme have already been prepared. Restoration of previous nesting areas has been carried out and further work is proposed for 1996. A group of ornithologists are developing a captive breeding plan.

Spain

The Lesser Kestrel is considered to be of "special interest" in the national legislation (Royal Decree 439/90) and it is listed as Vulnerable in the Red Data Book (Blanco and González 1992).

In 1988 and 1989 a national survey was carried out under the co-ordination of ICONA. A comprehensive research programme carried out by the Estación Biológica de Doñana has been going on for several years in Andalucía and Aragón, including population surveys (in Andalucía), limiting factors, foraging habitat selection, nest-site selection, reproductive strategies, breeding success, patterns of winter distribution, organochlorine and heavy metal contamination, etc. These studies have involved colour-ringing and radio-tracking of numerous individuals.

Zonal Programmes under European Union Regulation 2078/92 have been approved for steppe areas containing Lesser Kestrels in Castilla y León, Cataluña, Castilla-La Mancha, Madrid and Extremadura. A land management programme is in operation in Cataluña including the payment of subsidies for agricultural extensification and colony restoration.

In Barcelona and Lérida more than 100 young Lesser Kestrels are bred in captivity every year and a reintroduction project has been under way since 1989. Two private initiatives, FICAS in Madrid and CERCA in Extremadura, are also involved in captive breeding and reintroduction and have carried out environmental education, particularly CERCA.

Tunisia

The Lesser Kestrel is protected by the Tunisian Hunting Law. The population is divided between two main colonies with 30 and 40 pairs and smaller colonies of 2 to 5 pairs.

Turkey

All raptors are legally protected. The Lesser Kestrel is not included in the Draft Red List of Threatened Animals prepared by the Ministry of Environment. Only a very small portion of the Lesser Kestrel colonies in Turkey benefit from protected area status.

In 1992, some public awareness activities were carried out by DHKD near a colony in Eregli-Konya, with good coverage in press and television. In 1993, a baseline survey was carried out in central Turkey suggesting a population decline

probably due to increased pesticide use (Parr et al., 1995). As a follow-up of this study, a survey on food and habitat requirements at randomly selected sites was carried out in 1994 (Parr and Naveso, 1994).

Aims and objectives

Aims

1. In the short term, to maintain all known Lesser Kestrel breeding colonies at their 1994 levels or larger.

2. In the medium to long term, to increase the population size of the Lesser Kestrel to a level at which it no longer qualifies as a globally threatened species.

Objectives

1. **Policy and legislation**

1.1. *Agricultural policy*

The threats of habitat loss and food depletion in the breeding areas as well as during migration and in the winter quarters are similar for a number of threatened species. Conservation measures for the Lesser Kestrel are likely to have a positive effect also for the globally threatened Great Bustard *Otis tarda* as well as other declining species such as the White Stork *Ciconia ciconia*, Little Bustard *Tetrax tetrax*, Gull-billed Tern *Gelochelidon nilotica*, Pin-tailed Sandgrouse *Pterocles alchata*, Roller *Coracias garrulus*, Shrikes *Lanius* and other species hunting in the open landscape for large invertebrate prey. Thus steppe and dry grasslands are included in the Agricultural Conservation Strategy currently being prepared by BirdLife International (Tucker et al., in press.).

1.1.1. Promote agricultural policies which maintain and enhance Lesser Kestrel habitat

Lesser Kestrel conservation is largely dependent on practices which are heavily influenced by international or national agricultural policy. In the European Union, the Agri-environment Regulation 2078/92 should be promoted and EU range states should be encouraged to prepare zonal programmes under this regulation which will benefit the Lesser Kestrel. The European

Commission could assist by preparing guidelines for the implementation of this regulation, which should be applicable to farms bigger than 50 ha.

Funding for agri-environment measures is generally not available for countries in central and eastern Europe. EU and other funds, incentives and subsidies destined for support in these countries should promote specific measures to maintain or restore the Lesser Kestrel habitat through mechanisms such as environmentally sensitive areas and the setting-aside of agricultural land.

Co-ordination between agriculture and nature conservation administrations must be improved. Subsidies for extensive agriculture often clash with much bigger intensification programmes involving irrigation or monocultures. In Thessaly, Greece, a sudden change in cotton subsidies stimulated very sudden, widespread changes in land-use in 1995 (Hallmann, 1996) with probable negative consequences for Lesser Kestrels.

Priority: high
Time-scale: medium

1.1.2. Grazing levels on pasture land

Low-density grazing should be promoted in Lesser Kestrel areas and overgrazing must be avoided. Pastures should be maintained with reduced use of fertilizers and should be grazed non-intensively to allow for a high diversity of vegetation and consequently of prey insects. In areas with fast and abundant vegetation growth the grazing pressure should be strong enough to keep down vegetation so that invertebrate prey remain accessible. In steppe areas the recommended stocking density is 0.1 to 0.3 ULM which corresponds to 1.5 livestock units per hectare.

Priority: high
Time-scale: ongoing

1.1.3. Recommended cultivation practices

Uncultivated plots, road verges and edges between fields with short grass or steppe-like structure should be maintained within 4 km of colonies. In cultivated farmland, a fringe of at least 1 to 2 metres of uncultivated land with short grass and hedges should be provided and maintained between cereal fields and along roads and tracks to allow good populations of insects to

develop. Strips of short grass render prey easily accessible to Lesser Kestrels. Those agricultural practices which lead to high densities of prey, especially Orthoptera, should be promoted. Cultures of herbaceous Leguminosae should be maintained where they already exist. Fencing of fields should be avoided.

Priority: critical
Time-scale: ongoing

1.1.4. Pesticides

It is recommended that the use of agrochemicals in feeding habitats of the Lesser Kestrel should be strictly regulated and monitored.

Priority: medium
Time-scale: ongoing

1.2. *Promote forestry practices which do not conflict with Lesser Kestrel conservation*

In the European Union, afforestation under Regulation 2080/92 should be zoned so that sites important for the Lesser Kestrel are avoided. It is recommended that afforestation (and deforestation) programmes in Lesser Kestrel areas be subject to an environmental impact assessment. Better co-ordination is necessary between forestry and agriculture administrations responsible for the implementation of regulations 2080 and 2078.

Cutting of trees where Lesser Kestrels roost (before breeding, during migration or in the winter quarters) must be avoided.

Priority: high
Time-scale: short

1.3. *Promote the full legal protection of the species and important sites*

Ensure that the Lesser Kestrel is listed as a strictly protected species according to international agreements and national laws, and that legal instruments for the protection of the species and its habitats are being implemented.

Priority: high
Time-scale: medium

1.4. *All range states should be encouraged to produce a national action plan for the Lesser Kestrel*

Using this international action plan as a basis, each range state should be encouraged to prepare a national plan. The national action plan should set national targets and identify organisations which will be responsible for implementing different actions.

Priority: high
Time-scale: short

2. **Species and habitat protection**

2.1. *Promote the designation of protected areas for the Lesser Kestrel*

Agricultural surpluses in many parts of Europe offer a good opportunity to create new protected areas or to extend and improve existing ones. There is a need for more protected areas to be established in steppe and dry grassland habitats.

In the European Union, the designation of key breeding and foraging habitats of the Lesser Kestrel as SPAs should be encouraged and the enforcement of protective measures in existing SPAs should be promoted.

Acquisition or lease of land, or agreements with landowners, for conservation management by NGOs should be promoted.

Priority: high
Time-scale: medium

2.2. *Promote appropriate management at breeding colonies*

2.2.1. Co-operate with departments responsible for historic buildings

Conservation agencies and NGOs should pursue co-operation agreements with those departments dealing with the restoration of old or historic buildings in order to preserve Lesser Kestrel colonies. Such agreements already exist in some regions of Spain. Restoration work on buildings with nesting Lesser Kestrels should not take place during the breeding season. The competent authorities should consider technical and financial assistance to the owners of buildings in need of restoration with Lesser Kestrel colonies.

Priority: high
Time-scale: ongoing

2.2.2. Artificial nests

Artificial nests should be provided only where the feeding conditions are good and if there are no natural holes in the area. The design of the boxes and the materials used should be carefully chosen to avoid overheating, predation and inter-specific competition. Nest boxes should be installed outside the breeding season.

Priority: medium
Time-scale: ongoing

2.2.3. Protection of colonies in the countryside

Accidental and deliberate disturbance at colonies outside built-up areas should be prevented through provision of information and, in special cases, wardening.

Priority: high
Time-scale: ongoing

3. **Monitoring and research**

3.1. *Surveys*

Surveys of breeding, migration and wintering areas should be undertaken to get a better picture of population status and to identify important sites. In large countries the only possible method is to carry out surveys in pilot areas and then extrapolate the remaining suitable habitat. A standard methodology for Lesser Kestrel surveys should be developed and published.

Priority: Europe – high
         Africa – medium
Time-scale: short/medium

3.2. *Research into limiting factors*

More research is necessary on the factors limiting Lesser Kestrel populations, especially habitat requirements. This research is to take place in areas which are currently populated by Lesser Kestrels as well as in areas which have been abandoned. It is also important to carry out research and monitoring on habitat management to ensure the appropriate practices are being promoted.

Priority: high
Time-scale: short/ongoing

3.3. Reintroduction and recolonisation

Reintroduction attempts should only be carried out where conditions are suitable in accordance with IUCN criteria (Kleiman et al., 1994). These experiments provide a unique opportunity to study the process of recolonisation of empty areas and the establishment of new populations.

Priority: low
Time-scale: long

3.4. Pesticides

Pesticide and heavy metal residues in Lesser Kestrel eggs and tissue should be carried out routinely. The impact of pesticides on prey should be studied further.

Priority: medium
Time-scale: ongoing

3.5. Information exchange

Co-operation and information exchange between research institutions working on the Lesser Kestrel should be promoted, as well as exchange of workers. Training on research techniques and methodologies should be provided by those institutions which are carrying out intensive research programmes with the Lesser Kestrel.

Priority: medium
Time-scale: short/ongoing

4. Public awareness

4.1. Raise awareness of Lesser Kestrel feeding habitats

Public awareness campaigns targeted at local authorities, landowners, farmers, shepherds and hunters concerning the protection of feeding habitats should be carried out. The Lesser Kestrel should be used as a flagship species for the conservation of steppes, grasslands and traditional agricultural systems.

Priority: medium
Time-scale: short

4.2. Raise awareness of the importance of breeding colonies

Information and awareness campaigns should be carried out directed at householders, archaeological and historical building authorities, architects, construction companies, etc., responsible for the maintenance or restoration of buildings where the Lesser Kestrel breeds. A leaflet on restoration practices which favour the Lesser Kestrel and other birds should be produced.

Priority: medium
Time-scale: short

Annex
Recommended conservation actions by country

Albania

1.3. Promote legal protection.

3.1. Carry out surveys in order to establish the status of the Lesser Kestrel and identify key areas.

Algeria

3.1. Carry out surveys in order to establish the status of the Lesser Kestrel and identify key areas.

Armenia, Azerbaijan, Georgia, Kazakhstan and Uzbekistan

1.1.1. Encourage land management programmes to prevent overgrazing.

1.3. Promote the legal protection of the Lesser Kestrel.

3.1. Carry out surveys in order to establish the status of the Lesser Kestrel and identify key areas.

Bulgaria

1.1.4. Prevent the use of chemicals toxic to the Lesser Kestrel or its prey in breeding and foraging areas.

2.1. Seek legal protection for breeding sites.

2.2.1. Prevent the destruction of nest sites during building restoration.

2.2.2. Provide artificial nest boxes in suitable areas of the Trakia lowlands and the eastern Rhodopi mountains.

2.2.3. Prevent disturbance to colonies outside built-up areas.

2.2.3. Monitor quarrying activities at breeding sites.

3.1. Complete a national survey (starting in 1995).

3.1. Continue the current study of autumn migration along the Black Sea coast.

4.1./4.2. Undertake national public awareness campaigns about the Lesser Kestrel.

Croatia

1.3. Promote legal protection of the Lesser Kestrel.

2.1. Promote the establishment of a network of protected areas.

3.1. Carry out surveys in order to establish the status of the Lesser Kestrel and identify key areas.

Egypt

1.1.1./1.1.2./1.1.3. Promote extensive agriculture (pastures, fallow land and uncultivated margins of fields in areas of intensive agriculture).

1.3. Promote legal protection of the Lesser Kestrel.

France

2.1. Encourage the designation of the breeding area in La Crau as a protected area.

2.2./2.2.2. Promote the preparation and implementation of a management plan for La Crau, emphasising habitat measures (especially grazing) and provision of nest sites.

3.1./3.2. Continue current studies (ecological requirements) and monitoring of the species.

3.3. Undertake a feasibility study for reintroduction in Provence and Languedoc-Roussillon.

4.1./4.2. Undertake public awareness campaigns on the Lesser Kestrel with landowners, farmers, shepherds, hunters and tourists.

Greece

1.1./1.3. Promote better co-ordination among ministerial departments responsible for nature conservation.

2.1. Encourage the designation as protected areas of the key sites for breeding and foraging.

2.2.1. Prevent the destruction of nest sites during restoration work on buildings.

2.2.2. Provide new nest sites for breeding (holes in roofs, nest boxes, etc.).

3.1. Complete a national survey of the Lesser Kestrel.

3.2. Analyse conservation status and limiting factors in colonies and foraging habitat.

4.1./4.2. Undertake public awareness campaigns with local authorities, house- and landowners, farmers, shepherds, hunters and tourists.

Israel

1.1.1.3. Encourage control and reduction in the use of pesticides.

3.1. Carry out a national survey.

3.2. Investigate the reasons for the decline of the species and in particular analyse current conservation problems in colonies and foraging habitat.

Italy

1.1.1./1.3./2.1. Prevent habitat loss at important feeding areas through ploughing up, monocultures, construction, afforestation or other developments.

2.2.3. Prevent human disturbance at breeding sites (rocky slopes) in Sardinia and Sicily.

3.1. Undertake a national survey to assess population status and distribution and to locate important breeding and feeding areas.

3.1. Initiate a long-term monitoring scheme including ringing.

4.1. Use the Lesser Kestrel as a flagship species for the conservation of steppes and grasslands in Italy.

4.2. Undertake a public awareness campaign directed at authorities responsible for the historic heritage (especially in Puglia-Basilicata), architects, construction companies and householders.

Libya

1.3. Promote legal protection of the species.

3.1. Carry out surveys in order to establish the status of the Lesser Kestrel and identify key areas.

Moldova

1.3. Promote legal protection.

3.1. Carry out surveys in order to establish the status of the Lesser Kestrel and identify key areas.

Morocco

2.2.1. Prevent the destruction of old walls and buildings in old towns.

2.2.3. Prevent human persecution and disturbance at colonies.

3.1. Carry out a national survey and identify key areas.

3.1. Study migration through Morocco.

3.2./2.2.2. Study and prevent interspecific competition for nest sites with Jackdaws.

4.1./4.2. Undertake public awareness campaigns directed at the local population, especially schoolchildren.

Portugal

1.1.1. Promote the application of EU Regulation 2078/92 to farms larger than 50 ha to allow them to receive subsidies for extensive agriculture.

1.1.1. Encourage agriculture and trade policies which divert subsidies for intensive monocultures (sunflower, maize, etc.) away from Lesser Kestrel areas.

1.2. Encourage zoned afforestation under EU Regulation 2080/92 avoiding Lesser Kestrel areas.

2.1. Finalise the designation of the Convento de S. Francisco and surrounding area as a Protected Area of Legal Private Status.

2.2.2. Continue the artificial nest site experimentation in Mértola and Belver.

3.1. Undertake a population survey in the Alentejo.

3.1. Start a ringing programme in co-ordination with other countries.

3.2. Investigate limiting factors, notably feeding habitat, as a basis for appropriate land management schemes.

Romania

1.3. Promote legal protection of the Lesser Kestrel.

3.1. Carry out a national survey and identify key areas.

Russian Federation

1.3. Promote the inclusion of the Lesser Kestrel in the new edition of the Red Data Book.

3.1. Carry out a national survey and identify key areas particularly steppe and river bank IBAs with Lesser Kestrel colonies.

3.2. Study limiting factors and ecological constraints.

3.3. Develop a captive breeding and release programme if the IUCN criteria for reintroductions are met.

4.1./4.2. Undertake a public awareness campaign.

Slovenia

1.3. Promote legal protection of the species.

2.1. Encourage the establishment of a network of Nature Reserves.

3.1. Carry out a national survey and identify key areas.

Spain

1.1.1. Promote the preparation and submission to the European Union of regional zonal programmes under regulation 2078/92 and include the Lesser Kestrel in these programmes.

1.1.1./1.1.3. Use appropriate management prescriptions and incentive schemes to promote dry cultures in a one-year fallow rotation system within about 3 km of colonies containing more than 30 pairs.

1.1.1./1.2. Use appropriate management prescriptions and incentive schemes to prevent the abandonment of agriculture, natural succession and afforestation programmes in Lesser Kestrel areas.

2.2.2. Provide artificial nest boxes where necessary.

3.1. Design and implement a monitoring programme at national level.

3.1. Prepare guidelines for Lesser Kestrel surveys.

3.2. Continue current studies on breeding ecology, feeding ecology, population ecology and limiting factors.

3.3. Undertake reintroduction in areas suitable for the Lesser Kestrel outside urban areas if the IUCN criteria for reintroductions are met. Such reintroductions should be followed by research on recolonisation and the settlement of new colonies.

4.2. Undertake public awareness campaigns directed at town councils, householders and departments responsible for the historic heritage, in order to prevent damage to Lesser Kestrel nesting sites during restoration work.

Tunisia

1.3./2.1./2.2.2. Promote adequate protection of colonies.

3.1. Complete a national survey and collect data from foreign ornithologists visiting Tunisia in order to establish the status of the Lesser Kestrel and identify key areas.

3.4./1.1.4. Monitor and encourage reduced pesticide use in Lesser Kestrel areas.

4.1./4.2./2.2.1. Undertake a public awareness campaign and prevent disturbance of colonies at archaeological sites.

Turkey

1.1.1./2.2. Identify IBAs in central Turkey which hold important Lesser Kestrel populations and establish pilot conservation areas within the most important IBAs.

3.1. Carry out a large-scale survey of the Turkish population.

3.1. Undertake an inventory of semi-natural lowland habitats, marshes, pastures and dry grasslands with the help of satellite photography to help identify previously unknown breeding/foraging areas.

3.2./2.2. Assess the impact of development schemes on the Lesser Kestrel and its habitat.

4.1./4.2. Undertake public awareness campaigns to secure the availability of nest sites and to promote the ecological value of steppes and grasslands.

Ukraine

1.3. Promote the legal protection of the species.

3.1. Carry out a national survey and identify key areas.

Action plan
for the Corncrake (*Crex crex*) in Europe

Reviews

Progress towards implementation of actions and achievement of targets will be reviewed annually by BirdLife International. This document should be reviewed and updated by BirdLife International every three years. An emergency review will be undertaken if sudden major environmental changes, liable to affect the population, occur within the species range.

Geographical scope

This plan is intended for implementation in all 34 European breeding range states of the Corncrake:

Austria, Belarus, Belgium, Bosnia-Herzegovina, Bulgaria, Croatia, Czech Republic, Denmark, Estonia, Croatia, Finland, France, Germany, Hungary, Republic of Ireland, Italy, Latvia, Liechtenstein, Lithuania, Luxembourg, Republic of Moldova, Netherlands, Norway, Poland, Romania, Russian Federation (European part only), Serbia and Montenegro, Slovakia, Slovenia, Spain, Sweden, Switzerland, Ukraine, United Kingdom and Isle of Man.

Summary

The Corncrake *Crex crex* is a globally threatened species, classified as Vulnerable at both world and

---

Lietuviu liaudies daina/A Lithuanian folk song

Oi griezle, griezle mano,
Kur buvai sia vasarele?
Lankoj, lankoj,
Sieneli grebiau.

Oh Corncrake, my little corncrake,
Where were you this summer to stay?
In a meadow, until late,
I gathered in hay.

Uz arklio pedos tupejau,
Pro pradalgele ziurejau.
Greblys, greblys
Man lizda ardys.

I crouched in a horse's hoof print,
And watched from across a swath.
As a rake, a rake
My nest was to break.

Is rundo stikliuko geriau.
Is liusto mergyte vedziau
Truks plys, truks plys
Smuikelio styga.

I sipped from a small rounded glass.
And married a pretty young lass
One stroke, one stroke
My fiddle-string broke.

Translated by Mantas Zurba

A Latvian folk song

Grieze gieza rudztsos
Paipalina pjavina;
Atziet grieze no rudziem,
Paipalina no pjavinas

Corncrake craked in the rye
Little quail in meadow hay;
Corncrake leaves the rye field,
Quail is out when meadow yields.

Translated by Oskars Keiss

European level due to the long-term and very steep decline of the species across its range. It is listed in Annex I of the European Union's Wild Birds Directive and Appendix II of the Bern Convention, and it will be added to Appendix II of the Bonn Convention in 1997. The Corncrake's breeding range extends over much of northern and central Europe and into Asia. It migrates in autumn, especially through Egypt, to winter in sub-Saharan Africa. There are a few wintering records from Asia and Australasia, and one recent record of a recently captured bird on sale in Vietnam (E. Meek, *in litt.*). The estimate of the total European population is 92000 to 233000 singing males, breeding in 34 countries. Only 10 states, nine of which are in central and eastern Europe, now have populations of more than 1000 singing males, and only Russia, Belarus and Ukraine have more than 10000 males. Corncrakes have been declining in Europe since the last century, on average over the last 10 years by about 20% to 50%.

Threats and limiting factors

The mechanisation and earlier dates of mowing – high

Loss of suitable habitat: hay meadows and wetlands – high

Recreational disturbance and hunting – low

Ecological change in Africa – low/unknown

Pesticides and pollution – low/unknown

Increased predation rates – unknown

Conservation priorities

Encourage policies at international level to promote extensive, grass-based farming – high

Promote policies at national and regional (within-country) level that benefit Corncrakes including the production of a national Corncrake action plan – high

Encourage maximum legal protection of key sites and of the species – high

Development and implementation of a European survey and monitoring strategy – high

Establish and develop a corncrake research working group – high

Research to determine the impact of mowing on Corncrake populations and to indicate means of reducing the impact – high

Other research including monitoring of the effectiveness of conservation measures – high

Raise public awareness and support for the Corncrake across Europe – high

Introduction

The Corncrake *Crex crex* is a globally threatened species, listed as Vulnerable in *Birds to Watch 2* (Collar et al., 1994) and is considered as Rare by the IUCN (Groombridge, 1993). It is listed as Vulnerable at European level (Tucker and Heath, 1994) because of the long-term and very steep population decline across the continent – by about 50% over the last 20 years. The declines are thought to be due primarily to changes in grassland management on the breeding grounds associated with agricultural intensification together with loss of suitable breeding habitats, including losses through drainage.

The species is listed in Annex I of the European Union's Wild Birds Directive and Appendix II of the Bern Convention. In 1994 the Parties to the Bonn Convention agreed to list the Corncrake in Appendix II at their next conference in 1997, and until then to treat it as if already listed.

As part of the preparation of this action plan a questionnaire was sent to experts in 32 of the 34 known European breeding range states (Bosnia-Herzegovina and Serbia and Montenegro were not approached directly), asking questions about population size and trends, ecology, threats and conservation measures. Questionnaires were completed by all 32 range states and Croatian and German representatives supplied details for Bosnia-Herzegovina and Serbia and Montenegro. The results were collated in advance of a workshop in Gdansk (October, 1994) which was attended by 45 experts from 23 range states.

Background information

The information presented here is summarised from Green et al. (in press), which analyses the results of the completed questionnaires and other information received from the 34 breeding range states.

Distribution and population

Distribution

The Corncrake breeding range formerly extended over much of northern and central Europe between approximately 41°N and at least 65°N, extending into Asia in western Siberia up to 120°E. More than half the world population may breed in Asia (Russia, Georgia, Iran, Afghanistan, Tajikistan, Kyrgyzstan, Kazakhstan and China) (Collar et al., 1994). The distribution is now much restricted within the former range, and is fragmented in western Europe. In Europe, Corncrakes are found from sea-level up to 1400 metres in the Alps and 3000 metres in Russia.

The autumn passage of most of the world population appears to be concentrated through the Middle East and north-east Africa and especially Egypt (Stowe and Becker, 1992). Corncrakes winter mainly in the savannahs of south-central and south-east Africa, from southern Tanzania to northern South Africa; there are also some records from western Africa.

The Corncrake still breeds in 34 European states (its status in Albania is not known and it no longer breeds in the former Yugoslav Republic of Macedonia and breeds only irregularly in Turkey). Only 10 states now have populations of more than 1000 males. Nine of these are central and eastern European countries (CEEC), with more than 10000 singing males in Belarus, Russia and probably Ukraine, and several thousand in Bulgaria, Estonia, Latvia, Lithuania, Poland and Romania. France is the only country in western Europe with over 1000 males. Germany has the second-largest western population with about 800 singing males. Populations from Austria, Ireland, Italy, Sweden and United Kingdom are all significant in size, but those from other countries (Belgium, Denmark, Luxembourg, Netherlands, Norway, Spain and Switzerland) can only be considered relicts.

Population

The most recent European breeding population estimate is 92000 to 233000 singing males,

based on 1985 to 1994 data supplied in the questionnaires (Table 13. 1). This is similar to the estimate of 92000 to 200000 by Tucker and Heath (1994), despite the inclusion of more precise data for nine states.

Long-term trends

Corncrake populations in almost all European range states appear to have suffered long-term declines. Declines were reported as early as the latter half of the nineteenth century in Denmark (Kjærbølling, 1852) and Germany, and after 1880 in Britain and Ireland (Norris, 1947; Green, 1995). In France and Norway, as in other west European countries, declines were first noted in several regions early this century (Collett, 1921; Broyer, 1985). In central Russia declines were first reported around 1930, important declines becoming obvious in the 1950s and 1960s (Ptushenko and Inozemtzev, 1968; Malchevskiy and Pukinskiy, 1983; Kurochkin and Koshelev, 1987). Countries now showing stable or fluctuating trends either experienced large declines previously or have been properly surveyed only recently, and reliable comparisons thus cannot be made.

Recent trends

On average, Corncrake numbers fell by about 20% to 50% over the last 10 years in 22 European countries. Several countries such as Denmark, Ireland, Netherlands, Norway and Poland show very strong declines of more than 50%, whereas Belgium, Finland, Germany, Hungary, Italy, Sweden and Switzerland appear to have kept stable or fluctuating populations (Liechtenstein has an increasing, but very small, population). All other countries appear to have experienced declines of less than 50%.

Detailed surveys have demonstrated the alarming extent of declines in several countries. In Britain there was a 40% decline from 1978 to 1993, including a 17% decline from 1988 to 1993, and the declines in Ireland were even more severe, including 81% from 1988 to 1993. In France a reduction of about 40% in numbers and range occurred from 1984 to 1992. In western Ukraine probably more than 60% of the population has disappeared since 1976, including a 10% decline between 1988 and 1993. In the Netherlands the population has declined by more than 75% since the early 1980s. In Belarus, the decline has probably been greater than 10% to 15% in the last ten years.

Life history

Feeding

The diet in the breeding season includes a wide range of invertebrates found on plants, and on and within the soil. In Germany and Poland birds mainly take relatively large insects (length 5–12 mm) (N. Schäffer, unpubl.). Small vertebrates such as fish and amphibians are also taken occasionally. In Scotland and Ireland earthworms and molluscs are important in the diet (G. A. Tyler, unpubl. data). The principal prey (beetles, other large insects, earthworms, snails, slugs) are widespread in habitats other than those used by Corncrakes, so it appears that the species has specialised more in the structure of the vegetation that it occupies than in the food it takes. During autumn and winter the birds take mainly seeds.

Breeding

Most birds arrive on the breeding grounds in May, females slightly later than males. The mean date of arrival across 28 European range states is 21 May (30 April – 15 June).

Corncrakes are sequentially polygamous. Males advertise for mates, and probably defend territory, with a loud disyllabic song, given occasionally by day and almost continuously at night from tall ground vegetation. After being attracted to a singing male, the female associates closely with him for several days during which the male sings only infrequently (Schäffer and Munch, 1993; Tyler and Green, in prep.). The pair-bond breaks during egg-laying and the male then resumes singing, sometimes moving a considerable distance to a new singing area (Tyler and Green, in prep.). The mean date of ceasing to sing over 24 European states was 8 July (12 June – 19 July), several weeks before the southward migration starts. Calling is heard only occasionally as late as September. Females may lay a second clutch later

in the summer and may also move before doing so. Incubation and care of the chicks is done by the female alone.

The nest is on the ground in dense vegetation, constructed from dead stems and leaves. The average clutch size is around 10. Nests are recorded from the second half of May to the first half of July in over half of the 24 range states; in 12 states, nests are found over a period of two months or more. Chicks are recorded from the second half of June to the second half of July in more than half of the 21 states, with many states also reporting flightless chicks in August. The long period over which nests and chicks are reported suggests that production of two clutches per female may be widespread, while also being partly attributable to variations between states in the time at which breeding starts.

Observations in Scotland indicate that: incubation of first nests begins from around 20 May to 12 June and takes about 19 or 20 days; apart from the destruction of nests by mowing, nest success is remarkably high with 80% to 90% survival to hatching; chicks leave the nest soon after hatching and are fed by the female bill-to-bill; broods forage by day within 100 to 200 metres of the nest; about half of first-brood young survive to independence (10–15 days old, flying at about 35 days) in broods in which at least one chick survives; all females which rear their first brood before mid-July incubate a second clutch for 16 to 18 days, starting 12 days after leaving the first brood, with a similar nest success to first broods; most eggs hatch by the end of July or early August; females stay with their second broods longer (15–20 days) and overall productivity is higher than in first breeding attempts due to better chick survival, with 60% of chicks surviving to independence (T. Stowe et al., unpubl.).

At two weeks of age the distinctive calls of young birds and the females can be heard, giving reliable evidence of breeding (Schäffer, 1994).

Habitat requirements

Corncrakes breed in open or semi-open landscapes, mainly in meadows of tall grass. They almost always conceal themselves in tall ground vegetation. Their original breeding habitats would

Table 13. 1

The most recent Corncrake population estimates (singing males) in 34 European range states. Accuracy is assessed on a scale from 0 (a guess) to 3 (a census accurate to 10% of the true number). The population trend over the 10 years prior to the most recent estimate is given as −2 (decrease of >50%), −1 (decrease of 20%–49%), 0 (change of <20%), F (fluctuating, with changes of >20% but no clear trend)

Country	Number of singing males	Accuracy code	Year of estimate	Population trend
Austria	140–180	2	1989-91	(−1)
Belarus	26000–30000	2	1990	−1
Belgium	17–21	2–3	1992-94	F
Bosnia-Herzegovina	300–1,000	1	1987	?
Bulgaria	1000–2500	2	1980-94	−1
Croatia	400–1000	1	1990	?
Czech Republic	200–400	1	1985-89	−1
Denmark	6	3	1991	−2
Estonia	5,000	2	1993	−1
Finland	500–1000	2	1994	0
France	1100–1200	3	1991-92	−1
Germany	800	2	1994	0
Hungary	350–450	2	1993-94	F
Republic of Ireland	174	3	1993	−2
Italy	250–300	0	1994	?
Latvia	3000–10000	2	1993	−1
Liechtenstein	8	3	1994	0
Lithuania	3000–4000	2	1994	?
Luxembourg	<10	0	—	−1
Moldova	450	2	1985	−1
Netherlands	30–80	2	1990-95	−2
Norway	70	2	1995	−2
Poland	6600–7800	1	1993	−2
Romania	3000–6000	0–1	—	?
Russia	10000–100000	1	1994	−1
Serbia and Montenegro	>100	0	1991	
Slovakia	600–900	1	1992	?
Slovenia	>500	2–3	1992-93	−1
Spain	24–31	2	1993-94	−1
Sweden	250–1000	0	—	?
Switzerland	4	1	1993	0
Ukraine	25000–55000	1	1993	−1
United Kingdom and Isle of Man	489	3	1993	−1
Total	91668–233333			

almost certainly have been riverine meadows of *Carex-Iris-Typhoides* and other grasslands with few trees or bushes, including high-altitude meadows. Today Corncrakes are strongly associated with agricultural grassland managed for hay and silage (Cramp and Simmons, 1980). The ground vegetation of Corncrake breeding habitat needs to be over 20 cm tall in order to provide cover but not so dense that it is difficult for the birds to walk through. Most habitats selected by Corncrakes are subject to annual mowing, grazing or winter floods.

In parts of the breeding range the distribution, and probably abundance, of singing Corncrakes is strongly affected by the availability of suitable vegetation in spring. In western Scotland, where the meadow grass is too short to provide adequate cover until mid-June, on arrival Corncrakes use stands of tall herbs, such as *Urtica dioica* and *Anthriscus sylvestris*, and marsh vegetation such as *Iris pseudacorus*, *Phragmites* and *Phalaris arundinacea* (Cadbury, 1980). In Germany, singing males select tall ground vegetation with some robust or woody stems present, such as *Salix* bushes and the edges of reedbeds; neighbouring areas with shorter vegetation are used relatively early in the season as feeding habitats during daylight (Schäffer and Münch, 1993).

Corncrakes tend to avoid the following habitats because they are too dense: stands of dead grasses from the previous year's growth; vegetation with closely spaced and robust stems or leaves, such as tussock-forming species of *Juncus*; closely spaced grasses in fertilised meadows, especially if they are pushed to the ground by wind and rain; and vegetation on abandoned meadows and other farmland after a few years on nutrient-rich soils, but perhaps not for decades after abandonment if the soil is poor, as in the Bohemian forest of the Czech Republic.

Suitable habitats include moist, unfertilised grassland and regularly cut meadows in areas of low-intensity agriculture. Across their European range, hay or silage fields in valleys liable to flooding seem to be of highest importance, but the birds also breed in hay and silage fields in dry lowlands and in marshes, crops or in hay or silage fields in sub-alpine areas (listed in order of decreasing importance). Wetlands, in particular peatbogs

(e.g. in Bosnia-Herzegovina) and the edges of marshes, provide important habitats. They may act as refuges for Corncrakes when drier grasslands are unsuitable, for example, because the grass is too short during spring or after mowing in late summer. Wetland margins are also likely to be grazed or mowed late in summer, if they are managed at all, so the risk of damage to nests, chicks and flightless moulting adults is low.

In fertilised meadows or fields sown with cereals, successful breeding is believed to be infrequent, but herbaceous vegetation on field margins or fallow land may be used as alternative habitats during the harvest. Males are regularly found singing in clear-cut forests in Belarus, Belgium, Lithuania, Poland and Russia, in pastures in Latvia and Lithuania, in young conifer plantations in Belgium, and on abandoned land, including set-aside, in Austria, Belgium, Czech Republic, Germany and Slovenia.

Corncrakes breed in some grazed habitats in which vegetation grows tall in summer. In Scotland suitable habitat has been created by grazing grassland with cattle during autumn and winter (September to February), but carrying out no grazing or mowing in summer. Removal of cattle in very early spring allows time for patches of herbaceous vegetation (especially *Urtica dioica*) to grow tall enough to harbour corncrakes in May and early June when the grass is too short for them.

Movements

Autumn migration starts in August and continues until October. The main passage through Egypt is in September and the first half of October, with a peak in the third week of September (Goodman and Meininger, 1989). Southward movement through Africa lasts from September to December and is linked to the occurrence of rainfall and the growth of cover (Stowe and Becker, 1992).

Threats and limiting factors

Mechanisation and earlier mowing

The mechanisation of hay and silage mowing and the practice of starting it earlier in the year are the greatest threats to Corncrakes across Europe by reducing nest success and the survival of chicks and adults. It is likely that most rapid declines in Corncrakes have occurred following the mechanisation of mowing – the transition from hand scything to mowing machines, at first drawn by horses and then motorised. Mowing machines threaten Corncrakes as follows.

1. Reduced chance of nest and chicks avoiding destruction

Compared with hand scything, with mechanised mowing it is much more difficult:
a. for the mower to avoid destroying nests – virtually all nests in mowed meadows may be destroyed; and
b. for chicks to escape from the mower into uncut grass due to:
– the speed of operation of machinery; tractors are faster than horses, tractor-drawn mowers that cut in circles are faster than ones which mow in lines (N. Schäffer, in litt., 1994)
– the capability for large areas of hay/silage to be mowed in one session
– the cutting proceeding from the outside of the field inwards, trapping chicks in the centre where they are less likely to avoid destruction
– the increased chance that chicks which attempt to escape by crossing the open, already mowed area of the field may be taken by predators such as gulls Larus and White Storks Ciconia ciconia.

Adults are rarely killed, either during incubation or when with young or even when flightless during the moult in July and August. Adults and fledged young may fly out of the grass when close to the mower, but flightless chicks which do not break cover are often killed. In Scotland and Ireland at least 40% of chicks appeared to be killed when mowing took place from the edge of the meadow inwards. By comparison only up to 8% of chicks appear to be killed during mowing from the centre of the meadow outwards (Tyler, in prep.).

2. Increased proportion of Corncrake nests and chicks being at risk due to earlier mowing

Because it is more rapid, mechanised mowing allows the grass harvest to be completed within a shorter time. Hence, fields which would have been mowed in late summer if mowing was done by hand are harvested earlier, within the breeding period of the Corncrake. Earlier mowing also results from intensification of grass production, including a switch to silage production rather than hay.

3. Prevention of second clutches by early removal of tall ground vegetation

In many countries, hay mowing removes much of the tall vegetation suitable for Corncrakes before a second clutch can be produced.

According to the questionnaire returns, on average across Europe over 60% of the Corncrake population (17% to 100% in different states) may be affected by the management of hay and silage meadows. Mechanisation of mowing has occurred in most parts of the European range, and in most range states mowing with tractor-drawn mowers and forage or silage harvesters is the most common form of harvesting. However, harvesting of hay by hand or with hand-operated or horse-drawn machines is still an important method in some states (predominantly in central and eastern Europe) and high-density Corncrake populations have persisted longer here.

Most mowing of hay and silage in Corncrake areas takes place in June and July although there is considerable variation among states, some having most mowing in May and June and others in late July and August. Mowing earlier than late June will destroy the first nests and remove the tall vegetation necessary to allow the production of replacement nests and enhance the survival chances of adults and chicks. Hence, in most range states, mowing is sufficiently early so that there is little possibility of successfully producing a second brood in hay or silage and in some states even the production of the first brood is severely threatened.

In mechanised countries, Corncrakes are often confined to marginal areas, such as high altitudes or cold wet corners of the country, where grass growth is slower and mowing is thus delayed.

Importance: high

Loss of suitable habitat: hay meadows and wetlands

Loss of these habitats are important threats in many range states.

Wetland loss

Wetlands are threatened by drainage, flood alleviation schemes on rivers, peat extraction from peat bogs, etc. Indeed the extinction of breeding Corncrakes in the former Yugoslav Republic of Macedonia is attributed to the land-claim of wetlands in the last 15 to 20 years (V. Maletic, *in litt.*, 1994).

Meadow loss

Hay and silage meadows are threatened by drainage, flooding of river valleys through creation of reservoirs (e.g. in Ukraine), conversion to arable, forestry plantations and other developments. An example is the conversion of hay meadows in France to maize *Zea mais* and sunflower *Helianthus annuus* fields (due to European Union subsidies) and poplar *Populus* plantations.

Intensification

Intensification is the adoption of methods of farming that produce greater yields, with greater input of fertilisers and an increased number of agricultural operations. Intensification of management of mowed grassland includes the switch from hay to silage production and usually leads to faster grass growth and so to earlier harvesting. Intensification thus leads to increased risk of damage to Corncrakes and also to other changes that are less well understood. For example, increased fertiliser application and re-seeding could cause changes in plant species composition and physical structure of grasslands leading to reduced invertebrate prey availability and reduced penetrability of the grassland due to increased stem density. Also, the replacement of cattle and hay production by intensive sheep grazing (encouraged by sheep premium payments in the European Union) can lead to the loss of suitable tall vegetation, for example, in Scotland and parts of Ireland.

In the last five years, whereas most western European states have experienced increased agricultural intensification, most central and eastern European countries have undergone reductions in the intensity of farming, especially in the use of agrochemicals, resulting from the transition from state to private-run farming combined with the difficult economic situations. This trend towards extensification is likely to reverse when the economic situation in central and eastern Europe improves.

Abandonment

Abandonment, the converse of intensification, involves the withdrawal of centuries-old practices, such as hay making. In some states agricultural abandonment due to socio-economic factors – especially the exposure of rural communities to market forces – is a threat to habitats kept suitable for Corncrakes by traditional management. For example: the exodus of farmers from marginal and other rural areas (and areas contaminated with radioactivity from the accident at the Chernobyl nuclear power station, e.g. in Belarus), and ageing of the remaining population, causing abandonment of low-intensity grazing and hay making at wetland margins; the reduction in cattle farming leading to the abandonment of agriculture on dry grasslands which were previously grazed or mowed (in the European Union, declines in cattle, partly due to the limiting of milk production, may result in the conversion of meadows to arable or plantations). Through natural succession, abandonment can eventually lead to the development of vegetation (grass ground layer and scrub) which is too dense for Corncrakes, although initially a temporary increase in tall ground vegetation and large insects often benefits the species (N. Schäffer, unpubl.). The banning of all agricultural management following the establishment of strict nature reserves and "nature restoration projects" can thus be detrimental to Corncrakes.

Importance: high

Increased predation rates

Corncrakes tend to be more vulnerable to predators when they are located in small patches of tall cover or when they have to move between patches across short vegetation. Hence a decrease in the area and continuity of suitable tall cover could increase losses of adults to predators.

In Scotland and Ireland the main proximate cause of death of radio-tagged adults was predation by mammals (otter *Lutra lutra*, American mink *Mustela vison* and domestic/feral cat *Felis catus*). In addition, deaths and injuries to untagged Corncrakes caused by collisions with fences, overhead wires and road traffic were observed. Variation between areas in adult breeding season mortality was substantial, but did not correlate with variations in population trends. In fact adult mortality was higher in an increasing population than in one which was decreasing (G. A. Tyler, in prep.).

Importance: unknown

Recreational disturbance

Isolated populations may be vulnerable to disturbance from birdwatchers but in general Corncrakes are likely to be relatively resilient to human disturbance. For example, numbers in a Moscow city park remained stable between 1928 and 1994 despite heavy recreational pressure. An exception may be Switzerland where the relict population may be at risk from recreational disturbance (W. Müller, *in litt.*, 1995).

Importance: low

Hunting

The Corncrake is still a quarry species in at least two breeding range states, Russia and Ukraine. However, it is not usually a popular quarry: relatively few are taken and hunting is not considered likely to affect the species at population level.

An estimated 0.5% to 2.7% of the European Corncrake population (up to 14000 birds) is killed each autumn as a by-catch of the netting of Quail *Coturnix coturnix* and the trapping and shooting of other species on the north coast of Egypt (Baha el Din et al., in prep.). The birds killed include a high proportion of juveniles. This estimated proportion assumes that no Asian breeders are taken in Egypt, though Asian Corncrakes probably do pass through the country (Stowe and Becker, 1992) so the proportion of the European population at risk is even lower. Hence it seems unlikely that even the complete prevention of Corncrake killing in the coastal strip of Egypt would lead to an increase of more than 1%

of the probability of a European Corncrake surviving the non-breeding season.

Importance: low

Ecological change in Africa

A desk study has suggested that Corncrakes are not under threat in the sub-Saharan winter quarters (Stowe and Becker, 1992). Locally, burning of grasslands or overgrazing may have displaced birds, but no major threats have been identified, even from pesticide use. Indeed the area of suitable habitat may be increasing as woodlands are felled and cultivated areas abandoned. There is no evidence of an effect on Corncrakes of the recent droughts in sub-Saharan Africa, which are widely believed to have affected some species (e.g. Sand Martin *Riparia riparia*).

Importance: low/unknown

Pesticides and pollution

There is no hard evidence regarding the impact of pesticides or pollution in breeding, passage or wintering areas. It is possible that pesticides could reduce food availability. One possible impact of pollution is that nutrient enrichment, particularly by aerial deposition of nitrogen, could change the vegetation structure, making it too dense for Corncrakes to penetrate (N. Schäffer, *in litt.*, 1994). In central and east European countries there has been a reduction in the use of pesticides associated with the economic pressures of the political transition period.

Importance: low/unknown

Conservation status and recent conservation measures

Austria

Fully protected (including from shooting and disturbance; nest sites, eggs and young) under the nature conservation laws of all nine counties.

Important concentrations: Lower Austria, Styria and Vorarlberg.
• The first national Corncrake survey and the first conservation measures taken were in 1994; in two areas of eastern Austria, payments were made to farmers for Corncrake-friendly mowing.

•One quantitative study (unpublished) was undertaken in 1990 and 1991 to describe the calling habitats of Corncrakes on a military training area.

Belarus

Removed from the list of quarry species in winter 1994. Inclusion in the list of protected animals anticipated winter 1994-95.
Important concentrations: widespread.
•No conservation measures have been undertaken specifically for Corncrakes.

Belgium

Important concentrations: Fagne-Famenne.
A two-year programme, partly financed by the European Union LIFE programme which began in 1995. It entails the acquisition and management of land as well as (Wallonia only) population monitoring and public awareness.
Wallonia:
Full species protection under the Nature Conservation Law (Arrêté du Gouvernement wallon of 14 July 1994) and inclusion on the "Red List" of this law.
• RNOB manages over 80 ha of Corncrake habitat in Fagne and Famenne as nature reserves. Similar aquisition programmes are envisaged by the government.
• An annual magazine has been produced by P. Ryelandt to maintain contact between those concerned about Corncrakes, including farmers, foresters, etc.
Flanders:
Full species protection under the 1991 hunting decree.
• Corncrakes are now breeding in new nature reserves established primarily for breeding waders and wintering geese.

Bosnia-Herzegovina

Important concentrations: Livanjsko Polje.

Between 1992 and 1996 Livanjsko Polje has been affected by war. If and when information becomes available, it will be necessary to review the species status and that of the site, and take action as required.

Bulgaria

The species has been legally protected since 1962. The fine for any action against the species (trapping, killing, injuring, collecting eggs, chicks, etc.) was increased to 30000 leva (US$ 500) per specimen in 1995, from the fine initially imposed by a special act (342) of the Ministry of the Environment in 1986. Included as Endangered in the national Red Data Book (Boev, 1985).

Important concentrations: Sofia and Burgas regions, along the Black Sea coast, Smoljan region, the Balkans range (mainly 800–1400 metres), Dobrudja and Trakia plain.
• The Ministry of Environment is funding a BSPB project to conserve wet meadows in north-west Bulgaria.
• Four protected areas (Chokliovo Marsh, Aldomirovtzi and Dolni Bogrov, Dolni Bogrov and Vrachanski Balkan National Park) have been designated in core Corncrake areas and proposals have been made for further such designations.
• Habitat preferences were studied from 1992 to 1994.

Croatia

Fully protected (adults, young, eggs, habitat, against disturbance) in 1981 by a special act based on the Nature Conservation Law.

Important concentrations: alluvial wetlands of the Sava river (including Turopolje, Lonjsko, Mokro, Jelas Polje), Drava and Danube floodplains and north-east of Karlovac along the Kupa river.
• About 50000 ha of Lonjsko Polje and Mokro Polje is protected as a Nature Park.

Czech Republic

Fully protected by the Nature and Countryside Conservation Law No. 114/1992 and the appendix to Law No. 395/1992.

Important concentrations: Sumava, Krkonose, Jeseniky, Beskydy.
• Most of the main Corncrake populations are located in National Parks and Protected Landscape Areas.
• A detailed study on Corncrake habitat use is under way, involving vegetation analysis and intensive ringing and trapping, in abandoned meadows in the Sumava mountains.

Denmark

Protected from shooting and trapping since at least 1967. Included in the Red Data Book as Endangered (Skov-og Naturstyrelsen, 1991).

Important concentrations: Northern Jutland (Bornholm, Sealand) but the species no longer regularly breeds in Denmark.
• Environmentally Sensitive Areas were introduced in the mid-1980s with EU subsidies.
• In 1994 a conservation plan was introduced for the Ryå/Store Vildmose area in Northern Jutland (the last regular breeding site for Corncrakes, although irregular since 1984); the local authorities make agreements with the farmers for Corncrake-friendly management. Result: a male was heard singing on only one night.
• The 1992 Nature Protection Act revision provides better protection of meadows and their buffer zones to a minimum of 2500 m² in area.
• Most of the former important Corncrake localities have some form of national protection (e.g. under the 1992 Nature Protection Act), and Varde Ådal in south-west Jutland is a SPA, but due to lack of appropriate management this protection has been insufficient to maintain the Corncrake populations.

Estonia

No special protection, but not a quarry species. Protected only in nature conservation areas.

Important concentrations: widespread.
• Mowing has been delayed in Matsulu Nature Reserve.
• The Corncrake was the Estonian Bird of the Year in 1995: special attention was paid to clarifying habitat preferences, through the gathering of information on population size in different habitats, especially agricultural sites; widespread media promotion of Corncrakes will emphasise how farmers can help Corncrakes to survive.

Finland

Protected since 1962, classified as Vulnerable.

Important concentrations: south-east Finland, especially southern Karelia, and the south coast.
• No conservation measures have been undertaken specifically for Corncrakes.

France

Fully protected through the 1976 Nature Protection Law against shooting, capture, transport, use and persecution, including egg-collecting. Listed in the French Red Data Book as Vulnerable.

Important concentrations: Basses Vallées Angevines (BVA), Loire valley, Charente valley, Saone valley and Carentan marshes in Normandy.
• Although 80% of the national Corncrake population is concentrated in 10 IBAs, none of these sites has any legal protection.
• Voluntary schemes providing payments to farmers for Corncrake management were introduced in 1993 when 6 million French francs were spent on management over about 6000 ha (Marais de Carentan 3100 ha, BVA 1975 ha, Val de Soane 480 ha, Val de Meuse 400 ha) benefiting 10% to 20% of the national Corncrake population. The schemes are funded through the following programmes:
– Environmentally Sensitive Areas. Six ESAs have been established covering all the important concentrations mentioned above, except the Charente valley, Vallée de l'Oise and Vallée de la Meuse. Mowing is delayed (although sometimes not late enough for Corncrakes) and fertilisation regulated. Participation of farmers is variable, for example, in the Saone valley as much as one third of the habitat, but in the Meuse valley less than 10%.
– European Union ACNAT/LIFE. In four areas – Marais de Carentan, BVA, Val de Saone and Vallées du Nord-Est de la France (Meuse, Oise, Aisne, Chiers).
– In 1994 a LIFE nature programme was started to cover about 400 ha more through pilot programmes in five important areas in Val de Charente, Val de Loire, Val de Saone and Val de Seine.
– Through the CAP mechanism, beef grazed at less than 1.4 livestock units per ha receive a premium payment of 300 French francs per ha (approximately £35).
– The planting of poplars has been regulated in BVA.
– About 600 ha of land has now been acquired and is managed as nature reserves for

Corncrakes, including 180 ha by the Federation Departmentale de Chasseurs du Maine et Loire, 180 ha by Conservatoire Régional Rhône-Alpes, 200 ha by LPO and 70 ha by the Conservatoire des Sites Bourguignons.
• Experiment on Corncrake-friendly mowing (centre-out) in the Saone valley (1994, 1995).
• Research on Corncrake habitat use has been undertaken (relationship between mowing dates and quality of hay and Corncrake numbers); this has included funding from the EU LIFE programme (relationship between mowing dates and site fidelity, densities and population trends).
• EU LIFE-funded project with the Republic of Ireland and the United Kingdom.

Germany

Fully protected by the Nature Protection Law.

Important concentrations: Unteres Odertal in Brandenburg, Murnauer Moos and vicinity in Bayern, and north-west Niedersachsen.
• In a very few local areas, mowing has been stopped around the calling sites (NGOs and nature reserves).
• In Brandenburg Biosphere Reserves, National Parks and Landscape Parks (mainly in the Oder and Elbe valleys) farmers are paid 550 Deutschmarks per ha by the state authority to cut only small areas at a time (maximum 6 ha), and not more than 25% before 15 June, 50% before 30 June and 75% before 15 August. Together with four other similar programmes, the state of Brandenburg paid 18 million Deutschmarks in 1994 for bird-friendly management of 50000 ha of grassland.
• The two most important Corncrake areas have statutory protection, though not specifically for Corncrakes: Untere Oder National Park and Murnauer Moos Naturschutzgebiet nature protection area.
• In the Naturschutzgebiet "Lange Rhon" (17 calling males in 1993) 5% to 10% of management agreements from the "Bayerisches Naturschutzforderprogramme" delay mowing until 1 August (prior to 1992 the date was only 10 July). Also since 1992, farmers have voluntarily been leaving 5% to 10% of their meadows uncut under the "fallow-strip-concept". In November 1994 a new guideline for management agreements was introduced by the Bavarian State Ministry for the Environment providing much better possibilities for Corncrake management.
• Radio-tracking studies in 1991 on habitat use and breeding biology.
• Scientists from Germany and Poland undertook an intensive study from 1992 to 1994 including fieldwork in north-east Poland and also Czech Republic, Germany, Slovakia and Russia. Investigations covered: habitat use, mating system, breeding biology, vegetation structure, availability of food, feeding ecology, predation, biometry, migration, individuality of calls, calling groups and determination of sex and age. Methods include to date of writing trapping (700 birds), radio-tracking, counts of calling males, attracting migrating birds using tape-recorders, measurements of vegetation structure and food availabil-ity, DNA-fingerprinting and analysis of faeces. Six birds were kept in captivity and in 1994 the first successful captive breeding occurred.

Hungary

Strictly protected since 1988.

Important concentrations: Bodrogkoz, Hansag, Bodva-volgy.
• A new protected area has been designated.
• From 1990 to 1993, 100000 forint were spent on Corncrake conservation measures and a further 100000 forint on population surveys.

Republic of Ireland

Fully protected, being listed on Schedule 1 of the Wildlife Act 1976. Listed in the Irish Red Data Book as Endangered (Whilde, 1993).

Important concentrations: Shannon Callows, northern Donegal and Mayo.
• Introduction of Rural Environment Protection Schemes (ESA equivalent) from 1994, including specific management prescriptions (delayed and centre-out mowing, habitat creation measures) on Natural Heritage areas (statutory sites) important for Corncrakes.
• National Parks and Wildlife Service/IWC voluntary payment schemes to farmers for Corncrake management began in 1992 in northern Donegal (1992 £2785, 17% take-up; 1993 £2457, 20%

take-up; 1994 £5358, about 60% take-up) and were extended to the Shannon Callows (1993 £16638, 30% take-up; 1994 £70640, 80% take-up) and Moy valley (1994 £10215, about 55% take-up).
• IWC is acquiring land on the Shannon Callows (21 ha so far).
• Radio-tracking studies were undertaken by IWC/RSPB in the Shannon Callows from 1992 to 1994.
• EU LIFE-funded project with France and the United Kingdom.

Italy

Fully protected (from hunting, and taking and destruction of nests, eggs and chicks) under the National Law on Fauna Protection and Shooting Regulation (L. 157/92). The species was removed from the quarry list in 1978 prior to which it was mainly shot in August, during migration.

Important concentrations: province of Udine in Friuli-Venezia Giulia region, Veneto region especially Vicenza and Treviso provinces.
• The Osservatorio Faunistico for the province of Udine commissioned a preliminary report on the species in 1994. A researcher was funded to assist with the Italian national survey in 1995. LIPU is continuing survey work in other provinces in 1996.

Latvia

Fully protected since 1980 (including eggs, young and nests) by the regulation on particularly protected nature objects (territories and species). Included in the Latvian Red Data Book in category 2, "Declining" (Andrusaltis et al., 1985). (Proposed to be "Vulnerable with continuing declines": Lipsbergs et al., 1990.)

Important concentrations: widespread.
• A small proportion of the population breeds in existing and proposed protected areas.
• Surveys were carried out in some areas from 1989 to 1994 to determine numbers, trends, habitat selection and important sites for protection.
• Public awareness was raised in 1995, the European Nature Conservation Year, by depicting the Corncrake on postage stamps and by an associated information booklet.

Liechtenstein

Fully protected. Included in the Red Data Book as Endangered.

Important concentrations: Ruggeller Riet.
• No conservation measures have been undertaken specifically for Corncrakes.

Lithuania

Fully protected by the regulation on particularly protected nature objects. Included in the 1990 Red Data Book as an indeterminate, insufficiently studied species (fourth category).

Important concentrations: Nemunas valley and delta, Jura valley, central Lithuanian plain, Katra valley.
• In 1992 and 1993 surveys were carried out in about half of the administrative districts.
• In 1995 the first popular publication on Corncrake protection was produced.

Luxembourg

Fully protected by the National Bird Protection Law (1928). Listed in the National Red Data Book in Category 2.1, "Endangered with extinction" (Weiss 1992).

Important concentrations: near Fentage, Erpeldange/Bous and Pissange.
• No conservation measures have been undertaken specifically for Corncrakes.

Republic of Moldova

Protected, in other words, shooting is banned. Not included in the national Red Data Book.

Important concentrations: north-west, east and south-west Moldova, especially the middle Prut valley.
• Environmentally Sensitive Areas have been established in the middle Prut valley.
• The state has established the following reserves: Padurea Domneasca (seven males), Plaiul Fagilui (five males), Codrii (three males) and Prurul de Jos (two males).

Netherlands

Fully protected under the Bird Act 1936 (from shooting, damage to eggs and young, deliberate disturbance). Included in the Red Data Book as Endangered and Vulnerable (Osieck and Hustings, 1994).

Important concentrations: Rhine-Waal-Yssel river forelands and arable land in the north-eastern Groningen province (although the latter is declining sharply).
• Thirteen IBAs regularly hold 1 to 5 singing males, between them accounting for 32% of the national breeding population (23% in the five best sites) (Van den Tempel and Osieck, 1994). Only two of them (Oostvaardersplassen, Brabantse Biesbosch) are designated SPAs, holding 2% of the population. All 13 IBAs are at least partly protected by national law and/or owned by nature protection organisations. Although none are managed specifically for Corncrakes, managers usually take care when a singing male is present.
• Some small reserves have been established for Corncrakes, for example, in the early 1960s the Dutch State Forestry bought an area in the Sliedrechtse Biesbosch (no longer managed specifically for Corncrakes, but it had on average five singing males, 1989-91) and in the late 1970s and early 1980s it acquired land with singing Corncrakes in the Rhine area close to the German border (Ooypolders).
• From 1968 to 1986 over 500 birds were ringed, and research was undertaken on habitat use, territorial behaviour and movements (van den Bergh, 1991).
• From 1984 to 1987 an extensive study was made of numbers, distribution and habitat selection in the agricultural north-eastern part of Groningen province (Voslamber, 1989). Surveys continued to 1992 and were carried out again in 1995 (K. Koffijberg, pers. comm.).

Norway

Under the 1981 Species Protection Act as revised in 1993, Corncrakes are fully protected from shooting, nest destruction and disturbance, and adults, nests, eggs and young receive special protection during the breeding season. Included in the Norwegian Red List of vertebrates (Christensen and Eldøy, 1988) and the Norwegian Red List (DN rapport, 1992-96).

Important concentrations: Co. Rogaland, Møre and Romsdal, Akershus and Buskerud.
• Negligible numbers occur in protected areas.
• A national survey of Corncrakes was carried out in 1995, in which 70 calling males were found.
• A brochure promoting corncrake-friendly farming practices was widely distributed in 1995.

Poland

Fully protected under the Species Protection Act. Not listed in the Red Data Book for birds.

Important concentrations: Narew valley, Biebrza valley, Przemysl and Krosno areas and perhaps the foothills of the Bieszczady mountains.
• Most of the Biebrza valley was declared a National Park in 1993.
• German and Polish scientists undertook a major investigation on Corncrakes from 1992 to 1994 (see "Germany", above). Study sites included the Narew and Biebrza valleys. In 1994 about 200 ha of meadows were rented as a study area where early mowing was avoided.

Romania

Not protected under the 1973 nature protection law (9/1973). Included in the new Red Data Book published in 1995.

Important concentrations: widespread.
• No conservation measures have been undertaken specifically for Corncrakes.

Russian Federation

A quarry species, and not protected under any special laws. Will be included in the appendix of the Russian Red Data Book as a species requiring special control, but not special protection.

Important concentrations: widespread.
• No conservation measures have been undertaken specifically for Corncrakes although the species is protected within strict nature reserves (Zapovedniks) along with other bird species.
• In 1994 censuses were carried out in areas where there had been previous counts of Corncrakes. In addition, surveys in three river valleys (Oka, Moskva and Msta) showed that Corncrake densities were high enough for the valleys to qualify as IBAs.

Serbia and Montenegro

Important concentrations: in Serbia, Vojvodina, especially the Sava and Danube valleys; in Montenegro, Lake Plavsko jezero at the head of the Lim river.

Slovakia

Protected since 1 January 1995 (against trapping, and taking of eggs or young) by Law No. 287/94 of the Slovak Parliament on the conservation of nature and landscape. A special notice on the conservation of animals, connected to this general law, is currently in preparation and will include protection of nests, habitats and designation of special reserves for the Corncrake. Listed as Vulnerable in the former Czechoslovakian Red Data Book and also probably in the new Red Bird List for Slovakia (in preparation).

Important concentrations: widespread.
• During the last decade no special measures on research or protection of the Corncrake have been undertaken.
• The state nature conservation authorities have legal powers to restrict activities affecting the Corncrake, but these have not been implemented due to a lack of the necessary funds for Corncrake-friendly management.
• A management plan is being prepared for meadows in the Záhorie area.
• A group for the protection of the corncrake is currently being established by the Slovak Agency of Environment (under the auspices of the Ministry of Environment).

Slovenia

Fully protected (from hunting, and destruction of nests, eggs, chicks and habitat). Included in the Red Data Book as Endangered.

Important concentrations: Lake Cerknisko, Ljubljansko barje, west Julian Alps, Planinsko polje, Reka valley.
• A full national survey was carried out in 1992 and 1993 by DOPPS, plus some ringing.
• No conservation measures have been undertaken specifically for Corncrakes.

Spain

Legally protected (from shooting and harm to eggs, young and nest, but not from damage to habitat) and classified as "of special interest" in the National Catalogue of Threatened Species (Royal Decree 439/90). Included in the Red Data Book as Indeterminate (ICONA, 1986).

Important concentrations: Cinca basin, Ebro depression in Catalonia.
• The Catalonia Government has established two reserves: Llobregat delta (one male in 1984, 1993) and Montenegre mountain, Tordera (two males since 1990). No conservation measures have been undertaken specifically for Corncrakes.

Sweden

Fully protected from hunting and habitat damage under a schedule of the Wildlife Act.

Important concentrations: Oland, Gotland and Uppland.
• Radio-tracking studies were undertaken from 1992 to 1994 in South Oland to investigate the relationship between habitat, mowing and breeding success.

Switzerland

Protected under the *Bundesgesetz über die Änderung des Bundesgesetzes über Jagd und Vogelschutz vom 1962*. Protected under the federal law on hunting and bird protection, *Bundesgesetz über die Jagd und den Schutz der wildlebenden Säugetiere und Vögel vom 1986*, from shooting, damage to nests, eggs and young, and disturbance at the nest. Swiss Red Data Book, category 2, Endangered (Zbinden et al., 1994).

Important concentrations: Neuchatel and Vaud cantons of the Jura mountains.
• There has been a general change in agricultural policy to less intensive agricultural management of meadows.
• No Corncrakes breed in protected areas.

Ukraine

A quarry species, fully protected only in state Nature Reserves and partially protected in other nature protected areas. Not included in the new Red Data book of Ukraine.

Important concentrations: north-eastern and central Ukraine.
• No conservation measures have been undertaken specifically for Corncrakes.

United Kingdom

Fully protected under schedule 1 of the Wildlife and Countryside Act 1981 (in Britain) and Wildlife (Northern Ireland) Order 1985. A national action plan for this species was published in 1996 by the biodiversity steering group set up under the UK Biodiversity Action Plan (1994).

Listed in Red Data Birds in Britain (Batten et al., 1990).

Important concentrations: Western Isles, Inner Argyll Islands, Orkney.
• Through the European Union Common Agricultural Policy (CAP) mechanism, beef grazed at less than 1.4 livestock units per receive a premium payment.
• ESAs are established in the Western Isles, Inner Hebrides and Co. Fermanagh by government agriculture departments.
• Voluntary schemes are run throughout the range of the Corncrake to encourage delayed mowing and Corncrake-friendly mowing in strips or centre-out.
• SNH has established a scheme to promote the growing of late-cut hay in Skye. However this is not targeted particularly at Corncrakes and there are no options for the provision of early cover, so no Corncrakes are present in the area covered by the scheme despite the spending of £2002 over 51 ha in 1993 and £2500 over 60 ha in 1994.
• Around the RSPB reserve of Balranald, the RSPB established a hay scheme paying £2600 in 1993 and (with the addition of an option to increase early cover) £5600 in 1994. Numbers have increased from 11 in 1992 to 13 in 1994.
• The RSPB has established three reserves: Coll, 18 males in 1994; Balranald (North Uist), 13 males in 1994; Loch Gruinart, five males in 1994.

• Full surveys carried out in 1978 and 1979, 1988 and 1993, with annual population monitoring of the majority of the United Kingdom population

(since 1992 in Scotland and since 1990 in Northern Ireland).
• Radio-tracking studies carried out from 1985 to 1987 (the RSPB with Nature Conservancy Council funding) and 1993 and 1994 (RSPB) on habitat selection, timing of breeding and the effect of mowing on breeding success.
• The benefits to the crofting community of Corncrake-friendly management have been promoted (by the RSPB and the Scottish Crofters' Union).
• EU LIFE-funded project with the Republic of Ireland and France (see below).

Aims and objectives

Aims

1. To prevent any further declines below 1994 levels in the population size and distribution of the Corncrake in Europe (so removing the species from BirdLife International's World List of Threatened Birds (Collar et. al., 1994)).

2. To ensure the recovery of small breeding populations of Corncrake at risk of extinction.

Objectives

The policy objectives set out in this section should all be aimed at achieving the following detailed habitat measures.

Maintain or increase the area of habitats suitable for Corncrakes

•Natural habitats that require minimal human interference to maintain their suitability for Corncrakes (highest priority).
• Most habitats used by Corncrakes require low-intensity grassland farming management to keep the vegetation structure suitable.
•Land-claim, conversion to arable, intensification and abandonment of farmed habitats should be discouraged. Habitat restoration should be encouraged.

Manage suitable habitats in a Corncrake-friendly way

Sustainable extensive grass-based farming to benefit Corncrakes, which usually involves mowing, requires either:

• Continuation of traditional unmechanised methods (mainly in central and eastern European countries)
– maintain, as appropriate, farm size (small), type,(extensive, grass-based), and diversity (not monoculture); or
• Modification of mechanised methods (mainly in western Europe)
– reduce agrochemical inputs,
– grow late-cut hay or silage,
– discourage faster machinery such as circle mowers,
– Corncrake-friendly cutting (delay cutting; cut in small compartments over a long period; cut from centre to edges or in strips)

Both systems require sustainable rural communities with sufficient farmers to undertake the necessary management, which will be relatively labour-intensive, at least in unmechanised systems.

• Maintenance or development of tall ground vegetation throughout the season near or adjacent to hay meadows
• Careful control of the timing and stocking density of grazing.

1. Policy and legislation

1.1. *To encourage policies at an international level that benefit Corncrakes*

1.1.1. Encourage international agencies and governments in bilateral arrangements to promote extensive, grass-based farming through all their investment and agricultural policies, trade agreements and legislation

Organisations, particularly the World Bank, International Monetary Fund (IMF), World Trade Organisation (WTO), Organisation for Economic Co-operation and Development (OECD), Food and Agriculture Organisation (FAO), North Atlantic Treaty Organisation (Nato), European Bank for Reconstruction and Development (EBRD), European Union (EU) and Council of Europe (CoE), which have influence over recipient countries, national policy development should promote sustainable rural development which maintains Corncrake habitats and encourages Corncrake-friendly management practices.

Aid to countries in central and eastern Europe:
Agencies which provide aid to countries – especially the World Bank, EBRD, FAO, IMF, EU and also national governments in bilateral arrangements – should promote sustainable rural development which benefits Corncrakes. For example:

• Assess the environmental consequences of international aid for investment in agricultural and other development, for example, through EU strategic environmental assessment legislation.
• Minimise schemes and grants that could damage important sites or promote intensification, damaging changes to farm structure (e.g. size, type and diversity), or other damaging effects.
• Allocate a minimum 10% of support to rural areas for environmentally sensitive farming, with Corncrake habitats a clear priority. Direct funds to rural development projects that retain small-scale farming communities whose practices are extensive and specific farming schemes to benefit wildlife.
• Attach environmental conditions to aid, for example, conditional on signing the Biodiversity Convention (see 1.1.5).

Conditions attached to agreements on trade:
It is recommended that environmental conditions should be attached to all relevant trade agreements (e.g. the EU Association Agreements – the political and trade agreements between the EU and central and eastern European countries) which affect land use. Conditions which could harm extensive farming, such as those which require land privatisation as a condition of trade concessions, should be assessed and minimised.

Priority: high
Time-scale: ongoing

1.1.2. Encourage the development of sustainable agriculture and adequate nature conservation legislation, funding and action at the same time as economic development

Political and economic developments in Europe, including accession of more countries to the EU, will lead to further development of the economies of "marginal" areas through financial assistance, for example, the Structural Funds and PHARE (EU aid to central and eastern European countries). As central and eastern

European countries undergo transition to a market economy, prices and living standards will rise and farming and other industries will re-adjust to market conditions. This will mean pressure on natural and farmed habitats from land-claim and intensification or abandonment of farmed land. However, the rapid changes in farming expected in Europe will create opportunities for conservation as well as threats.

Enhance levels of nature protection:
The development of rural areas in Europe will need to be matched by increased environmental standards. Central and eastern European countries will need to adopt a similar level of nature protection legislation and policies to those of the EU, and to ensure channelling of adequate resources for nature protection institutions, science and projects.

Promote environmentally sensitive farming:
Policies that are being pursued to adjust farming structures, for example granting aid for farm amalgamation and development, should be used to benefit the environment, and avoid causing incidental damage.

Most scope for conservation action through influencing farmers financially in the short term is through payments for sympathetic management under policies such as those adopted in the EU under the Agri-environment Regulation 2078/92 and related measures. There is the potential in the medium term to have similar measures adopted in central and eastern European countries on their accession to the EU or through aid programmes.

It is recommended that EU agricultural policy be reformed to support extensive farming, shifting support for production towards support for environmental management, particularly through schemes based on Regulation 2078/92, but also through commodity reforms, Less Favoured Area policies, etc. The EU could draw up a list of potential ESAs which would benefit the Corncrake. The EU could also promote policies with low subsidies for production and high subsidies for environmental management within central and eastern European countries.

In central and eastern European countries, support (e.g. through capital grants for equipment) is needed to prevent abandonment and ensure continued agricultural management where this is required to maintain Corncrake habitats, and also to encourage the extensive management practices characteristic of good Corncrake habitats.

"Debt for nature" agreements, under which creditor states relieve the foreign debts of a country in exchange for appropriate conservation policies and their effective implementation, should be developed as an important potential source of funding for Corncrake conservation work, including reserve management costs (see 2.1.3.2).

Priority: high
Time-scale: ongoing

1.1.3. Encourage international agencies, especially the European Union, Council of Europe and national governments to co-operate to promote actions 1.1 and 1.2

Many governments and agencies have aid and assistance programmes in central and eastern European countries. These should be co-ordinated, and assistance given to developing environmentally sustainable policies and practices by using PHARE, TACIS etc., to support technical exchange and networks of policy specialists.

Experts throughout Europe, in agri-environment policy and agricultural land management for wildlife, particularly Corncrakes, should establish a network to: develop a strategic programme of policy analysis, development and promotion; exchange information; develop policy ideas for Corncrake conservation; monitor trends in agricultural policies affecting the central and east European countries in relation to potential risks and opportunities for Corncrakes.

Such a network should consist of western and eastern experts drawn from government agriculture and environment ministries, NGOs including BirdLife International and independent experts.

A conference to prepare an agri-environment action plan for transition to the European Union took place in May 1995, in Hungary, organised by BirdLife International, with support from the EU and from EU governments.

1.1.4. Consider the implications for Corncrakes of international flows of private capital investment in agriculture

Many EU (and United States) businesses are investing in central and eastern European countrie's agriculture (e.g. Bernard Matthews, Sentry Farming, Velcourt Farming) and are having a big impact on land use. This should be examined with a view to assessing the likely impacts on Corncrakes and the potential for influencing private capital investment in favour of Corncrakes.

Priority: medium
Time-scale: ongoing

1.1.5. Encourage all relevant international conventions to give Corncrakes maximum protection and all Corncrake range states to sign and ratify these

The Corncrake already receives maximum protection through the Bern Convention and the European Union's Wild Birds Directive. Protection could be strengthened, however, for example, through official addition of the species to Appendix II of the Bonn Convention (this will be addressed in 1997).

Ratification of these conventions represents the minimum level of protection necessary for a species such as the Corncrake which is widely dispersed and dependent on specific management. Hence, such commitments and legal agreements must be complemented by habitat management achieved through projects and policies (see 1.1.1–1.1.4, 1.2).

Priority: medium
Time-scale: medium

1.2. *To promote policies at national and regional (within the country) level that benefit Corncrakes*

1.2.1. Encourage all range states to prepare a national Corncrake action plan

Using this international action plan as a basis, each country should be encouraged to prepare a national plan. This should use the best available information on Corncrake populations, habitat requirements and ecology to determine measurable national population targets for Corncrakes and to define the conservation actions necessary to achieve these targets within an agreed timescale. The plans should specify clearly which organisations are to implement each action. Such action plans will contribute to each signatory country's commitments under the Biodiversity Convention. A strategic habitat approach is also to be encouraged. The Corncrake is a priority species for the forthcoming Habitat Strategy for Agricultural Habitats being prepared as one of eight habitat strategies for birds by BirdLife International (Tucker, in press). This will provide a framework for habitat action planning at national level.

Priority: high
Time-scale: short

1.2.2. Encourage all range states to give the maximum appropriate legal protection to Corncrakes and their habitats

National nature protection legislation should be maintained or enhanced to give the Corncrake full protection, including through adequate site protection legislation. Corncrakes already receive full protection in all EU states plus Belarus, Bulgaria, Croatia, Czech Republic, Latvia, Norway, Poland, Slovenia and Switzerland. Legal protection needs to be strengthened in Estonia, Lithuania, Romania and Slovakia and especially in Russia and Ukraine where the Corncrake is still listed as a quarry species. All range states should be encouraged to list the Corncrake as a species which justifies the designation of protected areas.

Priority: high
Time-scale: medium

1.2.3. Encourage national rural policies and legislation that are amended or introduced in an integrated manner to the benefit of Corncrakes

Government officials in agriculture, environment, water, forestry, rural and regional development departments and environment and nature conservation agencies should promote the reform of rural policies. Politicians in national governments and their advisers should be encouraged to lead this process. Agricultural advisory bodies, institutes, farmers' organisations and universities should also be lobbied to promote change (see also 4.1.2).

All rural land use policies should be closely integrated, with nature conservation objectives tied closely to other policy objectives. In particular, it is recommended that the emphasis of agricultural policies should change from food production only, to include conservation of the countryside, including nature conservation.

For the Corncrake to benefit from changes to rural policy, it could be used as a flagship species to promote extensive, grass-based farming (while keeping in mind the requirements of other priority species). It is recommended that specific targets for Corncrake conservation should be developed in national biodiversity plans and these should be supported within national rural policies for other economic sectors.

Within the European Union, the Structural Funds should promote rural development initiatives that will help sustain rural economies and communities in areas with Corncrake-friendly farming systems. Such initiatives could include marketing and processing of the produce of extensive farming systems, wildlife-based and other sensitive tourism (see 1.2.3.4), and other small-scale business development. It is recommended that all such EU-funded programmes should be subject to strategic environmental assessment to ensure that they have no adverse impacts on Corncrakes.

Priority: high
Time-scale: ongoing

1.2.3.1. Encourage national policies on land tenure (especially privatisation), farm restructuring and capital investment aid for agricultural "improvements" (meliorations) that favour Corncrakes

Many agricultural policies are determined at a national level, for example, land tenure (including privatisation) and capital grant aid to farmers. The potential of these policies to harm Corncrake habitat, especially through intensification, should be minimised. For example, grants for amalgamation of fields and farms should ensure that small-scale mosaics of grass-based farming are retained

and either that sufficient numbers of farmers are retained for continuation of traditional labour-intensive practices or that provision is made to compensate for loss of yield due to delayed mowing using Corncrake-friendly methods. However, governments should not normally provide capital funding for intensification of agriculture through land-claim, drainage, farm amalgamation and acquisition of machinery in any areas important for Corncrakes.

Priority: high
Time-scale: ongoing

1.2.3.2. Encourage national policies on taxation and employment legislation in relation to agriculture that include specific reference to balancing the needs of economic development with conservation

Many general policies that are not specific to agriculture (e.g., tax and employment legislation) have the potential to detrimentally affect the structure of farming and farming practices. One example is the saving of taxes by the purchase of agricultural machinery. Another is land taxes on hay meadows and wet grasslands (or even penalties to ensure intensive use or afforestation). Such policies encourage intensification and could be altered (e.g. by removing or reducing the taxes) to encourage the labour-intensive, grass-based farming systems needed by Corncrakes.

Priority: medium
Time-scale: ongoing

1.2.3.3. Encourage the allocation of funding to pay farmers for Corncrake-friendly management, targeted at key areas

In European Union member states, the agri-environment regulation 2078/92, extensification and ESA policies should be promoted and targeted at important areas for Corncrakes, with appropriate prescriptions. In countries about to, or planning to, join the EU, it is recommended that similar schemes should be developed, promoted and targeted at Corncrakes.

Management agreement schemes, designed specifically as hay meadow or Corncrake schemes, should aim to maintain, and where possible increase, the area of hay meadows and wetlands and manage these in a Corncrake-friendly way (see summary of main actions above). The schemes should have clear and measurable nature conservation targets, linked to international conventions, especially the Biodiversity Convention, and comprehensive monitoring of their results should be undertaken. To establish and successfully implement such schemes, publicity and campaigning, based on careful strategy, will be necessary to demonstrate the need for them, their feasibility, take-up of options by farmers, etc.

Funding for such schemes should come from agriculture budgets where possible, from within the Common Agricultural Policy (CAP) in the EU (especially regulation 2078) and from sources such as EU PHARE, World Bank, EBRD, IMF and bilateral aid in central and eastern European countries. Where funding from state agriculture departments is still under negotiation, the state nature conservation authorities, with assistance from conservation NGOs as appropriate, could introduce Corncrake grant schemes in strategically targeted areas (only where agricultural intensification is a problem). As well as protecting the local Corncrake populations the areas where these "pilot" or "model" schemes are taken up can act as trials and demonstrations of Corncrake-friendly practices.

Conservation organisations should identify priority areas, sources of funds and collaborators in farming organisations to implement the schemes (see 4.1.2, below). Sometimes, a Corncrake grant scheme will be a "top-up" of existing extensification or conservation schemes and sometimes it will be a separate scheme. It should be noted that in certain central and east European countries where farmers have suffered from recent economic crises, payment schemes are likely to be particularly effective.

Priority: high
Time-scale: ongoing

1.2.3.4. Sensitive development of ecotourism, where appropriate

In some important Corncrake areas, especially outside the central and eastern European countries, ecotourism could bring benefits, for example by providing funding for appropriate management as well as by raising public support for the Corncrake. However, this industry should be developed sensitively – promoting the Corncrake in the context of its landscape – and only where it is possible to carry it out with no detriment to Corncrakes or other wildlife.

Priority: low
Time-scale: ongoing

1.2.4. Ensure development of strong NGOs with competence in Corncrake conservation in all range states

Strong NGOs with expertise (well-trained staff) and resources (including well-informed members) are essential to ensure Corncrake conservation through, for example:
• Encouragement of, and co-operation with, governments in the funding and management of Corncrake-friendly practices (see 1.2.3.3).
• Reserve acquisition (2.1.3.1).
• Research to inform national policies and advice on Corncrakes (3.1–3.11).
• Undertaking education and awareness-raising work on the plight and requirements of the Corncrake (4.1–4.2).
• International liaison and co-operation on Corncrakes including:
– Corncrake research (see 3.11);
– exchanging experiences and advice on education and training of farmers, conservation officials, etc., and the preparation of management plans (see 2.2);
– raising awareness and generating international solidarity to encourage national governments to make commitments to Corncrake conservation (see 2.2).

Priority: high
Time-scale: ongoing

1.2.5. Re-creation of the Corncrake habitat in areas of former importance for the species

In several western European countries, much of the best Corncrake habitat has been destroyed through drainage, land-claim and conversion to arable, etc. In recent years, some governments (e.g. Denmark) have granted an annual sum for re-establishment of habitats formerly important for wildlife, and part of this should be targeted towards re-establishment of Corncrake habitats. It should be emphasised that Corncrake habitats also benefit other threatened species, for example, the White Stork, Garganey *Anas querquedula*, Black-tailed Godwit *Limosa limosa*, threatened amphibians, plants (e.g. orchids) and many others.

Priority: medium
Time-scale: ongoing

2.   Species and habitat protection

2.1.   *To encourage adequate protection for key Corncrake sites*

2.1.1. Identify key Corncrake sites that qualify as Important Bird Areas

It is essential to identify all key European sites for breeding Corncrakes and ensure that they are listed as Important Bird Areas (IBAs) according to agreed BirdLife International criteria (BirdLife International, in prep.). The most appropriate criterion for selecting Corncrake IBAs is that "the site holds significant numbers of one or more globally threatened species". A definition of "significant" has not yet been finalised. A conservative estimate of 1% of the European population is 900 calling males; only about a third of the range states (as few as 10) have a total population at that level, and, due to the dispersed distribution of this species, very few, if any, sites would have numbers which met this threshold.

New Corncrake IBAs should be identified in the light of results of the forthcoming European Corncrake survey (3.1.1). For large countries of apparent importance for Corncrakes but where Corncrake surveys have not yet been carried out at all, (e.g. Belarus), or have only just started (e.g. Russia), the following procedure for identifying Corncrake IBAs should be followed:

1. Set priorities by ranking habitats in order of Corncrake density and productivity on the basis of data from previous research in sample areas.

2. Get complementary preliminary information on Corncrake densities (and productivity where possible) in the different habitat types and regions including verification of rankings in 1, above. Existing distribution, or other data on Corncrakes from local people, including ornithologists, should be collated, even though little data may be available.

3. Identify potential IBAs on the basis of suitable Corncrake habitats (manual methods of map analysis, GIS, satellite images, etc.), making use of existing vegetation and land use maps as appropriate. Where it is impossible to undertake Corncrake surveys, IBAs could be identified solely on the basis of this habitat assessment. Otherwise:

4. Undertake special surveys in a sample of sites (selected to be a representative of the various Corncrake habitats, established in 2, above) to determine the number of Corncrakes included within each potential Corncrake IBA, and the boundaries of the site.

5. Rank IBAs according to Corncrake numbers and reassess the threshold population size used to identify IBAs if necessary (according to the current national population size and number of sites selected).

During this process the following should be taken into consideration:
• Sites with successful breeding and near-natural or natural habitats with small or no human impact and restricted management should be given priority (in the absence of data on breeding success the prevalence of late and Corncrake-friendly mowing should be taken to indicate probable breeding success).
• Widely standardised habitat definitions (as currently being developed by BirdLife International for IBAs) should be used to ensure comparable results across the range of the species (see also 3.6).

Priority: high
Time-scale: short

2.1.2. Encourage optimum statutory protection for important Corncrake sites

2.1.2.1. Identify and encourage the statutory designation, as appropriate, of all internationally and nationally important Corncrake sites

Each range state should be encouraged to identify all Corncrake sites, including IBAs, that qualify for statutory site protection under relevant existing international and national legislation. Each range state should determine the target proportion of the national Corncrake population to be encompassed by statutory site protection measures. This will depend on the Corncrake status, strength of statutory site protection in that country and adequacy of alternative means of securing requisite habitat management including wider countryside measures.

Range states should be encouraged to evaluate the adequacy of statutory site protection measures which can be applied to Corncrake sites, in terms of the range of controls over land use, efficacy of enforcement, scope of coverage of land types, etc. Any deficiencies in the system or its application should be rectified. National policies for statutory site designation should recognise that sites which are important for Corncrakes, and are in agricultural rather than natural biotopes, and which are not necessarily of very high biodiversity, should be considered for designation.

Important international site designations for Corncrakes under international legislation include Biosphere Reserves and IUCN Category 2 National Parks throughout the range and, in the European Union, SPA/Natura 2000. IUCN Category 2 National Park status may be preferable where Corncrakes occur in natural habitats, whereas Biosphere Reserve buffer zones may be more appropriate where their habitats depend on agriculture. Other relevant international designations are Ramsar and World Heritage Sites and Council of Europe biogenetic reserves. National (and regional, as appropriate) governments and statutory conservation agencies, with support from convention secretariats where necessary, are encouraged to ensure that all Corncrake sites which would benefit from statutory site protection are designated, including all IBAs. The particular mechanism(s) selected for each site should be that which affords it the strongest protection and best opportunities for Corncrake-friendly management. In some cases landscape conservation designations will be as relevant as those for biodiversity conservation purposes. It is recommended that the highest possible level of statutory protection should be secured for all IBAs listed for Corncrakes (see 2.1.1) by 2004.

Priority: high
Time-scale: long

2.1.2.2. Encourage Corncrake-friendly management policies and practices on all proposed and existing statutory sites for Corncrakes, taking account of the requirements of other high priority species (birds and others) where appropriate

It is essential that all relevant statutory sites – both biological and landscape – have management plans, preferably published, which include policies and prescriptions for Corncrakes to ensure that site management benefits Corncrakes as well as other priority species. As part of these management plans it is essential that managers of protected sites monitor trends in Corncrake populations in relation to management practices, and take account of their findings in modifying management where necessary. In central and eastern European countries, local NGOs and experts (supported as necessary by foreign governments, experts and international NGOs), should advise on legislation, policy and management to optimise the management of national protected sites for Corncrakes.

Priority: high
Time-scale: ongoing

2.1.2.3. Protect Corncrake sites from damaging developments

The statutory protection afforded to a site by its designation is only as good as the scope, application and enforcement of relevant legislation. Corncrake sites face a range of development threats such as individual land use development projects involving integrated rural development, industrial and housing developments, land drainage schemes, afforestation proposals and inappropriate tourist developments. Any potentially damaging developments which are on Corncrake sites or are otherwise likely to affect Corncrakes should be opposed or modified. Such developments and changes of land use should be subject to an adequate environmental impact assessment of both their individual and cumulative impacts.

Priority: high/medium
Time-scale: ongoing

2.1.2.4. Seek to obtain the maximum benefit from international conventions in protecting sites for Corncrakes

In addition to 1.1.5 above, international convention secretariats are encouraged to assist in ensuring that member states designate all key sites for Corncrakes under the relevant conventions, as appropriate, for example, Ramsar. Under such conventions the international status of sites designated should be used as a stimulus to strengthen national legislation and its implementation and enforcement and to raise public awareness of Corncrakes. Conventions (e.g. Ramsar, Bern, Bonn) should also be invoked in defending internationally important sites for Corncrakes (see 2.1.2.3 above).

Priority: high
Time-scale: ongoing

2.1.3. Acquire and appropriately manage nature reserves for Corncrakes

Nature reserves, defined here as areas owned and/or managed primarily for nature conservation, need to be acquired and managed for Corncrakes for the following reasons.
• To conserve a particular population of Corncrakes, especially core populations in countries with small populations by protecting its habitat from development threats, and ensuring optimal management to maximise productivity.
• To allow experiments in the development of optimal management techniques.
• To act as a demonstration site for optimal management techniques, including for managers of unprotected areas.
• To show Corncrakes to people to educate and raise awareness and public/political support for the species; this is especially relevant in countries with few Corncrakes.

The two actions below will apply especially to western European countries where Corncrakes tend to be more restricted to core areas. In central and eastern European countries, emphasis should be given to developing strong NGOs with expertise and resources to assist Corncrake conservation through reserve acquisition (see 1.2.4).

Priority: high/medium
Time-scale: ongoing

2.1.3.1. Consider acquisition of land with important Corncrake concentrations

Where there is a potential opportunity for statutory or voluntary nature conservation bodies to acquire land as a nature reserve to benefit Corncrakes, careful consideration should be given to whether acquisition is appropriate. It could, for example, be more cost-effective to protect the Corncrakes through payments (ideally from governments) to land managers for Corncrake-friendly management practices. Natural Corncrake habitats – as opposed to those maintained through agricultural management – should always be a priority for reserve acquisition as minimal management expenses need to be encountered.

Priority: high/medium
Time-scale: ongoing

2.1.3.2. Encourage appropriate management for Corncrakes in and around nature reserves of importance for the species

Management plans with clearly defined objectives and priorities should be considered essential for reserves important for Corncrakes, to ensure that their specific requirements are catered for in the general management of the reserve. Reserve managers should be provided with adequate advice to manage land optimally for Corncrakes. It is important to realise that continued agricultural management is often essential within a nature reserve to maintain habitat suitability.

Wherever possible, reserves, acting as core areas for Corncrakes, should be linked to Corncrake-friendly management (encouraged by financial incentives) in the surrounding wider countryside, enhancing the benefit of the reserve to Corncrakes as well as to the surrounding area.

On some reserves, especially in central and eastern Europe, ecotourism could bring benefits by providing funding for reserve management. However, this industry should be developed sensitively and only where it is possible to do so without detriment to Corncrakes or other wildlife (see 1.2.3.4). In some reserves with vulnerable Corncrake populations, especially in western Europe, human recreation should be managed to avoid disturbance to Corncrakes. Predator control may also be necessary on some reserves.

Priority: high/medium
Time-scale: ongoing

2.2. *Nature conservation organisations should ensure that they collaborate with each other and widely with relevant authorities and interest groups (apart from agricultural ones) regarding Corncrake conservation*

The nature conservation organisations leading Corncrake conservation action in their country should, as necessary, agree between themselves a division of labour regarding the Corncrake, and collaborate with local authorities, hunters, promoters of ecotourism and other conservation organisations to protect Corncrake habitats and promote Corncrake-friendly management.

Priority: medium
Time-scale: ongoing

2.3. *Nature conservation organisations should publish technical advice for administrators, land managers and their advisors responsible for delivering Corncrake-friendly management*

Nature conservation organisations are likely to have the best national expertise on Corncrake-friendly management. To disseminate this they should produce leaflets and technical manuals based on the best available scientific evidence. Funding for their production should be obtained from agricultural agencies where possible. The more technical manuals should be aimed at advisors of farmers – including fieldworkers deployed by the nature conservation and agricultural organisations; more simple guidance in the form of pamphlets should be provided for farmers (see 4.1.2). Technical publications should also be available for the administrative agencies responsible for land use policies, including payment schemes to farmers (see 4.1.1).

Priority: medium
Time-scale: ongoing

3. **Monitoring and research**

3.1. *To develop and implement a European survey and monitoring strategy for the Corncrake*

The three main objectives for a European Corncrake survey and monitoring strategy are:
• Identify the key Corncrake areas within each country.
• Provide a better estimate of total population size.
• Monitor trends in numbers across the range to detect significant changes.

Priority: high
Time-scale: medium

3.1.1. Ensure that comparable Corncrake surveys have been undertaken in all countries in the period 1995 to 2000

It is essential that during the period 1995 to 2000 national Corncrake surveys are undertaken in all European breeding range states, using standard methods. This will make it possible to identify key areas and establish a new European population estimate. Data on mowing dates and productivity (see 3.2.1) should also be collected. This might best be achieved through a pan-European Corncrake survey which could be co-ordinated – in terms of organisation and funding – by BirdLife International.

Priority countries:
The highest priority countries for future survey work, ranked in order (based partly on population sizes and partly on the lack of knowledge), are Russia, Ukraine, Belarus, Romania, Croatia, Bosnia-Herzegovina, Bulgaria and the Baltic states (Lithuania, Latvia, Estonia).

Pilot censuses:
Agreed methods and their practicalities should be tested by running one or two pilot projects in high-priority countries. Such trials were undertaken in 1995 in Russia and Bulgaria. It would be advisable for all high-priority countries to attempt small-scale experimental censuses to familiarise organisers with the methods and difficulties.

Implementation:
In many priority countries there is a shortage of skilled ornithologists to conduct surveys. Even

where such ornithologists exist they are often not in a position to participate in a survey. One solution could be to import birdwatchers into countries where local expertise is lacking, but this prevents creation of potential local job opportunities in conservation and may cause problems over language and lack of familiarity with the areas.

Priority: high
Time-scale: medium

3.1.2. Develop and implement an agreed pan-European monitoring strategy

A strategy for monitoring the European and national Corncrake populations is essential to detect population trends and the impact of conservation actions. Surveys should be repeated every five years where possible, with annual counts in some sample plots. However, in countries where no formal survey has been carried out prior to 1995, the first survey is likely to provide new data on areas of high density and/or productivity. These data can form the basis of an improved stratification as a basis for random sampling for repeat surveys.

Priority: high
Time-scale: ongoing

3.1.3. Establish and develop a Corncrake census working group

A working group is needed to organise census methods and sampling strategy across the Corncrake breeding range. At the Gdansk workshop it was agreed to form such a group under the chairmanship of R. Green (RSPB) to include about four Corncrake survey organisers from Russia and other high-priority countries. The first task of this group has already been accomplished: all 19 relevant range states have completed a questionnaire on the Corncrake census techniques previously used in each country. Following consideration of questionnaire returns, the working group should develop and recommend standard methods to be used for surveys, co-ordination of surveys at international level and evaluation of the results obtained.

Priority: high
Time-scale: ongoing

3.2. To encourage research to determine the impact of mowing on Corncrake populations and to indicate means of reducing the impact

3.2.1. Rapid assessment of the incidence and success of breeding

The presence of singing males in an area does not necessarily indicate successful breeding: males may fail to attract females; if females arrive and lay eggs it may be that virtually all nests fail or that virtually all chicks which hatch die before fledging. Detailed studies are required for full quantification of breeding success. However, some rapid methods can be used as an adjunct to surveys of singing males to identify areas where successful breeding is likely or unlikely to have occurred. During a census, such rapid assessment should be undertaken for at least a sample of areas in which surveys of singing males are carried out.

Priority: high
Time-scale: short

3.2.2. Determination of timing of reproduction and incidence of double-brooding across the Corncrake range

Radio-tracking of female Corncrakes in the United Kingdom has demonstrated that most females lay two clutches, the second of which hatches in mid- to late July. This behaviour has a strong influence on the degree to which delaying the time of mowing improves breeding success. More information is needed on the prevalence of this behaviour in sample areas throughout the breeding range.

Priority: high
Time-scale: medium

3.2.3. Correlation of population trends with habitats and the timing and method of mowing

Correlations have been found between Corncrake population trends and changes in the extent of tall ground vegetation habitats and the timing and method of mowing. Such studies are an essential test of hypotheses generated by more intensive work such as radio-tracking studies. Intensive studies may demonstrate the importance of particular habitats or farming practices in a few study areas, but hypotheses about population change derived from them are only convincing if confirmed by more extensive studies, such as those which compare the ecological circumstances associated with declining and stable populations.

Priority: high
Time-scale: long

3.2.4. Quantification of movements between geographical regions

The choice of an appropriate strategy for the conservation of Corncrakes is affected by the distances moved by individuals both within and between seasons. For example, if most individuals return to breed at some distance from their natal area then measures to increase populations by improving breeding success within small areas might be nullified by dispersal of locally produced recruits.

Priority: high
Time-scale: medium

3.3. To estimate annual survival rates of juveniles and adults

Estimation of survival rates is required for the construction of simulation models of Corncrake populations. Such models are of value in estimating the probable effect on population trends of varying survival and breeding success through conservation measures. Estimation of survival must take into account movements, so that estimates can be made of the number of birds that survive but do not return to particular intensive study areas.

Priority: high
Time-scale: medium

3.4. To investigate the ecological requirements of Corncrakes in habitats subject to infrequent management

Some Corncrakes occur in areas which are not often used for agriculture. Such areas could act as core reserves where Corncrakes would not be subject to adverse pressures from agricultural intensification. However, where agricultural activities have been abandoned relatively recently, such areas may soon become unsuitable for Corncrakes without further management. More information is required on habitat selection, diet,

breeding success and factors affecting important habitat characteristics in these areas.

Priority: high
Time-scale: medium

3.5. To quantify the effectiveness of conservation measures

Available research on Corncrake ecology suggests that several types of conservation action are likely to be effective in enhancing population levels. However, only a few studies have attempted to quantify the benefits of particular types of habitat management or modification of agricultural practice for Corncrakes. Such studies are essential in the design and implementation, with government support, of conservation measures. There is scope for studies of two distinct types: those that examine the effect of management on demographic rates (e.g. the effect of hay-mowing methods on chick survival) and those which aim to assess effects on population size at the level of a region or country.

As declining Corncrake populations may be affected by several interacting factors it is necessary to test the effect of a package of measures if positive results are to be expected at the population level. This should include assessment of the effects of: mowing method on chick survival; changing the time and/or method of mowing on the number of chicks fledged per female; increasing the area of tall ground vegetation; and changing fertiliser and pesticide inputs.

Priority: high
Time-scale: medium

3.6. To develop rapid methods for assessing the suitability of vegetation stands for Corncrakes

Monitoring of Corncrake habitats, including those resulting from experimental management, could be greatly improved if a standard method could be devised of measuring the characteristics of vegetation stands which are important to Corncrakes. Several studies of habitat selection by radio-tagged birds and the characteristics of singing sites and nest sites have identified correlates of habitat preference including species composition, vegetation height and mechanical resistance of the vegetation to passage by

Corncrakes. The results of these studies should be used to produce methods for recording vegetation structure which can be used in rapid field surveys.

Priority: high
Time-scale: short

3.7. To assess the importance of mortality caused by predators on the breeding grounds

There are few estimates of mortality rates of nests, chicks and adults caused by predators. Information is lacking on whether, in some areas, it might be possible to increase numbers of Corncrakes by reducing the proportion killed by predators. Studies should include evaluation of the importance of predation relative to other sources of mortality and whether modifications of habitats, for example increasing the area and quality of vegetation cover, could reduce predation.

Priority: medium
Time-scale: long

3.8. Association of the Corncrake with other wildlife

Areas with high densities of Corncrakes are often rich in other fauna and flora. The identification of important plant and animal species and assemblages in areas which also hold high densities of Corncrakes would be valuable in convincing governments to give protection to key Corncrake sites. This could be achieved by carrying out a review of knowledge of the fauna and flora of core Corncrake areas identified during the proposed survey and monitoring programme.

A related topic is the extent to which management techniques such as delayed hay mowing and/or mowing from the centre of meadows outwards benefit plants, particularly late-flowering species, and other animals. A review identifying the benefits to other wildlife of management prescriptions designed to benefit the Corncrake would be valuable in convincing governments to include such prescriptions in agri-environment measures and nature reserve management plans.

Priority: medium
Time-scale: long

3.9. To quantify mortality caused by hunting and trapping

Efforts should be made to improve estimates of the numbers of Corncrakes killed by hunting and trapping, especially during migration. At present the only recorded potentially significant trapping mortality is a by-catch associated with Quail-netting in Egypt.

Priority: medium
Time-scale: long

3.10. To assess factors adversely affecting Corncrake habitats outside Europe

A recent comprehensive review of the literature and unpublished information (Stowe and Becker, 1992) failed to identify any probable links between declines in Corncrake populations and ecological change in the main wintering areas in Africa. However, it would be valuable to update this study to take account of new information as it becomes available. Knowledge of distribution and timing of movements in winter has been improved by recent bird atlas projects in southern Africa, and there may be new information on the status in India. Advances in remote sensing are providing estimates of recent changes in the extent of biomes used by Corncrakes in Africa. A review of this and other new information should be carried out and updated regularly.

Priority: medium
Time-scale: long

3.11. To establish and develop a Corncrake research working group

Rapid progress in improving scientific knowledge relevant to the conservation of Corncrakes will be an important part of any strategy for stemming the species' decline. This progress will be facilitated by free exchange of ideas and information among scientists concerned, and it is proposed that an international Corncrake research working group be set up consisting of scientists directly involved in Corncrake research. The duties of this group would be as follows.
• Regular review of research requirements for Corncrake conservation.
• Dissemination and standardisation of research techniques such as habitat recording, ageing and

sexing, radio-tag attachment, etc.
• Co-ordination of international research projects such as studies of movements.
• Responding to queries from national or international bodies regarding scientific aspects of Corncrake conservation.
• Dissemination of scientific literature.
• Advice to postgraduate students on research projects relevant to Corncrake conservation.

In many countries, national Corncrake study groups should be formed and affiliated with the international group.

Priority: high
Time-scale: ongoing

4. Public awareness and training

4.1. *To raise awareness and support for the Corncrake across Europe*

Each target audience needs to be clearly defined in order to determine the best way to influence it, namely the key messages and the most effective way of successfully delivering them must be identified. All messages should explain why it is worth taking action to conserve the Corncrake: the fact that it is a globally threatened bird and why this is so; its national/local status; and a description of its most appealing characteristics. The messages should all emphasise what each target audience can do to help the Corncrake.

4.1.1. Convince decision-makers to support and undertake action for the Corncrake

International, national, regional and local politicians and other decision-makers need to be convinced to support and undertake action to conserve the Corncrake – especially through policy, legislation and the safeguarding of sites. Demonstration of their conviction by becoming active members of conservation NGOs should be encouraged.

The international and national legal and conservation status of the species and the international obligation to conserve it need to be emphasised together with its role as a flagship species for grassland and wetland conservation. All communications with this group must be based on sound technical (legal, economic, scientific) knowledge

but also convey measured emotion and conviction.

The messages should be relayed through personal contacts, meetings, symposia and concise technical publications. This should be set against a background of efforts to enhance public awareness (see 4.1.5) to demonstrate to politicians that this is a matter which the electorate cares about.

Priority: high
Time-scale: ongoing

4.1.2. Gain the commitment of farmers and their representative organisations and advisors to promoting and undertaking Corncrake-friendly policies and practices

Nature conservation organisations should liaise and collaborate closely with those who influence management decisions taken on the ground by farmers and agricultural contractors, including agricultural lobby groups, advisory bodies, training colleges, suppliers and agriculturalists. Conservation organisations should supplement as necessary the advice on Corncrakes given to farmers via agricultural groups with direct contact with individual farmers on the ground and at local meetings, together with information via the farming media. Supporting material should include leaflets, videos of farmers undertaking Corncrake-friendly mowing, etc., and concise technical manuals.

The most important messages to convey are detailed technical advice on how to undertake Corncrake-friendly mowing and management, where to obtain funding for undertaking this, where to obtain further management advice and, if appropriate, the possibility of income from eco-tourism. Background information on the natural history of Corncrakes and their local status should also be provided in order to promote understanding. In addition it is important to give feedback to farmers on the biological results of their own individual efforts at Corncrake-friendly management, as well as the results of efforts at a local and national level. This should be set against a background of efforts to enhance awareness about Corncrakes in the local community (see 4.1.3) to ensure that peer pressure supports the Corncrake-friendly efforts of farmers.

Priority: high
Time-scale: ongoing

4.1.3. Develop support for and a sense of ownership of Corncrakes in local communities where Corncrakes occur

Support for Corncrakes among people who share their local areas with them is important in encouraging local land managers to undertake their operations in a Corncrake-friendly manner; preventing hunting or birdwatching disturbance of Corncrakes and damage to Corncrake habitats; and involving local people in Corncrake surveys where appropriate. Key messages should aim to build a sense of affection, local pride and ownership for the species which can be achieved by providing vivid audiovisual illustration of the Corncrake call and appearance, interesting details about their natural history, and local facts about the Corncrake and any folklore associated with it. Simple details should also be given on what Corncrake-friendly management entails and how local people can prevent other threats to Corncrakes. The legal status of the bird should be made clear. Opportunities for income from ecotourism should be emphasised. It is important to provide feedback to the local community regarding the results of local and national conservation efforts for the Corncrake.

The messages can be conveyed by illustrated talks, local media, posters (in shops, bars, etc.), schools, adult education courses and churches. Locally targeted information leaflets should be supplied. Local authorities should also be targeted with these messages and asked to disseminate them further.

Priority: high
Time-scale: ongoing

4.1.4. Influence non-agricultural land managers and users, including hunters where necessary, to help conserve the Corncrake

In addition to farmers, others involved in land management can influence Corncrakes. The most obvious of these are reserve managers (see 2.1.3.2), but others include foresters, water management authorities, fishery managers, game managers and consultancies. Messages should be similar to those for farmers (see 4.1.2), with emphasis on providing detailed technical advice on what land managers can do for Corncrakes and any sources of remuneration. The legal status of the bird should be made clear to hunters, and where it is still a quarry species, voluntary shooting bans should be encouraged. Use should be made of the specialist media and meetings of interest groups to deliver the message.

Priority: medium
Time-scale: ongoing

4.1.5. Gain the support of the general public for Corncrake conservation

The general public, including children, birdwatchers and members of conservation NGOs, must be made aware of the Corncrake – its voice, appearance, habits and plight. A strong feeling must be engendered among the public that sufficient action must be taken to ensure the recovery of this species and thus its removal from the list of globally threatened species. The more people that write to politicians expressing this concern, the more likely it is that appropriate action will be taken. It is important that farmers are not blamed for the plight of the Corncrake, and that, where appropriate, the value of traditional farming systems for biodiversity conservation is emphasised. The message to the general public should be conveyed through:
• The media:
– Television: special programmes on the Corncrake scheduled for peak time, items in magazine programmes, short clips on the news, etc.,
– Radio: including Corncrake calls, live and recordings.,
– Newspapers.,
– Magazines: including countryside and birdwatching magazines.
• Schools, colleges, university and adult education classes (with support from the state education authority).
• Illustrated talks and film presentations (to the general public and members of conservation and birdwatching NGOs).
• Publicity materials promoting the Corncrake (e.g. leaflets, posters, calendars, postage stamps, games).

Priority: high
Time-scale: ongoing

4.2. *To ensure co-ordinated production of materials promoting Corncrakes and their requirements*

The conservation organisations of Europe should co-ordinate efforts to promote the Corncrake in order to maximise effectiveness of disseminating the message while minimising the cost of producing supporting materials. Organisations in each country should assess what materials they already have available, what additional materials are required, where they can be obtained and how they should be paid for. BirdLife International should then co-ordinate efforts to fill the gaps. Materials that could usefully be disseminated include:

• Videos aimed at land managers, showing farmers undertaking Corncrake-friendly management.

• Videos aimed at school children.
• Slide sets (e.g. birds alive and killed, mowing techniques).
• Leaflets.
• Games.
Translation services will also be required.

National publicity strategies (what, when, how, by whom) should be carefully planned before the start of each season, including consideration of having the Corncrake designated the national "Bird of the Year". Consideration should also be given to running a Corncrake campaign (public awareness and/or fund-raising) at a European level, probably linked to European Corncrake census or other pan-European conservation initiatives for the Corncrake.

Priority: high
Time-scale: medium

Annex
Recommended conservation actions by country

Austria

1.2.3. Encourage extensification of agriculture, including reduction in use of fertilisers, in Corncrake areas.

1.2.3.3. Encourage development and implementation of agri-environment measures to the maximum benefit of Corncrakes.

1.2.3.3. Encourage development and implementation of payment schemes in key areas to ensure late mowing.

1.2.3./2.1.2.3. Prevent canalisation, drainage and other damaging developments (road construction, etc.).

2.1.2.1. Promote statutory protection of IBAs.

2.1.3. Establish Nature Reserves in key Corncrake areas.

2.3./4.1.2. Provide advice to farmers on Corncrake friendly management.

3.1.1. Undertake a repeat national survey.

3.1.2. Develop and implement a regular Corncrake monitoring scheme.

3.2.1. Clarify reproductive status.

3.2.3. Undertake habitat surveys.

3.2.4. Undertake ringing studies to determine site faithfulness.

Belarus

1.2.2. Promote inclusion in the list of protected animals (anticipated winter 1994-95).

3.1.1. Undertake a national Corncrake census.

3.1.2. Develop and implement a regular monitoring programme.

3.2. Conduct research to assess the effect of agricultural activities on breeding success.

3.4. Conduct research on Corncrakes in the area abandoned due to the Chernobyl disaster.

Belgium

1.2.3.3. Wallonia: Encourage adoption of agri-environment measures in key Corncrake areas, especially funding for delayed mowing and

Corncrake-friendly mowing in SPAs; maintain unmown areas in key sites, including in nature reserves.

2.1.3. Acquire and manage Nature Reserves in key Corncrake areas.

2.3./4.1.2. Provide management advice to those who manage land with breeding Corncrakes, especially farmers.

3.1.2. Undertake full annual monitoring survey.

3.2.1. Wallonia: undertake an intensive survey of a sample of singing males to identify periods of low song intensity that could indicate mating and search for proof of breeding in key Corncrake areas using contact calls of juveniles.

3.2.4. Wallonia: undertake research using individual voice recognition to identify movements between sites within (and possibly between) breeding seasons.

3.4. Wallonia: undertake Corncrake research in the abandoned fields of the Marche-en-Famenne military camp.

2.1.5./4.1.2. Provide management advice to those who manage land with breeding Corncrakes, especially farmers, and provide information about funding and application of agri-environment measures in SPAs and nature reserves.

4.1.3. Raise public awareness about Corncrakes in local communities around Corncrake areas.

4.1.5. Produce leaflets on key Nature Reserves for Corncrakes.

Bosnia-Herzegovina

2.1.2.1. Encourage the designation of Livanjsko Polje as a protected site under the nature conservation law.

2.1.2.3. Encourage the protection of Livanjsko Polje from any further melioration programmes or peat extraction.

3.1.1. Undertake a national Corncrake census to identify key sites.

Bulgaria

1.1.2./1.2.3. Encourage the adoption of programmes for sustainable development in agricultural areas of importance to Corncrakes.

1.2.3.3. Promote the introduction of measures to encourage farmers to undertake Corncrake-friendly management.

1.2.3. Promote the extensification of agriculture, including reduction in use of fertilisers, in Corncrake areas.

1.2.3./2.1.2.3. Prevent canalisation and drainage of Corncrake areas.

2.1.2.1. Encourage the statutory protection of all IBAs identified for Corncrakes.

2.1.3. Establish Nature Reserves in key Corncrake areas.

2.3./4.1.2. Prepare a leaflet for farmers on Corncrake-friendly management.

3.1.1. Undertake a full national census as part of the co-ordinated European census, following the pilot survey in 1995.

3.1.2. Undertake annual surveys of core Corncrake areas.

3.2.3. Undertake habitat surveys.

3.2.2./3.4./3.5. Undertake radio-tracking studies to determine the timing of reproduction and incidence of production of second broods in mountain areas, species movements, key sites during migration, etc.

Croatia

1.2.1. Develop a national Corncrake action plan based on the European plan.

1.2.3./2.1.2.3. Prevent the planning and implementation of melioration and canalisation of the Sava and Drava rivers.

3.1.1. Undertake a national Corncrake survey.

3.1.2. Annually monitor the Corncrake population.

Czech Republic

2.3. Prepare guidelines for management of the Corncrake's breeding habitat.

3.1. Establish a national Corncrake working group to:

• Identify the key Corncrake areas and provide an exact estimate of population size.

• Monitor trends in numbers to detect significant changes.

• Undertake vegetational analysis of breeding habitats.

3.2.4. Intensive ringing in key areas to assess movements between regions.

3.4. Continue the study of habitat use within abandoned meadows in the Sumava mountains, and use radio-telemetry.

Denmark

1.2.1. Encourage the production of a national Corncrake action plan.

1.2.3./2.1.2.3. Discourage any further drainage of Corncrake habitats.

1.2.3.3. Encourage the continuation, evaluation and any necessary improvements in the Corncrake-friendly conservation plan introduced in 1994 in the Ryå/Store Vildmose area.

1.2.3.3. Seek to extend Corncrake-friendly farming to other former Corncrake localities and protected areas besides Ryå/Store Vildmose, delaying mowing until after 1 August, or at least 16 July, and cutting from the centre-out or in strips.

1.2.3.3. Encourage the inclusion of all suitable river valleys in the ESA scheme and that, where appropriate, these include government funding for Corncrake-friendly management.

2.2. Encourage close contact between the Ministries of Environment and Agriculture, the regional and local public administrations and DOF to exchange information on habitat preferences, prescriptions to achieve these and other information, including that emanating from the working groups mentioned under 3.1.3 and 3.1.1, below.

1.2.5. Seek to reverse drainage schemes where appropriate, as in the planned restoration of the Skjern Å river delta.

2.3. Produce specific agricultural guidelines for Corncrake-friendly management.

3.1.1. Undertake a national Corncrake survey as part of DOF's new atlas and bird site project, 1993-96.

3.5. Investigate the importance of permanent set-aside and encourage organic farming in relation to possible recolonisation by the Corncrake.

Estonia

1.2.1. Encourage the preparation of a national Corncrake action plan for the period 1996 to 2000.

1.2.2. Encourage the listing of the Corncrake as a legally protected species (Category II) and inclusion in the National Red Data Book.

1.2.3. Encourage the introduction of measures to stop the abandonment of traditional grassland management in river valleys and semi-natural alluvial meadows important for Corncrakes.

1.2.3.3. Encourage measures to ensure extensive land use in Corncrake areas.

2.3. Provide advice on Corncrake-friendly management.

3.1.1. Undertake a national survey.

3.1.2. Develop and implement a Corncrake monitoring scheme.

3.2. Undertake research on habitat use and population trends, starting in 1995.

4.1.2./4.1.4. Undertake a campaign to raise awareness and educate all relevant types of landowners about the requirements of Corncrakes.

Finland

1.2.3.3. Encourage the delay of mowing until August in Corncrake areas.

3.1.1. Undertake a national survey, including habitat description.

3.1.2. Develop and implement an annual monitoring programme.

3.2. Undertake research to determine habitat selection, proportion of paired males, site tenacity and breeding success.

4.1. Widely promote the needs of the Corncrake.

France

1.2.3.3./2.1.2.2. Encourage the adoption of agri-environment measures to promote late-cutting dates in the 10 IBAs which hold 80% to 90% of the national Corncrake population.

1.1.2./2.1.2.3. Encourage the production for each IBA of a land use plan agreed between French administration, farming authorities and conservation NGOs to prevent further loss of Corncrake habitat to crops or poplar plantations.

2.1.2.1. Encourage the designation of the 10 IBAs as SPAs.

2.1.3. Establish and manage reserves for Corncrakes in core areas.

3.1.1. National survey in 1997.

3.1.2. Annual surveys in key sample areas.

3.2.3. Continue research, through the LIFE programme, on the relationship between mowing dates, densities and population trend.

3.2.4. Research on site fidelity, movements and breeding biology.

Research on the relationship between densities, botanical parameters and timing and duration of flooding.

Germany

1.2.3.3. In Corncrake areas, seek later mowing dates than are necessary for breeding waders, extensive programmes to cut meadows in only small compartments, either in strips or from the centre to the edges, and encourage mowing machinery that moves more slowly.

2.1.2.2. Encourage appropriate management of statutory sites including the prevention of any unsuitable vegetational succession at Untere Oder National Park or ensure development of appropriate habitats as a substitute for any habitat lost to succession in core areas.

3.1.1. Undertake a national census.

3.2.1. Estimate breeding success.

3.2.3. Define the optimum size of patch to mow at one time to maximise the chances of Corncrake survival.

Determine the relationship between the speed of movement of mowing machines and the mortality of adult and juveniles.

Define the time it takes for meadows to become suitable for Corncrakes after mowing.

3.2.4. Identify source and sink populations through investigation of the relationship between populations from different biogeographical regions, including the migration of adult Corncrakes during the breeding period.

3.1.2./3.5. Monitor the effects of all conservation actions on Corncrakes.

3.7. Investigate the impact of predation and human disturbance on key Corncrake populations.

Hungary

1.2.3.3. Encourage wider adoption of agri-environment measures to promote late-cut grass.

2.1.3.1. Establish Nature Reserves in all core areas.

2.3./4.2. Prepare a leaflet on Corncrake-friendly management for Tokaj-Bodrogzug Landscape Protection Area (IBA 032).

3.1.2. Undertake annual monitoring in the key areas.

Republic of Ireland

1.2.3.3. Promote the uptake of the Rural Environment Protection Scheme in core Corncrake areas from 1995, and introduce targets and a monitoring programme to ensure that the scheme is effective in Corncrake conservation and habitat management.

1.2.3.3. Continue a separate Corncrake Grant Scheme (delayed mowing, centre-out mowing, early and late cover creation) until Corncrake conservation is adequately dealt with by agri-environment measures.

1.2.3.3. Examine the feasibility of drawing up management agreements in core Corncrake areas, for example, Donegal islands (Tory, Inisbofin).

2.1.2.1. Encourage the adequate protection of all important corncrake areas under the European Union's Wild Birds Directive and the revised Wildlife Act.

2.1.3.1. Establish Nature Reserves in core areas.

2.1.3.2. Finalise management plan for reserve in the Shannon Callows.

3.1.2. Undertake annual monitoring surveys in the key areas (Shannon Callows, Moy catchment, North Donegal).

Continue IWC/RSPB research project.

3.2.4./3.3. Continue IWC/RSPB research project, including ringing of adults and chicks, biometric and DNA studies and voice analysis.

Italy

1.2.3.3. Using EU Regulation 2078/92, encourage wider adoption of agri-environment measures to modify cutting techniques and prevent succession of abandoned habitats.

1.2.3.3. Encourage the establishment of annual schemes to pay farmers in Corncrake areas to delay cutting or to undertake Corncrake-friendly mowing.

2.3./4.1.1./4.1.2./4.1.4. Provide advice on methods of Corncrake management for local administrations.

3.1.1. Continue national surveying during the period 1996 to 1997.

3.2.3. Continue studies on habitat use.

3.2.4. Undertake studies of movements.

4.1.3. Encourage local politicians and fieldworkers to take action for Corncrakes.

Latvia

1.2.2. Promote the improvement of national nature protection legislation.

1.2.3. Promote measures to encourage sustainable agriculture.

2.3./4.1.2. Provide advice for farmers on Corncrake-friendly methods of management.

2.1.2.1. Encourage the improvement of the protected area system including designation of more flood plain meadows.

3.1.1. Undertake a national survey during the period 1995 to 2000.

3.1.2. Continue to develop and implement a Corncrake monitoring scheme.

3.2. Undertake detailed studies of habitat requirements.

Liechtenstein

1.2.3. Promote a change in agricultural policy towards extensification and reduction in use of fertilisers in potential Corncrake areas.

2.1. Encourage the production of a new nature conservation law with better possibilities for the financial support of extensification.

3.1.2. Undertake annual monitoring surveys.

Lithuania

1.2.1. Encourage the preparation of a national Corncrake action plan.

1.2.1./2.2/3.1.3/3.11. Organise a globally threatened species working group.

1.2.2. Encourage the updating of the Red Data List with information recently obtained for Corncrakes.

2.1.2.1./2.1.3. Promote the statutory protection and Nature Reserves of all important Corncrake areas not yet protected.

3.1.1. From 1995 to 1997 undertake Corncrake surveys in the IBAs of the Nemunas delta and the potential IBA in the Jura valley followed by a national Corncrake survey.

3.2.3. Study Corncrake biology and ecology in the Nemunas delta and two or three other sites with high Corncrake densities.

4.1.1. Convince decision-makers to support and undertake action for the Corncrake.

4.1.2. Undertake campaigns to raise awareness and educate farmers about Corncrakes and ecology in general.

4.1.3. Develop support and a sense of ownership for Corncrakes in local communities where Corncrakes occur.

4.1.5. Gain the support of the general public for Corncrake conservation.

Luxembourg

1.2.3.3. Encourage extensive farming methods.

2.1.1. Identify Corncrake sites.

2.1.2. Encourage optimum statutory protection for important Corncrake sites.

3.1.1. Corncrake survey in 1995 and 1996.

Moldova

1.2.3.3. Encourage the wider adoption of agri-environment measures to promote late-cut grass.

2.1.3. Establish reserves in core areas.

3.1.1. Undertake a full national survey in 1996.

3.1.2. Undertake annual monitoring surveys in the main areas.

3.2.4. Undertake studies of Corncrake movements.

Netherlands

1.2.3. Promote extensive use of river grasslands outside IBAs, including regular (annual) flooding.

1.2.3.3. Encourage adoption of agri-environment measures in areas that regularly hold singing male Corncrakes.

1.2.3.3. Encourage the development and implementation of payment schemes in key areas to encourage late mowing.

2.1.2.1. Encourage the designation as SPAs of the five existing IBAs of highest importance for Corncrakes (Sliedrechtse Biesbosch, Gelderse Poort, Heteren-Amerongen, Deventer-Zwolle, Ewijk-Waardenburg).

2.1.2.2. Encourage Corncrake-friendly management of all statutory sites and reserves, river forelands and other areas which hold Corncrakes.

3.1.1. Maintain the annual national Corncrake survey with special emphasis on habitat use and current land use.

3.5. Undertake a review of habitat use of singing Corncrakes in river flood plains in relation to current and future land use management.

4.1.2./4.1.5. Promote management advice to those who manage land with breeding Corncrakes, especially farmers and nature conservation bodies.

Norway

1.2.1. Encourage the preparation of a national Corncrake action plan by 1998.

1.2.2. Support legal protection, with practical measures each breeding season, to protect all proven and expected Corncrake nest sites, to an agreed radius around the nesting area.

1.2.3.3. Promote measures to extensify agriculture in Corncrake areas.

2.3./4.1.2. Provide advice for farmers on Corncrake-friendly management.

3.1.2. Follow up the 1995 national surveys with regular surveys and descriptions of habitat.

3.2. Analyse survey results to determine habitat use and population trends.

4.1. Undertake public awareness campaigns relating to the Corncrake.

Poland

1.2.2. Encourage the addition of the Corncrake to the next revision of the Polish Red Data Book.

1.2.3. Promote the introduction of measures to stop the abandonment of traditional grassland management in river valleys important for Corncrakes.

1.2.3.1. Promote measures to ensure that the value of Kombinat Wizna for Corncrakes is not diminished as 6000 ha of grassland is sold during the period 1994 to 1996.

2.1.2.2. Promote management of the Biebrza National Park to prevent natural succession of formerly mowed grasslands important for Corncrakes.

Encourage the completion of the management plan for the Kombinat Wizna collective farm to promote Corncrake-friendly mowing.

3.1.1. Undertake a national census.

3.2. Undertake the research outlined above (see "Germany"), including research to:
• Investigate the movements of flightless juveniles in relation to mowing, using radio-telemetry and trapping.
• Develop an optimum mowing regime for Corncrakes (and Aquatic Warblers *Acrocephalus paludicola*) at Kombinat Wizna.

3.4. Undertake research in the Biebrza National Park to determine the effects on Corncrakes of plant succession in response to cessation of mowing.

3.8. Undertake research to determine the possibilities for action to conserve Corncrakes, Aquatic Warblers and other species in the same habitat.

3.1.2./3.5. Monitor the effects of all conservation actions on Corncrakes.

Romania

1.2.1. Encourage the production of a national Corncrake action plan.

1.2.2. Encourage the legal protection of the species.

3.1.1. Undertake a national census in 1995 and 1996.

4.1. Raise public awareness.

Russian Federation

1.2.1. Encourage the production of a national Corncrake action plan.

1.2.3.3. Promote programmes to support traditional extensive management of meadows in model areas, namely some National Parks and regional temporary reserves (zakazniks).

1.2.3. Encourage stricter controls on the use of agrochemicals in river valleys and lake basins.

2.1.2.1. Promote statutory designation as regional temporary reserves (zakazniks) of most nationally and internationally important Corncrake areas.

2.1.3.1. Promote new regional temporary reserves (zakazniks) for Corncrakes.

3.1.1./3.2. Undertake a survey of European Russia in 1995 and 1996 to estimate the national population size, identify core Corncrake areas (IBAs) and describe associations with habitat and management.

3.1.2. Develop and implement a monitoring programme.

3.2.3. Undertake research on the impact of mowing on Corncrake breeding success.

Serbia and Montenegro

No information.

Slovakia

1.2.1. Encourage the production of a national Corncrake action plan.

1.2.2. Encourage full protection for the Corncrake under executive notices to the new law on the conservation of nature and landscape.

1.2.3.3. Encourage the introduction of schemes encouraging farmers to undertake Corncrake-friendly management.

1.2.4. Build up a strong NGO for the protection of birds, ensuring competence in the conservation of Corncrakes and other threatened species.

2.1.1. Revise and update the national IBA inventory to ensure that all qualifying Corncrake sites are included within the IBA network.

2.1.2.1. Promote statutory designation as Nature Reserves for all key Corncrake sites.

2.1.2.2. Encourage Corncrake-friendly management in protected areas.

2.1.2.4. Promote increased effectiveness in the implementation of the Ramsar Convention.

2.1.3. Consider acquisition and management of land with important Corncrake concentrations.

2.2. Promote the development of the Group for the Protection of Corncrakes and collaboration among nature conservation bodies and with other authorities regarding the conservation of Corncrakes.

3.1.1. Undertake a national Corncrake survey to estimate population size, distribution and key areas.

3.1.2. Develop and implement a Corncrake monitoring programme.

3.1.3./3.1.1. Become active members of the BirdLife Corncrake census and research working groups.

3.2./3.2.1. Undertake research to investigate habitat use by Corncrakes, including productivity in different habitats and the impact of timing and method of mowing.

3.5. Monitor the effectiveness of conservation measures.

4.1.2. Inform and educate farmers about the ecology and requirements of Corncrakes.

4.1.5. Organise a public campaign about the conservation of the Corncrake to gain wide public awareness.

4.1. Produce educational materials about Corncrake conservation.

Slovenia

1.2.1. Encourage the production of a national Corncrake action plan.

1.2.3. Promote a statutory national programme to support extensive meadow use.

1.2.3.3. Encourage measures to protect the main areas and develop and implement special Corncrake management programmes for each of the key areas.

2.1.2.1./2.1.3. Encourage the establishment of legally protected areas and Nature Reserves.

3.1.1. Undertake a full national survey before 1999.

3.1.2. Undertake annual monitoring (full and sample surveys) in the main areas, and occasional surveys at other sites.

3.2. Undertake research on habitat requirements, etc.

Spain

1.2.2. If breeding is confirmed (3.1.1, below) then the category of threat of the Corncrake in the National Catalogue of Threatened Species should be upgraded.

1.2.3.4. Maintain confidentiality of the location of the breeding sites to protect the birds from disturbance by birdwatchers.

2.1. Encourage the identification, protection and appropriate management of IBAs for Corncrakes.

3.1.1. Undertake a full survey in 1996 to confirm the existence of a breeding population and identify key areas most in need of protection.

3.1.2. Monitor the population annually.

4.1.2./4.1.3. Develop and implement a public awareness-raising programme targeted at farming communities.

Sweden

1.2.3. Encourage agricultural policies which favour Corncrakes.

2.3./4.1.2. Provide advice on Corncrake-friendly management.

3.1.2. Monitor the Corncrake population.

Continue radio-tracking studies in Oland.

Switzerland

1.2.1. Encourage the production of a national Corncrake action plan.

1.2.3. Encourage a change in agricultural policy to promote extensification in potential Corncrake areas.

1.2.3.3. Promote the introduction of payment schemes to encourage farmers to undertake Corncrake-friendly management.

2.1.2. Promote the introduction of special protection regulations for areas with Corncrakes: prevent early mowing at sites with singing males; if Corncrakes breed, ensure Corncrake-friendly management in the surrounding area.

2.3./4.1.2. Provide advice on Corncrake-friendly management for farmers and other managers.

3.1.2. Undertake annual monitoring surveys.

Ukraine

1.2.2. Promote the inclusion of the Corncrake in the National Red Data Book.

2.1.2. Encourage the protection and appropriate management of important Corncrake areas.

3.1.1. Undertake a national census to provide a national population estimate, and identify key areas.

3.1.2. Monitor Corncrake habitats.

3.2.1. Conduct research to determine population structure (sex ratio, etc.) and breeding success.

4.1. Raise awareness of the Corncrake, with nature protection and agricultural organisations as well as with the general public, and through secondary and higher education institutes.

United Kingdom

1.2.3.3. Continue the Corncrake Grant Scheme until it can be integrated into agri-environment measures.

1.2.3.3. Promote wider adoption of agri-environment measures to promote late-cut grass and reduce sheep numbers, increasing low-intensity beef.

2.1.3. Consider establishing further reserves in core areas.

3.1.1. Undertake a full survey in 1998.

3.1.2. Undertake annual surveys in the main areas.

3.2.2./3.2.3. Continue radio-tracking studies of timing of breeding and habitat selection.

3.2.4. Undertake studies of movements.

Action plan
for the Great Bustard (*Otis tarda*) in Europe

Reviews

This action plan should be reviewed and updated every three years. An emergency review will be undertaken if sudden major environmental changes, liable to affect the population, occur within the species range.

Geographical scope

The action plan needs implementation in Albania, Austria, Bulgaria, Croatia, Czech Republic, Germany, Hungary, Poland, Portugal, Romania, Russia, Slovakia, Spain, Turkey, Ukraine and Yugoslavia (Serbia).

Summary

The Great Bustard *Otis tarda* is a globally threatened species listed as Vulnerable by Collar et al. (1994). In Europe it is present in Austria, Bulgaria, Croatia, Czech Republic, Germany, Hungary, Italy, Moldova, Portugal, Romania, Russia, Slovakia, Spain, Turkey, Ukraine and the former Yugoslavia. The European population is estimated to be between 23790 and 30483 individuals (data gathered at the 1994 workshop) but there has been a rapid decline in much of central and eastern Europe. Its habitat is intensively used agricultural land and mixed extensive agricultural and pasture/fallow land. Conservation measures must focus on active habitat management and on the maintenance of large areas of non-intensive farming systems.

Threats and limiting factors

Habitat loss – critical

Low breeding – high/critical

Predation – medium/high

Collision with powerlines – medium/high in some areas

Human disturbance – medium

Application of pesticides – low/locally medium

Illegal hunting – low

Wire fences – low

Conservation priorities

Maintain open areas of non-intensive farmland through agricultural and forestry policies as well as protected areas and legislation – high/essential

Protection and management of breeding areas – essential

Maintain the ban on hunting – high

Ensure availability and quality of habitat in the winter quarters – high

Prevent collisions with powerlines – high

Monitoring of population size, trends and effects of habitat management – high

Research into mortality and factors limiting breeding success – high

Promote international co-operation on research and monitoring – high

Raise public awareness amongst farmers, landowners and the general public – high

Introduction

The Great Bustard *Otis tarda* is a grassland species that has changed its habitat preferences to agricultural habitats and pastures throughout its European range. It is globally threatened, classified as Vulnerable (Collar et al., 1994), and is included in Annex I of the European Union's Wild Birds Directive, Appendix II of the Bern Convention, Appendix I of the Bonn Convention and Appendix I of CITES.

A working group has been dealing with Great Bustard matters within BirdLife International (formerly the International Council for Bird Preservation) for about 20 years (this group has now been incorporated into the Steppe and Grasslands Bird Group). During a meeting held in

Vienna in 1988, recommendations were passed stressing that all efforts to preserve the species should be focused on its habitat rather than on the species itself, thus giving priority to habitat management over attempts to support populations by captive breeding or by rearing chicks in captivity.

In May 1994 a workshop took place in Hungary to discuss the European status of the Great Bustard and the conservation priorities for the future; this was organised by BirdLife International and the Hungarian Ornithological and Nature Conservation Society (MME, the BirdLife Partner in Hungary), and was attended by representatives from Bulgaria, Germany, Hungary, Portugal, Russia, Slovakia, Spain, Turkey and United Kingdom. This action plan is largely based on the results of that workshop.

In central Europe the Great Bustard is on the threshold of a minimum viable population. The current time lag for recruitment shows that any further delays would allow the species to decline below this threshold. Active habitat management is required if this situation is to be reversed.

Background information

Distribution and population

The Great Bustard occurs in highly fragmented populations across Europe, Morocco and Asia. The greatest part of the world's breeding population (c.50%) is now found in the Iberian peninsula, followed by Russia, Turkey and the Hungarian basin; several small populations, partly isolated, live in different central European countries (Table 14.1). The species became extinct in France, western Germany, Poland, the former Yugoslavia and United Kingdom.

Life history

Breeding

The nest is on the ground, generally on patches of bare soil in cereal fields or grassland. The location is chosen by the female, and is usually in the vicinity of the display grounds which are on open areas with low vegetation in agricultural land (often winter-sown). A low level of disturbance is essential for successful breeding.

Table 14.1

Estimated population of the Great Bustard in Europe, 1994. Based on data gathered during the workshop at Tiszafüred

Country	No. of birds
Austria	50–60
Bulgaria	10–15
Czech Republic	10–20
Germany	130
Hungary	1100–1300
Moldova	2–3
Portugal	1000
Romania	10–15
Russia	8000–10000
Slovakia	25–30
Spain	13500–14000
Turkey	800–3000
Ukraine	300–400
Yugoslavia (Serbia)	8–10
Total	24945–29983

The Great Bustard usually lays two eggs (more rarely one or three, exceptionally more), which are incubated for 25 to 27 days. The female is very likely to leave the clutch following disturbance, especially at the beginning of the breeding period. Chicks are led by the female parent during the first months of their life and may stay with females until the next courtship period.

Feeding

The chicks rely on insects for the first months of their life, and the adults eat insects and plants. During winter, birds feed mainly on Brassicaceae and alfalfa *Medicago sativa*, especially seeds which are found on the ground after harvesting. In spring and summer they eat mainly plant material (chiefly leaves and inflorescences, but also buds, shoots and seeds) as well as insects and even small vertebrates.

Migration and movements

Most populations are resident. Some migrate regularly, for example, part of the Russian population spends the winter in Crimea (Ukraine), and some fly ways are used during winter, for example, southwards from Austria and Slovakia to Hungary, and westwards from Hungary to northern Italy. Some populations in Spain make seasonal movements (Hidalgo and Carranza, 1990).

During severe winters, long-range displacements from eastern Europe westwards as far as the Netherlands and France occur. Since mortality is probably very high during such migration, and survival conditions in the wintering areas are not optimal, the species needs protection in the countries involved as well as those in which it breeds.

Habitat requirements

Great Bustards need wide, open and rather flat countryside. They seem to have moved from primeval landscapes like the Russian steppes to open agricultural land, especially traditional extensive farmland in dry regions. Birds in Iberia inhabit mixed forms of pasture, arable and fallow land, while those in Hungary live in pannonic grasslands, both pastures and secondary grassland (*puszta*), intermixed with agricultural land. Throughout the range the majority of clutches are found in agricultural habitats, often cereal crops. A certain amount of fallow land, such as fallow plots, set-aside plots, margins, etc., is necessary to provide food resources, especially insects, and for cover. Early-mown alfalfa, especially where intermixed with cereals, reduces breeding density.

The wintering habitat is mostly large fallow plains of alfalfa and rape *Brassica napus*.

Threats and limiting factors

Habitat loss

Ploughing of grasslands, afforestation, irrigation schemes, roads, highways, powerlines, fences, ditches, etc., affect Great Bustards in parts of Austria, Bulgaria, Germany, Hungary, Portugal, Russia and Spain. Changes of crops, for example, the reduction in alfalfa in Iberia and central Europe, can reduce breeding success and density. In eastern European countries, land privatisation can lead to further fragmentation of estates and to the intensification of agriculture.

Overgrazing and inappropriate grazing management may damage breeding grounds, for example, in Turkey (Baris, 1991) and in some areas of Spain. Habitats in the winter quarters can be adversely affected locally by a reduction in rape cultivation.

Importance: critical

Losses of eggs and chick

This is one of the key factors in all agricultural habitats due to direct damage by harvesting machinery (e.g. mowing of alfalfa), irrigation works, use of pesticides and fertilisers, lack of food, and increased stress due to disturbance (Litzbarski et al., 1987). It is especially relevant in Austria, Germany, Hungary and Slovakia and parts of Portugal, Russia and Spain. Changes in farming practices related to the cultivation of new crops generally produce threats to the young, for example, the early mowing of cereals in Extremadura (Spain).

Importance: high/critical

Predation

Eggs and chicks are predated by foxes, corvids and dogs. Adults may be predated by foxes and dogs. Some cases have been reported from Austria, Germany, Hungary, Russia, Slovakia and Spain, though the impact on the species is different for each population.

Importance: medium/high

Powerlines

Great Bustards are remarkably terrestrial, and are reluctant to fly in poor weather. Their poor manoeuvrability in flight renders them unable to evade poorly marked powerlines. Collision with overhead cables is a significant cause of death in some countries (Hungary, Portugal, Russia, Slovakia and Spain). Small populations can be totally destroyed by a single powerline. In some areas of Spain this is the prime cause of mortality in adult birds (Alonso et al., 1994).

Importance: medium/high in some areas

Human disturbance

Disturbance causes stress, desertion of clutches, escape flights during unfavourable weather and the associated risk of injuries (e.g. collision with powerlines), and, in the case of young birds, a reduction in time spent feeding. Disturbance at the display sites disrupts social behaviour and usually alters or aborts copulation. The problem is particularly relevant in areas of high human population, such as parts of Austria, Germany, Hungary, Slovakia and Spain.

Importance: medium

Pesticides

Application of pesticides adversely affects Great Bustard populations by lowering the reproduction rate. Massive applications can have a direct impact locally, for example, ill-timed locust control in parts of Spain (Hellmich, 1992). In 1996, the Government of Extremadura announced that aerial spraying with Malathion, for many years a serious problem in the Llanos de Cáceres and La Serena, would be replaced with more selective ground-based control through the implementation of a zonal programme under Regulation 2078/92/EEC approved by the European Commission in 1995.

Importance: low (locally medium).

Wire fences

In some parts of Spain wire fences on pasture land cause death of individuals as well as habitat fragmentation.

Importance: low

Illegal hunting

A few cases of poaching are reported every year across the range. This is still a problem in Russia, Spain, Turkey and Ukraine.

Importance: low

Conservation status and recent conservation measures

Austria

The species is strictly protected and included in the Austrian Red Data Book as Endangered. Hunting has been forbidden since 1969. A small-scale attempt during the 1960s and 1970s to breed and rear the species in captivity failed. In intensively used agricultural land some plots have been managed since 1979 especially as feeding and breeding areas. A reserve exists within the boundaries of Lake Neusiedl National Park, consisting of meadows and fallow land. The reproductive rate in all populations is still low (Kollar, 1991).

Bulgaria

The species has been protected under the Bulgarian Law for the Conservation of Nature since 1962 and by the 1986 Special Act 342 of the Ministry of the Environment which imposes a fine of US$ 460 for any bird killed, together with an additional penalty. It is included in the Red Data Book of 1985 as Endangered. The last confirmed breeding records date from 1983, but there are some summer observations in later years, including some in 1994. One area of primeval steppe in Dobrudja plateau (called "The Valley of the Bustards", 3 600 ha) which was protected in 1961 was deliberately ploughed up in 1962. There is no current monitoring of the population and no habitat management. A thorough survey of the species over the whole territory of Dobrudja (north-east Bulgaria) is urgently needed. Under a biodiversity conservation programme funded by the Swiss Government, set-aside schemes and programmes for leasing and acquiring land for agricultural extensification have begun in Dobrudja. Farmers are encouraged to adapt the timing of agricultural activities to the life cycle of the Great Bustard.

Czech Republic

The species is protected under the Law for the Protection of Nature and Landscape. There is one small population on the border with Austria for which there are no current protection schemes.

Germany

The species is legally protected and listed as Endangered in the German Red Data Book. In the former East Germany much effort was put into breeding, rearing and releasing Great

Bustards into the wild, first at Steckby, then at Buckow, and today a third of Germany's Great Bustard population consists of birds which came from the rearing programme. In addition, from the 1970s on, measures for restricting agriculture in Great Bustard areas were taken; these included delayed mowing and restricted use of pesticides and fertilisers; also, some eggs were collected from the wild for artificial incubation. Nowadays habitat management is carried out on a comparatively large scale, especially in Brandenburg where about 6600 ha of agricultural land has been leased or purchased and is now managed as meadows and set-aside plots (Block et al., 1993; Litzbarski, 1993). A total of 9500 ha is subject to a LIFE-funded scheme to rediversify agriculture following the break-up of collective farming, aimed at improving the Great Bustard's habitat.

Hungary

The Great Bustard is strictly protected under the Hungarian Law for the Conservation of Nature and is included in the Hungarian Red Data Book. Although the majority of *puszta* has been under protection for decades, either as National Parks or as Landscape Protection Areas, most breeding occurs outside these protected areas, and populations have thus further decreased due to loss of clutches as well as through the effects of severe winters. A rearing station was established at Dévaványa more than 10 years ago, but it has not been totally successful so far (Faragó, 1990). Winter feeding and the control of corvids in some areas have had a beneficial effect, but the most important task ahead is to concentrate all efforts towards habitat management in agricultural areas. Recent habitat protection programmes have been implemented in Dévaványa Landscape Protection Area, Hortobágy National Park, Kiskunság National Park and in the Moson Project near Mosonszolnok, covering approximately 11000 ha altogether. These programmes include habitat management and predator control.

Poland

The species is now extinct, the last breeding record dating from 1986. Up to 1989 there were a few individuals kept in captivity. The reasons for extinction were intensification and mechanisation

of agriculture, human disturbance and persecution (Bereszynski, in prep.).

Portugal

It is legally protected and included in the Red Data Book as Endangered. Hunting has been forbidden since 1967. Habitats in traditionally extensive agricultural land are being encroached upon and threatened by changes in land use, especially afforestation, because the subsidies for environmental agriculture are lower than those for afforestation. While there is a strong interest in the conservation of the species and its habitat, including application of agri-environment measures under EU Regulation 2078/92, the continuing decline demonstrates that these efforts are insufficient. So far there are no protected areas, SPAs or ESAs specific to the Great Bustard. LIFE funding has been used to intiate pilot programmes to encourage ESA take-up in Castro Verde, the most important Great Bustard area in Portugal.

Romania

Female Great Bustards are protected as National Monuments. The species has declined considerably in the last half-century to considerably less than 100 birds, found mostly outside protected areas.

Russian Federation

The species is included in the Red Data Book of 1985 as Vulnerable (Category II, rapid decline in numbers and habitat). After intensive ploughing programmes in the 1960s the range of the Great Bustard became highly fragmented. In the Saratov region there are four reserves covering more than 1000 km² in total where display and breeding sites are protected. In dry areas with poor soil, for example, in the Volgograd District, where agriculture is very extensive and a great part of the land is fallow, numbers seem to be stable or even increasing slightly. In regions with good soil, such as the Krasnodar District, numbers are declining because agriculture tends to be more intensive. There is a breeding and rearing station at Saratov, which has not been successful in increasing the population. A thorough survey of the species and an inventory of steppes are urgently needed.

Slovakia

The species is protected by the National Law for Nature Protection and listed as Endangered in the Red Data Book. Hunting has been forbidden since 1980. The core area of the former range has been designated as a protected area. A rearing and breeding station exists, so far without an impact on the population. Habitat management measures for arable land are in the planning stage.

Spain

The species has been protected since 1980. It is classified in the Red Data Book as Vulnerable and is officially listed as a species Of Special Interest under Royal Decree 439/90. Some of the most important Great Bustard sites have been included in zonal programme proposals under EU Regulation 2078/92, for example, Villafáfila, Madrigal-Peñaranda and Tierra de Campos. However, some of the main areas are still threatened by irrigation, land abandonment, afforestation, pesticides and overgrazing. In Extremadura, which alone holds about 15% of the world population (Hidalgo, 1990), habitat protection measures are restricted to Vicia cultivations, and there are plans for irrigation and afforestation schemes. Recently there have been attempts to re-establish hunting in some regions. Research on behaviour, breeding biology, habitat use and dispersal has been going on for several years in Extremadura and Castilla-León.

Turkey

The Great Bustard is classified as Rare in the Draft Red List of Threatened Animals. Hunting has been forbidden since 1977. A protected area of 20000 ha was established in 1993 by the National Parks and Game-Wildlife General Directorate. A thorough survey is planned for 1996 or 1997.

Ukraine

The species is legally protected and included in the Ukrainian Red Data Book. There are some reserves where breeding birds (Polessky Reserve) or wintering birds (Askania-Nova, Black Sea Reserve) are protected. In addition there is a project to create a reserve in the Crimea for the protection of the largest breeding Ukrainian population and for the wintering birds from Russia (Fedorenko, 1992). In Askania-Nova there was a breeding and rearing station, but its work has now ceased.

Aims and objectives

Aims

1. In the short term, to maintain the existing populations of the Great Bustard throughout its range.

2. In the medium to long term, to promote land use forms and habitat conservation schemes that allow for population growth and range expansion.

Objectives

1.   **Policy and legislation**

1.1.   *To promote national and international policies and legislation which favour the conservation of the Great Bustard and its habitat*

The threats of habitat loss and food depletion are similar for a number of threatened species. Conservation measures for the Great Bustard are likely to have a positive effect also for the globally threatened Lesser Kestrel *Falco naumanni* as well as other declining species such as the White Stork *Ciconia ciconia*, Kestrel *Falco tinnunculus*, Little Bustard *Tetrax tetrax*, Gull-billed Tern *Gelochelidon nilotica*, Pin-tailed Sandgrouse *Pterocles alchata*, Roller *Coracias garrulus*, Shrikes *Lanius* and other species hunting in the open landscape for large invertebrate prey. Thus steppe and dry grasslands are included in the Agricultural Conservation Strategy currently being prepared by BirdLife International (Tucker et al., in press).

1.1.1. Agricultural policies

In areas where traditional land uses still exist or are restorable, such as Portugal, Spain and parts of Hungary, policies should be developed or promoted at European level to enable these countries to maintain their "pseudosteppes" and *pusztas*. Within the European union, the concept of ESAs and zonal programmes should be further promoted. In countries outside the EU the policy mechanisms and funds may be lacking for such an approach. Funding from EU and other "western" sources should be encouraged to support farming practices compatible with bustard conservation in central and eastern Europe.

In intensively used farmland areas, agricultural policies and legislation should provide for the establishment of set-aside schemes, land leasing or acquisition programmes, extensification and special protection measures for Great Bustard breeding areas.

Priority: essential
Time-scale: short

1.1.2. Forestry policies

These should be subject to environmental impact assessment taking account not only of the economic benefits of reducing crop surpluses and carbon dioxide emissions but also the damage to globally threatened species such as the Great Bustard through the fragmentation of extensive farming habitats. Afforestation should be prevented in Great Bustard areas and replaced by appropriate incentive or compensation schemes.

Priority: high
Time-scale: short

1.1.3. Protected areas and legislation

The Great Bustard inhabits large areas of unbroken habitat in which farming is often the main land use. Thus a network of protected areas is not the best means of conserving the species. Even in wildlife reserves, the movements of juveniles and adults during dispersal exceed the boundaries of the protected areas. However, protected area status should be encouraged for those semi-natural habitats where the Great Bustard occurs (e.g. steppes, pseudosteppes, grasslands).

It is essential that the species gets full legal protection throughout its range to ensure that hunting will not be allowed and that key habitats will be maintained.

Priority: high/essential
Time-scale: short

1.1.4. Strategic environmental assessment

Strategic environmental impact assessment of strategies, policies and programmes should be promoted to evaluate their global impact on steppe and grassland habitats and species and to prevent damage due to the cumulative effects of individual projects. The Council of Europe and the European Commission are encouraged to support this approach and to facilitate information exchange between experts and competent authorities in this respect.

Priority: medium
Time-scale: medium

1.1.5. International co-operation

International treaties and conventions provide a framework for co-operation at governmental level. The signing and ratification of, among others, the Bern, Bonn and Biodiversity Conventions and CITES by Great Bustard range states should provide a basis for practical co-operation and exchanges of experience. A regional agreement on the conservation of palaearctic dry grassland birds under the Bonn Convention would be particularly desirable for central Europe. Bilateral agreements among Great Bustard range states should be promoted.

Priority: medium
Time-scale: medium

1.1.6. Hunting

It is recommended that hunting of the Great Bustard remain prohibited, irrespective of the numbers and trends of the species in each range state. The species should be removed from hunting legislation where this implies that the Great Bustard is a game species (even if hunting is not allowed). In all countries the species should be included in protected species legislation.

Priority: high
Time-scale: medium

2. Species and habitat protection

2.1. *To encourage adequate protection and management of the breeding areas and remove key factors adversely affecting breeding success*

2.1.1. Preserve traditional land use

Where land uses which are favourable to the Great Bustard, such as rotation of grazing plots and alternation between cultivation (cereals and legumes) and fallows, still exist (e.g. pseudo-steppes in Iberia and *puszta* in Hungary), these should be maintained and promoted through a system of incentives to farmers.

Priority: essential
Time-scale: short

2.1.2. Promote set-aside schemes and extensification programmes, and enable leasing and acquisition of land for Great Bustard conservation

The effective promotion and adoption of set-aside schemes (land taken out of production) in agricultural areas to protect Great Bustards and other wildlife is possible and promising, as shown by examples in Austria, Germany and Hungary. It should be encouraged and supported by official and private funds. Such schemes should stretch over a period of more than two years and should be thoroughly supervised and evaluated. Other types of set-aside such as extensively grazed rotational fallows (1–5 years) should be preserved and promoted.

Priority: essential
Time-scale: short

2.1.3. Adapt the timing of agricultural practices to the life cycle of the Great Bustard

Farmers should be made aware of the presence of Great Bustards in their fields and of the risk of destroying clutches. They must be encouraged to adapt their calendar of farming activities as much as possible to the breeding cycle of the Great Bustard. Mowing and irrigation should be postponed and carried out with special care, or dropped.

Priority: high
Time-scale: short/ongoing

2.1.4. Prevent disturbance at breeding and display sites

Since breeding females are especially vulnerable to disturbance, interference caused by farming activities, vehicles driving across the fields, hunting, birdwatching, photography, etc., should be minimised, especially in areas of low population density. Disturbance should generally be kept low in Great Bustard areas. Appropriate actions such as educating farmers, restricting access and wardening should be encouraged.

Priority: medium/high
Time-scale: short/ongoing

2.1.5. Undertake special measures for the protection of threatened breeding sites

The competent authorities and NGOs should be encouraged to take immediate action to manage those breeding sites where females regularly fail to raise young because of agricultural activities or other disturbance. In areas of high Great Bustard density, temporary protection schemes should be put in place to ensure appropriate breeding conditions. Adequate wardening is essential for the success of such schemes.

Priority: high
Time-scale: short/ongoing

2.1.6. Undertake captive management in emergency situations

If it is not possible to guarantee the successful breeding of Great Bustards at one particular site, the possibility of taking the eggs into captivity for artificial incubation should be carefully evaluated. Dummy eggs can be left in the nest instead and replaced by the real ones shortly before hatching. Rearing some young in captivity for release at a later stage is another possibility, although the risk of imprinting on humans is very high. Imprinted chicks will have difficulty in surviving under natural conditions. This kind of management should only be undertaken with the backup of well-equipped facilities and should be carried out only by well-trained professionals following the IUCN criteria for reintroductions (Kleiman et al., 1994).

Priority: low
Time-scale: long

2.1.7. Prevent predation

When predation is a continuous cause of breeding failure, appropriate measures should be undertaken to control the key predators. Foxes and feral dogs should be controlled and shepherds should be informed of the problem and encouraged to train their dogs not to chase or kill Great Bustards.

Priority: medium
Time-scale: short

2.2. *To improve habitat quality for the Great Bustard and prevent isolation and fragmentation of populations*

2.2.1. Ensure the availability and quality of the habitat in the winter quarters

Habitat preferences in winter are well known, as are the location of most wintering sites. In these areas, cultivation of rape and alfalfa should be maintained and promoted.

Priority: high
Time-scale: short

2.2.2. Prevent alterations that fragment or isolate the Great Bustard's habitat

The construction of new roads or highways, powerlines and railways, the planting of shelter belts, and irrigation and afforestation schemes should be prevented in Great Bustard areas. All these and other infrastructures should be subject to environmental impact assessments which consider viable alternatives, and take into account the special sensitivity of the Great Bustard to disturbance and habitat encroachment. Fences should either be avoided or constructed in a way that permits the free movement of chicks.

Priority: medium/high
Time-scale: short

2.2.3. Adopt corrective measures for powerlines

Collisions with overhead cables can be avoided or at least greatly reduced by appropriate marking. Existing lines which cross Great Bustard areas should be buried or marked prominently. New lines should not be built across Great Bustard areas.

Priority: high
Time-scale: short

3. **Monitoring and research**

3.1. *To monitor population parameters and the effects of management*

3.1.1. Standardise census methods

Methods used for counting Great Bustards in different regions of Europe cannot be applied to all parts of the range because of the different landscapes and the different densities of Great Bustard populations involved. For example, in Germany and other parts of central Europe (unlike in Spain), vegetation height from April onwards may not permit standing Great Bustards to be seen from a moving car or from fixed vantage points. In Russia, low Great Bustard densities would require a different census methodology. Despite these differences, standardised census methods should be used, at least within regions, to produce comparable results.

Priority: high
Time-scale: short

3.1.2. Monitor population size and population trends

Efforts to monitor the basic parameters of Great Bustard populations, such as size and trends, should be made at all sites.

Priority: high
Time-scale: short/ongoing

3.1.3. Monitor the effects of habitat management

Studies should be carried out on the effects of habitat protection measures, implementation of agri-environment regulations, etc. These studies should preferably be done at sites where the population has been well monitored for a number of years.

Priority: high
Time-scale: short/ongoing

3.1.4. Monitor the success of release programmes

The survival of chicks bred in captivity and of chicks hatched from artificially bred clutches should be closely monitored, as well as the survival and breeding performance of adults released in the wild. Release programmes should be permanently reassessed and discontinued if birds are failing to survive under natural conditions.

Priority: high
Time-scale: ongoing

3.1.5. Carry out co-ordinated and comparable national surveys as a basis for cross-border protection measures

Those Great Bustard populations which are shared by two or more countries, such as Austria/Hungary/Slovakia or Portugal/Spain should be the subject of bilateral or trilateral agreements to ensure that there is appropriate co-ordination for research, monitoring and conservation activities.

Priority: medium
Time-scale: short

3.2. *To promote research which is of direct application to the conservation of the Great Bustard*

3.2.1. Undertake comparative studies

Great Bustard populations in western Europe (Iberia) and eastern Europe (Hungary, Russia) live under different ecological conditions. A comparative analysis of the existing data on population dynamics, habitat requirements, effects of habitat changes and causes of decline between the populations would be most useful in redefining conservation strategies in the future.

Priority: medium
Time-scale: medium

3.2.2. Promote studies on mortality factors in areas with different land uses

All individuals found dead should be examined for the causes of mortality. This, together with field studies and monitoring of marked individuals, should help to identify the direct or indirect impact of land use on Great Bustard mortality.

Priority: high
Time-scale: short/ongoing

3.2.3. Investigate factors limiting breeding success

The ecology of core Great Bustard populations in extensive agro-pastoral systems should be studied, giving priority to the analysis of those factors which may have an influence on breeding success. These should include the use of habitat and space, home range and dispersal patterns.

Priority: high
Time-scale: short/medium

3.2.4. Carry out international studies on migration

The migration patterns of the Great Bustard are still poorly understood. Studies involving satellite telemetry should be planned to locate wintering areas and to clarify migration routes.

Priority: medium/high
Time-scale: medium

3.3. *To improve international co-operation in the monitoring of breeding and wintering populations*

3.3.1. Promote information exchange

The Great Bustard working group should act as a forum for information exchange and discussion about international initiatives. The group should meet once a year, preferably in combination with bigger conferences. A bibliography on the Great Bustard should be compiled and distributed to all those involved in research or management.

Priority: medium
Time-scale: medium

3.3.2. Promote international teams and joint projects

Where the range of Great Bustard populations stretches across neighbouring countries, joint research projects for combining and improving conservation efforts should be promoted.

Priority: high
Time-scale: short

3.3.3. Provide support for high-priority projects

Funds for projects of highest conservation priority should be sought from international funding agencies, governments, NGOs and individuals.

Priority: high
ime-scale: short

4. Public awareness and training

4.1. To increase public awareness of the need to protect Great Bustards and their habitat

Being a conspicuous and impressive species, the Great Bustard should be used as a flagship for the protection of steppes, dry grasslands and agricultural landscapes across Europe. The whole biological community which depends on such habitats will benefit from this protection.

Priority: medium/high
Time-scale: short

4.2. To enhance farmers' and landowners' understanding of the Great Bustard

Farmers should be the target audience of specific campaigns designed to raise awareness of the international importance of the Great Bustard. They should also be provided with information on the biological characteristics of the species and the timing of breeding in order to prevent damage by farming activity.

Priority: high
Time-scale: short

4.3. To inform the public about the problems of the Great Bustard and the need for its protection

The media should be used regularly to raise the profile of the Great Bustard as an outstanding feature of the European plains and as an invaluable asset of the European natural heritage.

Priority: high
Time-scale: ongoing

4.4. To provide training for staff working in conservation bodies

Personnel working regularly in Great Bustard areas (agronomists, biologists, wardens, etc.) should receive specific training on Great Bustard matters, especially census techniques and management practices which enhance the survival of the species.

Priority: medium/high
Time-scale: short/ongoing

5. Bustards in captivity

5.1. To set up a working group and initiate a studbook of Great Bustards in captivity

Priority: medium
Time-scale: medium

5.2. To create criteria for evaluating the success of breeding stations

Priority: medium
Time-scale: medium

5.3. To undertake feasibility studies, following the IUCN criteria (Kleiman et al., 1994) for reintroduction in France, Poland and United Kingdom.

Priority: low
Time-scale: long

5.4. To provide support for successful captive management stations

Priority: medium
Time-scale: medium

Annex
Recommended conservation actions by country

Austria

2.1.2. Encourage the extension of the ongoing set-aside and habitat management schemes to other areas and increase the total area of set-aside plots.

2.2.1. Promote the growing of rape and alfalfa at wintering sites.

2.2.2. Prevent habitat alterations which may have adverse effects within the Great Bustard's range.

3.1.5. Carry out co-ordinated surveys with Hungary and Slovakia.

3.3.2. Improve and strengthen cross-border co-operation for Great Bustard protection, research and monitoring with the Czech Republic, Hungary and Slovakia.

Bulgaria

1.1.2. Urge the forestry authorities to cancel afforestation projects to set up shelter belts in the key sites for the species in Dobrudja.

1.1.3. Encourage maximum legal protection and maximum penalties to those who kill Great Bustards and enforce the conservation legislation at the "Valley of the Bustards".

1.1.4. Promote the preparation of an environmental impact assessment prior to all large-scale projects (highways, powerlines, railways, irrigation or afforestation schemes).

2.1.2. Continue the development of set-aside schemes and programmes for the leasing and acquisition of land for extensification through the Bulgarian-Swiss programme for the conservation of biodiversity, and encourage farmers to adapt the timing of their agricultural activities to the life cycle of the Great Bustard.

2.1.2. Carry out special protection measures in intensively used farmlands in Dobrudja and in Zlatiata.

2.1.4. Take special measures for minimising disturbance during breeding.

2.1.5. Promote use of existing legal instruments in Bulgaria in order to designate the species' breeding sites as temporarily protected areas.

2.2.1. Increase the quality of wintering habitats by promoting the cultivation of rape and alfalfa.

3.1.2. Monitor population size and population trends.

3.1.3. Monitor the effects of habitat management.

3.1.5. Carry out cross-border co-ordinated surveys in Dobrudja between Bulgaria and Romania.

4.1. Use the Great Bustard as a flagship species for the conservation of steppes and agricultural habitats.

4.2. Undertake an educational campaign stressing the cultural and scientific value of the Great Bustard.

Czech Republic

2.1.2. Promote set-aside schemes and extensification programmes in the Great Bustard area near Brno.

2.2.1. Promote the cultivation of rape and alfalfa to improve habitat quality at wintering sites.

3.1.5. Carry out co-ordinated surveys as a basis for cross-border conservation programmes.

Germany

2.1.7. Undertake measures to minimise predation.

2.2.2. Mitigate the adverse effects of the railway line that is planned across the Great Bustard area in Buckow.

Hungary

1.1.1. Consider changes in agricultural policy so that it is compatible with the Great Bustard's habitat needs, stressing incentives and land use regulations.

1.1.3. Encourage the provision of a legal background for ESAs and apply ESA schemes to the most important Great Bustard areas.

1.1.5. Promote a regional agreement on the conservation of the Great Bustard under the Bonn Convention.

2.1.2. Encourage the lease or purchase of grasslands and arable land in breeding and wintering areas and undertake habitat management.

2.1.3. Promote agricultural practices that do not cause disturbance or damage to Great Bustards during the period of display and breeding.

2.1.6. Undertake emergency protection measures for individual breeding females and chicks; improve the technology for artificial incubation; release and monitor captive-reared birds.

2.1.7. Undertake predator control where predation (especially by foxes and corvids) is a limiting factor.

2.2.1. Encourage farmers to cultivate rape in wintering areas and provide supplementary food during periods of thick snow cover.

2.3.1. Promote the submission of all possibly damaging alterations to Great Bustard habitats to environmental impact assessment.

3.1.2. Organise two synchronised counts in winter and in spring to monitor population size and trends.

3.1.3. Monitor effects of habitat management and of measures for nest protection.

3.1.4. Monitor and evaluate the success of Great Bustard releases.

3.1.5. Carry out co-ordinated surveys with Austria and Slovakia.

3.2.1. Improve international co-operation (especially with Spain) for monitoring Great Bustard breeding populations.

3.2.2. Evaluate the effects of predators.

3.2.3. Investigate space and habitat use in core populations.

3.2.4. Carry out studies on migration including mortality factors.

3.3.2. Carry out a synchronised census in the Kisalföld region in collaboration with Austria and Slovakia.

4.1. Use the Great Bustard as a flagship species for the protection of dry grasslands and extensive agricultural areas.

4.2. Prepare and distribute leaflets to raise awareness among farmers about appropriate practices to protect Great Bustards.

4.3. Provide adequate information for the public and for decision-makers about the needs and problems of Great Bustard conservation.

4.4. Provide training for the staff of conservation bodies about the principles and techniques of Great Bustard protection.

5.1. Undertake experiments on captive breeding.

Portugal

1.1.1. Encourage application of potentially conflicting EU agricultural policies in such a way as to prevent the spread of crops which adversely affect the Great Bustard (e.g. sunflower monocultures).

1.1.2. Prevent afforestation in Great Bustard habitats (e.g. *Eucalyptus* plantations).

1.1.3. Promote the protection of the Great Bustard and its habitat within and outside protected areas and in areas which are subject to management schemes.

1.1.4. Encourage the submission of all new infrastructures in bustard habitat to environmental impact assessment.

2.1.1. Promote the preservation of traditional land uses by establishing a system of EU-supported incentives to farmers.

2.1.2. Promote set-aside schemes and the leasing and buying of land on a scale that is effective for the maintenance of Great Bustard populations.

2.1.5. Increase wardening in breeding areas.

2.2.2. Prevent the siting of fences, afforestation, irrigation schemes, and the planting of orchards in Great Bustard areas.

2.2.4. Promote the installation of markers on overhead powerlines crossing key Great Bustard areas.

3.1.5. Carry out annual surveys and undertake co-ordinated surveys and monitoring in border areas with Spain.

3.2.3. Undertake studies on population dynamics, habitat requirements, the effects of habitat changes and causes of decline.

3.3.2. Establish collaborative research programmes and joint teams with Spain to combine and strengthen conservation efforts.

4.1. Use the Great Bustard as a flagship species to raise awareness of the importance of grasslands and arable land as a habitat for wildlife.

4.2. Increase farmers and landowners understanding of the value and importance of the Great Bustard as an indicator of habitat quality.

Romania

1.1.3. Clarify and reinforce the protection status of male Great Bustards. Encourage maximum legal protection for the species as a whole.

2.1.2. Carry out special protection measures in farmland in Dobrudja.

2.2.1. Increase the quality of wintering habitats by promoting the cultivation of rape and alfalfa.

3.1.2. Monitor population size and population trends.

3.1.3. Monitor the effects of habitat changes and management.

3.1.5. Carry out cross-border co-ordinated surveys in Dobrudja between Bulgaria and Romania.

4.1. Use the Great Bustard as a flagship species for the conservation of steppes and agricultural habitats.

4.2. Undertake an educational campaign stressing the cultural and scientific value of the Great Bustard.

Russian Federation

1.1.2. Encourage the Forestry Department of the region of Saratov to drop afforestation projects in important Great Bustard areas.

1.1.5. Undertake bilateral agreements for Great Bustard protection between Russia and those countries which host wintering populations (e.g. Ukraine).

2.1.2. Encourage the establishment of protected areas of different rank across the Great Bustard's range and promote enforcement of protection status at designated sites.

2.1.3. Propose, to the agricultural authorities, changes in the timing of farming practices (e.g. dates of cultivation and hay harvesting) to be applied where agricultural pressure is high.

2.1.6. Improve the conditions of the Saratov station for breeding and rearing Great Bustards and encourage farmers to rescue abandoned clutches.

2.1.7. Control the number of predators in areas where they have a significant effect on Great Bustards.

3.1.1. Carry out surveys in co-operation with trained and informed farmers, schools and professional hunters.

3.1.2. Establish a network of experts involving scientific institutes from Saratov, Volgograd, Rostov and Orenburg, ecological committees at district and county level, and hunting boards at district and county level.

3.1.5. Design and carry out a national survey through a network of experts and create a Great Bustard database.

3.2.3. Study sex and age structure of local populations and undertake marking of individual birds.

3.2.4. Carry out international studies to locate wintering grounds and investigate the possibility of satellite tracking.

3.3.1. Promote information exchange between Russian and foreign scientists.

4.1. Raise public awareness through the mass media; support Russian NGOs in carrying out environmental educational programmes; strengthen environmental educational programmes for local communities.

4.2. Work with the local authorities and stress the problem of disturbance and destruction of Great Bustard nests; inform farmers, provide them with educational materials and involve their children in conservation activities.

Slovakia

2.1.2. Promote set-aside schemes and agricultural extensification programmes.

2.1.5. Encourage increased wardening to prevent disturbance at key sites and undertake emergency measures for the protection of individual nesting birds and clutches.

2.2.2. Promote the submission of all new developments and infrastructures affecting Great Bustard areas to environmental impact assessment.

2.2.3. Promote installation of ball markers on the powerline near Kolarovo.

3.1.2. Monitor population size and trends at all sites.

3.1.5. Carry out co-ordinated surveys with Hungary and Austria.

3.3.2. Promote information exchange and co-operation in joint research and conservation projects (especially wardening) with the Czech Republic, Hungary and Austria.

3.3.3. Provide financial support to habitat management schemes.

4.1. Increase awareness of the general public and of decision-makers.

5.1.1. Improve the effectiveness of captive breeding attempts and set up a studbook of Great Bustards in captivity.

Spain

1.1.1. Promote development and implementation of zonal programmes already approved by the European Union and discourage crops which are detrimental to the Great Bustard (e.g. sunflower monocultures).

1.1.2. Promote the submission of regional forestry plans to environmental impact assessment (especially in Extremadura) and encourage zonation of forestry, including that carried out under EU Regulation 2080/92, avoiding Great Bustard areas.

1.1.3. Encourage the competent authorities to declare as protected areas key grassland areas and pseudosteppes (e.g. Monegros, Bardenas, La Serena).

1.1.5. Promote the development of an agreement for the conservation of grassland birds under the Bonn Convention. A bilateral agreement for Great Bustard protection between Portugal and Spain should be pursued.

1.1.6. Resist pressure to legalise the hunting of Great Bustards and to change national and international legislation. Illegal hunting should be prevented and summer hunting seasons for other species limited in certain areas.

2.1.1. Maintain and promote wide-scale traditional land uses through a system of incentives to

farmers; new agricultural policies should be carefully examined to assess their impact on the Great Bustard.

2.1.2. Encourage an increase in the total area of set-aside in Great Bustard areas.

2.1.3./2.1.5. Replace late, aerial spraying of locusts in key grasslands with earlier, more localised, ground-based applications of pesticides.

2.1.4. Promote the setting up of temporary protection schemes to ensure appropriate breeding conditions at key sites, restrict access and increase wardening.

2.2.1. Promote the dry-farming cultivation of sweet-peas and alfalfa at wintering sites.

2.2.2. Barbed-wire fences, overhead cables, the planting of orchards, and irrigation and afforestation schemes should be prevented in Great Bustard areas.

2.2.3. Promote adequate marking of overhead cables and wires that cross Great Bustard areas.

3.1.1. Provide training on survey and management techniques for personnel in charge.

3.1.2. Undertake a series of monthly counts at core areas every five years.

3.1.5. Undertake cross-border census work and joint habitat conservation measures with Portugal.

3.2.1. Carry out a comparative analysis of the existing data on population dynamics, habitat requirements, effects of habitat changes and causes of decline for the east European and Iberian populations.

3.2.2. Carry out examination of corpses, including the study of stomach contents; use the network of wardens to collect carcasses and arrange for analysis by the appropriate institutions.

3.3.2. Provide support for a joint Spanish-Portuguese conservation project.

Turkey

1.1.1. Encourage improved grassland protection legislation and promote agricultural policies which favour extensification; irrigation projects in central and south-east Anatolia should be assessed for possible impact on the Great Bustard and other species.

1.1.3. Promote establishment of special reserves for the Great Bustard and ensure adequate protection; encourage technical and financial support to the Turkish National Parks and Wildlife Authority for the maintenance of the Great Bustard protection area in Kütahya.

3.1.1. Encourage birdwatchers visiting Turkey to fill in the site recording and casual records forms available from DHKD.

3.1.5. Carry out a national Great Bustard survey in the very near future and identify the key areas; establish a network of contacts as a basis for survey and conservation work.

4.1. Use the Great Bustard as a flagship species to increase public awareness of the international importance of steppes and dry grasslands in Turkey.

Ukraine

2.1.2. Encourage the extension of the ongoing set-aside and habitat management schemes to other regions; promote the establishment of an ornithological reserve on the Kerch peninsula (Crimea).

2.1.6. Consider the feasibility of creating a Great Bustard breeding and rearing centre.

2.2.1. Collaborate with local hunting organisations to prevent illegal hunting at wintering sites and provide supplementary feeding.

Action plan for the Houbara Bustard in the Canary Islands
(Chlamydotis undulata fuertaventurae)

Reviews

This document should be reviewed by BirdLife International every four years. An emergency review will be undertaken if sudden major environmental changes, liable to affect the population, occur within the species' range.

Geographical scope

The islands of Fuerteventura, Lobos, Lanzarote and Graciosa in the east of the Canary Islands archipelago.

Summary

The Canary Islands' Houbara Bustard *Chlamydotis undulata fuertaventurae* is a sub-species endemic to the Canary Islands, and is found on the islands of Fuerteventura, Lobos, Lanzarote and Graciosa. The total population is estimated at 700 to 750 birds (300–350 on Fuerteventura and Lobos and 400 on Lanzarote and Graciosa). The species is protected under Spanish legislation and classed as Endangered in the national Red Data Book (Blanco and González, 1992); there has been a recovery plan in existence since 1985. It is also listed in Annex I of the European Union's Wild Birds Directive.

Threats and limiting factors

Habitat loss – critical

Disturbance and habitat change due to tourism – high

Abandonment of traditional agriculture – medium/high

Disturbance from military activity – medium

Disturbance due to truffle collecting – low

Illegal hunting – unknown, potentially high

Collisions with powerlines – unknown, potentially medium

Overgrazing – unknown

Predation – unknown

Parasitic disease – unknown

General increase in the number of people – unknown

Desertification and climatic factors – unknown

Conservation priorities

Adoption as royal decree of an updated recovery plan – essential

Enforce restrictions on vehicle use in key areas and launch a public awareness campaign on this issue – essential

Prevent habitat loss in key areas – essential

Purchase key areas – essential

Continue research and monitoring – essential

Provide adequate protection under the new Countryside Law and Wildlife Protection Law – high

Designate additional SPAs – high

Encourage management to benefit Houbaras under the European Union's agri-environment regulation – high

Eradicate illegal hunting – high

Avoid the use of key Houbara areas for military manoeuvres – high

Increase wardening – high

Introduction

The Houbara Bustard *Chlamydotis undulata* is not considered threatened at world level in *Birds to Watch 2* (Collar et al., 1994) due to the fact that large numbers are found in Asia and North Africa, but it is considered a Vulnerable species by the IUCN (Groombrige, 1993). In Europe, it is present only in the Canary Islands (Spain) where the endemic sub-species *fuertaventurae* occurs, and it was provisionally classified as Endangered

(Tucker and Heath, 1994). The sub-species is listed in Annex I of the European Union's Wild Birds Directive and in Appendix II of the Bern Convention. The populations of north-east Africa are listed in Appendix I of the Bonn Convention.

This action plan incorporates the discussions and conclusions of a workshop held in La Laguna in July 1993 which was attended by those involved in the conservation of the species and its habitat: the other four threatened species found in the Canary Islands were also discussed. This document recommends priority actions for the conservation of the Canary Islands' Houbara Bustard and it is hoped that it will serve as a stimulus for the approval of a legally binding recovery plan in accordance with current Spanish legislation.

Background information

Distribution and population

The Houbara is found in suitable areas on Fuerteventura and Lanzarote although it has also recently been recorded on Graciosa (A. Martín, pers. comm.) and is occasionally observed on Lobos. The total population in the Canary Islands is estimated at 700 to 750 birds; 300 to 350 on Fuerteventura and Lobos (ORNISTUDIO, 1992) and 400 on Lanzarote/Graciosa (Martín et al., in

press). Census studies carried out in December 1993 on Lanzarote (Martín et al., in press) show that the Houbara population there is much bigger than was thought; these authors consider that the Fuerteventura population must also be larger and has been underestimated. Table 15.1 shows the results of censuses carried out to date.

Life history

Taxonomic status

Taxonomists recognise three sub-species of Houbara: *C. u. macqueenii* in the deserts of Russia, Asia and the Middle East; *C. u. undulata* in North Africa; and *C. u. fuertaventurae* in the eastern Canary Islands (Collar and Goriup, 1983). The Canary Islands sub-species, first described in 1894, is the most threatened and is distinguished by its smaller size, darker and more extensive markings on its back and by its generally less sandy colouring than other sub-species.

Breeding

In the Canary Islands the males defend separate territories of around 500 to 1000 metres. Both sexes tend to be solitary during the breeding season and only come together for mating. The

Table 15.1

Summary of the censuses and population estimates of the Houbara Bustard in Fuerteventura (F) and Lanzarote (L)

Year	No. of birds observed	Estimated population		Author
1979	42	80–100	(F)	Lack, 1983
	7	15–20	(L)	Lack, 1983
1981	—	59–90	(F)	Collins, 1984
1984	24	69–86	(F)	Osborne, 1986
	6	—	(L)	Osborne, 1986
1988	127	262–318	(F)	ORNISTUDIO, 1989a
1989	124	262–318	(F)	ORNISTUDIO, 1989b
1989	153	153–378	(F)	ORNISTUDIO, 1990
1991	67	—	(L)	ORNISTUDIO, 1991
1992	—	300–350	(F)	ORNISTUDIO, 1992
1993	146	400	(L)	Martín et al., in press

males are probably polygynous and do not take part in rearing the young (Collins, 1984). Courtship takes place from December to March and consists of the male ruffling his head and neck feathers while moving over a distance of about 100 to 200 metres in a straight line or circle. The female lays two or three eggs between February and April in a small scrape she makes on the ground. The chicks are nidifugous and follow the female after hatching.

The *macqueenii* sub-species has been bred in captivity in the Al Ain Zoo in Abu Dhabi (Ramadan-Jaradi and Ramadan-Jaradi, 1989), and at Taif in Saudi Arabia there are also captive breeding facilities for Houbaras and other bustards (Renaud, 1989).

Feeding

Information from other parts of the world suggests that the Houbara is a very versatile species as regards its diet. In Baluchistan 31.5% of its prey consists of beetles and ants as well as 21 plant species (Mian, 1986). In the Canary Islands the birds feed alone or in small groups, taking both animal matter (beetles, grasshoppers, ants, larvae, snails, small lizards) and plant material (cereal seeds, peas, lentils, *Lycium, Ononis, Launaea* berries). The chicks need insects to grow properly (Collar and Goriup, 1983).

Habitat requirements

The houbara's habitat in the Canary Islands is made up of plains and rocky slopes of a semi-desert type, coastal plains and immobile dunes. The vegetation cover is made up of bushes with a predominance of *Launaea arborescens, Lycium intricatum* and *Salsola vermiculata* (Domínguez and Díaz, 1985). On Lanzarote the birds select areas with taller vegetation (Martín et al., in press). They occasionally feed in cereal and legume fields early in the morning or towards dusk, but avoid forested areas, human settlements, cornfields and lava flows.

Threats and limiting factors

Habitat loss in critical areas

Recent examples of developments causing loss of Houbara habitat include the Jandía Wind Energy Park and the gravel quarries in Lajares. These developments also give rise to other associated impacts such as the construction of new roads and tracks, increased human presence, establishment of new tracks through the use of vehicles off-road, noise, etc.

Importance: critical

Disturbance and habitat change due to tourism

The increase in the number of tourist developments (such as Costa Calma on the isthmus of Jandía and Corralejo) over the last few years has led to an increase in the number of tourist vehicles using tracks and travelling cross-country in Houbara areas. This is linked to the fact that four-wheel-drive rental companies organise safaris through the most remote parts of the islands. Frequent vehicle movements disturb the Houbaras directly and cause habitat change through the establishment of new tracks. In Fuerteventura this problem is especially serious in Corralejo, Jandía and Lajares.

Importance: high

Disturbance from military activity

Some areas, such as Llanos de Lajares, are especially suitable for military manoeuvres. These activities cause direct disturbance to the birds in the breeding season. These areas are still open to use by the public so military activity does not bring a reduction in disturbance from other activities.

Importance: medium

Disturbance from truffle collecting

The collecting of truffles ("criadas"), takes place during the breeding season and seems to have increased over the last few years. The presence of people searching the ground causes direct disturbance to the Houbara and may lead to breeding failure in incubating birds.

Importance: low

Abandonment of traditional agriculture

The Canary Islands' countryside has witnessed the progressive abandonment of arable and livestock agriculture during the twentieth century. In the eastern islands, traditional cereal and legume crops produced via the "gavias" system (small terraces adapted to this type of farming) were formerly very widespread and provided an additional food source for the Houbara. The abandonment of this type of farming is positive in the sense that some of these areas have seen the return of natural vegetation, but the negative side is that they are no longer valuable food sources. A return to this type of farming could increase the likelihood of a rise in Houbara numbers.

Importance: medium/high

Overgrazing

The grazing of goats in Fuerteventura and Lanzarote has generally had negative effects on the vegetation and has contributed to soil loss and desertification on the islands. Following a steep decline over the last few decades, the number of goats is increasing in some parts of Fuerteventura due to subsidies from the local government and the livestock farmers are organising themselves into co-operatives. In the sixteenth and seventeenth centuries there was much more livestock than at present but despite this there were quite a lot more Houbaras. It is currently thought that grazing has a negative effect on the vegetation and may have repercussions on the Houbara, although it is not clear to what extent. The use of vehicles by shepherds contributes to disturbance to the species.

Importance: unknown

Illegal hunting

This has probably been the reason for the Houbara's disappearance from some parts of Fuerteventura and Lanzarote. It is currently very difficult to quantify the extent to which illegal hunting affects populations and there are no estimates of the number of birds killed annually. The problem appears to be associated mainly with some areas where poaching is a deeply rooted tradition, for example, Tuineje in Fuerteventura.

Importance: unknown, potentially high

Collisions with powerlines

Several cases of Houbara deaths due to collisions with powerlines have been recorded. The inci-

dence among steppe-living birds of this type is generally well known and it would not be surprising to find that such collisions are more frequent than is so far apparent.

Importance: unknown, potentially medium

Transmission of parasitic diseases

It is increasingly common for farm-bred game species such as Red-legged Partridge Alectoris rufa and Barbary Partridge A. barbara to be released into the countryside without adequate sanitary supervision. This situation makes more likely the spread of parasitic diseases to which the Houbara is not resistant, and this has the potential for severe effects on the population.

Importance: unknown

Predation

Houbara predators include the Raven Corvus corax, possibly Barbary Falcon Falco pelegrinoides and Buzzard Buteo buteo. Normally only one chick survives from each clutch, occasionally two. Potential egg predators include rats Rattus, the Algerian hedgehog Atelerix algirus, Egyptian Vulture Neophron percnopterus and Raven. The Barbary ground squirrel Atlantoxerus getulus, an introduced species, does not appear to have any contact with the Houbara (Collar and Goriup, 1983; Domínguez and Díaz, 1985) although it may compete for some prey such as snails (M. Nogales, in litt., 1994).

Predation by feral dogs and cats is a potential threat, although it has not been proved to affect the Houbara.

Importance: unknown

General increase in the numbers of people

The population of Fuerteventura has tripled in recent years. If this trend continues, it may have very negative long-term repercussions on the Houbara although, at the moment, it is difficult to evaluate what the impact will be.

Importance: unknown

Desertification and climatic factors

This is another factor that could effect the Houbara in the long term although at the moment it is impossible to predict to what extent. The prolonged drought affecting the eastern Canary Islands could affect the Houbara reducing food availability and breeding success.

Importance: unknown

Conservation status and recent conservation measures

The species is classified as Endangered in both the Red Data Book of the Canary Islands' Land Vertebrates (Martín et al., 1990) and in the Red Data Book of Spanish Vertebrates (Blanco and González, 1992). In current legislation it is classified as Endangered by Royal Decree 439/90.

The history of the Houbara Bustard in the Canary Islands up to 1978 has already been summarised by Collar (1983). Recent conservation measures are summarised below in chronological order:

1979. ICBP (subsequently to become BirdLife International) organised Expedition Houbara to Fuerteventura during which the first population census, including on Lanzarote, was carried out, and the results were published in the first issue of *Bustard Studies*.

1981. D. R. Collins completed his Masters thesis on the behaviour and ecology of the Houbara in Fuerteventura, including an estimate of population size (Collins, 1984).

1984. ICBP carried out a general survey of the birds of Fuerteventura together with a census of the Houbara both there and on Lanzarote (Osborne, 1986).

1985. In view of the alarming results of the censuses mentioned above, ICONA (now DGN) decided that a recovery plan should be drawn up which included guidelines on the setting up of reserves, experimental captive breeding (Domínguez and Díaz, 1985) and education and awareness-raising among the local people. As part of the implementation of this plan the following actions were undertaken: three reserves in Fuerteventura (Jandía Isthmus, Lajares and Tesjuate Lagoon) and two in Lanzarote (Rubicón and Teguise) were declared under the

law that regulates the close season; census work was carried out in Fuerteventura in 1988, 1989, 1991 and 1992 (ORNISTUDIO 1989a,b, 1990, 1991, 1992); the La Oliva facilities were built and specimens caught for captive breeding; a poster about the Houbara was prepared; and a joint project with farmers was undertaken to promote a return to former farming methods (Domínguez 1993).

1986. Since Spain's entry into the European Union in this year, three SPAs containing Houbaras have been declared: Jandía, Dunas de Corralejo and Lobos and Lajares.

1987. The Canary Islands' Countryside Law was passed, making two important areas for the Houbara into natural (regional) parks (Corralejo and Jandía).

1989. The Countryside and Wildlife Conservation Law 4/89 was passed establishing measures necessary to guarantee wildlife conservation and giving priority to endemic species and sub-species.

1993. EU funding under LIFE regulation was granted for a habitat restoration project in Lajares which is an important area for Houbara.

1994. The new Canary Islands' Countryside Law was passed.

The Vice-Council for the Environment organised a census covering the whole of the Houbara's range.

Aims and objectives

Aims

In the short term to maintain the range and population of the Canary Islands' Houbara Bustard at no less than the 1994 levels. In the medium to long term to promote an increase in the population and an expansion of its range

Objectives

1. **Policy and legislation**

1.1. *To ensure the adoption and publication as Royal Decree of an updated recovery plan for the Canary Islands' Houbara Bustard*

The Recovery Plan drawn up in 1985 by F. Domínguez and G. Díaz may be considered ideal for its time, but it needs to be revised and updated in the light of the new political and administrative situation in the Canary Islands.

Current Spanish legislation on nature conservation includes recovery plans for the species listed as Endangered (Law 4/89, Art. 31.2) which include the Canary Islands' Houbara Bustard (R.D. 439/1990), and specifies that it is the regional government's responsibility to prepare and pass these recovery plans. The Vice-Council for the Environment should review the Houbara recovery plan and prepare an updated version. The adoption and publishing of this document as a Royal Decree with legal status by the Canary Islands' Regional Government would represent political support for the recovery plan and help ensure adequate staffing and the financial means to implement it.

Priority: essential
Time-scale: short

1.2. *To ensure that regulations on the use and management of protected countryside in the Canary Islands cover the conservation of the Houbara and its habitat*

Law 12/1987, which declared Natural Areas in the Canary Islands, has been inadequate to conserve the Houbara's habitat due to its almost exclusively urban emphasis and to the lack of resources. The new Canary Islands' Countryside Law passed in 1994 includes use and management plans, master plans (*planes directores*), conservation regulations and special plans as planning guidelines for the different protected areas. The regulations for areas containing Houbaras must guarantee that the uses to which they are put and the activities that take place there are compatible with conservation requirements for the species and its habitat. These plans could be used to address the problem of overgrazing, for example. Nature conservation organisations must be represented on the island's boards of management of the protected Natural Areas.

Priority: high
Time-scale: medium

1.3. *To complete the network of Special Protection Areas (SPAs) in the Canary Islands*

The European Commission has assigned to the Houbara a "high" threat category which means that at least 80% of the population should be included in SPAs. Present coverage for the Houbara in the SPA network is far from this figure, especially in Lanzarote where it is recommended that priority is given to the designation of Tache-Guanapay and Rubicón. On Fuerteventura the areas of Lajares and Los Alares should also be considered a priority for SPA designation.

The administration should ensure that effective measures to prevent changes in the Houbara's habitat are taken in existing SPAs.

Priority: high
Time-scale: short

1.4. *To ensure a suitable general protection framework for the Houbara Bustard under the new Canary Islands' Wildlife Protection Law*

The draft of the new wildlife law is at the consultation stage and includes the Regional List of Endangered Species and the new status of Biological Refuge as a precautionary protection measure. This legislation should ensure that the Houbara is protected throughout its distribution in the Canary Islands, both inside and outside the protected areas, in accordance with Law 4/89 (Articles 26 and 27).

Priority: high
Time-scale: short

1.5. *To encourage appropriate management in key Houbara areas through the use of schemes under EU agri-environment regulation 2078/92*

Ecologically Sensitive Areas are included in the Canary Islands' Law on the Prevention of Ecological Impact and may be declared if Houbaras are present. The declarations in the ESAs are binding and the environmental discipline mechanisms (if it is desired that they be implemented) are conclusive.

This mechanism could be used to encourage a return to traditional farming techniques and to reduce grazing pressure through fencing and removal of animals from key areas. Experience from the restoration of former "gavias" presently taking place in Lajares highlights how important this type of agriculture is for this species. It might be advisable to fence restored plots to keep goats and rabbits out.

Priority: high
Time-scale: medium

1.6. *To enforce the ban on off-road driving*

The possibility of establishing a penalty system for those using four-wheel drive vehicles incorrectly in Houbara areas should be explored.

Priority: essential
Time-scale: short

2. **Species and habitat protection**

2.1. *To prevent non-natural mortality*

2.1.1. Eradicate illegal hunting

In the short term the best way of dealing with illegal hunting is by increasing surveillance, especially in hunting reserves established under the Annual Close Season Order where hunting is not permitted. The current wardening levels in the eastern islands are too low to meet conservation needs. It is important to involve the civil guard in wardening work and formally request the setting up of a SEPRONA unit (civil guard wildlife service) in Fuerteventura. It would be advisable to set up new hunting reserves in areas with Houbaras such as Los Llanos de Tao and Los Llanos de Triquivijate.

As yet, there have been no prosecutions for killing Houbaras but it is important that, should there be one, the strong penalties included in current legislation be applied in full (one million pesetas fine, Order of 14 September 1988 on the Updating of the Value of Game and Protected Species).

Priority: high
Time-scale: short

2.1.2. Prevent collisions with powerlines

The first step in eliminating this cause of death is to find out where this type of accident most frequently occurs. To do so it is necessary to patrol the powerlines in Houbara areas searching for dead birds. Once the places are identified, the company owning the line must be invited to take the necessary preventive measures. As a precaution, all new lines in Houbara areas should be laid below ground, or their routing altered with the lines appropriately marked.

Priority: medium
Time-scale: medium

2.1.3. Prevent predation by non-natural predators

2.1.3.1. Control of feral dogs and cats

Although it has not been proved that there is a problem with feral dogs and cats, it would be advisable to remove animals that are regularly detected in the same area as Houbaras as a precautionary measure. Given the frequent use of dogs for hunting and the increase in numbers of people, feral animal numbers will probably increase.

Priority: low
Time-scale: medium

2.1.3.2. Control of rats in Houbara Bustard areas

It is suspected that rats may take Houbara eggs and chicks, but more information is needed before embarking on control programmes (see 3.1.5).

Priority: low
Time-scale: long

2.2. *To prevent human disturbance*

2.2.1. Restrict and control vehicle movement in critical areas

Vehicle movement along tracks in protected Natural Areas and SPAs where Houbaras are found needs to be restricted via the 1989 Order on Regulation of the Use of Tracks on Public Land and Other Areas For Tourist/Recreational Purposes. It will also be necessary to ban traffic from tracks and roads. These measures must be accompanied by an increase in surveillance, especially in Corralejo and Matas Blancas.

Priority: essential
Time-scale: immediate

2.2.2. Avoid holding military manoeuvres in critical areas

It is necessary to establish direct contact with military authorities to provide them with information on areas in which it is recommended that manoeuvres should not be carried out, and to suggest alternatives in areas less important for wildlife.

Priority: high
Time-scale: ongoing

2.2.3. Increase the number of wardens

Warden numbers in the eastern islands are too low to meet current needs. On Fuerteventura the estimated number of rangers needed is 10 and on Lanzarote five with temporary help during the breeding season (December to April) and the peak of the hunting season (September). The wardening service needs to be rationalised and optimised.

Priority: high
Time-scale: short

2.3.   To ensure the appropriate management of Houbara Bustard areas

2.3.1. Prevent habitat loss in critical areas

Proposals for building or commercial projects (gravel extraction, new roads, windpower facilities, etc.) in critical Houbara areas will need to be accompanied by an environmental impact assessment including the effects on Houbaras and their habitat and measures to be taken to minimise these effects. It would be advisable to include this requirement in the updated version of the official recovery plan. Protected countryside, rural parks and peripheral protection areas containing Houbaras would have to be considered as Ecologically Sensitive Areas as laid down in the legislation on environmental ecological impact.

Priority: essential
Time-scale: short

2.3.2. Acquire key Houbara Bustard areas

The critical areas are those used for nesting and feeding. Once these have been identified (some are already known see 3.1.1), acquisition of at least some of them should be considered as the best way to ensure that they are managed effec-

tively to ensure the species' survival. Such areas could be use to reintroduce traditional farming techniques and measures to control grazing.

The possibility of temporarily leasing the land prior to acquisition should not be ruled out.

Priority: essential
Time-scale: short

2.4.   To review the captive breeding programme

The review currently under way will consider if it is appropriate for the programme to continue. Facilities at the experimental captive breeding centre at La Oliva Biological Station seem to be adequate to breed Houbaras, but the centre lacks the funds required to fulfil its objectives. It would require a qualified biologist or veterinarian with some captive breeding experience and resident in Fuerteventura to be directly responsible for the technical side. Individual birds would also have to be ringed to permit individual identification.

If the centre is to continue operating it should have a work plan, clear objectives and some way of measuring the degree of success or failure. Some aspects that should be carefully considered are: factors preventing breeding, difficulty of rearing of chicks without imprinting, expected time needed to achieve success, the use to which captive bred birds will be put (see 3.2.3), selection of release site, monitoring after release. Information should be exchanged with the captive breeding programmes in Saudi Arabia and Abu Dhabi.

Captive breeding and subsequent releases should only be carried out if the IUCN criteria for reintroductions are met (Kleiman et al., 1994).

Priority: medium
Time-scale: ongoing

3.   Monitoring and research

3.1.   To have up-to-date information on conservation status and population trends

3.1.1. Continue the inventory and mapping of the Houbara's distribution

The objective of this basic study is to define the nesting areas and distribution of the different groups. This information is indispensable for evaluating the possible ecological impact of new roads, powerlines, building projects, etc.

Priority: essential
Time-scale: short

3.1.2. Clarify population status and distribution in Lanzarote and Graciosa

Fuerteventura has been the subject of almost all the studies, censuses and conservation efforts carried out to date. The Lanzarote population is much more restricted and, therefore, more vulnerable to any kind of disturbance or habitat change and so should receive urgent attention from those responsible for wildlife conservation in the Canary Islands.

Priority: high
Time-scale: ongoing

3.1.3. Improve census methodology

The transect method currently employed seems to be the most suitable as it is easy to use and has the advantage that the results are comparable with census results from previous years. However, it would be useful to combine this method with another (e.g. counting breeding males) in order to have another reference marker on population size. Observers who take part in the transect work should be equipped with radiotelephones so that they can communicate with each other.

Priority: high
Time-scale: ongoing

3.1.4. Repeat censuses every 3 to 4 years

The censuses provide indispensable information on population trends. The methodology currently used is a standardised version of the line transect in which groups of eight people walk 200 metres apart. Census work should be done simultaneously on all the islands to find out the total population at a given moment and to avoid possible errors due to bird movements between islands.

Priority: high
Time-scale: ongoing

3.1.5. Improve knowledge of breeding biology and factors leading to breeding failure

Almost nothing is known about the species' breeding biology in the Canary Islands. Among other things, this study should establish baseline data for periodic monitoring of breeding in pilot areas and for information on population dynamics. The impact of predators such as rats and feral dogs and cats should be monitored.

Priority: essential
Time-scale: short

3.1.6. Regular monitoring of breeding success

Every two years monitoring of breeding parameters should be carried out in a series of previously selected areas with subsequent analysis of the factors responsible for variations in breeding success.

Priority: high
Time-scale: medium

3.2. *To promote the development of applied research to ensure effective management of the species and its habitat*

3.2.1. Define the extent of Houbara movements and use of space and habitat

The most effective way of carrying out this study is by fitting some individuals with transmitters and monitoring them. Conditions in Fuerteventura and Lanzarote are ideal for radiotelemetry: the land is flat and unforested so the signal can be received at great distances, allowing birds to be located and followed without disturbance. Such studies would enable home ranges of individuals to be defined and would lead to a better understanding of causes of death.

Priority: high
Time-scale: short

3.2.2. Initiate a study on the effects of grazing on the Houbara's habitat

This study could be carried out when some of the plots have been fenced in to compare the regrowth of vegetation both outside and inside or to extrapolate the results of other studies on the effects of grazing in desert areas (see 1.5 and 2.3.2).

Priority: medium
Time-scale: long

3.2.3. Take advantage of facilities at La Oliva Biological Station in order to carry out basic research on the Houbara

The existence of this captive population offers an excellent opportunity to study the bustard's reaction to different marking techniques (wing tags, radio transmitters, harnesses, etc.). Information could also be obtained on microbiology, parasites, blood parameters, etc. It would be very interesting to analyse the genome of the current stock and check its variability as well as to compare the genetic make-up of the Canary Islands' Houbara with that of other sub-species.

Priority: medium
Time-scale: medium

3.2.4. Set up a study grant for the Houbara in the Canary Islands

This possibility will be explored with the Steppe and Dry Grasslands group of BirdLife International, and contacts with possible sponsors will be established.

Priority: low
Time-scale: long

4. **Public awareness and training**

4.1. *To inform and increase awareness about the need to protect the Houbara Bustard and its habitat in the eastern Canary Islands*

4.1.1. Campaign to raise awareness of the ban on off-road driving

This campaign would involve a leaflet with a code of conduct for vehicle users in Houbara areas emphasising both the need to use the tracks correctly and the ban on driving off the tracks and disturbing the birds. Other publicity measures would also be used.

Priority: essential
Time-scale: immediate

4.1.2. Build a hide for observation of the Houbara Bustard in the wild

An ever-increasing number of birdwatchers come to the eastern islands to see the Houbara and other endemic species. This demand could be controlled via the construction of a permanent hide in the vicinity of an area which Houbaras visit regularly for feeding, preferably in one of the protected areas. In this way, public access could be managed and birds in other areas would benefit from decreased disturbance. The possibility of observing the species in the wild would increase the tourist value of the islands and would help to educate the local population.

Priority: medium
Time-scale: long

4.1.3. Undertake an educational campaign directed at young people and groups important for Houbara conservation

This campaign would include a video and a educational notebook about the species. There would also be a series of talks for arable and livestock farmers, hunters, tour companies and the civil guard using local media to publicise the cause of the Houbara and emphasise the need to conserve it.

Priority: medium
Time-scale: medium

4.2. *To establish a local monitoring network*

By making use of the new infrastructure of the Spanish Ornithological Society (SEO) in Tenerife, a network of contacts with people interested in bird conservation will be set up to obtain direct information on any disturbance to the Houbara's habitat and to take part in conservation work related to this action plan.

Priority: low
Time-scale: long

International action plan for the Slender-billed Curlew *(Numenius tenuirostris)*

Reviews

This action plan should be reviewed and updated by BirdLife International every two years. An emergency review will be undertaken if sudden major environmental changes, liable to affect the population, occur within the species range.

Geographical scope

The action plan needs to be implemented in: Albania, Algeria, Bulgaria, Croatia, Greece, Hungary, Iran, Iraq, Italy, Kazakhstan, Morocco, Romania, Russian Federation, Spain, Tunisia, Turkey, Ukraine and the former Yugoslavia.

Summary

The conservation status of the Slender-billed Curlew *Numenius tenuirostris* is classified as Critical at a global level (Collar et al., 1994). It is almost certainly the rarest and most poorly known bird species in Europe, where it occurs as a passage migrant. The population is estimated at 50 to 270 birds. The first action plan, covering nine range states, was included in the BirdLife International monograph on the species (Gretton, 1991).

Conservation of the Slender-billed Curlew is a truly formidable task. Although major gaps remain in our knowledge of the species in large parts of its range, certain actions can be taken immediately (and some have already been achieved). Effective conservation action will depend largely on a high degree of co-operation and commitment among those responsible, and on medium- to long-term funding of the necessary activities.

Threats and limiting factors

Habitat loss – low/high (breeding areas), medium/high (passage and wintering areas)

Hunting – medium (historically high)

Breakdown of social behaviour patterns – medium/high (following initial decline)

Other factors – unknown

Conservation priorities

Effective legal protection for the Slender-billed Curlew and its look-alikes – essential/high

Locate the breeding grounds – essential

Promote international and national policies which protect the Slender-billed Curlew and its habitat – high

Appropriate protection and management of all passage, wintering and breeding grounds – high

Locate and study key wintering and passage sites – high/medium

Increase public awareness of the species critically threatened status amongst politicians, decision-makers and hunters – high

Introduction

The Slender-billed Curlew is arguably the most threatened bird species in the western Palaearctic; it is certainly the least known of the region's threatened birds, which greatly adds to the difficulty of conserving it. It appears to be the only bird species of the western Palaearctic whose breeding grounds have remained unknown for the last 70 years. Thus, although its current population size is comparable with that of Zino's Petrel *Pterodroma madeira* and Bald Ibis *Geronticus eremita*, because the Slender-billed Curlew's present breeding grounds are unknown (as well as most of the wintering areas), there is much less that can be done to help it. The conservation challenge is compounded by the fact that the identification of the species is not straightforward and that it is a medium- to long-range migrant, crossing many countries in which conservation action is needed.

The species is globally threatened, and has a Critical threat status (Collar et al., 1994), with a population recently estimated at 50 to 270 individuals (Gretton, 1994). It is listed in Annex I of the European Union's Wild Birds Directive and in CITES, and in Appendix I of the Bonn Convention and Appendix II of the Bern Convention. A memorandum of understanding for the conservation of the species was developed during 1993 and 1994 by the Bonn Convention Secretariat. A wide range of activities was carried out from 1992 to 1994 across much of the species range, under the European Union (ACNAT) project "Preparation of a rescue plan for the Slender-billed Curlew" (European Commission, 1994).

A workshop to identify priority actions necessary for the species in the west Mediterranean was held at Merja Zerga, Morocco, on 21 and 22 January 1994. This was attended by 30 people from the five relevant range states (Italy, Spain, Morocco, Algeria, Tunisia) as well as France, Belgium and UK. The main output was an action plan covering the five west Mediterranean range states. In addition, the 1988-90 BirdLife International project covered the whole range of the species, involving detailed research and identification of priority actions in each of the (then) nine range states. The action plan resulting from this project (included in Gretton, 1991) has been used as the basis, after revision, for the recommendations given here for Romania, Hungary, Turkey and Greece. For the remaining range states, new recommendations have been drafted, either because of political changes (the former Yugoslavia and the former Soviet Union), or because of new information or re-interpretation of the importance of countries for the species (Bulgaria, Iran, Iraq). During the IWRB Black Sea meeting in Odessa in October 1993, discussions were held on actions necessary for the Slender-billed Curlew with the four Black Sea range states. In 1994 an agreement of co-operation was drawn up between the Novosibirsk Institute, the Dutch Government, Vogelbescherming Nederland and BirdLife International for future surveys in south-west Siberia.

Background information

The information given below is a summary of the available material; see Gretton (1991) for further details.

Distribution and population

The only fully confirmed breeding records of the Slender-billed Curlew were established between 1914 and 1924 near Tara, to the north of Omsk in Siberia (Ushakov, 1916; 1925). There are a number of historical records of summering birds from elsewhere in south-west Siberia and northern Kazakhstan which may refer to breeding birds, though there is no hard evidence of nesting.

From the breeding area the main migration route is in a WSW direction, north of the Caspian and Black seas through south-east and southern Europe to north-west Africa. There are also records of wintering birds in the Middle East, but because of the low density of observers in much of this area it is not clear whether these records represent a second wintering area or whether they refer to vagrants. Iran and Iraq may be of particular importance for wintering birds, but unfortunately it has been impossible to carry out surveys there in recent years.

The situation in North Africa is also rather unclear at present. Historically this area supported considerable numbers of wintering Slender-billed Curlews, with large flocks reported in Algeria and Tunisia at the end of the nineteenth century. Indeed the species was described as the most common curlew species in Tunisia (Stresemann and Grote, 1943) and in Morocco and Algeria (Glutz von Blotzheim et al., 1977). As late as the 1960s and the 1970s, flocks of over 100 birds were seen in Morocco. In recent years, however, despite increasing interest in the species, only one regular wintering site for it has been identified: Merja Zerga in Morocco, which had supported just two individuals in the previous two winters but only one during the winter of 1994-95. There is thus almost as much mystery concerning the current winter quarters as the breeding area. During the late 1980s there were claimed observations of 30 to 90 Slender-billed Curlews in Algeria, but unfortunately these records could not be confirmed and have not been repeated.

The population of the species was estimated in 1990 at 80 to 400 individuals; this may have been too optimistic and the estimate was recently reduced from 50 to 270 birds (see Gretton, 1994, for the background of this estimate). This estimate is based mainly on the number of passage birds; several difficulties exist in producing a population estimate from such data, notably uncertainty regarding the proportion of passage birds that are likely to be seen and whether the same birds would be seen in different locations. Since 1980, however, there have been (on average) almost 10 confirmed records of the species per year, involving some 15 to 22 individuals, and many birds are likely to go unseen. Clearly birds are also wintering elsewhere than in the known site in Morocco.

Life history

Breeding

Little detailed information can be given on breeding ecology and behaviour, since the only confirmed observations come from just one site and were reported at least 70 years ago (Ushakov, 1916, 1925). This site, near Tara, is close to the northern limit of the forest-steppe zone. Ushakov described the habitat as "an extensive quaking peatbog with a dense cover of sedge...", with willow, birch and pine present. The habitat appeared largely unchanged during surveys in 1990 and 1994, and was closer to a taiga marsh than a typical forest-steppe marsh. It is possible that the habitat at this site was not typical of that used by the species, and thus the species may nest further north (in true taiga habitat) or south (in steppe habitat).

In May 1914, Ushakov found a single Slender-billed Curlew nest, with four eggs. (Eurasian Curlews were also nesting nearby). He shot the female, thus curtailing any further observations. Ten years later, however, Ushakov found a colony of the species, containing 14 nests (within a few metres of each other); at the same site south of Tara. With so few observations there is no way of knowing how common such colonial

nesting is, but it is notable that Ushakov had not recorded colonial nesting previously.

Feeding

There is little information available on diet. The birds at Merja Zerga have been recorded as eating earthworms and tipulid larvae, while elsewhere other insects (grasshoppers, an earwig and a beetle), molluscs and crustaceans have been recorded as prey. The most detailed observations of foraging behaviour have been made in recent years at Merja Zerga (Van den Berg, 1988; Gretton, 1991) where the species uses two contrasting habitats, brackish grazing marsh and sandy agricultural land on higher ground nearby. In both areas the birds often feed with Eurasian Curlews and the feeding behaviour is broadly similar to that species: the birds walk slowly, occasionally pecking at the surface or probing the soil; if a food item is located, intensive probing results until the item is extracted. On average 1.5 to 2.75 food items were obtained per minute, and feeding was concentrated in mid-morning and mid-afternoon, with the birds roosting in the lagoon at other times.

Habitat requirements

The breeding habitat (as far as it is known) is discussed above. On migration a wide variety of habitats is used, including saltmarsh, steppe grassland, fishponds, saltpans and brackish lagoons. There is a similar degree of variation in the known wintering habitats, with some records from tidal mudflats (Tunisia), others from semi-desert "sebkhets" (temporary brackish wetlands in Tunisia and Algeria), and others from brackish marsh and sandy farmland (such as at Merja Zerga). In view of the species' rather broad choice of habitat on passage and in winter, it is unlikely that habitat loss in these areas has played a major part in the decline (particularly since many other wader species using the same region have not suffered such a decline). Loss of breeding-ground habitat, which may be much more specialised, would better explain such a drastic collapse. It has been argued (e.g. by Belik, 1994) that the species may nest primarily in steppe areas; if so, then the massive loss of such habitat (notably in Kazakhstan) may have played a part in its decline.

Threats and limiting factors

Habitat loss

Due to the lack of knowledge concerning the location of the breeding grounds, it is not possible to assess the scale of threat posed by their modification/loss. In general the taiga has been little modified, the forest-steppe partly cultivated (but with many wetlands remaining), and much of the steppe severely modified by intensive agriculture. The importance of this factor could thus range from low to high, depending on which habitat is used for nesting.

Much of the passage route has been greatly modified by man, for example the Aral Sea area and the steppe areas of central and eastern Europe. There has also been a general loss of wetlands throughout the western Palaearctic. The loss of traditional stopover sites may have had serious effects on the Slender-billed Curlew, but, as noted above, it can use a range of passage habitats and yet has still suffered a much greater decline than other waders crossing the same region.

Parts of the winter quarters (e.g. the Rharb plain of north-west Morocco) have been greatly affected by man, with large-scale drainage of wetlands. In Tunisia also, temporary freshwater marshes (e.g. Kairouan) have been seriously damaged by the construction of dams for flood control and the provision of water supplies. Elsewhere in North Africa, however, other types of wetland have been less affected, such as coastal sites and inland sebkhets/chotts (temporary brackish wetlands, e.g. those near Constantine in Algeria). The situation is hard to assess as long as Merja Zerga remains the only known, current regular wintering site for the species. In the Middle East, the marshes of Iraq are potentially a very important wintering site, but are rapidly being destroyed. By 1991 to 1992, the area of the central (Qurnah) marshes had been reduced to 67% of its 1984-85 area, while the area of permanent marshes overall had been reduced to 40% of the 1984-85 area (from 1 133 000 ha to 457 000 ha). If drainage plans proceed as at present, the marshes will probably be lost in 10 to 20 years (Maltby, 1994).

Importance: low/high (breeding areas), medium/high (passage and wintering areas)

Hunting

In the early part of the twentieth century, across much of Europe, hunting of waders took place on a large scale (principally for food), with curlews (as the largest waders) being a favoured quarry. Significant numbers of Slender-billed Curlew specimens, notably from Hungary and Italy, date from this time, the birds often being from markets (Gretton, 1991). Because the Slender-billed Curlew is often tamer than its congeners (Gretton, 1991), it could have suffered very heavily at this time. Indeed there is considerable evidence that hunting may have been the key cause of its decline, with habitat loss an important secondary factor – though it is hard to imagine habitat loss affecting this one species more than any other European wader. The selective threat posed by hunting is clear: curlews were the prime wader targets for food, and Slender-billed Curlews (according to much evidence) were the tamest curlew. It would be difficult, perhaps impossible, to prove absolutely that hunting was the key factor some 60 to 100 years after the main period of decline, but the available evidence points in this direction.

At least up to the 1970s there was also strong hunting pressure in parts of North Africa. At present the threat is generally less, but between 1962 and 1987, 17 Slender-billed Curlews are known to have been shot (13 of these in Italy and the former Yugoslavia). With the world population so low, this number is highly significant; the loss of even a single further bird to hunting is unacceptable.

Importance: medium (but historically high)

Breakdown of social behaviour patterns

This is very much a secondary factor, not responsible for the original decline, but likely to be important in keeping numbers low following the main decline (i.e. during the last 30 to 50 years). Early records often referred to large flocks of the species on migration and in winter, and it is possible that the experience of older birds was important in guiding such flocks. As Slender-billed Curlew numbers fell, individuals would be more likely to join flocks of other species, notably the Eurasian Curlew. The chances of Slender-billed Curlews meeting each other on the breeding grounds would become increasingly low, as was graphically described for the Eskimo Curlew by Bodsworth (1954). Without drastic (and probably unfeasible) intervention, there is little that can be done to ameliorate these effects.

Importance: medium to high (following initial decline)

Other factors

Many other possible causes of the decline have been considered (Gretton, 1991), but very few are thought plausible. Two factors, affecting parts of Kazakhstan potentially used by the species, are highly speculative but warrant mention, although it is difficult to obtain precise information on either. The level of agricultural chemicals used in the Aral Sea area (since the 1950s) has caused widespread concern, and has been held responsible for widespread human illness and high levels of child mortality. The lack of water in the area would serve to concentrate such chemicals still further, and could contaminate Slender-billed Curlews via their food, or directly in drinking water.

There are (unconfirmed) reports of nesting Slender-billed Curlews from Ust-Kamenogorsk and Semipalatinsk (Gavrin et al., 1962) in the 1920s and 1930s. The main nuclear testing ground of the former Soviet Union is just west of Semipalatinsk, and was used until very recently. In earlier years atmospheric tests were conducted here, presumably causing major contamination. Summer records of the species are also known from the Chelyabinsk region (Gavrin et al., 1962), and in recent years very high levels of radioactivity have been found in the environment near Chelyabinsk -40 (E. Nowak, verbally). At present we do not have enough information to assess whether such factors could have affected the Slender-billed Curlew, but the possibility cannot be entirely ruled out.

Importance: unknown

Conservation status and recent conservation measures

International

There have been several international initiatives for the species, briefly summarised in the introduction to this plan. These include the 1988-90 BirdLife International project (Gretton, 1991), the European Union (ACNAT) project (European Commission, 1994), the Bonn Convention memorandum of understanding which has been signed by 14 range states with a further four or five expected by the end of 1995, and the agreement of co-operation for breeding-ground searches. A European Union LIFE project commencing in 1996 envisages co-operation between Greek and foreign scientists, including links between Greek and Russian research.

Albania

2 records, 1992-93 (maximum five birds).

The species is likely to have been greatly underrecorded during much of the twentieth century, and therefore it is included here as a potential range state (further surveys are a high priority). Little is known about the current hunting situation, but in view of the economic situation, curlews are likely to be at some risk.

Algeria

7 records, 1977-90 (maximum 37 birds), plus three unconfirmed records.

The Slender-billed Curlew has been protected since 1983, but other *Numenius* species and godwits *Limosa* are not protected. For the last two years, since the political situation has deteriorated, hunting has been entirely banned; prior to that, hunting was allowed on just one day per week. There are some 40000 licensed hunters. There is not thought to be a serious problem with the poaching of waders, as tourist hunters mainly hunt wild boar.

The RSPB carried out surveys for the Slender-billed Curlew in 1990 and 1992 (Chown and Linsley, 1994), resulting in one record of the species; IRSNB also surveyed selected areas in November 1992, as part of the ACNAT project.

Bulgaria

19 records, 1903-93 (maximum four to seven birds), plus 10 unconfirmed records.

Key site: Lake Atanasovo (six records).

All *Numenius* and *Limosa* species are protected, along with most other waders (Ordinance 342, 21/4/86); the penalty for shooting a Slender-billed Curlew has been increased to the maximum (30000 leva = c. US$ 450). The penalties for shooting all other curlew and godwit species are also high (10000 leva). Among waders, only Snipe and Woodcock are legal quarry. There are some 90000 licensed hunters, plus from 700 to 800 foreign hunters per year. There is a problem with poaching in some areas (including Lake Atanasovo) and a serious problem with largely uncontrolled foreign hunters shooting globally threatened species (e.g. Red-breasted Goose, White-headed Duck).

The Slender-billed Curlew was not included in the 1985 Red Data Book. Bulgaria was not included as a full range state in the 1988-90 BirdLife International project, as only seven records of the species were then known to BirdLife International. In 1993 surveys for the species were carried out by BSPB and D. Nankinov under the EU ACNAT project, and recommendations for conservation action were made; these have been included in the proposals below. A preliminary management plan for Lake Atanasovo has been produced by RSPB and BSPB. A second site used by the Slender-billed Curlew, Chengene skele, is now legally protected, following efforts by BSPB. A national plan for the conservation of wetlands has been compiled by the Ministry of the Environment,the BSPB, scientific institutes, etc.

Croatia

5 records, 1970-87 (maximum two birds), plus 11 unconfirmed records.

Included in the 1988-90 BirdLife International project (as part of the former Yugoslavia); the species was given considerable publicity by the Croatian Institute for Ornithology. Five Slender-billed Curlews are known to have been shot between 1970 and 1987 (three by Italian

hunters). There has been little conservation action since 1990, due to the political situation. (Information on current hunting laws is awaited.)

Greece

70 records, 1918-93 (maximum c. 150 birds), plus seven unconfirmed records.

Key sites: Evros delta (SPA), Porto Lagos (SPA), Axios delta (SPA).

Curlews and godwits are legally protected throughout the year (penalty c.US$ 300 – 3000) but illegal hunting remains problematic in Greece. Intense hunting pressure occurs in the small hunting zones within the Evros and Axios deltas. These exclude areas used by Slender-billed Curlews but the risk of disturbance or illegal encroachment by hunters remains. There are some 300000 licensed hunters, but only a small proportion are said to pursue waterfowl and/or waders. The Slender-billed Curlew is listed in the Red Data Book (Handrinos, 1992) as endangered.

Surveys for the Slender-billed Curlew (and Lesser White-fronted Goose) were carried out at the Evros delta in 1987-88, by RSPB and the Hellenic Ornithological Society; subsequently a poster was produced for these two species. BirdLife International, with V. Goutner, carried out surveys in northern Greece in 1988 and 1989. WWF has been supporting the conservation of key Greek wetlands through the Red Alert project and their support of the Greek Wetland centre, established near Thessaloniki in 1991. A management plan for the Evros delta has been produced and a joint ministerial decision to delineate the site is in preparation. Further work on the species was carried out during 1993-94 under the ACNAT project (Handrinos, in European Commission, 1994) and under another EU contract (Vangeluwe and Handrinos, 1995). Moreover, a LIFE project started in 1996 to be implemented at six key wetland sites for the species.

Hungary

85 records, 1903-91 (maximum 36 birds), plus one unconfirmed record.

Key sites: Hortobágy, Kardoskut.

All three curlew species (and godwits) have been protected since 1954, and the legislation is well-respected and enforced. The fine for killing a Slender-billed Curlew is now 250000 forint (close to the maximum) and potentially one year in jail. Among waders, only Snipe *Gallinago gallinago* and Woodcock *Scolopax rusticola* are legal quarry, and all hunting is forbidden at the key sites. There are some 45000 licensed hunters and about 25000 visiting hunters; there have been some problems with visiting Italians not respecting Hungarian hunting laws (e.g. some Great White Egret *Egretta alba* were shot).

Hungary was fully involved in the 1988-1990 BirdLife International project and the recent ACNAT project. The penalty for shooting Slender-billed Curlew was recently increased (it was previously only 1000 forint). The staff of the Hortobágy National Park are well aware of the species and its needs. Detailed management recommendations for the Hortobágy and Kardoskut were included in the ACNAT report.

Iran

6 records, 1963-73 (maximum seven birds), plus 35 unconfirmed records.

There is apparently virtually no wader hunting, at least for food, as the meat is considered unclean by Muslims (B. Behrouzi-Rad, *in litt.*). No information is available on current hunting laws and penalties. BirdLife International supported surveys in 1990, which resulted in four unconfirmed records of the species. D. A. Scott and M. Smart visited Iran in the 1992-93 winter, but did not record the species and were unable to fully evaluate the previous records (D. A. Scott, *in litt.*, 1994).

Iraq

3 records, 1917-79 (maximum six birds).

Probably greatly under-recorded; the marshes of Iraq have never been fully surveyed for birds, yet they are (or were) the largest area of freshwater marsh in the western Palaearctic. Efforts were made by BirdLife International to carry out joint surveys in 1988 and 1989; although an invitation

was received from Baghdad, it was almost immediately postponed. Subsequent developments have unfortunately made the prospect of any surveys in the near future remote. No specific conservation measures for the Slender-billed Curlew are known; meanwhile the destruction of the marshes continues apace (see above, under habitat loss).

Italy

76 records, 1900-93 (maximum seven birds), plus six unconfirmed records. In winter 1994-95 a flock of up to 20 birds was recorded.

Key sites: Viareggio area, Golfo di Manfredonia (part SPA); Valli di Comacchio/Ravenna coast (part SPA); Circeo National Park (SPA); Laguna di Orbetello/Maremma National Park (both SPAs).

Curlews are not listed as legal quarry species, and are thus to be considered protected. Legislation is nevertheless needed for their strict protection, with substantial penalties applicable; this would best be achieved by including the species on the special protection list. The Black-tailed Godwit was removed from the quarry list in 1991-92, but is now listed again. During 1994 there was considerable confusion concerning hunting proposals (N. Baccetti, *in litt.*). On the one hand there was a proposal (a circular from the Minister of Agriculture, No. 16, 15/7/94) to again remove Black-tailed Godwit from the list of quarry species, specifically in order to avoid confusion with the Slender-billed Curlew. On the other hand some hunting organisations proposed the addition of the Eurasian Curlew and the Bar-tailed Godwit *Limosa lapponica* to the list of quarry species; the first proposal in June 1994 was stopped following intervention by LIPU.

There are 1.5 million registered hunters, with much uncontrolled hunting occurring next to (and even within) protected areas. Italy (Istituto Nazionale per la Fauna Selvatica, (INFS)) took a full part in the BirdLife International project and the recent ACNAT project. A workshop was held on the species at Arosio, 27 to 29 March 1992, and produced a declaration for intended circulation among hunting organisations.

Discussions between LIPU and government representatives on the preparation of a national action plan for the Slender-billed Curlew have already begun in view of the possible return of the flock observed in 1994-95. This flock mainly frequented wetlands in the Golfo de Manfredonia which are formally protected, but which are regularly shot over.

Kazakhstan

4 records, 1921-91 (maximum three birds), plus 31 records, including 17 summering, mapped in Gavrin et al. (1962).

The Slender-billed Curlew is included in the Kazakhstan Red Data Book, and is thus presumably protected, but the exact situation is not known. No other specific conservation measures are known to date.

Morocco

53 records, 1939-94 (maximum 500 to 800 birds), plus three unconfirmed records.

Key site: Merja Zerga.

All curlew species are protected, but not godwits; prior to 1990 all curlews, including Slender-billed, were listed as quarry species. In 1979 there were 50000 hunters, with the number rising annually, plus visiting hunters (Bergier, 1987). Hunting has been permitted at Merja Mellah, in the northern part of the Merja Zerga Biological Reserve (poaching also occurs elsewhere in the reserve). In December 1989 one of the three Slender-billed Curlews was shot and wounded near Merja Mellah, adding considerable pressure to the calls for hunting to be banned from the whole area (this is expected to occur before the end of 1994: Eaux et Forêts staff, verbally).

The species has occurred widely along the Atlantic coast of Morocco, but the areas in the south, such as Khnifiss, were rarely monitored until recently. A considerable amount of work has been put into surveys and research on the species. BirdLife International supported work in the 1987-88 winter (Van den Berg, 1988), and made visits to Merja Zerga in January 1989 and 1990 (Gretton, 1991). Peace Corps volunteers, notably H. Cooper, also made observations

during this winter. Several surveys were carried out in the 1993-94 winter, under the ACNAT project (Agbani and Dakki, Franchimont, in European Commission, 1994).

Romania

16 records, 1966-89 (maximum 30 birds).

Key site: Danube delta.

The Bern Convention entered into force in 1993 following ratification by Romania, but there is no implementing law and the Slender-billed Curlew is not protected by specific legislation. Other species of large wader remain legal quarry (open season mid-August to mid-March). There is apparently little interest in shooting waders, however, among the 60000 hunters in Romania. In 1989 the fine for shooting a curlew out of season was about £5. All records of the species but one have been from the Danube delta, particularly the saltmarsh areas at Istria and Razelm-Sinoie. Since 1989 the conservation prospects of the delta have improved dramatically, with several agencies now involved in protecting and managing the delta, which is now a Biosphere Reserve.

Russian Federation

9 records, 1908-91 (maximum three birds), plus Ushakov's records near Tara.

The species was included in the Red Data Book of the USSR and is included in the Russian Red Data Book. It is in theory therefore protected, but in some areas this seems to apply only during the breeding season. New hunting laws are being prepared at present. Members of the Russian Federation are also free to introduce their own laws. Other curlews and godwits are legal quarry.

Searches for the breeding grounds were carried out annually from 1989 to 1995 by A. K. Yurlov, in co-operation with BirdLife International and the Dutch Government (G. Boere, Ministry of Agriculture). Searches were also carried out near Barnaul (Chupin et al., 1994) and Chelyabinsk. This work will continue until at least 1996, under an agreement of co-operation signed in 1994 (see introduction above).

Spain

6 records, 1962-80 (maximum 13 birds), plus up to 35 unconfirmed observations, all but three from Coto Doñana, January 1990 to February 1992.

Potential key site: Coto Doñana National Park (SPA).

The Slender-billed Curlew is listed as Insufficiently Known in the Spanish Red Data Book (Blanco and Gonzaléz, 1992). It is not, however, included in the national inventory of endangered species (Royal Decree 439/1990) and thus is not legally considered as belonging to the Spanish avifauna. All other curlews and godwits are protected and there is not thought to be a problem with the hunting of large waders (R. Martí, verbally and in litt., 1994). Among waders, only Lapwing Vanellus vanellus, Jack Snipe Lymnocryptes minimus, Snipe and Woodcock are legal quarry (Royal Decree 1095/1989). Surveys for the species were carried out in Doñana and other selected sites on the Andalucian coast, between November 1993 and January 1994, under the ACNAT project. No Slender-billed Curlew records resulted from these surveys, but a full report was produced on the past occurrence and conservation of the species (Urdiales, in European Commission, 1994).

Tunisia

26 records, 1915-92 (maximum 32 birds), plus two unconfirmed records.

Key areas: Kairouan–Monastir Gulf of Gabès.

Curlews and godwits are not listed as quarry species, and curlews, but not godwits, are explicitly protected under Article 7, Arrêté de Chasse (curlews were listed in June 1994 following a request from BirdLife International). There were some 15000 registered hunters in 1992-1993 (the highest number to date) plus almost 2000 tourist hunters. Existing laws are generally respected, although there may be some poaching at certain sites. During February and March 1992 surveys of coastal wetlands were carried out by RSPB, following similar surveys in Algeria (Chown and Linsley, 1994); 25 sites were checked, but no Slender-billed Curlews were seen. Further sur-

veys were carried out the following winter (November 1992 and January 1993) by the Institut Royal des Sciences Naturelles de Belgique, under the ACNAT project, and a paper was written evaluating the probability of Slender-billed Curlew occurring with Eurasian Curlew in Tunisia (Ledant and Lafontaine, in European Commission, 1994).

Turkey

29 records, 1946-90 (maximum four birds), plus three unconfirmed records.

Potential key sites: Göksu delta (three records), Tuz Gölü, Seyfe Gölü.

The Slender-billed Curlew is protected; other curlew species and Bar-tailed Godwit have been protected since 1992. Black-tailed Godwit is still a legal quarry species (open season 15 September-28 February). Although only 12 wader species are not strictly protected, in practice almost all waders are liable to be shot, as there is very little awareness or enforcement of existing laws. There are some 4–5 million hunters, of whom only 2 million are licensed (Magnin, 1989; M. Yarar, in litt.). DHKD helped with the 1988-90 BirdLife International project, and issued a request to visiting birdwatchers in April 1990 for information on Slender-billed Curlew and other threatened species. The DHKD also widely distributed information and recommendations for conservation efforts among government officials. International Wader and Waterfowl Research Group (WIWO) carried out several surveys at major wetlands in the late 1980s and early 1990s, but only recorded one probable Slender-billed Curlew (Çukurova delta, 1986). The potential key sites are not fully protected.

Ukraine

15 records, 1908-93 (maximum 48 birds), plus 18 unconfirmed records.

Key areas: Danube delta, northern Black Sea, Azov Sea and Sivash lagoon; partly protected (as Zapovedniks or Zakazniks), but large areas unprotected.

The Slender-billed Curlew is listed in the Red Data Book and is protected (penalty five times the minimum monthly wage), as are the Eurasian Curlew and the Whimbrel *Numenius phaeopus* (penalty four times the minimum monthly wage), under the Law of 19 April 1993 (Appendix 1/6/93). Godwits are not protected, however, and there is little enforcement of existing laws. There are 530000 hunters, about 1% of the population. Surveys for the species were carried out in 1993 under the ACNAT project, and WIWO has also carried out detailed work on waterbirds at Sivash (Van der Have et al., 1992). The IWRB Black Sea meeting in Odessa in October 1993 afforded a useful opportunity to discuss Slender-billed Curlew conservation issues in the region.

The former Yugoslavia

38 records (32 from Vojvodina), 1900-84 (maximum 50 birds).

Key site: Soskopo.

The Slender-billed Curlew was unprotected in the former Yugoslavia, but apparently is now protected (IRSNB, 1994). In 1988, in the former Yugoslavia, there were 264000 registered hunters, as well as many visiting hunters from abroad, particularly Italy. Two Slender-billed Curlews are known to have been shot in Vojvodina in 1962 and 1968. Surveys for the species were carried out, mainly in Vojvodina, between 1988 and 1990, under the 1988-90 BirdLife International project. Due to the political situation no further work has been carried out.

Aims and objectives

Aims

1. In the short term, to prevent the extinction of the Slender-billed Curlew.

2. In the medium term, to prevent any further decrease in the Slender-billed Curlew population caused by threats in either the breeding, passage or wintering grounds.

3. In the long term, to secure a significant increase in the number of Slender-billed Curlews.

Objectives

1. **Policy and legislation**

1.1. *To promote broad national and international policies which will ensure the long-term conservation of the Slender-billed Curlew and its habitats.*

1.1.1. Encourage the maximum level of protection for the Slender-billed Curlew and its habitat under international conventions

During 1993 and 1994, the Bonn Convention Secretariat (in discussion with BirdLife International and others) developed a memorandum of understanding "concerning conservation measures for the Slender-billed Curlew" for signing by the Slender-billed Curlew range states. The memorandum of understanding will provide a framework for range state government action, while this action plan sets targets for the BirdLife International Network and NGOs, as well as governments. All Slender-billed Curlew range states should be encouraged to sign this.

Priority: medium
Time-scale: medium

1.1.2. Encourage international policies that promote the conservation of Slender-billed Curlew sites

Although the key sites for the Slender-billed Curlew are all IBAs (Grimmett and Jones, 1989), and are mostly protected as Reserves or National Parks, the species also occurs occasionally at a wide range of wetland sites. Only very broad policies can promote the conservation of the range of such sites. Initiatives such as MED-WET and the ESA concept (within the EU) should be promoted where possible. Any use of international funds (e.g. from the World Bank or EU structural funds) must be carefully assessed to ensure that wetlands are not damaged.

Priority: high
Time-scale: ongoing

1.1.3. Promote international co-operation and funding from bilateral sources and other agencies

The sharing both of experience and skills, and of the necessary funds to allow project work, is vitally important. Because the Slender-billed Curlew is little known and poses identification problems, the involvement of those with experience of the species in countries with limited knowledge of it (e.g. Albania, Iran, Iraq, Kazakhstan) can be of great value. Without outside support and funds, little will be achieved in many range states. Bilateral support can be highly effective (such as the Dutch government programmes in Ukraine and Russia) as can wider programmes such as those funded by the European Union/World Bank).

Priority: medium
Time-scale: ongoing

1.1.4. Encourage national policies for all protected areas which ensure that all Slender-billed Curlew key sites are fully and effectively protected (including sites where the species has been seen only occasionally)

Any loss of (or damage to) wetland habitat within the Slender-billed Curlew key sites, should be avoided and it is recommended that hunting should be banned at these sites. National wetland inventories (and conservation strategies) should be produced by each range state to provide a framework for setting wetland conservation priorities.

Priority: high
Time-scale: ongoing

1.2.   To promote the full and effective legal protection for the Slender-billed Curlew and its "look-alikes" throughout its range

1.2.1. Encourage legal protection of the Slender-billed Curlew

Encourage the listing of the Slender-billed Curlew in each range state as a strictly protected species, with maximum applicable penalties for contravention of the law. Countries where the species is not specifically protected in this way include Italy, Spain (not included in Royal Decree 439/1990), Tunisia and Ukraine (fine too low); the situation is unclear in Kazakhstan, Iran, Iraq and Russia.

Priority: essential
Time-scale: short

1.2.2. Encourage legal protection of look-alike species

Encourage the listing of other Numenius and Limosa species (and Limnodromus in Russia) as protected species. This is necessary due to the problem of identifying the Slender-billed Curlew; few hunters would be able to make the correct identification in time. This objective applies to Albania, Algeria, Croatia, Kazakhstan, Iran, Iraq, Italy (Black-tailed Godwit, and perhaps the Eurasian Curlew and the Bar-tailed Godwit if these are listed as quarry species), Morocco (Limosa), Romania, Russia, Tunisia (specific protection needed), Turkey (Black-tailed Godwit), Ukraine (Limosa) and the former Yugoslavia. Thus only Bulgaria, Greece, Hungary and Spain have the necessary legislation on look-alike species.

Priority: high
Time-scale: short

2.   **Species and habitat protection**

2.1.   To promote the appropriate protection and management of all Slender-billed Curlew passage, wintering and breeding grounds

2.1.1. Promote the statutory protection of key sites

Encourage the highest category of protection – as IBAs, Ramsar Sites, Strict Reserves, National Parks, etc. for all existing key sites (and others as they become known). The establishment of buffer zones and no-hunting areas should also be encouraged where necessary. No damaging developments should be considered inside such areas.

Priority: high
Time-scale: medium

2.1.2. Promote the enforcement of legislation

Encourage enforcement of legislation which will involve measures appropriate to each country, for example, mass hunter education efforts (aided by national and international hunting organisations), intensive wardening of key sites, arrests to demonstrate that laws will be fully applied, and the creation of no-hunting buffer areas. Considerable effort will be necessary to achieve this in many countries.

Priority: high
Time-scale: medium

2.1.3. Promote prevention of disturbance

At all key sites, but especially at wintering sites, disturbance (intentional and unintentional) should be kept to a minimum. Where serious disturbance is being caused to Slender-billed Curlews, reserve wardens should have the power to close certain areas to visitors.

Priority: medium
Time-scale: short

2.1.4. Promote appropriate management of key sites

Encourage the provision of all necessary resources – financial and manpower – for the effective protection and management of such sites. Where countries do not have sufficient resources for essential management, international organisations, including BirdLife International, should help raise funds. Management plans will be needed for key sites, taking into account the Slender-billed Curlew's needs, such as the creation of wet areas, drained fishponds, appropriate grazing levels and, where necessary, reserve maintenance should be fine-tuned to the needs of the Slender-billed Curlew, such as the appropriate timing of fishpond drainage in the Hortobágy.

Priority: high
Time-scale: ongoing

2.1.5. Promote protection of breeding grounds

Should the breeding grounds be found, all necessary steps will need to be taken to give the species total protection from any disturbance, or threat of predation. Decisions on conservation actions on the breeding grounds should be taken by a specialist Slender-billed Curlew working group (involving those searching for the breeding grounds under the agreement of co-operation with Novosibirsk). Great care should be taken with distribution of information. If necessary such information should be kept completely confidential.

Priority: high (when breeding grounds are found)
Time-scale: ongoing

3.   **Monitoring research**

3.1. *To locate and study the current breeding grounds*

3.1.1. Undertake ground surveys to locate breeding grounds

Due to the present lack of transmitters small enough to undertake satellite tracking (see 3.1.2) ground searches for the breeding grounds should continue.

Priority: essential
Time-scale: ongoing

3.1.2. Develop technology to enable use of satellite tracking (from a wintering site) to pinpoint the breeding area

Such a technique will be feasible only if transmitter weight comes down to 10 to 12 g and the process must be carried out with every possible care and precaution. If battery power allows, such tracking could also provide information on the spring migration route and stopover sites. In the event of the technology becoming available, it may be necessary to establish an international protocol as to the use of the technique for this species.

Priority: high
Time-scale: medium/long

3.1.3. Studies in the summering/breeding area, if located

Only 2 to 3 experienced researchers should be involved, with wardens available if necessary to protect the site. If nesting birds are seen, the maximum possible amount of information should be obtained, using all available techniques (including video monitoring, if feasible). Following such research, any necessary management measures should be carefully introduced (habitat management, predator control, supplementary feeding, etc. see 2.1.5).

Priority: high (when breeding grounds are found)
Time-scale: medium

3.2. To locate and study further key wintering and passage sites

3.2.1. Ground surveys

In the absence of the necessary satellite-tracking transmitters at present, ground surveys should be continued, particularly in the least-known countries. Much time has already been spent on such surveys and a good deal of useful information has resulted. Observers must be sufficiently experienced and training sessions organised where necessary. The use of a good telescope is essential in almost all cases. Ground surveys will be difficult in some countries (e.g. Algeria and Iraq) until the political situation improves.

Priority: high (wintering areas: Algeria, Iran, Iraq, southern Morocco, Spain), medium (passage sites: Croatia, Kazakhstan, south-west Russia, Turkey, Ukraine)

Time-scale: ongoing

3.2.2. Satellite-tracking

If this can be carried out (and if it works well), unprecedented information will result on at least the spring migration route. If Slender-billed Curlews rest for a few days at stopover sites, observers on the ground could be alerted and could gather detailed information, as has been successfully achieved for the Lesser White-fronted Goose *Anser erythropus* in some countries. At present it is unlikely that autumn and wintering sites could be located by this means, due to limitations on battery life.

Priority: high (if possible)
Time-scale: medium to long

3.2.3. Monitor known (and any further identified) key sites

Where possible, such monitoring should be carried out by on-site (or local) reserve staff/ornithologists. Full details should be recorded of all sightings (on Slender-billed Curlew record sheets) and if possible detailed observations should be made. A full research programme should be carried out at wintering sites (Merja Zerga is currently the only regular site known) and, using such research, recommendations for beneficial management should be made. A central register of sightings of the species should be kept pending greater understanding of key sites and migration routes.

Priority: medium
Time-scale: ongoing

3.3. Monitor hunting activity (and poaching) at sites where it occurs

Simple techniques, such as shot-counting, have been useful in Italy. This information should be used to take appropriate action to control such hunting (see 2.1.1. and 2.1.2.)

Priority: medium
Time-scale: ongoing

4. Public awareness

4.1. To increase awareness of the species critically threatened status among politicians and decision-makers

Further efforts are needed to ensure that concern about the Slender-billed Curlew's plight does not remain limited to ornithologists, but is fully shared by the relevant decision-makers. The essential message to convey is that the Slender-billed Curlew is the most threatened bird species in the western Palaearctic and will face a real threat of extinction in the next 10 to 20 years. The lack of detailed knowledge, particularly concerning the breeding grounds, greatly increases the problem of conserving the species, and greater financial resources are needed if real advances are to be made. The contrast with the amount spent on certain threatened bird species in countries such as the United States is striking (e.g. US$ 17 million spent on the California Condor to date). BirdLife International and other NGOs should provide advice and encouragement to governments and others, whether at national or regional level.

Priority: high
Time-scale: ongoing

4.2. To increase awareness of the Slender-billed Curlew among the public, particularly in range states

As the most threatened western Palaearctic bird species, the Slender-billed Curlew is of great potential interest to the public, and deserves effective publicity. A well-made film would probably be the best way to achieve wide awareness (good video footage was recently obtained at Merja Zerga), and the publication of articles in each range state would also be very useful.

Priority: medium
Time-scale: ongoing

4.3. *To increase awareness among hunters*

There is an urgent need to increase greatly the awareness of the species and the part played by

hunting in its decline, together with the problem of look-alike species. In general, national hunters' organisations should play a key role in this (and should fund the necessary actions), aided by groups such as FACE and CIC.

Priority: high
Time-scale: short

Annex
Recommended conservation actions by country

Albania

1.2.1./1.2.2./2.1.2. Promote the legal protection of the Slender-billed Curlew and other large waders and enforce this legislation.

3.2.1. Carry out surveys for the species in order to identify key sites, in co-operation with foreign ornithologists.

Algeria

1.2.2/3.3./2.1.2. Promote the inclusion of the other *Numenius* and *Limosa* species on the list of species protected by Presidential decree; monitor the hunting situation and enforce restrictions where necessary.

2.1.1. Promote the safeguard of any sites found to be important for the species through declaration as strictly protected areas and Ramsar Sites, with no hunting permitted.

3.2.1. Carry out surveys for the species in known and potential areas, using international co-operation where possible and necessary. Through training in identification skills, set up an informal "Slender-billed Curlew network" of 6 to 12 reliable observers.

4.2./4.3. Increase public awareness of wetland conservation issues and the plight of the Slender-billed Curlew through appropriate NGOs. Hunters' groups, schools and the wider public could all be targeted by such a programme.

Bulgaria

1.1.4. Promote the implementation of the parts of the national plan for wetland conservation that concern sites used by the Slender-billed Curlew.

2.1. Promote the protection of all sites where the species has been recorded more than once.

2.1.1. Encourage and increase the extent of the protected area at Lake Atanasovo (particularly the northern and north-eastern parts).

2.1.2. Improve the enforcement of existing hunting legislation and the control of hunting in protected areas, notably Lake Atanasovo. It is recommended that no temporary decrees prolong the hunting season in the Burgas region during winter.

2.1.3. Provide wardening for the areas used by the species at Lake Atanasovo and other Burgas wetlands in winter.

2.1.4. Promote the provision of the necessary resources for the effective management and protection of Lake Atanasovo and other wetlands in the Burgas area (including full-time wardens with vehicles). Develop and implement the management plan for Lake Atanasovo and compile such plans for Poda and Chengene skele.

3.2.3./3.3. Monitor the occurrence of the Slender-billed Curlew at Lake Atanasovo and the Burgas area, and monitor the hunting situation at these sites.

4.2. Increase awareness among the general public of the plight of the Slender-billed Curlew (and other threatened species).

4.3. Develop and implement an education programme aimed at hunters to promote the conservation of the Slender-billed Curlew, waders and other wetland birds.

Croatia

1.2.1./1.2.2. Encourage the full protection of all *Numenius* and *Limosa* species, with maximum penalties for the shooting of a Slender-billed Curlew, and effectively enforce this law. Activities of any foreign hunters must be effectively controlled; visiting hunters breaking the law should be banned from hunting in Croatia.

3.2.1. Survey suitable wetlands (particularly those with past records) for the species, in order to identify any key sites.

4.1./4.3. Increase awareness of the species among politicians and hunters.

Greece

2.1.1./2.1.4. Encourage full and effective protection for key sites, ensuring that no adverse developments occur. Promote adoption through a joint ministerial declaration of the management plan for the Evros delta and fully implement its recommendations, with the necessary resources being made available.

2.1.2. Encourage the enforcement of existing laws, especially at key sites (ideally there should be total hunting bans in and around such sites).

3.2.3./3.3. Monitor the key sites to determine to what extent the species is still occurring on passage (e.g. the last records from the Evros delta were single birds in 1988 and 1995; in Porto Lagos in 1988 and 1993), and monitor the hunting situation at such sites.

4.2./4.3. Increase awareness among the public and hunters, especially at the key sites.

Hungary

2.1.1. Promote the full protection of all key sites with the adequate resource available for their management. At the Hortobágy careful rotation in the draining of fishponds in autumn is important, and some pusztas could usefully be flooded and new salt lakes made (Kovács, 1994). At Kardoskut extra water is needed to flood the salt lakes; a new artificial salt lake is planned at Kardoskut, which should be beneficial (Nagy, in European Commission, 1994 and *in litt.*).

3.2.3. Monitor the existing key sites and other suitable wetlands during passage seasons for the presence of the species.

3.3/ 2.1.2. Monitor the hunting situation, particularly near key sites, and ensure that the efficient existing legislation is fully enforced. There have been problems with visiting hunters, so strong action may be needed; those breaking the law should be banned from hunting in Hungary.

Iran

1.2.1./1.2.2/2.1.2. Promote the listing of the Slender-billed Curlew and its look-alikes as protected species, with high penalties for infringement and effective enforcement (regardless of whether or not waders are commonly shot).

2.1.1./2.1.4. If key sites are identified, encourage their full protection, with the necessary resources available for their management.

3.2.1. Carry out surveys for the species, using trained and experienced staff, to locate any key sites (the Miankaleh peninsula and the Mehran delta may both be key sites, but confirmation of records is needed). If necessary and feasible, foreign ornithologists could co-operate in such surveys.

Iraq

The activities listed below can be achieved only if the political situation in Iraq changes considerably; it is to be hoped that the marshes will not have been entirely destroyed by this time.

1.2.1./1.2.2./2.1.2. Encourage the listing of the Slender-billed Curlew and its look-alikes as protected species, with high penalties for infringement, and effective enforcement, of such laws.

2.1.1. Encourage the protection of the Iraqi marshes, particularly areas suitable for waders, such as temporary marshes and areas fringing waterbodies.

3.2.1. Carry out surveys for the species, using trained and experienced staff, to locate any key sites; if possible and necessary, this could be done in co-operation with visiting ornithologists.

Italy

1.2.1./1.2.2. Encourage stronger specific legislation to protect the Slender-billed Curlew and other *Numenius* and *Limosa* species (the Black-tailed Godwit may currently be unprotected if the July 1994 circular of the Minister of Agriculture has not yet taken effect). If large waders continue to be shot, then further species, notably Ruff *Philomachus pugnax*, should also be protected.

2.1.2. Encourage enforcement of legislation on hunting, through the appointment at each key site of from three to five armed wardens responsible solely for hunting control. It is recommended that no-hunting buffer zones should be established around key sites, within which even the carrying of a gun would be an offence.

2.1.1./2.1.2./2.1.3/2.1.4. Encourage the full protection of key sites from development, and provide the resources necessary for their management. Recommended actions include the designation of the Viareggio wetlands as a Ramsar Site, SPA and Strict Nature Reserve, the banning of hunting in the entire area and its surroundings, and the provision of wardens. The other key sites should be designated as Ramsar Sites (smaller sites should be joined to form single large sites), with buffer zones around them. Restore the boundaries originally proposed for Gargano National Park, with buffer zones and from two to three anti-poaching wardens. The Carabinieri and Forest Guards should be deployed to intervene whenever and wherever migrating groups occur; and birdwatchers' access should be carefully controlled.

3.2.3. Monitor key sites and other suitable areas for the species and monitor hunting activity at key sites.

4.1./4.2./4.3. Increase awareness of the plight of the species among politicians, hunters and the general public. In particular, provide and disseminate scientifically based information in order to stress the importance of reducing the hunting of

large waders as a direct measure for the protection of the Slender-billed Curlew.

Kazakhstan

1.2.1./1.2.2. Encourage the full protection of the Slender-billed Curlew and its look-alikes, with high penalties for offenders.

3.2.1./3.2.2./2.1. Carry out surveys for the species to locate any key sites; the species might even be found nesting in Kazakhstan. If technically possible, satellite-tracking would be by far the best method of locating such sites, as the country is huge, travel is difficult, and the density of ornithologists is very low. Any key sites identified should be fully protected.

Morocco

1.2.1./1.2.2. Promote an increase in the penalty for shooting a Slender-billed Curlew to the maximum possible level, and substantially increase the fine for shooting other curlew species.

1.2.2./3.3. Promote the protection of both *Limosa* species with substantial penalties for contravention, and monitor the hunting situation.

2.1.3. Prevent significant disturbance to the species at Merja Zerga and any other key sites.

2.1.1./2.1.4. Promote the strengthening of the level of protection afforded to Merja Zerga, with a total ban on adverse developments within the reserve. Hunting should be banned permanently in the whole reserve, including Merja Mellah. Further resources should be made available for the site's management, including the appointment of more wardens, each with their own vehicle. A study of agricultural practices around the lagoon would yield valuable information on the management of the reserve. A management plan is needed for the reserve and an information centre should be built.

3.2.1. Survey the coast for Slender-billed Curlews, and continue to monitor occurrences at Merja Zerga. While this site remains the only known regular wintering area for Slender-billed Curlew there is a strong case for an intensive study of the species to be carried out here.

4.1./4.2./ 4.3. Increase awareness of the species among decision-makers, hunters and the general public.

Romania

1.2.1. Promote the approval and implementation of the bill (No. 501, 14 July 1993) intended to protect the Slender-billed Curlew.

1.2.2./2.1.2. Promote the protection of other *Numenius* and *Limosa* species, with effective penalties, and ensure the law is enforced.

2.1.1./2.1.2./2.1.4. Promote the full protection of the Danube delta and ensure that only sustainable use is allowed. Considerable resources are needed for the management of the area, and much work is ongoing, including staff training and the production of a management plan for the delta. Those responsible for the delta must be fully aware of the importance of the Istria and Razelm-Sinoie areas for the Slender-billed Curlew and other threatened birds; hunting must be totally banned here, and in much of the delta proper.

3.2.3. Continue to monitor the Slender-billed Curlew, particularly in the Danube delta (no records have been made since 1989).

Russia

1.2.1./2.1.2. Encourage the strict protection of the Slender-billed Curlew throughout its Russian range, with heavy penalties for contravention.

1.2.2./2.1.2. Encourage the full protection of other *Numenius, Limosa* and *Limnodromus* species throughout the Slender-billed Curlew's range (i.e. west of the River Yenisey). Legislation must include heavy penalties and must be widely publicised, particularly among hunting organisations and through the network of hunting inspectors.

3.1.1./3.1.2./3.1.3. Locate the breeding grounds and protect them effectively. The most effective means of finding them would be satellite-tracking of birds from the wintering grounds. In the absence of suitable transmitters, ground surveys will continue at least until 1996, co-ordinated by A. K. Yurlov in Novosibirsk. If located, all neces-

sary resources must be devoted to the study and protection of the site and the birds.

3.2.1. Identify key passage sites, through increased publicity and survey efforts, especially on the Russian coasts of the Black, Azov and Caspian seas, and protect effectively, as Zapovedniks, any sites thus identified.

Spain

2.1.1./2.1.3./2.1.4. If Coto Doñana is confirmed as a key wintering site, specific management recommendations should be identified and implemented by the national park authorities, including increased wardening to prevent disturbance, and the creation of a strict no-hunting zone of 2 to 3 km around the area used by the species.

3.2.1. Carry out special surveys for the species in autumn and winter, particularly in areas where the species has been recorded (Balearic Island wetlands, Mediterranean coast wetlands and Andalucian wetlands, notably Doñana). All resulting records of the species should be submitted to the Iberian Rarities Committee and to BirdLife International.

3.3./2.1.2. Monitor the situation concerning the hunting of large waders, particularly near any key sites identified; if problems are apparent enforcement efforts will need to be increased.

4.2. Increase awareness of the species among ornithologists and the general public, by popular articles and possibly the production of a leaflet to aid identification. Accurate illustrations would be an important part of such a leaflet.

Tunisia

1.2.2./3.3./2.1.2. Promote the protection of godwits by listing them in Article 7 of the Arrêté de Chasse (curlews were listed in June 1994). The situation concerning the hunting of large waders should be monitored, and measures taken for increased enforcement if necessary, particularly at key sites.

2.1.1. Encourage the declaration of any Slender-billed Curlew key sites as fully protected areas and Ramsar Sites, with total bans on hunting in the area and its immediate surroundings. Such areas can be declared permanent Hunting Reserves in the Arrêté Annuel de la Chasse, as determined by the Conseil Superieur de la Chasse.

2.1.4 Initiate a study of the Kairouan wetlands (other than Kelbia) to investigate the hydrology of the system and the effect of up-river dams. This would contribute to the development of a conservation management plan for the area.

3.2.1. Continue and increase monitoring of potential key sites, with particular emphasis on areas where the species has been recorded in the past (Kairouan-Monastir and Gulf of Gabès). The main aim of such surveys would be the identification of precise sites where conservation action could be taken; expeditions could be organised, if necessary, in co-operation with visiting ornithologists.

3.3./4.3. Monitor the shooting of large waders. If the shooting of large waders is more widespread than currently thought, the production of posters combined with articles in hunters' magazines would help to raise awareness of the species. At the 1994 meeting of the hunting council a request was made by the regional hunting association of Tunis and the hunting federation for such a programme.

Turkey

1.2.2./2.1.2. Promote the inclusion of the Black-tailed Godwit on the list of protected species. Encourage better understanding and enforcement of hunting legislation, particularly at potential key sites.

2.1.1. Promote the full protection of key sites, once these have been identified with full resources for effective management. No hunting should be allowed in or near such sites (no-hunting buffer zones will be needed).

3.2.1. Carry out surveys during passage and winter to establish which, if any, sites are used regularly. The highest priority sites for such surveys are the Göksu delta, Çukorova delta, Apolyont Gölü, Eregli marshes, Çamalti Tuzlasi and Büyük Menderes delta. Foreign observers

and expeditions should be encouraged to look for the species.

4.1./4.3. Raise awareness of the species (and the law protecting it) with relevant politicians and hunters' groups.

Ukraine

1.2.1./1.2.2./2.1.2. Encourage an increase in the penalty for shooting a Slender-billed Curlew to the maximum level, and that for shooting other curlews to a more significant amount. Protect godwits, and ensure that all such laws are well-publicised and enforced.

2.1.1. Encourage the effective protection of a network of major wetland sites along the northern shores of the Black and Azov seas.

3.2.1./3.2.2. Identify key sites used by the species. Satellite-tracking would greatly facilitate this process, but with international co-operation and funding, substantial ground survey efforts could be made. Any sites thus identified should be fully protected (see 2.1.1.), and total hunting bans should be introduced at these sites.

4.3. Publicise the plight of the species with hunters.

The former Yugoslavia

1.2.1./1.2.2./2.1.2. Promote the listing of the Slender-billed Curlew and its look-alikes as protected species, with high penalties for infringement, and effective enforcement. Foreign hunters must also be fully controlled, perhaps by a lifetime ban on returning to hunt in the former Yugoslavia if caught breaking the law.

2.1.1./2.1.4. Encourage effective protection and management of key sites, notably Soskopo.

3.2.1. Carry out further surveys for the species, particularly in Vojvodina.

4.1./4.3. Increase awareness of the species among the relevant politicians and hunters.

International action plan for Audouin's Gull (*Larus audouinii*)

Reviews

This action plan should be reviewed and updated every three years. An emergency review will be carried out if sudden major environmental changes or threats, liable to affect the population, occur within the species' range.

Geographical scope

The action plan needs implementation in Algeria, Cyprus, France, Greece, Italy, Lebanon, Mauritania, Morocco, Senegal, Spain, Tunisia and Turkey.

Summary

Audouin's Gull *Larus audouinii* is a rare and localised species with a breeding population of about 15 000 pairs limited to the Mediterranean Sea. Because of the population increase in the western Mediterranean in the last twenty years it is now classified as Conservation Dependent (Collar et al., 1994). Most breeding sites are rocky cliffs and offshore islands or islets, the exception being the colony in the Ebro delta (Spain) which is on a saltmarsh/sandy seashore habitat. The most important colonies (c.90% of the total population) lie within protected areas. Wintering areas are poorly known and include Algeria, Mauritania, Morocco and Senegal.

Threats and limiting factors

Habitat alterations at breeding sites – high

Changes in fishing practices – high

Competition with the Yellow-legged Gull and other species – locally high

Egg collection and human persecution – low

Human disturbance – low

Depletion of food resources – unknown, potentially high

Chemical pollution and oil spills – unknown

Conservation priorities

Policies (including fishing and shipping) compatible with the conservation of the species – high

Legal protection for the species and its habitat – high

Preparation of national species action plans – high

Prevent habitat alterations at breeding sites – high

Prevent and reduce human disturbance – high

Survey and monitor the population particularly determining the status in the eastern Mediterranean – high

Carry out research into population dynamics and impact of fishing – high

Identify the most important passage and wintering sites – high

Improve international co-operation for research and monitoring – high

Involve tourists and fishermen in preventing disturbance – high

Introduction

The world distribution of Audouin's Gull *Larus audouinii* is confined to the Mediterranean basin. It is classified as Conservation Dependent at a global level (Collar et al., 1994) and as Localised at European level (Tucker and Heath, 1994). It is also included in Annex I of the European Union's Wild Birds Directive, in Appendix II of the Bern Convention and in Appendix I of the Bonn Convention. The population increase which has taken place in the western Mediterranean during the last 10 years has led to its removal from the list of globally threatened species (Collar et al., 1994).

A workshop on the conservation and management of Audouin's Gull in the Mediterranean was held on 28 and 29 April 1994 on the island of Montecristo (Italy). The meeting was organised by LIPU and BirdLife International, with the aims of: (1) pooling new information about the population status and conservation problems of Audouin's Gull, (2) discussing an action plan to secure its future and (3) creating a working group. In all, 16 participants represented Algeria, Germany, Italy, Morocco, Spain, Tunisia and UK. This action plan relies largely on the discussions held during this workshop and on written contributions received afterwards.

Background information

Distribution and population

Audouin's Gull breeds in Algeria, Cyprus, France, Greece, Italy, Morocco, Spain, Tunisia and Turkey. The most northerly colony is on the island of Gorgona (Tuscan archipelago, Italy, 43°2'35"N). Population figures are given in Table 17.

Table 17.1

Breeding population of Audouin's Gull, 1993. Figures are based on recent published data (de Juana, 1994) and communications presented at the workshop in Montecristo

Country	No. of pairs	No. of colonies
Algeria	600–600	4
Cyprus	10–20	1
France	90–90	2
Greece	200–300	min. 16
Italy	550–650	10
Morocco	50–50	1
Spain	14000–14000	8
Tunisia	70–70	4
Turkey	50–50	1
Total	15620–15830	48

The central western Mediterranean (west of Sicily) holds more than 95% of the world breeding population. Two breeding colonies include c.14000 pairs (86.7% of the world breeding population): 9400 pairs in the Ebro delta (Spain) and

3600 pairs in the Chafarinas Islands (Spain) (Ruiz et al., 1993).

The world population has increased dramatically in the last 20 years from an estimated 1000 pairs in 1975 (Witt, 1977) to c.15 000 pairs now. A 10% population increase per year has been estimated (de Juana and Varela, 1993). Information about the species is good for the western Mediterranean (with the exception of Algeria), but is still fragmentary for the eastern part.

After the breeding season, Audouin's Gulls migrate south and west, and winter along the coasts of Algeria, Mauritania, Morocco, Senegal and Spain (Cantos and Gómez-Manzaneque, 1993; Oró and Martínez-Villalta, 1994b).

Life history

Breeding

Audouin's Gull breeds in colonies ranging from a few pairs to several thousand. Large or medium-sized colonies are often divided into distinct sub-colonies.

The colony-site fidelity is very high (Ruiz et al., 1993; Oró and Martínez-Villalta, 1994b), while year-to-year fluctuation in nest-site selection and number of breeding pairs has been recorded in almost all colonies. Site fidelity is likely to be related to previous breeding success. On the Chafarinas Islands birds returned to nest in successive years at successful sites but deserted those which were unsuccessful (P. Bradley, verbally, 1994).

Even if the location of nesting sites varies very much in subsequent years, breeding occurs quite regularly within traditional areas (e.g. an island or an archipelago) (Lambertini, 1993). New colonisation sometimes occurs, as happened in the Ebro delta (Spain) where the colony went from 36 pairs in 1981 to 9400 pairs in 1994.

Egg-laying takes place from the second half of April until the beginning of May; this is almost one month later than in the sympatric Yellow-legged Gull L. cachinnans. A colony's laying period is spread over about two weeks. Fledging is mostly in the first two weeks of July (Witt, 1977; Mayol,

1978; de Juana et al., 1979; Guyot, 1985; Lambertini, 1993). The degree of egg-laying synchrony may depend on factors such as food availability (Oró et al., 1994).

Breeding failures due to bad weather are reported (Lambertini et al., 1988). Yellow-legged Gulls can be responsible for high chick mortality (Bradley, 1986) and nest-site competition (Monbailliu and Torre, 1986), but this is not the case at all colonies or in all years (Ruiz et al., 1993; Oró and Martínez-Villalta, 1994a). At present the main cause of chick mortality is food scarcity resulting from trawl-fishing moratoria in waters around the Ebro delta colony (Ruiz et al., 1993, in press).

Feeding

It has long been thought that Audouin's Gull was a pelagic bird feeding mainly offshore, but more recent observations show that it feeds regularly along the coast. Their diet is mostly fish (especially clupeids) and cephalopods, but small mammals, arthropods, birds and plant material are also eaten. The concentration of breeding colonies in the western Mediterranean could be related to the lower water salinity and higher abundance of clupeids (Witt et al., 1981; Witt, 1982). Birds from the Ebro delta feed extensively on discarded food from the local fishing fleet (Oró and Martínez-Villalta, 1992; Paterson et al., 1992; Ruiz et al., in press).

Habitat requirements

Colonies are located on rocky cliffs and on offshore islands or islets, with the exception of the Ebro delta colony which is on saltmarsh and sandy seashore.

Characteristics of habitats used differ from region to region and even within the same areas in different years: for example, altitude ranges from close to sea level to over 100 metres, vegetation cover varies from bare rocks to 85% bush cover, and slope from 0° to 90°.

Medium vegetation cover is preferred, and this probably allows chicks to find shelter from heat and predators. Chicks on bare sites leave the nest significantly earlier than those in areas with vegetation cover (Bradley, 1986).

Threats and limiting factors

Habitat alterations at the breeding sites

Houses, hotels and marinas for tourism are spreading in many areas occupied by the species and can destroy the habitat as well as increased disturbance during the breeding season. The problem is especially acute in the Balearic Islands, Sardinia, Tuscan Isles and in many areas in the eastern Mediterranean.

Importance: high

Changes in fishing practices

The increase in numbers at the colony in the Ebro delta is apparently linked to the exploitation by Audouin's Gull of fish waste dumped from boats fishing nearby (Beaubrun, 1983; Oró and Martínez-Villalta, 1994b). The industrial use of fish waste to produce animal food, as occurs in other areas of the Mediterranean, could pose a great and immediate threat to the maintenance of the colony at the Ebro delta, which relies largely on this food resource.

Importance: high

Depletion of food resources

Food availability is considered a major cause of population fluctuations and mobility of seabirds (Hunt, 1972; Springer et al., 1986). Large-scale human-induced alterations in river discharges to the sea, as has occurred with the Nile and the Aswan dam in the eastern Mediterranean, can affect marine productivity. The regulation of the Ebro river (Spain) by a series of dams could result in a decrease of nutrients in one of the most productive fishing areas of the Spanish Mediterranean coast, affecting severely the breeding success of Audouin's Gull.

Importance: unknown, potentially high

Interference with other species

Interaction with the Yellow-legged Gull has been recognised as a limiting factor in several Mediterranean colonies. This includes competition for nesting sites and predation of eggs

(Oró and Martínez-Villalta, 1994a) and predation of nestlings and adults (Bradley, 1986; Monbailliu and Torre, 1986).

Stray cattle and dogs can also damage nests and young, and this is a major problem in several Italian colonies (Asinara, Piana, Mortorio, Caprera, Molara, etc.) (X. Monbailliu, *in litt.*, 1995). Rats, foxes, cats and some reptiles could also pose a threat to the species.

Importance: locally high

Human disturbance

The breeding period of Audouin's Gull overlaps with the tourist season on the Mediterranean coasts, and the increasing disturbance which this causes may represent a major future hazard for the species (Mayol, 1986; Thibault and Guyot, 1989) and for other sympatric seabirds. The easy accessibility of many colonies and the conspicuousness of the gulls makes them very vulnerable to disturbance by tourists, either by boating near the shore or by direct intrusion on the nesting areas. Birdwatching and research activities can also cause serious disturbances. Illegal fishing with dynamite may be a problem locally. Man's negative effects on a nesting colony are well reviewed by Burger (1981).

Importance: low

Egg collection and human persecution

Direct human impact such as the killing and/or collecting of eggs and chicks by local people and fishermen was formerly widespread but at present is of very little significance, although Audouin's Gull eggs are still highly regarded in North Africa for confectionery.

Importance: low

Chemical pollution

Chemical contamination is heavy in Mediterranean waters and represents a serious hazard for seabirds (Lambertini and Leonzio, 1986). High levels of heavy metals and chlorinated hydrocarbons (including dioxins, coplanar PCBs and dibenzofurans) have been found in Audouin's Gull samples. Among these, coplanar PCBs show higher toxicological incidence when concentration levels are expressed as I-TEF (International Toxicity Equivalent Factors) (Pastor et al., in press). High mercury levels were found in chicks in Asinara (Sardinia), and for several years the colony had a very low breeding success which finally led to its total disappearance (X. Monbailliu, *in litt.*, 1995).

Importance: unknown

Oil spills

The high level of recorded oil pollution in the Mediterranean could have lethal and sub-lethal effects on adults and eggs through eggshell smearing. A serious oil spill during the breeding season near the two largest breeding colonies could be disastrous for Audouin's Gull.

Importance: unknown

Conservation status and recent conservation measures

Algeria

Audouin's Gull went unrecorded in Algeria until the 1970s when the first colonies were discovered on the west coast of Orán (Jacob and Courbet, 1980). Four colonies are still located in this area with c.400 pairs altogether (Boukhalfa, in prep.). Overall, the breeding population in the past 15 years has declined by c.50%, but new sites have been colonised. The total breeding population is estimated at c.600 pairs and recently 100 pairs have settled in the Habibas islands (Boukhalfa, 1990; 1992), the largest breeding colony in Algeria. The breeding sites are mainly rocky islands which remain undisturbed because of the difficult access.

In the winter of 1978, 824 individuals were counted (Jacob, 1979). Audouin's Gull is protected under national legislation (Decree No. 83–509) but enforcement is poor. A good opportunity for the protection of the species and its breeding areas should be the creation of a network of marine nature reserves.

Cyprus

The species breeds in small numbers and was first recorded in 1960 (COS, 1960). In subsequent years the colony had 6 nests in 1961, none in 1966, 1 in 1968 and 15 in 1987 (de Juana and Varela, 1993). Breeding is confined to the Klidhes islands (IBA 001) which are currently included in the Zafer Burnu National Park.

France

The species is legally protected by measures implemented in 1976 and 1981. Audouin's Gull has been recorded in Corsica since the nineteenth century, and regular censuses have been carried out from 1979 (Thibault and Guyot, 1989). The Cerbicales islands are the best known historical breeding site (IBA 145) but since 1988 the colony has been deserted because of competition with the increasing Yellow-legged Gull. The islands around Cape Corse (Finocchiarola) (IBA 153) hold the current breeding population which has fluctuated from 18 to 90 pairs over the past 15 years. In 1980 the Yellow-legged Gull bred on only one of the three islands of Cape Corse, but between 1980 and 1987 there was a 12% annual increase in the number of pairs, and in 1988 all three islands were occupied. The breeding failure in recent years is related to predation on chicks by Yellow-legged Gulls. An eradication program of that species is currently underway on the two islands which hold Audouin's Gull colonies, together with rat control (Thibault and Guyot, 1989). The high number of non-breeding Yellow-legged Gulls greatly reduces the effectiveness of these actions (J. C. Thibault, in litt., 1994).

All the occupied breeding sites in the islands of Finocchiarola as well as the historically occupied areas on the Cerbicales have been designated as Nature Reserves. Other potential sites benefit from Prefecture and French Navy restrictions of access.

Greece

There is little information about the past and present status of the species but surveys of uninhabited islands in the Aegean were carried out by HOS during 1995. It occurs in small colonies on the islands of Crete (IBA 101 Nissi Dionisiades, Lasithi), Dodecaneso (IBA 102 Nissos Kasos), Cicladas (IBA 105 Northern Syros) and Sporades (IBA 107 Nissi Kyra/Panaghia/Ghioura/Piperi/

Skantzoura). Most of the sites are unprotected. The currently supposed size of the breeding population is around 235 pairs, of which 135 are newly discovered in colonies in the Aegean. This total is probably an underestimate (Halmann in Grimmett and Jones, 1989; de Juana and Varela, 1993; HOS, in litt.). The main threats are tourist development of the islands and disturbance from fishermen. Audouin's Gull is specially protected by Decision 414985/85 (Handrinos, 1992).

Italy

The status of Audouin's Gull remained relatively unknown until the 1980s, when more detailed surveys and investigations started. In c.10 years the breeding population had probably increased slightly but more slowly than in other parts of the range. The species breeds in Sardinia (IBAs 108, 109, 110, 113, 118 and 125) and the Tuscan archipelago, and since 1992 a small colony became established along the Puglia coast. In 1984 c.550 pairs were counted (Shenk and Meschini 1986) and in 1992 new surveys confirmed a breeding population of 600 to 700 pairs (M. Lambertini's own data).

Fluctuation and mobility of the colonies is normal within each traditional area. In 1993 many colonies disappeared (e.g. 20 pairs instead of the previous 180 in the Tuscan islands). No relationship was found between population changes on the Tuscan and Corsican islands.

Audouin's Gull is specially protected under national legislation. Three of the five islands frequented in the Tuscan archipelago are already protected by a newly established National Park which may soon be enlarged. A good proportion of the islands and archipelagos in Sardinia where the species breeds will soon be included in regional or national protected areas. For some years (1984-88) the local municipality of Capraia Island (Tuscan archipelago) limited access to the colonies during the tourist season.

Lebanon

A colony of c.10 pairs has been recorded since the nineteenth century on the Palm Islands (IBA 001, Marine Nature Reserve) off the port of Tripoli (de Bournonville, 1964); 18 adults were present in April 1973 but none in 1975 (Evans, 1994). In 1993 there were no Audouin's Gulls on the islands, which are disturbed by line fishermen and Sunday visitors. The area is of scientific interest for coastal flora and infralittoral organisms (X. Monbailliu, *in litt.*, 1995).

Morocco

A single colony has recently been recorded in the Bokoyas Islands, with 29 pairs in 1989 (M. Dakki, verbally, 1994), but no data are available on other historical sites. Audouin's Gull winters along both the Mediterranean and Atlantic coasts of Morocco and the estimated total of wintering birds is 6000 (M. Dakki, verbally, 1994); in 1993 over 1000 were counted at Dakla alone. The most important wintering sites have been proposed for inclusion in the new list of protected areas. The Bokoyas Islands are included in the planned Al-Hoceima National Park. The species is protected by Moroccan law.

Spain

Audouin's Gull is included in the Spanish Red Data Book as Rare (Blanco and González, 1992) and legally protected under Law 4/1989 for the Conservation of Natural Areas and Wildlife. It is listed as Of Special Interest in the National Catalogue of Threatened Species (Royal Decree 439/90).

In 1993 the total number of breeding pairs was 13724 in four main colonies: the Ebro delta (9373), the Chafarinas Islands (3540), the Columbretes Islands (102) and the Balearic Islands (709). All these colonies are now protected: the Ebro delta as a Natural Park; the Chafarinas as a Hunting Refuge; the Columbretes as a Natural Park; Cabrera (Baleares) as a National Park; other Balearic islets as Natural Areas of Special Interest (though in this last case protective measures are not ensured).

In 1987 a conservation action plan was started involving the regional governments of the Baleares, Cataluña, Valencia and Andalucía under the co-ordination of ICONA (now DGN). Activities undertaken within this plan have included surveys, monitoring of breeding success, culling of Yellow-legged Gulls (Chafarinas, Balearic

and Medas islands), rat control, colour ringing and monitoring of dispersal (ICONA, 1993).

Tunisia

Audouin's Gull has been reported as a breeding species only since the early 1980s (Gaultier and Ayache, 1986). The more recent available data confirm two major breeding areas in La Galite archipelago and in Zembra National Park, with a total of 70 pairs (Essetti, no date). There is strong competition with the Yellow-legged Gull on the island of Zembra and control measures are needed. Audouin's Gull is a protected species in Tunisia.

Turkey

A single breeding colony of c.30 pairs was recorded in the 1970s along the south coast (Witt, 1976) (IBA 048). In 1995 field surveys are to be carried out along the Mediterranean coast (M. Yarar, *in litt.*, 1995).

Aims and objectives

Aims

1. In the short term, to maintain the current population of Audouin's Gull throughout its range.

2. In the medium to long term, to conserve suitable habitats in order to promote the expansion of the species' range and numbers particularly in smaller colonies.

Objectives

1.   **Policy and legislation**

1.1.   *To influence European Union fisheries policies and regulations for the benefit of biodiversity conservation in the Mediterranean*

Fishing moratoria should be set up in a way that is compatible with the subsistence of the major breeding colonies of Audouin's Gull.

Priority: high
Time-scale: ongoing

1.2. To develop national coastal strategies

The European Union coastal strategy, currently in draft, has the potential to set targets for coastal management across the EU requiring member states to establish integrated processes to manage their coasts sustainably. Appropriate legal and financial instruments must accompany the strategy if it is to be effective. The targets set must ensure benefits for Audouin's Gull and its habitat.

All countries around the Mediterranean should develop and implement coastal strategies which plan and manage development and use of the coasts in a sustainable manner. Important coastal habitat must be safeguarded including all Audouin's Gull colonies and major roosting sites. Protection of important Audouin's Gull sites in Europe will be of limited value for safeguarding numbers and distribution if the key sites which they depend on elsewhere are lost.

Priority: medium
Time-scale: medium

1.3. To ensure that Audouin's Gull and its habitat receive full protection through national and international legislation

Many Mediterranean islands are not protected and are the subject of housing and tourism development plans. It is essential to seek policies that promote sustainable development of inhabited Mediterranean islands through ecotourism and full protection of deserted offshore and coastal islands.

Annex I of the European Union's Habitats Directive lists Mediterranean cliffs as a habitat in need of protection; governments must ensure that this habitat is adequately covered under the network Natura 2000 and that all the islands where Audouin's Gull occurs or has occurred recently are designated as SACs. The same should happen under the European Union Wild Birds Directive through the establishment of SPAs.

Similar actions must be extended to coastal West African countries (Mauritania and Senegal), and also to North African and eastern Mediterranean countries which are not part of the European Union.

Audouin's Gull must be considered as a protected species in the national legislation of all countries within its breeding, wintering and migration range. All breeding and wintering areas should be protected.

Priority: high
Time-scale: short/medium

1.4. Prevent chemical pollution of the sea and oil spills

National and international legislation on chemical pollution and industrial treatment should be enforced and appropriate action undertaken to avoid chemical release from both offshore and land-based sources.

The use of agricultural chemicals near breeding colonies should be carefully monitored, as should the release of chemicals in the feeding waters.

The IMO and shipping insurance brokers (Veritas, Lloyds) should be lobbied to establish a system of incentives for those oil tanker companies which agree to avoid sensitive marine ecosystems. Heavy fines should be imposed for the cleaning of oil tankers outside the areas especially designated for that purpose.

Priority: high
Time-scale: short/ongoing

1.5. To promote the preparation of national action plans

National action plans for Audouin's Gull should be prepared with the co-operation of GOs, NGOs and research institutions. Once finished, these plans should be endorsed by the national authorities for nature conservation.

Priority: high
Time-scale: short

1.6. To involve international conventions in the conservation of the species and its habitat

The Agreement on the Conservation of African-Eurasian Migratory Waterbirds under the Bonn Convention provides a valuable framework for international co-operation on the conservation of Audouin's Gull and its habitat.

The Ramsar Convention should seek ways and means to review its criteria for the inclusion of coastal and island areas, particularly those which harbour colonial waterbirds.

The Barcelona Convention should seek to include all Audouin's Gull colonies in the Mediterranean as SPAs.

National strategies drawn up under the Biodiversity Convention should promote the conservation and sustainable management of coastal and island ecosystems.

Priority: medium
Time-scale: medium

1.7. *To promote international co-operation and funding from bilateral agencies*

Bilateral agreements for establishing and managing protected areas and for research and monitoring of Audouin's Gull should be promoted among governments of Mediterranean countries. International NGOs should assist national NGOs to carry out projects for the conservation of globally threatened species.

Priority: high
Time-scale: short/ongoing

2.   **Species and habitat protection**

2.1. *To ensure adequate protection of breeding sites and remove major threats to breeding habitat*

2.1.1. Designate all key sites as protected areas

All IBAs where Audouin's Gull breeds should be designated as protected areas. In islands and archipelagos with high colony mobility, temporary protection schemes should be promoted, preventing disturbance and avoiding human access to the colony year by year. Management plans should be prepared and implemented at all designated sites.

Priority: high
Time-scale: short/medium

2.2.2. Prevent habitat alteration at all regular breeding sites

Enforcement of the legal protection status of all sites already designated must be ensured. Where protection has not been completed, other land-use planning instruments should be brought into force to prevent development. The existence of breeding Audouin's Gulls should be taken into account when preparing planning regulations. All proposed land-use changes threatening occupied and traditional breeding sites should be submitted to environmental impact assessment.

Priority: high
Time-scale: short/ongoing

2.2. *To undertake appropriate management at breeding colonies*

2.2.1. Prevent and reduce human disturbance

The control of human access to colonies is essential in order to prevent breeding failure and site desertion. Whenever trekking, boating, seabathing, birdwatching or any other activity is seen to disrupt the breeding gulls it should be reported to the authorities responsible for the area. If legal status is lacking, specific protection measures must be urged on local and national authorities. Wardening by volunteers or paid staff is strongly recommended at the colonies most sensitive to human disturbance.

Priority: high
Time-scale: short/ongoing

2.2.2. Control competitors and predators and assess effectiveness of control measures

Humane population control of Yellow-legged Gulls should be undertaken if there is evidence of competition and predation as a limiting factor for Audouin's Gull. The causes of the population increase of Yellow-legged Gull should be investigated.

If rats are known to be feeding upon eggs and/or the young on a scale that seriously threatens the viability of a colony, a control programme should be undertaken immediately using rodenticide in specially designed boxes. Predators such as foxes *Vulpes* which could cause great damage to particular colonies should be eliminated or relocated. Stray cattle and dogs should be removed.

Priority: medium
Time-scale: medium/ongoing

2.2.3. Prevent egg-collecting

The location of Audouin's Gull colonies which are not adequately protected should be treated with confidentiality. In the already known colonies the best way to prevent egg-collecting is through surveillance during the breeding period and enforcement of existing sanctions.

Priority: low
Time-scale: short/ongoing

2.3.   To protect Audouin's Gull and its habitat in the winter quarters and along the migration route

2.3.1. Seek protection for all regular wintering sites

All sites which regularly hold more than 200 Audouin's Gulls should receive legal protection. In the meantime, housing and industrial developments, pollution or any other kind of habitat alteration should be prevented. The fishing industry in the vicinity of the major wintering sites should be monitored and overfishing avoided.

Priority: medium
Time-scale: medium

3.   Monitoring and research

3.1.   To set up and implement a monitoring programme

3.1.1. Monitor population status and range trends

Monitoring of Audouin's Gull already takes place in several range states within the framework of wider monitoring programmes. However, better international co-ordination is necessary to ensure an overall view of population and range trends. It is suggested that the working group for Audouin's Gull meets every 2 to 3 years to co-ordinate monitoring activities and review progress with the implementation of the action plan.

Priority: high
Time-scale: short/ongoing

3.1.2. Determine current distribution and population status

The eastern and southern Mediterranean regions need more detailed population surveys; the current number of breeding pairs in this region is unknown and there may be a few colonies still to be discovered. An accurate census of the world population should be undertaken and repeated every three years. An effort should be made to identify all breeding sites.

Priority: high
Time-scale: short

3.1.3. Determine the extent and location of discrete populations

A colour-ringing scheme at selected colonies should be undertaken to ascertain the relationship between different colonies and the degree of population interchange. Colour-ringing is regularly done at some Spanish colonies but should be extended to other Mediterranean countries. Good international co-ordination is essential for the success of such a scheme, and one particular organisation has to be appointed to centralise information, decide on colour codes, store data and disseminate results; Medmaravis is suggested as a likely organisation to undertake this task. Colour-ringing should be prevented at colonies where disturbed chicks can flee to the sea and at those with a low reproductive rate.

Priority: medium
Time-scale: ongoing

3.2.   To undertake research on dispersal patterns and winter ecology

3.2.1. Identify the most important passage sites and wintering areas

Intensive ringing (including colour-ringing) campaigns should be promoted in order to permit a better understanding of movements and migration routes; these campaigns should be carefully planned to minimise disturbance. The winter quarters must be defined geographically and data on numbers and dispersal of the wintering population are needed. One point of special importance is the determination of survival rates of young and adult birds in winter.

Priority: high
Time-scale: medium

3.2.2. Feeding ecology and habitat use in winter

Very few data exist on the winter ecology of Audouin's Gull, as on the species' habits outside the breeding season. A better knowledge of habitat selection and habitat use can provide useful information for conservation management. There is also very little baseline information about possible threats in the winter quarters.

Priority: medium/high
Time-scale: short/medium

3.3. To promote research which is of direct application to the conservation and management of Audouin's Gull

3.3.1. Study population dynamics

The factors that influence and regulate breeding success and survival should be determined, and the patterns and mechanisms of action of those factors analysed. Colour-ringing can also be used to ascertain survival rates of different age groups, especially adults and sub-adults. The results of this and other related studies should be used to build a predictive population model.

Priority: high
Time-scale: short/medium

3.3.2. Undertake comparative studies of breeding biology and colony-site selection in different habitats

High colony mobility can compromise many conservation efforts. A protected-area network could be invalidated by colony displacement from year to year. It is important to know the mechanisms of site selection and to evaluate breeding success in different habitats. It is also necessary to establish site-selection preferences of young Audouin's Gulls born and raised in atypical habitats for the species, such as the saltmarshes of the Ebro delta.

Priority: medium
Time-scale: medium

3.3.3. Determine the diet in different parts of the Mediterranean

The diet of adults and chicks can be studied through pellet analysis or food regurgitation. Inter-colony and inter-individual variability within colonies should be taken into account. These studies should be compared with the abundance and availability of food at sea during different periods of time.

Priority: medium
Time-scale: medium

3.4. To assess major threats and their effects

3.4.1. Chemical pollution and oil spills

Blood and tissue samples should be collected to assess levels of heavy metals, PCBs and other pollutants.

Priority: medium
Time-scale: medium

3.4.2. Fishing policies

The effects of fishing policies and regulations should be evaluated. In particular, data about fishing methods, fishing effort, fishing periods and captures should be collected from different parts of the Mediterranean and compared with the species' population status and breeding success.

Priority: high
Time-scale: medium

3.4.3. Habitat requirements

Habitat selection studies should be undertaken to ascertain the habitat requirements of Audouin's Gull. The results will be applied directly in the management of the sites.

Priority: medium
Time-scale: medium

3.4.4. Human disturbance

Effects of human disturbance on breeding failure and egg/chick mortality should be evaluated. Given the difficulty of obtaining data for such studies it is recommended that researchers working on Audouin's Gull colonies undertake self-assessments of the disturbance they provoke.

Priority: medium
Time-scale: medium

3.4.5. Competitors

Studies of population dynamics, feeding and habitat selection of the Yellow-legged Gull are necessary in order to evaluate that species' impact on Audouin's Gull. Attempts at control of Yellow-legged Gulls should be based on sound scientific evidence that the species is a limiting factor for Audouin's Gull.

Priority: medium
Time-scale: medium

3.4.6. Predators

The impact of predation by foxes, dogs, cats, reptiles, rodents, etc., should be estimated and monitored. Control programmes should be undertaken in the event of predation becoming a threat for the survival of a colony. The possibility of providing artificial refuges to Audouin's Gull chicks should be explored.

Priority: medium
Time-scale: medium/ongoing

3.4.7. Monitor fishing activities for possible impact on breeding and wintering Audouin's Gulls

In the long term, depletion of fish stocks could have a strong negative impact on Audouin's Gull, which relies mainly on clupeids and other seafood. The impact of the fishing industry and the methods used must be monitored and restricted for the sustainability of the industry itself and of seabird populations. Policies must be developed and implemented which prevent a direct impact of overfishing on Audouin's Gull.

Priority: high
Time-scale: short/ongoing

3.5. To agree on a protocol for low-disturbance monitoring and research

Negative effects of intensive field studies on the breeding of colonial waterbirds have been reported by several authors. Audouin's Gull must be considered a highly sensitive species in this respect because of its restricted range and its exceptional colony mobility. A protocol for low-disturbance monitoring and research must be agreed by all involved in research or management of the species.

Priority: medium
Time-scale: short

4.   Public awareness and training

4.1. To provide information and increase awareness

4.1.1. Increase awareness about Audouin's Gull among politicians and decision-makers

In many range states it is necessary to influence decision-makers, local authorities, landowners, landscape planners and others involved in deci-

sions and activities which could have an influence on the conservation of the species.

Priority: medium
Time-scale: short/ongoing

4.1.2. Inform the general public about the plight of Audouin's Gull

National and international NGOs should play a major role in increasing public awareness of Audouin's Gull, a species which is still largely unknown and ignored by people, even those living near the breeding colonies.

Priority: medium
Time-scale: short/ongoing

4.1.3. Involve tourists and fishermen in preventing disturbances

Some colonies are very close to human settlements and frequently visited by tourists in summer, thus suffering heavy disturbance. Education campaigns should be undertaken at such sites, intended to inform tourists and local people (especially fishermen) about the sensitivity of Audouin's Gull and to prevent disturbance. Local municipalities must also be involved and asked for legal measures for the temporary or long-term protection of breeding sites.

Priority: high
Time-scale: short/ongoing

4.1.4. Prepare and distribute educational material

Information and educational services to the public should be provided in areas frequented by Audouin's Gull. Leaflets, videos and posters should be made available, including information on the species and its habitat, as well as guidelines and rules to prevent disturbance.

Priority: medium
Time-scale: short/ongoing

4.1.5. Use the media to increase awareness

Information on the species, the threats to it and the need for protection should be made available to newspapers, magazines and other media. This should be combined with lectures and slide/video presentations in areas in which breeding colonies are found.

Priority: medium
Time-scale: short/ongoing

4.2. *To use Audouin's Gull as a flagship species*

As a rare and elegant bird, endemic to the Mediterranean, Audouin's Gull should be used as a flagship species when campaigning for the conservation of Mediterranean coastal habitats and islands. Its importance as an indicator of healthy marine ecosystems and unspoilt rocky sea cliffs and islands should be highlighted. An international awareness campaign and a specific event should be organised to attract the attention of the international community.

Priority: medium
Time-scale: medium

4.3. *Promote information exchange*

A meeting to exchange information, debate problems, update the action plan and co-ordinate fieldwork should be organised every 2 to 3 years. Proceedings of the meetings should be published and disseminated.

Priority: high
Time-scale: short/ongoing

Annex
Recommended conservation actions by country

Algeria

1.3. Encourage appropriate measures to enforce the status of protection afforded by Decree No. 83–509.

1.3. Promote enforcement of the environmental national law No. 83 and seek the designation of coastal and marine nature reserves, particularly on the Habibas islands.

2.2.2. Promote control measures for rodents at the main colonies.

3.1.2. Assess the status and distribution of the breeding population through adequate and extensive field work.

3.2. Undertake research on population numbers and habitat use during winter.

4.1.1. Increase awareness among decision-makers and the public about the rarity and vulnerability of Audouin's Gull.

Cyprus

3.1.2. Undertake a survey of suitable sites and confirm breeding at the Klidhes islands.

France

2.2.2. Undertake active control of the Yellow-legged Gull near the breeding areas of Audouin's Gull, especially the closing of all open refuse dumps.

Greece

1.2. Promote the formulation of a national coastal strategy in accordance with the EU coastal strategy and ensure that areas where Audouin's Gull occurs are managed sustainably.

1.3. Encourage the designation of all breeding colonies as SACs within the network Natura 2000 of the EU Habitats Directive.

3.1.2. Undertake field surveys to assess current distribution and population status.

Italy

1.2. Promote the formulation of a national coastal strategy in accordance with the EU coastal strategy and ensure that areas where Audouin's Gull occurs are managed sustainably.

1.3. Encourage designations of all colonies as SACs within the network Natura 2000 of the EU Habitats Directive.

1.4. Promote a ban on tankers in the Bocche di Bonifacio Straits between Sardinia and Corsica, and around the Tuscan Islands.

2.1.1. Encourage the designation of all breeding sites which are not already protected as protected areas under Italian law 394/91 on National Parks and Protected Areas.

2.1.2. Prevent housing and development plans which would adversely affect the Audouin's Gull in the Tuscan and Sardinian Islands.

2.2.1. Prevent disturbance to those colonies in the Sardinian and Tuscan Islands which are close to human settlements and tourist resorts, involving local authorities, fishermen, tourists and volunteers.

3.4.1. Undertake research on the effects of chemical pollutants, crude oil and human disturbance.

3.5. Promote the formulation of a protocol on low-disturbance monitoring and research among INFS, CISO, the universities involved in research on colonial waterbirds and LIPU-BirdLife Italy.

4.1.4. Seek support from public and private organisations to prepare educational materials (including a video tape) and organise local and national events and communications through press and other media.

Lebanon

2.1.2./2.2. Promote management of the Nakhl Islands (Palm Islands), especially the restoration of the natural drainage system and of the abandoned saltpans. No landing facilities should be built on the Nature Reserve.

Morocco

2.3.1. Promote inclusion of the most important wintering sites in the developing protected areas network.

3.1.2. Undertake extensive fieldwork to assess the status and distribution of the breeding population.

3.2.1. Undertake more regular counts of wintering birds and define geographically the most important sites for migration and wintering.

Spain

1.1. Ensure that fishing moratoria are set up in a way which is compatible with the subsistence of the breeding colonies.

1.2. Promote the formulation of a national coastal strategy in accordance with the EU coastal strategy and ensure that areas where Audouin's Gull occurs are managed sustainably.

1.3. Encourage the review and updating of the National Catalogue of Threatened Species.

1.5. Encourage the formulation of regional action plans.

3.1.1. Continue with regular monitoring of the population and review management activities in the light of the latest research findings.

4.3. Update and reinforce the existing co-ordinated action plan.

Tunisia

2.1.1. Promote the declaration of La Galite archipelago as a National Park and enlarge the buffer marine zone around Zembra.

2.2.1. Promote restriction of access to Zembra and Zembretta and submit the plans for development of tourism on Zembra to impact assessment.

3.1.2. Assess the status and distribution of the breeding population through adequate and extensive fieldwork.

3.2.1. Undertake regular counts of wintering Audouin's Gulls and define geographically the most important sites for migration and wintering.

3.2.2. Promote research on habitat use and distribution patterns of the wintering population.

3.4.5. Undertake research on the effects of competition and predators, particularly on Zembra, and define control measures.

4.1. Publish and distribute educational materials and raise public awareness.

Turkey

2.1.1. Promote the designation as protected areas of all Audouin's Gull breeding sites.

2.2.2. Promote the prevention of grazing on the islands off the south-east coast where Audouin's Gull breeds.

3.1.2. Undertake a survey of the Mediterranean coast and determine the current distribution and population status.

Action plan for the Madeira Laurel Pigeon (*Columba trocaz*)

Reviews

This document should be reviewed and updated by BirdLife International every five years. An emergency review will be undertaken if sudden major environmental changes, liable to affect the population, occur within the species' range.

Geographical scope

The island of Madeira (Portugal).

Summary

The Madeira Laurel Pigeon *Columba trocaz* is an endemic bird of the island of Madeira and is under strict national and international protection.

In the earlier days of man's colonisation of the island it was a very abundant bird but due to very heavy persecution and dramatic loss of its habitat (85%) it has become a threatened species. The remaining 15% of the laurel forest (an area of about 12 000 ha) is now under the jurisdiction of the Parque Natural da Madeira (Madeira Natural Park). Thanks to the very intense management carried out by this Natural Park, the population of the Madeira Laurel Pigeon is now increasing, and has reached numbers that give great optimism for its future if, and only if, management, protection and research are continued.

Threats and limiting factors

Illegal poisoning and shooting – medium

Unpopularity – medium

Livestock grazing – medium

Forest fires – low

Habitat loss – low, historically high

Predation – unknown

Conservation priorities

Establish a management plan for the Natural Park of Madeira – high

Seek funds from relevant international organisations, especially the EU – high

Prevent the illegal killing of Madeira Laurel Pigeons – high

Promote the use of bird scarers to reduce agricultural damage – high

Prevent further habitat loss through livestock grazing or fires – high

Identify and protect new areas of laurel forest – high

Continue research, especially annual monitoring of the population – high

Undertake an education campaign to overcome the species unpopularity – high

Introduction

The Madeira Laurel Pigeon or Long-toed Pigeon *Columba trocaz* is endemic to the island of Madeira. It is listed as Rare in the African Red Data Book (Collar and Stuart, 1985) and in the *IUCN Red List of Threatened Animals* (Groombridge, 1993) and is classified as Conservation Dependent in *Birds to Watch 2* (Collar et al., 1994). It is also included in Annex I of the European Union's Wild Birds Directive and in Annex III of the Bern Convention. In the Portuguese Red Data Book it is listed as Vulnerable (Cabral et al., 1990).

The Madeira Laurel Pigeon formerly occurred also on the neighbouring island of Porto Santo (Pieper, 1985); the reduction of its range there and on Madeira is associated with the cutting of laurel forest for wood, agriculture, grazing and human settlements. The species also used to be very heavily hunted both for sport and because of the damage it causes to crops.

The establishment of the Natural Park of Madeira has afforded legal protection to almost all of the laurel forest which is a priority habitat listed in

Annex I of the European Union's Habitats Directive (45.61 to 45.63 Macaronesian Laurel Forests). The inclusion of the Madeira Laurel Pigeon in Annex I of the European Union's Wild Birds Directive in 1986 has assured and reinforced the ban on hunting that was established in 1989 through the Decreto-Lei 75/91 which adapts the directive to Portuguese law. The future of the species is now secure and the main tasks ahead are to monitor population trends and to promote expansion of its range through the regeneration of laurel forest.

Background information

Distribution and population

The Madeira Laurel Pigeon is restricted to areas of native forest on the mountainous northern slopes and a few isolated pockets in the south of Madeira. It was probably exceptionally plentiful before the first settlement of the island but the loss of laurel forest and perhaps also over-hunting have led to a severe decrease. Population size has been estimated at 3500 to 4900 individuals and is increasing (Oliveira and Jones, in press).

Life history

Breeding

Madeira Laurel Pigeons build their nest with dry twigs in a forest tree, and occasionally on the ground or in cavities in cliffs (Zino, 1969). Normally one egg is laid, occasionally two, though no nest with two chicks has ever been found (P. Oliveira, in litt, 1994). Incubation takes from 19 to 20 days and the fledging period is up to 28 days (Zino, 1969). Captive breeding has been achieved (Zino and Zino, 1986).

Feeding

Food consists mainly of the fruits of *Laurus azorica* and *Ocotea foetens*, but also flowers and leaves of *Sonchus* spp., *Apium nodiflorum*, *Nastasium officinale*, and a wide variety of other plants (Zino and Zino, 1986; Jones, 1988). The crop contents and state of the gonads of 25 pigeons were examined in 1985 and compared to a sample of 29 birds in 1988. In 1985 only agricultural food remains were found

in the pigeons and the gonads were inactive; in 1988 only berries from laurel forest trees were found and, of the 25 birds, 19 were sexually active, three were juveniles and three had undeveloped gonads (Zino and Biscoito, 1993).

Habitat requirements

There is strong evidence that the pigeons move from valley to valley all year round, and that they look for different areas at different times of the year (Oliveira, 1992; Oliveira and Jones, in press). Habitat selection has been studied in summer when the pigeons show a strong preference for laurel forest at low altitudes, especially high-canopy forest on steep slopes (Jones, 1988). In places not altered by housing and agriculture, pigeons may occur very near the coast (Zino and Zino, 1986; Jones, 1990). The biotopes that are preferred are those dominated by *Ocotea foetens*, although those with exotic vegetation are in relatively high demand all year round if compared with some of the laurel forest habitats. Pigeons occur within the whole altitudinal range of the laurel forest but they show a much higher preference for forests under 850 metres (Oliveira, 1992; Oliveira and Jones, in press).

Threats and limiting factors

Illegal hunting

Hunting was prohibited in 1989 but still occurs illegally in a few well-defined areas, especially when pigeons leave the forest to feed on agricultural land. These movements out of the forest may be associated with a lack of natural foods (Zino and Zino, 1986) or with the existence of predictable food sources in close proximity to the pigeon's natural habitat (Oliveira and Jones, in press). In 1985, because of damage caused to crops by the pigeons, a special legal shooting period was established, covering five consecutive Sundays in January and February: over 300 birds were shot, with the possibility of a further 150 to 200 killed by poison; one party of four guns at Chão da Ribeira shot 64 birds in four days and over 140 were shot in this valley during the five Sundays (Zino and Zino, 1986).

Importance: medium

Poisoning

Poisoning is illegal but occurs nevertheless in a few well-defined areas. In 1985, it was estimated that from 150 to 200 birds were killed by poison (Zino and Zino, 1986) and now that shooting is illegal, there is an increased threat from the use of poison.

Importance: medium

Unpopularity

Apart from having a great effect on the extent to which the birds are shot, people's attitude towards the species can have a negative influence on the enforcement of conservation and management actions undertaken by the Natural Park in the field.

Importance: medium

Livestock grazing

In some particular areas overgrazing is a threat to laurel forest because it does not allow regeneration.

Importance: medium

Forest fires

Regenerating areas, or areas above the treeline, may be affected but fire is not a significant threat to mature laurel forest.

Importance: low

Habitat loss

Madeira was largely covered by laurel forest when discovered in 1419. Since then, much of it has been cleared for its valuable timber and this was the most important factor for the decline of the species in the past. Laurel forest now covers only 15% of the island but is recovering well in several areas through natural regeneration made possible by the legal protection afforded to these areas.

Importance: low, historically high

Predation by rats

Rats (*Rattus rattus* and *Rattus norvegicus*) are likely to be a significant limiting factor since they have an impact on breeding success (Zino and Zino, 1986). In the forest, competition for food with rats can also be significant, but only at local level (P. Oliveira, *in litt.*, 1993).

Importance: unknown

Conservation status and recent conservation measures

In Portugal, the Madeira Laurel Pigeon is a protected species under Decreto-Lei 75/91, which adapts the EU Wild Birds Directive to Portuguese law. At present there are seven important bird areas in the island of Madeira (Grimmett and Jones, 1989) and five of these include the Madeira Laurel Pigeon. All five have been designated as Special Protection Areas under Article 4 of the EU Wild Birds Directive. Hunting of this species is now illegal following its inclusion in 1986 in Annex I of the Directive.

Almost the entire pigeon population is included within areas controlled by the Natural Park of Madeira, which is part of the Secretaria de Agricultura, Florestas e Pescas do Governo Regional da Madeira. The Natural Park includes practically all the laurel forest and was fully established in May 1993. There are currently eight different types of protected areas: (1) Reserva Natural Integral (Strict Nature Reserve); (2) Reserva Natural Parcial (Partial Nature Reserve); (3) Paisagem Protegida (Protected Landscape); (4) Reserva de Recreio e Montanha (Leisure and Mountain Reserve); (5) Zona de Repouso e Silêncio (Silence and Rest Zone); (6) Zona de Caça (Hunting Zone); (7) Zonas de Pastagem (Pasture Zone); (8) Reserva Geológica e de Vegetaçao de Altitude (Geological and High Altitude Vegetation Reserve).

The areas of laurel forest within the Natural Park have been designated as a Biogenetic Reserve by the Council of Europe.

In 1988 a survey of the distribution, density and habitat preferences of the Madeira Laurel Pigeon was undertaken by ICBP (Jones, 1988), and a monitoring scheme is currently being implemented by the Natural Park.

Some experiments have been carried out to identify ways of scaring pigeons away from crops. In 1989 a bird scarer was placed on a property near Faial, where about 650 walnut trees had been planted. The pigeons were eating the newly formed walnuts and young shoots, and were breaking the small branches on which they settled. The scarecrow, a bright red and white doll which was inflated at regular intervals and produced a piercing sound audible at a distance of about 200 metres away, was placed in the middle of the walnut plantation. The effects of the scarer were immediate and no pigeons were seen in the field after it started operating (Biscoito and Zino, 1989).

In 1993 the Natural Park used five other scarers in agricultural fields with different characteristics. In open fields with fruit trees the success was 100%; in open fields with cabbages the success was acceptable; in fields which were not very open the success was not acceptable (compared with the cost). Sound scarers have proved most effective and are reasonably cheap. At the moment, a new and inexpensive method is being tried, consisting of nylon strands laid across the fields above the cabbages (Oliveira, 1993). The Direção Regional da Agricultura is carrying out a rat control programme in agricultural areas surrounding laurel forest, with the aim of reducing crop damage from rats and also for public health purposes.

There is also a LIFE-funded project running from October 1994 to December 1996: Conservação e Recuperação de Espécis e Habitats na Madeira covering a range of complementary conservation activities in the National Park.

Aims and objectives

Aims

In the short term, to maintain the population of the Madeira Laurel Pigeon at no fewer than 3500 individuals. In the medium term, to ensure its continued increase towards occupying all suitable habitats in Madeira. In the long term, to enable the recolonisation of areas of its former range through habitat restoration.

Objectives

1. **Policy and legislation**

1.1. *To ensure an adequate legal and financial framework for the conservation of laurel forests and the Madeira Laurel Pigeon*

1.1.1. Establish the management plan for the Natural Park of Madeira

A comprehensive management plan should be developed for approval by the regional authorities, and an adequate budget allocated for species and habitat conservation. Ideally, the Madeira Laurel Pigeon action plan would become part of this management plan as would the action plan for the Zino's Petrel.

Priority: high
Time-scale: short

1.1.2. Attract funding from relevant international organisations, especially the EU

To ensure that the park has a budget commensurate with its size and global importance, a general application for the conservation and management of the Natural Park of Madeira should be submitted to the EU under LIFE regulation. This would benefit the two endemic bird species as well as the laurel forest, a priority habitat in the EU and other endemic flora.

Priority: high
Time-scale: ongoing

1.1.3. Incorporate species recovery plans into regional and national legislation

Recovery plans are included as legal measures in other countries. Consideration should be given to incorporating the action plan for the Madeira Laurel Pigeon into appropriate legislation.

Priority: low
Time-scale: long

1.1.4. Recognise the global importance of the Natural Park of Madeira

The designation of the Natural Park of Madeira as a World Heritage Site under Unesco should be pursued.

Priority: medium
Time-scale: ongoing

1.1.5. To upgrade the protection status of the Madeira Laurel Pigeon under the Bern Convention

The species is currently listed as protected under Appendix III. The Portuguese Government is encouraged to pursue its upgrading to Appendix II as a strictly protected species, which implies the adoption of appropriate and necessary legislative and administrative measures to ensure the conservation of its habitat. Both species of the Laurel Pigeon in the Canary Islands are included in Appendix II of the Bern Convention.

Priority: low
Time-scale: long

1.1.6. Promote the regeneration of laurel forest through abandonment in key areas

Laurel forest is now recovering well in a number of areas through natural regeneration. This applies particularly to the more recently degraded areas dominated by tree heath and non-native forest. The abandonment of agriculture contributes in a very significant way to the regeneration of the laurel forest, and should be encouraged through the appropriate policy mechanisms in key areas around existing forest.

Priority: medium
Time-scale: ongoing

2. Species and habitat protection

2.1. *To reduce human predation*

2.1.1. Prevent hunting and poisoning within the laurel forest and on agricultural land

The killing of the Madeira Laurel Pigeons should not be allowed under any circumstances. This prohibition should be enforced by the Natural Park authorities, and the existing penalty applied to punish violators. The number of wardens in areas where killing is a problem should be increased.

Those hunters who specialise in shooting pigeons (usually when the birds gather in large berry-laden trees) should be identified and their movements observed by the wardens of the Natural Park and those of the Direcção Regional das Florestas.

Priority: high
Time-scale: short

2.1.2. Promote the use of bird-scaring devices

A variety of devices should be available from the Natural Park to be loaned on request to farmers suffering crop damage from pigeons. A variety of methods should be used in order to prevent familiarisation by the pigeons. The work that the Natural Park is doing with scarers is important in preventing illegal shooting because it persuades farmers that there is an alternative to killing the birds and it increases the presence of the park's staff in the problem areas.

Priority: high
Time-scale: ongoing

2.1.3. Provide support for farmers affected by the pigeons

An evaluation of the cost of crop damage should be undertaken yearly, and a compensation plan prepared for emergency cases, based on a system of rapid notification and verification. Compensation should take the form of payments in kind (e.g. seed for the next season) rather than cash, and should be accompanied by free advice on measures to minimise pigeon damage.

Priority: medium
Time-scale: long

2.2. *To enforce current habitat protection through the implementation of the Natural Park regulations*

2.2.1. Preserve the existing laurel forest

A great majority of the laurel forest in Madeira is included within the Natural Park, the regulations of which should be fully implemented. All dense, high-canopy laurel forest below 950 metres should receive the maximum status of protection; this includes Ribeira de Janela, Ribeira Grande, Ribeira do Inferno, Faja da Nogueira and the forest between Ribeiro Frio and Lamaceiros.

Priority: high
Time-scale: ongoing

2.2.2. Identify and protect new laurel forest areas

A detailed inventory of laurel forest in Madeira was started by the Natural Park in 1992 and will take at least three years to complete. Any new areas of laurel forest identified outside the boundaries of the Natural Park should be protected either by extending the park boundaries or designating new protected areas.

Priority: high
Time-scale: ongoing

2.3. To improve breeding success

2.3.1. Prevent predation by rats

There is evidence to suggest that rats can pose a threat to pigeons during the breeding season. The magnitude of this threat has to be assessed and, if necessary, action undertaken to reduce it. The Natural Park authorities should promote a "take your litter home" policy and provide waste receptacles in tourist areas in such a way that garbage is not accessible to rats. There has to be a close co-operation with the Secretaría Regional da Educaçao of the regional government of Madeira to provide advice on and guidelines for adequate waste management.

Priority: medium
Time-scale: medium

2.3.2. Prevent disturbance from tourism

Madeira is increasingly popular as a tourist resort and the presence of large numbers of tourists in the laurel forest could result in some disturbance to the birds. It is important that the Natural Park authorities keep records of the number of visitors and their preferred areas, and that visitor numbers are restricted if necessary. The first steps to monitor visitor numbers have already been taken.

Priority: medium
Time-scale: ongoing

2.4. To encourage the spread of the Madeira Laurel Pigeon into suitable habitat

2.4.1. Prevention of livestock grazing

Livestock grazing mainly affects areas that are regenerating or areas above the treeline. Areas of tree heath and non-native forest are those which might most easily return to native forest. The feasibility of gradually eliminating sheep and goats from these areas should be assessed, and if possible a suitable programme implemented.

Priority: high
Time-scale: short

2.4.3. Prevent fire damage to regenerating laurel forest

Forest fires do not occur very often in Madeira, and laurel forest does not burn easily. However, under certain weather conditions fire can cause very serious damage, particularly in areas where the vegetation is regenerating through natural succession. Fires are generally started intentionally by shepherds, and this should be prevented. Instructions should also be provided to tourists and campers to avoid casual fires. The Natural Park should have the appropriate means to extinguish fires.

Priority: high
Time-scale: short

3. Monitoring and research

3.1. To obtain regular information on the size, range and trends of the Madeira Laurel Pigeon population

3.1.1. Continue to monitor population numbers

A monitoring scheme, following the methodology in Jones (1990), but improved with estimates of distance between bird and observer, was conducted during 1992 and 1993 with very good results. Surveys were carried out on a monthly basis but the method has been refined and from 1994 they will be done every three months. The Natural Park is encouraged to continue with this effort, which allows for a much better understanding of the pigeon's numbers and the way in which they fluctuate.

Priority: high
Time-scale: ongoing

3.1.2. Monitor reproductive parameters

Efforts should concentrate on breeding success, but other aspects to be monitored are chronology, seasonality and number of broods per year. The effects of rat predation on breeding success needs to be clarified and the existing data analysed. Information should be exchanged on a regular basis with those carrying out work on Laurel Pigeons in the Canaries.

Priority: high
Time-scale: short

3.1.3. Identify habitat preferences and habitat selection

Habitat preference has been studied previously (Jones, 1988, 1990; Oliveira, 1992; Oliveira and Jones, in press) but further research is needed to identify habitat selection on a finer scale.

Priority: high
Time-scale: ongoing

3.2. *To promote better knowledge of the effect of rats on the general ecology of laurel forest.*

3.2.1. Study interactions between rats and laurel forest

A study should be undertaken to establish rat densities and population cycles in laurel forest, stressing the potential role of the rat as a disrupting agent in the process of co-evolution between frugivorous birds and berries. It should include practical recommendations to prevent the increase of the rat population in the future.

Priority: medium/high
Time-scale: long

3.2.2. Monitor the current control programme

Ensure that the rat control programme undertaken by the Direcçao Regional da Agricultura takes into account the effect of rats on the overall ecosystem and that it is carried out under strict scientific control and the results monitored.

Priority: medium
Time-scale: short

4.   **Public awareness and training**

4.1. *To increase public awareness of the Madeira Laurel Pigeon and its habitat*

4.1.1. Provide information about the species and the laurel forest to visitors of Madeira and the local population

An interpretation centre is necessary to explain to local people and visitors the different biotopes of the Natural Park, stressing the importance and special value of the Madeira Laurel Pigeon and its habitat. Information materials should be prepared and distributed in schools (especially in the north of the island), government buildings, tourist centres, etc., as part of a broader education campaign.

Priority: high
Time-scale: ongoing

Action plan for the Dark-tailed Laurel Pigeon (*Columba bollii*)

Reviews

This document should be reviewed by BirdLife International every four years. An emergency review will be undertaken if sudden major environmental changes, liable to affect the population, occur within the species' range.

Geographical scope

The islands of Tenerife, La Palma, La Gomera and El Hierro in the Canary Islands archipelago.

Summary

The Dark-tailed Laurel Pigeon *Columba bollii* is endemic to the Canary Islands, and occurs in the laurel forests of Tenerife, La Palma, La Gomera and El Hierro with an estimated population of 1700 individuals (Emmerson, 1985; Emmerson et al., 1993). It is classified as Vulnerable in the *Red Data Book of Spanish Vertebrates* (Blanco and González, 1992) and also at world level (Collar et al., 1994). The species is included in Annex I of the European Union's Wild Birds Directive and its habitat is considered a priority habitat listed in Annex I of the European Union's Habitats Directive (45.61 to 45.63 Macaronesian Laurel Forest).

The range of this species has contracted substantially since the nineteenth century. Emmerson et al. (1986) commented that on Tenerife, the Dark-tailed Laurel Pigeon now occupies just 35% to 40% of its original area, which gives an idea of the scale of the destruction and alteration of laurel forest on the island.

Threats and limiting factors

Habitat loss – critical

Habitat change – critical

Illegal hunting – high

Lack of drinking areas – high

Placing of snares and traps – low

Newcastle disease – unknown

Predation – unknown

Conservation priorities

Avoid further damage to laurel forest from commercial forestry – essential

Control illegal hunting – essential

Carry out a full census and initiate a monitoring programme – essential/high

Investigate factors affecting breeding performance – essential

Ensure the adequate legal protection of the species – high

Implement a programme of alternatives to commercial forestry – high

Promote restoration and expansion of laurel forest – high

Purchase of important sites – high

Establish new hunting reserves – high

Undertake a public awareness campaign – high

Promote dialogue between different bodies – high

Training of wardens – high

Introduction

The Dark-tailed Laurel Pigeon is endemic to the Canary Islands. It is classified as Rare by IUCN (Groombridge, 1993) and is considered Vulnerable at world level (Collar et al., 1994) and at European level (Tucker and Heath, 1994). The species is listed in Annex I of the European Union's Wild Birds and in Appendix II of the Bern Convention. Its habitat is listed in Annex I of the European Union's Habitats Directive as a priority habitat (45.61 to 45.63 Macaronesian Laurel Forests).

This action plan incorporates the discussions and conclusions of the meeting held in July 1993 at La Laguna (Tenerife) which was attended by those involved in the conservation of the Dark-tailed Laurel Pigeon and its habitat: the situation of the other four threatened bird species in the Canary Islands was also discussed. This plan addresses the actions that should be carried out to maintain and boost the population of the species.

Background information

Distribution and population

This species is found on Tenerife, La Palma, La Gomera and El Hierro. On Gran Canaria the remains of a pigeon that used to inhabit the island have been found. Its bones are similar to those of Laurel Pigeons, but it has not been possible to identify the species due to lack of comparative material (Alcover and Florit, 1986). Moreover, Tristam (1889) recorded three Laurel Pigeons on the island which he thought possibly belonged to this species.

The estimated minimum total population of the Dark-tailed Laurel Pigeon is 1150 to 1300 individuals (Emmerson, 1985) However, recent studies suggest that the population is about 1700 individuals (Emmerson et al., 1993). The numbers on each island are as follows:

La Palma: 250 to 300 birds in very restricted areas. The highest densities occur in the north-west (San Andrés and Sauces);

Tenerife: 350 to 400 minimum. Anaga and Los Silos and the small forest patches between these two sites are important areas;

La Gomera: 550 to 600 individuals mainly concentrated in Garajonay National Park, although more recent studies suggest that the population in the park is over 1000 individuals (Emmerson et al., 1993);

El Hierro: the first observation of the Dark-tailed Laurel Pigeon on the island was made in 1985 (Martín, 1985) and nesting was recorded in 1993 (Martín et al., 1993). The population is estimated to be over 30 birds with up to 12 pigeons recently observed together at a drinking station (A. Martín, pers. comm., 1994). The low number

may be due to poor plant diversity within the laurel forest on this island with "fayas" and predominant heath (Emmerson, 1985).

Life history

Breeding

Nesting occurs exclusively in trees within laurel forest. The height of the nest varies, the most frequently used tree species being *Erica arborea*, *Laurus azorica*, *Myrica faya* and *Ilex canariensis* (Emmerson, 1985). Nests appear well camouflaged by foliage, possibly to protect them from aerial predators such as Sparrowhawk *Accipiter nisus*, Buzzard *Buteo buteo* or Raven *Corvus corax*. They can be re-used for successive clutches and successive years. The most common nest material is small branches of heath *Erica arborea* (Emmerson, 1985).

The breeding season extends from October to July (Emmerson, 1985) although it is very possible that birds breed all year round. The long breeding season must be related to the continuous availability of fruit, the main food of this species.

The clutch is a single egg incubated for 18 to 19 days (Koenig, quoted in Emmerson, 1985) and the chicks spend from 30 to 35 days in the nest (Emmerson, 1985).

Feeding

The diet is mainly made up of fruit (*Laurus* sp., *Persea indica*, etc.) the precise composition varying with the timing of fruiting of different tree species (Emmerson, 1985).

Besides fruit, the birds feed on leaves, shoots and leaf and flower buds, and they may, if the opportunity presents itself, supplement their diet with small invertebrates (Emmerson, 1985). Some cereals (wheat, rye) are also eaten (Cramp, 1985). Birds have been observed feeding both on the ground and in the trees.

Habitat requirements

The species principally inhabits areas of closed-canopy laurel forest, particularly ridges and passes where the forest reaches its greatest development in terms of both tree size and plant diversity. In summer, when food is scarce, the birds will use the lower areas of laurel forest and agricultural fields where most of the trees in fruit at this time are found (*Myrica faya*, etc.) (Emmerson, 1985). However, this species avoids farmed or degraded forest areas to a greater extent than the White-tailed Laurel Pigeon *Columba junoniae*.

Threats and limiting factors

Habitat loss

With the arrival of the Spanish in the fifteenth century, laurel forests were subject to intensive exploitation. Extensive areas of forest were razed to create farmland and large trees were felled for timber and fuel, greatly reducing the area of original forest.

These activities have decreased considerably but even today laurel forest is still exploited, especially in La Palma, and its conservation is therefore cause for concern.

Importance: critical

Habitat change

Apart from the enormous decrease in its extent, laurel forests have also been profoundly changed and fragmented due to the increase over the last few decades in the demand for wooden poles and tool handles used in the cultivation of tomatoes, bananas and vines.

This wood is obtained by coppicing laurel trees so that a large number of shoots sprout from the remaining stump. This results in a thick layer of vegetation, mainly consisting of "fayas" and heath, which over time becomes extensive (Emmerson, 1985). This is carried out along horizontal or vertical bands, depending on the slope, and results in the partitioning of the woods into plots with vegetation at different stages of growth. The best preserved areas of laurel forest are now restricted to inaccessible points.

Importance: critical

Illegal hunting

Hunting is almost certainly one of the factors that most affects the Dark-tailed Laurel Pigeon today. Since the total ban on hunting under Royal Decree 3181/80 the number of hunters has decreased considerably, but those who persist cause significant damage to the population. The birds are hunted from hides placed at feeding and drinking points.

Importance: high

Placing of snares and traps

Snares and traps are known to have been placed at drinking and feeding areas.

Importance: low

Lack of drinking areas

Due to a massive demand for water in the Canary Islands, all natural water sources in the forest have been artificially channelled at source. This has meant that there are now only a few open drinking places used by pigeons and other animals. These sites are well known to illegal hunters.

Importance: high

Newcastle disease

This virus, increasingly common in domestic pigeons, is transmitted through air as well as in the eggs and meat of infected birds, resulting in a high mortality rate. Danger comes from the introduction of infected birds, eggs and poultry products or from existing sources of infection on the islands. The disease has so far not been reported in the wild.

Importance: unknown

Predation

Although it is thought that predation by rats could be a limiting factor on the species, no specific study has been carried out on their impact on eggs and chicks. However, in other studies carried out on the biology and ecology of this species (Emmerson, 1985; A. Martín and E. Hernández, pers. comm.) it has been shown that rats do eat eggs and chicks.

In a study of the feeding habits of Sparrowhawks on Tenerife, it was found that the Dark-tailed Laurel Pigeon made up 1.2% (seven items) of 565 prey items identified (Delgado et al., 1988).

Predation by feral dogs and cats may be affecting the population, but the effect is thought to be minimal (K. Emmerson, pers. comm., 1994).

Importance: unknown

Conservation status and recent conservation measures

Nationally the species is classified as Vulnerable in the *Red Data Book of Spanish Vertebrates* (Blanco and González, 1992) and has been declared of Special Interest by Royal Decree 439/90. Regionally it is classified as Endangered on El Hierro, Vulnerable on Tenerife and La Palma and Rare on La Gomera in the *Red Data Book of Land Vertebrates of the Canary Islands* (Martín et al., 1990).

Recent conservation measures are listed below in chronological order:

1970: hunting this species on Tenerife was banned under the General Close Season Order (1970 only);

1974: hunting was banned by the General Close Season Order in the areas of Las Mercedes, Mina and Yedra, San Andrés, Pijaral, Igueste and Anaga (Tenerife);

1980: Royal Decree 3181/80 banned hunting, capture, trade, collecting of eggs or young, and preparation of and trade in parts, including stuffed specimens, throughout the country;

1981: Garajonay National Park (La Gomera) was established. It is the most important area in the Canary Islands for Dark-tailed Laurel Pigeon;

1984: the estate of El Canal and Los Tiles (Los Sauces, La Palma) was declared a Biosphere Reserve under Unesco's Man and Biosphere programme. This area is important for the Dark-tailed Laurel Pigeon population on La Palma;

1986: since Spain's accession to the European Union in this year, the following areas important for this species have been designated as SPAs: Garajonay (La Gomera); Tigaiga, Teno and Anaga (Tenerife); Monte de los Sauces and Punta Llana, and Pinar de Garafía (La Palma) and El Hierro Natural Park (El Hierro);

1987: The Canary Islands Countryside Law was passed and in accordance with this, the following important Dark-tailed Laurel Pigeon areas have been declared Natural Parks: Anaga, Laderas de Santa Ursula, Los Silos and Tigaiga (Tenerife), Barranco de los Hombres and Fagundo, Monte de los Sauces and Punta Llana, Cumbre Vieja and Teneguía (La Palma), and El Hierro Natural Park (El Hierro);

1989: The Countryside and Wildlife Conservation Law 4/89 was passed, establishing a method of cataloguing nationally threatened species (Articles 29-32) and giving conservation priority to endemic species and sub-species (Article 27.c);

1993: Approval was given for EU funding under LIFE regulation for a project submitted by the Gran Canaria Government to restore an area in Doramas where the species might be reintroduced at some point in the future;

1994: European Union funding under LIFE regulation was approved for a project for the conservation of both species of Laurel Pigeon submitted by the Vice-Council for the Environment of the Canary Islands regional government.

The new Canary Islands Countryside Law was also approved.

Aims and objectives

Aims

In the short term, to conserve the Dark-tailed Laurel Pigeon population at no less than its 1993 level and in the medium term, to promote the expansion of its range.

Objectives

1. **Policy and legislation**

1.1. *To ensure the Dark-tailed Laurel Pigeon is given adequate legal protection*

1.1.1. Ensure that the new Canary Islands Countryside Law adequately protects this species and its habitat

The Canary Islands Countryside Law, passed in 1994, does not designate any new protected areas but reclassifies existing ones into new protection categories. In addition to seeking to achieve the designation of all areas important for the species, the planning instruments for such protected areas – use and management plans, master plans (*planes directores*), conservation regulations and special plans – should aim to address all threats.

Priority: essential
Time-scale: short

1.1.2. Ensure that the new Canary Islands wildlife protection law adequately protects this species

The draft of the new wildlife law is at the consultation stage and includes the Regional Checklist of Threatened Species and the new status of Biological Refuge as a precautionary measure. This legislation should address the protection of the species, in the wider countryside as well as in protected areas, as required under Law 4/1989 on the Conservation of the Countryside, Wildlife and Plants.

Priority: high
Time-scale: short

1.2. *To ensure, through countryside-planning plans, that exploitation of the countryside is compatible with the conservation of the species and its habitat*

1.2.1. Avoid damage to laurel forest by commercial forestry

In the short term, commercial forestry (felling or planting) in mature laurel forest should be discouraged and guided towards suitable alternative areas. Regeneration should be favoured over commercial forestry in areas of degraded laurel forest with the aim of eliminating all damage to laurel forest from commercial forestry in the medium term.

Priority: essential
Time-scale: short

1.2.2. Implement a programme of alternatives to present commercial forestry practices

Alternatives to commercial forestry are needed, such as the promotion of alternative materials for poles and tool handles (poles have already been manufactured using galvanised metal tubing) to meet farmers' needs. Consideration should also be given to replanting areas adjacent to laurel forest so that they can subsequently be used for commercial forestry.

Priority: high
Time-scale: short

1.3. *To establish new Hunting Reserves*

Consideration should be given to establishing new Hunting Reserves in areas such as El Rejo (La Gomera), Barranco del Agua, Barranco de la Herradura, Barranco de Fagundo and Barranco de los Hombres (La Palma), and Barranco de Cochinos and Cuevas Negras (Tenerife). Other human activity in these areas, likely to have a negative effect on the species and its habitat, should be modified or diverted away to a suitable location.

Priority: high
Time-scale: medium

1.4. *To increase health controls on birds imported to the Canary Islands*

These measures must be applied to all living birds being imported, whether for exhibition or consumption, in order to prevent the spread of Newcastle disease. It is also important that controls are carried out on bird rearing facilities to detect the presence of this virus.

Priority: low
Time-scale: short

2. Species and habitation protection

2.1. *To control illegal hunting*

Hunting continues to be a serious threat to the Dark-tailed Laurel Pigeon. The number of wardens, especially on the smaller islands (La Gomera, La Palma, and El Hierro) needs to be increased to provide greater surveillance of important areas, particularly hunting reserves established under the Annual Close Season Order. The support of SEPRONA (Civil Guard Wildlife Service) could be sought and they could be provided with information on the places most frequented by hunters. It is important that the penalties imposed under current law (700 000) be applied when charges are brought (Order

14/1988 on the Updating of the Value of Game and Protected Species).

Priority: essential
Time-scale: immediate

2.2. *To promote the restoration and expansion of laurel forest*

The main introduced-tree species in laurel forest in the Canary Islands are: chestnut *Castanea sativa*, eucalyptus *Eucalyptus globulus* and Monterey pine *Pinus radiata*. The latter is a rapidly growing Californian species with little resistance to fire which was used to replant large deforested areas of Tenerife in the 1940s. The eradication of this species would allow 10% of laurel forest on this island to recover.

The Vice-Council for the Environment of the Canary Islands regional government recently began implementing the Annual Forestry Plan which includes the felling of 2000 ha of Monterey pine on Tenerife and replanting with native species. Plans that include felling and reafforestation would be more effective if prior analysis were carried out to select forestry practices which would most benefit the environment. Laurel forest regeneration is slow, therefore extensive reafforestation with native species might be needed in suitable areas.

Priority: high
Time-scale: ongoing

2.3. *To purchase important sites*

The purchase of some of the important areas for this species currently in private ownership, both within and outside protected areas, would make it possible to carry out the optimum management for this species and its habitat.

Priority: high
Time-scale: medium

2.4. *To provide additional drinking points*

This should be done to reduce the number of pigeons gathering at existing natural drinking areas so that they are not such easy prey for hunters. Additional drinking points would also make it easier for the birds to find water.

Priority: medium
Time-scale: medium

2.5. *To initiate a captive breeding programme*

This is not a priority at the moment. However, it would be useful to contact recognised and prestigious zoological collections that would be interested in breeding the species should the need arise. This information can be obtained through the IUCN Captive Breeding Specialist Group.

Priority: low
Time-scale: long

3.   Research and monotoring

3.1. *To carry out a full census of the species*

Existing information mainly comes from work carried out between 1983 and 1985 (Emmerson, 1985) with more recent information available only for Garajonay (Emmerson et al., 1993). New data on all the different breeding groups in the Canary Islands, including El Hierro, are now needed. A recent inventory of all breeding areas would allow better targeting of conservation action.

Priority: essential
Time-scale: short

3.2. *To improve monitoring methods*

The Madeira Laurel Pigeon *C. trocaz* is monitored through fixed transects every three months in several biotopes where the species is found (Oliveira and Jones, in press). Using this and other studies as a basis, a similar methodology suited to the particular requirements of the Canary Island Dark-tailed Laurel Pigeon should be designed. Exchange of information between Laurel Pigeon researchers in Madeira and the Canary Islands is highly recommended.

Priority: high
Time-scale: short

3.3. *To monitor the population regularly*

The overall census should be repeated every four years with annual estimates in areas of high density to detect population fluctuations and trends.

Priority: high
Time-scale: short

3.4. *To study breeding success and the factors affecting it*

A study must be carried out urgently on the factors affecting breeding success, especially predation (rats, cats) and food availability. The results will make informed decisions possible on the need for measures to control predators, particularly rats.

Priority: essential
Time-scale: immediate, ongoing

3.5. *To undertake a socioeconomic study of commercial forestry*

The main aim of this study would be to evaluate the economic importance of commercial forestry for the local population, and its repercussions on the conservation of the biotope. This study should address alternatives to current forestry practices hindering the conservation of the species and its habitat.

Priority: medium
Time-scale: medium

4. Public awareness and training

4.1. *To undertake a public awareness campaign aimed at local people*

This campaign should be aimed mainly at those living near areas important for this species, particularly children and young people, using different kinds of publicity material to raise awareness of the importance of the species and its habitat.

There is also the need to target the hunting fraternity to gain their support for the control of illegal hunting.

Priority: high
Time-scale: short, ongoing

4.2. *To promote ongoing dialogue between the different bodies involved in the conservation of the pigeon and its habitat*

The promotion of constant communication between the different bodies responsible for the protection of this species and its habitat is a priority. This would help ensure the efficient use of resources. The formation of a Laurel Pigeon working group is a possible means of achieving this.

Priority: high
Time-scale: short

4.3. *To increase the effectiveness of wardens*

Staff motivation should be emphasised during the selection process for additional wardens and ongoing training should be provided through short courses and job exchanges.

Priority: high
Time-scale: short

Action plan for the White-tailed Laurel Pigeon (*Columba junoniae*)

Reviews

This document should be reviewed by BirdLife International every four years. An emergency review will be undertaken if sudden major environmental changes, liable to affect the population, occur within the species' range.

Geographical scope

The islands of Tenerife, La Palma and La Gomera in the Canary Islands archipelago (Spain).

Summary

The White-tailed Laurel Pigeon *Columba junoniae* is a species endemic to the Canary Islands archipelago, and is found only on the islands of Tenerife, La Palma and La Gomera. It occurs in laurel forest and has an estimated population of about 1200 to 1480 birds (Emmerson, 1985). The species is considered as Globally Threatened (Collar et al. 1994; Tucker and Heath 1994) and is classified as Vulnerable in the Red Data Book of Spanish Vertebrates (Blanco and Gonzalez 1992). It is included in Annex I of the European Union's Wild Birds Directive and its habitat is considered a priority habitat listed in Annex I of the European Union's Habitats Directive (45.61 to 45.63 Macaronesian Laurel Forests).

The enormous reduction in laurel forest cover over the last 500 years (Ceballos and Ortuño, 1976) has resulted in a substantial contraction of the species range. Numbers are, however, believed to have been stable from 1970 to 1990 although sufficient data are not available to confirm this.

Threats and limiting factors

Habitat change – critical

Habitat loss – high

Illegal hunting – high

Lack of drinking water – high

Changes in agriculture – medium

Newcastle disease – unknown

Trapping – low

Predation – unknown

Conservation priorities

Avoid further damage to laurel forest by commercial forestry – essential

Control illegal hunting – essential

Carry out a full census and initiate a monitoring programme – essential/high

Investigate factors affecting breeding performance – essential

Ensure the adequate legal protection of the species – high

Implement a programme of alternatives to commercial forestry – high

Promote restoration and expansion of laurel forest – high

Purchase important sites – high

Establish new hunting reserves – high

Undertake a public awareness campaign – high

Promote dialogue between different bodies – high

Training of wardens – high

Introduction

The White-tailed Laurel Pigeon *Columba junoniae* is endemic to the Canary Islands and is classified as Vulnerable at global and European level (Collar et al., 1994; Tucker and Heath, 1994) and is classified as Rare by IUCN (Groombridge, 1993). It is also listed in Annex I of the European Union's Wild Birds Directive and in Appendix II of the Bern Convention. Its main habitat, laurel forest is a priority habitat listed in Annex I of the European Union's Habitats Directive (45.61 to 45.63 Macaronesian Laurel Forests). This species also feeds in pinewoods which are also listed in Annex I of the Directive (42.9 Macaronesian Pine Forests (endemic)).

This action plan includes the conclusions of a workshop held in 1993 in La Laguna (Tenerife) which was attended by organisations involved in the conservation of the pigeon and its habitat; the situation of the other four threatened Canary Island species was also discussed. This plan covers the actions that should be carried out to maintain and boost population of the White-tailed Laurel Pigeon.

Background information

Distribution and population

This species is found on the islands of Tenerife, La Palma and La Gomera, with an estimated population of 1200 to 1480 birds (based on minimum estimates made by Emmerson, 1985). A new population estimate is needed. Details of the population on each island are as follows:

La Palma: has the largest population with around 1000 to 1200 individuals. The species is mainly found in the north-east of the island, being quite abundant in areas such as El Canal and Los Tilos as well as in Barranco de la Herradura.

Tenerife: 80 to 120 birds with the highest densities occurring in Monte del Agua (Los Silos), and Laderas de Tigaiga.

La Gomera: 120 to 160 birds mainly in the north of Garajonay National Park and surrounding areas.

Life history

Breeding

Nests are constructed on the ground, on small ledges or crevices, or beneath trunks or stones, always within the cover of laurel forest. The nest is built mainly of branches, twigs and ferns. The breeding season extends at least from March to September although it is quite possible that nesting actually occurs throughout the year (A. Martín and E. Hernández, pers. comm., 1994). The clutch consists of just one egg and the incubation period lasts from 18 to 20 days (Emmerson, 1985). The chick leaves the nest at 22 to 24 days old but at first remains nearby. This is a critical time for chicks as they are exposed to predators (rats, Sparrowhawks,

Accipiter nisus). Juveniles remain in the company of the adults for the first few weeks (Emmerson, 1985).

Feeding

Despite the fact that no thorough studies of its diet have been carried out, the White-tailed Laurel Pigeon is thought to be a fruit-eater feeding on *Ocotea foetens*, *Laurus azorica*, *Persea indica*, *Apollonias barbujana*, *Rhamnus glandulosa* and cultivated species such as apricots, cherries, etc. (Emmerson, 1985). In farming areas it supplements its diet with some cereals (wheat, flax, barley) and some flowers (Meade-Waldo, 1889; Koenig, 1890). Birds have also been observed eating pine seeds in pinewoods (Emmerson, 1985).

The fruit of *Ocotea foetens* is important in the White-tailed Laurel Pigeon's diet (particularly on La Palma where these trees are more abundant) as it is available almost all year round. On La Gomera, the White-tailed Laurel Pigeon is restricted to laurel forest as there are no mixed pinewoods. The modified areas within the forest contain cultivated fruit trees that the pigeons occasionally use.

Habitat requirements

The species occurs in areas with steep slopes, large escarpments and deep canyons, where it prefers mature laurel forest (Emmerson, 1985), but also occurs in degraded laurel forest, scrubbier areas with *Myrica faya* and tree heath *Erica arborea* (generally along the lower edges of major stands of laurel forest), in Canary pine woods *Pinus canariensis*, mixed pine stands (generally found along the upper edges of laurel forest) and cultivated areas.

Threats and limiting factors

Habitat loss

With the arrival of the Spanish in the fifteenth century, laurel forest was subjected to intensive exploitation. Extensive areas of forest were razed to create farmland and large oak trees were felled for timber and fuel, greatly reducing the area of original forest.

These activities have decreased considerably but even today laurel forest, especially on La Palma, is still exploited and its conservation is therefore cause of concern.

Importance: high

Habitat change

Apart from the enormous decrease in its extent, laurel forests have also been profoundly changed and fragmented due to the increased demand for wooden poles and tool handles for the cultivation of recently introduced crops (tomatoes, bananas and vines).

This wood is obtained by coppicing laurel trees so that a large number of shoots sprout from the remaining stump. This results in a thick layer of vegetation mainly consisting of "fayas" and heath that over time becomes extensive (Emmerson, 1985). This is carried out along horizontal or vertical strips, depending on the slope, and results in the partitioning of the woods into plots with vegetation at different stages of growth. The best preserved areas of laurel forest are now restricted to inaccessible areas.

Importance: critical

Changes in agriculture

Recent years have seen a change in agriculture, most evident on La Gomera where fruit farming has decreased. Availability of this food source has thus declined.

Importance: medium

Illegal hunting

Hunting is almost certainly one of the factors that most affects the White-tailed Laurel Pigeon today. Since the total ban on hunting under Royal Decree 3181/80, the number of hunters has decreased considerably but those who persist cause significant damage to the population. The birds are hunted from hides placed at drinking sites.

Importance: high

Traps and snares

Traps and snares are known to have been placed at drinking and feeding places.

Importance: low

Lack of drinking water

Due to massive demand for water in the Canary Islands, all natural water sources in the forests have been artificially channelled at source. This has meant that there are now only a few open drinking places used by pigeons and other animals. These sites are well known to illegal hunters.

Importance: high

Newcastle disease

This virus, increasingly common in domestic pigeons, is transmitted through air as well as in the eggs and meat of infected birds, resulting in a high mortality rate. Danger comes from the introduction of infected birds, eggs and poultry products or from existing sources of infection on the islands.

Importance: unknown

Predation

Although it is thought that predation by rats could be a limiting factor on the species, no specific study has been done of the impact on eggs and chicks. However, in other studies carried out on the biology and ecology of this species (A. Martín and E. Hernández, pers. comm., 1994), it has been shown that rats do eat eggs and young.

In a study of the feeding habits of Sparrowhawk on Tenerife, remains of a single White-tailed Laurel Pigeon were found among 565 prey items identified (Delgado et al., 1988).

Predation by feral dogs and cats might occur but it is thought that the impact must be minimal (K. W. Emmerson, pers. comm., 1994).

Importance: unknown

Conservation status and recent conservation measures

Nationally, the species is classed as Vulnerable in the *Red Data Book of Spanish Vertebrates* (Blanco and González, 1992) and regionally it is considered to be Endangered on Tenerife, Vulnerable on La Gomera and Rare on La Palma according to the *Red Data Book of Canary Island*

Terrestrial Vertebrates (Martín et al., 1990). Legally, it is classed as being of Special Interest in Royal Decree 439/90 on which the National Endangered Species List is based.

Recent conservation measures are listed below in chronological order:

1970: hunting this species on Tenerife was banned under the General Close Order Season (1970 only);

1980: Royal Decree 3181/80 banned hunting, capture, trade, collecting of eggs or young, and preparation of and trade in parts, including stuffed specimens, throughout the country;

1981: Garajonay National Park (La Gomera) was established. It is the single most important area in the Canary Islands for the White-tailed Laurel Pigeon;

1984: the estate of El Canal y Los Tiles (Los Sauces, La Palma) was declared a Biosphere Reserve under Unesco's Man and Biosphere programme. This is an important area for this species;

1986: since Spain's accession to the European Union this year, the following areas important for White-tailed Laurel Pigeon have been designated as SPAs: Garajonay (La Gomera); Tigaiga, Teno and Anaga (Tenerife); Monte de los Sauces and Punta Llana, and Pinar de Garafía (La Palma);

1987: The Canary Islands Countryside Law was passed and in accordance with this, the following important White-tailed Laurel Pigeon areas were declared Natural Parks: Laderas de Santa Ursula, Tigaiga and Teno (Tenerife); Barranco de los Hombres and Fagundo, Monte de los Sauces and Punta Llana, Cumbre Vieja and Teneguía, Barranco Quintero, El Río, and La Madera and Dorador (La Palma);

1989: The Countryside and Wildlife Conservation Law 4/89 was passed, establishing a method of cataloguing nationally threatened species (Articles 29-32) and giving conservation priority to endemic species and sub-species (Article 27c);

1993: the Order of 13 July 1993 which establishes the limitations on hunting and open season includes important pigeon areas such as: Barranco de Liria on La Gomera; El Canal and Los Tiles Biosphere Reserve (San Andrés and Sauces) in La Palma; Laderas de Tigaiga (Los Realejos) and Monte del Agua (Los Silos) on Tenerife;

1994: European Union funding under LIFE regulation was approved for a project for the conservation of both species of Laurel Pigeon submitted by the Vice-Council for the Environment of the Canary Islands regional government.

The new Canary Islands Countryside Law was also approved.

Aims and objectives

Aims

In the short term, to conserve the White-tailed Laurel Pigeon population at no less than its 1985 level and in the medium to long term, to promote the expansion of its range.

Objectives

1. **Policy and legislation**

1.1. *To ensure that the White-tailed Laurel Pigeon is given adequate legal protection*

1.1.1. Ensure that the new Canary Islands Countryside Law adequately protects this species and its habitat

The Canary Islands Countryside Law, passed in 1994, does not designate any new protected areas but reclassifies existing ones into new protection categories. In addition to seeking to achieve the designation of all areas important for the species, planning instruments for such protected areas – use and management plans, master plans (*planes directores*), conservation regulations and special plans – should aim to address all threats.

Priority: high
Time-scale: short

1.1.2. Ensure that the new Canary Islands wildlife protection law adequately protects this species

The draft of the new wildlife law is at the consultation stage and includes the Regional Checklist of Threatened Species and the new status of Biological Refuge as a precautionary measure. This legislation should address the protection of the species, in the wider countryside as well as in protected areas, as required under Law 4/1989 on the Conservation of the Countryside, Wildlife and Plants.

Priority: high
Time-scale: short

1.2. *To ensure, through countryside-planning plans, that exploitation of the countryside is compatible with the conservation of this species and its habitat*

1.2.1. Avoid damage to laurel forest by commercial forestry

In the short term, commercial forestry (felling or planting) in mature laurel forest should be discouraged and guided towards suitable alternative areas. Regeneration should be given priority over commercial forestry in areas of degraded laurel forest with the aim of eliminating commercial forestry in laurel forest areas in the medium term.

Priority: essential
Time-scale: short

1.2.2. Implement a programme of alternatives to present commercial forestry practices

Alternatives to commercial forestry are needed such as the promotion of substitute materials for poles and tool handles (poles have already been manufactured using galvanised tubing) to meet farmers' needs. Consideration could also be given to replanting areas adjacent to laurel forest so that they can subsequently be used for commercial forestry.

Priority: high
Time-scale: short

1.3. *To establish new hunting reserves*

Consideration should be given to establishing new Hunting Reserves in areas such as El Rejo (La Gomera), Barranco del Agua and Barranco de la Herradura (La Palma), and Barranco de Cochinos and Cuevas Negras (Tenerife). Other human activity likely to have a negative impact on

the species and its habitat should be modified or diverted away from these areas.

Priority: high
Time-scale: medium

1.4. *To increase health controls on birds imported to the Canary Islands*

These measures must be applied to all live birds being imported, whether for exhibition or for consumption, in order to prevent the spread of Newcastle disease. It is also important that controls are carried out on bird rearing facilities to detect the presence of this virus.

Priority: low
Time-scale: short

2. Species and habitat protection

2.1. *To control illegal hunting*

Hunting continues to be an important threat to the White-tailed Laurel Pigeon. The number of wardens needs to be increased so that surveillance can be stepped up, especially in hunting reserves set up under the Annual Close Season Order. The support of SEPRONA (Civil Guard Wildlife Service) could be sought and they could be supplied with information on the places most frequented by hunters. It is important that sanctions imposed under current law (700 000 pesetas) be applied when charges are brought (Order 14/1988 on the Updating of Values of Game and Protected Species).

Priority: essential
Time-scale: immediate

2.3. *To promote the restoration and expansion of laurel forest*

The main introduced-tree species in laurel forests in the Canary Islands are: chestnut *Castanea sativa*, eucalyptus *Eucalyptus globulus* and Monterey pine *Pinus radiata*. The latter is a fast-growing Californian species with little resistance to fire which was used to replant large deforested areas of Tenerife in the 1940s. The eradication of this species would allow about 10% of the laurel forest on this island to recover.

The Vice-Council for the Environment of the Canary Islands regional government recently began implementing the annual forestry plan which includes the felling of 2000 ha. of Monterey pine on Tenerife and replanting with native species. Plans that include felling and replanting with other species would benefit from prior analysis to select forestry practices which would most benefit the environment. Laurel forest regeneration is slow, therefore extensive reafforestation with native species might be needed in suitable areas.

Priority: high
Time-scale: ongoing

2.3.   To purchase important sites

The purchase of some of the important areas for this species currently in private ownership, both within and outside designated areas, would make it possible to carry out the optimum management for this species and its habitat.

Priority: high
Time-scale: medium

2.4.   To provide additional artificial drinking points for the pigeons

This should be done mainly to reduce the number of pigeons gathering at existing natural drinking areas so that they are not such easy prey for hunters. Drinking stations would also make it easier for the birds to find water.

Priority: medium
Time-scale: medium

2.5.   To initiate a captive breeding programme

This is not a priority. It would be useful to establish contacts with recognised and prestigious zoological collections that would be interested in breeding this species should the need arise. This information can be obtained from the IUCN Captive Breeding Specialists Group which brings together the main experts and zoological collections.

Priority: low
Time-scale: long

3.   Research and monitoring

3.1.   To carry out a full census of the species

Existing information comes mainly from work carried out by K. W. Emmerson between 1983 and 1985, and new data on the different breeding groups are now needed. A recent inventory of breeding areas would allow better targeting of conservation action.

Priority: essential
Time-scale: short

3.2.   To improve monitoring methods

The Madeira Laurel Pigeon C. trocaz is monitored every three months through fixed transects in several biotopes where the species is found (Oliveira and Jones, in press). Using this and other studies as a basis, a similar methodology suited to the particular requirements of the Canary Island White-tailed Laurel Pigeon should be designed. Exchange of information between Laurel Pigeon researchers in Madeira and the Canary Islands is highly recommended.

Priority: high
Time-scale: short

3.3.   To monitor the population regularly

An overall census should be carried out every four years with annual estimates in areas of high density in order to detect population fluctuations and trends.

Priority: high
Time-scale: short

3.4.   To study breeding success and the factors affecting it

A study must be carried out urgently on the factors affecting breeding success especially predation (rats, cats) and food availability. The results will make informed decisions possible on whether it is necessary to start measures to control predators, particularly rats.

Priority: essential
Time-scale: immediate, ongoing

3.5. *To undertake a socio-economic study of commercial forestry*

The main aim of this study would be to evaluate the economic importance of commercial forestry for the local population, and its repercussions on the conservation of the biotope. This study should address alternatives to current practices hindering the conservation of the species and its habitat.

Priority: medium
Time-scale: medium

4.   Public awareness and training

4.1. *To undertake a public awareness campaign aimed at local people*

This should be aimed at those living near areas important for this species, particularly children and young people, using different types of publicity material to raise awareness of the importance of the species and its habitat. There is also a need to target the hunting fraternity to gain their support for the control of illegal hunting.

Priority: high
Time-scale: short, ongoing

4.2. *To promote ongoing dialogue between the different bodies involved in the conservation of the pigeon and its habitat*

The promotion of constant communication between the different bodies responsible for the protection of this species and its habitat is a priority. This would help ensure the efficient use of resources. The formation of a Laurel Pigeon working group is a possible means of achieving this.

Priority: high
Time-scale: short

4.3. *To increase the effectiveness of wardens*

Staff motivation should be emphasised during the selection process for additional wardens and ongoing training should be provided through short course and job exchanges.

Priority: high
Time-scale: short

Action plan for the Aquatic Warbler (*Acrocephalus paludicola*) in Europe

Reviews

This action plan should be reviewed and updated by BirdLife International every four years. An emergency review will be undertaken if sudden major environmental changes, liable to affect the population, occur within the species' range.

Geographical scope

The action plan needs implementation in Belarus, Belgium, France, Germany, Hungary, Latvia, Lithuania, Netherlands, Poland, Russian Federation (European part), Ukraine and United Kingdom.

Summary

The Aquatic Warbler *Acrocephalus paludicola* is a globally threatened species which breeds in Belarus, Germany, Hungary, Latvia, Lithuania, Poland, Russian Federation and Ukraine. The European population is provisionally estimated at 5 600 to 10 700 singing males, with major populations in Belarus, Poland, Hungary and Russia. On migration it has been recorded in 13 European countries, mainly in the west and south-west of the continent. It winters in West Africa, south of the Sahara, but little more is known about the species during winter. There is also a lack of knowledge about its habitat requirements during migration.

Threats and limiting factors

Habitat loss including drainage – critical

Breeding habitat changes due to abandonment – high

Breeding habitat changes due to uncontrolled burning – high

Disturbance – low and localised

Loss of habitat in the winter quarters – unknown

Habitat change at migration sites – unknown

Eutrophication – unknown

Conservation priorities

Promote national and international policies and legislation which favour the conservation of the Aquatic Warbler and its habitat – high

Promote adequate protection of the breeding sites – high

Habitat management at breeding sites – high

Promote the protection of the species and its habitat in its winter quarters and along the migration route – high

Habitat restoration – high

Develop and implement a monitoring programme – high

Continue ongoing research into the species and its habitat – high

Develop a strong network for Aquatic Warbler conservation – high

Use the Aquatic Warbler as a flagship species – high

Prepare educational materials to increase public awareness – high

Introduction

The Aquatic Warbler is a marshland specialist which has suffered a very severe decline in western Europe due to habitat loss. It is classified as Vulnerable at a global level (Collar et al., 1994) and is listed as Insufficiently Known in the *IUCN Red List of Threatened Animals* (Groombridge, 1993). At European level it is classified as Endangered (Tucker and Heath, 1994). It is also included in Annex I of the European Union's Wild Birds Directive, in Appendix II of the Bern Convention and in Appendix II of the Bonn Convention.

On 13 and 14 March 1993 a workshop took place at Ruda Milicka (Poland) to discuss the situation of the Aquatic Warbler in Europe and agree upon a conservation strategy for the future. The workshop was organised by OTOP, the BirdLife Partner in Poland, in co-operation with the University of Wroclaw. It was attended by experts from Germany, Hungary, Poland, Spain, Ukraine and United Kingdom. This action plan is based largely on the discussions held during the workshop, and also on the comments received from other experts at a later stage.

Given the European scope of the project, the action plan highlights the actions necessary to protect the Aquatic Warbler on its breeding grounds in Europe. However, those countries with more than 100 records of birds on migration during the period 1879 to 1987 (de By, 1990) have also been included within the geographic scope of the plan. It is expected that, as more information becomes available, future versions of the action plan will be extended to cover the whole of the species' flyway.

This action plan identifies some important areas of imbalance in our knowledge of this species, one of which is the great difference in current understanding of the species' biological requirements in the breeding areas as compared with the wintering grounds. Some very good research has been carried out on reproduction and mating systems, but almost nothing is known about the species during winter. Dramatic habitat changes in the Sahelian wetlands could be a very important limiting factor, but the extent to which this is affecting the population dynamics remains unknown.

Differences in knowledge also occur from west to east across the breeding range. While occurrence and numbers are quite well known in Germany, Poland, Hungary and, to a lesser extent, the Baltic states, we know almost nothing about these same aspects in Belarus, Ukraine or Russia. This action plan is also intended to stimulate basic surveys in these countries, which can then form the basis for a thorough conservation strategy for the species in the near future.

Background information

Distribution and population

The breeding range is restricted to the western Palaearctic between 50° and 60°N, although the eastern and southern limits are not well known. Breeding occurs in Germany, Poland, Hungary, Latvia, Lithuania, Ukraine, Belarus, Russia and possibly Bulgaria (D. Nankinov, pers. comm., to A. Dyrcz and L. Tomialojc), and population figures are given in Table 21.1.

Table 21.1

Population of the Aquatic Warbler in Europe. Figures for Germany, Hungary and Poland are from actual surveys; the remaining figures are estimates and are shown in parentheses

Country	No. of singing males
Belarus	(1 500–5 000)
Germany	40–50
Hungary	400–425
Latvia	(10–50)
Lithuania	(50–200)
Poland	3 500–4 500[2]
Russian Federation	(100–500)
Ukraine	(1–10)
Total	5 600–10 700

1. Surveys during 1995 indicate that the breeding population in Belarus could be over 5 000 males and may be as high as 20 000 males. Further surveys are planned in 1996 (M. Flade, pers. comm).

2. A. Dyrcz and L. Tomialojc, pers. comm.

The breeding distribution is fragmented because of habitat constraints. The species became extinct in western Europe during the twentieth century and has declined dramatically in central Europe. It formerly bred in France, Belgium, Netherlands, former West Germany, former Czechoslovakia, the former Yugoslavia, Austria and Italy (Cramp, 1992).

Aquatic Warblers have been recorded on migration in 13 European countries. Birds from Poland and eastern Germany migrate on a westerly heading along the Baltic coast in Poland and eastern Germany, then along the North Sea coast of western Germany, Netherlands, Belgium and sometimes England, thereafter heading south along the French and Iberian Atlantic coast (Schulze-Hagen, 1993).

The winter quarters lie in West Africa, south of the Sahara, and include wetlands and floodplains of Mauritania, Mali, Ghana and Senegal, but little more is known about the species during winter.

Life history

Breeding

The mating system combines polygyny and promiscuity, and territories are exceptionally large compared with other similar species. At 15 to 16 days, the nestling period is the longest of all European *Acrocephalus*. Nesting success is very high, up to 83%, and losses caused by predators affect around 10.7% of nests. The main predators are harriers *Circus*, and probably small mammals such as rodents and carnivores (weasel, stoat *Mustela*) (Dyrcz, 1993; Dyrcz and Zduneck, 1993). In some places, such as the Biebrza marshes (Poland), there are large, local annual variations in nesting density, which may be related to changes in habitat structure and arthropod density rather than to losses in the winter quarters. In the Biebrza marshes, the best conditions for breeding are created one to three years after the controlled burning of a sedge area (M. Flade, *in litt.*, 1994).

Feeding

Their diet comprises large insects, especially dragonflies (Odonata) and caterpillars (*Lepidoptera*), and spiders. Compared with other *Acrocephalus* species, the nestlings are fed with relatively large insects. A rich supply of arthropods in the vegetation seems to be a prerequisite for the Aquatic Warbler (Dyrcz and Czeraszkiewicz, 1992).

Habitat requirements

The Aquatic Warbler is a habitat specialist. During the breeding season it occurs mainly in continental lowland marshes with a water depth of from 1cm to 10 cm. In primeval landscapes it depends on relatively short-lasting plant succession stages, especially in non-flooded areas. It has been recorded in:

1. Fen mires in river valleys, comprising open sedge moorland with medium and large tuft-forming and scattered *Carex* (Biebrza and lower Odra river marshes in Poland) with taller *Molinia caerulea* which serves as a singing post for the male;

2. Calcareous marshes with Cladium mariscus (Chelm);

3. Seasonally flooded, brackish marshes characterised by very weak and low reed stands 80 to 120 cm high in summer (in Germany and at the Swina river mouth in Poland);

4. Wet boggy grasslands covered by high grass and clumps of sedge (in Hungary and in the Narew valley in Poland);

5. Wet hay meadows of *Alopecurus pratensis* and *Phalaris* cut once or twice a year, with sedge patches mainly of *Carex gracilis* and *C. nigra* (Narew valley and lower Odra floodplains in Germany).

During migration, Aquatic Warblers strongly favour low stands of sedges and reeds near open water, normally along rivers, estuaries and coastal lagoons (de By, 1990). The habitat in winter is thought to resemble strongly that of the breeding grounds, including *Salicornia* associations, large inundated grasslands and reedbeds, etc. (Schulze-Hagen, 1993).

Threats and limiting factors

Loss of breeding habitat

This is usually related to drainage, unfavourable water management (e.g. water extraction) and canalisation of rivers. Currently there are problems at some Polish sites with drainage affecting small areas at Chelm, Biebrza and Narew valley, and larger proportion of Kramsk (Konin) and Mazuria.

Importance: critical

Breeding habitat changes related to plant succession

This is an important factor in Poland (Biebrza and to some extent on the Odra river), where, if a stop is put to the grazing of cattle and horses or to the cutting of vegetation at intervals of no more than two to three years, natural succession will take place and the habitat may become unsuitable. In the past, reeds used to be occasionally harvested with scythes in the Biebrza marshes for use on floors and for thatching, etc., together with the more important harvesting of sedges as poor quality hay and the active elimination of bushes. These traditions have now stopped. Also in the past there was a special breed of small reddish cows which ate *Carex* and was adapted to this ecosystem.

Importance: high

Habitat change and loss at migration sites

The extent of this problem and its impact on the population are unknown but could be affecting the population.

Importance: unknown

Habitat changes in wintering areas

Drought and habitat alteration in the winter quarters could be true bottlenecks for the Aquatic Warbler. The main threats which have been identified are: drying up due to periods of drought; drainage projects to enable irrigation and farming; increasing human population; over-grazing of grasslands by cattle; succession of grass associations into scrub; increasing desertification as well as salinisation of irrigated soils.

Importance: unknown

Disturbances caused by man

In Biebrza, birdwatchers tend to leave the paths and locally trample around the nesting habitat. This is also a potential problem in smaller places such as Chelm. There have also been some attempts at egg-collecting but these have general-ly been prevented. Disturbance from mowing is a problem in Hungary and also in some sites of the Odra and Narew rivers in Poland and Germany.

Importance: low and localised

Eutrophication

Mineralisation due to the lowered water levels leads to minerals being washed downstream to flooded Aquatic Warbler areas, thus speeding up the rate of vegetation succession. This could be an important factor.

Importance: unknown

Uncontrolled burning

Often used as a management tool in pastoral agriculture. In Biebrza, there was a 3 000-ha fire which caused a great deal of soil mineralisation, but uncontrolled burning is more often a direct threat, especially (to birds and nests) in the breeding season.

Importance: high

Conservation status and recent conservation measures

Belarus

The precise status and distribution were not well known but several sites were surveyed in 1995 and further survey work is planned for 1996 (M. Flade, pers. comm.). The population is recorded as stable or declining. Drainage of vast areas of marshes and wetlands has substantially reduced the amount of habitat available.

A survey in 1995 of the primaeval Dekoe bog suggests a population of 1 500 – 3 000 males in 5 000 ha which are currently unprotected (M. Flade, *in litt.*). Three State Reserves have been established: the Berezinsky Biosphere Reserve, the Pripyat Biological and Landscape Reserve and Belovezhskaya Pushcha State National Park (Vyazovich, 1993).

France

Large reedbeds on the coast (Channel, Atlantic and Mediterranean) or inland are regularly used during migration. The species is more numerous during the autumn passage than in spring. The number of birds ringed has remained fairly stable despite an increase in the ringing effort (Euring Acro Project). The number varies between 110 to 200 individuals caught each year.

Germany

The Aquatic Warbler is classed as Endangered in the German Red Data Book and is legally protected. The population is the westernmost and smallest of all the European countries. In 1992 there were only two isolated sites, both in the north-east corner of Germany close to the Polish border: near Greifswald and in the polders of the Odra river near Schwedt and

Friedrichsthal. The two sites are separated by about 100 km and numbers have been stable in recent years. Both populations are considered to be satellites of the nearby Polish breeding area, and to be unviable without it. One of the sites is within the Lower Odra Valley National Park and the other within the Freesendorfer Wiesen Nature Reserve. There are also small and fluctuating numbers of outlying pairs which are not protected (Schulze-Hagen and Wawrzyniak, 1993).

Hungary

The species is strictly protected under the Hungarian law for the conservation of nature and is listed as Endangered in the Hungarian Red Data Book. The only breeding population is in the Hortobágy National Park, where it is increasing slightly (Kovács, 1991). A monitoring scheme has been in effect for 15 years, longer than in any other country. There may be further small populations still to be discovered in Hortobágy.

Latvia

The species is listed as Rare in the Latvian Red Data Book, having been recorded as a breeder at four coastal wetland sites: Lake Pape and adjoining marshland, Lake Liepaja, Bog Sarnate/Uzava and Lake Kanieris (Viksne, 1994). Lake Pape is a shallow lake separated from the sea by a spit of dunes; due to the absence of cattle grazing since the 1960s, meadow areas surrounding the lake have decreased significantly; in the recent past there was cattle grazing and reed cutting, which influenced the succession of vegetation, but this is being abandoned now (EUCC, 1993).

Lithuania

The Red Data Book classifies the species as Insufficiently Known (Paltanavicius, 1992). There are two known breeding localities, the Nemunas delta and Zuvintas Nature Reserve. The Nemunas delta comprises an area of 20 000 ha on the eastern side of the Curonian lagoon, including rivers, lakes, wet woodlands, fishponds, marshes, reedbeds, meadows and shallow waters. Part of the area has been protected as a Nature Reserve (EUCC, 1993). Cutting of vegetation in

the breeding season has been identified as a problem for Aquatic Warblers (P. Mierauskas, verbally, 1993). In Zuvintas Nature Reserve sedge, meadows are no longer cut for hay, thus reducing the amount of suitable habitat (Pranaitis, 1993).

Poland

The Aquatic Warbler is protected under the Nature Conservation Law of 1991 and is listed in the Polish Red Data Book as Endangered (Glowacinski, 1992). There are three main populations:

1. Biebrza is the most important breeding area, with an estimated 3 000 to 3 500 singing males (A. Dyrcz and L. Tomialojc, pers. comm.). A National Park has been established recently. A research project on the Aquatic Warbler led by A. Dyrcz of Wroclaw University has been going on for several years;

2. Chelm is part of the Lublin marshes, and the Aquatic Warbler is present in four neighbouring blocks, totalling 15 km². The total estimate is from 200 to 400 singing males (A. Dyrcz and L. Tomialojc, pers. comm.) and the highest density is from 4 to 6 males/ha; there could be further birds breeding in neighbouring areas. A management plan has been produced by OTOP. Two specific management actions have been carried out: the cutting of scrub to create more open habitat and promote colonisation by the Aquatic Warbler (by OTOP); and the cutting of trees to clear the habitat (by the Lublin Forest Authority);

3. At the Odra estuary the number of recorded singing males is 383 but the estimated total is c.400 (A. Dyrcz and L. Tomialojc, pers. comm.). There may be more populations still unknown. There are 10 sub-sites holding Aquatic Warblers which are at present unprotected. Nearby is Wolinski National Park which could be extended to cover two islands of the Swina mouth. There is also a proposal to declare a Landscape Park in the Inter Odra region, the first step for a future National Park to the south of Szczecin. OTOP has established a private reserve on the island of Karsiborska Kepa.

In the north-east lake district (Mazury) there is a further known breeding site with 10 singing males, but there might be a more important population yet to be discovered.

Russian Federation

The Aquatic Warbler is not included in the Red Data Book of 1985 but it is proposed for inclusion, as Vulnerable, in the new edition. The species is rare and of erratic occurrence in the European part of Russia, except in the Kaliningrad region where there is a stable population (A. L. Mischenko, verbally, 1994). In a preliminary inventory of Important Bird Areas it is recorded only in the floodplains of the upper Mologa and Osen' rivers (Tver region) which is a partly unprotected Nature Monument.

Ukraine

It will be included in the new edition of the Red Data Book which is now being prepared. An estimated 10 to 15 pairs breed along the Desna river (Sumy and Chernigov regions) and a population could exist in the Pripyat marshes near the border with Belarus (I. Gorban, verbally, 1993). There is very little information about the species in eastern Ukraine.

United Kingdom

Not included in the UK Red Data Book (Batten et al., 1990). Southern Britain lies within the migration route, and the species is recorded almost exclusively in autumn, chiefly in southern England. Numbers were apparently maintained to at least 1985, despite the population decline (Cramp, 1992). A national action plan is already in preparation by RSPB and English Nature.

Aims and objectives

Aims

In the short term, to maintain the current population of the Aquatic Warbler throughout its range. In the medium to long term, to promote the expansion of the breeding population to other suitable areas.

Objectives

1. Policy and legislation

1.1. *To promote national and international broad policies and legislation which favour the conservation of the Aquatic Warbler and its habitat*

1.1.1. Seek national or international policy incentives to maintain traditional farming practices at breeding sites

It is assumed that traditional farming practices such as hand-scything, grazing with particular low-intensive breeds of cow, and late mowing, which have characterised important Aquatic Warbler breeding sites, are required to maintain the habitat in a condition suitable for the birds. However, in many areas within the species' range these practices are rapidly disappearing as uneconomic. Without intervention, agriculture in many sites may have completely ceased within 5 to 6 years. It is therefore essential to seek policies that enable people to maintain these traditional methods of farming while still enjoying a reasonable standard of living. National or supra-regional agricultural land-use policies that increase incentives for damaging management of Aquatic Warbler habitat should be opposed or modified.

The concept of Environmentally Sensitive Areas, currently being applied in the European Union, promotes environmentally friendly farming. Consideration should be given to developing a similar scheme for eastern Europe with international funding.

Priority: high
Time-scale: medium

1.1.2. Promote the full protection of the Aquatic Warbler and its habitats through national and international legislation

Given its status as a globally threatened species, action should be taken to ensure that the Aquatic Warbler receives the fullest possible legislative protection in all range states. These countries should be encouraged to adopt a listing process for all the threatened species and produce recovery plans or action plans for those that are threatened.

Steps should also be taken to ensure that in all range states effective national legislation is in place to protect Aquatic Warbler breeding habitat, including the prevention of potentially damaging drainage, for example, local water supply, mineral extraction, industry, etc.

Environmental impact assessment regulations should be promoted. It is recommended that the use of insecticides in water catchments should be regulated and limited. Range states should be encouraged to prepare national wetland action plans for the sustainable use of all wetland resources in their territory. Legislation that provides for management agreements with landowners/managers who manage their land for the species' benefit should be encouraged and promoted.

Priority: high
Time-scale: medium

2.   Species and habitation protection

2.1.   *To promote adequate protection of the breeding sites and remove key factors adversely affecting the breeding habitat*

2.1.1. Seek designation as protected areas of all sites regularly holding breeding Aquatic Warblers

Protection of Aquatic Warbler sites including appropriate management should be encouraged. When designating protected areas, the protection of buffer zones around core Aquatic Warbler sites should be considered.

Management plans for the protected areas should be produced, taking into account the species' habitat requirements. These areas should be provided with sufficient human resources and equipment for their adequate management.

The renting or acquisition of important sites should be considered, and these reserves should be managed appropriately in terms of habitat and visitors.

Priority: high
Time-scale: ongoing

2.1.2. Prevent habitat alteration, pollution and other factors that could be detrimental to the Aquatic Warbler in its breeding sites

The enforcement of legal protection at sites already designated as national or international protected areas must be ensured. Where legal designation of an important site has not been completed, damaging developments should be opposed as far as possible.

Drainage, water extraction and other kinds of detrimental water management should be avoided. Burning should also be controlled and turf fires prevented. Waste disposal at breeding sites must not be authorised and alternative sites should be suggested.

Priority: high
Time-scale: ongoing

2.2.   *To manage the breeding habitat to increase numbers, productivity and distribution*

2.2.1. Prevent natural succession of the vegetation by undertaking management in specially selected plots

To maintain their suitability for Aquatic Warblers, several thousand hectares of breeding habitat require active management, especially in unflooded plots. Within five to six years, agriculture at many sites may have ceased completely. Traditional farming practices at breeding sites should be maintained and promoted.

Priority: high
Time-scale: ongoing

2.2.2. Hand-scything and mowing

Due to access problems, the only practicable means of keeping the vegetation down in many plots is hand-scything. In the past, vegetation was scythed every year, though the effects of this practice on the Aquatic Warbler are still poorly understood. A 7- to 10-year rotation of scything on small blocks of 50 ha should be enough to maintain suitable nesting habitat, cutting every year in different plots, though this prescription needs to be tested experimentally. Hand-scything should be done in early autumn, when the water level is low.

Management could also be done with small mowing engines or by low-density cattle grazing. Hay meadows should not be mowed before the end of June. Sedge cutting in July should continue, removing the sedge after mowing. Growth of bushes should be prevented.

Priority: medium/high
Time-scale: ongoing

2.2.3. Grazing

The effect of grazing on Aquatic Warbler habitat is not as important as mowing/scything. The general agricultural trend is to abandon grazing, which is maintained only on flooded meadows immediately adjacent to rivers. In some areas, there are breeds of small red marsh cows specially adapted to this environment, and these should be bred for conservation management purposes.

Populations of native wild ungulates (elk *Alces alces*, roe deer *Capreolus capreolus*) should be conserved and encouraged in order to keep down bush growth, but overgrazing should be avoided in all cases.

Priority: medium/high
Time-scale: ongoing

2.2.4. Controlled burning

Fire can be a very effective management tool though its effects are still poorly understood. While considered to be beneficial, further investigation is needed on the effects on invertebrates and the ecosystem in general. In newly grown areas, arthropod density drops by five to seven times after burning in early spring, compared to adjacent unburnt areas.

In some areas rotational burning takes place every four to five years but could be done in January and February when the marshes are frozen but there is not much snow.

Uncontrolled fires should be stopped. This means the employment of wardens and local farmers in early spring to control burning. Larger bushes are not controlled by this sort of burning and should be removed by hand.

Priority: medium/high
Time-scale: ongoing

2.2.5. Regulate water levels and restore natural water conditions

This is especially necessary in those places where drainage and canalisation have had a severe impact on the wetlands.

Priority: low/medium
Time-scale: ongoing

2.2.6. Disseminate habitat management recommendations to land managers

Guidelines for the management of breeding habitat should be prepared, and disseminated among managers of protected areas and landowners. Appropriate management should be encouraged.

Priority: high
Time-scale: ongoing

2.3.   To protect the Aquatic Warbler and its habitat in the winter quarters and along the migration route

2.3.1. Promote the protection of wintering and passage sites

All sites in Europe used regularly by birds on passage should be protected. Development proposals that could have a detrimental effect on these sites should be opposed or modified, for example, those that have the potential to damage or destroy habitat, cause pollution, or increase disturbance.

Priority: high
Time-scale: ongoing

2.4.   To restore habitats for the Aquatic Warbler

2.4.1. Undertake the ecological restoration of areas no longer used for agriculture

The extensification of farming practices in some parts of Europe provides the opportunity to create suitable areas for the Aquatic Warbler. This should be pursued especially where nearby breeding populations exist, as a means of promoting range expansion.

Priority: high
Time-scale: ongoing

3. Monitoring and research

3.1. To develop and implement a monitoring programme enabling population trends to be tracked

3.1.1. Design a methodology for counting Aquatic Warblers

The recommended methodology is transects through various habitats, eventually combined with point counts. The best dates are from 15 May to 10 June, when the numbers of singing males are stable, starting one hour before sunset until 45 minutes after. Transects have to be long enough not to be affected by local successional changes; the ideal length is about 3 km (or three hours). In some places with thick vegetation, listening stations could be visited in plots of about 150 ha, a technique less time-consuming than transects.

Some elementary training is required to learn identification features of the Aquatic Warbler, and how to differentiate it from look-alike species such as the Sedge Warbler A. schoenobaenus.

It is essential that monitoring is done regularly at as many sites as possible, for example counts during two consecutive years every five years. Organisers of the surveys should remain constant at particular sites.

Priority: high
Time-scale: ongoing

3.1.2. Undertake national surveys to estimate breeding populations

Such surveys should be co-ordinated internationally over a period of five years from 1994. Surveys in Russia, Latvia, Lithuania, Belarus, Ukraine and Moldova are needed particularly urgently. An effort should be made to identify all breeding localities, using aerial photographs as a guide to potential sites. It is desirable that the same survey techniques be used at every site, and that these be compatible with the monitoring techniques.

Priority: high/essential
Time-scale: medium

3.1.3. Identify major passage sites and wintering areas

Intensive ringing by fully trained and responsible workers should be promoted. The use of a tape recorder during the night at potential migration sites made possible the capture of approximately 300 to 400 birds in Belgium and France from 1989 to 1991. However, use of recordings should be restricted to daytime only. Use of recordings at night could cause birds to stop at inappropriate sites which they would not have used otherwise (this species migrates only at night) distorting the results of ringing projects. It is also possible to catch birds during the breeding season by playing the song of the Sedge Warbler, to which Aquatic Warblers react aggressively.

Priority: medium
Time-scale: ongoing

3.1.4. Research into habitat characteristics at migration and wintering sites

Once sites have been identified, research is needed into the habitat requirements of the species outside the breeding season and any threats these sites may face. This information is needed before actions to protect these sites can be planned if necessary.

Priority: medium
Time-scale: ongoing

3.2. To promote research useful for the conservation of the Aquatic Warbler in the future

3.2.1. Undertake comparative studies of breeding biology in different habitats

The breeding biology is quite well studied at some sites (such as the Hortobágy or Biebrza marshes) but there is not much information from other areas. A comparative study is required to assess variation in breeding density and success between different habitat types and sites.

Priority: medium
Time-scale: medium

3.2.2. Assess the effect of burning, scything, mowing, grazing and water conditions on breeding populations

An international working party should be set up to investigate potential burning techniques in

Biebrza/Chelm, taking into account the danger of turf fires in Biebrza.

Priority: high
Time-scale: short

3.2.3. Develop collaborative research and monitoring programmes between range states

The existing co-operation between Germany and Poland should be extended to the Baltic republics, Belarus, Ukraine, Moldova and Russia. Financial support from Germany for Aquatic Warbler surveys in these countries would be desirable.

Priority: high
Time-scale: short

4. Public awareness

4.1. *To ensure development of a strong network of organisations and individuals committed to the conservation of the Aquatic Warbler*

NGOs play an essential role in the conservation of threatened species and habitats and also contribute to increasing the awareness of the general public. International conservation organisations such as BirdLife International, IUCN, IWRB and WWF should continue to provide technical and financial help for national and local initiatives in Aquatic Warbler countries. They can also play a role in co-ordinating the efforts of volunteer ornithologists.

Priority: high/essential
Time-scale: ongoing

4.2. *To use the Aquatic Warbler as a flagship species*

Being Europe's rarest migratory passerine the Aquatic Warbler should be used as a key species for the inventory and protection of lowland marshes and wet meadows. It should be elected as "bird of the year" in several range states simultaneously, as a means of increasing awareness and for fund raising.

Priority: high
Time-scale: short

4.3. *To prepare educational materials promoting and informing about the Aquatic Warbler*

Information and educational services to the public should be provided in protected areas. These should include leaflets, stickers, T-shirts, etc. A promotional film about the species and the areas where it lives should be made, and the inclusion of Aquatic Warbler sequences in nature films and documentaries promoted.

Priority: high
Time-scale: short

Annex
Recommended conservation actions by countries

Belarus

2.1.1. Investigate the options for protected area designation in the Dekoe bog and any other area that emerges as a key site for the species.

3.1.2. Undertake a national survey as soon as possible.

4.1. Promote a strong bird conservation NGO.

Germany

2.1.1. Prepare and implement habitat management plans in Brandenburg, especially on the lower Odra river, and encourage the authorities of Mecklenburg-Vorpommern to prepare a management plan for Freesendorfer-Wiesen.

2.2.6. Encourage low-density grazing (1–2 cattle per ha) with the native breed of cows at Aquatic Warbler sites after June.

2.4. Promote habitat restoration in Mecklenburg-Vorpommern (especially at potential breeding sites such as Peenetalmoor, Grosser Wotig, Struck and Kooser Wiesen) and Brandenburg, where at least 2 000 ha is suitable for recolonisation. The managers of the Lower Odra National Park should restore habitats for the Aquatic Warbler, in particular because this species could suffer from habitat losses following restoration of alluvial forests.

3.1. Monitor the population.

Hungary

2.2. Maintain the water level in Kunkápolnási mocsár and Nagyret marsh (Hortobágy National Park) by artificial flooding, for example, in case of lack of winter precipitation.

2.2.4. Promote a ban on mowing and burning in areas where they cause disturbance to breeding birds.

3.1. Monitor the population in the Hortobágy National Park.

3.1.2. Survey unprotected areas in search of new breeding populations.

Latvia

2.1.1. Prepare a management plan for Lake Pape and adjoining marshland as soon as possible. Management is necessary to prevent the spread of reedbed monocultures following land abandonment. The area needs adequate water management to ensure the maintenance of its value for Aquatic Warblers.

2.1.2. Prevent urban development, increased human disturbance, and pollution by industrial and urban sewage and agricultural run-off from affecting Lake Liepaja. The protected status of Lake Liepaja, Bog Sarnate and Uzava coast should not be diminished.

Lithuania

2.1.1. Prepare a management plan for Nemunas Delta Regional Park.

2.2.1. Undertake habitat management at Zuvintas Nature Reserve, particularly the mowing of the sedge meadows for hay-making.

3.1.2. Monitor the population regularly.

Poland

Biebrza and Narew marshes:

1.1.2. Encourage the establishment of a buffer zone with low-intensity farming and restricted use of insecticides around the Biebrza National Park.

2.1.1. Purchase grassland areas in the Narew valley which are likely to be sold to private entrepreneurs for intensification (e.g. Kombinat Wízna).

2.1.2. Prevent further illegal drainage in the upper basin of the Biebrza river.

2.2.1. Stop scrub encroachment and seek to restore herds of the native breed of cows characteristic of the area.

2.2.4. Undertake experimental controlled burning during winter in habitats where succession has taken place.

2.2.5. Where possible, raise the water table (especially in the middle basin where drainage has had a severe impact) and restore natural water conditions.

3.1. Evaluate and monitor the Aquatic Warbler population in the area.

3.2. Support continuing research on the species' ecology.

Chelm marshes:

2.1.1. Seek adoption and implementation of OTOP's management plan by the local authorities. Conservation prescriptions of this plan include:

1. Declaration of all the marshes as Nature Reserves.

2. Building of a new well system for the city of Chelm to prevent extraction of ground water.

3. Damming and depth reduction of all main channels draining the marshes.

4. Employment of wardens to protect the marshes against uncontrolled fires and human disturbance.

Odra river:

2.1.1. A network of Nature Reserves needs to be established in order to protect the Aquatic Warbler habitat. The existing Volinski National Park should be extended to include two Aquatic Warbler sites on islands in the Swina estuary. The declaration of a Landscape Park in the southern part of the Swina estuary should be promoted, seeking to include two sites in the buffer zone. In the medium to long term, this area should be declared a National Park as part of the Polish-German Lower Odra National Park.

2.1.2. Evaluate the environmental impact on the Lower Odra National Park of the projected deepening of the Odra river and prevent dumping of waste from the chemical plant in the meadows near Jasienica and pumping of water at Skoszewskie meadows.

2.2.1. Undertake active management to halt the expansion of dense reedbeds at most sites on the Odra river. Low-intensity mowing and grazing of Aquatic Warbler habitat should be encouraged.

Russian Federation

1.1.2. Encourage the state authorities to give legal protection to the Aquatic Warbler.

2.1.1. Promote the protection of those areas holding permanent breeding populations of more than 100 singing males.

3.1.2. Status and distribution of the Aquatic Warbler in Russia have to be precisely determined by a national survey. Schemes such as the Important Bird Areas programme should be promoted as a means of identifying Aquatic Warbler sites.

3.2. Investigate the processes and reasons for population fluctuations and the periodic changes of nesting places.

United Kingdom

1.1.2. Promote the preparation and implementation of a national action plan.

Ukraine

1.1.2. Promote the preparation of a national wetland action plan.

3.1.2. Undertake a national survey to clarify distribution and numbers.

4.1. Promote a strong bird conservation NGO with financial support from international organisations.

Action plan for the Blue Chaffinch (*Fringilla teydea*)

Reviews

This document will be reviewed and updated by BirdLife International every four years. An emergency review will be undertaken if sudden major environmental changes, liable to affect the population, occur within the species' range.

Geographical scope

The islands of Tenerife and Gran Canaria in the Canary Islands archipelago (Spain).

Summary

The Blue Chaffinch *Fringilla teydea* is endemic to the Canary Islands and comprises two sub-species, one found on Tenerife (*F. t. teydea*) and the other on Gran Canaria (*F. t. polatzeki*). Its habitat is Canary pine *Pinus canariensis* woodland which is listed in Annex I of the European Union's Habitats Directive. Although there has not been a census of the Tenerife population, its situation is thought to be stable, while the estimated population on Gran Canaria is from 185 to 260 birds (Moreno, 1991), which means that the latter sub-species is classified as Endangered both nationally and internationally.

Threats and limiting factors

Tenerife Blue Chaffinch:

Illegal trade – unknown

Gran Canaria Blue Chaffinch:

Habitat loss and fragmentation – critical

Forest fires – high

Small population size – medium

Social demand for recreation space in Gran Canaria – medium

Natural predation and predation by feral cats – low

Lack of water – low

Conservation priorities

Include the Blue Chaffinch in CITES – high

Ensure adequate protection under the new Countryside Law and Wildlife Protection Law – high

Complete the National Endangered Species List – high

Eradicate illegal trade – high

Gran Canaria Blue Chaffinch:

Undertake habitat restoration – essential

Prevent forest fires – essential

Continue the current monitoring programme – high/essential

Continue and expand the current research programme – high/essential

Draw up an official action plan – high

Introduction

The Blue Chaffinch is endemic to the Canary Islands and comprises two sub-species *Fringilla teydea teydea* on Tenerife and *F. t. polatzeki* on Gran Canaria. The status of the Tenerife sub-species is good, while the Gran Canaria sub-species presents serious conservation problems.

The species is classified as Rare by IUCN (Groombridge, 1993) and as Conservation Dependent in *Birds to Watch 2* (Collar et al., 1994). At European level the species is classified as Vulnerable (Tucker and Heath, 1994) and it is listed in Annex I of the European Union's Wild Birds Directive and in Appendix II of the Bern Convention. Its habitat is included in Annex I of the European Union's Habitats Directive (42.9 Macaronesian Pine Forest (endemic)).

This action plan incorporates the conclusions of the workshop held in July 1993 in La Laguna (Tenerife) which considered the situation of the Blue Chaffinch and the four other globally threatened Canary Island species. It also includes the measures established in the Gran Canaria

Blue Chaffinch Conservation Programme which is being implemented by the Vice-Council for the Environment of the Canary Islands Government. The action plan is aimed at all those involved in the conservation of the Blue Chaffinch and includes measures needed to maintain and boost the populations of this species. Some of the actions are already being implemented.

Except where otherwise specified, any information or recommendations apply to both sub-species.

Background information

Distribution and population

The Blue Chaffinch is found on Tenerife and Gran Canaria. Until now no full census of the population has been made but the population is estimated to be around 1000 to 1500 pairs (Tucker and Heath, 1994).

It appears that by dispersing and/or being patchily distributed or concentrated in its pine forest habitat, this species has given varying impressions of its abundance to different observers over the last 100 years on Gran Canaria and Tenerife, ranging from Rare to Common (Collar and Stuart, 1985).

Tenerife Blue Chaffinch:

The habitat covers a wooded belt between 1000 and 2000 metres around the whole island. The pinewoods in the north, and those of Vilaflor and Arico in the south, are particularly noteworthy (Martín, 1987).

Although no full census has been carried out, this sub-species is not considered as threatened (Blanco and González, 1992).

Gran Canaria Blue Chaffinch:

This sub-species is restricted to just a few woods. The current population is estimated at 185 to 260 birds (Moreno, 1991) which justifies its status as an Endangered sub-species. It is mainly found in the pinewoods of Ojeda, Inagua and Pajonales with a few pairs thought to inhabit the woods of Tamadaba (Moreno, 1991).

Life history

Taxonomic status

The Blue Chaffinch comprises two sub-species, one found on Tenerife (nominate teydea) and the other on Gran Canaria (sub-species polatzeki). The Gran Canaria birds are up to 10% smaller and have duller plumage (Cramp and Perrins, 1994).

Breeding

Birds on Tenerife pair up in April (Martín, 1979) and breeding lasts until the end of July or the beginning of August. The nest is built by the female, usually located in pine trees or sometimes heath Erica arborea or laurel Laurus azorica (Martín, 1979). Nests are formed from pine needles and branches of broom Chamaecytisus proliferus and lined with moss, feathers, grasses and rabbit hair (Martín, 1979). The clutch generally consists of two eggs; in the case of the Tenerife sub-species, they are laid during the first fortnight in June although in the south they may be laid as early as April (A. Martín, pers. comm.). In Gran Canaria, eggs are laid in the last half of April and the first half of June (Rodríguez and Moreno, 1993). The female incubates for 14 to 16 days (Martín, 1979; Rodríguez and Moreno, 1993). The chicks are blind and covered in down on hatching and are fed by both the male and the female. The chicks remain in the nest from 17 to 18 days (Martín, 1979).

Feeding

Canary pine seeds constitute the main food source. The birds feed both in the trees and on the ground, extracting the seeds from the half-open cones by breaking them open with their thick, powerful bills. They occasionally feed on other types of fruit and also eat a large amount of insects (mainly nocturnal butterflies and some beetles) taken from cracks in pine bark. In the breeding season, the birds eat more insects and larvae than at other times, probably due to the rich source of protein that this provides for the chicks.

Habitat

The area of pinewoods on Gran Canaria has decreased due to various factors, especially past felling of trees and forest fires. They currently cover approximately 10875 ha (Nogales, 1985). Reafforestation has been going on since the 1940s and Blue Chaffinches have colonised areas planted with Canary pine where these fall within the area of the tree's natural distribution (Martín, 1979).

Chaffinches will occasionally feed outside the pinewoods during severe weather conditions, and during the breeding season they are found in high pinewood areas with a high proportion of broom in the undergrowth where they search for insects and seeds.

Threats and limiting factors

Tenerife Blue Chaffinch:

Illegal trade

The species is still kept as a cage-bird on the island. Birds are also illegally caught and exported to other European countries (Italy, Belgium, Germany are thought to be the main destinations) and this may have an effect on population levels.

Importance: unknown

Gran Canaria Blue Chaffinch:

Habitat loss and fragmentation

In the past the pinewoods were subjected to intense commercial exploitation. This led to a substantial decrease in the area of pinewood on Gran Canaria which inevitably affected the Blue Chaffinch population. These commercial activities also caused habitat fragmentation and, therefore, population isolation.

Importance: critical

Forest fires

Forest fires have in the past played an important role in the destruction of Gran Canaria's pinewoods. At present, a fire in one of the critical Blue Chaffinch areas could have catastrophic results due to the small areas and population involved.

Importance: high

Small population size

The current population is so small that the sub-species runs the risk of becoming extinct due to random population fluctuations. The smallness of the population must also have led to reduced genetic variability.

Importance: medium

Social pressure on the habitat

The lack of space for recreation and leisure on Gran Canaria has led to a lot of pressure against the limitations on use of the protected natural areas (e.g. pinewoods) for leisure purposes.

Importance: medium

Natural predation

Predation does not appear to be limiting the Blue Chaffinch population, although some species are known to feed on it occasionally: Long-eared Owl *Asio otus* (Nogales et al., 1986; Rodríguez and Moreno, 1993), Great Spotted Woodpecker *Dendrocopos major* (A. Moreno and F. Rodríguez, pers. comm.) and Raven *Corvus corax* (Rodríguez and Moreno, 1993).

Rodríguez and Moreno (1993) observed that nests within 20 metres of the nearest clearing were subject to a greater predation of eggs and chicks than were others, suggesting that nests near the edge of woodland are more vulnerable to predation than those in its interior.

Importance: low

Predation by cats

Although feral cats are relatively frequent in Ojeda, Inagua and Pajonales pinewoods, studies of their feeding habits (Nogales, 1985; Rodríguez and Moreno, 1993) have revealed little evidence of Blue Chaffinches being eaten.

Importance: low

Lack of water

The natural lack of water in summer could be a limiting factor. Some authors give it as a possible reason for the bird's scarcity on Gran Canaria (Bannerman, 1963; Collar and Andrew, 1988). The piping of water on forested slopes has led to a decrease in the number of drinking places available.

Importance: low

Conservation status and recent conservation measures

At national level, the Blue Chaffinch is classified as Not Threatened and the sub-species *F. t. polatzeki* as Endangered in the *Red Data Book of Spanish Vertebrates* (Blanco and González, 1992). At regional level *F. t. polatzeki* is considered to be Endangered (Martín et al., 1990). Under current Spanish law the Blue Chaffinch is classed as Of Special Interest in Annex II of Royal Decree 439/90 on which the National List of Threatened Species is based.

Recent conservation measures are listed below in chronological order:

1980: Royal Decree 3181/80 banned hunting, capture, trade, collecting of eggs or young, and the preparation of and trade in parts, including stuffed specimens;

1982: Royal Decree 1740/1982 declared the hills of Inagua, Ojeda and Pajonales a National Refuge;

1987: The Canary Islands Countryside Law was passed and included the declaration of Natural Parks and Natural Areas in the following important Blue Chaffinch areas: El Teide forest (Tenerife), Inagua, Ojeda and Pajonales, Ayagaures and Pilancones, Tamadaba and the Macizo de Tauro (Gran Canaria);

1988: Work began on the designation of SPAs. To date three Blue Chaffinch areas have been designated: one on Tenerife (the Tenerife forest) and two on Gran Canaria (Tamadaba and Ojeda/Inagua/Pajonales);

1989: The Countryside and Wildlife Conservation Law 4/89 was passed establishing the National Threatened Species List thereby giving priority to endemic species and sub-species;

1990: The Vice-Council for the Environment of the Canary Islands regional government prepared drafts of recovery plans for five threatened Canary Island species, including the Gran Canaria Blue Chaffinch, as well as a subsequent revision;

1991: The Vice-Council initiated a Gran Canaria Blue Chaffinch Conservation Programme based on the Recovery Plan which includes research studies and the implementation of conservation and management measures both *in situ* and *ex situ*. A study was carried out on the distribution, biology and essential habitat characteristics of the Gran Canaria Blue Chaffinch (Moreno, 1991), since there was very little information. These studies continued in subsequent years together with others on population, breeding, habitat and the effect of predation. The results of these studies were compiled by Rodríguez and Moreno (1993);

Four artificial drinking points, each with a capacity of 2000 litres, were installed in the Inagua, Ojeda and Pajonales pinewoods as part of this conservation programme. These drinking points were used in the summer of 1993 by the birds in the pinewoods, including Blue Chaffinches;

1992: The Vice-Council prepared a plan for experimental captive breeding of the Blue Chaffinch with birds taken from Tenerife. The breeding facilities came into operation in 1993;

1994: The Vice-Council implemented the following as part of the conservation programme:

– captive breeding attempts;

– continuation of research on population, breeding success and habitat use;

– evaluation of potential habitat;

– control of non-natural predators;

– installation of more drinking points;

– approach to CITES authorities;

– a publicity campaign.

That same year the Vice-Council for the Environment of the Canary Islands regional government received funding from the EU under LIFE regulation to finance the Gran Canaria Blue Chaffinch Conservation Programme. This project includes the following objectives:

– improvement of the infrastructure needed to carry out the captive breeding programme;

– provision of the infrastructure needed for reintroductions;

– habitat improvement in current and potential distribution areas;

– increase in the survival chances of current populations.

The new Canary Islands Countryside Law was also approved.

Aims and objectives

Aims

In the short term, to conserve the Blue Chaffinch range and populations in the Canary Islands at no less than the present level and in the medium to long term, to increase the Gran Canaria population to the level where it is no longer classified as an endangered sub-species.

Objectives

1. **Policy and legislation**

1.1. *To draw up an official action plan for the Gran Canaria Blue Chaffinch*

Spanish wildlife conservation legislation (Law 4/80) provides for four kinds of legally binding action plans according to the degree of threat to the species or sub-species: recovery plans, habitat conservation plans, conservation plans and management plans. As the Blue Chaffinch is classified as Of Special Interest, it deserves at least a management plan that will determine the measures necessary to maintain populations at a suitable level.

Priority: high
Time-scale: short

1.2. *To complete the National Endangered Species List*

Law 4/89 established the National Endangered Species List which classified species, sub-species and populations under various categories of threat. As a preliminary step in the drawing up of the law, Royal Decree 439/90 was passed classifying endangered species and including all the rest in the category Of Special Interest. The current classification of Blue Chaffinch as Of Special Interest does not reflect the extent to which the Gran Canaria population is threatened. As five years have passed since the passing of the law, it is advisable now to complete the classification process and initiate the legally binding action plans that the law provides for.

Similarly, it is recommended that the Regional List of Threatened Species be drawn up in accordance with Article 30.2 of Law 4/89.

Priority: high
Time-scale: short

1.3. *To ensure that the new Canary Islands wildlife protection law adequately protects this species*

The draft of the new wildlife law is at the consultation stage and includes the Regional List of Threatened Species and the new status of Biological Refuge as a precautionary measure. This legislation should ensure the protection of the species, in the wider countryside as well as within protected areas, as required under Law 4/1989 on the Conservation of the Countryside, Wildlife and Plants.

Priority: high
Time-scale: short

1.4. *To ensure that Blue Chaffinch habitat is adequately covered under the new Canary Islands Countryside Law*

The new Canary Islands Countryside Law has just been passed, reclassifying the existing areas but not creating any new ones. The planning instruments for such areas – use and management plans, master plans (*planes directores*), conservation regulations and special plans – should aim to address all threats to species' habitat and promote its recovery.

Priority: high
Time-scale: short

1.5. *To include the Blue Chaffinch in CITES*

The inclusion of the Blue Chaffinch in CITES would provide a legal tool at international level for the protection of this species and would help in the control of illegal trade. Steps towards this have already been made by the Vice-Council for the Environment of the Canary Islands and its approval is imminent. TRAFFIC's European offices should also be aware of the existence of this illegal trade.

Priority: high
Time-scale: immediate, ongoing

2. Species and habitat protection

2.1. To eradicate illegal trapping and trade

Illegal trade in this species must be thoroughly investigated, with increased surveillance of Blue Chaffinch areas and periodic monitoring of specific pet shops, animal collections, zoos, etc. International action to identify the trade routes and the destinations of Canary Island birds is equally necessary. The collaboration of Italy, Belgium and Germany is needed, as these countries are thought to be the main destinations of exported birds.

Priority: high
Time-scale: short

Gran Canaria Blue Chaffinch:

2.2. To initiate a habitat recovery programme

This programme would consist of an intense reafforestation campaign to join up the different patches of forest that represent the current and potential habitat of the sub-species. This would enable birds to recolonise and settle in other potential areas. Replanting should include open areas in the Inagua, Ojeda and Pajonales pinewoods which would possibly reduce the risk of nest predation near woodland edge as well as providing additional habitat.

European Union Regulation 2080/92 which established an aid system for forestry activities related to agriculture could be a useful instrument in achieving this objective.

Priority: essential
Time-scale: medium

2.3. To prevent forest fires

Fires are a major risk as they could result in the total extinction of the Gran Canaria Blue Chaffinch. For this reason, it is essential to carry out an intensive fire prevention programme and have available suitable means to fight fires when they occur. The LIFE project for the Blue Chaffinch includes a section which seeks to increase the surveillance and fire prevention measures within the pine forests.

Priority: essential
Time-scale: short

2.4. To provide the people of Gran Canaria with recreation and leisure areas

Pressure for leisure areas should be deflected away from the pinewoods where the Blue Chaffinch lives, and current access restrictions maintained. In order to do this it would be advisable to set aside several recreation areas in places where integral habitat protection is not needed.

Priority: low
Time-scale: medium

2.5. To monitor and limit the movement of people through the Ojeda, Inagua and Pajonales pinewoods

Enforcement of the current access restrictions should contribute to the reduction of the number of people in the pinewoods with a consequent reduction in the risk of fire, nest robbing, disturbance, etc. The rubbish and waste that attract crows (which may prey on Blue Chaffinch nests) would also decrease. Monitoring access to the woods will provide the information needed to decide if further restrictions are necessary.

Priority: medium
Time-scale: short

2.6. To control the cat population in the Ojeda, Inagua and Pajonales pine forests as a precautionary measure

Potential predation by feral cats should be prevented. They may be controlled be either by shooting or by trapping the cats alive. Traps of proved efficiency exist which have been used by the hunting lobby on Gran Canaria over the last few years with good results.

Priority: low
Time-scale: medium

3. Monitoring research

Tenerife Blue Chaffinch:

3.1. To carry a full census of the population followed by regular monitoring

It would be advisable to set up a monitoring system utilising transects, listening stations or other means to determine variations in population density and size. An accurate population estimate for this species is not available and is needed to confirm its present status of "not threatened".

Priority: medium
Time-scale: short

3.2. To better understand its biology and ecology

Some specific aspects which call for a thorough investigation are habitat requirements and feeding habits. As the population of this sub-species is larger, detailed studies including individual marking could be carried out. The experience and information gained would be useful for the conservation of the Gran Canaria sub-species.

Priority: medium
Time-scale: short

Gran Canaria Blue Chaffinch:

3.3. To continue census work and periodic monitoring

The size and state of the population should be assessed regularly and in the different distribution areas. This will provide information on the effect of conservation measures as well as other factors.

Priority: high/essential
Time-scale: ongoing

3.4. To continue with the study of limiting factors

Especially those factors that are having a negative effect on breeding with particular attention given to identifying any predators that may have an impact on eggs and chicks.

Priority: high/essential
Time-scale: ongoing

3.5. To continue and complete studies of habitat selection

It is important to know what the Blue Chaffinch's optimum habitat is so that areas of potential habitat can be identified which could be the target of a reintroduction programme should the IUCN criteria for reintroductions be satisfied (Kleiman et al., 1994).

Priority: high
Time-scale: short, ongoing

3.6. To implement a captive breeding programme

This is not a priority at the moment but would be needed if the population declined further. Some steps are already being taken under the conservation programme for this species.

Priority: low
Time-scale: long, ongoing

4.   Public awareness and training

4.1. To prepare educational and publicity information

Such a campaign would involve various kinds of publicity material (posters, stickers, etc.) as well as a programme of talks and lectures to inform people about the Blue Chaffinch's conservation problems and emphasise the need to protect and improve its habitat.

Priority: medium
Time-scale: medium

4.2. To initiate an awareness-raising campaign

People's attention should be drawn to the Blue Chaffinch as something unique to the Canary Islands and the conservation activities that are being carried out should be publicised. The need for restricted access to pinewoods should be explained to overcome resistance to these measures.

Priority: medium
Time-scale: medium

Action plan for the Azores Bullfinch (*Pyrrhula murina*)

Reviews

This document should be reviewed and updated by BirdLife International every four years. An emergency review will be undertaken if sudden major environmental changes, liable to affect the population, occur within the species' range.

Geographical scope

The island of São Miguel (Azores, Portugal).

Summary

The Azores Bullfinch *Pyrrhula murina* is a very distinct form occurring in the east of the island of São Miguel. It was a locally abundant pest of fruit orchards in the nineteenth century but became rare after 1920. The present population of about 120 pairs is largely confined to native vegetation, which has been reduced and invaded by aggressive exotic plants: *Pittosporum undulatum*, *Cryptomeria japonica*, *Hedychium gardneranum* and *Clethra arborea*.

A three-year study of its population and ecology revealed that native vegetation is preferred all year round but exotic vegetation with open patches is used to some extent in summer. Birds feed on seeds of herbaceous plants in summer, seeds of fleshy fruits in autumn, tree seeds and fern sporangia in winter, and flower buds in spring. A mosaic of vegetation types is thus necessary. Seeds of exotic plants are important from May to July and from October to March, but during periods of food scarcity (late March to early May) the birds are heavily dependent on flower buds of *Ilex perado*. Apart from *Clethra arborea* the seeds of common exotics are ignored.

This action plan is based on the results of a project which received European Union funding through a LIFE grant and aims to restore and expand the area of laurel forest and increase the population of Azores Bullfinch to about 150 to 200 pairs.

Threats and limiting factors

Habitat loss – critical

Food shortage during late winter – critical

Food shortage in summer – low/medium

Random demographic and environmental factors – low/medium

Predation – unknown

Low breeding success and natural mortality – unknown

Conservation priorities

Control the expansion of exotic flora – critical

Protect and increase the population of key food plants – critical

Promote the regeneration of laurel forest – high

Provide supplementary feeding – high

Continue population monitoring – high

Introduction

The Azores Bullfinch *Pyrrhula murina*, also known as the São Miguel Bullfinch or Priolo, is a very distinct form occurring only in the east of the island of São Miguel in the Azores archipelago (Portugal). It is listed as Endangered in IUCN's *Red List of Threatened Animals* (Groombridge, 1993) and in the Portuguese Red Data Book (Cabral et al., 1990). It is included in Annex I of the European Union's Wild Birds Directive. Laurel forest, the habitat of this species, is listed as a priority habitat in Annex I of the European Union's Habitats Directive (45.61 to 45.63 Macaronesian Laurel Forests).

Godman identified the bullfinch in 1866 and described it as being characteristic of mountainous areas. It once had a wider range since it was regarded as a pest in orange orchards around Furnas and was easily collected for museums (Bannerman and Bannerman, 1966 and references cited there; Le Grand, 1983). The reduction of its range is associated with the cutting of the laurel forest for grazing and agriculture, afforestation with *Cryptomeria japonica*, and the introduction of aggressive exotic plants that are now widespread: *Pittosporum undulatum* on slopes along streams up to 500 metres, *Hedychium gardneranum* on disturbed ground and streams, and *Clethra arborea* which is scattered widely through the whole of the native forest.

Habitat change due to the spread of exotic vegetation is the main conservation threat facing this bird. Between 1991 and 1993 a study was undertaken to evaluate this threat (Ramos, 1993) and this action plan draws on the results of that study. It is now virtually impossible to eradicate the exotic plants, some of which have become naturalised. However, action should be taken to control them and to restore and enlarge the remaining patches of the laurel forest. It should be noted that native plants are slow growing and positive results may thus be seen only in the long term.

Background information

Distribution and population

The Azores Bullfinch is largely confined to native vegetation in eastern São Miguel, from 300 to 800 metres above sea-level. It has never been recorded in the western part of the island. Two main patches of native vegetation are present within its range: the largest, centred on Pico da Vara summit, where birds occur all year round, and Salto do Cavalo, on the west of the range, where birds have been observed from September to December (Ramos, in press a). Only juveniles have been seen at Salto do Cavalo suggesting post-fledging dispersal. Azores Bullfinches range widely within the main area. The largest movements were of about 3 km, recorded in May along streams.

The population was estimated at 30 to 40 pairs in the late 1970s (Le Grand, 1983), 100 pairs in 1989 (Bibby and Charlton, 1991; Bibby et al., 1992) and between 60 and 200 pairs (mean 120) in 1991, 1992 and 1993 (Ramos, in press a).

Life history

Taxonomic status

Azores Bullfinches differ from their mainland counterparts and seem likely to merit the species rank which they are accorded here. The sexes are virtually identical in colour, though males sometimes show the slightest suffusion of reddish-tawny on the abdomen and flanks (Bibby et al., 1992; Ramos, 1994a). Preliminary studies of phylogenetics show the Azores Bullfinch to differ consistently from British and north European Bullfinches *P. pyrrhula* on two bases of the mitochondrial DNA (Ramos, 1993). These differences are greater than those amongst crossbill *Loxia* species in Britain (R. Dawson, pers. comm.), but a full evaluation of this point must include DNA from Iberian birds.

Breeding

Breeding occurs from mid-June to late August. During the recent study, two nests were found 3 metres above the ground on a *Cryptomeria japonica* tree, both surrounded by dense vegetation (*Cryptomeria japonica* and *Clethra arborea*). Nests are like those of mainland bullfinches, with two layers. Nest materials include twigs of *Clethra arborea* and *Erica azorica*, grass, rootlets and moss. Clutch size is unknown. Young fledge from mid-July. Adults moult from September onwards (Ramos, 1994a).

Feeding

The diet shows marked monthly variation and comprises at least 37 different plants, of which only 13 are known to be important. In summer birds take herbaceous seeds (*Polygonum capitatum*, *Prunella vulgaris*, *Hypericum humifusum*, *Leontodon filii*); in autumn, seeds of fleshy fruits (*Vaccinium cylindraceum*, *Rubus* sp., *Leicesteria formosa*); in winter, tree seeds (*Clethra arborea*) and fern sporangia (*Woodwardia radicans*, *Culcita macrocarpa*); in spring, flower buds (*Ilex perado*), fern sporangia (*Osmunda regalis*) and fern fronds (*O. regalis*, *Pteridium aquilinum*) and moss tips (Ramos, 1995a).

Native vegetation comprises the majority of the diet in August and September (*L. filii* and *V. cylindraceum*) and April (*I. perado*). The fact that birds are heavily dependent on flower buds of

I. perado in April and that large ferns are important food from November to March (Ramos, 1995a) may explain why birds are not present in the area of native vegetation at Salto do Cavalo in winter, since these plants are present there in much lower densities than around Pico da Vara (Ramos, 1995a).

Observations in the field and trials with captive birds showed that all fleshy fruits are greatly preferred to *Clethra arborea* seeds. These seemed preferable to fern sori in autumn. In April, birds preferred *I. perado* over fern sori, and these over *Clethra arborea*. Seeds of *Clethra arborea* are ignored once flower buds reach a length of about 2.8 to 3.0 mm. Seeds of *Hedychium gardneranum* and *Cryptomeria japonica* (birds do not extract seeds from cones) were consumed only very rarely and *Pittosporum undulatum* was never taken (Ramos, in press b). Fern fronds were only taken when other food items were scarcer (Ramos, 1994b).

Habitat requirements

In the nineteenth century this species was considered a locally abundant pest of fruit orchards but at present orchards are very small and far from forest cover so they are no longer used by the species.

Native vegetation is always greatly preferred but there are some important seasonal variations in habitat selection. In summer, birds select bare ground, short vegetation (less than 2 metres high) and forest margins. Plantations of *Cryptomeria japonica* (especially those less than 6 metres high) and copses of *Pittosporum undulatum* within 200 metres of the native forest are used to some extent from May to November. From January to April about 90% of the bird records were in native vegetation (Ramos, in press a).

To complete the annual cycle birds need a mosaic of several vegetation types. This is reflected in their home ranges, which are wide around a regular base. Birds move from area to area following the fruiting of food plants. They are more mobile during summer (June to September) because they have to cross areas of mature forest that are unsuitable for foraging. Longer movements (up to 3 km, down from 700 metres to about 300 metres) were recorded in early May when birds moved to feed on ripening herbaceous seeds (Ramos, in press a).

Threats and limiting factors

Habitat loss

The remaining native forest (about 580 ha) supports about 120 pairs of Azores Bullfinches. Loss of native forest and its large-scale invasion by exotics seem to be the major factors explaining the gradual contraction of the Azores Bullfinch range and present small population levels. Exotic vegetation is of limited use because it does not provide food. Exotic forests could be of some value if they were less dense, allowing the development of an understorey with herbaceous plants and shrubs. Forest margins at lower altitudes with herbaceous plants and fleshy-fruit-producing shrubs should be considered as valuable habitats for this bird (Ramos, in press a). Fruit orchards are no longer important as a habitat for this species as they are small and far from forest cover.

Importance: critical

Food shortage in winter

Seeds of *Clethra arborea* and sori of large ferns are the main foods from November to March. In April birds feed on flower buds of *I. perado* (though *Clethra arborea* seeds are still present, but presumably too dry and indigestible). An experiment with netted trees showed that most buds are consumed, and Azores Bullfinches may thus face food shortage in late winter (Ramos, 1995a). A higher proportion of fern fronds and moss tips was consumed in 1993 when larger buds and herbaceous seeds became available about 20 days later than usual. These foods are of low quality and birds may not survive when feeding on them alone (Ramos, 1994b). Thus higher mortality due to shortage of good-quality food may occur from mid-March to mid-May.

Importance: critical

Food shortage in summer

There is no evidence of a lack of herbaceous seeds in summer. Several species are present and some may replace others. However, they occur on disturbed ground, which, at some sites, may become carpeted by exotics, especially *Hedychium gardneranum*. Most food resources appear to have been consumed in the 1991 and 1992 summers (Ramos, 1995a). Openings in the vegetation will be formed naturally every year since the ground is very steep. However, if these are very far apart there may be an increased cost for breeding birds and breeding success may be reduced. The area at Salto do Cavalo is less steep and openings are consequently less frequent.

Importance: low/medium

Random demographic and environmental factors

Such a small population may be affected by random environmental and demographic factors. The effect of inbreeding is unknown but it may have lowered the reproductive output of individuals.

Importance: low/medium

Predation

There are no avian predators in the Azores which would take finches. Predation of adult Azores Bullfinches by cats has been recorded twice when birds were feeding on *Polygonum capitatum* on a road (Ramos, 1994a). Some cats are now wandering in the area occupied by the finches following the abandonment of a garbage site at 350 metres above sea-level. They are seen mainly at lower altitudes, however, and do not seem to have an impact on the population. Rats have been seen near nest sites but it is not known if they prey on eggs or chicks.

Importance: unknown

Low breeding success and natural mortality

Juveniles comprise 50% to 60% of the total population during the last 10 days of August. Breeding productivity is about two young per pair. Annual mortality is 45% to 60%. There is little information on recruitment: very small sample sizes indicate a value similar to that of mortality (Ramos, 1994a). Information on post-fledging mortality is needed to evaluate whether recruitment matches mortality.

Importance: unknown

Conservation status and recent conservation measures

The Azores Bullfinch is a protected species under Decreto/Lei 75/91, which adapts the European Union's Wild Birds Directive to Portuguese Law. The only terrestrial Iimportant Bird Area (IBA) in the Azores (Grimmett and Jones, 1989) includes the area of native vegetation centred on Pico da Vara which is the main area for the Azores Bullfinch. The area around Salto do Cavalo, Pico Bartolomeu and the mountain slopes above Monte Simplicio (Povoação) are not included in the IBA.

Pico da Vara was designated a Natural Forest Reserve (Reserva Florestal Natural) by the regional government of the Azores. It was also designated a Special Protection Area (Zona de Protecção Especial) by the Azorean Government (DRA, 1991) under the EU Wild Birds Directive. No other laurel forest fragments have been designated although those fragments above Monte Simplicio hold birds all year round. All areas are owned and managed by the forestry service (direcção regional dos recursos florestais).

A broad ecological research programme, which looked at feeding resources, limiting factors and habitat restoration, was carried out between 1991 and 1993 (Ramos, 1993), laying solid foundations for practical conservation work. Habitat management (the control of invasive exotics and the planting of native species raised in nurseries) began in early 1995 following the recent approval of EU funding for this work through a LIFE grant. The main aim of this project is to re-establish and improve the laurel forest in order to ensure that in the long term the Azores Bullfinch reaches a viable population size. Native plants are very slow growing and effects will be seen only in the long term. Areas planted with native species will need to be checked regularly to control invasion by *Hedychium gardneranum*.

A 50-page booklet on the special value of the Azores Bullfinch, its habitat, diet, feeding behaviour and conservation (Ramos, 1995b) has been published by the Town Hall of Nordeste and will be distributed to all schools of São Miguel.

Aims and objectives

Aims

To increase the Azores Bullfinch population to between 150 and 200 pairs by the year 2010 and to extend the area of the laurel forest by 80 ha, reversing its continuing large-scale deterioration through the invasion of exotic flora.

Objectives

1. Policy and legislation

1.1. *To ensure the adequate legal protection of the Azores Bullfinch and its habitat*

1.1.1 Increase the area of the Natural Forest Reserve and Special Protection Area

The Azorean Government is encouraged to increase the area of the Pico da Vara Natural Forest Reserve to include all laurel forest patches between Pico Bartolomeu and Salto do Cavalo. These areas should also be included in the Special Protection Area of Pico da Vara.

Priority: medium
Time-scale: long

1.1.2. Legislate on the planting of exotic species

The Convention on Biological Diversity clearly states that exotic species should not be introduced and that they should be controlled or eradicated when they threaten ecosystems, habitats or species. These principles should be adequately reflected in domestic legislation. The Azorean Government is encouraged to clearly define the areas that are suitable for the planting of exotics, leaving a wide buffer zone between the laurel forest and such plantations and severely restricting afforestation with *Cryptomeria japonica* within the range of the Azores Bullfinch.

Priority: high
Time-scale: long

1.1.3. Incorporate species recovery plans into regional and national legislation

Recovery plans are included as legal measures in other countries. Consideration should be given to incorporating the action plan for the Azores Bullfinch into appropriate legislation.

Priority: low
Time-scale: medium/long

1.1.4. Review international and national legislation in light of taxonomic research

If, as expected, the Azores Bullfinch is shown to be a full species it will be necessary to add it to Annex II of the Bern Convention and Annex I of the EU Birds Directive.

Priority: medium
Time-scale: medium

1.2. *To ensure an adequate framework for the management of the Natural Forest Reserve*

For effective management the reserve should be provided with a management body, a management plan, adequate regulations and continued funding.

Priority: high
Time-scale: medium

2. Species and habitat protection

2.1. *To control the expansion of exotic flora and promote the regeneration of the laurel forest*

The expansion of *Pittosporum undulatum*, *Hedychium gardneranum* and *Clethra arborea* should be controlled either by physical removal or by use of arboricides (*Hedychium gardneranum*) or tree trunk injections (*Pittosporum undulatum* and *Clethra arborea*).

The control of *Clethra arborea* is controversial since this is the best food-option available to the birds between December and March (Ramos, 1995a). However, it is outcompeting native species, notably *I. perado* and many areas may turn into monospecific stands of *Clethra arborea*. Control should therefore be carried out progressively as areas of native vegetation are restored and expanded. Financial resources must be allocated for continuing long-term control of exotics.

The control of exotics allows native seedlings to develop and helps the recovery of the laurel forest through natural regeneration. This applies to most areas in Pico da Vara and Salto do Cavalo which have recently been degraded by goats and pigs, and by the extraction of topsoil by local people.

Areas that are now dominated by exotics should be converted to their original vegetation, including several areas densely carpeted by *Hedychium gardneranum* and slopes that are not suitable for the planting of *Cryptomeria japonica* because of their exposure to strong winds. Restoration should start around the valley of Ribeira do Guilherme, within the main range of the Azores Bullfinch, and continue progressively towards the west.

Priority: critical
Time-scale: ongoing

2.2. *To protect and increase the population of plants that provide key food sources*

Populations of native plants should be re-established within and around the main area of native vegetation by planting seedlings. There is an urgent need to increase the population of flower- and bud-producing species (*I. perado* and *Prunus lusitanica*, now extremely rare), because this is the only food available in spring, a time of food scarcity. This is especially important at lower altitudes where trees will produce larger buds earlier. Populations of the following species should also be increased: *Woodwardia radicans, Culcita macrocarpa* and *Rubus hochstetterorum.*

Priority: critical
Time-scale: ongoing

2.3. *To provide supplementary feeding*

This involves the installation of feeding stations where sunflower seeds will be placed from February to April, with a view to boosting winter survival. This should be carried out until food availability ceases to be a limiting factor.

Priority: high
Time-scale: ongoing

2.4. *To supplement the wild population with captive bred individuals*

Captive breeding should only be attempted if the population in the wild decreases dramatically as birds kept in captivity will not accept new foods easily and their normal food sources are difficult to find (Ramos, 1993).

Priority: low
Time-scale: long

3.   **Monitoring and research**

3.1. *To continue the monitoring of population size and reproduction*

It is essential to continue with the monitoring scheme started in 1990 using point counts (Bibby and Charlton, 1991). Population size and breeding success should be estimated once a year, in May/June and end of August/early September respectively. The key period of mortality appears to be March/April but this, and the importance of predation, requires further study.

Priority: high
Time-scale: ongoing

3.2. *To study the large-scale invasion of the laurel forest by exotic flora*

The continuing invasion by *Hedychium gardneranum* and *Clethra arborea* is especially worthy of study. The results may be valuable in the control of such invasion.

Priority: medium
Time-scale: long

3.3. *To promote studies of taxonomy*

It is important to continue studies on the phylogenetics of mainland European Bullfinches, including Iberian birds, to clarify the taxonomic position of the Azores Bullfinch.

Priority: medium
Time-scale: short

4.   **Public awareness and training**

4.1. *To provide information about the Azores Bullfinch and its habitat to the local people of São Miguel and to visitors*

A booklet about the Azores Bullfinch and its habitat will be distributed to all schools on the island (Ramos, 1995b). Several placards will be placed at the main entrances of the Natural Forest Reserve so that the local population understands and supports the conservation measures carried out for this species and its habitat.

Priority: medium
Time-scale: ongoing

Appendix I
Acronyms and abbreviations

AAO	Association "Les Amis des Oiseaux"
ACNAT	Action by the Community relating to Nature Conservation: Council Regulation (EC) 3907/91
AEWA	African Eurasian Migratory Waterbirds Agreement
AMA	Agencia de Medio Ambiente
ASPBM	Albanian Society for the Protection of Birds and Mammals
Bern Convention	Convention on the Conservation of European Wildlife and Natural Habitats
BNVR	Belgische Natuur- en Vogelreservaten (RNOB)
Bonn Convention	Convention on the Conservation of Migratory Species of Wild Animals
BOS	Belarusian Ornithological Society
BSPB	Bulgarian Society for the Protection of Birds
BVCF	Black Vulture Conservation Foundation
CAP	EU Common Agricultural Policy
CEECs	Central and Eastern European Countries
CEMO	Centre d'Etude des Migrations d'Oiseaux
CIC	Conseil International pour la Chasse
CISO	Italian Centre for Ornithology
CITES	Convention on International Trade in Endangered Species
CMS	Convention on Migratory Species (Bonn Convention)
CNPI	Czech Nature Protection Institute
CoE	Council of Europe
COS	Cyprus Ornithological Society
CPCN	Comité des Programmes de Conservation de la Nature
CSIC	Consejo Superior de Investigaciones Científicas
CSO	Czech Society for Ornithology
CSPBN	Croatian Society for the Protection of Birds and Nature
CSRLGMNR	Central Scientific Research Laboratory of Game Management and Natural Resources
DDRA	Danube Delta Reserve Authority
DGBC	Dévaványa Great Bustard Centre

DGN	Dirección General para la Conservacion de la Naturaleza (formerly ICONA), Spain
DHKD	Turkish Society for the Protection of Nature
DOF	Dansk Ornitologisk Forening
DOPPS	Bird Watching and Bird Study Association of Slovenia
EBD	Estación Biológica de Doñana
EOS	Estonian Ornithological Society
ESA	Environmentally Sensitive Area
EU	European Union
EU Habitats Directive	Directive on the conservation of natural habitats and of wild fauna and flora (92/43/EEC)
FACE	European Federation of Hunters' Associations
FAO	Food and Agriculture Organisation
FIR	Fonds d'Intervention pour les Rapaces
GBC	Great Bustard Centre
GBWC	Greek Biotopes and Wetlands Centre
GFV	Gesellschaft für Vogelkunde
GIS	Geographic Information System
GOMAC	Groupe Ornithologique du Maroc
GREPOM	Groupe Recherche Protection Oiseaux Maroc
GWC	Greek Wetlands Centre
HOS	Hellenic Ornithological Society
IBA	Important Bird Area
IBR	Institute for Biological Research
ICBP	International Council for Bird Preservation (now BirdLife International)
ICN	Institute for Nature Conservation
ICONA	Instituto Nacional para la Conservacion de la Naturaleza/National Institute for the Conservation of Nature, Spain (now DGN)
IMO	International Maritime Organization
INFS	National Institute for Wild Animals (Italy)
INP	Institute for Nature Protection
IPRMCP	International Pelicans Research, Management and Conservation Programme
IRSNB	Institute Royale des Sciences Naturelles de Belgique
IUCN	International Union for Conservation of Nature and Natural Resources

IWC	International Waterfowl Census
IWC	Irish Wildbird Conservancy
IWRB	International Waterfowl and Wetlands Research Bureau
JNCC	Joint Nature Conservation Committee, UK
KMNCD	Körös–Maros Nature Conservation Directorate
LFN	Latvian Fund for Nature
LFN	Lithuanian Fund for Nature
LIFE	L'Instrument Financiere pour l'Environment/Financial Instrument for the Environment: Council Regulation (EEC) 1973/92
LIPU	Lega Italiana Protezione Uccelli
LNVL	Lëtzebuerger Natur- a Vulleschutzliga
LOB	Latvian Ornithological Society
LOD	Lithuanian Ornithological Society
LPA	Landscape Protection Area
LPN	Liga para a Protecção da Natureza
LPO	Ligue pour la Protection des Oiseaux
MAPA	Ministerio de Agricultura, Pesca y Alimentación
MEAT	Ministere de l'Environnement et de l'Aménagement du Territoire
MEDWET	Mediterranean Wetlands Initiative
MEPNRRF	Ministry for Environment Protection and Natural Resources of the Russian Federation
MEPNSU	Ministry of Environmental Protection and Nuclear Safety of Ukraine
MME	Hungarian Ornithological and Nature Conservation Society
MNCN	Museo Nacional de Ciencias Naturales
MOPTMA	Ministerio de Obras Públicas, Transporte y Medio Ambiente
MOS	Moldavian Ornithological Society
NABU	Naturschutzbund Deutschland
NATO	North Atlantic Treaty Organization
NCO	National Conservation Office
NCSPBN	North Cyprus Society for the Protection of Birds and Nature
NGO	Non-governmental organization
NOF	Norwegian Ornithological Society
NPGWD	National Parks, Game and Wildlife Department
ONC	Office Nationale de la Chasse

OSME	Ornithological Society of the Middle East
OTOP	Polish Society for the Protection of Birds
PHARE	EC Programme for the Economic Reconstruction of Eastern Europe: Council Regulation (EEC) 3906/89 as amended by 2698/90 and 3800/91
PND	Parque Nacional de Doñana
PNRC	Parc Naturel Régionel de Corse
PNZ	Parc National de Zembra
PSGBP	Pannonic Society for Great Bustard Protection
PTOP	Póknonopodlaskie Towarzystwo Ochrony Ptaków
Ramsar Convention	Convention on Wetlands of International Importance especially as Waterfowl Habitat
RAS	Russian Academy of Sciences
RBCU	Russian Bird Conservation Union
RDWG	Ruddy Duck Working Group
RNOB	Réserves Naturelles et Ornithologiques de Belgique (BNVR)
ROS	Romanian Ornithological Society
RRINC	Russian Research Institute of Nature Conservation
RSPB	The Royal Society for the Protection of Birds (UK)
SAC	Special Area for Conservation (EU Habitats Directive)
SAS	Slovak Academy of Sciences
SEO	Sociedad Española de Ornitología/BirdLife Spain
SNH	Scottish Natural Heritage (statutory conservation agency)
SOR	Romanian Ornithological Society
SOS	Slovak Ornithological Society
SOVS	Society for the Protection of Birds in Slovakia
SPA	Special Protection Area under the EU Wild Birds Directive and/or Barcelona Convention
SPAG	State Property Agency
SPEA	Sociedade Portuguesa para o Estudo das Aves
SPNI	Society for the Protection of Nature in Israel
SPNZH	Service des Parcs Nationaux et Zones Humides
SPP	Society for the Protection of Prespa
TVH	Nature Conservation Authority (Hungary)
UNEP	United Nations Environment Programme

Unesco	United Nations Educational, Scientific and Cultural Organization
UOS	Ukrainian Ornithological Society
UTOP	Ukrainian Union for Bird Conservation
UUBC	Ukrainian Union for Bird Conservation
WTO	World Trade Organization
WWF	World Wide Fund for Nature
WWT	Wildfowl and Wetlands Trust

Appendix 2
Globally threatened species by country

Based on references in the action plans

Albania

Pygmy Cormorant *Phalacrocorax pygmeus*
Dalmatian Pelican *Pelecanus crispus*
Lesser Kestrel *Falco naumanni*
Slender-billed Curlew *Numenius tenuirostris*

Algeria

Marbled Teal *Marmaronetta angustirostris*
White-headed Duck *Oxyura leucocephala*
Lesser Kestrel *Falco naumanni*
Slender-billed Curlew *Numenius tenuirostris*
Audouin's Gull *Larus audounii*

Armenia

Marbled Teal *Marmaronetta angustirostris*
Cinereous Vulture *Aegypius monachus*
Imperial Eagle *Aquila heliaca*
Lesser Kestrel *Falco naumanni*

Austria

White-headed Duck *Oxyura leucocephala*
Corncrake *Crex crex*
Great Bustard *Otis tarda*

Azerbaijan

Lesser White-fronted Goose *Anser erythropus*
Red-breasted Goose *Branta ruficollis*
Marbled Teal *Marmaronetta angustirostris*
White-headed Duck *Oxyura leucocephala*
Cinereous Vulture *Aegypius monachus*
Imperial Eagle *Aquila heliaca*
Lesser Kestrel *Falco naumanni*

Belarus

Corncrake *Crex crex*
Aquatic Warbler *Acrocephalus paludicola*

Belgium

White-headed Duck *Oxyura leucocephala*
Corncrake *Crex crex*

Bosnia-Herzegovina

Corncrake *Crex crex*

Bulgaria

Pygmy Cormorant *Phalacrocorax pygmeus*
Dalmatian Pelican *Pelecanus crispus*
Lesser White-fronted Goose *Anser erythropus*
Red-breasted Goose *Branta ruficollis*
White-headed Duck *Oxyura leucocephala*
Cinereous Vulture *Aegypius monachus*
Imperial Eagle *Aquila heliaca*
Lesser Kestrel *Falco naumanni*
Corncrake *Crex crex*
Great Bustard *Otis tarda*
Slender-billed Curlew *Numenius tenuirostris*

Croatia

Imperial Eagle *Aquila heliaca*
Lesser Kestrel *Falco naumanni*
Corncrake *Crex crex*
Slender-billed Curlew *Numenius tenuirostris*

Cyprus

Imperial Eagle *Aquila heliaca*
Audouin's Gull *Larus audounii*

Czech Republic

Corncrake *Crex crex*
Great Bustard *Otis tarda*

Denmark

White-headed Duck *Oxyura leucocephala*
Corncrake *Crex crex*

Egypt

Marbled Teal *Marmaronetta angustirostris*
Lesser Kestrel *Falco naumanni*

Estonia

Corncrake *Crex crex*

Federal Republic of Yugoslavia (Serbia and Montenegro)

Dalmatian Pelican *Pelecanus crispus*
• Lesser White-fronted Goose *Anser erythropus*
Corncrake *Crex crex*
Slender-billed Curlew *Numenius tenuirostris*

Finland

White-headed Duck *Oxyura leucocephala*

France

White-headed Duck *Oxyura leucocephala*
Lesser Kestrel *Falco naumanni*
Corncrake *Crex crex*
Audouin's Gull *Larus audouinii*

Georgia

Marbled Teal *Marmaronetta angustirostris*
Cinereous Vulture *Aegypius monachus*
Imperial Eagle *Aquila heliaca*
Lesser Kestrel *Falco naumanni*

Germany

Lesser White-fronted Goose *Anser erythropus*
White-headed Duck *Oxyura leucocephala*
Corncrake *Crex crex*
Great Bustard *Otis tarda*
Aquatic Warbler *Acrocephalus paludicola*

Greece

Pygmy Cormorant *Phalacrocorax pygmeus*
Dalmatian Pelican *Pelecanus crispus*
Lesser White-fronted Goose *Anser erythropus*
Red-breasted Goose *Branta ruficollis*
White-headed Duck *Oxyura leucocephala*
Cinereous Vulture *Aegypius monachus*
Imperial Eagle *Aquila heliaca*
Lesser Kestrel *Falco naumanni*
Slender-billed Curlew *Numenius tenuirostris*
Audouin's Gull *Larus audounii*

Hungary

Lesser White-fronted Goose *Anser erythropus*
White-headed Duck *Oxyura leucocephala*
Imperial Eagle *Aquila heliaca*
Corncrake *Crex crex*
Great Bustard *Otis tarda*
Slender-billed Curlew *Numenius tenuirostris*
Aquatic Warbler *Acrocephalus paludicola*

Iceland

White-headed Duck *Oxyura leucocephala*

Iran

Slender-billed Curlew *Numenius tenuirostris*

Iraq

Slender-billed Curlew *Numenius tenuirostris*

Ireland

Corncrake *Crex crex*
White-headed Duck *Oxyura leucocephala*

Israel

Marbled Teal *Marmaronetta angustirostris*
White-headed Duck *Oxyura leucocephala*
Imperial Eagle *Aquila heliaca*
Lesser Kestrel *Falco naumanni*

Italy

White-headed Duck *Oxyura leucocephala*
Lesser Kestrel *Falco naumanni*
Corncrake *Crex crex*
Slender-billed Curlew *Numenius tenuirostris*
Audouin's Gull *Larus audounii*

Kazakhstan

Lesser White-fronted Goose *Anser erythropus*
Red-breasted Goose *Branta ruficollis*
Lesser Kestrel *Falco naumanni*
Slender-billed Curlew *Numenius tenuirostris*

Latvia

Corncrake *Crex crex*
Aquatic Warbler *Acrocephalus paludicola*

Lebanon

Marbled Teal *Marmaronetta angustirostris*
Audouin's Gull *Larus audounii*

Libya

Lesser Kestrel *Falco naumanni*

Liechtenstein

Corncrake *Crex crex*

Lithuania

Corncrake *Crex crex*
Lesser White-fronted Goose *Anser erythropus*
Aquatic Warbler *Acrocephalus paludicola*

Luxembourg

Corncrake *Crex crex*

Middle East

Imperial Eagle *Aquila heliaca*

Moldova

Pygmy Cormorant *Phalacrocorax pygmeus*
Imperial Eagle *Aquila heliaca*
Lesser Kestrel *Falco naumanni*
Corncrake *Crex crex*

Morocco

Marbled Teal *Marmaronetta angustirostris*
White-headed Duck *Oxyura leucocephala*
Lesser Kestrel *Falco naumanni*
Slender-billed Curlew *Numenius tenuirostris*
Audouin's Gull *Larus audounii*

Netherlands

White-headed Duck *Oxyura leucocephala*
Corncrake *Crex crex*

Norway

Lesser White-fronted Goose *Anser erythropus*
White-headed Duck *Oxyura leucocephala*
Corncrake *Crex crex*

Poland

Corncrake *Crex crex*
Aquatic Warbler *Acrocephalus paludicola*

Portugal

Fea's Petrel *Pterodroma feae*
Zino's Petrel *Pterodroma madeira*
White-headed Duck *Oxyura leucocephala*
Lesser Kestrel *Falco naumanni*
Great Bustard *Otis tarda*
Madeira Laurel Pigeon *Columba trocaz*
Azores Bullfinch *Pyrrhula murina*

Romania

Pygmy Cormorant *Phalacrocorax pygmeus*
Dalmatian Pelican *Pelecanus crispus*
Lesser White-fronted Goose *Anser erythropus*
Red-breasted Goose *Branta ruficollis*
White-headed Duck *Oxyura leucocephala*
Imperial Eagle *Aquila heliaca*
Lesser Kestrel *Falco naumanni*
Corncrake *Crex crex*
Slender-billed Curlew *Numenius tenuirostris*

Russian Federation

Pygmy Cormorant *Phalacrocorax pygmeus*
Dalmatian Pelican *Pelecanus crispus*
Lesser White-fronted Goose *Anser erythropus*
Red-breasted Goose *Branta ruficollis*
Marbled Teal *Marmaronetta angustirostris*
White-headed Duck *Oxyura leucocephala*
Cinereous Vulture *Aegypius monachus*
Imperial Eagle *Aquila heliaca*
Lesser Kestrel *Falco naumanni*
Corncrake *Crex crex*
Great Bustard *Otis tarda*
Slender-billed Curlew *Numenius tenuirostris*
Aquatic Warbler *Acrocephalus paludicola*

Slovakia

Imperial Eagle *Aquila heliaca*
Corncrake *Crex crex*
Great Bustard *Otis tarda*

Slovenia

Lesser Kestrel *Falco naumanni*
Corncrake *Crex crex*

Spain

Marbled Teal *Marmaronetta angustirostris*
White-headed Duck *Oxyura leucocephala*
Cinereous Vulture *Aegypius monachus*
Spanish Imperial Eagle *Aquila adalberti*
Lesser Kestrel *Falco naumanni*
Corncrake *Crex crex*
Great Bustard *Otis tarda*
Houbara Bustard (Canary Islands) *Chlamydotis undulata fuertaventurae*
Slender-billed Curlew *Numenius tenuirostris*
Audouin's Gull *Larus audounii*
Dark-tailed Laurel Pigeon *Columba bollii*
White-tailed Laurel Pigeon *Columba junoniae*
Blue Chaffinch *Fringilla teydea*

Sweden

Lesser White-fronted Goose *Anser erythropus*
White-headed Duck *Oxyura leucocephala*
Corncrake *Crex crex*

Switzerland

White-headed Duck *Oxyura leucocephala*
Corncrake *Crex crex*

Syria

Marbled Teal *Marmaronetta angustirostris*
White-headed Duck *Oxyura leucocephala*

The former Yugoslav Republic of Macedonia

Pygmy Cormorant *Phalacrocorax pygmeus*
Dalmatian Pelican *Pelecanus crispus*
Corncrake *Crex crex*
Imperial Eagle *Aquila heliaca*

Tunisia

Marbled Teal *Marmaronetta angustirostris*
White-headed Duck *Oxyura leucocephala*
Lesser Kestrel *Falco naumanni*
Slender-billed Curlew *Numenius tenuirostris*
Audouin's Gull *Larus audounii*

Turkey

Pygmy Cormorant *Phalacrocorax pygmeus*
Dalmatian Pelican *Pelecanus crispus*
Red-breasted Goose *Branta ruficollis*
Marbled Teal *Marmaronetta angustirostris*
White-headed Duck *Oxyura leucocephala*
Cinereous Vulture *Aegypius monachus*
Imperial Eagle *Aquila heliaca*
Lesser Kestrel *Falco naumanni*
Corncrake *Crex crex*
Great Bustard *Otis tarda*
Slender-billed Curlew *Numenius tenuirostris*
Audouin's Gull *Larus audounii*

Ukraine

Pygmy Cormorant *Phalacrocorax pygmeus*

Dalmatian Pelican *Pelecanus crispus*

Lesser White-fronted Goose *Anser erythropus*

Red-breasted Goose *Branta ruficollis*

White-headed Duck *Oxyura leucocephala*

Cinereous Vulture *Aegypius monachus*

Imperial Eagle *Aquila heliaca*

Lesser Kestrel *Falco naumanni*

Corncrake *Crex crex*

Great Bustard *Otis tarda*

Slender-billed Curlew *Numenius tenuirostris*

Aquatic Warbler *Acrocephalus paludicola*

United Kingdom

White-headed Duck *Oxyura leucocephala*

Corncrake *Crex crex*

Aquatic Warbler *Acrocephalus paludicola*

Uzbekistan

Lesser Kestrel *Falco naumanni*

Appendix 3
Contributors

Steering Committee

Laurence Rose (Chairman)
The Royal Society for the Protection of Birds, UK

Borja Heredia (project co-ordinator)
BirdLife International, UK (now DGN, Spain)

Stefano Allavena
Ministry of Forest and Agriculture, Italy

Nicola Crockford
The Royal Society for the Protection of Birds, UK

Dr Colin A. Galbraith
Joint Nature Conservation Committee, UK

Eladio Fernández Galiano
Council of Europe (Bern Convention on the Conservation of European Wildlife)

Richard Geiser
DG XI/B2, Commission of the European Communities

Douglas Hykle
Bonn Convention on the Conservation of Migratory Species of Wild Animals

Zbigniew Karpowicz
IUCN

Oscar Merne
National Parks and Wildlife Service, Republic of Ireland

Dr Alexander Mischenko
Russian Scientific Research and Nature Reserves Institute

Manuel Nogales
Universidad de la Laguna, Spain

Valentin Serebryakov
Ukrainian Ornithological Society

António Teixeira
Instituto da Conservação da Natureza, Portugal

Ianine Van Vessem
Wetlands International

Murat Yarar
Dogal Hayati Koruma Dernegi, Turkey

Fea's Petrel
(Pterodroma feae)

Compiled by:

Francis Zino
(Freira Conservation Project, Madeira)

Borja Heredia
(BirdLife International, UK) and

Manuel J. Biscoito
(Museu Municipal do Funchal, Madeira)

With contributions from:

B. Bell
(Wildlife Management International, New Zealand)

C. J. Bibby
(BirdLife International, UK)

W. R. P. Bourne
(Aberdeen University, Scotland)

A. Buckle
(ICI Public Health, UK)

H. Costa Neves
(Parque Natural da Madeira)

T. Gerrard
(Madeira)

J. P. Granadeiro
(Instituto da Conservação da Natureza, Portugal)

R. F. A. Grimmett
(BirdLife International, UK)

P. Oliveira
(Parque Natural da Madeira)

L. Rose
(Royal Society for the Protection of Birds, UK)

A. Swash
(Ministry of Agriculture, Fisheries and Food, UK)

Zino's Petrel
(Pterodroma madeira)

Compiled by:

Francis Zino
(Freira Conservation Project, Madeira)

Borja Heredia
(BirdLife International, UK) and

Manuel J. Bliscoito
(Museu Municipal do Funchal, Madeira)

With contributions from:

B. Bell
(Wildlife Management International, New Zealand)

C. J. Bibby
(BirdLife International, UK)

W. R. P. Bourne
(Aberdeen University, Scotland)

A. Buckle
(ICI Public Health, UK)

H. Costa Neves
(Parque Natural da Madeira)

T. Gerrard
(Madeira)

J. P. Granadeiro
(Instituto da Conservação da Natureza, Portugal)

R. F. A. Grimmett
(BirdLife International, UK)

P. Oliveira
(Parque Natural da Madeira)

A. Swash
(Ministry of Agriculture, Fisheries and Food, UK)

Pygmy Cormorant
(Phalacrocorax pygmeus)

Compiled by:

A. J. Crivelli
(Station Biologique de la Tour du Valat, France)

T. Nazirides
(University of Thessaloniki, Greece)

H. Jerrentrup
(Society for Protection of Nature and Ecodevelopment, Greece)

With contributions from:

M. Anagnostopoulou
(Greek Biotope/Wetland Centre)

C. Athanasiou
(WWF-Greece)

G. Catsadorakis
(Greece)

E. Daroglou
(Society for Protection of Nature and Ecodevelopment, Greece)

B. Hallmann
(Greece)

G. Handrinos
(Wetlands International National Delegate, Ministry of Agriculture, Greece)

D. Hatzilakou
(Greece)

B. Heredia
(BirdLife International, UK)

S. Kouvelis
(WWF-Greece)

M. Malakou
(Society for the Protection of Prespa, Greece)

M. Marinov
(Danube Delta Institute, Romania)

T. Michev
(Institute of Ecology, Bulgaria)

C. Papaconstantinou
(Hellenic Ornithological Society, Greece)

N. Peja
(Univerity of Tirana, Albania)

N. Petrov Dilchev
(Institute of Ecology, Bulgaria)

P. Rose
(Wetlands International, UK)

G. Sarigul
(Turkish Society for the Protection of Nature, Turkey)

V. Taylor
(Wetlands International, UK)

J. van Vessem
(Wetlands International, UK)

Dalmatian Pelican
(Pelecanus crispus)

Compiled by:

A. J. Crivelli
(Station Biologique de la Tour du Valat, France)

With contributions from:

M. Anagnostopoulou
(Greek Biotope/Wetland Centre)

C. Athanasiou
(WWF-Greece)

G. Catsadorakis
(Society for the Protection of Prespa, Greece)

G. Daoutopoulos
(University of Thessaloniki, Greece)

E. Daroglou
(Society for Protection of Nature and
Ecodevelopment, Greece)

T. Dimalexis
(University of Thessaloniki, Greece)

B. Hallmann
(Greece)

G. Handrinos
(International Wetlands and Waterfowl Research
Bureau National Delegate, Ministry of Agriculture,
Greece)

D. Hatzilakou
(Greece)

B. Heredia
(BirdLife International, UK)

H. Jerrentrup
(Society for Protection of Nature and
Ecodevelopment, Greece)

S. Kouvelis
(WWF-Greece)

M. Malakou
(Society for the Protection of Prespa, Greece)

M. Marinov
(Danube Delta Institute, Romania)

T. Michev
(Institute of Ecology, Bulgaria)

T. Nazirides
(University of Thessaloniki, Greece)

C. Papaconstantinou
(Hellenic Ornithological Society, Greece)

N. Peja
(University of Tirana, Albania)

N. Petrov Dilchev
(Institute of Ecology, Bulgaria)

M. Pyrovetsi
(University of Thessaloniki, Greece)

P. Rose
(International Wetlands and Waterfowl Research
Bureau, UK)

L. Rose
(Royal Society for the Protection of Birds, UK)

G. Sarigul
(Turkish Society for the Protection of Nature)

V. Taylor
(International Wetlands and Waterfowl Research
Bureau, UK)

J. van Vessem
(International Wetlands and Waterfowl Research
Bureau, UK)

Lesser White-fronted Goose
(Anser erythropus)

Compiled by:

Jesper Madsen
(National Environmental Research Institute,
Denmark)

With contributions from:

T. Aarvak
(Norwegian Ornithological Society)

Å. Andersson
(Swedish Hunters' Society)

A. Andreev
(Research Centre Eastern Palearctic Wetlands, Russian Federation)

T. Ardamatskaya
(Azov Black Sea Ornithological Station, Ukraine)

T. Bø
(Noreland Region, Norway)

A. Bylin
(Tovetorp Zoological Research Station, Sweden)

M. Ekker
(Directorate for Nature Management, Norway)

S. Farago
(University of Forestry and Wood Sciences, Hungary)

E. H. Sultanov
(Azerbaijan)

G. Handrinos
(Ministry of Agriculture, Greece)

P. Herkenrath
(Naturschutzbund Deutschland)

P. Iankov
(Bulgarian Society for the Protection of Birds)

B. Ivanov
(Bulgarian Society for the Protection of Birds)

H. Jerrentrup
(Society for the Protection of Nature and Ecodevelopment, Greece)

T. Larsson
(Swedish Environmental Protection Agency)

J. Lu
(China)

J. Markkola
(Finland)

T. Michev
(Institute of Ecology, Bulgaria)

V. Morozov
(Russian Research Institute of Nature Conservation)

D. Munteanu
(Romanian Ornithological Society)

I. J. Øien
(Norwegian Ornithological Society)

V. Serebryakov
(Shevchenko University, Ukraine)

E. Syroechkovski, Jr.
(Institute of Evolutionary Morphology and Animal Ecology, Russian Federation)

L. von Essen
(Swedish Hunters' Society)

A. Z.-U. Zhatknabayev
(Institute of Zoology, Kazakhstan)

Other collaborators:

T. Fox
(Denmark)

B. Ebbinge
(Institute for Forestry and Nature Research, Netherlands)

H. Meltofte
(Denmark)

D. Vangeluwe
(Institut Royal des Sciences Naturelles de Belgique)

Red-breasted Goose
(Branta ruficollis)

Compiled by:

Janet M. Hunter
(Wildfowl and Wetlands Trust, UK)

Jeffrey M. Black
(Wildfowl and Wetlands Trust, UK)

With contributions from:

T. Ardamatskaya
(Azov Black Sea Ornithological Station, Ukraine)

O. Biber
(Schweizerische Vogelwarte)

N. Crockford
(Royal Society for the Protection of Birds, UK)

G. Dändliker
(Schweizer Vogelschutz-BirdLife)

V. Flint
(Institute for Nature Conservation, Russian Federation)

G. Handrinos
(Ministry of Agriculture, Greece)

B. Heredia
(BirdLife International, UK)

P. Iankov
(Bulgarian Society for the Protection of Birds, Bulgaria)

B. Ivanov
(Bulgarian Society for the Protection of Birds)

I. Kostin
(Central Scientific Research Laboratory of Game Management and Natural Resources, Russian Federation)

V. Krivenko
(Institute for Nature Conservation, Russian Federation)

J. Madsen
(National Environmental Research Institute, Denmark)

T. Michev
(Le Balkan Foundation, Institute of Ecology, Bulgaria)

J. Mooij
(Zentrale für Wasservogelforschung und Feuchtgebietsschutz in Deutschland)

W. Müller
(Schweizer Vogelschutz-BirdLife)

D. Munteanu
(Romanian Ornithological Society)

M. Owen
(Wildfowl and Wetlands Trust, UK)

M. Patrikeev
(Canadian Wildlife Service, Canada)

P. Rose
(International Waterfowl and Wetlands Research Bureau, UK)

Y. Schadilov
(Institute for Nature Conservation, Russian Federation)

P. Simeonov
(Le Balkan, Bulgaria/France)

W. I. Sutherland
(University of East Anglia, UK)

E. Syroechkovski, Jr.
(Institute for Ecology and Evolution, Russian Federation)

V. Taylor
(International Waterfowl and Wetlands Research Bureau, UK)

D. Vangeluwe
(Institut Royal des Sciences Naturelles de Belgique)

A. Z.-U. Zhatknabayev
(Institute of Zoology, Kazakhstan)

Other collaborators:

A. Belousova
(Institute for Nature Conservation, Russian Federation)

V. Chetverikov
(Ministry for Environment Protection and Natural Resources, Russian Federation)

B. Ebbinge
(Institute for Forestry and Nature Research, Netherlands)

V. Morozov
(Institute for Nature Conservation, Russian Federation)

E. V. Rogacheva
(Academy of Sciences, Russian Federation)

V. Serebryakov
(Shevchenko University, Ukraine)

D. E. Sergeant
(Canada)

E. E. Syroechkovski, Sr.
(Academy of Sciences, Russian Federation)

Marbled Teal
(Marmaronetta angustirostris)

Compiled by:

A. Green
(Wildfowl and Wetlands Trust, UK)

With contributions from:

D. Alon
(Israel Raptor Information Center)

G. Aydemir
(Turkish Society for the Protection of Nature)

A. Belemih
(Comité des Programmes de Conservation de la Nature, Morocco)

D. Boukhalfa
(Service des Parcs Nationaux et Zones Humides, Algeria)

V. van den Berk
(National Reference Centre for Nature Management, Netherlands)

N. J. Crockford
(Royal Society for the Protection of Birds, UK)

M. Dakki
(Centre d'Etudes des Migrations des Oiseaux)

J. Franchimont
(Groupe Ornithologique du Maroc)

H. Hamrouni
(Association "Les Amis des Oiseaux", Tunisia)

D. Hoffmann[1]
(Comité des Programmes de Conservation de la Nature, Morocco)

J. Hunter
(Wildfowl and Wetlands Trust, UK)

A. Khan
(Ornithological Society of Pakistan)

G. Kirwan
(Ornithological Society of the Middle East, UK)

F. Maamouri
(WWF, Tunisia)

M. Maghnouj
(Eaux et Forêts, Morocco)

R. Martí
(SEO/BirdLife Spain)

P. L. Meininger
(Ministerie van Verkeer en Waterstaat, Netherlands)

J. D. Navarro Medina
(Sociedad Ornitológica Marmaronetta, Spain)

E. Nowak
(Bonn Convention Secretariat, Germany)

M. Patrikeev
(Canadian Wildlife Service, Canada)

F. Robledano
(Sociedad Ornitológica Marmaronetta, Spain)

P. Rose
(Wetlands International, UK)

E. Shy
(Nature Reserves Authority, Israel)

V. Taylor
(Wetlands International, UK)

M. Yarar
(Turkish Society for the Protection of Nature)

White-headed Duck
(Oxyura leucocephala)

Compiled by:

A. Green
(Wildfowl and Wetlands Trust, UK)

B. Hughes
(Wildfowl and Wetlands Trust, UK)

With contributions from:

J. A. Aguilar-Armat
(Doñana Biological Station, Spain)

F. J. Aguilar Delgado
(SEO/BirdLife Spain)

A. Alcalá-Zamora Barrón
(AMA, Córdoba, Spain)

D. Alon
(Israel Raptor Information Center)

B. Asensio
(DGN, Spain)

J. M. Ayala Moreno
(SEO/BirdLife Spain)

G. Aydemir
(Turkish Society for the Protection of Nature)

H.-G. Bauer
(Vogelwarte Radolfzell, Germany)

Z. Benaïssa
(Association "Les Amis des Oiseaux", Tunisia)

V. van den Berk
(National Reference Centre for Nature Management, Netherlands)

1. Now Royal Society for the Protection of Birds, UK.

D. Boukhalfa
(Service des Parcs Nationaux et Zones Humides, Algeria)

J. Criado
(SEO/BirdLife Spain)

N. J. Crockford
(Royal Society for the Protection of Birds, UK)

M. Dakki
(Centre d'Etudes des Migrations des Oiseaux, Morocco)

G. Dändliker
(Swiss Association for the Protection of Birds)

G. Engblom
(Swedish Ornithological Society)

E. Fernández-Galiano
(Council of Europe, France)

A. Fox
(National Environmental Research Institute, Denmark)

J. Franchimont
(Groupe Ornithologique du Maroc)

H. Garrido
(Doñana National Park, Spain)

I. Gorban
(L'viv University, Ukraine)

H. Hamrouni
(Association "Les Amis des Oiseaux", Tunisia)

G. Handrinos
(Ministry of Agriculture, Greece)

B. Heredia
(BirdLife International, UK)

J. Holmes
(Joint Nature Conservation Committee, UK)

J. Hunter
(Wildfowl and Wetlands Trust, UK)

P. Iankov
(Bulgarian Society for the Protection of Birds)

B. Ivanov
(Bulgarian Society for the Protection of Birds)

H. Jerrentrup
(Society for the Protection of Nature and Ecodevelopment, Greece)

J. Jiménez
(Cabañeros Natural Park, Spain)

A. Khan
(Ornithological Society of Pakistan)

G. Kirwan
(Ornithological Society of the Middle East, UK)

J. M. López Martos
(SEO/BirdLife Spain)

M. Máñez
(Doñana National Park, Spain)

R. Martí
(SEO/BirdLife Spain)

J. J. Matamala
(SEO/BirdLife Spain)

J. Mayol
(Wildlife Service, Mallorca, Spain)

B. Moreno Arroyo
(AMA, Córdoba, Spain)

C. Morillo
(DGN, Spain)

D. Munteanu
(Romanian Ornithological Society)

J. C. Nevado
(Environmental Agency, Almería, Spain)

O. K. Nielsen
(Icelandic Museum of Natural History)

H. Opitz
(German Society for the Protection of Nature)

M. Patrikeev
(Canadian Wildlife Service)

P. Pereira
(Doñana National Park, Spain)

J. Quero Fernández de Molina
(Agencia de Medio Ambiente, Spain)

P. Rose
(International Waterfowl and Wetlands Research Bureau, UK)

E. Shy
(Nature Reserves Authority, Israel)

J. A. Torres Esquivias
(Agencia de Medio Ambiente, Spain)

C. Urdiales
(Doñana National Park, Spain)

M. Vitaloni
(WWF, Italy)

M. Yarar
(Turkish Society for the Protection of Nature)

Cinereous Vulture
(Aegypius monachus)

Compiled by:

Borja Heredia
(BirdLife International, UK)

With contributions from:

A. Abuladze
(Institute of Zoology, Georgia)

M. Bijleveld
(Black Vulture Conservation Foundation,
Switzerland)

E. Bikos
(Souflion Forest Service, Greece)

V. Ciochia
(Romanian Ornithological and Nature
Conservation Society)

J. Criado
(SEO/BirdLife Spain)

N. J. Crockford
(Royal Society for the Protection of Birds, UK)

R. Faust
(Frankfurt Zoological Society, Germany)

H. Frey
(University of Veterinary Medicine, Austria)

V. Galushin
(Moscow Pedagogical University)

J. Garzón
(European Nature Heritage Fund, Spain)

L. M. González
(DGN, Directorate-General for Nature
Conservation, Spain)

B. Grubac
(Institute for Nature Protection, Serbia)

B. Hallmann
(Black Vulture Conservation Foundation,
Greece)

P. Iankov
(Bulgarian Society for the Protection of Birds)

J. Jimenez
(Cabañeros National Park, Ciudad Real, Spain)

S. Kladara
(WWF, Greece)

F. Lamani
(Albania)

S. Marin
(Green Balkans Movement, Bulgaria)

P. Matsoukas
(WWF, Greece)

J. Mayol
(Mallorca Wildlife Service, Spain)

B.-U. Meyburg
(World Working Group on Birds of Prey,
Germany)

M. Panayotopoulou
(Hellenic Ornithological Society)

T. Petrov
(Bulgarian Society for the Protection of Birds)

K. Pistolas
(Dadiá Reserve, Greece)

K. Poirazidis
(WWF, Greece)

L. Profirov
(Ministry of the Environment, Bulgaria)

D. Rallis
(Dadiá Council, Greece)

J. J. Sanchéz
(Black Vulture Conservation Foundation,
Mallorca)

R. Spiropoulou
(Ministry of the Environment, Greece)

G. Susic
(Institute of Ornithology, Croatia)

M. Terrasse
(Fonds d'Intervention pour les Rapaces, France)

E. Tewes
(Wildlife Service, Mallorca)

M. Tsolakidis
(Evros Directorate of Forestry, Greece)

S. Yotov
(Birds of Prey Protection Society, Bulgaria)

Imperial Eagle
(Aquila heliaca)

Compiled by:

Borja Heredia
(BirdLife International, UK)

With contributions from:

A. Abuladze
(Institute of Zoology, Georgia)

J. Bagyura
(Hungarian Ornithological and Nature
Conservation Society)

V. Belik
(Rostov, Russian Federation)

N. J. Crockford
(Royal Society for the Protection of Birds, UK)

J. Chavko
(Slovak Agency for the Environment)

S. Danko
(Slovak Ornithological Society)

V. Galushin
(Moscow Pedagogical University)

A. Gretton
(UK)

B. Hallmann
(Hellenic Ornithological Society)

L. Haraszthy
(Hungarian Ornithological and Nature
Conservation Society)

P. Iankov
(Bulgarian Society for the Protection of Birds)

L. Kalabér
(Romanian Ornithological Society)

P. Kanuch
(Society for the Protection of Birds in Slovakia)

S. Marin
(Green Balkans Movement, Bulgaria)

B.-U. Meyburg
(World Working Group on Birds of Prey,
Germany)

T. Mikuska
(Croatian Society for the Protection of Birds and
Nature)

T. Petrov
(Bulgarian Society for the Protection of Birds)

R. F. Porter
(BirdLife International, UK)

L. Profirov
(Ministry of Environment, Bulgaria)

M. Terrasse
(Fonds d'Intervention pour les Rapaces, France)

V. Vetrov
(Ukrainian Union for Bird Conservation)

Z. Waliczky
(BirdLife International, UK)

M. Yarar
(Society for the Protection of Nature, Turkey)

N. Zubcov
(Institute of Zoology, Moldova)

Spanish Imperial Eagle
(Aquila adalberti)

Compiled by:

Luis Mariano Gonzámez
(DGN, Directorate-General for Nature
Conservation, Spain)

With contributions from:

J. Caballero
(Spain)

R. Cadenas
(Doñana National Park, Spain)

B. Heredia
(BirdLife International, UK)

I. Oria
(Spain)

A. Sánchez
(Environmental Agency, Extremadura, Spain)

Lesser Kestrel
(Falco naumanni)

Compiled by:
Jean-Pierre Biber
(Bureau NATCONS, Switzerland)

With contributions from:
(including those who contributed to the 1990 action plan)

A. Abuladze
(Institute of Zoology, Georgia)

A. Araújo
(Instituto da Conservação da Natureza, Portugal)

L. Brun
(CEEP/FIR, Arles, France)

J. Bustamante
(Estación Biológica de Doñana, Spain)

P. Campredon
(IUCN, Guinée-Bissau)

O. Ceballos
(Grupo de Estudios Biológicos Ugarra, Pamplona, Spain)

M. Charalambides
(Cyprus Ornithological Society)

J. Criado
(SEO/BirdLife Spain)

A. Davygora
(Orenburg Pedagogical Institute, Russian Federation)

J. A. Donázar
(Estación Biológica de Doñana, Spain)

I. Essetti
(Association les Amis des Oiseaux, Tunisia)

G. Fernández Alcàzar
(Consellería d'Agricultura i Pesca, Palma de Mallorca, Spain)

J. Franchimont
(Groupe d'Ornithologie du Maroc)

U. Gallo Orsi
(Lega Italiana Protezione Uccelli)

G. González Jurado
(SILVEMA, Spain)

B. Hallmann
(Hellenic Ornithological Society, Greece)

B. Heredia
(BirdLife International, UK)

F. Hiraldo
(Estación Biológica de Doñana, Spain)

P. Iankov
(Bulgarian Society for the Protection of Birds)

J. P. Ledant
(Institut Royal des Sciences Naturelles de Belgique)

S. León Rodríguez
(SILVEMA, Spain)

H. Mendelssohn
(University of Tel-Aviv, Israel)

D. Munteanu
(Romanian Ornithological Society)

J. Muzinic
(Croatian Society for Bird and Nature Protection)

M. A. Naveso
(SEO/BirdLife Spain)

J. J. Negro
(Estación Biológica de Doñana, Spain)

D. Pepler
(Nature Conservation, South Africa)

A. L. Pérez Lara
(SILVEMA, Spain)

M. Pomarol
(Generalitat de Catalunya, Spain)

M. de la Riva
(Estación Biológica de Doñana, Spain)

P. Rocha
(Instituto da Conservação da Natureza, Portugal)

L. Rose
(Royal Society for the Protection of Birds, UK)

A. Sigismondi
(Comitato Italiano Protezione Rapaci)

J. Sultana
(BirdLife Malta)

J. L. Tella
(Estación Biológica de Doñana, Spain)

M. Yarar
(Turkish Society for the Protection of Nature)

Corncrake
(Crex crex)

Compiled by:

N. Crockford
(Royal Society for the Protection of Birds, UK)

R. Green
(Royal Society for the Protection of Birds, UK)

G. Rocamora
(Ligue pour la Protection des Oiseaux France)

N. Schäffer
(Max-Planck-Institut für Verhaltenphysiologie, Germany)

T. Stowe
(Royal Society for the Protection of Birds, UK)

G. Williams
(Royal Society for the Protection of Birds, UK)

With contributions from:

L. van den Bergh
(Institute for Forestry and Nature Research, Netherlands)

J. Broyer
(Office National de la Chasse, France)

R. Budrys
(Department of Zoology, Vilnius University, Lithuania)

P. Burger
(South Bohemian Museum, Czech Republic)

C. Casey
(Irish Wildbird Conservancy, Republic of Ireland)

G. Chacón
(Centre Catalá d'Ornitología, Spain)

P. Cempulik
(Department of Natural History, Upper Silesian Museum, Poland)

T. Conzemius
(Lëtzebuerger Natur- a Vulleschutzliga, Luxembourg)

J. Coveney
(Irish Wildbird Conservancy, Republic of Ireland)

M. Czyzak
(Ornithological Station IEPAS, Poland)

V. Delov
(Bulgarian Society for the Protection of Birds)

M. Demko
(Society for the Protection of Birds in Slovakia, Slovakia)

J. Dewyspelaere
(Natuurreservaten BNVR, Belgium)

J. Dixon
(Royal Society for the Protection of Birds, UK)

M. Dvorak
(BirdLife, Austria)

J. Elts
(Estonian Ornithological Society, Tartu)

I. Farronato
(GVSO Nisoria, c/o Museo Naturalistico di Vicenza, Italy)

M. Flade
(Landesanstalt für Grosschutzgebiete Brandenburg, Germany)

A. Folvik
(Norwegian Ornithological Society)

C. Gache
(SOR-Iasi, Laboratory of Zoology, University of Iasi, Romania)

B. Godert
(Lëtzebuerger Natur- a Vulleschutzliga, Luxembourg)

I. Gorban
(L'viv State University, Ukraine)

M. Grell
(Dansk Ornitologisk Forening, Denmark)

M. F. Heath
(BirdLife International, UK)

B. Heredia
(BirdLife International, UK)

J. Hora
(National Museum, Czech Republic)

R. Horváth
(Hungarian Ornithological and Nature
Conservation Society)

J. Huysecom
(Réserves Naturelles et Ornithologiques de
Belgique)

P. Iankov
(Bulgarian Society for the Protection of Birds)

W. Kania
(Ornithological Station IEPAS, Poland)

P. Kanuch
(Society for the Protection of Birds in Slovakia)

D. Karaska
(Society for the Protection of Birds in Slovakia)

O. Keiss
(Latvian Fund for Nature)

K. H. Kolb
(Rhoen Biosphere Reserve, Germany)

J. Kornan
(Society for the Protection of Birds in Slovakia)

P. Koskimies
(BirdLife Finland)

T. Kulakowski
(Bialystok, Poland)

A. Kuresoo
(Institute of Zoology and Botany, Estonia)

A. Kürthy
(Society for the Protection of Birds in Slovakia)

P. Lina
(National Reference Centre for Nature
Management, Netherlands)

V. Maletic
(University of Skopje, the former Yugoslav
Republic of Macedonia)

A. Mikityuk
(Ukrainian Union for Bird Conservation)

T. Mikuska
(Croatian Society for the Protection of Birds and
Nature)

I. Mirowski
(Foundation Ecofund, Poland)

A. Mischenko
(Russian Research Institute of Nature
Conservation)

T. Mokwa
(Ornithological Station IEPAS, Poland)

A. Mosalov
(Moscow State Pedagogical University)

W. Müller
(Schweizer Vogelschutz)

A. Munteanu
(Institute of Zoology, Moldova)

D. Munteanu
(Societatea Ornitologica Romana)

I. Øien
(Norwegian Ornithological Society)

E. Osieck
(Vogelbescherming Nederland)

R. Ottvall
(Ottenby Bird Observatory, Sweden)

F. Perco
(Osservatorio Faunistico del FV6 – Udine, Italy)

A. Petryshyn
(L'viv Ornithological Club, Ukraine)

J. Pettersson
(Ottenby Bird Observatory, Sweden)

J. Priednieks
(Latvian Fund for Nature)

J. Pykal
(Czech Institute of Nature Conservation)

J. Radovic
(State Institute for the Protection of Cultural
and Natural Heritage, Croatia)

M. Remisiewicz
(Polish Society for the Protection of Birds)

P. Ryelandt
(Réserves Naturelles et Ornithologiques de
Belgique)

P. Sackl
(Stmk Landesmuseum Joanneum, Austria)

E. Sérusiaux
(Réserves Naturelles et Ornithologiques de
Belgique)

A. Sikora
(Ornithological Station IEPAS, Poland)

I. Skilsky
(Museum of Natural History, Ukraine)

K. Standring
(Royal Society for the Protection of Birds, UK)

M. Strazds
(Latvian Ornithological Society)

A. Tishechkin
(Belarusian Ornithological Society)

P. Tout
(Collegio del Mundo Unito dell'Adriatico, Italy)

P. Trontelj
(Birdwatching and Bird Study Association of
Slovenia)

F. Vassen
(Réserves Naturelles et Ornithologiques de
Belgique)

Y. Vergeles
(State Academy of Urban Economy, Ukraine)

Z. Waliczky
(BirdLife International, UK)

G. Willi
(Bot.-Zool. Ges. Liechtenstein-Sargans-
Werbenberg, Liechtenstein)

J. Wilson
(National Parks and Wildlife Service, Republic of
Ireland)

J. Winkelman
(Vogelbescherming Nederland)

M. Zielinski
(Ornithological Station IEPAS, Poland)

K. Zub
(Mammal Research Institute, Poland)

M. Zurba
(Lithuanian Ornithological Society)

Great Bustard
(Otis tarda)

This action plan is dedicated to the late Julia
Antonchikova, who contributed so much to
Great Bustard conservation in the Russian
Federation.

Compiled by:

Hans Peter Kollar
(Austria)

With contributions from:

J. A. Alonso
(University of Madrid)

J. C. Alonso
(National Museum of Natural Sciences, Spain)

J. Antonchikova
(Russian Bird Conservation Union)

V. Belik
(Russian Antiplague Institute, Rostov)

J. Chavko
(Slovak Nature Protection Agency, Bratislava
District)

J. Chobot
(Slovak Nature Protection Agency, Nitra
District)

S. Faragó
(University of Forestry and Wood Sciences,
Hungary)

I. Fatér
(Hungarian Ornithological and Nature
Conservation Society)

D. Georgiev
(Bulgarian Society for the Protection of Birds)

I. Gorban
(L'viv University, Ukraine)

P. Goriup
(Nature Conservation Bureau, UK)

J. Hellmich
(Asociación para la Defensa de la Naturaleza y
los Recursos de Extremadura, Spain)

B. Heredia
(BirdLife International, UK)

S. Hidalgo de Trucios
(University of Extremadura, Spain)

P. Iankov
(Bulgarian Society for the Protection of Birds)

Z. Kalotás
(Agency for Nature Conservation, Hungary)

P. Kanuch
(Society for the Protection of Birds in Slovakia)

I. Kurpé
(Dévaványa Landscape Protection Area,
Hungary)

N. Lindsay
(Zoological Society of London, UK)

H. Litzbarski
(Landesumweltamt Brandenburg, Germany)

F. Márkus
(WWF, Hungary)

S. Nagy
(Hungarian Ornithological and Nature
Conservation Society)

M. A. Naveso
(SEO/BirdLife Spain)

F. Petretti
(WWF, Italy)

M. Pinto
(Instituto da Conservação da Natureza,
Portugal)

L. Rose
(Royal Society for the Protection of Birds, UK)

L. Szabó
(Hortobágy National Park, Hungary)

A. Teixeira
(Instituto da Conservação da Natureza,
Portugal)

M. Vlasín
(Czech Institute for Nature Protection)

Z. Waliczky
(BirdLife International, UK)

H. Wurm
(Pannonic Society for Great Bustard Protection,
Austria)

M. Yarar
(Society for the Protection of Nature, Turkey)

Houbara Bustard (Canary Islands)
(Chlamydotis undulata fuertaventurae)

Compiled by:

Borja Heredia
(BirdLife International, UK)

With contributions from:

J. Carrillo
(University of La Laguna, Tenerife)

G. Delgado
(Natural History Museum, Tenerife)

G. Díaz
(Vice-Council for the Environment, Gran
Canaria)

F. Domínguez
(Vice-Council for the Environment, Tenerife)

K. W. Emmerson
(ORNISTUDIO, Tenerife)

C. González
(SEO/BirdLife Spain, Tenerife)

P. Goriup
(Nature Conservation Bureau Ltd., UK)

E. Hernández
(Vice-Council for the Environment, Tenerife)

J. A. Lorenzo
(University of La Laguna, Tenerife)

A. Machado
(DGN, Tenerife)

A. Martín
(University of La Laguna, Tenerife)

A. Moreno
(Vice-Council for the Environment, Gran
Canaria)

M. Nogales
(University of La Laguna, Tenerife)

V. Quilis
(Vice-Council for the Environment, Tenerife)

F. Rodríguez
(Vice-Council for the Environment, Gran
Canaria)

J. L. Rodríguez
(Vice-Council for the Environment, Tenerife)

L. Rose
(Royal Society for the Protection of Birds, UK)

A. Sánchez
(SEO/BirdLife Spain)

C. Sunyer
(SEO/BirdLife Spain)

Slender-billed Curlew
(Numenius tenuirostris)

Compiled by:

Adam Gretton
(BirdLife International, UK)

With contributions from:

(including those involved as national coordinators in the BirdLife International
(then ICBP) project 1988-90)

F. Ayache
(Ministry of Environment and Land Use Planning, Tunisia)

N. Baccetti
(Istituto Nazionale per la Fauna Selvatica, Italy)

S. Baris
(Society for the Protection of Nature, Turkey)

V. Belik
(Russian Bird Conservation Union, Rostov)

B. Chalabi
(Institut National Agronomique, Algeria)

M. Dakki
(Institut Scientifique, Morocco)

A. Errahioui
(Eaux et Forêts, Morocco)

T. Gaultier
(Laboratoire d'Ornithologie, Tunisia)

V. Goutner
(Thessaloniki University, Greece)

B. Heredia
(BirdLife International, UK)

D. Hoffmann
(BirdLife International/CPCN, Morocco)

P. Iankov
(Bulgarian Society for the Protection of Birds)

A. Ignatov
(Bulgarian Society for the Protection of Birds)

H. Kachiche
(Eaux et Forêts, Morocco)

G. Kovács
(Hortobágy National Park, Hungary)

A. Kovshar
(Zoological Institute, Alma-Ata, Kazakhstan)

M. Lambertini
(Lega Italiana Protezione Uccelli)

G. Magnin
(Society for the Protection of Nature, Turkey)

F. Márkus
(Hungarian Ornithological and Nature Conservation Society)

R. Martí
(SEO/BirdLife Spain)

A. Mikityuk
(Ukranian Union for Bird Conservation)

A. Mischenko
(Russian Bird Conservation Union, Moscow)

V. Morozov
(Russian Bird Conservation Union, Moscow)

D. Munteanu
(Romanian Ornithological Society)

J. Muzinic
(Institute for Ornithology, Croatia)

S. Nagy
(Hungarian Ornithological and Nature Conservation Society)

L. Profirov
(Ministry of Environment, Bulgaria)

L. Rose
(Royal Society for the Protection of Birds, UK)

C. Urdiales
(Doñana National Park, Spain)

D. Vangeluwe
(Institut Royal Sciences Naturelles de Belgique)

M. Yarar
(Society for the Protection of Nature, Turkey)

A. K. Yurlov
(Institute of Systematics and Animal Ecology,
Novosibirsk, Russian Federation)

Audouin's Gull
(Larus audouinii)

Compiled by:

Marco Lambertinio
(Lega Italiana Protezione Uccelli)

With contributions from:

G. Allport
(BirdLife International, UK)

G. Alvarez
(Instituto Nacional para la Conservación de la
Naturaleza, Spain)

N. Bacetti
(Istituto Nazionale per la Fauna Selvatica, Italy)

D. Boukhalfa
(Agence Nationale de Conservation de la Nature,
Algeria)

P. Bradley
(Royal Society for the Protection of Birds, UK)

M. Dakki
(Centre D'Etude des Migrations d'Oiseaux,
Morocco)

I. Essetti
(Association les Amis des Oiseaux, Tunisia)

M. Fasola
(University of Pavia, Italy)

B. Heredia
(BirdLife International, UK)

L. Jover
(Universitat de Barcelona, Spain)

B. Lombatti
(Lega Italiana Protezione Uccelli)

X. Monbailliu
(MEDMARAVIS, France)

X. Ruiz
(Universitat de Barcelona, Spain)

J. C. Thibault
(Parc Naturel Régionel de Corse, France)

H.-H. Witt
(Germany)

M. Yarar
(Society for the Protection of Nature, Turkey)

Madeira Lurel Pigeon
(Columba trocaz)

Compiled by:

Borja Heredia
(BirdLife International, UK)

Paulo Oliveira
(Parque Natural da Madeira)

With Contributions from:

M. J. Biscoito
(Museu Municipal do Funchal, Madeira)

H. Costa Neves
(Parque Natural da Madeira)

N. J. Crockford
(Royal Society for the Protection of Birds, UK)

R. F. A. Grimmett
(BirdLife International, UK)

M. J. Jones
(Manchester Metropolitan University, UK)

F. Zino
(Freira Conservation Project, Madeira)

Dark-tailed Laurel Pigeon
(Columba bollii)

Compiled by:

Cristina González
(SEO/BirdLife Spain, Tenerife)

With contributions from:

J. Carrillo
(University of La Laguna, Tenerife)

G. Delgado
(Natural History Museum, Tenerife)

G. Díaz
(Vice-Council for the Environment, Gran
Canaria)

F. Domínguez
(Vice-Council for the Environment, Tenerife)

K. W. Emmerson
(ORNISTUDIO, Tenerife)

A. Fernández
(Garajonay National Park, La Gomera)

B. Heredia
(BirdLife International, UK)

E. Hernandez
(Vice-Council for the Environment, Tenerife)

J. A. Lorenzo
(University of La Laguna, Tenerife)

A. Machado
(DGN, Tenerife)

A. Martín
(University of La Laguna, Tenerife)

A. Moreno
(Vice-Council for the Environment, Gran Canaria)

M. Nogales
(University of La Laguna, Tenerife)

V. Quilis
(Vice-Council for the Environment, Tenerife)

F. Rodríguez
(Vice-Council for the Environment, Gran Canaria)

J. L. Rodríguez Luengo
(Vice-Council for the Environment, Tenerife)

L. Rose
(Royal Society for the Protection of Birds, UK)

C. Sunyer
(SEO/Birdlife, Spain)

White-tailed Laurel Pigeon
(Columba junoniae)

Compiled by:

Cristina González
(SEO/BirdLife Spain, Tenerife)

With contributions from:

J. Carrillo
(University of La Laguna, Tenerife)

G. Delgado
(Natural History Museum, Tenerife)

G. Díaz
(Vice-Council for the Environment, Gran Canaria)

F. Domínguez
(Vice-Council for the Environment, Tenerife)

K. W. Emmerson
(ORNISTUDIO, Tenerife)

A. Fernández
(Garajonay National Park, La Gomera)

B. Heredia
(BirdLife International, UK)

E. Hernandez
(Vice-Council for the Environment, Tenerife)

J. A. Lorenzo
(University of La Laguna, Tenerife)

A. Machado
(DGN, Tenerife)

A. Martín
(University of La Laguna, Tenerife)

A. Moreno
(Vice-Council for the Environment, Gran Canaria)

M. Nogales
(University of La Laguna, Tenerife)

V. Quilis
(Vice-Council for the Environment, Tenerife)

F. Rodríguez
(Vice-Council for the Environment, Gran Canaria)

J. L. Rodríguez Luengo
(Vice-Council for the Environment, Tenerife)

L. Rose
(Royal Society for the Protection of Birds, UK)

C. Sunyer
(SEO/Birdlife Spain)

Aquatic Warbler
(Acrocephalus paludicola)

Compiled by:

Borja Heredia
(BirdLife International, UK)

With contributions from:

N. J. Crockford
(Royal Society for the Protection of Birds, UK)

R. Czeraszkiewicz
(Szczecin Ornithological Station, Poland)

A. Dyrcz
(University of Wroclaw, Poland)

M. Flade
(Landesanstalt für Grosschutzgebiete, Germany)

I. Gorban
(L'viv University, Ukraine)

A. Gretton
(BirdLife International, UK)

L. Halupka
(University of Wroclaw, Poland)

S. Konyhás
(Hortobágy National Park, Hungary)

G. Kovács
(Hortobágy National Park, Hungary)

J. Krogulec
(University Marie-Curie Sklodowskiej, Poland)

C. Martín-Novella
(BirdLife International, UK)

M. Niziol
(Institute of Biology, Lublin, Poland)

D. Ochrymiuk
(Póknonopodlaskie Towarzystwo Ochrony
Ptaków, Poland)

E. Raneszek
(Milicz, Poland)

Y. Ravkin
(Biological Institute, Novosibirsk, Russian
Federation)

Y. Salyga
(L'viv University, Ukraine)

N. Schäffer
(Vogelwarte Radolfzell, Germany)

K. Schulze-Hagen
(Germany)

K. Standring
(Royal Society for the Protection of Birds, UK)

J. Szostakowski
(Ogólnopolskie Towarzystwo Ochrony Ptaków,
Poland)

J. Viksne
(Latvian Ornithological Society)

Z. Waliczky
(BirdLife International, UK)

Blue Chaffinch
(Fringilla teydea)

Compiled by:

Cristina González
(SEO/BirdLife Spain, Tenerife)

With contributions from:

J. Carrillo
(University of La Laguna, Tenerife)

G. Delgado
(Natural History Museum, Tenerife)

G. Díaz
(Vice-Council for the Environment, Gran Canaria)

F. Domínguez
(Vice-Council for the Environment, Tenerife)

K. W. Emmerson
(ORNISTUDIO, Tenerife)

B. Heredia
(BirdLife International, UK)

E. Hernández
(Vice-Council for the Environment, Tenerife)

J. A. Lorenzo
(University of La Laguna, Tenerife)

A. Martín
(University of La Laguna, Tenerife)

A. Moreno
(Vice-Council for the Environment, Gran Canaria)

M. Nogales
(University of La Laguna, Tenerife)

V. Quilis
(Vice-Council for the Environment, Tenerife)

F. Rodríguez
(Vice-Council for the Environment, Gran Canaria)

J. L. Rodríguez
(Vice-Council for the Environment, Tenerife)

L. Rose
(Royal Society for the Protection of Birds,UK)

C. Sunyer
(SEO/Birdlife, Spain[1])

Azores Bullfinch
(Pyrrhula murina)

Compiled by:

Jaime A. Ramos
(Universidade dos Açores, Portugal)

With contributions from:

C. J. Bibby
(Birdlife International, UK)

B. Heredia
(BirdLife International, UK)

---

1. Now Jorge Manrique 1, 28240 La Navata, Madrid.

Appendix 4
References

Aarvak, T. and Øien, I. J. (1994) Dverggås *Anser erythropus* - en truet art i Norge. *Vår Fuglefauna* 17: 70-80.

Aarvak, T. and Brøseth, H. (1994) *Prosjekt dverggås. Årsrapport 1994.* Norwegian Ornithological Society (Rep. 1-1994).

Abuladze, A. (1994) Birds of prey in Georgia in the 20th century. In Meyburg B. -U. and Chancellor, R. D., eds. *Raptor conservation today.* WWGBP Pica Press.

Abuladze, A. (in prep.) Ecology of the Imperial Eagle in Georgia. *Eagle Studies.*

Abuladze, A. and Shergalin, Y. E. (in prep.) On new threats for the Imperial Eagles. *Eagle Studies.*

Adamyan, M. S. (1989) [Breeding of *Anas angustirostris* in the Armenian SSR.] *Biol. J. Armenia* 8: 778-780. (In Russian.)

Aigare, V., Andrúaitis, G., Lipsbergs, J., Lodzina, I. and Tabaka, L. (1985) Pp.328-329 in *Latvijas PSR sarkana gramata.* Riga: Zinatne. (In Latvian, in Russian.)

Albanis, T. (1993) *Pesticide residues and their accumulation in wildlife of wetlands in Thermaikos and Amvrakikos Gulfs.* WWF project 4680-Greece, report.

Alcover, J. A. and Florit, X. (1986) Els ocells del jaciment archeologic de la Aldea, Gran Canaria. *Butll. Inst. Cat. Hist. Nat.* 56: 47-55.

Alonso, J. C., Alonso, J. A., and Muñoz-Pulido, R. (1994) Mitigation of bird collisions with transmission lines through groundwire marking. *Biol. Conserv.* 67: 129-134.

AMA Córdoba (1991) Evolución de la población ibérica de Malvasía (*Oxyura leucocephala*). Pp.145-151 in M. Jesús Martos J. and Fernández Palacios, eds. *Plan Rector de Uso y Gestión de las Reservas Naturales de las Lagunas de Cádiz.* Junta de Andalucía: Consejería de Cultura y Medio Ambiente, Agencia de Medio Ambiente.

Amat, J. A. and Sanchez, A. (1982) Biología y ecología de la malvasía *Oxyura leucocephala* en Andalucía. *Doñana Acta Vert.* 9: 251-320.

Ambiental, S. A. (1992) *Plan de recuperación de la Cerceta Pardilla en la Comunidad Valenciana.* Conselleria de Medi Ambient de la Generalitat Valenciana.

Andalus (1993) *Boletín Monográfico Buitre Negro.* Sevilla: Andalus.

Andone, G., Almasan, H., Rudu, D., Andone, L., Chirac, E. and Sclarletescu, G. (1969) Cercetare asupra pasarilor ichiofage din delta Dunarii. *Inst. Cercet. Pisc. Studi si Cercetari* 27: 133-183.

Anon. (1993) An international *Oxyura jamaicensis* workshop. *IWRB Threatened Waterfowl Res. Group Newsletter.* 4: 3-5. Anstey, S. (1989) The status and conservation of the White-headed Duck *Oxyura leucocephala.* Slimbridge, UK: International Waterfowl and Wetlands Research Bureau (IWRB Spec. Publ. 10).

Anon. (1978) European news. *Brit. Birds* 71: 582-587.

Anon. (1995) National Bank for Ornithological Information, Bulgarian Society for the Protection of Birds, Sofia, Bulgaria.

Anon. (1985) *Red Data Book of the People's Republic of Bulgaria, 2.* Sofia: Bulgarian Academy of Sciences.

Anon. (1992) *Conservation status of the Danube delta. 4.* Gland, Switzerland: IUCN East European Programme Environmental Status Reports.

Appak, B. A. (1992) Status of the Cinereous Vulture population in Crimea. In *Protection and study of rare and endangered animal species in Nature Reserves.* Moscow: Collection of Scientific Papers.

Arenas, R. and Torres, J. A. (1992) Biología y situación de la Malvasía en España. *Quercus* 73: 14-21.

Asensio, J. M. (1991) Impacto de la captura del Cangrejo Rojo sobre otras poblaciones de animales del Brazo del Este. *J. Zonas Húmedas Andaluzas* 1190: 107-115.

Ash, J. S. and Miskell, J. E. (1983) Birds of Somalia: their habitat, status and distribution. *Scopus* (Special Supplement) 1.

Audouin's Gull in two Spanish colonies in 1991. *Brit. Birds* 85: 97-100.

Aukes, P., van den Berk, V. M., Cronau, J. P., van Dorp, D., Özesmi, U. and van Winden, A. C. Bagyura, J. (1993) *The project of the Eastern European Imperial Eagle Working Group.* Unpublished.

Bannerman, D. A. (1963) *Birds of the Atlantic Islands, 1.* Edinburgh: Oliver and Boyd.

Bannerman, D. A. & Bannerman, W. M. (1966) *Birds of the Atlantic islands. 3: A history of the birds of the Azores.* Edinburgh, U.K.: Oliver and Boyd.

Barbieri, F., Bogliani, G. and Prigioni, C. (1986) Note sull' ornitofauna dell' Albania. *Riv. ital. Orn.* 56: 53-66.

Baris, Y. S. (1991) Conservation problems of steppic avifauna in Turkey. Pp.93-96 in P. D. Goriup, L. A. Batten and J. A. Norton, eds. *The conservation of lowland dry grassland birds in Europe.* Peterborough, UK: Joint Nature Conservation Committee.

Bartzoudis and Pyrovetsi, M. (1994) Efficient use of irrigation water from Lake Kerkini. Report.

Batten, L. A., Bibby, C. J., Clement, P., Elliott, G. D. and Porter, R. F., eds. (1990) *Red data birds in Britain: action for rare, threatened and important species.* London: T. and A. D. Poyser.

Bauer, H.-G. (1994) Ruddy Duck (*Oxyura jamaicensis*) and White-headed Duck (*O. leucocephala*) in Germany: occurrence and legal status. *Oxyura* 7:49-60.

Baumgart, W. (1991) Raptor problems in Syria. *WWGBP Newsl.* 14: 15-16.

Beaman, M. (1986) Turkey: Bird Report 1976-81. *Sandgrouse* 8: 1-41.

Beaubrun, P.-C. (1983) Le Goéland d'Audouin (*Larus audouinii* Payr.) sur les côtes du Maroc. *Oiseau et R.F.O.* 53: 209-226.

Beaubrun, P., Thévenot, M. and Baouab, R. E. (1986) Recensement hivernal d'oiseaux d'eau au maroc Janvier 1985. *Documents de l'Institut Scientifique,* Rabat no. 10.

Belik, V. P. (1994) Where on earth does the Slender-billed Curlew nest? Information from the *Wader Study Group,* No. 7, published by the Menzbir Ornithological Society, pp. 30-32 (translated by G. H. Harper).

Bell, B. (1993) *Feasibility study of removal of problem animals from islands of Madeira.* BirdLife International/Wildlife Management International LTD.

van den Berg, A. B. (1988) *Moroccan Slender-billed Curlew survey, winter 1987-88.* Cambridge, U.K.: International Council for Bird Preservation (Study Rep. 29).

van den Berg, L.M.J. (1991) Status, distribution and research on Corncrakes in the Netherlands. *Vogelwelt* 112:78-83.

Bergier, P. (1987) *Les rapaces diurnes du Maroc: statut, repartition et ecologie.* Aix en Provence: Centre d'etudes sur les ecosystemes de Provence (Annales du CEEP 3).

Berrevoets, C. and Erkman, A. (1991) *Count of White-headed Duck* Oxyura leucocephala *in Burdur Gölü,* February 1991. Unpublished report.

Bibby, C. J. & Charlton, T. D. (1991) Observations on the Sao Miguel Bullfinch. *Açoreana* 7: 297-304.

Bibby, C. J. & del Nevo, A. J. (1991) A first record of *Pterodroma feae* from the Azores. *Bull. Brit. Orn. Club* 111: 183-186.

Bibby, C. J., Charlton, T. D. & Ramos, J. A. (1992) Studies of West Palearctic birds, the Azores Bullfinch. *Brit. Birds* 85: 677-680.

Biber, J.-P. (1990) *Action plan for the conservation of western Lesser Kestrel* Falco naumanni *populations.* Cambridge, UK: International Council for Bird Preservation (Study Rep. 41).

Biber, J.-P. (1994) Lesser Kestrel *Falco naumanni*. Pp.292-293 in G. M. Tucker and M. F. Heath *Birds in Europe: their conservation status*. Cambridge, UK: BirdLife International (BirdLife Conservation Series No. 3).

Bijlsma, S., Hagemeijer, E. J. M., Verkley, G. J. M. and Zollinger, R. (1988) *[Ecological aspects of the Lesser Kestrel* Falco naumanni *in Extremadura (Spain).]* Nijmegen: Vakgroep Experimentele Zoölogie, Katholieke Univ. (Report Werkgroep Dieroecologie 285). (In Dutch.)

BirdLife International (1995) *IBAs within the European Union and Globally threatened Birds: a provisional list*. Unpubl. report to the European Commission.

Biscoito, M. & Zino, F. (1989) *Short report on the use of an automatic bird scarer in Madeira*. Unpublished.

Black, J. M. (1991) Reintroduction and restocking: guidelines for bird recovery programmes. *Bird Conserv. Internatn.* 1: 329-334.

Black, J. M. and Madsen, J. (1993) Red-breasted Goose: conservation and research needs. *IWRB Goose Res. Group Bull.* 4: 8-15.

Blanco, J. A. and González, J. L., eds. (1992) *Libro Rojo de los vertebrados de España*. Madrid: Instituto Nacional para la Conservación de la Naturaleza.

Blitzblau, S. (1992) *Breeding waterbirds in northern Israel spring/summer 1990*. Israel Ornithology Center (Spec. Rep. 1).

Block, B., Block, P., Jaschke, W., Litzbarski, B., Litzbarski, H. and Petrick, S. (1993) Komplexer Artenschutz durch extensive Landwirtschaft im Rahmen des Schutzprojektes "Großtrappe". *Natur und Landschaft* 68: 565-576.

Bodsworth, F. (1954) *The last of the curlews*. New York: Dodd, Mead and Company.

Boev, N. (1985) Lesser White-fronted Goose (*Anser erythropus*). P.58 in B. Botev and T. Peshev, eds. *Red Data Book of Bulgaria*. Sofia: BAS.

Boev, N. (1985) The Corncrake *Crex crex*. Pp.104-105 in B. Botev and T. Peshev, eds.

Red Data Book of Bulgaria. Sofia: Bulgarian Academy of Sciences. (In Bulgarian.)

Bondarev, D. V. (1975) On the nesting of the Pygmy Cormorant. *Uchenye ap Permsk Gos Pedagog Inst.* Pp.89-92. (In Russian.)

Bondarev, D. V. (1976) Rafts for nesting *Pelecanus crispus*. The Volga River delta. In *Manual of wetland management*. Slimbridge, UK: International Waterfowl and Wetlands Research Bureau.

Borodin, A. M., ed. (1984) *Red Data Book of the USSR: rare and endangered species of animals and plants*, 1: *animals*. Second edition. Moscow: Promyshlennost. (In Russian.)

Boswall, J. and Dawson, R. (1975) Spring notes on the birds of southern Montenegro with special reference to wetlands. *Bull. Brit. Orn. Club* 95: 4-15.

Botev, B. and Peshev, T., eds. (1985) *Red Data Book of the People's Republic of Bulgaria*, 2. Sofia: Bulgarian Academy of Sciences. (In Bulgarian.)

Boukhalfa, D. (1990) Observation de quelques especes d'oiseaux de mer nicheurs sur la côte ouest d'Oran (Algerie). *Oiseaux et R.F.O.* 60 (3): 248-251.

Boukhalfa, D. (1992) Le Goéland d'Audouin aux îles Habibas (Oran, Algérie). *Faune et Nature* 34: 14-15.

Boumezbeur, A. (1992) Le statut de l'érismature à tête blanche et du fuligule nyroca dans le complexe d'El Kala, Algeria, de 1990 à 1992. *IWRB Threatened Waterfowl Res. Group Newsl.* 2: 4-5.

Bourne, W. R. P. (1983) The Soft-plumaged Petrel, the Gon-gon and the Freira, *Pterodroma mollis, Pterodroma feae* and *Pterodroma madeira*. *Bull. Brit. Orn. Club* 103(2): 52-58.

Bradley, P. (1986) The breeding biology of Audouin's Gull on the Chafarinas Islands. Pp.221-230 in MEDMARAVIS and X. Monbailliu, eds. *Mediterranean marine avifauna*. Berlin and Heidelberg: Springer-Verlag (NATO ASI Ser. G. 12).

Brichetti, P., de Franceschi, P. and Baccetti, N., eds. (1992) Fauna d'Italia, 29. *Aves* 1: Gaviidae-Phasianidae. Bologna: Edizioni Calderini.

Brown, L. H. and Amadon, D. (1968) *Eagles, hawks and falcons of the world.* London: Country Life.

Broyer, J. (1985) *Le râle de genêts en France* (Crex Crex). Lyon: Union Nationale des Associations Ornithologiques.

Burger, J. (1981) Effects of human disturbance on colonial species, particularly gulls. *Colonial Waterbirds* 4: 28-36.

Buzun, V. A. and Grinchenko, A. B. (1991) About nesting birds of the Oysul lagoon: *Phalacrocorax pygmeus, Casarca ferruginea* and *Tadorna tadorna* in the Crimea. Pp.182-193 in A. I. Koshelev and I. I. Chernichko, eds. *Rare birds of the Black sea coastal area.* Kiev: Lybid. (In Russian.)

Cabral, M. J., Magalhães, C. P., Oliveira, M. E. and Romão, C. (1990) *Livro vermelho dos vertebrados de Portugal*, I. Lisboa: Serviço Nacional de Parques, Reservas e Conservação de Natureza.

Cadbury, C. J. (1980) The status and habitats of the Corncrake in Britain 1978-79. *Bird Study* 27: 203-218.

Cade, T. J. (1982) *The falcons of the world.* London: Collins.

Cadenas, R. (1992) *Informe de resultados de las campañas de reproducción del aguila imperial en el Parque Nacional de Doñana.* Huelva: ICONA (unpublished report).

Cadenas, R. (1995) El Plan de manejo del aguila imperial ibérica *(Aquila adalberti)* en Doñana. Congreso Biología y Conservación de Rapaces Mediterráneas. Palma de Mallorca 1994.

Calderón, J., Castroviejo, J., García, L. and Ferrer, M. (1988) El Aguila Imperial *(Aquila adalberti)*: dispersión de los jovenes, estructura de edades y mortalidad. *Doñana Acta Vert.* 15: 79-98.

Cambridge, UK: International Council for Bird Preservation (Techn. Publ. 5).

Cambridge, UK: BirdLife International.

Cantos, F. J. and Gómez-Manzaneque, A. (1993) Informe sobre la campaña de anillamiento de aves en España. Año 1992. *Ecología* 7: 299-374.

Carp, E. (1980) *A directory of western Palaearctic wetlands.* Gland, Switzerland: International Union for Conservation of Nature and Natural Resources and United Nations Environment Programme.

Castari, R. (1958) Notes de Tunisie. *Alauda* 25: 56-62.

Castroviejo, J. (1993) *Memoria–Map of the Doñana National Park.* Andalucía: Consejo Superior de Investigaciones Científicas and Agencia de Medio Ambiente de la Junta de Andalucía.

Catsadorakis, G., Malakou, M. and Crivelli, A. J. (in press) The effects of the 1989-1990 drought on the colonial waterbirds nesting at Lake Mikri Prespa with special attention on pelicans. *Colonial Waterbirds.*

Catuneanu, I. I., Korodi, G., Munteanu, P., Pascovschi, S. and Vespremeanu, E. (1978) Fauna republicii Socialiste Romania: *Aves* 15 (1): 266-279.

Ceballos, O. & Ortuño, F. (1976) *Study of the vegetation and forest flora of the western Canary Islands.* Santa Cruz de Tenerife: Excmo. Cabildo Insular. (In Spanish.)

Chalabi, B. (1990) *Contribution a l'étude de l'importance des zones humides Algériennes pour la protection de l'avifaune: cas du Lac Tonga.* Algeria: Institut National Agronomique.

Chappuis, J. L., Bousses, P. & Barnaud, G. (1994) Alien mammals, impact and management in the French subantarctic islands. *Biol. Conserv.* 67: 97-104.

Cheylan, G. (1990) *Historique de la régression du Faucon crécerellette en France.* Unpublished.

Cheylan, G. (1991) Le Faucon crécerellette *(Falco naumanni)* en France: statut actuel et régression. *Faune de Provence* (CEEP) 12: 45-49.

Chown, D. and Linsley, M. (1994) *Wetlands in northern Algeria and coastal Tunisia.* RSPB report.

Christensen, H. R. and Eldøy, S. (1988) *Truede virveldyr i Norge.* DN-rapport 1988-82.

Chupin, I., Nowak, E. and Yurlov, A. K. (1994) Search project of the breeding area of the

Slender-billed Curlew in SW Siberia. In *European Commission 1994* (Annex 35).

Ciochia, V. and Hafner, H. (1969) Observations sur quelques espèces d'oiseaux qui hivernent sur le littoral de la mer Noir at dans le delta de Danube. *Lucr. Stat. Cerc. Mar.* 3: 307-313.

Collar, N. J. (1983) A history of the Houbara in the Canaries. *Bustard Studies* 1: 9-30.

Collar, N. J. and Andrew, P. (1988) *Birds to watch: the ICBP world check-list of threatened birds.* Cambridge, UK: International Council for Bird Preservation (Techn. Publ. 8).

Collar, N. J. and Goriup, P.D. (1983) The ICBP Fuerteventura Houbara Expedition: introduction. *Bustard Studies* 1: 1-8.

Collar, N. J. and Stuart, S. N. (1985) *Threatened birds of Africa and related islands: the ICBP/IUCN Red Data Book.* Cambridge, UK: International Council for Bird Preservation and International Union for Conservation of Nature and Natural Resources.

Collar, N. J., Crosby, M. J. and Stattersfield, A. J. (1994) *Birds to watch 2: the world list of threatened birds.* Cambridge, UK: BirdLife International (BirdLife Conservation Series No. 4).

Collins, D. R. (1984) *A study of the Canarian Houbara Bustard* Chlamydotis undulata fuerta-venturae, *with special reference to its behaviour and ecology.* University of London (M.Phil. thesis).

Cook, R. T. (1992) *Trace metals and organochlorines in the eggs and diets of Dalmatian Pelicans* (Pelecanus crispus) *and Spoonbills* (Platalea leucorodia) *in Northern Greece.* M.Sc. thesis, University of Manchester, UK.

Coombes in Bannerman, D. A. (1957) *The birds of the British Isles,* 6. Edinburgh: Oliver and Boyd.

COS (Cyprus Ornithological Society) (1960) Klidhes expedition. *Cyprus Orn. Soc. Bull.* 8:1-3.

Cowles, G. S. (1981) The first evidence of Demoiselle Crane Anthropoides virgo and Pygmy Cormorant Phalacrocorax pygmaeus in Britain. *Bull. Brit. Orn. Club.* 101: 383-386.

Cracknell, G. (1990) Reports and news. *IWRB Goose Res. Group Newsl.* 3: 4-10.

Cramp, S., ed. (1985) *The birds of the western Palearctic,* 4. Oxford: Oxford University Press.

Cramp, S., ed. (1992) *The birds of the western Palearctic,* VI. Oxford: Oxford University Press.

Cramp, S. and Perrins, C. M., eds. (1994) *The birds of the western Palearctic,* 8. Oxford: Oxford University Press.

Cramp, S. and Simmons, K. E. L., eds. (1977) *The birds of the western Palearctic,* 1. Oxford: Oxford University Press.

Cramp, S. and Simmons, K. E. L., eds. (1980) *The birds of the western Palaearctic,* 2. Oxford: Oxford University Press.

Crivelli, A. J. (1987) *The ecology and behaviour of the Dalmatian Pelican,* Pelecanus crispus Bruch, *a world-endangered species.* Arles, France: Commission of the European Communities and Station Biologique de la Tour du Valet.

Crivelli, A. J. (1994) The importance of the former U.S.S.R. for the conservation of pelican populations nesting in the Palearctic. Pp.1-4 in A. J. Crivelli, V. G. Krivenko and V. G. Vinogradov, eds. *Pelicans in the former USSR.* Slimbridge, UK: International Waterfowl and Wetlands Research Bureau (Spec. Publ. 27).

Crivelli, A. J. and Vizi, O. (1981) The Dalmatian Pelican Pelecanus crispus Bruch 1832, a recently world endangered bird species. *Biol. Conserv.* 20: 297-310.

Crivelli, A. J., Grillas, P. and Lacaze, B. (1995a) *Responses of vegetation to a rise in the water level at the Kerkini reservoir (1982-1991), a Ramsar site in northern Greece.* J. Environmental Management.

Crivelli, A. J., Krivenko, V. G. and Vinogradov, V. G., eds. (1994) *Pelicans in the former USSR.* Slimbridge, UK: International Waterfowl and Wetlands Research Bureau (IWRB Spec. Publ. 27).

Crivelli, A. J., Jerrentrup, H., Nazirides, T. and Grillas, P. (1995b) *Effects on fisheries and waterbirds of raising the water level at the Kerkini reservoir, a Ramsar site in northern Greece.* I. Environmental Management.

Crivelli, A. J., Mitchev, T., Catsadorakis, G. and Pomakov, V. (1991b) Preliminary results on the wintering of the Dalmatian Pelican, *Pelecanus crispus*, in Turkey. Zool. Middle East 5: 11-20.

Crivelli, A. J., Catsadorakis, G., Jerrentrup, H., Hatzilacou, D. and Michev, T. (1991a) Conservation and management of pelicans nesting in the Palearctic. Pp.137-152 in T. Salathé, ed. *Conservation of migratory birds*. Cambridge, UK: International Council for Bird Preservation (Tech. Publ. 12).

Crivelli, A. J., Focardi, S., Fossi, C., Leonzio, C., Massi, A. and Renzoni, A. (1989) Trace elements and chlorinated hydrocarbons in eggs of *Pelecanus crispus* a world endangered bird species nesting at Lake Mikri Prespa, north-western Greece. *Environ. Pollut.* 61: 235-247.

Curry-Lndahl, K. (1959) *Våra fåglar i Norden*. Stockholm.

Danko, S. (1993) *Schutz und management der Greifvögel in der Ostslowakei*. Unpublished.

Daoutopoulos, G. A. and Pyrovetsi, M. (1990) Comparison of conservation attitudes among fishermen in three protected lakes in Greece. J. *Environmental Management* 31: 83-92.

de Bournonville, D. (1964) Observations sur une importante colonie de Goéland d'Audouin - *Larus audouinii* Payr. - a large de la Corse. *Gerfaut* 54: 439-453.

de By, R. A. (1990) Migration of Aquatic Warbler in western Europe. *Dutch Birding* 12: 165-181.

de Juana, E. (1994) Audouin's Gull. Pp.286-287 in G.M. Tucker and M. F. Heath Birds in Europe: their conservation status. Cambridge, UK: BirdLife International (BirdLife Conservation Series No. 3).

de Juana, E. and Varela, J. M. (1993) The world breeding population of the Audouin's Gull *Larus audouinii*. Pp.71-85 in J. S. Aguilar, X. Monbailliu and A. M. Paterson, eds. *Status and conservation of seabirds*. Madrid: Sociedad Española de Ornitología/Birdlife/Medmaravis. (In Spanish.)

de Juana, E., Bueno, J. M., Carbonell, M., Mellado, V. P. and Varela, J. (1979) Aspectos de la alimentación y biología de reproducción de *Larus*

audouinii Payr. en su gran colonia de cría de las Islas Chafarinas (año 1976). *Bol. Estación Central de Ecología* 8: 53-65.

Delgado, G., Martín, A., Quilis, V. and Emmerson, K. (1988) Alimentación del Gavilán (*Accipiter nisus*) en la Isla de Tenerife. *Doñana Acta Vert.* 15: 193-199.

Dementiev, G. P. and Gladkov, N. A., eds. (1952) *Birds of the Soviet Union*, 4. Moscow: Sovetskaya Nauka. (In Russian.)

DHKD and Burdur Municipality (1993) *Proceedings of the international symposium on Burdur Lake and the White-headed Duck, 3-4 December 1991, Burdur, Turkey*. Istanbul, Turkey: Dogal Hayati Koruma Dernegi and Burdur Municipality. (In Turkish.)

van Dijk, G., van and Ledant, J. P. (1983) La valeur ornithologique des zones humides de l'est Algérie. *Biol. Conserv.* 26: 215-226.

Dijksen, A. J., Lebret, T., Ouwened, G. L. and Philippona, S. (1973) Ornithological observations in the lagoons of the Dobrodgea, Rumania, in autumn and winter of 1969, 1970 and 1971. *Ardea* 61: 159-178.

Dolz, J. C., Ripoll, M. G. and Pedrero, J. H. (1991) Status of some threatened anatidae species in the Comunidad Valenciana, East Spain. *IWRB Threatened Waterfowl Res. Group Newsl.* 1:7-8.

Domínguez, F. and Díaz, G. (1985) *Plan for the recuperation of the Canarian Houbara*. Santa Cruz de Tenerife: Servício Provincial del ICONA. (In Spanish.)

Domínguez, F. (1993) *Recovery plan for the Houbara*. Unpublished. (In Spanish.)

Donázar, J. A., Negro, J. J. and Hiraldo, F. (1993) Foraging habitat selection, land-use changes and population decline in the Lesser Kestrel *Falco naumanni*. J. *Appl. Ecol.* 30: 515-522.

Donázar, J. A., Bustamante, J., Negro, J. J. and Hiraldo, F. (1994) *Estudio del cernícalo primilla en el suroeste de España: factores determinantes de la distribución y densidad de población*. Madrid: Sociedad Española de Ornitologia.

DRA (1991) *Zonas de Protecção Especial.* Horta (Açores): Secretaría Regional do Turismo e Ambiente, Direcção Regional de Ambiente.

Dyrcz, A. (1993) Nesting biology of the Aquatic Warbler Acrocephalus paludicola in the Biebrza marshes (NE Poland). *Vogelwelt* 114: 2-15.

Dyrcz, A. and Zdunek, W. (1993) Breeding ecology of the Aquatic Warbler *Acrocephalus paludicola* on the Biebrza marshes, northeast Poland. *Ibis* 135: 181-189.

Dyrcz, A. and Czeraszkiewicz, R. (1992) Report concerning numbers, distribution, conservation and threats of the Aquatic Warbler *Acrocephalus paludicola* in Poland. Gdansk: Ogólnopolskie Towarzystwo Ochrony Ptaków. (Unpublished report).

Ekman, S. (1922) *Djürvärldens Utbredningshistoria på den Skandinaviska halvön.* Stockholm.

Emmerson, K. W. (1985) Estudio de la biología y ecología de la Paloma Turqué y la Paloma Rabiche con vistas a su conservación, 1 and 2. Tenerife: Ornistudio S.L.

Emmerson, K. W., Barone, R. B., Lorenzo, J. A. & Naranjo, J. J. (1993) *The census and analysis of the ornithological community of the National Park of Garajonay.* Santa Cruz de Tenerife: ORNISTUDIO S. L. (unpublished). (In Spanish.)

Emmerson, K. W., Martín, A., Delgado, G., and Quilis, V. (1986) Distribution and some aspects of the breeding biology of Bolle's Pigeon (*Columba bollii*) on Tenerife. *Vogelwelt* 107: 52-65.

ESPARVEL (1993) Proponen proteger a la Malvasía en Castilla-la Mancha. *Quercus* 94: 39.

Essetti, I. (no date) *Le Goéland d'Audouin en Tunisie. Etat actuel et tendances évolutives de la population nicheuse du Goéland d'Audouin en Tunisie.* Tunis: Association "Les Amis des Oiseaux".

EUCC (1993) *Baltic Coastal Corridor Programme.* Leiden: European Union for Coastal Conservation. Unpublished.

European Commission (1994) *Preparation d'un plan de sauvetage pour Numenius tenuirostris, Rapport final,* Tome 2, Annexes. Brussels.

Evans, M. I. (1994) *Important Bird Areas in the Middle East.* Cambridge, UK: BirdLife International (BirdLife Conservation Series No. 2).

Faragó, S. (1990) Evaluation of the ten-year work at the Dévaványa Conservation Area Bustard Rescue Station. *Scient. Publ. Forest. Timb. Ind.* 1989/1: 81-143.

Farago, S., Kovacs, G. and Sterbetz, T. (1991) Goose populations staging and wintering in Hungary 1984-1988. *Ardea* 79: 161-164.

Fasola, M. and Barbieri, F. (1981) Prima nidificazione di Marangone Minore Phalacrocorax pygmeus in Italia. *Avocetta* 5: 155-156.

Fedorenko, A. P. (1992) The reasons for the decline in numbers of bustards and means of their conservation in the Ukraine Soviet Socialist Republic. *Bustard Studies* 5: 8-15.

Ferrer, M. (1992) Regulation of the period of postfledging dependence in the Spanish Imperial Eagle Aquila adalberti. *Ibis* 134: 128-133.

Ferrer, M., Migens, E. and Cepeda, J. M. (1990) Reducción de la mortalidad por electrocución del águila imperial ibérica. Manuscrito inédito. Agencia del Medio Ambiente. Junta de Andalucía.

Flint, P. R. and Stewart, P. F. (1992) *The birds of Cyprus.* Second edition. Tring, UK: British Ornithologists' Union (Check-list 6).

Flint, V. and Sorokin, A. G. (1992) The legal situation of birds of prey in the former USSR. *WWGBP Newsl.* 16/17: 7-8.

Flint, V. E., Boehme, R. L., Kostin, Y. V. and Kuznetsov, A. A. (1984) *A field guide to birds of the USSR.* Princeton, New Jersey: Princeton University Press.

Flint, V. Y. and Krivenko, V. G. (1990) The present status and trends of waterfowl in the USSR. In G. V. T. Matthews, ed. *Managing waterfowl populations.* Proc. IWRB Symp., Astrakhan 1989. Slimbridge, UK: International Waterfowl and Wetlands Research Bureau (Spec. Publ. 12).

Fossi, C., Focardi, S., Leonzio, C. and Renzoni, A. (1984) Trace metals and chlorinated hydrocarbons in birds' eggs from the Danube delta. *Environ. Conserv.* 11: 345-350.

Fouarge, J. P. (1992) Observation de deux aigles imperiaux iberiques (*Aquila heliaca adalberti*) dans la region de Chechaouen. *Porphyrio* 4(1/2): 25-28.

Galushin, V. M. (1995) Long-term changes in birds of prey populations within European Russia and neighbouring countries. In W. Hagemeijer and T. Verstrael, eds. *Bird Numbers 1992: distribution, monitoring and ecological aspects.* Proceedings 12th International Conference of IBCC and EOAC. Voorburg: SOVON-CBS.

Galushin, V. and Abuladze, A. (in press) *The Black Vulture in the eastern part of the range.*

Garzón, J. (1972) Especies en peligro: el Aguila imperial. *Adena* 4: 8-12.

Garzón, J. (1974) Contribucion al estudio del status, alimentacion y proteccion de las Falconiformes en España Central. *Ardeola* 19: 279-330.

Gaultier, T. and Ayache, F. (1986) *Rapport faunistique sur l'ile de la Galite et ses ilots.* Tunis: Association "Les Amis des oiseaux".

Gavrin, V. F., Dolgushin, I. D., Korelov, M. N. and Kuzmina, M. A. (1962) *Ptitsy Kazakhstana,* 2. Alma-Ata: Izdat. Akad. Nauk Kazakhskoy SSR.

Georgiev, D., Stoikov, S., Marinov, M. and Stoyanova, S. (1994) Lesser White-fronted Goose (*Anser erythropus*). *Neophron* 1/94: 11.

Géroudet, P. (1977) Coup d'oeil au "Paradis des Oiseaux" et au lac Manyas, en Turquie. *Nos Oiseaux* 34: 23-30.

Gjiknuri, L. and Peja, N. (1992) Albanian lagoons: their importance and economic development. Pp.130-133 in M. Finlayson, T. Hollis and T. Davis, eds. (1992) *Managing Mediterranean wetlands and their birds: proceedings of an International Waterfowl and Wetlands Research Bureau international symposium,* Grado, Italy, February 1991.

Glowacinski, Z. (1992) Polska czerwona ksiega zwierzat: *Polish Red Data Book of animals.* Warsaw: Polish Academy Sciences.

Glutz von Blotzheim, U. N., Bauer, K. M. and Bezzel, E. (1977) *Handbuch der Vogel Mitteleuropas,* 7. Wiesbaden: Akademische Verlagsgesellschaft.

González, J. L., Garzón, P. and Merino, M. (1990) Censo de la población española de Cernicalo Primilla. *Quercus* 49: 6-12.

González, L. M. (1990) Censo de las poblaciones reproductoras de Aguila Imperial y Buitre Negro en España. *Quercus* 58: 16-22.

González, L. M. (1991) *Historia natural del Aguila Imperial Iberica (Aquila adalberti Brehm,1861): taxonomia, población, anális de la distribución geográfica, alimentación, reproducción y conservación.* Madrid: ICONA, Ministerio de Agricultura (Colección Técnica).

González, L. M. (1994) Cinereous Vulture. Pp.24-25 in G. M. Tucker and M. F. Heath *Birds in Europe: their conservation status.* Cambridge, UK: BirdLife International (BirdLife Conservation Series No. 3).

González, L. M., Bustamante, J. and Hiraldo, F. (1990) Factors influencing the present distribution of the Spanish Imperial Eagle *Aquila adalberti. Biol. Conserv.* 51: 311-320.

González, L. M., Alonso, J. C., González, J. L. and Heredia, B. (1985) *Exito reproductor, mortalidad, período de dependencia y dispersión juvenil del Aguila Imperial Ibérica (Aquila adalberti) en el Parque Nacional de Doñana (1984).* Madrid: ICONA (Monogr. 36).

González, L. M., González, J. L., Garzón, J. and Heredia, B. (1987) Censo y distribución del Aguila Imperial Ibérica, *Aquila (heliaca) adalberti,* Brehm,1861, en España durante el periodo 1981-1986. *Bol. Est. Cent. Ecol.* 16: 99-109.

González, L. M., Heredia, B., González, J. L. and Alonso, J. C. (1989a) Juvenile dispersal of the Spanish Imperial Eagle (*Aquila adalberti*). *J. Field Orn.* 60: 369-379.

González, L. M., Hiraldo, F., Delibes, M. and Calderón, J. (1989) Zoogeographic support for the Spanish Imperial Eagle as a distinct species. *Bull. Brit. Orn. Club* 109: 86-93.

González, L. M., Hiraldo, F., Delibes, M. and Calderón, J. (1989b) Reduction in the range of the Spanish Imperial Eagle (*Aquila adalberti*) since AD 1850. *J. Biogeogr.* 16: 305-315.

Goodman, S. M. and Meininger, P. L. (1989) *The birds of Egypt.* Oxford: Oxford University Press.

Goriup, P. D. and Batten, L. (1990) The conservation of steppic birds: a European perspective. *Oryx* 24: 215-223.

Green, A. G. (1992) Wildfowl at risk. *Wildfowl* 43: 160-184.

Green, A. J. (1993) *The status and conservation of the Marbled Teal* Marmaronetta angustirostris. Slimbridge, UK: Wetlands International (IWRB Spec. Publ. 23).

Green, A. J. (1994) Estatus mundial de la Malvasía *Oxyura leucocephala. Oxyura* 7: 75-87.

Green, A. J. and Anstey, S. (1992) The status of the White-headed Duck *Oxyura leucocephala. Bird Conserv. Internatn.* 2: 185-200.

Green, A. J., Hilton, G. M., Hughes, B., Fox, A. D. and Yarar, M. (1993) *The ecology and behaviour of the White-headed Duck* Oxyura leucocephala *at Burdur Gölü, Turkey, February-March 1993.* Slimbridge, UK: Wildfowl and Wetlands Trust.

Green, A. J., Fox, A. D., Hilton, G. M., Hughes, B., Yarar, M. and Salathé, T. (in press) *The conservation status of Burdur Lake, Turkey and its population of the White-headed Duck.*

Green, I. A., Moorhouse, C. N. and West, S. (1989) White-headed Duck in Turkey: a study of their breeding status and distribution (unpublished report).

Green, R. E. (in press) The decline of the Corncrake *Crex crex* continues. *Bird Study.*

Gretton, A. (1994) An estimate of the current population of the Slender-billed Curlew. In European Commission: *Preparation d'un plan de sauvetage pour* Numenius tenuirostris. *Rapport final,* Tome 2, Annexes (Annex 5).

Gretton, A. (1991) *The ecology and conservation of the Slender-billed Curlew* (Numenius tenuirostris). Cambridge, UK: International Council for Bird Preservation (Monogr. 6).

Grimmett, R. F. A. and Jones, T. A. (1989) *Important Bird Areas in Europe.* Cambridge, UK: International Council for Bird Preservation (Techn. Publ. 9).

Groombridge, B., ed. (1993) *1994 IUCN Red List of threatened animals.* Gland, Switzerland, and Cambridge, UK: International Union for Conservation of Nature and Natural Resources.

Gürpinar, T. and Wilkinson, W. H. N. (1970) Wildfowl status in Turkey. Pp.174-176 in Y. A. Isakov, ed. *Proceedings of the International Regional Meeting on Conservation of Wildfowl Resources, Leningrad, USSR., 25-30 September 1968.* Moscow.

Guyot, I. (1985) Quelques donnes sur la nidification du Goéland d'Audouin Larus audouinii en Corse. Pp.82-85 in *Oiseaux marine nicheurs du Midi et de la Corse.* Aix-en-Provence: Annales C.R.O.P. 2.

Hagemeijer, W. J. M., ed. (1994) Wintering waterbirds in the coastal wetlands of Albania, 1993. Zeist, Netherlands: Werkgroep Internationaal Wad-en Watervogelonderzoek (WIWO Report 49).

Hallmann, B. (in prep.) *The Black Vulture situation in Greece.*

Hallmann, B (1985) The status and conservation of birds of prey in Greece. pp 55-59 in I. Newton and R. D. Chancellor eds. *Conservation studies on raptors.* Cambridge, UK: International Council for Bird Preservation.

Hallmann, B (1986) *Raptor surveys in Greece.* Report to WWF/IUCN.

Hallmann, B (1996) *Lesser Kestrel Survey of Thessaly.* Report to the Hellenic Ornithological Society and RSPB.

Handrinos, G. (1992) Birds. Pp.125-243 in M. Karandrinos and A. Legakis, eds. *The Red Data Book of Greek vertebrates,.* Athens: Hellenic Zoology Society and Hellenic Ornithological Society. (In Greek.)

Handrinos, G. (1993) Midwinter numbers and distribution of Great Cormorants and Pygmy Cormorants in Greece. Pp.147-159 in J. S. Aguilar, X. Montbailliu and A. M. Paterson, eds. *Status and conservation of seabirds.* Madrid: Sociedad Española de Ornitología and Medmaravis.

Handrinos, G. I. (1991) The status of geese in Greece. *Ardea* 79: 175-178.

Handrinos, G. I. (1995) The White-headed Duck *Oxyura leucocephala* in Greece. *IWRB Threatened Waterfowl Res. Group Newsl.* 7.

Handrinos, G. L. and Goutner, V. (1990) On the occurrence of the Lesser White-fronted Goose Anser erythropus in Greece. *J. Orn.* 131: 160-165.

Haraszthy, L., Bagyura, J., Szitta, T., Petrovics, Z. and Viszló, L. (in prep.) Biology, status and conservation of the Imperial Eagle in Hungary. *Eagle Studies.*

Hatzilacou, D. (1993) *The distribution of the globally endangered Dalmatian Pelican Pelecanus crispus in Greece: threats pertaining to its habitats and recommendations for protection.* Sandy, UK: Royal Society for the Protection of Birds.

van der Have, T. M., van de Sant, S., Verkuil, Y. and van der Winden, J., eds. (1993) *Waterbirds in the Sivash, Ukraine, spring 1992.* Zeist: Foundation Working Group International Wader and Waterfowl Research (WIWO Rep. 36).

Hazevoet, C. J. (1994) Status and conservation of seabirds in the Cape Verde Islands. Pp.279-293 in D. N. Nettleship, J. Burger & M. Gochfeld, eds. *Seabirds on islands: threats, case studies and action plans.* Cambridge, UK: BirdLife International (BirdLife Conservation Series No. 1).

Heim de Balsac, H. and Mayaud, N. (1962) *Les oiseaux du nord-ouest de l'Afrique.* Paris: Paul Lechevalier.

Heins, J.-U., Rüsler, S. and Brinkmann, R. (1990) Situation des Krauskopfpelikans *Pelecanus crispus* Bruch 1832 in Menderes delta/SW Türkei. Kartierung mediterr. *Brutvögel* 4: 3-11.

Hellmich, J. (1992) Impacto del uso de pesticidas sobre las aves: el caso de la Avutarda. *Ardeola* 39: 7-22.

Hidalgo, J. (1991) The Marbled Teal in the Marismas del Guadalquivir, Spain. *IWRB Threatened Waterfowl Res. Group Newsl.* 1: 6.

Hidalgo, S. J. (1990) World status of the Great Bustard with special attention to the Iberian peninsula populations. *Misc. Zool.* 14: 167-180.

Hiraldo, F. (1974) Colonias de cría y censo de los buitres negros (*Aegypius monachus*) en España. *Naturalia Hispanica* 2: 3-31.

Hiraldo, F. (1976) The diet of Black Vulture *Aegypius monachus* in Iberian peninsula. *Doñana Acta Vert.* 3: 19-31.

Hiraldo, F. (1983) Breeding biology of the Cinereous Vulture. Pp.197-213 in S. R. Wilbur and J. A. Jackson, eds. *Vulture biology and management.* Berkeley: University of California Press.

Hiraldo, F., Delibes, M. and Calderón, J. (1976) Sobre el status taxonómico del águila imperial ibérica. *Doñana Acta Vert.* 3: 171-182.

Hidalgo, S. J. and Carranza, J. (1990) *Ecología y Comportamiento de la Avutarda.* Servicio de Publicaciones de la Universidad de Extremadura.

Holmes, J. and Galbraith, C. A. (1994) The UK Ruddy Duck (*Oxyura jamaicensis*) Working Group. *Oxyura* 7:61-65.

Hora, J. and Kanuch, P. (1992) *Important Bird Areas in Europe: Czechoslovakia.* Prague: Czechoslovak ICBP Section.

Hudson, R. (1975) *Threatened birds of Europe.* London: Macmillan.

Hughes, B. (1991) The status of the North American Ruddy Duck *Oxyura jamaicensis* in Great Britain. Pp.162-163 in D. Stroud and D. Glue, eds. *Britain's birds in 1989-1990: the conservation and monitoring review.* Thetford, UK: British Trust for Ornithology and Nature Conservancy Council.

Hughes, B. and Grussu, M. (1994) The Ruddy Duck (*Oxyura jamaicensis*) in the United Kingdom: distribution, monitoring, current research and implications for European colonisation. *Oxyura* 7: 29-47.

Hughes, R. H. and Hughes, J. S. (1992) A directory of African wetlands. Cambridge, UK: World Conservation Union, United Nations Environment Programme and World Conservation Monitoring Centre.

Hume, A. A. and Marshall, C. H. T. (1880) Gamebirds of India, Burmah and Ceylon. Calcutta.

Hunt, G. L. (1972) Influence of food distribution and human disturbance on the reproductive success of Herring Gulls. *Ecology* 53: 1051-1061.

Hustings, F. and van Dijk, K. (1994) *Bird census in the Kizilirmak delta, Turkey, in spring 1992*. Zeist: Foundation Working Group International Wader and Waterfowl Research.

Iankov, P. (1993) Project "Black Vulture Bulgaria 1993-2002". Unpublished.

Iankov, P. (1994) IBA: a step forward that BSPB has already made. Neophron 1/94: 4-5.

Iankov, P., Khristov, K. and Avramov, S. (1994) Changes in status of the Black Vulture *Aegypius monachus* in Bulgaria for the period 1980-1990. Pp.139-142 in B.-U. Meyburg and R. D. Chancellor, eds. *Raptor conservation today*. Berlin: World Working Group on Birds of Prey and Pica Press.

Iankov, P., Petrov, T., Michev, T. and Profirov, L. (1994) Past and present status of the Lesser Kestrel *Falco naumanni* in Bulgaria. Pp. 133-137. Meyburg, B. -U. and Chancellor, R. D., eds. *Raptor Conservation Today*. WWGBP, The Pica Press.

ICBP/IUCN Red Data Book. Cambridge, UK: International Council for Bird Preservation, and International Union for Conservation of Nature and Natural Resources.

ICONA (1993) *Plano coordinado de actuaciones para la conservación de la Gaviota de Audouin*. Co-ordinated action plan for the conservation of Audoin's Gull (unpublished report).

ICONA (1993) The spread of the Ruddy Duck in Spain and its impact on the White-headed Duck. *IWRB Threatened Waterfowl Res. Group Newsl.* 3: 3-4.

ICONA (1994) *IV Censo Nacional del Aguila Imperial Ibérica*.

ICONA/CCAA (1995) *Espacios Naturales Protegidos en España*. Servicio de Parques Nacionales.

Imber, M. J. (1989) Report on visit to Madeira in 1989 and comments on the *P. madeira* and *P. deserta* conservation projects. Unpublished report to ICBP.

Inskipp, T. and Collins, L. (1993) *World checklist of threatened birds*. Peterborough, UK: Joint Nature Conservation Committee.

Institut Royal des Sciences Naturelles de Belgique (IRSNB) (1994) *Preparation d'un plan de sauvetage pour* Numenius tenuirostris: *rapport final*, 2. Brussels.

Ivanov, B. E. and Pomakov, V. A. (1983) Wintering of the Red-breasted Goose (*Branta ruficollis*) in Bulgaria. *Aquila* 90: 29-34.

Ivanov, G. K. (1983) The White-headed Duck *Oxyura leucocephala*. Pp.195-196 in A. M. Kolosov, ed. *Red Data Book of the RSFSR: animals*. Moscow: Rossel 'khozizdat. (In Russian.)

IWRB Database of the International Waterfowl Census (IWC). Accessed 1994. Slimbridge, UK: International Waterfowl and Wetlands Research Bureau.

J. (1988) The Çukurova deltas: geomorphology, hydrology, climate, biotopes and human impact. Pp.13-32 in T. M. van der Have, V. M. van der Berk, J. P. Cronau and M. J. Langeveld, eds. *South Turkey Project: a survey of waders and waterfowl in the Çukurova deltas, spring 1987*. Zeist, Netherlands: Working Group International Wader and Waterfowl Research (WIWO Rep. 22).

Jacob, J. P. (1979) Resultats d'un recensement hivernal de Larides en Algerie. *Gerfaut* 69: 425-436.

Jacob, J. P. and Courbet, B. (1980) Les oiseaux de mer nicheurs sur la côte algerienne. *Gerfaut* 70: 385-401.

Jacobs, P. and Ochando, B. (1979) Répartition géographique et importance numérique des anatides hivernants en Algérie. *Gerfaut* 69: 239-251.

Jerrentrup, H., Gaethlich, M., Holm Joensen, A., Nohr, H. and Brogger-Jensen, S. (1988) *Urgent action plan to safeguard three endangered bird species in Greece and the European Community: Pygmy Cormorant (*Phalacrocorax pygmaeus*); Great white egret (*Egretta alba*); White-tailed eagle (*Haliaeetus albicilla*)*. Arhus: Naturhistorisk Museum.

Jiménez, J. (1990) Censo de las poblaciones de Aguila Imperial y Buitre Negro en Ciudad Real. Ciudad Real: Consejeria de Agricultura.

Jiménez, J. (1990) Estudio de las poblaciones de Buitre Negro (Aegypius monachus) y Aguila Imperial (Aquila adalberti) en la provincia de Ciudad Real: descripción y problemática. Toledo: Servicio de Publicaciones, Junta de Comunidades de Castilla-La Mancha.

Johnsgard, P. A. (1993) Cormorants, darters, and pelicans of the world. Washington: Smithsonian Institution Press.

Johnson, A. and Hafner, H. (1970) Winter wildfowl counts in south-east Europe and western Turkey. Wildfowl 21: 22-36.

Jones, M. J. (1988) A survey of the distribution, density and habitat preferences of the Long-toed Pigeon Columba trocaz in Madeira. Cambridge, UK: International Council for Bird Preservation (Study Rep. 32).

Jones, M. J. (1990) A survey of the distribution, density and habitat preferences of the Long-toed Pigeon. Bol. Mus. Mun. Funchal 42 (219):71-86.

Kalabér, L. (in prep.) Data about the Imperial Eagle in Romania. Eagle Studies.

Kasparek, M. (1992) Die Vögel der Turkei: eine Übersicht. Heidelberg: Max Kasparek Verlag.

Katsadorakis, G., Poirazidis, K., Gatzoyiannis, S., Adamakopoulos, T., Tsekouras, G. and Matsoukas, P. (in prep.) The management of vulture's population and habitat in Dadiá Forest Reserve: a conceptual framework.

Kazakov, B. A., Khokhlov, A. N., Pishvanov, Y. V. and Yemtyl, M. K. (1994) Pelicans on wetlands of the Predkavkaz'e region (north of the Caucasus). Pp. 9-16 in A. J. Crivelli, V. G. Krivenko and V. G. Vinogradov, eds. (1994) Pelicans in the former USSR. Slimbridge, UK: International Waterfowl and Wetlands Research Bureau (IWRB Spec. Publ. 27).

Khokhlov, A. N. (1995) Recent status of birds of prey in Stavropol and Karachevo-Cherkessk regions. Birds of prey and owls in the Northern Caucasus. Stavropol.

Khokhlov, A. I. and Melgunov, I. L. (1994) Pelicans on wetlands of the Stavropol Region. Pp.17-19 in A. J. Crivelli, V. G. Krivenko and V. G. Vinogradov, eds. (1994) Pelicans in the former USSR. Slimbridge, UK: International Waterfowl and Wetlands Research Bureau (IWRB Spec. Publ. 27).

Kirwan, G. (in press) The breeding status and distribution of the White-headed duck Oxyura leucocephala on the central plateau, Turkey. Sandgrouse.

Kjærbølling, N. (1852) Danmarks fugle. Copenhagen.

Kleiman, D. G., Stanley Price, M. R. and Beck, B. B. (1994) Criteria for reintroductions. Pp. 287-303. Olney, P. J. S., Mace, G. M. and Feistner, A. T. C. (eds.) Creative Conservation: Interactive management of wild and captive animals. London: Chapman & Hall.

Koenig, A. (1890) Ornitologische Forschungsergebnisse einer Reise nach Madeira und den Kanarischen Inseln. J. Orn. 38: 257-488.

Kohl, I. (1958) The Red-necked Goose (Branta ruficollis) in Romania. Larus 9-10: 184-187.

Kollar, H. P. (1991) Status of lowland dry grasslands and great bustards in Austria. Pp 77-80 in P. D. Goriup, L. A. Batten and J. A. Norton (Eds), The conservation of lowland dry grassland birds in Europe. Joint Nature Conservation Committee. UK.

Korodi, G. J. (1962-1963) Data on the Dalmatian Pelicans, territorial extension, biometry and nutrition in Romania. Aquila 69-70: 71-79.

Kovács, G. (1994) Management proposals for protecting the Slender-billed Curlew at Hortobágy National Park (Hungary). Unpublished.

Kovács, G. (1995) The Birdlife of the Hortobágy fishponds (in Hungarian). In Alfoldi Mozaik. Min. Env. and Reg. Policy, Budapest.

Kovács, G. (1994) Population increase and expansion of the Aquatic Warbler (Acrocephalus paludicola) in the Hortobágy between 1974 and 1994. Aquila 101: 133-143.

Kovács, G. (1991) *The Aquatic Warbler in Hungary*. Unpublished.

Krivenko, V. G. (1983) *The Red Data Book of the RSFSR*.

Krivenko, V. G. and Vinokurov, A. A. (1984) Marbled Teal. In A. M. Borodin, ed. *The Red Data Book of the USSR*. Vol. I. Second edition. Moscow: Lesnaya Promyshlennost. (In Russian Federation).

Krivenko, V. G., Crivelli, A. J. and Vinogradov, V. G. (1994) Historical changes and present status of *Pelecanus crispus* and *Pelecanus onocrotalus* numbers and distribution in the former USSR: a synthesis with recommendations for their conservation. Pp.132-151 in A. J. Crivelli, V. G. Krivenko and V. G. Vinogradov, eds. (1994) *Pelicans in the former USSR*. Slimbridge, UK: International Waterfowl and Wetlands Research Bureau (IWRB Spec. Publ. 27).

Krivonosov, G. A. and Rusanov, G. M. (1990) Wintering waterfowl in the north Caspian. In G. V. T. Matthews, ed. *Managing waterfowl populations*. Proc. IWRB Symp., Astrakhan 1989. Slimbridge, UK: International Waterfowl and Wetlands Research Bureau (Spec. Publ. 12).

Krivonosov, G. A., Rusanov, G. M. and Gavrilov, N. N. (1994) Pelicans on the northern Caspian Sea. Pp.25-31 in A. J. Crivelli, V. G. Krivenko and V. G. Vinogradov, eds. (1994) *Pelicans in the former USSR*. Slimbridge, UK: International Waterfowl and Wetlands Research Bureau (IWRB Spec. Publ. 27).

Kurochkin, E. N. and Koshelev, A. I. (1987) Family Rallidae. Pp.335-464 in V. D. Ilyichev and V. E. Flint, eds. *Birds of the USSR*: Galliformes, Gruiformes. Leningrad: Nauka. (In Russian.)

Lack, P. C. (1983) The Canarian Houbara: survey results, 1979. *Bustard Studies* 1: 45-50.

Lamani, F. (1989) Données sur la distribution et la zoogéographie des Pelecaniformes et des Ciconiiformes en Albanie. *Biologia Gallo-Hellenica* 13: 111-118.

Lambertini, M. (1993) The ecology and conservation of Audouin's Gull (*Larus audouinii*) at the northern limit of its breeding range. Pp.261-272 in J. S. Aguilar, X. Monbailliu and A. M. Paterson, eds. *Status and conservation of seabirds*. Madrid: Sociedad Española de Ornitología/Birdlife/Med maravis.

Lambertini, M. and Leonzio, C. (1986) Pollutant levels and their effects on Mediterranean seabirds. Pp.359-378 in MEDMARAVIS and X. Monbailliu, eds. *Mediterranean marine avifauna*. Berlin and Heidelberg: Springer-Verlag (NATO ASI Ser. G. 12).

Lambertini, M., Lakeberg, H. and Witt, H.-H. (1988) Brutausfall der Korallenmowe (Larus audouinii) an ihren Nistplatzen im Nordlichen Tyrrenischen meer. Vogelwelt 4/87.

Lambertini, M., Gustin, M., Faralli, U. and Tallone, G (1991) IBA – Italia. *Aree di Importanza Europea per gli Uccelli Selvatici in Italia*. Parma: LIPU.

Le Grand, G. (1982) O Priôlo, a ave mais interessante de S. Miguel. *Açoreana* 6: 195-211.

Le Grand, G. (1983) Der wiederentdeckte Azorengimpel. *Wir und Vogel* 15(1): 37-38.

Lebret, T. (1978) Roemeens dagboek op zoek naar de laatste Roodhalsganzen. *Lepelaar* 55: 14-17.

Ledant, J.-P., Jacob, J.-P., Jacobs, P., Malher, F., Ochando, B. and Roche, J. (1981) Mise à jour de l'avifaune algérienne. Brussels: *Gerfaut* 71: 295-398.

Ledant, J. P., Roux, F., Jarry, G., Gammell, A., Smit, C., Bairlein, F. and Wille, H. (1986) Aperçu des zones de grand intérêt pour la conservation des espèces d'oiseaux migrateurs de la Communauté en Afrique. Unpublished.

Lehmann, H. (1974) Brutkolonien im Hochland Zentralanatoliens. *Jahrb. Naturwiss. Ver. Wuppertal* 27: 80-104.

Linkov, A. B. (1984) *Oxyura leucocephala* ecology in Eastern Manych. Pp. 85-86 in *Present status of waterfowl resources. Proceedings of the All-Union Seminar, Moscow, 20-23 October 1984*. (In Russian.)

Linkov, A. B. (1994) *Pelecanus onocrotalus* and *Pelecanus crispus* in Kalmykia. Pp. 20-24 in A. J. Crivelli, V. G. Krivenko and V. G. Vinogradov, eds.

(1994) *Pelicans in the former USSR*. Slimbridge, UK: International Waterfowl and Wetlands Research Bureau (IWRB Spec. Publ. 27).

Lipsbergs, J., Kacalova, O., Ruce, I. and Sulcs, A. (1990) Pp.106-107 in *Popularzinatniska sarkana gramata, dzivnieki*. Riga: Zinatne.

Litvinova, N. A. (1994) Trends in pelican numbers on the south-west shore of the Caspian Sea. Pp.122-123 in A. J. Crivelli, V. G. Krivenko and V. G. Vinogradov, eds. (1994) *Pelicans in the former USSR*. Slimbridge, UK: International Waterfowl and Wetlands Research Bureau (IWRB Spec. Publ. 27).

Litzbarski, B., Litzbarski, H. and Petrick, S. (1987) Zur Ökologie und zum Schutz der Großtrappe im Bezirk Potsdam. *Acta Ornithoecol.*, Jena 1, 3: 199-244.

Litzbarski, H. (1993) Das Schutzprojekt "Grosstrappe" in Brandenburg. *Ber. Vogelschutz* 31: 61-66.

Lorentsen, S.-H. and Madsen, J (1995). *Recommendations on Urgent Action for the Conservation of the Lesser White-fronted Goose*. Unpublished report of Wetlands International Goose Research Group.

Lorentsen, S.-H. and Spjøtvoll, Ø. (1990) Note on the food choice of breeding Lesser White-fronted goose *Anser erythropus*. Fauna Norv. Ser. C., *Cinclus* 13: 87-88.

Louette, M. (1973) Ornithological observations near fresh- and brackish water in Morocco during summer 1971. *Gerfaut* 63: 121-132.

Louette, M. (1981) *The birds of Cameroon: an annotated checklist*. Brussels: Palais der Academien.

Lucchesi, J. L. (1990) *Reproduction du Faucon cré-cerellette Falco naumanni en Crau, Bouches-du-Rhône*. Unpublished.

Lysenko, V. I. (1990) Current status of waterfowl in Ukraine. Pp.43 in G. V. T. Matthews, ed. *Managing waterfowl populations*. Slimbridge, UK: International Waterfowl and Wetlands Research Bureau (Spec. Publ. 12).

Lysenko, V. I. (1994) The Dalmatian Pelican (*Pelecanus crispus*) in the Ukraine. P.5 in A. J. Crivelli, V. G. Krivenko and V. G. Vinogradov, eds. (1994) *Pelicans in the former USSR*. Slimbridge, UK: International Waterfowl and Wetlands Research Bureau (IWRB Spec. Publ. 27).

Lysenko, V. I. (1991) *Fauna of Ukraine: birds: Anseriformes*, 5 (3). Kiev: Naukova Dumka.

Mace, G. and Stuart, S. (1994) *Draft IUCN Red List* categories. Species 21-22: 13-24.

Madge, S. and Burn, H. (1988) Wildfowl. London: Christopher Helm.

Madsen, J. (1994) Red-breasted Goose *Branta ruficollis*. Pp.116-117 in G. M. Tucker and M. F. Heath, *Birds in Europe: their conservation status*. Cambridge, UK: BirdLife International (BirdLife Conservation Series No. 3).

Madsen, J., Komdeur, J. and Cracknell, G. (1993) International action for the Lesser White-fronted Goose *Anser erythropus*. Proc. 7th Nordic Orn. Congress: 120-123.

Magnin, G. (1989) *Falconry and hunting in Turkey during 1987*. Cambridge, UK: International Council for Bird Preservation (Study Rep. 34).

Malchevskiy, A. S. and Pukinskiy, Y. B. (1983) *Ptitsy Leningradskoy oblasti i sopredelnykh territoriy*,1. Leningrad: Leningradskogo University.

Maltby, E., ed. (1994) *An environmental and ecological study of the marshlands of Mesopotamia*. Exeter, UK: AMAR Appeal Trust.

Máñez, M. (1991) Estado actual en el Parque Nacional de Doñana de aves incluidas en la "Lista Roja de los vertebrados de España" dentro de las categorias de "En peligro" y "Vulnerable". *J. Zonas Húmedas Andaluzas* 1990: 41-49.

Martí, R. (1993) *The spreading of the Ruddy Duck Oxyura jamaicensis in Europe and its effect on conservation of the White-headed Duck Oxyura leucocephala in Spain*. Madrid: SEO/BirdLife Spain.

Martín, A. (1979) Contribution to the study of the Canarian avifauna: the biology of the Blue Chaffinch (*Fringilla teydea teydea* Moquin-

Tandon). Tenerife: Universidad de La Laguna (thesis). (In Spanish.)

Martín, A. (1985) Première observation du Pigeon Trocaz (Columba trocaz bollii) a l'île de Hierro (Iles Canaries). *Alauda* 53: 137-140.

Martín, A. (1987) *Atlas of the breeding birds of the island of Tenerife.* Santa Cruz de Tenerife: Instituto de Estudios Canarios (Monogr. 32). (In Spanish.)

Martín, A., Hernández, M. A. and Rodríguez, F. (1993) Première nidification du Pigeon Trocaz Columba bollii a l'île du Hierro. *Alauda* 61: 148.

Martín, A., Hernández, E., Nogales, M., Quilis, V., Trujillo, O. and Delgado, G. (1990) *El Libro Rojo de los vertebrados terrestres de Canarias.* Santa Cruz de Tenerife: Servicio de Publicaciones de la Caja General de Ahorros de Canarias.

Martín, A. M., Nogales, M., Hernández, M. A., Lorenzo, J. A., Medina, F. M. and Rando, J. C. (in press) *Status, conservation and habitat selection of the Houbara Bustard in Lanzarote.*

Matamala, J. J., Aguilar, F. J., Ayala, J. M. and López, J. M. (1994) La Malvasía (*Oxyura leucocephala*). Algunas referencias históricas, situación, problemática y distribución en España. Importancia de los humedales almerienses para la recuperación de una especie amenazada. Pp.35-84 in *Especies singulares almerienses, La Malvasía Comun.* Almería, Spain: Agencia de Medio Ambiente.

Mathews, G. M. (1934) Remarks on the races of Pterodroma mollis. *Bull. Brit. Orn. Club* 54: 178-179.

Mayol, J., ed. (1978) Observaciones sobre la gaviota de Audouin, Larus audouinii Payr., en el Mediterráneo occidental (primavera de 1978). Madrid: Publicaciones del Ministerio de Agricultura Secretaria General Tecnica (*Naturalia Hispanica* 20).

Mayol, J. (1994) La Malvasía en Mallorca, consideraciones en torno a una reintroducción. *Oxyura* 7: 109-118.

Mayol, J. (1986) Human impact on seabirds in the Balearic Islands. Pp.379-396 in MEDMARAVIS and X. Monbailliu, eds. *Mediterranean marine avi-fauna.* Berlin and Heidelberg: Springer-Verlag (NATO ASI Ser. G. 12).

Meade-Waldo, E. G. (1889) Further notes on the birds of the Canary Islands. *Ibis* (6)1: 503-520.

Meinertzhagen, R. (1930) *Nicoll's birds of Egypt.* London: Hugh Rees.

Meininger, P. L., Wolf, P. A., Hadoud, D. A. and Essghaier, M. F. A. (1994) *Ornithological survey of the coast of Libya, July 1993,* with notes on some wetlands in Tunisia. Zeist, Netherlands: Working Group International Wader and Waterfowl Research (WIWO Rep. 46).

Meyburg, B.-U. and Meyburg, C. (1984) Distribution et statut actuels du vautour moine *Aegypius monachus. Rapin. Med.* 2: 26-31.

Mian, A. (1986) A contribution to the biology of the Houbara: some studies on gizzard contents from 1983-84 wintering population in western Baluchistan. *Pakistan J. Zool.* 18 (49): 363-370.

Michev, T. (1981) The Dalmatian Pelican (*Pelecanus crispus*): its numbers and population dynamics in the Srébarna Nature Reserve, south Dobrodgea. Pp.516-527 in *Proceedings of the regional Symposium MAB-UNESCO, 20-24 October 1980, Blagoevgrad, Sofia.* (In Bulgarian with English summary.)

Michev, T. M., Naninkov, D. N., Ivanov, B. E. and Pomakov, V. A. (1981) *Midwinter numbers of geese in Bulgaria.* IWRB Symposium on Population Ecology of Geese. Hungary 26-30 October 1981.

Ministère de l'Environnement de Bulgarie (1993) *Plan National d'Actions Prioritaires de Conservation des Zones Humides les Plus Importantes de Bulgarie.* Rapport du Ministère de l'Environnement de Bulgarie.

Monbailliu, X. and Torre, A. (1986) Nest-site selection and interaction of Yellow-legged and Audouin's Gulls at Isola dell'Asinara. Pp. 245-263 in MEDMARAVIS and X. Monbailliu, eds. *Mediterranean marine avifauna.* Berlin and Heidelberg: Springer-Verlag (NATO ASI Ser. G. 12).

Montes, C., Bravo, M. A., Baltanás, A. and Gutiérrez, P. J. (1993) *Bases ecológicas para la gestión del Cangrejo Rojo en el Parque Nacional de*

Doñana. Parque Nacional de Doñana, ICONA and Universidad Autónoma de Madrid.

Moreau, R. E. (1972) *The Palaearctic-African bird migration systems*. London and New York: Academic Press.

Moreno, A. C. (1991) *Distribution, biology and essential habitat requirements of Blue Chaffinch on Gran Canaria*. Gran Canaria: Gobierno de Canarias, Viceconsejería de Medio Ambiente (unpublished). (In Spanish.)

Morgan, N. C. (1982) An ecological survey of standing waters in North West Africa: II. Site descriptions for Tunisia and Algeria. *Biol. Cons.* 24: 83-113.

Mukhina, Y. A. and Lukashevich, R. V. (1989) Waterbirds and waterfowl of the Karshi steppe. Pp.123-135 in *Bird fauna and bird ecology of Uzbekistan*. Samarkand.

Munteanu, D., Tonuic, N., Weber, P., Seabo, J. and Marinov, M. (1989) Evaluarea efetivelor pasarilov acvatice in cartierele lor de ierare din Romania (1988-1989). *Ocrot. Nat.* 33: 105-112.

Munteanu, D., Weber, P., Szabó, J., Gogu-Bogdan, M. and Marinov, M. (1991) A note on the present status of geese in Romania. *Ardea* 79: 165-166.

NABU (1991) Die Europäischen Vogelschutsgebiete (IBA) in den fünf neuen Bundesländern. *ICBP IBA Report* No. 5.

Nankinov, D. (1989) Früherer und jetziger Stand der Bestandsentwicklung der Zwergscharbe *Phalacrocorax pygmaeus* in Bulgarien. *Faun. Abh. Staatl. Mus. Tierk. Dresden* 17: 79-84.

Nankinov, D. N. (1993) A new wintering area of the Lesser White-fronted Goose *Anser erythropus* in Bulgaria. *Ornis Svecica* 3: 165-166.

Navarro, J. D. and Robledano, F., eds. (in press) *La Cerceta Pardilla (Marmaronetta angustirostris) en España*. Madrid: Instituto Nacional para la Conservación de la Naturaleza (Colección Técnica).

Nazirides, T. and Papageorgiou, N. (in press) *The breeding biology of Pygmy Cormorants (Phalacrocorax pygmeus), a vulnerable bird species, at Lake Kerkini, northern Greece*. Colonial Waterbirds.

Negro, J. J. and Hiraldo, F. (1993) Nest-site selection and breeding success in the Lesser Kestrel *Falco naumanni*. Bird Study 40: 115-119.

Negro, J. J., de la Riva, M. and Bustamante, J. (1991) Patterns of winter distribution and abundance of Lesser Kestrels (*Falco naumanni*) in Spain. *J. Raptor Res.* 25: 30-35.

Negro, J. J., Donázar, J. A., Hiraldo, F., Hernández, L. M. and Fernández, M. A. (1993) Organochlorine and heavy metal contamination in non-viable eggs and its relation to breeding success in a Spanish population of Lesser Kestrels (*Falco naumanni*). *Environ. Pollut.*: 201-205.

Nielsen, O. K. (1994) The Ruddy Duck (*Oxyura jamaicensis*) in Iceland. *Oxyura* 7: 67-73.

Nielsen, O. K. (1995) The Ruddy Duck colonisation in Iceland. *Bliki* 15: 1-15. (In Icelandic with English summary.)

Nikolskyi, A. M. (1891) Vertebrates of Crimea. Add. to Vol. 68 "Notes of Empire Academy of Sciences". St Petersburg.

Nogales, M. (1985) *Contribution to the study of the flora and fauna of the Pajonales, Ojeda and Inagua mountains (Gran Canaria)*. Tenerife: Universidad de La Laguna (thesis). (In Spanish.)

Nogales, M., Suarez, C. and Diaz, G. (1986) Blue Chaffinch of El Teide (*Fringilla teydea*): presence of Fringilla teydea polatzeki in Asio otus pellets. *Ardeola* 33: 213. (In Spanish.)

Norderhaug, A. and Norderhaug, M. (1982) Anser erythropus in Fennoscandia. *Aquila* 89: 93-101.

Norderhaug, A. and Norderhaug, M. (1984) Status of the Lesser White-fronted Goose, Anser erythropus, in Fennoscandia. *Swedish Wildl. Res.* 13: 171-185.

Norris, C. A. (1947) Report on the distribution and status of the Corncrake. *Brit. Birds* 40: 226-244.

Øien, I. J. and Aarvak, T. (1993) *Status for dverggs* Anser erythropus *in Fennoskandia*. Norwegian Ornithological Society.

Oliveira, P. (1992) Alguns aspectos da ecologia, biologia e comportamento do Pombo Trocaz, Columba trocaz. Lisbon, Portugal: Faculdade de Ciencias, Universidad de Lisboa (relatório de estágio para a licenciatura em Recursos Faunisticos e Ambiente). Unpublished.

Oliveira, P. (1993) *O uso de espantalhos automáti-cos como medida de conservação e proteção do Pombo Trocaz*, Columba trocaz. Relatório efectua-do para a CE no ambito do projecto "A Conservaçao da Avifauna da Laurisilva da Madeira e Açores". Unpublished.

Oliveira, P. and Jones, M. J. (in press) *Population numbers, habitat preferences and the impact of the Long-toed Laurel Pigeon on agricultural fields: pros-pectives for future management*. Symposium on flora and fauna of the Atlantic islands, Madeira, October 1993.

ORNISTUDIO (1989a) *Census of the Canary Island Bustard in Fuerteventura (December 1988)*. Unpublished. (In Spanish.)

ORNISTUDIO (1989b) *Census of the Canary Island Houbara Bustard in Fuerteventura (July 1989)*. Unpublished. (In Spanish.)

ORNISTUDIO (1990) *Census of the Canary Island Bustard in Fuerteventura (December 1989)*. Unpublished. (In Spanish.)

ORNISTUDIO (1991) *Census of the Canary Island Houbara Bustard in Lanzarote (April 1991)*. Unpublished. (In Spanish.)

ORNISTUDIO (1992) *Census of the Canary Island Houbara Bustard in Fuerteventura (January 1992)*. Unpublished. (In Spanish.)

Oró, D. and Martínez-Vilalta, A. (1992) The colo-ny of Audouin's Gull at the Ebro delta. *Avocetta* 16: 36-39.

Oró, D. and Martínez-Vilalta, A. (1994a) Factors affecting kleptoparasitism and predation rates upon a colony of Audouin's Gull (*Larus audouinii*) by Yellow-legged Gulls (*Larus cachinnans*). *Colonial Waterbirds* 17: 35-41.

Oró, D. and Martínez, A. (1994b) Migration and dispersal of Audouin's Gull *Larus audouinii* from the Ebro delta colony. *Ostrich* 65: 225-230.

Oró, D., Jover, L. and Ruiz, X. (1994) *Effects of food shortage on some breeding parameters of the Audouin's Gull*. Poster, XXI International Ornithological Congress.

Ortali, A. (1981) Il Marangone Minore *Phalacrocorax pygmaeus* nel ravennate: possibile stanziale e probabile nidificare. *Gli Uccelli Italia*: 210-212.

Osborne, P. E. (1986) *Survey of the birds of Fuerteventura, Canary Islands, with special reference to the status of the Canarian Houbara Bustard* Chlamydotis undulata. Cambridge, UK: International Council for Bird Preservation (Study Rep. 10).

Osieck, E. R. and Hustings, F. (1994) *Red data and important birds in the Netherlands*. Zeist: Vogelbescherming Nederland (Techn. Rep. 12). (In Dutch.)

Pain, D. J., ed. (1992) *Lead poisoning in waterfowl*. Proc. IWRB Workshop, Brussels, Belgium, 1991. Slimbridge, UK: Wetlands International (IWRB Spec. Publ. 16).

Palma, L. (1985) The present situation of birds of prey in Portugal. Pp.3-14 in I. Newton and R. D. Chancellor, eds. *Conservation studies on raptors*. Cambridge, UK: International Council for Bird Preservation (Techn. Publ. 5).

Paltanavicius, S. (1992) *Red Data Book of Lithuania*. Vilnius: Environmental Protection Department of the Republic of Lithuania.

Parr, S. and Naveso, M. (1994) *Interim report on Lesser Kestrel research in central Turkey*. Unpublished.

Parr, S., Collin, P., Silk, S., Wilbraham, J., Williams, N. P. and Yarar, M. (1995) A baseline survey of Lesser Kestrels *Falco naumanni* in central Turkey. *Biol. Conservation* 72: 45-53.

Paspaleva, M., Botond Kiss, J. and Talpeanu, M. (1985) Les oiseaux coloniaux dans le delta du Danube. *Trav. Mus. Histoire nat. "Grigore Antipa"* 27: 289-304.

Pastor, D., Jover, L., Ruiz, X. and Albaiges, J. (in press) Monitoring organochlorine pollution in Audouin's Gull eggs: the relevance of sampling procedures. The Science of Total Environment.

Paterson, A., Martínez-Vilalta, A. and Dies, J. I. (1992) Partial breeding failure of Audouin's Gull in two Spanish colonies in 1991, Brit. Birds 85:97-100.

Patrikeev, M. (1993) Preliminary inventory of Important Bird Areas in Azerbaijan. Unpublished.

Paz, U. (1987) The birds of Israel. London: Christopher Helm.

Pearce, F. (1993) Draining life from Iraq's marshes. New Scientist 17 April: 11-12.

Peja, N., Sarigul, G., Siki, M. and Crivelli, A.J. (in press) The Dalmatian pelican, Pelecanus crispus, nesting in Mediterranean lagoons: Karavasta (Albania), Camalti Tuzlasi and Menderes delta in Turkey. Colonial Waterbirds.

Pereira, P. (1991) Resultados del seguimiento de Malvasías procedentes del programa de cría en cautividad durante el año 1990. Pp.135-143 in M. Jesús Martos and J. Fernández Palacios, eds. Plan Rector de Uso y Gestión de las Reservas Naturales de las Lagunas de Cádiz. Junta de Andalucía: Consejería de Cultura y Medio Ambiente, Agencia de Medio Ambiente.

Perennou, C. and Cantera, J.-P. (1993) Etude de faisabilité sur la réintroduction de l'Erismature à tête blanche sur l'étang de Biguglia, Haute Corse. AGENC and Station Biologique de la Tour du Valat.

Perennou, C., Mundkur, T., Scott, D. A., Follestad, A. and Kvenild, L. (1994) The Asian Waterfowl census 1987-1991: Distribution and Status of Asian Waterfowl. Kuala Lumpur, Malaysia: AWB (Publ. 86) and Slimbridge, UK: International Waterfowl and Wetlands Research Bureau (Publ. 24).

Petrov, T. and Iankov, P. (1993) Imperial Eagle project: Bulgaria. Unpublished.

Petrov, T., Iankov, P., Darakchiev, A., Nikolov, K., Michev, T., Porfirov, L. and Milchev, B. (in prep.) State of the Imperial Eagle Aquila heliaca in Bulgaria in the period between 1890 and 1993 (unpublished report). Eagle Studies.

Phalacrocorax pygmeus (Pallas 1773) from Lake Skadar (Yugoslavia). Glasnik Rep. Zav. Zast Prirode Muzeju Titogradu 14: 65-70.

Phillips, J. (1923) A natural history of ducks, 1. Boston: Houghton Mifflin.

Pieper, H. (1985) The fossil land birds of Madeira and Porto Santo. Bocagiana 88: 1-6.

Pintos, R. and Rodríguez de los Santos, M. (1992) Presencia de las Malvasía Cariblanca en Andalucía; sus efectos sobre Oxyura leuco cephala. IWRB Threatened Waterfowl Res. Group Newsl. 2: 16-18.

Porter, R. (1991) Priority bird species in Turkey. Orn. Soc. Middle East Bull. 26: 1-8.

Poslavski, A. (1992) The status of the Marbled Teal and White-headed Duck in Turkmenistan and Uzbekistan. IWRB Threatened Waterfowl Res. Group Newsl. 2: 8-10.

Pranaitis, A. (1993) Changes in abundance and species composition of birds breeding in overgrowing marshy meadows in Zuvintas Nature Reserve. Abstract. Palanga: Baltic Birds 7 Conference.

Pritchard, D. E., Housden, S. D., Mudge, G. P., Galbraith, C. A. and Pienkowski, M. W. (eds) (1992) Important bird areas in the United Kingdom including the Channel Islands and the Isle of Man. RSPB.

Psilovikos, A. (1992) Research on the sedimentation problem of Lake Kerkini: recommendations, solution. Report.

Ptushenko, E. S. and Inozemtsev, A. A. (1968) Biologiya i khozyaistvennoye znacheniye ptits Moskovskoy oblasti i sopredelnykh territoriy. Moscow: Moskovskogo University. (In Russian.)

Puscariu, V. (1983) La présence de Branta ruficollis pendant l'hiver en Roumanie. Aquila 90: 23-27.

Puscariu, V. (1977) Roumanie. IWRB Bull. 43/44: 32-33.

Pyrovetsi, M. (1990) Conservation and management of the biotopes of the Dalmatian pelican (Pelecanus crispus) in northern Greece. Thessaloniki, Greece: Commission of European

Communities (DG XI) and Aristotelian University of Thessaloniki.

Pyrovetsi, M. and Crivelli, A. J. (1988) Habitat use by water-birds in Prespa National Park, Greece. *Biol. Conserv.* 45: 135-153.

Pyrovetsi, M. and Daoutopoulos, G. A. (1990) Educational response to differences in environmental attitudes among fishermen. Pp.497-506 in M. Marchand and H. A. Udo de Haes, eds. *The people's role in wetland management.* Leiden: Centre for Environmental Studies, Leiden University.

Pyrovetsi, M. and Daoutopoulos, G. A. (1991) Educational response to differences in environmental attitudes among lake fishermen. *Landscape Urban Planning* 20: 167-172.

Pyrovetsi, M. and Dimalexis, A. (1994) *Physical factors controlling breeding performance of the Dalmatian Pelicans* (Pelecanus crispus). *Proceedings of VI International Congress on Ecology, Manchester, UK* .

Pyrovetsi, M. and Papastergiadou, E. (1992) Biological conservation implications of water-level fluctuations in a wetland of International Importance: Lake Kerkini, Macedonia, Greece. *Environ. Conserv.* 19: 235-244.

Pyrovetsi, M. and Papazahariadou, M. (in press) *Mortality factors of wintering Dalmatian pelicans* (Pelecanus crispus) *in Macedonia, Greece.*

Pyrovetsi, M., Dimalexis, A. and Stamou, G. (1993a) Factors affecting breeding success of Dalmatian Pelicans at Lake Mikri Prespa. Pp.174-176 in *Proceedings of 15th Panhellenic Conference of the Greek Society of Biological Science, Florina.*

Pyrovetsi, M., Psalidas, V. and Vokou, D. (1993b) Contribution of the environmental education in changing high school students knowledge and attitudes towards a wetland ecosystem. In *Proceedings of 15th Panhellenic Conference of Greek Society of Biological Science, Florina.*

Ramadan-Jaradi, G. and Ramadan-Jaradi, M. G. (1989) Breeding the Houbara Bustard at the Al Ain Zoo and Aquarium Abu Dhabi U.A.E. *Zool. Garten* 59: 229-240.

Ramos, J. A. (in press b) The influence of size, shape and phenolic content on the selection of winter foods by the Azores Bullfinch. *J. Zool.*

Ramos, J. A. (in press a) The introduction of exotic plants as a threat to the Azores Bullfinch population. *J. Appl. Ecol.*

Ramos, J. A. (1995a) The diet of the Azores Bullfinch *Pyrrhula murina* and floristic variation within its range. *Biol. Conserv.* 71: 237-249.

Ramos, J. A. (1993) *Status and ecology of the Priolo or Azores Bullfinch.* Oxford, UK: University of Oxford (Ph.D. thesis).

Ramos, J. A. (1995b) *O Priôlo: sua relação com a floresta natural de altitude.* Nordeste (Açores): Câmara Municipal de Nordeste.

Ramos, J. A. (1994b) Fern frond feeding by the Azores Bullfinch. *J. Avian Biol.* 25: 344-347.

Ramos, J. A. (1994a) The annual cycle of the Azores Bullfinch. *Arquipelago. Ser. Cien. Nat.* 12A: 101-109.

Ramsar Convention Bureau (1990) *Directory of wetlands of international importance.* Ramsar Switzerland Conference 1990. Gland, Switzerland: International Union for Conservation of Nature and Natural Resources.

Renaud, J. (1989) Captive propagation of Houbara Bustards at the National Wildlife Research Centre, Taif. Pp.335-339 A. H. Abu-Zinada, P. D. Goriup and I. A. Nader, eds. *Wildlife conservation and development in Saudi Arabia: proceedings of the first symposium on the potential for wildlife conservation and development in Saudi Arabia, Riyadh, February 1987.* Riyadh: National Commission for Wildlife Conservation and Development (National Commission for Wildlife Conservation and Development Publications 3).

Rocamora, G. (1993) Les Zones Importantes pour la Conservation des Oiseaux en France. LPO.

Rodríguez, F. and Moreno, A. C. (1993) Conservation programme for the Blue Chaffinch *Fringilla teydea polatzeki* (Hartert, 1905) on Gran Canaria 1991-1993. 1: Populations, reproduction, habitat characteristics and predation. Gran

Canaria: Gobierno de Canarias, Viceconsejería de Medio Ambiente (unpublished). (In Spanish.)

Rogacheva, H. (1992) *The birds of central Siberia.* Husun Druck- und Verlagsgesellschaft.

Romashova, A. T. (1994) Breeding biology and feeding ecology of *Pelecanus crispus* and *Pelecanus onocrotalus* in the northern Caspian. Pp.99-114 in A. J. Crivelli, V. G. Krivenko and V. G. Vinogradov, eds. (1994) *Pelicans in the former USSR.* Slimbridge, UK: International Waterfowl and Wetlands Research Bureau (IWRB Spec. Publ. 27).

Rose, P. (1992) *Western Palearctic Waterfowl Census 1992.* Slimbridge, UK: Wetlands International.

Rose, P., ed. (1993) *Ruddy Duck European status report – 1993.* Slimbridge, UK: International Waterfowl and Wetlands Research Bureau.

Rose, P. M. and Scott, D. A. (1994) *Waterfowl population estimates.* Slimbridge, UK: International Waterfowl and Wetlands Research Bureau (IWRB Spec. Publ. 29).

Rudescu, L. (1955) Pelicanii din Delta Dunarii. *Ocrotirea Nat. Bucuresti* 1: 107-120.

Rufino, R., ed. (1989) *Atlas das aves que nidificam em Portugal continental.* Lisbon: CEMPRA/SNPRCN.

Ruiz, X., Oró, D., Martínez-Vilalta, A. and Jover, L. (in press) *Feeding ecology of Audouin's Gulls (Larus audouinii) in the Ebro delta.* Colonial Waterbirds.

Ruiz, X., Jover, L., Oró, D., González-Solís, J., Pedrocchi, V. and Bosch, M. (1993) *Ecología y dinámica de la población de la Gaviota de Audouin, Larus audouinii: primera memoria de resultados.* ICONA/Universitat de Barcelona. Unpublished.

Salathé, T. and Yarar, M. (1992) *Towards a management plan for Lake Burdur.* Dogal Hayati Koruma Dernegi and Tour du Valat (unpublished report).

Sánchez, A. and Rodríguez, A. (1992) *Censo y reproducción del Aguila Imperial en Extremadura (1988-1992).* Mérida Bádajoz: Consejería de Obras Públicas y Medio Ambiente.

Sapetin, Y. V. (1968) Material on ringing of *Pelecanus onocrotalus* and *Phalacrocorax pygmeus* in the Terek delta. *Animal Migration* 5: 113-117 (In Russian.)

Schäffer, N. (1994) Methoden zum Nachweis von Bruten des Wachtelkönigs *Crex crex. Vogelwelt* 115: 69-73.

Schäffer, N. and Münch, S. (1993) Untersuchungen zur Habitatwahl und Brutbiologie des Wachtelkönigs *Crex crex* im Murnauer Moos/Oberbayern. *Vogelwelt* 114: 55-72.

Schenk, H. (1976) Analisi della situazione faunistica in Sardegna. Uccelli e mammiferi. Pp.465-556 in *SOS fauna, animali in pericolo in Italia.* Camerino: World Wildlife Fund-Italy.

Schulze-Hagen, K. (1993) *Winter quarters of the Aquatic Warbler and habitat situation: short review of recent knowledge.* Unpublished.

Schulze-Hagen, K. and Wawrzyniak, H. (1993) *Recent situation of the Aquatic Warbler in Germany and conservation activities.* Unpublished.

Scott, D. A. (1980) *A preliminary inventory of wetlands of international importance for waterfowl in west Europe and northwest Africa.* Slimbridge, UK: International Waterfowl and Wetlands Research Bureau (Spec. Publ. 2).

Scott, P. (1939) *Wild chorus.* Glasgow: University Press.

Scott, P. (1970) Redbreasts in Romania. *Wildfowl* 21: 37-41.

SEO (1992) *Areas Importantes para las aves en España.* Report to the European Commission.

Shenk, H. and Meschini, E. (1986) Gabbiano corso *Larus audouinii* Payraudeau 1826. *Ric. Biol. Selvaggina* 11: 41-51.

Shirihai, H. (1995) *Birds of Israel.* London: Academic Press.

Simeonov, S., Michev, T. and Nankinov, D. (1990) *The fauna of Bulgaria.* 1: Aves 20. Sofia: BAS Publ. House. (In Bulgarian.)

Simeonov, S. D. and Petrov, T. H. (1980) Studies on the food of the Imperial Eagle *Aquila heliaca,* the Buzzard *Buteo buteo* and the Rough-legged Buzzard *Buteo lagopus. Ecology* 7: 22-30.

Skov- og Naturstyrelsen, Miljøministeriet Ministry of the Environment, National Forest and Nature Agency (1991) *Rødliste '90. Red Data List '90.* (In Danish.)

Slimbridge, UK: *International Waterfowl and Wetlands Research Bureau* (IWRB Spec. Publ. 20).

Smart, M. (1970) Status of the species of wildfowl occurring in Tunisia. Pp.163-168 in Y. A. Isakov, ed. *Proceedings of the international regional meeting on conservation of wildfowl resources (Europe, western Asia, Northern and tropical Africa). Leningrad, USSR 25-30 Sept. 1968.* Moscow.

Smith, K. D. (1968) Spring migration through southeast Morocco. *Ibis* 110: 452-492.

Soikkeli, M. (1973) Decrease in numbers of migrating Lesser White-fronted Geese *Anser erythropus* in Finland. *Finnish Game Res.* 33: 28-30.

Soti, J., Vizi, O. and Krsmanovic, L. (1981) Weight and measures of Pygmy Cormorant *Phalacrocorax pygmeus* (Pallas 1773) from Lake Skadar (Yugoslavia) *Glasnik Rep. Zav. Prirode Muzeju Titogradu* 14: 65-70.

Springer, A. M., Roseneau, D. G., Denby, S. L., McRoy, C. P. and Murphy, E. C. (1986) Seabird responses to fluctuating prey availability in the eastern Bering Sea. *Mar. Ecol. Prog. Ser.* 32: 1-12.

Sterbetz, I. (1980) Occurrence of the Red-breasted Goose (*Branta ruficollis*) at Kardoskut in 1978-1979. *Aquila* 87: 141-142.

Sterbetz, I. (1968) Der Zug der Zwerggans auf der Ungarischen Puszta. *Ardea* 56: 259-266.

Sterbetz, I. (1990) Variations in the habitat of the Lesser White-fronted Goose (*Anser erythropus* L., 1758) in Hungary. *Aquila* 96-97: 11-17.

Sterbetz, I. (1986) Percentage of juvenile Lesser White-fronted Geese (*Anser erythropus* L., 1758) in Hungary. *Aquila* 92: 81-88.

Sterbetz, I. (1982) Migration of *Anser erythropus* and *Branta ruficollis* in Hungary 1971-1980. *Aquila* 89: 107-114.

Sterbetz, I. (1982) Migration of *Anser erythropus* and *Branta ruficollis* in Hungary 1971-1980. *Aquila* 89: 107-114.

Stowe, T. J. and Becker, D. (1992) Status and conservation of Corncrakes *Crex crex* outside the breeding grounds. *Tauraco* 2: 1-23.

Straka, U. (1990) Beobachtungen an überwinternden Zwergsarben (*Phalacrocorax pygmeus* Pallas 1773) an der niederösterreichischen Donau im Winter 1989-1990. *Egretta* 33: 77-85.

Stresemann, E. and Grote, H. (1943) Ist *Numenius tenuirostris* im Aussterben begriffen? *Orn. Monatsber.* 51: 122-127.

Swash, A. R. H. & Zino, F. (1991) *Protecting the Freira from predation by rodents.* Unpublished report to ICBP (1990-1991).

Tariel, I. (1993) Apres 100 ans d'absence le vautour moine est de retour. *Revue 23*: 21. Fonds d'Intervention pour les Rapaces.

van den Tempel, R. and Osieck, E. R. (1994) *Important Bird Areas in the Netherlands.* Zeist: Vogelbescherming Nederland (Techn. Rep. 13). (In Dutch.)

Tewes, E. (1994) The European Black Vulture *Aegypius monachus* Project in Mallorca. Pp.493-498 in B.-U. Meyburg and R. D. Chancellor, eds. *Raptor conservation today.* Berlin: World Working Group on Birds of Prey and Pica Press.

Thibault, J. C. and Guyot, I. (1989) *Le Goéland d'Audouin en Corse: synthèse pour la gestion d'une espèce menacée.* Ajaccio: Association des Amis du Parc Naturel Regional Corse.

Torres, J. A. and Arenas, R. (1985) Nuevos datos relativos a la alimentación de *Oxyura leucocephala. Ardeola* 32: 127-131.

Torres, J. A., Arenas, R. and Ayala, J. M. (1986) Evolución histórica de la población Española de Malvasía (*Oxyura leucocephala*). *Oxyura* 3: 5-19.

Torres, J. A., Arenas, R. and Ayala, J. M. (undated) Pp.173-176 in: *La regeneración de la Laguna del Rincón.* Zonas Húmedas Ibéricas. Ponencias de las II Jornadas Ibéricas sobre estudio y protección de las zonas húmedas. Federación de Amigos de la Tierra.

Torres, J. A., Moreno, B. and Alcalá-Zamora, A. (1994a) Resultados del programa de control de la Malvasía Canela. *Quercus* 104: 15-18.

Torres, J. A., Moreno, B. and Alcalá-Zamora, A. (1994b) La Malvasía Canela (*Oxyura jamaicensis*) en España y su relación con la Malvasía Cabeciblanca (*Oxyura leucocephala*). *Oxyura* 7: 5-27.

Tristram, H. B. (1884) *The fauna and flora of Palestine*. London.

Tristram, H. B. (1889) Ornithological notes on the island of Gran Canaria. *Ibis* (6)1: 13-32.

Tuaien, D. G. and Kurbanov, N. I. (1984) Quantitative characteristics of breeding Anseriformes in Azerbaidzhan. Pp.98-100 in *Present status of waterfowl resources in USSR. Proceedings of All-Union Seminar, October 1984*. Moscow. (In Russian.)

Tucker et al. (1996 in press) *Habitats for Birds in Europe: a conservation strategy.*

Tucker, G. M. and Heath, M. F. (1994) *Birds in Europe: their conservation status*. Cambridge, UK: BirdLife International (BirdLife Conservation Series No. 3).

Urdiales, C. and Pereira, P. (1993) *Identification key of O. jamaicensis, O. leucocephala and their hybrids*. Madrid: Instituto Nacional para la Conservación de la Naturaleza.

Ushakov, V. E. (1916) Nest and eggs of *Numenius tenuirostris*, Vieill. *Orn. Vestnik* 3: 185-187.

Ushakov, V. E. (1925) Colonial nesting of the Slender-billed Curlew in Tara district of Omsk government. *Ural'skiy okhotnik* 2: 32-35.

Uspenski, S. M. (1965) *Die Wildgänse nordeurasiens*. Wittenberg-Lutherstadt: Neue Brehm-Bücherei.

Uspenski, S. M. (1966) Verbreitung and ökologie der Rothalsgans. *Falke* 13: 83-85.

Uspenski, S. M. and Kishko, Y. K. (1967) Winter range of the Red-breasted Goose in eastern Azerbaidzhan. *Problemy Severa* 11: 235-243.

Valkh, B. S. (1900) Materials for ornithology of Ekaterinoslov Province. Observations of 1892-1897. *Works of Natural Society*, Chakkiv Univ. 34: 1-90.

Valverde, J. (1964) Datos sobre Cerceta Pardilla en las Marismas. *Ardeola* 9: 121-132.

Vangeluwe, D. and Handrinos, G. (1995) *Urgent measures for the protection of the Slender-billed Curlew*, Numenius tenuirostris *on the migration sites of Porto Lagos and the Evros Delta*. Report to the European Commission.

Vangeluwe, D. and Snethlage, M. (1992) *Rapport des investigations sur l'écologie et la conservation de la Bernache à cou roux* Branta ruficollis *en Dobroudja (Roumanie et Bulgarie) Janvier 1992*. Institut Royal des Sciences Naturelles de Belgique.

Vangeluwe, D. and Stassin, P. (1991) Hivernage de la Bernache à cou roux *Branta ruficollis* en Dobroudja septentrionale, Roumanie et revue du statut hivernal de l'espèce. *Gerfaut* 81: 65-99.

Vangeluwe, D., Beudels, M.-O. and Lamani, F. (in press) *Conservation status of Albanian coastal wetlands and their colonial waterbird populations* (Pelecaniformes and Ciconiiformes). *Colonial Waterbirds*.

Vasic, V., Grubac, B., Susic, G. and Marinkovic, S. (1985) The status of birds of prey in Yugoslavia with particular reference to Macedonia. Pp.45-53 in I. Newton and R. D. Chancellor, eds. *Conservation studies on raptors*. Cambridge, UK: International Council for Bird Preservation (Techn. Publ. 5).

Vetrov, V. and Gorban, I. (1994) *Imperial Eagle Project: Ukraine 1994-2004*. Unpublished.

Vielliard, J. (1968) Résultats ornithologiques d'une mission à travers la Turquie. *Rev. Faculté Sci. Univ. Istanbul (B)* 33: 67-171.

Viksne, J. (1994) *Putniem Nozímígás Vietas Latvijá*. Riga: Latvijas *Ornitologijas biedríba*.

Vinogradov, V. (1990) *Anser erythropus* in the USSR. Pp.199-203 in G. V. T. Matthews, ed. *Managing waterfowl populations*. Proc. IWRB Symp., Astrakhan, 1989. Slimbridge, UK: International Waterfowl and Wetlands Research Bureau (IWRB Spec. Publ. 12).

Vinokurov, A. A. (1990) Branta ruficollis in the USSR. Pp.197-198 in G. V. T. Matthews, ed. *Managing waterfowl populations.* Proc. IWRB Symp., Astrakhan, 1989. Slimbridge, UK: International Waterfowl and Wetlands Research Bureau (IWRB Spec. Publ. 12).

Vitaloni, M. (1994) *Progetto Oxyura.* WWF Italia (unpublished report).

Vizi, O. (1981) The Dalmatian Pelican of Lake Skadar. Pp.419-424 in G. S. Karaman and A. M. Beeton, eds. *The biota and limnology of Lake Skadar, Titograd.*

Vizi, O. (1979a) Ishrana pelikana kudravog *Pelecanus crispus* Bruch 1832 na Skadarskom jezeru i njegov znacaj za ribarstvo. *Podjoprivreda i sumarstvo* 25: 45-57.

Vizi, O. (1975) O gnezdenju pelikana kudravog (*Pelecanus crispus* Bruch 1832) na Skadarskom jezeru is problem njegove Zastite. *Glas. Republ. Zavoda Zast. Prir. Prirodnajackog Muzeja* 8: 5-13.

Vizi, O. (1979b) New data on breeding of Dalmatian Pelican (*Pelecanus crispus* Bruch 1832) on Lake Skadar. *Glas. Republ. Zavoda Zast. Prir. Prirodnajackog Muzeja* 12: 125-139.

Vizi, O. (1979) The nesting of Common Heron (*Ardea cinerea*) on Skadar Lake in the periods 1972-1975 and 1977-1978. Proceedings of a meeting of the Association of ecological Societies of Yugoslavia, Zagreb: 1705-1716.

von Essen, L. (1993) *Projekt Fjällgås. Projektbeskrivning och resultat intill 1992.* 10.31. Report from Swedish Hunters' Association.

von Essen, L. (1991) A note on the Lesser White-fronted Goose *Anser erythropus* in Sweden and the results of a re-introduction scheme. *Ardea* 79: 305-306.

Voslamber, B. (1989) De Kwartelkoning *Crex crex* in het Oldambt: aantallen en biotoopkeuze. *Limosa* 62: 15-21.

Vyazovich, Y. (1993) *Wetlands in the Republic of Belarus and their inventory under the international project.* Unpublished.

Warham, J. (1990) *The petrels: their ecology and breeding systems.* New York: Academic Press.

Watzman, H. (1993) Israel floods drained swamp to bring in tourists. *New Scientist* 17 April: 9.

Weiss, J. (1992) Rote Liste der Brutvöel Luxemburgs 5 Fassung/Stand: Herbst 1991. *Regulus Wiss. Ber.* 10: 23-29.

Whilde, A. (1993) Threatened mammals, birds, amphibians, and fish in Ireland. *Irish Red Data Book 2:* Vertebrates. Belfast: HMSO.

Whistler, H. (1936) Further observations from Albania. *Ibis* 13: 335-356.

Wink, M. and Seibold, I. (1994) *Molecular systematics of Mediterranean raptors: summary.* VI Conference on Biology and Conservation of Mediterranean Raptors, Palma de Mallorca.

Witt, H.-H. (1977) Zur Biologie der Korallenmöwe *Larus audouinii*, Brut und Ernährung. *J. Orn.* 118: 134-155.

Witt, H.-H. (1976) Beobachtungen zum Vorkommen und zur brut einiger non-Passeres au der turkischen Südkuste bei Silifke. *Vogelwelt* 97: 139-145.

Witt, H.-H. (1982) Ernährung und Brutverbreitung der Korallenmöwe *Larus audouinii* im Vergleich zur Mittelmeersilbermöwe *Larus argentatus michahellis*. *Seevögel* 3 suppl.: 87-91.

Witt, H.-H., Crespo, J., de Juana, E. and Varela, J. (1981) Comparative feeding ecology of Audouin's Gull *Larus audouinii* and the Herring Gull *Larus argentatus* in the Mediterranean. *Ibis* 123: 519-526.

Zbinden, N., Glutz von Blotzheim, H. And Schifferli, L. (1994) Liste der Schweizer Brutvögel mit Gefährdungsgard in den einzelnen Regionen. Pp.24-30 in P. Duelli *Rote Listen der gefährdeten Tierarten der Schweiz.* Bern: Buwal.

Zino, F., Biscoito, M. J. & Costa Neves, H. (1993) *The Freira Conservation Project.* Poster presented at the First Symposium on Flora and Fauna of Atlantic Islands, Funchal.

Zino, F., Biscoito, M. J. & Costa Neves, H. (1989) *Madeira Freira Project.* Unpublished report, Funchal.

Zino, F., Biscoito, M. J. and Zino, P. A. (1994) Zino's Petrel Pterodroma madeira. Pp.62-63 in G. M. Tucker, M. F. Heath. *Birds in Europe: their conservation status*. Cambridge, UK: BirdLife International (BirdLife Conservation Series No. 3).

Zino, P. A. and Zino, F. (1986) Contribution to the study of petrels of the genus *Pterodroma* in the archipelago of Madeira. *Bol. Mus. Mun. Funchal* 38(180): 141-165.

Zino, P. A. (1969) Observations sur *Columba trocaz. Oiseaux et R. F. O.* 39:261-264.

Zino, F. (1991) The Madeira Freira Conservation Project. *World Birdwatch* 13(2): 8-9.

Zino, F. and Biscoito, M. J. (1994) Breeding seabirds in the Madeira archipelago. Pp.172-185 in D. N. Nettleship, J. Burger and M. Gochfeld, eds. *Seabirds on islands: threats, case studies and action plans*. Cambridge, UK: BirdLife International (BirdLife Conservation Series No. 1).

Zino, F (1992) Cats amongst the Freiras. *Oryx* 26: 174.

Zino, F. and Zino, P. A. (1986) An account of the habitat, feeding habitats, density, breeding and need of protection of the Long-toed Wood Pigeon, *Columba trocaz. Bocagiana* 97:1-16.

Zino, F. and Biscoito, M. J. (1993) Interrelation of food availability and reproduction in *Columba trocaz*. Funchal: Abstracts, First Symposium on Fauna and Flora of the Atlantic Islands.

Zino, F. (1992) Cats amongst the Freiras. *Oryx* 26: 174.

Sales agents for publications of the Council of Europe
Agents de vente des publications du Conseil de l'Europe

AUSTRALIA/AUSTRALIE
Hunter publications, 58A, Gipps Street
AUS-3066 COLLINGWOOD, Victoria
Fax: (61) 34 19 71 54

AUSTRIA/AUTRICHE
Gerold und Co., Graben 31
A-1011 WIEN 1
Fax: (43) 1512 47 31 29

BELGIUM/BELGIQUE
La Librairie européenne SA
50, avenue A. Jonnart
B-1200 BRUXELLES 20
Fax: (32) 27 35 08 60

Jean de Lannoy
202, avenue du Roi
B-1060 BRUXELLES
Fax: (32) 25 38 08 41

CANADA
Renouf Publishing Company Limited
5369 Canotek Road, Unit 1
CDN-OTTAWA ONT K1J 9J3
Fax: (1) 613 745 76 60

DENMARK/DANEMARK
Munksgaard
PO Box 2148
DK-1016 KØBENHAVN K
Fax: (45) 33 12 93 87

FINLAND/FINLANDE
Akateeminen Kirjakauppa
Keskuskatu 1, PO Box 218
SF-00381 HELSINKI
Fax: (358) 01 21 44 50

GERMANY/ALLEMAGNE
UNO Verlag
Poppelsdorfer Allee 55
D-53115 BONN
Fax: (49) 228 21 74 92

GREECE/GRÈCE
Librairie Kauffmann
Mavrokordatou 9, GR-ATHINAI 106 78
Fax: (30) 13 23 03 20

HUNGARY/HONGRIE
Euro Info Service
Magyarorszag
Margitsziget (Európa Ház),
H-1138 BUDAPEST
Fax: (36) 1 111 62 16

IRELAND/IRLANDE
Government Stationery Office
4-5 Harcourt Road, IRL-DUBLIN 2
Fax: (353) 14 75 27 60

ISRAEL/ISRAËL
ROY International
17 Shimon Hatrssi St.
PO Box 13056
IL-61130 TEL AVIV
Fax: (972) 3 546 1423

ITALY/ITALIE
Libreria Commissionaria Sansoni
Via Duca di Calabria, 1/1
Casella Postale 552, I-50125 FIRENZE
Fax: (39) 55 64 12 57

MALTA/MALTE
L. Sapienza & Sons Ltd
26 Republic Street
PO Box 36
VALLETTA CMR 01
Fax: (356) 233 621

NETHERLANDS/PAYS-BAS
InOr-publikaties, PO Box 202
NL-7480 AE HAAKSBERGEN
Fax: (31) 542 72 92 96

NORWAY/NORVÈGE
Akademika, A/S Universitetsbokhandel
PO Box 84, Blindern
N-0314 OSLO
Fax: (47) 22 85 30 53

POLAND/POLOGNE
Główna Księgarnia Naukowa im. B. Prusa
Krakowskie Przedmiescie 7
PL-00-068 WARSZAWA
Fax: (48) 22 26 64 49

Internews
Ul. Kolejowa 15/17
PL-01-217 WARSZAWA
Fax: (48) 22 632 55 21/66 12

PORTUGAL
Livraria Portugal
Rua do Carmo, 70
P-1200 LISBOA
Fax: (351) 13 47 02 64

SPAIN/ESPAGNE
Mundi-Prensa Libros SA
Castelló 37, E-28001 MADRID
Fax: (34) 15 75 39 98

Llibreria de la Generalitat
Rambla dels Estudis, 118
E-08002 BARCELONA
Fax: (34) 343 12 18 54

SWEDEN/SUÈDE
Aktiebolaget CE Fritzes
Regeringsgatan 12, Box 163 56
S-10327 STOCKHOLM
Fax: (46) 821 43 83

SWITZERLAND/SUISSE
Buchhandlung Heinimann & Co.
Kirchgasse 17, CH-8001 ZÜRICH
Fax: (41) 12 51 14 81

BERSY
Route du Manège 60, CP 4040
CH-1950 SION 4
Fax: (41) 27 31 73 32

TURKEY/TURQUIE
Yab-Yay Yayimcilik Sanayi Dagitim Tic Ltd
Barbaros Bulvari 61 Kat 3 Daire 3
Besiktas, TR-ISTANBUL

UNITED KINGDOM/ROYAUME-UNI
HMSO, Agency Section
51 Nine Elms Lane
GB-LONDON SW8 5DR
Fax: (44) 171 873 82 00

**UNITED STATES and CANADA/
ÉTATS-UNIS et CANADA**
Manhattan Publishing Company
468 Albany Post Road
PO Box 850
CROTON-ON-HUDSON, NY 10520, USA
Fax: (1) 914 271 58 56

STRASBOURG
Librairie Kléber
Palais de l'Europe
F-67075 STRASBOURG Cedex
Fax: (33) 03 88 52 91 21

Council of Europe Publishing/Editions du Conseil de l'Europe
Council of Europe/Conseil de l'Europe
F-67075 Strasbourg Cedex
Tel. (33) 03 88 41 25 81 - Fax (33) 03 88 41 27 80